THE PHILOSOPHY OF
MARJORIE GRENE

THE LIBRARY OF LIVING PHILOSOPHERS

Paul Arthur Schilpp, Editor
THE PHILOSOPHY OF JOHN DEWEY (1939, 1971, 1989)
THE PHILOSOPHY OF GEORGE SANTAYANA (1940, 1951)
THE PHILOSOPHY OF ALFRED NORTH WHITEHEAD (1941, 1951)
THE PHILOSOPHY OF G. E. MOORE (1942, 1971)
THE PHILOSOPHY OF BERTRAND RUSSELL (1944, 1971)
THE PHILOSOPHY OF ERNST CASSIRER (1949)
ALBERT EINSTEIN: PHILOSOPHER-SCIENTIST (1949, 1970)
THE PHILOSOPHY OF SARVEPALLI RADHAKRISHNAN (1952)
THE PHILOSOPHY OF KARL JASPERS (1957; AUG. ED., 1981)
THE PHILOSOPHY OF C. D. BROAD (1959)
THE PHILOSOPHY OF RUDOLF CARNAP (1963)
THE PHILOSOPHY OF C. I. LEWIS (1968)
THE PHILOSOPHY OF KARL POPPER (1974)
THE PHILOSOPHY OF BRAND BLANSHARD (1980)
THE PHILOSOPHY OF JEAN-PAUL SARTRE (1981)

Paul Arthur Schilpp and Maurice Friedman, Editors
THE PHILOSOPHY OF MARTIN BUBER (1967)

Paul Arthur Schilpp and Lewis Edwin Hahn, Editors
THE PHILOSOPHY OF GABRIEL MARCEL (1984)
THE PHILOSOPHY OF W. V. QUINE (1986, AUG. ED., 1998)
THE PHILOSOPHY OF GEORG HENRIK VON WRIGHT (1989)

Lewis Edwin Hahn, Editor
THE PHILOSOPHY OF CHARLES HARTSHORNE (1991)
THE PHILOSOPHY OF A. J. AYER (1992)
THE PHILOSOPHY OF PAUL RICOEUR (1995)
THE PHILOSOPHY OF PAUL WEISS (1995)
THE PHILOSOPHY OF HANS-GEORG GADAMER (1997)
THE PHILOSOPHY OF RODERICK M. CHISHOLM (1997)
THE PHILOSOPHY OF P. F. STRAWSON (1998)
THE PHILOSOPHY OF DONALD DAVIDSON (1999)

Lewis Edwin Hahn, Randall E. Auxier, and Lucian W. Stone, Jr., Editors
THE PHILOSOPHY OF SEYYED HOSSEIN NASR (2001)

Randall E. Auxier and Lewis Edwin Hahn, Editors
THE PHILOSOPHY OF MARJORIE GRENE (2002)

In Preparation:
THE PHILOSOPHY OF ARTHUR C. DANTO
THE PHILOSOPHY OF MICHAEL DUMMETT
THE PHILOSOPHY OF JAAKKO HINTIKKA
THE PHILOSOPHY OF HILARY PUTNAM
THE PHILOSOPHY OF RICHARD M. RORTY

Marjorie Grene

THE LIBRARY OF LIVING PHILOSOPHERS
VOLUME XXIX

THE PHILOSOPHY OF
MARJORIE GRENE

EDITED BY

RANDALL E. AUXIER

AND

LEWIS EDWIN HAHN

SOUTHERN ILLINOIS UNIVERSITY CARBONDALE

CHICAGO AND LA SALLE, ILLINOIS • OPEN COURT • ESTABLISHED 1887

To order books from Open Court, call 1-800-815-2280.

THE PHILOSOPHY OF MARJORIE GRENE

Open Court Publishing Company is a division of Carus Publishing Company.

Library of Congress Cataloging-in-Publication Data

    The Philosophy of Marjorie Grene / edited by Randall E. Auxier, Lewis Edwin Hahn.
       p. cm.— (The Library of Living Philosophers; v. 29)
    "Bibliography of Marjorie Grene": p.
    Includes bibliographical references and index.
    ISBN 0-8126-9527-5 (trade) —ISBN 0-8126-9526-7 (cloth)
      1. Philosophy. 2. Grene, Marjorie Glicksman, 1910– I. Grene, Marjorie Glicksman, 1910– II. Auxier, Randall E., 1961– III. Hahn, Lewis Edwin, 1908– IV. Series.

B945.G734 P47 2002
191—dc21

                            2002034570

The Library of Living Philosophers is published under the sponsorship of Southern Illinois University Carbondale.

GENERAL INTRODUCTION
TO
THE LIBRARY OF LIVING PHILOSOPHERS

Since its founding in 1938 by Paul Arthur Schilpp, the Library of Living Philosophers has been devoted to critical analysis and discussion of some of the world's greatest living philosophers. The format for the series provides for setting up in each volume a dialogue between the critics and the great philosopher. The aim is not refutation or confrontation but rather fruitful joining of issues and improved understanding of the positions and issues involved. That is, the goal is not overcoming those who differ from us philosophically but interacting creatively with them.

The basic idea for the series, according to Professor Schilpp's general introduction to the earlier volumes, came from the late F.C.S. Schiller, who declared in his essay on "Must Philosophers Disagree?" (in *Must Philosophers Disagree?* London: Macmillan, 1934) that the greatest obstacle to fruitful discussion in philosophy is "the curious etiquette which apparently taboos the asking of questions about a philosopher's meaning while he is alive." The "interminable controversies which fill the histories of philosophy," in Schiller's opinion, "could have been ended at once by asking the living philosophers a few searching questions." And while he may have been overly optimistic about ending "interminable controversies" in this way, it seems clear that directing searching questions to great philosophers about what they really mean or how they think certain difficulties in their philosophies can be resolved while they are still alive can produce far greater clarity of understanding and more fruitful philosophizing than might otherwise be had.

And to Paul Arthur Schilpp's undying credit, he acted on this basic thought in launching the Library of Living Philosophers. It is planned that each volume in the Library of Living Philosophers include an intellectual autobiography by the principal philosopher or an authorized biography, a bibliography of that thinker's publications, a series of expository and critical essays written by leading exponents and opponents of the philosopher's thought, and the philosopher's replies to the interpretations and queries in these articles. The intellectual autobiographies usually shed a great deal of light on both how the philosophies of the great thinkers developed and the major philosophical movements and issues of their time;

and many of our great philosophers seek to orient their outlook not merely to their contemporaries but also to what they find most important in earlier philosophers. The bibliography will help provide ready access to the featured scholar's writings and thought.

With this format in mind, the Library expects to publish at more or less regular intervals a volume on one of the world's greater living philosophers.

In accordance with past practice, the editors have deemed it desirable to secure the services of an Advisory Board of philosophers as aids in the selection of subjects of future volumes. The names of nine prominent American philosophers who have agreed to serve appear on the page following the Founder's General Introduction. To each of them the editors are most grateful.

Future volumes in this series will appear in as rapid succession as is feasible in view of the scholarly nature of this library.

Throughout its career, since its founding in 1938, the Library of Living Philosophers, because of its scholarly nature, has never been self-supporting. We acknowledge gratefully that the generosity of the Edward C. Hegeler Foundation has made possible the publication of many volumes, but for support of future volumes additional funds are needed. On 20 February 1979 the Board of Trustees of Southern Illinois University contractually assumed sponsorship of the Library, which is therefore no longer separately incorporated. Gifts specifically designated for the Library, however, may be made through the Southern Illinois University Foundation, and inasmuch as the latter is a tax-exempt institution, such gifts are tax-deductible.

RANDALL E. AUXIER
LEWIS E. HAHN

DEPARTMENT OF PHILOSOPHY
SOUTHERN ILLINOIS UNIVERSITY CARBONDALE

FOUNDER'S GENERAL INTRODUCTION*
TO
THE LIBRARY OF LIVING PHILOSOPHERS

According to the late F.C.S. Schiller, the greatest obstacle to fruitful discussion in philosophy is "the curious etiquette which apparently taboos the asking of questions about a philosopher's meaning while he is alive." The "interminable controversies which fill the histories of philosophy," he goes on to say, "could have been ended at once by asking the living philosophers a few searching questions."

The confident optimism of this last remark undoubtedly goes too far. Living thinkers have often been asked "a few searching questions," but their answers have not stopped "interminable controversies" about their real meaning. It is nonetheless true that there would be far greater clarity of understanding than is now often the case if more such searching questions had been directed to great thinkers while they were still alive.

This, at any rate, is the basic thought behind the present undertaking. The volumes of the Library of Living Philosophers can in no sense take the place of the major writings of great and original thinkers. Students who would know the philosophies of such men as John Dewey, George Santayana, Alfred North Whitehead, G.E. Moore, Bertrand Russell, Ernst Cassirer, Karl Jaspers, Rudolf Carnap, Martin Buber, et al., will still need to read the writings of these men. There is no substitute for first-hand contact with the original thought of the philosopher himself. Least of all does this Library pretend to be such a substitute. The Library in fact will spare neither effort nor expense in offering to the student the best possible guide to the published writings of a given thinker. We shall attempt to meet this aim by providing at the end of each volume in our series as nearly complete a bibliography of the published work of the philosopher in question as possible. Nor should one overlook the fact that essays in each volume cannot but finally lead to this same goal. The interpretive and critical discussions of the various phases of a great thinker's work and, most of all, the reply of the thinker himself, are bound to lead the reader to the works of the philosopher himself.

---

*This General Introduction sets forth in the founder's words the underlying conception of the Library. L.E.H.

At the same time, there is no denying that different experts find different ideas in the writings of the same philosopher. This is as true of the appreciative interpreter and grateful disciple as it is of the critical opponent. Nor can it be denied that such differences of reading and of interpretation on the part of other experts often leave the neophyte aghast before the whole maze of widely varying and even opposing interpretations. Who is right and whose interpretation shall he accept? When the doctors disagree among themselves, what is the poor student to do? If, in desperation, he decides that all of the interpreters are probably wrong and that the only thing for him to do is to go back to the original writings of the philosopher himself and then make his own decision—uninfluenced (as if this were possible) by the interpretation of anyone else—the result is not that he has actually come to the meaning of the original philosopher himself, but rather that he has set up one more interpretation, which may differ to a greater or lesser degree from the interpretations already existing. It is clear that in this direction lies chaos, just the kind of chaos which Schiller has so graphically and inimitably described.[1]

It is curious that until now no way of escaping this difficulty has been seriously considered. It has not occurred to students of philosophy that one effective way of meeting the problem at least partially is to put these varying interpretations and critiques before the philosopher while he is still alive and to ask him to act at one and the same time as both defendant and judge. If the world's greatest living philosophers can be induced to cooperate in an enterprise whereby their own work can, at least to some extent, be saved from becoming merely "desiccated lecture-fodder," which on the one hand "provides innocuous sustenance for ruminant professors," and on the other hand gives an opportunity to such ruminants and their understudies to "speculate safely, endlessly, and fruitlessly, about what a philosopher must have meant" (Schiller), they will have taken a long step toward making their intentions more clearly comprehensible.

With this in mind, the Library of Living Philosophers expects to publish at more or less regular intervals a volume on each of the greater among the world's living philosophers. In each case it will be the purpose of the editor of the Library to bring together in the volume the interpretations and criticisms of a wide range of that particular thinker's scholarly contemporaries, each of whom will be given a free hand to discuss the specific phase of the thinker's work that has been assigned to him. All contributed essays

---

1. In his essay "Must Philosophers Disagree?" in the volume of the same title (London: Macmillan, 1934), from which the above quotations were taken.

will finally be submitted to the philosopher with whose work and thought they are concerned, for his careful perusal and reply. And, although it would be expecting too much to imagine that the philosopher's reply will be able to stop all differences of interpretation and of critique, this should at least serve the purpose of stopping certain of the grosser and more general kinds of misinterpretations. If no further gain than this were to come from the present and projected volumes of this Library, it would seem to be fully justified.

In carrying out this principal purpose of the Library, the editor announces that (as far as is humanly possible) each volume will contain the following elements:

First, an intellectual autobiography of the thinker whenever this can be secured; in any case an authoritative and authorized biography;

Second, a series of expository and critical articles written by the leading exponents and opponents of the philosopher's thought;

Third, the reply to the critics and commentators by the philosopher himself; and

Fourth, a bibliography of writings of the philosopher to provide a ready instrument to give access to his writings and thought.

PAUL ARTHUR SCHILPP
FOUNDER AND EDITOR, 1939–1981

DEPARTMENT OF PHILOSOPHY
SOUTHERN ILLINOIS UNIVERSITY CARBONDALE

ADVISORY BOARD

ACKNOWLEDGMENTS

The editor hereby gratefully acknowledges his obligation and sincere gratitude to all the publishers of Marjorie Grene's books and publications for their kind and uniform courtesy in permitting us to quote—sometimes at some length—from Professor Grene.

RANDALL E. AUXIER
LEWIS EDWIN HAHN

Added to Board after the subject of this volume was chosen.

TABLE OF CONTENTS

II. PHILOSOPHY OF BIOLOGY

PREFACE

We are pleased and regard ourselves as fortunate to bring you a new volume in our series on Marjorie Grene's philosophy. Readers will discover quickly in surveying the contents of this volume that Professor Grene has not only lived an interesting and varied life, but that she has been willing to tell us about that life with both humor and engaging familiarity. Indeed, the charm and dry wit of Professor Grene's writing might hold for us a certain danger, namely a tendency to underestimate the difficulties she faced as a woman in the middle portion of the twentieth century in gaining the professional positions and recognition for her ideas—recognition that men with only a fraction of her talent and learning could easily have commanded. Apart from a few indomitable pioneering souls of slightly earlier years, such as Mary Whiton Calkins, Professor Grene was a member of the first generation of women in America and Europe to blaze the path into academic philosophy, in particular, and the Western academies more generally. But the personal struggle associated with gaining recognition for her philosophical ideas, courageous though it has been, is not the reason the Advisory Board of the Library chose to devote a volume to Professor Grene. Rather, it is the value of the ideas themselves that has warranted the broad and far-reaching assessment contained in the pages that follow.

Professor Grene has written about a wide variety of philosophical topics and issues over her long career. Particularly she made and continues to make major contributions to the philosophy of biology, a field in which she has been an important voice in the community of biological theorists in their on-going discussion of evolution and its various possible interpretations. Professor Grene has been instrumental in changing the way historians of philosophy read and write about the figures they study, having insisted that a grasp of historical context is required for an adequate understanding of the arguments one wishes to consider. Yet, Grene has also opposed antiquarianism, arguing instead that the best way to bring historical thinkers to bear on our own problems is to understand them first in their own contexts so that we can appreciate how their problems have come to be our own problems through many mutations. Professor Grene's personalist stance and her collaborations with the late Michael Polanyi have staked out for her an epistemological position that is broadly naturalistic and contextualist, and yet empirical and rigorous. This combination is not usual in the present philosophical climate, dominated as it is by rationalist philosophies of consciousness, but Grene's able defense of her approach has been one of the main reasons that a personalistic and contextualist epistemology remains a viable part of the contemporary conversation. Professor Grene, then, has been among the few who refuse to approach problems of perception and experience by appealing first to consciousness as both *explanandum* and *explanans*. Rather Grene's account begins with the living creature in its environment and understands perception on a Gibsonian model of orientation and affordances.

In her often well-publicized and pointed disputes with the philosophers of consciousness, Professor Grene has come to have a daunting reputation as a philosopher who can disarm or slay an opponent with a single phrase or question. Many more philosophers than would confess it have approached with considerable trepidation a public disputation with Professor Grene, and not a few have quietly declined the opportunity to argue with her altogether. In short, it must be said that Professor Grene is not now and never has been a philosopher to be trifled with, who does not suffer fools lightly, and her colleagues know this and respect it. Some of the reasons for this reputation will become evident in Professor Grene's replies to her critics within the covers of this volume. The discussion is often colorful and sharp, but that is in keeping with the character of this philosopher, and it ought to appear here just as it has elsewhere throughout her long career. Yet, I would not leave the readers of this volume with the false impression that there is a deficiency of kindness, gentle guidance, or even philosophical mercy in Professor Grene's style of philosophizing. The testimonials of those among her former students who have, in fear and trembling, placed a criticism before their former teacher in this volume will make plain enough their loyalty to Professor Grene as a teacher, a philosophical guide, a person of considerable wisdom and humility, and as that rarest of finds in the contemporary world, a true human being. We are pleased to present to you this volume, and we have every confidence you will find it worth your effort to have studied.

We at the Library of Living Philosophers office are grateful to Professor Grene and her able critics for their efforts in creating this volume, and we hope that our efforts in their behalf have adequately repaid their time and creativity.

The LLP staff is happy to acknowledge once more the warm support, encouragement, and cooperation of our publisher, Open Court Publishing Company, especially M. Blouke Carus, David R. Steele, and Kerri Mommer. And we also very much appreciate continued support, understanding, and encouragement from the administration of Southern Illinois University Carbondale, especially the College of Liberal Arts and Dean Shirley Clay Scott. As always, moreover, we are grateful for the friendly and unfailing help in a variety of ways from the staff of Morris Library at SIUC. It is invaluable for our work and that of our fellow scholars. Without the on-going and unflagging support of the Department of Philosophy at Southern Illinois University Carbondale, and its Chair Kenneth W. Stikkers, these volumes could not be published, and we want to thank them for their support. As Editor, my warm gratitude also goes to Christina Martin and the Philosophy Department secretariat for help with numerous projects; to Frances Stanley who does nearly everything related to creating these volumes, such as creating the camera-ready proofs, helping with manuscripts, catching many editing points I have missed, and keeping the constant correspondence with contributors moving and well-ordered. I would also like to thank James Russell Couch, who is a doctoral student at SIUC, for his excellent research, library work, and tireless efforts in tracking down and verifying quotations and citations. Lucian W. Stone also has to be heartily thanked for similar work earlier in the Grene project, and Nicholas Barron for library research.

Professor Lewis Hahn, who was Editor of the Library of Living Philosophers from 1981 until June of 2001, has now taken a well-earned retirement in the great Lone Star State of his origin and youth, but at our urging has consented to remain Editor Emeritus of LLP. Professor Hahn launched the present volume several years ago, along with five others that will follow this one, those treating the thought of Michael Dummett, Jaakko Hintikka, Richard Rorty, Hilary Putnam, and Arthur Danto. These are in various states of completion at present. While Professor Hahn's health has prevented him from taking an active role in producing these volumes for some time now, nevertheless they each bear his mark, largely in the care with which the main figures and many contributors have been selected. Those who have worked with the Library of Living Philosophers over the years and the members of the Philosophy Department and wider academic community at Southern Illinois University Carbondale simply stand in awe of Lewis Hahn's achievements in academic life. But even more than that, the work of a true philosopher will genuinely show itself in the achievement of a rich, wise, humble, and irreproachable character. If that is the work of the true philosopher, and it is, then Lewis Hahn is among the greatest philosophers of his generation. The list of persons whose lives have been materially and spiritually bettered because of contact with Lewis Hahn would fill a hundred volumes the size of this one, my own name all but lost among them. We all fondly dedicate this volume to Lewis Edwin Hahn in the knowledge that whatever good we may do in the future is only possible because of what he has already selflessly done for us.

RANDALL E. AUXIER
EDITOR

DEPARTMENT OF PHILOSOPHY
SOUTHERN ILLINOIS UNIVERSITY CARBONDALE
AUGUST 2002

PART ONE

INTELLECTUAL AUTOBIOGRAPHY OF MARJORIE GRENE

From Descartes' mechanistic thinking spring both his
agreement with and his difference from Harvey on
the heart and blood. The evidence chiefly of Harvey's
De Motu Cordis (1628) and Second Disquisition to Riolan
(1648-9?) and of Descartes' Discours de la Methode
(1637) Pt. V and Description du Corps Humain (1648)
suggest the following contrast:

I. As to their general conception of method: Descartes
(though not the simple _a priorist_ he is often alleged
to be) puts his reliance, in the manner of mathematicians,
on the _intelligibility_ of his explanation: mechanical
principles have the ~~required~~ clarity and simplicity
requisite for truth, and it is no surprise if the
evidence of the senses conforms to their fundamental
self-evidence. Harvey, on the other hand, in opposing
the Cartesian physiology, insists that his ultimate
authority is sense. His proofs, he says, are after the
fashion of anatomists, not astronomers with their
hypothetical reasoning (no one has seen the other side
of the moon; Harvey has ~~seen~~ the heart beating and
the blood spurting). Even geometry, he feels, needs,
in the last analysis, the support of ocular evidence
what Harvey ~~(think of~~ Descartes with his piece of wax!); anatomy
not only needs, but revels in it. Thus Descartes
uses the theory of the circulation as a helpful
corollary of his mechanical theory, (the heart works like a furnace). but rejects the
Harveyan muscular motion of the heart (an unin-
telligible suggestion when the conception of involuntary
muscles is wanting) and, accepting instead the
traditional "fact" of the "fire without light" in
the heart (like the fire in badly cured hay), confirmed by the "fact" that the heart is never empty of
explains the heart's motion mechanically in terms
of the rarefaction of the blood as it enters that organ.
But Harvey _sees_ the heart contracting like a

Marjorie Grene

INTELLECTUAL AUTOBIOGRAPHY

In my *Philosophical Testament*, published in 1995, I loudly declared that that collection of philosophical reflections was *not* a memoir in the autobiographical sense. In fact I went so far as to say: "I find it incredible that ordinary and often rather silly people write their memoirs, as if anybody should be interested in such humdrum and boring lives, or even such neurotic and 'Oh, tell me who I am' lives. What does it matter, except to them? So I wouldn't dream of writing my memoirs, in the usual sense; that would be ego-inflated and stupid."[1] Words I must now eat! The invitation to become a subject (or object?) for a volume in the Library of Living Philosophers was too improbable and too flattering to reject. Mostly, I hope, what intrigues me about this project is the opportunity to read and comment on appraisals of my work, but, meantime, I am committed also to the ego-inflated, if not "stupid," undertaking of telling my life story. I confess to the habit of expressing my opinions too harshly, and this time it turns out that what I hurled was a boomerang. However, if, as I sometimes think, our tradition in philosophy is a conversation going back to Thales, any teacher of philosophy and writer in philosophy, however ordinary, has a place in that conversation and may accordingly tell his or her story insofar as it is a story of philosophical discourse.[2] I will certainly try to keep the following account within that framework.

As has long been the case with most women, and still holds today for very many, my personal history has had a very important influence on my professional work, keeping me from it in large measure for many years and encouraging me (I won't say "forcing me" since I don't know to what extent it is weakness of character rather than circumstance that has made me run from one topic to another) to work in areas I would not myself have chosen. But the particulars of that history are irrelevant to the present story. It is not my life as growing girl, wife, mother, farmer's wife, and farmer that belongs in this volume, but only my life in philosophy, patchy though it happens to have been.

The patchiness is not only temporal but thematic. As to the former: I was officially outside the profession of philosophy from 1944, when I lost my job as instructor at the University of Chicago, until 1959, when I stumbled by chance into a temporary lectureship at Leeds. In 1960 I became lecturer in philosophy at Queen's University, Belfast and then in 1965 professor at University of California at Davis, retiring from there at the then mandatory retirement age in 1978. As to thematic patchiness: as my bibliography shows, I have worked in a number of areas in the history of philosophy, Greek and early modern; in so-called continental philosophy; in the philosophy of science, especially the philosophy of biology; in the theory of knowledge, especially the problem of perception; in philosophical anthropology; even, briefly, in aesthetics, ethics, philosophy of law. There seems to be little coherence in such an assortment.

Nevertheless, when I look back at nearly seven decades in and out of philosophy, I do find one persistent strand implicit or explicit in much of my work (even though I was not always aware of it). As a teenager I thought I might be interested in philosophy, but failed to understand what I tried to read. When I entered Wellesley College as a freshman in 1927 I was told I must wait till sophomore year to take the introductory course. Meantime I had become interested in zoology, which I had started as my required science course, and in fact I majored in zoology, but what really put me off philosophy when I tried it (apart from the dull lectures and true and false exams) was the instructor's insistence that I accept the *cogito*: that is, accept the notion that, setting aside all my everyday beliefs, I could have some special awareness of myself as something purely subjective, apart from my bodily existence. Again, in the fall of 1931 in Freiburg im Breisgau, in Werner Brock's proseminar on Descartes, I had the same problem. I remember coming out after the seminar remarking: "Was wär' ich ohne meine Umwelt?" This refusal to accept the *cogito*, and all it implies, as the unique starting point of philosophy has been, I believe, a persistent theme in much of my work, insofar as I have been trying to think through philosophical problems for myself and not simply expounding the ideas of others. A recent example is my contribution to Ulric Neisser's symposia on the self, "The Primacy of the Ecological Self" (1993). Of course a refusal alone doesn't get one anywhere. Refusing to start with the *cogito* means starting somewhere else, as, indeed, many others have tried to do throughout the past century—though without altering by one whit the Cartesian alternative still regnant in much of establishment philosophy: the choice between a meaningless physical basis out there and secret inner somethings in here. I'll return to this claim in due course, as well as to what seems to me the best hope for a fruitful way out of the old alternative.

Meantime, let me try to recall—or reconstruct—some of the landmarks along my way. In 1931 I was sent as a German-American exchange student to Freiburg, where—with hundreds of others—I sat at the feet of Martin Heidegger, and heard his lectures on "the essence of truth" and on "the

beginning of Western philosophy." In the second semester I also participated (silently!) in his seminar on the *Phaedrus*. What did I learn from this
experience? In my *Philosophical Testament* I tried to come to terms with
Heidegger from my present point of view, but now I want to try to assess
what it was like then, and also what difference these semesters made later
on to my own thought.

As to the lectures: I returned to the U.S. in the summer and painstak-
ingly typed up my notes from them. What did they mean to me? Really, I
think, very little. A few years later, in my positivist reaction to German
profundities, I published an article on Heidegger in which I gave what still
seems to me a faithful account of those occasions:

> It should be added . . . that the forcefulness of Heidegger's "aristocratic"
> arguments depends in large part on the personality of the lecturer. One is
> caught as in a political rally by the slow intensity of his speech. The contemp-
> tuous epigrams with which he dismisses the protests of logic or good sense
> sting the listener's ears with their acidity; and his prophetic solemnity when he
> invokes the quest for being ties one as spellbound as if one were a novice
> taking his first step into the rituals of the Eleusinian mysteries. One sits on the
> edge of one's chair and agrees breathlessly—no point-of-viewlessness, only
> courage of point of view—and oh, were one but among the blessed few who
> have it![3]

Admittedly, there were parts of the lectures that did teach me something:
the reading of Parmenides, for example, provided a reasonable introduction
to the fragments. But for the most part it was a question of dazzlement, not
of understanding.

The *Phaedrus* seminar was another matter. Some of the time
Heidegger's students made comments, allegedly in his language, for which
they were promptly slapped down; but for the most part, we read the text
(second part first and speeches thereafter) with great care and devotion. It
was not only an excellent exercise in reading a philosophical text; it was
also the start of my life under the guidance of the *Phaedrus* and the
Symposium—but that is decidedly not the story I am telling here.

During the same summer, on shipboard and then at home in Madison,
Wisconsin between two academic years in Germany, I read *Sein und Zeit*
for the first time, again, I suspect, with minimal understanding—certainly
with no grasp of the great question of Being for the sake of which the
account of human being was undertaken. I can only report here what I
gleaned eventually from that work, although since I taught it many times
much later, I find it hard to sort out what I gathered then from later insights.
In the analysis of *Dasein* there was the emphasis on the future as the

primary tense of human existence, but at the same time the importance of historicity, in effect, of contingency, as well as of the triviality of many of our preoccupations in our addiction to the everyday. (The stress on contingency ties in, in my own case, with the acceptance of organic evolution, in more or less Darwinian mode; in a Heideggerian context, that has certainly no connection whatsoever with Dasein's historicity.)

There was also the contrast of the inauthentic with authenticity, to which I returned later, when asked to talk about existentialism (see "Authenticity, an Existential Virtue," 1952). I didn't at the time understand, as I believe I now do, Heidegger's overly Teutonic reading of authenticity (the German soldier risking his life for the Fatherland as the exemplar of being-to-death), and I could as well have found a related concept in Goethe's *Wilhelm Meister*, or, philosophically best of all, in Spinoza's *Ethics* (which Heidegger would never have so much as mentioned, and of which at the time I certainly knew nothing). But whatever we made of it, we all bowed down to authenticity as an ideal. Then, of course, I also appreciated Heidegger's critique of *res extensa* in its guise of *Vorhandenheit* and the rejection of a philosophy centered in the notion of "consciousness."

In 1932–33, since Heidegger was on leave, I went to Heidelberg to study with Jaspers. Although I read his three-volume *Philosophie*, and later wrote a few essays about him when requested to do so, I cannot say that his philosophy influenced my thinking in any way. However, both his seminar on Hegel and his lectures on the *Critique of Pure Reason* were important landmarks in my intellectual development. We read Hegel's lectures on the philosophy of history and I wrote a paper (long since lost) called "Der Begriff der Vergänglichkeit in der Geschichtsphilosophie Hegels," in which I expressed a (reasoned) contempt for Hegel and Hegelianism that has never left me. Indeed, any kind of programmatic idealism has long seemed to me simply nonsense. The lectures on Kant I found magnificent. Jaspers had a gift for catching the general bent of what a philosopher was after, and putting it in a way that was both pedagogically useful and original. Or so I thought at the time. I don't remember the details, but it was certainly Jaspers's lectures that started me on a lifelong devotion to the First Critique—and particularly to the "Transcendental Analytic." I know that what I later made of that beginning wasn't exactly Kant, but the starting point was important, and in any case the Analytic is one of the texts I'm always happy to return to. I once heard Carnap remark, "I am an unhistorical man." An honest confession, but I do believe that philosophical reflection is better for being rooted in tradition. In my time, that meant just knowing certain texts; by now, the tradition is beginning to be examined with more attention to context. That's an improvement, in my view, but at least the texts were much better than nothing. Indeed, an interest in various figures, or periods, in our philosophical tradition has been a conspicuous feature in my work. My bibliography attests to that, and I will have occasion to refer to some of this material—although my chief focus here is rather on immediately philosophical than on historical issues.

In 1933, after a truncated semester (the time of Hitler's ascendancy to power and the so-called "Nationale Erhebung"), I moved to Radcliffe College—the nearest a woman could get to Harvard in those days—to work for a doctorate. The first year I studied for my preliminaries and the second year wrote a hasty and atrocious dissertation on the concept of *Existenz* in contemporary German philosophy. I hasten to say that it is buried somewhere, I hope very deep and inaccessible, in the Radcliffe library. It was not that I was interested in the topic, but that I foolishly thought if I did something quickly I could get out and get a teaching position. This was in the Depression, however, and in any case women were not considered suitable candidates for positions in philosophy.

Except for the requirement of prelims in the standard areas, the Harvard program seems to me to have been far from rigorous. But I did find inspiration in three teachers, David Prall, Alfred North Whitehead, and C. I. Lewis. Prall's course on Spinoza instilled in me a lifelong admiration for that transcendently great thinker. Whitehead's lecture course on cosmologies contrasted the *Timaeus* with Hume's *Dialogues* as two opposite roots of our tradition. At the same time, Whitehead insisted that the whole of Western philosophy consisted of a series of footnotes to Plato, a view with which I found myself in sympathy. Not that I was ever a "Platonist" in the crude sense in which many understand that epithet; but I did find in the dialogues an inexhaustible fund of thought-provoking insights as well as equally inexhaustible mysteries. Whitehead himself, of course, was a most eloquent and inspiring lecturer. I tried, in the years that followed, to understand *Process and Reality*, but was always stumped by eternal objects, and, indeed, by the bewildering technical vocabulary in which his metaphysic was couched. But I did take *Science and the Modern World* very much to heart, and especially the little work *Nature and Life* (lectures delivered in 1933 and published in 1935), which, some years later, I suppose helped to confirm my anti-Cartesian bias, as well as my dissatisfaction with logical positivism (or logical empiricism, as it came to call itself).

At the same time, almost schizophrenically, if you like, the chief influence on my thinking in those years came from a very different direction, from the epistemology of C. I. Lewis. His introduction to epistemology convinced me, for a time, of his position of conceptual pragmatism, probably in part because of the way he related his views to those of Kant. In fact, if I remember correctly, what I did in that terrible thesis was to try to justify a Lewis-like epistemology in existentialist terms.

It was Lewis, also, who stimulated my interest in the new movement of logical positivism. I read the first volumes of *Erkenntnis* with devotion; indeed, I thought of writing a dissertation on Schlick's ethics. But Lewis, to whom I suggested it, said, "No. In ethics I am a Kantian!" So that was out and I devised my "Existenz" topic, with an alleged supervisor whom I met twice for twenty minutes each time. Needless to say, at this point I had no inkling that logical positivism itself was, as I later came to understand, one of the ultimate outcomes of the Cartesian starting point I distrusted, of what Helmuth Plessner called "the Cartesian alternative."

If it is odd to come under the influence at one and the same time of Whitehead and Lewis (let alone, of Plato and positivism!), I should say that there was one lesson to be learned from both those thinkers, as well as from Cassirer's *Substanzbegriff und Funktionsbegriff*, which I also read in that period, and that was: that a twentieth-century metaphysics must focus somehow on events or processes rather than on "substance." However much one admires Spinoza in his time and place, or even as a thinker somehow greater than any time or place (like Eriugena in the ninth century), one must admit that substance metaphysics is over and done with. What there is is a host of happenings, neither a cluster of minimal things nor one great overarching one. This belief does, of course, agree well with the notion that a thinker is far from being a self-contained entity, or that thinking is a self-referential act divorced from its bodily and social setting. Not that I made that connection then, but at least it was possible!

From 1935, when I received my doctorate, until 1937, when I became a teaching assistant at the University of Chicago, in order to participate in Carnap's research seminar, my intellectual history is a blank, or worse. It occurred to me, foolishly, that since I was writing about "existentialism," I should apply for a postdoctoral fellowship to go to Denmark and study Søren Kierkegaard. I did in fact receive the Alice Freeman Palmer Fellowship from Wellesley and spent the year, first in Copenhagen learning Danish and reading all the works and journals of that very melancholy Dane, and then back in Madison writing a (happily unpublished) book about Kierkegaard and writing to numerous academic institutions in search of a job. There was in the book, I think, a not bad chapter on S. K. on modalities whose loss I regretted when I came to try to compare Kierkegaard with Sartre on history; but since I so loathed its subject, it must have been a bad book. While in Copenhagen I did try to pursue the study of symbolic logic, but I got no help from the university, where there was a logic requirement with three alternatives: traditional syllogistic logic, Hegelian logic, or symbolic logic. But the last-named was provided at a level too elementary even for me. So, philosophically, I think that year was just a blank.

The next year was worse. I did somehow contrive to get a job—as Assistant Director of Residence in a women's junior college (formerly ladies' seminary) in southern Illinois and taught a very little philosophy, sort of, as well as typing and occasional bits of biology. In 1937, however, I was able to move to the University of Chicago as a teaching assistant in order to participate in Carnap's research seminar, where the late and much lamented Carl (Peter) Hempel was his assistant.

Apart from some summer lectures Carnap had given at Harvard in 1936, that was my official initiation into logical positivism, and after a few weeks, the beginning of my disappointment in it. As a rudimentary zoologist and a former student of C. I. Lewis, I didn't understand how one could construct a philosophy of science with a purely extensional logic. Carnap, too, admittedly, had eventually to abandon that aspect of his program, but at the time he was adamant about it, and I hadn't anything like his patience in slowly modifying whatever proved untenable in one's over-all enterprise. Besides, I hope I was already having misgivings about the notion of an exact, all-explaining "scientific method." However, since I have no records and memories only of incidents, not of any sweeping conversion experience, I can't be sure. My only evidence, which I shall report in due course, comes from thirteen years later.

Meantime, what is clear is that I was becoming thoroughly disillusioned with the positivist program, and also skeptical about the nature of philosophy as a profession in our time (since all the subject matters had left us). I thought I might try law school and audited the course in Contracts—hence the paper in the *Law Review*. But I had been officially a student for too long—straight through from four to twenty-four—and in addition, I was becoming interested, through teaching, in the history of philosophy.

In 1940 I published, with T. V. Smith (though it was entirely my work), the anthology *From Descartes to Kant*, which was widely used for years to come. Looking at it now, I find it defective in a number of respects, but I certainly learned something from producing it. Indeed, as I mentioned in passing at the start of this story, philosophy is, in my view, in one sense at least, a dialogue with our past. I have certainly continued to work in the history of philosophy, for the most part, early modern; and however much I focus here on my own philosophizing, the historical perspective is always present, and still, even at this late date, an essential feature of the development of my own thought. It is difficult to specify just how this works; but my *Descartes* (1985, repr. 1998) is a good example of the kind of thing I have in mind. It was written for a series called "Philosophers in Context." I specified two contexts: Descartes in his own time, and Descartes in relation to our present philosophical situation. My seventeenth-century work since then, *Descartes among the Scholastics* (1991) and several essays, two written with Roger Ariew, has pursued the seventeenth-century context in more detail. Yet I hope that the same bi-contextual point of reference remains. Granted, it is important, or so I believe, not to import the arguments of earlier thinkers too hastily or too arbitrarily into the framework of our currently fashionable debates, and it is certainly inappropriate to read our current debates directly into earlier thinkers. At the same time, since we are histories, and Western philosophy is a history, locating our own concerns judiciously within that history illuminates and enriches our own beliefs and our own arguments.

Apart from the *Law Review* essay, which led no farther, my publications in this period were on Hume and, oddly, on Gerard's *Essay on Taste*. I had already developed a weakness for Hume—(at Radcliffe, of course; Hume was referred to only sneeringly by Jaspers, in contrast to the greatness of Kant), and I had been puzzled, in particular, by the problem of accounting for taste on an empiricist foundation. I read a number of the texts in this tradition—Burke, Reynolds, and others—but focused on Gerard. I am much more a pedagogue than a scholar, and can never support propositions about "all" the thinkers of a period or movement, so I try to settle on one or a few who seem typical. In any case, I presume I was here following out a little an interest in Hume's problems, rather than pursuing an interest of my own in aesthetics. Certainly, I never (except once or twice, when invited to) returned to that topic, although I always return to Hume.

In 1944, after several years as instructor at Chicago, I was told my services were no longer wanted. It was still wartime, with few jobs and few students, and I was tied down to family and farm; so, as I have said, I was exiled from philosophy officially until 1959, living in the country in Illinois until 1952 and after that in Ireland. An outsider, looking at my publications during these years, would say this was my existentialist period. I suppose that's fair enough, in that I did study and write about the so-called existentialists (both Heidegger and Jaspers rightly abjured the title). When existentialism came into fashion after World War II, I was asked to write about it, and my policy was not to reject any offer that was professionally respectable. I even continued to write about Sartre, on and off, after my return to teaching, but, again, usually because I was asked to do so. To leap ahead: I also found *Being and Nothingness* a magnificent text to teach. It is so gloriously mistaken, and shows you what a dead end—or one of the dead ends—Cartesianism leads to, in this case mixed with a generous dose of Husserl, Heidegger, and Hegel.

I have few pertinent recollections of the years from 1945 to 1950. However, my few publications apart from the existentialist material—and even that in small part—do suggest some continuing themes. A little paper,

"An Implicit Premise in Aristotle's *Ethics*" (1946) presents, I still think, a valid criticism of those who would apply Aristotle's views directly to our society: for the doctrine to work, it is necessary that all agree who the wisest are, and that certainly does not hold for our situation, if it ever did. What is striking when I look back at this essay, however, is the degree to which my own thinking was steeped in the reading, not of Aristotle—who really swam into my ken only rather later—but of Plato. It is Plato's anguish about a divided society that seemed to me closer to us, and to reality, than Aristotle's serene confidence in identifying his practically wise man.

Another reminder of old interests and disappointments that I find suggested, as a matter of fact in one of my existentialism essays, concerns pragmatism, especially of the Deweyan mode. I think there must have been still at Chicago in the 1940s, alongside the pseudo-Aristotelianism of the reigning ideology, some remnant of the pragmatist tradition of Dewey and Mead. I was probably looking for some philosophical alternative to positivism; in any case, I venture to quote part of what I said about pragmatism in an essay on Kierkegaard. "It may be said," I wrote then:

> that it is unnecessary to go back to Kierkegaard for a new impulse in philosophy: that such a movement as pragmatism, for example, has already effected what existential philosophy aims at;—that is, it has rebelled against the arid technicality of metaphysics, and has brought philosophy closer to the living problems of real people. But has it?[4]

Then, after looking at an example from Dewey, about the man who builds a house for the enjoyment of building, since after all he might die before coming to live in it, I continued:

> Pragmatism was directed against a number of things, but it contained nothing positive beyond the pleasant desire to make things comfortable. Whatever is uncomfortable—death, sin, despair—it passes by on the other side. As has been said a number of times, pragmatism is afraid to face evil. And it is afraid, too, to face the ultimate puzzle of human individuality. To be sure, the individual and the activities of the individual are what pragmatism, like existential philosophy, is supposed to devote itself to. But it is the "adjusted" individual, the stereotyped individual, the individual who has forgotten how to be an individual that pragmatism celebrates. Pragmatism is indeed the philosophy of our society: a society whose cult is to forget all the unpleasant-nesses and therewith most realities, a society in which . . . the big bad wolf refrains with incredible decency from eating up the little pigs.[5]

In view of the fact that, when my colleagues mention James or Dewey, I simply scream or gnash my teeth, it seems worth recalling that I did have my reasons.

There is some evidence, also, that I was still looking—or at least hoping—for some alternative to the Cartesian starting point in philosophy. In 1947, the same year as my first existentialism essays, I published a little piece called "On Some Distinctions between Men and Brutes," in which I considered the approach to human uniqueness of Descartes, Hobbes, and Hume, finding them all inadequate, but suggesting no way out. (We still talked of "men" in those long ago times when we meant "human beings.") Although, as I said at the start, I am here abstracting from my personal history, I may remark in passing that this essay does show clearly the influence on my philosophical reflections of two aspects of my life: maternity and farming. A close acquaintance with infants, as well as with members of other species, does make a difference. (Four decades later, in my book on Descartes, I noted his unfairness to children, and I hope we all recognize how unfair he was to nonhuman animals.) At the same time, this essay presents a complaint, not a program; in this way it contrasts sharply (not only in nomenclature!) with my Davis research lecture of 1971, "People and Other Animals" (published in 1973), which owes a great deal to Plessner's philosophical anthropology—and probably also to my work in the philosophy of biology in the intervening years. I'll return to that later in this story.

1950 is a special year in my *vita*: the year I met Michael Polanyi, eminent physical chemist turned philosopher, who asked me to work with him in the development of his Gifford Lectures—eventually the book *Personal Knowledge*, published in 1958.[6] I had managed, with some difficulty, to attend one of his lectures at Chicago, and when I remarked to him afterward that he had said what I had tried vainly to express years before about the weakness of logical positivism, he replied, "That is just what I said in my book, *Science, Faith and Society*."[7] I hurried off and found the last available copy at a Chicago bookstore. Looking at the book now, I find it a very crude, and even partly misleading, anticipation of the major work. Nor do I recall the content of the lecture in question, but I think what Polanyi must have been referring to in *Science, Faith and Society* was the first lecture, or even the first few pages, in which he points out the impossibility of finding natural laws "by applying some explicitly known operation to the given evidence of measurements."[8] There is always (what he later came to call) a "logical gap" between data and conclusion (of course, Hume knew that too; it's what the argument on cause amounts to). Polanyi proposes to think of science on the model of what he calls "the theory of the burglar." Let me quote part of this passage:

Suppose we wake up at night to the sound of a noise as of rummaging in a neighboring unoccupied room. Is it the wind? A burglar? A rat? . . . We try to guess. Was it a foot-fall? That means a burglar! Convinced, we pluck up courage, rise and proceed to verify our assumption.

... The theory of the burglar—which represents our discovery—does not involve any definite relation of observational data from which further new observations can be definitely predicted. It is consistent with an infinite number of possible future observations. Yet the theory of the burglar is substantial and definite enough; it may even be capable of proof beyond any reasonable doubt in a court of law. In the light of common sense there is nothing curious in this: it merely makes it clear that the burglar is being assumed to be a real entity; a real burglar. So that we may even reverse this by saying that science is assuming something real whenever its propositions resemble the theory of the burglar. In this sense an assertion concerning the path of a planet may be said to be a proposition concerning something real, it being open to verification but only by some definite but also by many as yet quite undefined observations. . . . It appears of the essence of scientific propositions that they are capable of bearing such distant and unexpected fruit; and we may conclude, therefore, that it is also of their essence to be concerned with reality.

A second significant feature of the discovery of the burglar, closely connected with what has just been said, is the way in which it is made. Curious noises are noticed; speculations about wind, rats, burglars, follow, and finally one more clue being noticed and taken to be decisive, the burglar theory is established. We see here a consistent effort at guessing—and at guessing right. The process starts with the very moment when, certain impressions being felt to be unusual and suggestive, a "problem" is presenting itself to the mind; it continues with the collection of clues with an eye to a definite line of solving the problem; and it culminates in the guess of a definite solution.

But there is a difference between the solution offered by the burglar theory and that offered by a new scientific proposition. The first selects for its solution a known element of reality—namely burglars—the second often postulates an entirely new one. The vast growth of science in the last 300 years proves massively that new aspects of reality are constantly being added to those known before. Whence can we guess the presence of a real relationship between observed data, if its existence has never before been known?[9]

These remarks already contain a number of the theses later developed: realism, fallibilism, and the importance of the unspecifiable and of the unexpected. The lectures also stress the significance of the premises of science: the fundamental beliefs entailed in any process of scientific exploration, as well as the importance of tradition and of community in what we now call scientific practice.

Polanyi's Gifford Lectures were delivered in 1951–52, but it was not until 1958 that the resulting volume was published. During that period, chiefly through correspondence, I acted partly as Polanyi's research assistant and chiefly, I think, as editor and as advisor in the history of philosophy. I was deeply committed to what he came to call his "fiduciary program": a kind of lay Augustinianism, in which we recognize that our reasoning always rests on the attempt to clarify, and to improve, something we already believe, but believe, of course, in such a way that we recognize that we might be mistaken.

At a more everyday level, the most important feature of *Personal Knowledge*, as Polanyi himself remarked after the book's completion, was the distinction he had introduced between focal and subsidiary awareness. This was later developed, in *The Tacit Dimension*[10] and other essays, in the account of tacit knowing: of the thesis that all our knowledge, however theoretical, always entails a from-to structure. We rely on less than explicit clues from which we attend to the focus of our attention. Polanyi is often cited as a thinker who claims there is some tacit knowledge in addition to what is made explicit; but what is important in his claim is the relation of the two, that is, the dependence of the explicit on the tacit. Moreover, knowledge as from-to reaches primarily outward. I am reaching out toward something other than myself. Although one can also rely on clues beyond oneself to focus on oneself, that is by no means the usual, or most fruitful order. I am somewhere in a world that presents me with a problem. I attack that problem by assimilating to myself clues bearing on it, in such a way that I can look from, and through, those clues to features out there in the problem area. It is I who am attending to my problem, and even assimilating myself to it, in the process Polanyi called "indwelling." Still, I am out there with it; my search is mine, and so personal, but not subjective. And it is some aspect of the world itself that presents my problem; so the world itself carries meanings. This was a good platform, I think, on which to build a vision of science, of knowledge, and of human reality against and beyond the divided *res cogitans* and *res extensa* bequeathed to us by Descartes. Indeed, it was in the introduction to *Knowing and Being* (1969), a collection of Polanyi's essays which I edited, that I first formulated the slogan "All knowledge is orientation." This seems to answer my question of 1931 (although it is emphatically not the case that all orientation is knowledge!).

If 1950 presents a clear dividing line in my philosophical activity, so does 1960, though perhaps not quite so abruptly, since what I would count as one new field of interest is expressed in publications as early as 1958. Three things happened then, or thereabouts. First, since I was appointed at Belfast to teach Greek philosophy, I embarked, for the first time in my life, on a systematic study of Aristotle. Secondly, I began to investigate questions in the philosophy of biology—strictly speaking, a little earlier, in the late fifties, but still, I would date my systematic interest in this field from my move to Belfast in 1960. And finally, I read for the first time Merleau-Ponty's *Phenomenology of Perception*. Let me look a little more closely at some of the consequences of these events.

First: Aristotle. Following the tradition established by D'Arcy Thompson, I interpreted Aristotle as a metaphysician motivated by his researches in biology. This was in itself a significant enrichment in my philosophical perspective. Since I accept as what Polanyi would have called a fundamental belief the thesis of the primacy of history, I believe that anyone coming to develop a relatively serious interest in any one of the major thinkers of our tradition is so much the wiser for that development. Yet Aristotle taught me a great deal also in relation to current problems in the philosophy of biology and, if only by contrast, in the philosophy of science. My most conspicuous contribution in this area was my *Portrait of Aristotle* (1963, reissued 1998). The nearest I came to a substantive contribution to the technical literature on Aristotle was in a paper on the relation of genus to species and matter to form, published in 1974. Oddly, what I then thought a rather frivolous essay, "Aristotle and Modern Biology" (1972), I now find expresses rather well what I had learned from studying and teaching Aristotle in the preceding decade. The concluding paragraphs should give a fair idea of its tenor. I had found, I said, "three important methodological lessons to be derived from the study of Aristotle":

> Through the concept of form as an analytical tool, correlative with matter, Aristotle can remind us of the many-levelled structure both of inquiries into complex systems and of the systems themselves, and thus of the inadequacy of a one-levelled atomism for the understanding of such systems. In conjunction with the grounding of form in the . . . ["being-what-it-is"] of each kind of thing, further, he can remind us of the falsity of two other modern misconceptions: the unity of science concept on the one hand, the claim that the subject-matter and method of science are everywhere the same, and, on the other, the insistence that science must renounce any claim to seeking contact with reality: that theories float, as pure constructs, on the surface of the phenomena, with no mooring in the real nature of . . . real events or things.
>
> The first of these reminders is plainly related to the concept of organization or information and hence (as I have already argued) to the subject-matter of biology, and to the question of its reducibility or irreducibility to chemistry and physics. The second reminder, of the plurality of science, a reminder of the good Kantian principle that we can have no systematic knowledge of the whole of nature, should help also to liberate biology, or thinking about biology, from the overabstract and reductive demands of taking one science, classical physics, as the ideal of all. And lastly, the acknowledgement of scientific realism should release the biologist to admit the insights into the concrete manifold of his subject-matter, from which his work originates and in which,
>
> Nor, finally, as I emphasized at the outset, is this a plea for a return to Aristotelianism. It is a plea for us to listen, despite our fundamental differences

of metaphysic and of method, to some of the tenets that Aristotle, as a biologist-philosopher, advocated long ago, and to try to interpret them in ways that could be useful to us as we attempt to articulate and revise our conception of what the investigation and the knowledge of living nature are.[11]

Although the problem of "reductionism" is no longer much debated, at least among philosophers, as it was twenty or thirty years ago, there is still some point, I think, in questioning the thesis that biological explanation consists entirely in considering least parts—as some molecular biologists have been inclined to do. It's no longer a question of physico-chemical nothing-buttery, but rather of reducing every biological question purely to one of specifying particular macromolecules. Nor is the unity of science any longer a fashionable catchword; we hear more of plurality these days than of unity. But I think the point I was making does bear on the turn from an abstract conception of "science as such" to the investigation and analysis of scientific practice that has characterized the most promising literature in this area at the turn of the century. Finally, also, I am confident that the study of scientific practices in biology is helping to introduce, or to restore, a reasonable attitude of realism, rather than phenomenalism, to the principles of the philosophy of science.

Perhaps I should repeat, however, the warning that I was not recom-mending some kind of wholesale "return to Aristotle." Indeed, one of the rewards of teaching Aristotle, I found, was the opportunity this provided for looking at some of the characteristics of science as it has developed since the Renaissance by contrasting them with the strikingly different features of the Aristotelian enterprise: on certainty, on induction, on the rigid segregation of the sciences, and so on. (In opposing the positivist program with its unity of science, one is not, of course, suggesting that scientific disciplines are wholly segregated, but their interrelations are neither total and systematic nor in any way fixed in advance of developing research.)

Second: the philosophy of biology. When I look back at it, my work in this area seems to fall into three parts. The first, which has persisted for forty years, is a concern with the structure of evolutionary theory. Polanyi had asked me earlier to look into heresies in evolution. His understanding of Darwinian theory was minimal, or worse, and I'm afraid mine at the time was not much better. In any event, I had written two papers on the conceptual structure of evolutionary theory, "Two Evolutionary Theories" and "Statistics and Selection," published in 1958 and 1961 respectively, although both had already been written while I was at Leeds from 1958 to 1960. I would still defend both these papers as reasonable pieces of conceptual analysis, even though some of what I published somewhat later on evolution now seems to me at least in large part indefensible, especially a really bad chapter on "The Faith of Darwinism" in *The Knower and the Known* (published in 1966, but written in Belfast in the early sixties). I realized later that what I had been trying to criticize was what Stephen Jay Gould calls "the hardened synthesis," a singularly narrow doctrine current in many quarters in the celebratory year of 1959.[12] I encountered its odd circularity a number of times. At one centenary session in Leeds, for example, when I asked, skeptically, how a phenomenon like Kettlewell's industrial melanism explained the origin of moths, as against darker rather than paler moths, I was told: "Don't be so dogmatic!" And much of the literature of the time confirmed this impression. Of course, after I moved to Davis in 1965, I did learn better, thanks to colleagues like G. L. Stebbins and Theodosius Dobzhansky—and thanks, over the years, to the magnificent accomplishments of the "Darwin Industry." Not that the hardened synthesis was not in fact as narrow and self-congratulatory as it seemed, but that there is very much more to the Darwinian tradition in evolutionary theory than that particular view allowed.[13]

At the same time, there was something in my original uneasiness with the stock (neo-)Darwinian position. It does tend to turn into what Georges Canguilhem would have called a scientific ideology. For example, my 1961 analysis of the multiple senses of "improvement" in Fisher's *Genetical Theory* correctly singled out one feature of this tendency. Or, much later, in a 1990 paper, "Evolution, Typology and Population Thinking," I pointed out the oversimplistic nature of the standard contrast between the evil "typology" that preceded Darwin and the wholesome "population thinking" that allegedly reigned among the virtuous thereafter. Supposedly before Darwin everybody was a Platonist, who thought there were eternal "natures" and after Darwin the enlightened saw there were no natures whatsoever, only individuals. But since it is populations that evolve—that is, aggregates of individuals—and not individuals at all, this leaves us in a pickle. And how anyone can practice any science, or carry on everyday life, for that matter, as a pure nominalist, I really don't know. That natures change doesn't mean there are none. I also suggested in that paper that a more ecological approach to evolutionary processes as well as attention to the hierarchical, and more than singly hierarchical, character of evolutionary events would help to enrich the over-narrow perspective of some forms of neo-Darwinism.

On Darwin himself, I think the best thing I have written was my Gildersleeve Lecture at Barnard in 1987, "Darwin's Great Tree of Life: Roots and Ramifications," most of which was assimilated in the second chapter of Eldredge and Grene, *Interactions* (1992). The separation of two evolutionary hierarchies, genealogical and economic, I owe to Niles Eldredge, who was in turn inspired by David Hull's ground-breaking paper,

"Individuality and Selection."[14] It is paradoxical that Hull, to whom we owe the distinction between replicators and interactors, is at the same time one of the fiercest defenders of the thesis that in the living world there are no natures whatsoever, only individuals. The premise for this argument is that everything is either a class, which is characterized by some property or properties, and must be eternal, or an individual, which has a history but no nature at all. I tried, in the first chapter of my book with Eldredge, to criticize the strange consequence of this thesis: that species are individuals, so that I can't say, this tiger is a member of the species *Felis tigris*, but only a part of it,[15] and I suggested that we refer to species as "historical entities," in order to avoid the confusions of the species–individuals debate. I regret to say, however, that, due to a computer glitch, some of Niles's pronouncements on species as necessarily "classes or individuals" were retained in a later chapter. Unless they are Hegelians, philosophers are not supposed to contradict themselves; what I wanted us to say on this subject appears in the passage already referred to.

Evolutionary theory was the first area, and has continued to be a major area, in my concern with the philosophy of biology. Another area of interest was suggested, shortly after I moved to Belfast, when someone (I have no idea who) asked me for a bibliography in the philosophy of biology. I consulted the *Repertoire Philosophique de Philosophie de Louvain* and thus discovered a number of writers, chiefly from the continent of Europe, whose work gave me a broader perspective on philosophical questions connected with biology. These thinkers held my attention for a number of years; indeed, in 1968 I published a book about several of them, *Approaches to a Philosophical Biology*, which I later came to think I should have left unwritten. Not only did no one want to hear about my authors, but by now I myself wonder what, with one exception, I thought I had learned from them. The exception is Helmuth Plessner's philosophical anthropology, or, more generally, his view of the nature of living things and of ourselves in particular as odd examples of living things. He based his account on the concept of "positionality," the way in which an organism sets between itself and its surroundings a boundary that is both outside and within itself. He went on to distinguish between the open positionality of plants, the closed positionality of animals, and the eccentric positionality of human beings, who can take a stand over and against their own bodily existence. My lecture, "People and Other Animals," which I referred to earlier is still, I think, the best statement I have made about the character of persons in relation to nature and culture.[16] And my argument there is heavily Plessnerian.

Perhaps I am being unfair to my other subjects. Adolf Portmann's work comparing the rates of maturation of human infants and the newborn of other species was certainly important. And so was Erwin Straus's discussion of the upright posture. Both these writers—one a zoologist, who started as a marine invertebratist, the other a psychiatrist—demonstrated clearly how our very biological make-up suits us for life in language and in the artifacts of culture. Of course, such demonstration does not absolutely rule out a traditional mind-body dualism. Kant reviewed a work by one Moscati, who used the oddities of our urinogenital systems to show that we were descended somehow from quadrupeds, and found it comforting to learn that we are botched animals—made, not to be vitally efficient, but to gaze on the starry heavens above and the moral law within. Still, if one is looking for clues on what it is to be a person—clues that take due account of our situatedness, both in nature and in culture (itself within nature)—Portmann and Straus, as well as Plessner, do provide useful evidence. In fact, I did find the three essays, on Plessner, Portmann, and Straus, worth reprinting in *The Understanding of Nature* (1974). Even then I was doubtful about the other two, F. J. J. Buytentijk and Kurt Goldstein. Goldstein was an important influence on Merleau-Ponty, but I found it difficult to discover philosophical coherence in his work.

In addition to conceptual problems in evolutionary theory and my excursion into the work of more peripheral thinkers, I came to participate in the decades following 1960 in the then current debates in the developing field of philosophy of biology—and sometimes, more generally, of philosophy of science. The opportunity to develop a course in the philosophy of biology at Davis contributed strikingly to my work in this area. Indeed, I have always learned from teaching. Two problems were prominent in those days, perhaps successively, though they are clearly interrelated: reductionism (is biology reducible to chemistry and physics?) and the question of hierarchies in biology.[17]

Reflection on the philosophy of biology led to speculations about the philosophy of science in general. Classic philosophy of science, from the Vienna Circle onwards, was based, notoriously, on physics, or on a particular conception of physics, as its model. Attention to biology leads, I came to believe, to a different philosophical perspective on science, its history and its achievements. In an invited address to the Philosophy of Science Association in 1976, "Philosophy of Medicine: Prolegomena to a Philosophy of Science," I took for a case study a work, *The Normal Lung*, by physician John Murray,[18] and listed fifteen respects in which our conception of science would have been different if, as I suggested, we had had the physic, rather than the physics, of Padua as our model. One reader at least took me to be arguing about the oddity of biology as a science. On the contrary, I was proposing a much revised conception of the philosophy of science as such in the light of a reliance on biology as subject matter.

I have carried this notion further in later work, for example, in such essays as "Perception and Interpretation in the Sciences."[19] There, and later, in a still unpublished piece titled "Two and a Half Thought Styles in the Philosophy of Science,"[20] I developed further a number of principles which I find important in the philosophical assessment of scientific practice. These include: the primacy of history, the primacy of perception, the ubiquity of interpretation, the social nature of science, the plurality of scientific subject matters, and so on. None of this, of course, is original; but I hope I have put together some of the themes that colleagues, too, both historians and philosophers of science, are beginning to find significant as perspectives for their work.

So much for two of the spheres of interest that have kept my attention, more or less continuously, since 1960. I also mentioned a third 1960 landmark; that's another story. My reading of Merleau-Ponty's *Phenomenology of Perception*, belatedly, some time during that academic year, constituted for me something like a revelation. For one thing, Merleau-Ponty seemed to me to be saying, in a different order, what Polanyi was saying, independently, in *Personal Knowledge*. Since I had worked too closely with Polanyi, and I suppose, too much in isolation from any philosophical community, I found it difficult simply to adopt his language. But existentialist discourse was, in a way, what I had started from, so this almost twenty-year-old text, new to me, gave me a voice. It showed me, also, that I had somehow learned something from the "existentialist" writers I had reluctantly studied and written on. And most fundamentally, Merleau-Ponty's thesis of the primacy of perception, of his reflection on human perception in particular, gave me a starting point, not made explicit in Polanyi's account of from-to knowing, for a radically post-Cartesian conception of persons as part of living nature, but with a difference. In short, in reading Merleau-Ponty, I found myself, as Kierkegaard would have put it, "his reader." That is, of course, apart from the early Marxist work, which is wholly foreign to me.

At the same time, studying and teaching Merleau-Ponty's texts (I remember teaching one course in Davis in which we read all three of his major works), affects one's rhetoric, perhaps for the worse. As I confessed in "Merleau-Ponty and the Renewal of Ontology," "[t]hinking about him produces a kind of verbal vertigo."[21] When I reread them now, I find both that essay and the lecture "The Sense of Things" filled with surprising truths that I had forgotten I had ever thought of; yet they seem in the way they are written to express rather intellectual inebriation than insight.[22] The first was the Presidential Address to the Metaphysical Society of America in 1976; the second was the first Mandel Lecture delivered to the American Society for Aesthetics in 1979. Neither of these fields is one to which I have since contributed; perhaps I was drunk with novelty. But rhetoric aside, there is nevertheless something in both these addresses that bears on my counter-Cartesian *leitmotif*: Merleau-Ponty's "centrifugal pluralism," as I called it, in the first case, and, in the second, his reliance on the situation of the painter, who "brings his body with him," as the appropriate model for the way in which we are all bodily with, yet still over against, things in the world, in such a way that we make a world as it makes us. Merleau-Pontyan rhetoric again, perhaps, but there's something in it.

My landmarks go by decades. The next, and presumably the last, occurs only in 1980. Granted, my return to teaching in the United States in 1965, at the University of California at Davis, made an immense difference to my intellectual life. It had been stimulating to return to teaching in the United Kingdom, but returning to our system, where instructors are relatively at liberty to develop their own courses and where students actually like to ask questions, was positively exhilarating. After my retirement I continued teaching at a number of institutions; I am grateful to all of them, but it would be tedious to list them here.

It was also a delight to return to being part of a philosophical community (in Belfast, I found, everyone had to cross the Irish sea to find someone to talk to). At Davis, I would like to acknowledge, in particular, my indebtedness to a much younger colleague, the late Fred Berger; our interests were quite different, but it was always immensely helpful to talk through with him any work one was engaged in. I owe a similar debt to a less immediate colleague, Alan Donagan, whom I met through his contributions to a volume on Spinoza that I edited for Doubleday, and who continued to offer philosophical inspiration until his death in 1991. From 1988 on I have had the good fortune to be affiliated with the department at Virginia Tech (as adjunct professor and honorary distinguished professor); I am deeply grateful to my colleagues there, and in particular to the successive department heads, Richard Burian, Joseph Pitt, and Roger Ariew, for their help and hospitality. I am especially fortunate in having had as a colleague Patrick Croskery, who possesses in the nth degree the gift I acknowledged in Berger. If philosophy is not always contemporary dialogue, it is certainly improved by being so. My debt to my colleague Roger Ariew is different: as well as being current head of the department (as of this writing), he is my guide through the labyrinth of seventeenth-century philosophy, especially its scholastic aspect. I owe a great deal to his scholarship and his encouragement. I should say the same for Richard Burian in the philosophy of biology; up to recently, I have not done as much work in that field as in early modern philosophy since coming to Blacksburg, but our association, and my debt to him, go a long way back.

The years 1965 to 1980 and even the years since have allowed me, in the main, to continue along lines already initiated, especially in the history of philosophy. However, as I have said, there is one more landmark I must touch on, one that is difficult to describe in brief. J. J. Gibson's *Ecological Approach to Visual Perception*[23] was published in 1979. I had read his *The Senses as Perceptual Systems*[24] some years earlier, but, apart from appreciating its rich approach to evolution, had not understood it very well. It was when I read the 1979 work, probably some time late in 1980, that I came to see, or rather to glimpse, some of the implications of this new perceptual psychology for my problems: the nature of persons, of knowledge, of the practices of the sciences. In 1981 I taught a month-long seminar at the University of Waterloo on Merleau-Ponty and Gibson, but found that it was Gibson I most wanted to focus on. I had long accepted a principle of the primacy of perception—see, for example, my Mellon Lecture at Tulane in 1978, "Knowledge, Belief and Perception."[25] But my previous mentors, Polanyi and Merleau-Ponty, had both lacked an adequate theory of perception on which to base their views. Plessner's physical anthropology, although it lays an appropriate foundation for a new understanding of perception, does, so far as I recall, little if anything about that particular problem. It is that new foundation that Gibson, or better, the Gibsons, were able to supply. (Gibson's wife, Eleanor J. Gibson, was an important contributor in her own right to the ecological approach, and she has continued its development since her husband's death in 1979.) Unfortunately, ecological psychology is still a minority "school" within experimental psychology, and, as far as I can tell, with very little, if any, influence in current philosophical debate. When it is referred to at all it is, in my experience, usually misinterpreted.[26] I shall try to give some notion of its import here, although I find it difficult to present convincingly in a few paragraphs a summary of a truly innovative approach that few of my colleagues are willing to take seriously.

Back once more to my old friend, or enemy, the *cogito* and the *res cogitans* we reach from it. Descartes emphasizes, in the *Principles*, that our sensory awareness holds only as purely subjective. That follows from the *cogito*, since if we can, and ought to, start from such a self-contained moment of self-awareness, we will inevitably continue, in further exploration of ourselves and our possible place in an "external world," to find ourselves cut off from any direct, reality-based contact with that alien otherness. We have what Wittgenstein was to call little "secret inner somethings" which in themselves tell us nothing about a real world, and it must be we who somehow read "meanings" or "values" into that desert-like stuff out there. Both major traditions in Western thought have been haunted by this Cartesian theme. If the idealist tradition was to build a whole world out of "consciousness," the "external" world itself was reduced, in the outcome of empiricism, to equally private, equally meaningless "minimum sensibles." But is that really what experience is like? J. J. Gibson, working for the air force as an experimental psychologist during World War II, discovered that if pilots relied on the usual model of sense perception, they would all crash. Thirty years of experiment and reflection led him to a radically new theory, which expresses much more adequately the way in which animals, including ourselves as oddly enculturated animals, find our way around in the world we in fact inhabit.

Forget sensations, which are relatively unimportant in our communion with the world around us, and consider what is going on when an animal perceives something: for example, food, a mate, danger, the solution to a problem. Every animal has developed, in the course of evolution, *perceptual systems* that enable it to cope both with the threats and the opportunities offered by its environment. That is the perspective suggested by Gibson's 1966 book. We should consider animal behavior as expressive of an evolutionary process that is thoroughly interactive. True, population geneticists can, if they like, express these interactions in terms of their outcome as differential gene frequencies. But what has been going on that results in such numbers is the activities of phenotypes, not genes or even genotypes, in the environments they have to face—and to whose alteration and very existence they contribute through their activities. Traditionally, perceptions were arbitrary guesses, "inferred" from pinpoint, meaningless sensations. According to the psychologist Richard Gregory, for example, perceptions are not even hypotheses, but illusions, which natural selection has taught us to follow, since otherwise it would eliminate us. A relatively linear, non-ecological view of evolution is consistent with such a view. But if we consider what goes on in the history of life more concretely, in terms of organisms in their "conditions of existence," as Darwin put it, we get a different picture. Those little inner somethings now appear relatively unimportant. What we have, again, are animals whose perceptual systems have enabled them to pursue successfully the opportunities offered them in a complex environment, and to avoid its dangers. The experience mediated by such systems—our visual system, a dog's olfactory system, for example—is itself an organized whole, and the environment to which it is directed is itself a system of a sort, an "ambient array," as Gibson calls it. It is not a bare *res extensa*, but a complex as much of interconnections, and even of meanings, as of "bare facts."

Against the background of this evolutionary view, Gibson stated in his last book, in 1979, a more fully developed account of his "ecological approach" to perception, and in particular his theory of *affordances*. What happens when an animal perceives something? (In trying to answer that question, I am following, roughly, an analysis by Eleanor Gibson.) In describing such an activity (and perception is an activity, not a mere passive reception), we must include three levels. First, there are things and events occurring in the animal's environment. Gibson rightly considered his account emphatically that of a philosophical realist. Second, there is

information available in the environment that the animal has the capacity
to pick up. Such information, however, be it noted, does not consist of
"information-theoretical" bits, but of actual structures or ratios in the
environment, for example, for terrestrial animals, the layout of the ground,
the horizon, and so on. Different kinds of information will of course be
picked up, in the light of their evolutionary history, by animals of different
species or varieties; but it is information that is *there*, really, in a real world.
It consists, in each case, of what Gibson calls *invariants*: constancies in the
flow of stimulation that the perceptual systems of the particular animal
enable it to pick out. A dog can pick up olfactory information beyond our
powers. Our visual system, on the other hand—not just upside-down images
on the retina, which in ordinary life we never see, but the systematic efforts
of our eyes, eye movements, slight movements of the head, and so on—our
visual system provides us, or most of us, with a fund of information about
events and objects around us. Thirdly, these environmental invariants
permit the animal to perceive what Gibson came to call the *affordances* of
the environment: opportunities offered it, or dangers threatened, or the like.
The rabbit, for example, affords dinner for the hunter, while the hunter
affords danger to the rabbit. Thus sense perception is direct, active as well
as passive, bearing on real entities or events so structured that the animal
can pick up, through its sensory systems, information that in turn enables
it to grasp in this particular situation some affordance pertinent to its day-to-
day concerns. There are events going on, there is information to be picked
up that signals them to us, and it is what those events *afford* us that is
perceived. When we ask how any animal finds its way around, all these
aspects, or all these levels, must be taken into account.

What about our case? If we want to understand persons, or persons as
knowers, or our practices in attempting to develop what we call "scientific"
knowledge about nature, or even about ourselves, our perceptual orientation
needs to be taken into account. Human beings are still animals, still within
nature. Our perceptions, however, Gibson points out, acquire a certain
indirectness through the devices of language, tools, and pictures (or
picturing). From birth (in the case of language, perhaps even earlier),
human perceptions are saturated by these cultural ingredients. But again,
culture is still, and always, within nature, and in all our enterprises the
threefold structure of events or entities, information and affordances
persists.

Given this substructure, I find, we can consider more fruitfully what
persons are without being haunted by the specter of "consciousness."
Further, Gibson's "ecological approach" provides, it appears to me, a solid
basis, both epistemological and ontological, for current efforts to understand
the practices of science, in place of the outworn abstractions of "logical
reconstruction." Within a relatively stable experimental tradition, for

example, a new piece of evidence may provide information that allows the investigator to grasp—whether more or less cerebrally—the solution to a problem, or it may instead suggest a new problem, previously unforeseen. The seeker within any human tradition—I would suppose, artistic or technological, for example, as well as scientific—once assimilated to his or her acquired environment, learns to pick up information that enables him or her to "perceive" the affordances of that environment. There is no single formula for such efforts and achievements, but in general, I should think, they can be best understood as extensions of, or analogues to, the dimensions of perceptual exploration and perceptual learning that we share with our distant cousins—different, of course, in our case, as in every case. In deeply enculturated situations such as ours, Eleanor Gibson speaks of "nested affordances." It would be worthwhile, I believe, to try to carry such a conception further in some detail.

It should be clear even from this choppy summary how the perspective of ecological psychology contributes to my old puzzle about the *cogito*. The error that has haunted modern philosophy has been the supposition that we have some hidden subjective awareness, or self-awareness, set against a spread-out, meaningless external world. When we understand that it is not sensations—those secret, inner somethings—that are the fabric of our experience, but affordances that a real environment presents to us as real exploring individuals; when we understand this, we can rid ourselves also of the notion—equally misguided—that the physical world, the nature that surrounds us and of which we are particular expressions, itself carries no meanings: that reality itself is normless, and it is only our conventions that seem to impose norms.

Looking back, I can see that my earlier (contemporary) guiding lights, Polanyi, Merleau-Ponty, and Plessner, have also contributed to this insight, anticipating some aspects of Gibson's ecological realism. First, Polanyi's concept of commitment, or of his "fiduciary program," places the seeker for contact with reality in a concrete, historical situation in which he or she already accepts certain starting points, not proven, but assimilated in the hope that they may serve as guides—Gibsonian information?—to genuine insights: to the perception of affordances offered by the environment that the belief system in question supports, or even constitutes. The distinction between subsidiary and focal awareness, developed further in the theory of tacit knowing, confirms this kinship between the two doctrines. Indeed, when I wrote *The Knower and the Known*, which was intended to show some guidelines in the history of philosophy that might help lead to a philosophy like Polanyi's, I thought of describing my own view as "an ecological epistemology." However, the adjective seemed to me too trendy to adopt; it survives only, as I noted earlier, in my slogan "all knowledge is orientation . . . "

Secondly, and more directly, if you like, Merleau-Ponty's thesis of the primacy of perception, with its stress on embodiment, cries out for a foundation in a theory of perception such as Gibson was later to supply. Plessner's concept of positionality, and of our eccentric positionality—in which, through the mediation of language, instruments, and pictorial devices, we can put ourselves at a distance from our own embodiment while at the same always continuing to express it—is also enriched, and given solidity, by Gibson's new and illuminating theory of perception and of the way in which the structure of perception persists as the basis for all our "higher," or more cerebral activities, whether in science or the arts.

Thus, looking back over very many years, I can see now that, as I have just been suggesting, a number of influences and interests have helped me discover what appears to be a promising framework for reflection on the problems that have engaged me: the nature of the person, the character of knowledge claims, problems in the philosophy of science, not only in biology, but more generally as well. And of course my sorties into a number of areas in the history of philosophy have helped me toward not so much a set of conclusions, as of premises: I have been, it seems, as Polanyi thought one should do, trying to clarify, and improve, my fundamental beliefs.

So in a way this may sound like a tale with a happy ending. I wish it were. But philosophy, like other practices, depends on communities for its existence and its development. And those who share my philosophical predilections are few and far between. In fashionable philosophical circles, particularly in much of what is called cognitive science, it is still Cartesianism, even a hyper-Cartesianism, that appears to reign supreme. There is the brain, which simply does what it does (not even the whole of the central nervous system, let alone the whole organism, or rather the organism-in-its-environment, as both maker of that environment and made by it), and there is "consciousness"—once more, the congeries of secret inner somethings—that has somehow to be explained. It is a dreary and depressing picture. Have we entered a new millennium still inhabiting a world that consists, as Whitehead put it, of "a mystic chant over an unintelligible universe"?

MARJORIE GRENE

BLACKSBURG, VIRGINIA
JANUARY, 2001

I would like to thank Roger Ariew, Patrick Croskery, David Depew, Moti Feingold, and Doris Zallen for their comments on earlier versions of this document.

Of course, I also want to express my gratitude to all the contributors, as well as to series editor Dr. Randall E. Auxier, to the indefatigable secretary of the series, Ms. Frances Stanley, and to Open Court editor Dr. Kerri Mommer, for their diligence in putting together a coherent volume on my scattered and patchy work—none of it, I fear, thorough enough—in a strange variety of areas. It has been a pleasure to work with them, and to reply to (almost) all my commentators and critics.

NOTES

1. Marjorie Grene, *A Philosophical Testament* (Chicago: Open Court, 1995), p. 2.
2. For this view of philosophy, see my "Epilogue" in *Descartes and his Contemporaries: Meditations, Objections and Replies*, ed. Roger Ariew and Marjorie Grene, (Chicago: University of Chicago Press, 1995).
3. Marjorie Grene, "A Note on The Philosophy of Heidegger," *The Journal of Philosophy* 35 (1938): 99.
4. Marjorie Grene, "Kierkegaard: The Philosophy," *Kenyon Review* 9 (1947): 57.
5. Ibid., p. 58.
6. Michael Polanyi, *Personal Knowledge* (Chicago: University of Chicago Press, 1958).
7. Michael Polanyi, *Science, Faith and Society* (London: Oxford University Press, 1946).
8. Ibid., p. 8. Republished (Chicago: University of Chicago Press, 1964), p. 22.
9. Ibid., pp. 8–10.
10. Michael Polanyi, *The Tacit Dimension* (New York: Doubleday, 1966).
11. Reprinted in *The Understanding of Nature* (Dordrecht and Boston: Reidel Publishing Company, 1974), pp. 103–4.
12. See "Changing Concepts of Darwinian Evolution," *The Monist* 14 (April 1981): 195–213.
13. See for example, "Is Evolution at a Crossroads?," *Evolutionary Biology* 24 (1990): 51–81.
14. David Hull, "Individuality and Selection," *Annual Review of Ecology and Systematics* 11 (1980): 311–32.
15. Niles Eldredge and Marjorie Grene, *Interactions* (New York: Columbia University Press, 1992), pp. 23–24.
16. Delivered in 1971, published in 1973, and reprinted in *Understanding*, 1974.
17. See for example my "Hierarchies in Biology," *American Scientist* 75 (1987): 504–10.
18. John Murray, *The Normal Lung* (Philadelphia: Saunders, 1976).
19. (1987; the 1985 version was badly botched by the copy editors—in my experience, an infernal race!).
20. In press in French in a rather different form as "La Vie des sciences et les science de la vie" (Brussels: Ousia).
21. Marjorie Grene, "Merleau-Ponty and the Renewal of Ontology," *Review of Metaphysics* 29 (1976): 622.

22. Marjorie Grene, "The Sense of Things," *The Journal of Aesthetics and Art Criticism* 38 (1980): 377–89.

23. J. J. Gibson, *Ecological Approach to Visual Perception* (Boston: Houghton Mifflin, 1979).

24. J. J. Gibson, *The Senses as Perceptual Systems* (Boston: Houghton Mifflin, 1966).

25. Reprinted as chapter 1 of my *Philosophical Testament* in 1995.

26. I have written about it in chapter 8 of my *Descartes* (1985) and in chapter 7 of *A Philosophical Testament* (1995); see also "The Primacy of the Ecological Self," *The Perceived Self: Ecological and Interpersonal Sources of Self-Knowledge* (Cambridge: Cambridge University Press, 1993).

PART TWO

DESCRIPTIVE AND CRITICAL ESSAYS WITH REPLIES

1

Phil Mullins

ON PERSONS AND KNOWLEDGE: MARJORIE GRENE AND MICHAEL POLANYI

This work owes much to Dr. Marjorie Grene. The moment we first talked about it in Chicago in 1950 she seemed to have guessed my whole purpose, and ever since she has never ceased to help its pursuit. Setting aside her own work as a philosopher, she has devoted herself for years to the service of the present enquiry. Our discussions have catalyzed its progress at every stage and there is hardly a page that has not benefitted from her criticism. She has a share in anything I may have achieved here.[1]

These words of high praise for Marjorie Grene come from the acknowledgments section of Michael Polanyi's *magnum opus, Personal Knowledge: Towards a Post-Critical Philosophy*, published in 1958. Although she has done many things as a philosopher, a significant part of the life and philosophical work of Marjorie Grene has been entwined with the work of Polanyi, a physical chemist who in middle age became a philosopher. In this essay, I attempt in three ways to explore this link between Grene and Polanyi. In the next two sections below, I outline historical aspects of the connection between Grene and Polanyi that have some bearing on philosophy. Grene's long friendship and working partnership with Polanyi are in part revealed in the Grene-Polanyi correspondence in the archival Papers of Michael Polanyi; other details emerge in a few of Grene's essays and books. Clearly, Grene helped shape some of Polanyi's philosophical views and publications. Since Polanyi was not trained as a professional philosopher, he relied on Grene to direct him through twists and turns in the history of Western philosophy and to help him see his own ideas in this context. Grene frequently tried to show Polanyi ideas of contemporary thinkers that complemented those he was developing. Polanyi died in 1976 and Grene, of course, produced many philosophical articles and books both before and after Polanyi's death. A few of her essays and books comment on Polanyi's philosophical work. In the third section below, I argue that Grene, in fact, is one of Polanyi's best interpreters and sharpest critics. Finally, in the last section, I suggest what is obvious to those who work with Polanyi texts: not only did Grene influence Polanyi, but also Polanyi influenced Grene. Some of Grene's important philosophical themes, especially her discussions of persons and knowledge, are very much akin to Polanyi's discussions.

THE LUCK OF HISTORY

Marjorie Grene notes, but underplays, many of the biographical details of her own life that shaped her sixty-plus-year career as a philosopher. In her 1995 book, *A Philosophical Testament,* which she somewhat tentatively identifies as an *apologia pro philosophia sua,* she proclaims "a straightforward 'story of my life as a philosopher' would be rather dreary. . . ."[2] She provides a mere paragraph in the introduction to place herself in her historical context,[3] a modest but ironic contribution for a philosopher who takes the historical, as well as the natural, environment so seriously. The early phase of her academic life is worth an initial review since it accounts for her coming to work with Michael Polanyi.

After taking an undergraduate degree in zoology in 1931 at Wellesley, she went to Freiburg as an exchange student and heard Heidegger's lectures; the next year she went to Heidelberg and studied with Jaspers, but then came back to the United States and took an M.A. and Ph.D. in philosophy at Radcliffe from 1933 to 1935. In 1935–36, since she could not get a job, she went to Denmark on a fellowship to study Kierkegaard, a thinker about whom she was unenthusiastic. She then returned to her family's home in Madison to write and job-hunt until she moved on to a short stint as Director of Residence in a junior college in southern Illinois. Because she wanted to participate in Carnap's research seminar at the University of Chicago, she managed to move into a teaching assistant position in Chicago. Her successful application, she was told, came because someone urged the department to try the noble experiment of hiring a woman philosopher. She moved from an assistant to instructor in her several years at Chicago, but her academic life there was nipped in the bud when, as she unceremoniously puts it, "McKeon had me fired in 1944."[4] By this time, Grene already had a complicated life outside of the academy. She was a farmer in Illinois from 1940 until 1952, and then in Ireland from 1952 until she returned to the United States and a philosophy job at the University of California, Davis, in 1965. After she was fired by McKeon, except for a few lectures, translations, and bits of writing, as she summarizes it, "most of my time was taken with marriage, family and farming."[5]

In 1950, Grene was still at least on the periphery of the University of Chicago academic circles and there, by a happy coincidence, became acquainted with Polanyi. Polanyi came to the University of Chicago as the Alexander White Visiting Professor for spring term of 1950 where he gave at least eleven lectures, most of which were from material in the soon to be published collection of essays *The Logic of Liberty*.[6] In May 1947, Polanyi had been invited to give the next series of Gifford Lectures; these two cycles of lectures in Aberdeen were originally scheduled to begin in the fall of 1949, but were several times postponed, and Polanyi did not deliver them until the spring of 1951 and the late fall of 1952. By the time Polanyi arrived in Chicago in spring 1950, he already had been working on his Gifford Lectures and had begun to dig more deeply into the history of philosophy as part of his preparation. Grene heard one of Polanyi's 1950 Chicago lectures, introduced herself, and met with Polanyi later.[7] Apparently, Grene was quite interested in Polanyi's developing philosophical projects[8] and Polanyi very quickly came to appreciate Grene's background and skill as a philosopher. This was the beginning of a friendship that lasted until Polanyi's death in 1976; for at least eighteen of these years, Grene undertook several philosophical projects that were distinctly linked to Polanyi. One of the most important of these was her work on the Gifford Lectures and *Personal Knowledge*, the book to which the Gifford Lectures led. Below I first discuss this early phase of Grene's work with Polanyi, matters about which there are only sketchy historical details. Then I outline Grene's role in some later Polanyi projects.

Grene describes her 1950 meeting with Polanyi as a venue back into something like academic work and a return, after twenty years, to her study of biology and thinking about evolution:

Michael Polanyi, a distinguished physical chemist turned philosopher, had come to lecture at the University of Chicago and though I was marooned on the farm I managed to hear one of his lectures. As I remarked earlier, I found his argument against positivism thoroughly convincing; in fact I thought he had found the very refutation of that movement that I had been unable to articulate twelve years earlier in Carnap's seminar. So when he asked me to help him with the preparation of his Gifford lectures—the work that would be published in 1958 as *Personal Knowledge*—I was delighted to do so. It seemed to me that if I had any talent for philosophy, the best I could do with it in my isolated situation would be to help Polanyi in his struggle, as he called it then, "to articulate the inarticulate." I remember his telling me this as we walked a bare eroded field . . . on our Cook County farm. One of the jobs he set me soon thereafter was to look up heresies in evolutionary theory, specifically critics of the evolutionary synthesis, which was then, if one takes the centennial year of 1959 as its apotheosis, in its chief period of flowering. And once I started reading that literature I was unable to stop.[9]

The working relationship between Grene and Polanyi certainly took some crazy bounces in the early years. The patchy historical record suggests that, soon after meeting him, Grene became an important advisor to Polanyi. After his 1950 lectures in Chicago, Polanyi returned to Manchester where he very recently had exchanged his chair in chemistry for a new chair in social studies (an exchange designed to give him more time to prepare his Gifford Lectures). At some point in 1950, Polanyi was offered and accepted a permanent chair (to commence in the fall of 1951) at the University of Chicago through the Committee on Social Thought. He resigned his Manchester position, and prepared, in 1951, to move to Chicago. However, he never actually came to the United States because his visa application, filed in March 1951, was not approved until June 1953! Although Polanyi's case was widely publicized, his plans were mangled by the McCarthy era scrutiny of his past affiliations. Polanyi was lucky enough to reclaim his unfilled social studies position at Manchester in November of 1951. When he was still planning to come to Chicago, Polanyi had already secured a Rockefeller Foundation grant that had some funding earmarked to the University of Chicago for Grene to be his research assistant in 1951. Either this or another Rockefeller Foundation grant did bring Grene to Manchester for six weeks in the spring of 1952 to work with Polanyi on his second series (fall of 1952) of Gifford Lectures. She may also have come to Manchester in late 1950 or early 1951 to work with him on the first series Gifford Lectures.[10]

After Grene moved to Ireland in 1952, working with Polanyi was no longer a transcontinental exercise. Polanyi spent a month in the summer of 1953 in Ireland working with Grene.[11] After completing the Gifford Lectures, although Polanyi was involved with many other projects, he apparently soon started to work trying to turn his lectures into *Personal Knowledge*. But this proved to be a much bigger project than he originally anticipated. Grene was apparently involved in this six-year endeavor at every stage and seems to have been in Manchester frequently until the publication of *Personal Knowledge* in June 1958.[12] She gathered material for chapters, discussed it with Polanyi, and reviewed and criticized drafts as they were written.[13] Although she was not the only hand involved, she likely played an important role in revising the final draft after Polanyi completed it in March 1957.[14] She and her children put together the index for *Personal Knowledge*.[15] Along the way to 1958, Grene seems also to have done other things with Polanyi. In January and February of 1954, Polanyi gave lectures at the University of Chicago. Grene also came to Chicago to help Polanyi and gave lectures herself for the Committee on Social Thought, including a lecture on Polanyi's ideas and their setting in history.[16]

In sum, what does all of this historical detail about matters long ago point to? I believe that it strongly suggests that Grene was an absolutely central figure in the development of the philosophical ideas in Polanyi's Gifford Lectures and in *Personal Knowledge*. When Polanyi turned in earnest to philosophy, he was very lucky to have found Grene as his supporter. This is, of course, a speculative thesis whose implications will always remain unclear. I doubt that Grene, who is generous with her praise for Polanyi and quite self-effacing, will approve even of my putting forward this thesis. I do not put such a claim forward to detract in any way from Polanyi's achievements, but simply to make clear that Grene was deeply involved in those achievements. When Polanyi says in his acknowledgments to *Personal Knowledge* (quoted at the opening of this essay) that Grene "has a share in anything I have achieved here," this is not mere hyperbole but should be taken quite literally. Polanyi was a polymath, but even polymaths sometimes need direction, and that is what Grene seems to have provided, at least as far as Polanyi's philosophical work goes. This does not mean Grene always knew where the germs of Polanyi's early philosophical ideas would lead—clearly, she did not.[17] Grene reports, for example, that for Polanyi unspecifiability was a constant preoccupation while writing *Personal Knowledge*. Polanyi "seemed just hypnotized by it, to the exclusion of what philosophers might have considered much more substantive problems."[18] She could not discern why Polanyi took a year drafting the "Articulation" chapter of his book in which unspecifiability is a central theme. But later she came to appreciate the philosophical importance of the matter with which Polanyi was wrestling:

> I recall being puzzled by this delay—some time about 1953 or 1954. Although I collected a vast number of extracts to assist in the composition of the chapter, I did not really understand at the time why just this problem: the grounding of articulation in the inarticulate, should need to be spelled out so painfully. But it is indeed the heart of the matter—not, again, because Polanyi was developing an "irrationalism" (a "neo-obscurantism," as one reviewer called it), but

because the understanding of understanding, of rationality itself, demands an understanding of the way in which the subsidiary supports the focal, in particular of the way in which the ineffable supports the activities of voice or pen.[19]

The poet Elizabeth Sewell, a friend of both Polanyi and Grene who saw much of both in Manchester from 1955 to 1957 and who, like Grene, read the emerging chapters of *Personal Knowledge,* had a window on what she termed the "close and constant professional connection"[20] between Grene and Polanyi. Perhaps Sewell best captures the kind of role Grene played for Polanyi's work:

> During my first two years in Manchester, 1955–57, Marjorie's whole work time was devoted to the *Personal Knowledge* enterprise. A professional philosopher and a born teacher, explicator, *rédacteur*, (she could make some philosophy clear even to my cloud-swirling poetic mind), one had the sense of her constant presence in Michael's day-to-day endeavours, checking and suggesting references, discussing the work with him, arguing, extricating as far as possible the Germanic touches in his style. . . . In those Manchester years she was integral to Michael's professional life, I watching [sic] this with admiration and some astonishment.[21]

THE CONTINUING CONNECTION

After the publication of *Personal Knowledge* in 1958, Grene remained a close friend of Polanyi and was involved in several important joint endeavors; however, Grene seems to have devoted more and more energy to philosophical writing of her own. Nevertheless, until after the publication of *Knowing and Being: Essays by Michael Polanyi*[22] in 1969, which Grene edited, Grene served as a catalyst who organized or contributed to many things related to Polanyi and the perspectives articulated in *Personal Knowledge.* Grene contributed an essay to a 1961 *festschrift, The Logic of Personal Knowledge,*[23] for Polanyi's seventieth birthday and helped organize the celebration.[24] She contributed another essay to a second *festschrift, Intellect and Hope,*[25] in 1967. She was involved with Polanyi for a number of years in a group that originated in 1964 and eventually came to be called the Study Group on the Unity of Knowledge.[26] Much of the archival Grene-Polanyi correspondence is concerned with this group's affairs. Polanyi, Grene, and Edward Pols organized this group which was funded by the Ford Foundation and held a series of meetings over several years on particular themes. The organization's general purpose is summarized in one publication as follows: "Convinced that there is an unsuspected convergence of ideas separately developed in various fields, we propose a meeting of a number of persons who actively oppose in their work the scientism, and the related methodological and ontological over-simplification, which in one or another form are ascendant in every field of scholarly and creative endeavor."[27] Although Polanyi was the official chairman of this group, correspondence suggests that, at least in the early stages, Grene seems to have provided most of the energy and organizational savvy to get things done. The meetings involved a number of scholars whose writings reflect interest in issues and themes that Polanyi treated in *Personal Knowledge. The Anatomy of Knowledge* and *Interpretations of Life and Mind*, the publications that Grene edited for the Study Group, included papers prepared for meetings of the Study Group between 1965 and 1970.[28]

The ten or twelve years after the publication of *Personal Knowledge* were important years in the development of Polanyi's philosophical perspective. This is the period in which Polanyi worked out his theory of tacit knowing which is only nascent in *Personal Knowledge*. Polanyi produced a number of short articles and delivered several different sets of public lectures. Two of these are turned into short books, *The Study of Man* (1959) and *The Tacit Dimension* (1966). There is an interesting correspondence between Grene and Polanyi that frequently comments on Polanyi's writing (and sometimes, on Grene's writing) in the period after 1958. At least some articles and lectures that Polanyi wrote underwent Grene's scrutiny before they were published or were the subject of Grene's comments (sometimes quite blistering) after they were published. Two examples show that Grene's later interest in Polanyi's philosophical writing was sometimes much like the care she put into the *Personal Knowledge* project. In 1962, Polanyi gave the Terry Lectures and he continued to work on this material for several years until *The Tacit Dimension* was published in 1966. In a 1963 letter, Grene comments to Polanyi,

> I've worried again about the Terry lectures—Michael, you must not publish the expanded T 1 [first Terry Lecture] without very considerable revision. The brief version was brilliant; the present text is so bogged down & cluttered up with stuff that it obscures what you had before made clear.[29]

In a 1967 letter, Grene sharply hits a soon-to-be-published Polanyi essay[30] for confusions about the history of philosophy and for failing consistently to apply his own philosophical distinctions:

> Incidentally, this is *not* something you could alter at this stage, but I do want to say that I'm very uneasy about your passage on mind and body. 1) As I hope I tried to say earlier, this is NOT Cartesian dualism, which is a *2-substance* view, but that's a minor detail. More important, 2) there is surely something

radically wrong with the distinction as you make it. When I see an external object, I rely on subsidiaries in my body to see the object out there—this is my mind at work, but not, as such, *known* by me. My brain, on the other hand, as observed by a neurologist, is known by him.[31]

In fact, in her 1977 article on Polanyi's thought, Grene is quite clear that Polanyi's effort to attack behaviorism leads him into claims about mind and body that are fundamentally at odds with his own most important philosophical innovations. She claims, with good warrant, that in some ways Polanyi "gravely misunderstood his own place in contemporary philosophy":

> Polanyi believed that he was reviving dualism, when in fact he was helping to refute it. For the theory of mind mediated by the doctrine of tacit knowing is a theory of mind as fundamentally and irrevocably incarnate. In fact, Polanyi is one of the few thinkers of this century to have found adequate concepts through which to overcome Cartesian dualism, and to philosophize outside the impoverished traditions of empiricism and rationalism that it had generated.[32]

As noted above, Grene pulled together a collection of Polanyi essays, *Knowing and Being*, published in 1969, that included only things written after *Personal Knowledge*. The correspondence regarding this project is lively. Grene chose Polanyi essays that she thought were philosophically his best. She successfully resisted Polanyi's push to include some pieces that she regarded as confused or poorly written.[33] She insisted upon some editorial revisions of several pieces previously published. She sometimes did the revisions herself and went to great pains to get Polanyi not to try further revisions. What is most important is that Grene recognized that Polanyi's philosophical ideas were developing in interesting ways in the decade after *Personal Knowledge*. Her collection was designed primarily to show this, as her remarks on the third group of essays in the collection show:

> *Personal Knowledge* was directed not so much to tacit knowing as to the problem of intellectual commitment, the question how I can justify the holding of dubitable beliefs. The theory of tacit knowing is indeed the foundation of the doctrine of commitment, but while the latter probes deeper into the foundation of human personality, the former is more far-ranging. It reveals a pervasive substructure of all intelligent behavior.[34]

At least in part, the ways in which Polanyi's ideas developed in the decade after *Personal Knowledge* are a reflection of his continuing interaction with Grene. Clearly, Polanyi relied on Grene for help in understanding and mining the history of Western philosophy. A letter dated 4 September 1960 that Polanyi dubbed a "violent appeal" designed to evoke reaction from Grene amply illustrates this. After musing about the bearings of what he termed "two kinds of knowing" on traditional philosophical problems and asking what Grene thought of some books he had recently read by Pieper, Gilson, and Langer, Polanyi put his case this way:

> All this goes to say: You (Marjorie) are a philosopher, intent on finding out how things stand and you accept the framework of dual knowing; *you* have all the knowledge of philosophy, past and present that I lack—what is your reason for leaving this enormous body of thought unleavened by the new insights which you share with me?[35]

Grene also tried in the period following *Personal Knowledge* to make Polanyi aware of the kinship between his own ideas and those of other contemporary thinkers. This is clear in their correspondence in the sixties. Frequently, Polanyi seems to have read Grene's suggestions; often he seems to have resisted Grene's comparisons, but there are sometimes animated discussions about particular figures. Grene's recommendations included not only Merleau-Ponty, but also Erwin Strauss, Kurt Goldstein, Helmuth Plessner, and others.[36] Polanyi often does include in his writing after *Personal Knowledge*, especially in prefatory material, some suggestions about overlap with other thinkers.[37]

Polanyi continued to publish and make presentations in the early seventies, after the publication of *Knowing and Being*. Grene was aware of at least most of Polanyi's work, but she seems to have found a bit baffling Polanyi's late effort to produce a general account of meaning in art, symbol, myth, and religion. Such a synthesis was too grand, and particular elements, such as Polanyi's explanation of symbols, were not very well grounded in careful analysis.[38] In her 1977 article on Polanyi's philosophical ideas, she straightforwardly points out that Polanyi worked hard to link art and science in *Personal Knowledge* but seems in his late ideas to have forgotten this: "Polanyi's later work on art, especially on metaphor, moreover, seemed to me tragically misguided, a betrayal, in its separation of art and science, of his own best insights. I tried repeatedly to tell him this, to no avail."[39] Ultimately, Polanyi's late lectures and writing on these topics from the late sixties and the early seventies were published, with the help of another American philosopher/collaborator, Harry Prosch, as *Meaning*.

What is most apparent in the very late correspondence between Grene and Polanyi is that Polanyi's strength and his intellectual powers were waning. Grene recognized this and addressed Polanyi more and more as simply an old friend rather than as a fellow philosopher on whose work she needed to comment. Unquestionably, Polanyi greatly respected Marjorie Grene. As his own powers declined, he hoped to have her come to England and pull together the fragments of his last years' work. In one late letter, he

notes, "I think I have got the outlines of my last works fairly well in front
of me; but who can give me the ways and here goes once more my appeal
on the lines of your possible past ways."[40] In another, he says, "I need the
deep community with you for the end of my still intended work."[41]
Polanyi's late hopes were memories of the good Manchester years from
1950 until 1958. But Marjorie Grene recognized that the days for collaboration had passed.

GRENE AS POLANYI INTERPRETER

Already in some of the account above, I have suggested that Grene has been
a perceptive interpreter of Polanyi's philosophical thought. These suggestions need some amplification. Certainly, Grene knew, perhaps better than
anyone else, that Polanyi was a maverick, who gravitated to philosophy
only after early training as a physician, after working many years as a
renowned research chemist, and after writing about economics and politics.
Grene herself has been a maverick who sometimes produced humorous but
insightful and biting comments about professional philosophical inquiry and
academic philosophers. Some gems, in fact, are in her recent book, *A
Philosophical Testament*:

> In my experience, the professionalization of fundamental questions so often
> leads to triviality, that I hasten to neglect what, as a kind of professional, I
> suppose (or others suppose) I ought to read. . . . Most philosophers, I have
> found, live in a philosopher's room, where all apertures have been hermetically
> sealed against reality and only recent copies of a few fashionable philosophical
> journals are furnished to the inhabitants.[42]

Grene has appreciated many of the philosophical ideas of Polanyi as the
kind of insights an outsider can bring. She seems to have recognized
reasonably early that Polanyi's effort to create what he called a "post-
critical philosophy" was an effort that might transform many of the sup-
positions and interests of modern philosophers. This is a delicate point
worth exploring, for on the surface, it seems the height of pretension even
to aim at the kind of transformation of philosophy that Polanyi did aspire to.

Grene's several discussions of Polanyi's philosophical contributions
might be summarized by pointing to two themes Polanyi develops in his
Gifford Lectures and in *Personal Knowledge*. First, it is clear that Grene
appreciates what Polanyi dubbed in his Gifford Lectures the "restrictions of
objectivism."[43] Second, Grene's discussions of Polanyi's thought have
emphasized that when Polanyi called for "the rehabilitation of overt

belief,"[44] he was not advocating subjectivism and irrationality. To the contrary, Grene shows that Polanyi affirms the importance of reason. Further, his account of reason is a fallibilistic one that is grounded in a new appreciation of the inarticulate.

Grene met Polanyi at a stage in his life when he was already deeply engaged in an effort to understand how the scientific community worked. He already had published *Science, Faith and Society* which linked perception, specialized skills, tradition, and scientific discovery and provided perspectives on science that probably today would be called sociology of science. He was deeply troubled by what he took to be the real threats to science from social and political philosophy and practical politics on both the left and right. He had fled two countries by this time and was keenly aware of and disturbed by Stalinist persecution of scientists. He was unsatisfied with Marxist-Communist accounts of science that obliterated the distinction between pure and applied science and saw no virtue in theoretical matters. He had led a movement to resist "planned" science in England and Europe and had done a fair bit of analysis of the problems of centrally planned economies. Perhaps most importantly, Polanyi was thoroughly unsatisfied with what he thought contemporary Western philosophy and philosophy of science said about science. Nor did he like what scientists themselves often said about the nature of science. Polanyi thought that most philosophical accounts of science were insufficiently grounded in scientific practices and history. Such philosophers did not adequately treat scientific discovery and the matter of the positive development of scientific ideas. They were often naively empiricist. They misrepresented the fragile relationship between the scientific community and the political and cultural order and therefore left science as vulnerable as it had shown itself in the Soviet Union. In sum, the Western philosophical discussions of science did not provide any better justifications for science than did Marxist accounts. This is the context in which Polanyi took on the opportunity to give the Gifford Lectures.[45] It is also the context in which Polanyi and Grene joined forces.

It is something like this quickly sketched set of convictions that is the background for Polanyi's identification of the "restrictions of objectivism" as the problem his constructive philosophy must overcome. In the process of articulating his constructive alternative, with the help of Grene, Polanyi solidifies, also with the help of Grene, his case against the status quo. Admittedly, in the closer foreground, there lie some particular philosophical movements, figures, and ideas that Polanyi found quite objectionable. To put it very generally, views advanced by philosophers of science or epistemologists that ignore or deny the importance of the personal participation of the knower in shaping the known (or of the scientist in his or her discovery), Polanyi thought to be profoundly mistaken. Polanyi seems to use "objectivism" rather broadly and somewhat interchangeably with "positivism," which, Grene has pointed out, for Polanyi covers much more than the thought of Carnap.[46] But, as Grene has made clear, Polanyi thinks all of the "objectivists" and "positivists" fail to appreciate the role of the inarticulate; and what Polanyi is fundamentally concerned with is the paradoxical business of trying "to articulate the significance of the inarticulate."[47] Further, as Grene also has shown, the "objectivists" are what Polanyi refers to as "the critical tradition"[48] or as partisans of "the 'critical' thought style."[49] And "the critical tradition" is fundamentally misguided because it overvalues doubt and reduces all belief to subjectivity.

This brings me to the second theme of the Gifford Lectures and *Personal Knowledge* noted above, namely the "the rehabilitation of overt belief." Grene has been one of the clearest voices showing that what Polanyi is up to should not be read—as it often has been—as advocating subjectivism and irrationality. To clarify this matter, however, requires a review of a few other things Grene has discussed about Polanyi's thought. In the August 1957 preface (the original preface) to *Personal Knowledge*, Polanyi comments on the personal participation of the knower in the known and on his view that "personal knowledge" is not merely subjective but is an act of comprehension described as a "responsible act claiming universal validity."[50] In the June 1964 preface to the Torchbook Edition of *Personal Knowledge*, Polanyi identifies the objective of *Personal Knowledge* as "the task of justifying the holding of unproven traditional beliefs"; he points out that "more than forty declarations of belief" in the book are listed in the index under "fiduciary program."[51] Grene has confirmed that when she and her children were preparing this index that Polanyi "had specially requested that I stress all passages that showed the book to be a *credo*" and she contends that this reflects how "Polanyi himself set great store by the fiduciary programme."[52]

The "fiduciary program" is the key to Polanyi's early account of "personal knowledge" and Grene's publications on Polanyi have tried to explain in some detail the substance of this odd locution (i.e., the "fiduciary program" or, in the Gifford Lectures, the "fiduciary mode" and "fiduciary philosophy").[53] Grene has succinctly described the nature of the "fiduciary program" by pointing out that Polanyi's constructive argument in *Personal Knowledge* is based on an analogical foundation. Polanyi's method in his *magnum opus* "consisted essentially in broadening and stabilizing the interpretive circle through a series of analogies, by showing that human activities of many kinds are structures in the same hopeful yet hazardous fashion as those of science."[54] That is, Polanyi links his account of commitment in science to a broader range of human committed endeavor:

the account of commitment, expanded to a fiduciary programme, showed us science as one instance of the way in which responsible beings do their best to make sense of what is given them and yet what they, by their active powers, have also partly already enacted.[55]

Grene has explained Polanyi's notion of commitment in science and elsewhere as the human obligation "to fulfil demands made on us by something that both defines and transcends our particular selves"; she identifies it as "what Polanyi called the paradox of self-set standards. We accept with universal intent principles or patterns of behavior that we have at one and the same time both happened to develop and enacted as responsibly our own."[56]

Grene is right on target in her description of Polanyi's "fiduciary program." If I were attempting to supplement her assessment in any way, I would add one small point that I suspect that she assumes: Polanyi's account of commitment expanded to a fiduciary program presupposes a realist stance. That is, Polanyi believes that scientists (as well as other animals) can and do make contact with reality and our beliefs generated from that contact, though often wrong, are concerned essentially with understanding and making our way in a real world.[57]

Grene does an outstanding job of showing how Polanyi's ideas develop from interest in the "fiduciary program" to his more philosophically significant theory of tacit knowing. Polanyi starts philosophizing with "[t]he problem of the administration of science,"[58] and this leads him to seek an "epistemology of science"[59]; he works out his case for the justification of dubitable belief (that is, the "fiduciary program") in *Personal Knowledge*. Then, further reflection on unspecifiability leads Polanyi to the theory of tacit knowing. As I have noted in the last section, Grene acknowledges that even though she was working closely with Polanyi, she did not foresee this development. But she is quite clear that this development is Polanyi's most significant philosophical contribution; it is a "conceptual instrument for a one hundred and eighty degree reversal in the approach of philosophers to the problems of epistemology."[60] She affirms:

> Polanyi was not only right to call the distinction between two kinds of awareness the most important feature of *Personal Knowledge*; he was righter than he knew. For in the development of his thought that followed *Personal Knowledge*, it was the strengthening and extension of his conception of the tacit foundation of knowledge that, in my view at least, proved most fruitful.[61]

Grene also has been very keen on clarifying common misunderstandings of the theory of tacit knowing that Polanyi articulates in *The Tacit Dimension* and other essays in the period after *Personal Knowledge*. She warns against misconstruing Polanyi as merely arguing for a kind of subjectivism that claims only "that for any given cognitive statement or body of knowledge there is some residue that resists formulation."[62] She insists that in the theory of tacit knowing "what is essential is not the existence of the tacit, but the *relation* of the tacit to the explicit":

> The tacit component is not a residuum, but an indispensable foundation. What matters is not *that* there is something unspecifiable, for example, in science, but how unspecifiability works and what it accomplishes. It is the *function* of the tacit in all knowledge, however exact and "objective," that the tradition had neglected or denied, and that Polanyi's epistemology allows us to accept and articulate.[63]

She makes the same points elsewhere about the essentials of Polanyi's theory of tacit knowing when she says Polanyi offers an "ecological epistemology"[64] which is developed "in terms of his conception of knowledge as 'from-to' in structure."[65] Referring back to her earlier introduction to *Knowing and Being*, she points out that for Polanyi "all knowing . . . is orientation."[66] This, incidentally, is quite close to the way in which Grene, after sixty years as a philosopher, describes, in her 1995 book, her own approach to knowing.[67]

Grene's discussions of "the fiduciary program" and Polanyi's "from-to" structure of knowing are incisive and eloquent efforts to show why Polanyi focused on belief and what later are called tacit factors underlying and shaping all explicit knowledge. A fairly recent article, "The Personal and the Subjective," that was originally an address to a conference on Polanyi's thought, is perhaps, one of Grene's most direct efforts to show that Polanyi was not advocating subjectivism and irrationality; this is a particularly interesting essay both for its treatment of its main theme and because it articulates a "new" (that is, based on her rereading *Personal Knowledge* twenty years after the last reading) criticism of Polanyi's *magnum opus*. The essay is organized as a careful walk through the chapters of *Personal Knowledge* in which she argues that the distinction between the personal and the subjective is "fundamental to Polanyi's philosophy of science and, more generally, to his theory of knowledge."[68]

Grene thinks philosophers have often missed the careful delineation of Polanyi's distinction. Thus, she tries in the course of her discussion to "suggest reasons for the neglect of this work by the philosophical community in general. . . ."[69] What Grene shows is the way in which Polanyi's argument both sharply separates the personal and "subjectivity," understood in one sense, and yet links the personal, objectivity, and "subjectivity," understood in another sense. I cannot here tease out the intricacy of Grene's extended discussion, but the following sentence does capture much of her point: "The subjective, as just my passive experience, is other than the personal; but the personal contains an aspect of subjectivity, of mineness, in fusion with objectivity, the thrust toward something other than myself."[70] Grene goes on to argue that in her recent reading of *Personal Knowledge* she now suspects that Polanyi introduced, late in *Personal Knowledge*, "a third concept of subjectivity"[71] and that at least one footnote (what she dubs later a "treacherous footnote"[72]) on page 374 of *Personal Knowledge* is very disturbing. It implies that Polanyi, using this third concept of subjectivity ("commitments made to a mistaken system"[73]), advocated a position that undercut the emphasis upon commitment and fallibility that she regards as central to Polanyi's argument in his *magnum opus*. In *A Philosophical Testament*, she says, "I must admit, sadly, that Polanyi in part undercut the position he had developed in the account of implicit beliefs"[74] (that is, the subsection of *Personal Knowledge* [pp. 286–88] discussing implicit beliefs). To this reader, Grene makes an interesting case in her careful exegesis of *Personal Knowledge* that has ferreted out this conceptual problem, but it is a case based largely on one footnote. It is a case, at best, of inconsistency: it is the very sort of thing that Grene in her correspondence with Polanyi often pointed out to him and which he sometimes eliminated in other writing.

Grene's new question about subjectivity in *Personal Knowledge* cannot, in my mind, finally be completely separated from her more general dissatisfaction, made plain in publications for over twenty years, with the fourth section of *Personal Knowledge*, and particularly the last chapter of the book. What is objectionable here? There are many things, too many to discuss fully and therefore I will limit myself to only a few points.

Grene has never approved of the way Polanyi weaves into *Personal Knowledge* theistic hints and sounds "Christian over- or undertones."[75] Many of these notes or tones (Polanyi's use of the fall and redemption scheme, the analogy between Augustine's faith and the scientist's faith, and so on) come before the fourth section of the book, but certainly similar elements come back in the last chapter. Surely Grene is correct when she points out that Polanyi's weaving of a theistic theme did alienate philosophers of science.[76] But the same theistic elements that have led some philosophers to ignore and dismiss Polanyi also have intrigued other readers. Polanyi's comments on religious elements remain quite ambiguous.[77] They have inspired a veritable cottage industry of speculation about Polanyi's personal religious beliefs. But a postcritical perspective has also helped produce constructive reflection on religion as a constant in human affairs. Although Grene finds Polanyi's interest (which admittedly is sometimes an uncritical interest) in and openness to religion strange, that Polanyi had such interests is historically quite understandable. Polanyi participated, from 1944 until some time in the sixties, in discussion groups convened by the Christian activist J. H. Oldham. Here he interacted with many intellectuals interested in religion; Polanyi was quite clear that Oldham and his circle were important in shaping his ideas.[78]

Grene seems most upset by the prospect that a sense of historical contingency and fallibility might have been lost at the end of *Personal Knowledge* (particularly if one takes the "treacherous footnote" seriously) and that the discussion here becomes cosmologically overambitious. In her 1991 article, she says that she now suspects that Polanyi slipped into "ontological dogmatism" and she finds "the hopelessly anthropocentric evolutionism of the final chapter, as well as its closing Christian apologetic, must be discouraging, . . . to supporters of the model of commitment for epistemology and the philosophy of science."[79] Grene does allow that "Polanyi's later work on tacit knowledge, being cosmologically less ambitious, may help to correct this imbalance."[80] Clearly, Grene is very disenchanted with most of Polanyi's treatment of evolution and his discussion of emergence in his last section:

> while these chapters raise some important points against reduction in biology, the effort to locate *homo sapiens* as the apex of evolution is hopelessly mistaken. The ontological aspect of tacit knowing, proposed in *The Tacit Dimension*, being more limited in its import, is much more convincing. Commitment, however, has, I should think, to retain its precarious ontological position as the stance of a given embodied person, cast ephemerally into the flow of history, and pre- and posthistory, self-obliged to obey a calling that takes him (her) beyond the confines of subjective preference.[81]

As Grene well knows, much of the biology that Polanyi used in discussions of evolution and emergence is dated.[82] Nevertheless, I find important elements here that are germane to Polanyi's constructive philosophizing. I suspect that Grene worries too much about anthropocentrism.[83] Primarily, I understand these late chapters in terms of two related elements. First, Polanyi wanted to offer antireductionist criticisms of much of the thought in biology. Grene seems to accept this, although it remains unclear where she thinks antireductionist views in biology should lead us philosophically, if not in the direction Polanyi sketches. I suspect that Polanyi is basically correct when he remarks that evolution or philosophical accounts of evolution must make sense of what he terms, in *The Tacit Dimension*, an "afterthought to five hundred million years of pure self-seeking."[84] What he is pointing to in this phrase is the human "moral sense and our respect for it" which "presuppose an obedience to commands accepted in defiance of the immemorial scheme of self preservation. . . ."[85] Second, it seems that Polanyi's cosmological vision and rather grand rhetoric in Part Four of *Personal Knowledge* is part of—and largely inseparable from—the elements of a *Lebensphilosophie* that come to a conclusion here. The "fiduciary program" that is articulated in *Personal Knowledge* is woven from the beginning with a *Lebensphilosophie*. This also seems to me to be true of much that Polanyi says after *Personal Knowledge* about the theory of tacit knowing. One of the broader aims of Polanyi's constructive philosophy is to develop a panoramic vision of responsible humanity at home in the universe. He does this by recasting evolutionary theory as a story reflecting not only the kinship of living beings, but also the growth of complexity and the potential for responsibility among living beings. Polanyi angles to portray human beings as capable creatures responsibly serving self-set standards and challenged to explore the unknown. What Polanyi calls evolutionary emergence is an analog of discovery, and discovery, Polanyi thinks, is central to science. Discovery represents the paradigm case of human knowing (prefigured in perception), but also human excellence and responsibility.

As I see it, Polanyi's account of persons and personal knowledge ends on the note that human beings are members of communities of inquiry, like the scientific community. Human beings are called to use unspecifiable powers to indwell and discover aspects of reality that may transform them and their social companions. None of these final notes in Polanyi's discussion seems to me to move, as Grene fears, into a stance in which commitment loses "its precarious ontological position as the stance of a given embodied person, cast ephemerally into the flow of history, and pre- and posthistory, self-obliged to obey a calling that takes him (her) beyond the confines of subjective preference."[86]

SOME POLANYIAN THEMES IN GRENE'S PHILOSOPHICAL THOUGHT

To conclude, I shall comment very briefly on the connection between some of Grene's own philosophical work and that of Polanyi. I limit my reflection to Grene's *A Philosophical Testament*, a 1995 book that pulls together many of her interests. My general conclusions can be put succinctly: there is little in Grene's book that I find sharply at odds with the main themes in Polanyi's work; to the contrary, much that is in Grene's book develops ideas—sometimes in quite interesting ways—that are also found in Polanyi's writings. I have tried to show in the opening sections above that I believe Polanyi should be taken rather literally when he says that Grene has a share in anything achieved in the *Personal Knowledge* project. It is no surprise that *A Philosophical Testament* is a philosophical discussion that continues in the groove of that earlier project. Also, in the last section, I have tried to make clear that Grene regards the theory of tacit knowing as resolving a number of modern philosophical problems; *A Philosophical Testament* reflects this conviction.

Grene summarizes her lifelong philosophical interests at the beginning of *A Philosophical Testament* in this way:

> The problems that have interested me most persistently in philosophy have, at their core, to do with the problem of knowledge: *what is it to make a knowledge claim?* And since science is the most conspicuous example of knowledge in our society, it is a problem continuous with questions in the philosophy of science. The epistemic question, in turn, however, needs to be asked with due attention to historical contexts.[87]

A little later she expands this summary modestly to clarify that questions about knowledge in historical context mean knowing and being-a-person are bound together: "I have got myself entangled with epistemic questions in the context of questions about what persons can do. . . ."[88] In fact, Grene confesses at the end of *A Philosophical Testament* that she originally intended to title the book *Persons*:

> When I first thought of writing this book, in fact, I meant to call it *Persons*. But then it turned out to be about a cluster of other topics, focussed especially on matters related to the problem of knowledge, and bringing in a lot of what professional philosophers call necessary conditions for our ways of knowing, or claiming to know, but not very directly about the concept of the person as such. Still, "Persons" is the title I thought of for this concluding chapter. Now I'm not sure why. I've rambled on about evolution, and reality, and perception and symboling and heaven knows what.[89]

Grene gives here a brief but fair summary of topics covered in her book. Although her book is not tightly focused on a philosophical account of the person, it does treat the topic broadly, as she suggests, and insightfully by addressing, "epistemic questions in the context of questions about what persons can do." She touches the set of topics related to an account of persons—evolution, reality, perception, and symboling—that have interested her in her long career.

Chapter 1 in *A Philosophical Testament* directly treats epistemic questions in terms of "the traditional problem of the relation of knowledge to opinion and of the role of perception in knowledge."[90] Grene argues that the assumed categorical difference between knowledge and belief, running through the Western philosophical tradition since Plato, is problematic:

philosophers must give up the presumption that knowledge is necessary and universal and belief is contingent and parochial, and that the two have no connection with one another. As an alternative, Grene argues, we must "look at the knowledge claims we make and see how they are structured if we take them, not as separate from, but as part of, our system of beliefs."[91] If knowledge is a class of beliefs, what class is it? Grene does not wish merely to argue that knowledge is justified true belief. Like Polanyi, she thinks justification is the real issue; we must continue to make truth claims but as historical and bodily beings. Ultimately, she states her position as follows: "Knowledge is justified belief, rooted in perception, and depending for its possibility on the existence in reality itself of ordered kinds of things, including the kind that claims to hold justified beliefs."[92]

The formal discussion of the problem of knowledge in Grene's first chapter is a discussion sympathetic to Polanyi's positions. But it should be clear that Grene links her views not to Polanyi alone, and she shapes her discussions (somewhat unlike Polanyi) in ways that professional philosophers are likely to find familiar. In particular, this chapter and the entire book reflect the ways in which Grene has linked Polanyian themes with ideas developed further or somewhat differently by other thinkers. Grene has collected a whole set of figures who have reformulated philosophical problems on a post-Cartesian basis, the foremost of whom is Merleau-Ponty. Although she could never convince Polanyi that Merleau-Ponty was truly an ally, much of Grene's discussion seamlessly weaves together Merleau-Ponty and Polanyi, as this comment on belief and perception shows:

> As there is no sharp cut between belief and knowledge, so there is no sharp cut between perception and belief. Perception is both primordial—the most primitive kind of knowledge—and pervasive: the milieu, on our side, within which we develop such information as we can obtain, such beliefs as we can articulate, concerning the places, things and processes among which we live, move and have our being. That is, I think, something like what Merleau-Ponty meant by "the primacy of perception." It is also the necessary foundation for Polanyi's doctrine of tacit knowing.[93]

In her book, Grene also comments on several figures in the history of philosophy that she has earlier written about. But her comments here are circumscribed and directed to ways these figures support or fail to support an adequate account of persons. She proposes, for example, to transform key Kantian claims:

> But what if the T. U. A. were, neither on the one hand a mere fact . . . , nor on the other a self-knowing, thinking substance such as Descartes claimed to have

discovered by the Sixth Meditation, but something more ordinary: a real, live, breathing, perceiving, exploring *animal*, destined to seek, and find, its way in a real, existent, challenging, but up to a point manageable environment?[94]

All in all, however, Grene thinks Kant got many important things right or partially right: "What remains in all this of Kant's laboriously elaborated argument? Three essentials remain, it seems to me: the active role of the knower in making experience objective, the inexhaustibility of the known, and the indissoluble connection between knower and known."[95]

In her own words, what Grene has always struggled to articulate is an "ecological epistemology,"[96] a phrase, as noted above, she earlier applied to Polanyi:

It should also be clear by now that both the justified belief formula and the thesis of the primacy of perception must be understood in a realistic sense. We dwell in human worlds, in cultures, but every such world is itself located in, and constitutes, a unique transformation of, some segment of the natural world, which provides the materials for, and sets the limits to, its constructs.[97]

Or as she later puts the matter, in terms of a focus upon the living biological and social person:

To be alive, however, is to be somewhere, responding somehow to an environment, and in turn shaping that environment by our way of coping with it. To study human practices, including language, as forms of life is to study them as activities of the particular sort of animal we find ourselves to be.[98]

Certainly one of Grene's most interesting chapters is the one titled "Darwinian Nature." After earlier discussions of "being-in-the-world" in Heidegger, Sartre, and Merleau-Ponty, Grene shifts to what she terms "a very crude and overabstract run at what we might mean by 'Darwinian nature' as our habitat."[99] Her study of the literature of evolution has led her to believe that "a balance of structure and alternation are needed to produce any episode in evolution, much less the sweep of the whole history of life on earth."[100] The emphasis upon form has sometimes been almost totally repressed by the Darwinian emphasis upon change. In her chapter, Grene provides a long and detailed discussion of the role of chance in Darwinian nature. She emphasizes the importance of mutation or chance variation in evolution (since something must be heritable) and she points out parallels between modern biology discussions and responses to chance in the ancient philosophical tradition. Repeatedly, Grene emphasizes that her philosophical thinking has steadfastly sought to place humans in an evolving nature. Her probing of biology has always aimed to discern what difference biology makes in what can be said about human capacities. For Grene, philosophical questions about the nature of freedom emerge from within the Darwinian frame:

> it does appear that different organisms differ in the extent to which they can learn from experience. And it is that space for learning, and, where there are traditions, like ours of speaking our strange languages . . . it is that space for learning or tradition that sets the stage for freedom.[101]

She also works out ways to emphasize responsibility within the context of a steadfastly natural vision: "a human being is a biological individual capable of becoming a responsible person through participation in (or as one unique expression of) a culture."[102] She argues that human knowledge is fundamentally orientational, since in essence it is concerned with knowing one's way about in the world. And she believes "the most significant epistemological consequence of an evolutionary metaphysic" is "an unwavering and unrepentant realism."[103] All in all, "Darwinian Nature" is an interesting chapter that makes clear how Grene's study of biology has refined her philosophical commitments, and particularly her commitments about persons. It is not the broader type of cosmological discussion that is found in Part Four of *Personal Knowledge*, but it is true that Grene's account reflects the conviction that the problem of knowledge is what Polanyi called *ultrabiology*.[104] Grene does, like Polanyi, tie her account of nature to discussion of human freedom and responsibility.

Grene's discussion of Darwinian nature makes plain another important philosophical conviction: she is a realist. She defines her realist position as built on two theses: human beings exist within a real world and are surrounded by it and shaped by it, and human beings are real. These fundamental affirmations, she says, are essentially an effort to get beyond the subject-object split and the split between in-here and out-there which "makes nonsense of a world that is living, complicated, messy as you like, but real. I am myself one instantiation of that world's character, one expression of it, able also, in an infinitesimal way, to shape and alter it."[105] Grene argues that much of the philosophical discussion of realism is overly formalistic (in its conception of knowledge) and harbors misguided ideas about perception. Something like Polanyi's from-to account of knowledge is needed, Grene contends.

The final unit of Grene's book includes three chapters that she locates under the rubric "coping." These chapters are about "how we manage. As natural beings made what, or who, we are by the givens of a culture, how does each of us, as a responsible person, cope with the world around us, including, of course, our peers of the human world?"[106] Grene's chapter on

perception mines the work of J. J. and Eleanor Gibson; she accepts that
there is no strong distinction between sensation and perception and this
leads to a more relational and biological approach to perception. Perception
needs to be considered in terms of particular organisms in particular
environments. Where Grene takes this ecological approach to perception
ultimately links up nature and culture in the human world: "as human
reality is one version of animal reality, so human knowledge is one species-
specific version of the ways that animals possess to find their way around
their environments."[107]

Grene's discussion of culture per se offers a rich foray into philosophical anthropology where she makes use of works like Peter Wilson's *The
Promising Primate*. She outlines her basic ideas about "coping" through
human use of symbols. Through language, the products of language and
ritual, human groups set forth and enforce a particular system of symbols
and symbolic behavior which makes a group distinct. As symbol users, we
are the creatures who promise; we pledge in the present to certain behaviors
in the future. Symbols allow humans to take on social roles and create
social spaces and, in turn, to be shaped by them:

> Other animals of course have "houses" and territories; other animals of course
> assume various social roles. Ants, for example, build whole cities, and act as
> foragers, guardians or garbage collectors, as the case may be. But we
> systematically construct such places and such roles, and are constructed by
> them, through the activities of symboling that make our particular society—and
> thereby our particular selves—the societies and the selves that they historically
> proclaim themselves to be.[108]

The human lifestyle is distinguished from the life forms of other kinds of
organisms in that it must be characterized in terms of "systematic self-
creation."[109]

Grene comments upon pluralism and relativism at the end of her
discussion. She admits that she finds it "unlikely that there is one great
system of standards adherence to which defines humanity."[110] But Grene
thinks that Polanyi's ideas about commitment rescue one from the horns of
the dilemma occupied by skepticism and absolute dogmatism. She affirms
that her position (and that of Polanyi) is different from that of "careless
relativism."[111] Grene articulates an account of commitment that also
respects tradition and recognizes that, in Polanyi's language, human beings
at their best dwell in tradition in order to break out and reconstitute it:

> we know that we hold our beliefs, as, indeed, the Azande do theirs, responsibly
> and with universal intent. Given such self-knowledge, further, we can school
> ourselves to approach other cultures with understanding while recognizing our

own allegiance to our own. From within our own system of ritual, myth, and language we can describe and appraise the practices of others. Indeed, it is one of the characteristics of our particular tradition that, within limits, we are able to do this—as well as to appraise and amend some features of the tradition in which we ourselves were reared.[112]

Put in another way, what Grene is pointing to is what Polanyi calls the paradox of self-set standards, as she acknowledges:

We enter into obligations which compel us—not biologically or physically, but personally and morally—to act as we do. The intellectual passions that drive the life of science, the aspirations that compel the artist to paint or write or carve or build or compose: all these strivings express commitments, obligations to fulfil demands made on us by something that both defines and transcends our particular selves. . . . [T]he point is to recognize what Polanyi called the paradox of self-set standards. We accept with universal intent principles or patterns of behavior that we have at one and the same time both happened to develop and enacted as responsibly our own.[113]

Grene argues that a sense of obligation is fundamental not only to ethical decision making but to the quest for knowledge and this seems to be central to being a person in the strong sense of that term:

I do want to accept from Kant the notion of obligation, or, in Polanyi's terms, of commitment, as a necessary, and even central, ingredient of our existence as persons. To act freely, as a responsible center of decision and performance, is in some sense to give oneself, of one's own accord, to some principle or task or standard that obliges one's obedience or one's assent.[114]

Her effort to sort out exactly what constitutes a person turns, at the end of her book, to her own person. Surely this last note is vintage Grene:

When I am asked what my speciality is in philosophy, I stammer and say, "Oh, well, this and that." I admitted earlier that while I was semi-, or better, about ninety percent detached from my profession, I did a lot of jobs I was asked to do because I thought that if I refused any offers with any professional respectability I would disappear altogether. But I think I also suffer from a tendency to run at this and that and fail to stick with it. Self-knowledge is difficult; I don't know. It's also boring; I don't much care. For the moment, at any rate, this is the best I can do at seeing, or saying, how the question, what it is to be a person, was involved in such work as I have been doing over the years, and decades.[115]

As I suggested at the beginning of this section, *A Philosophical Testament* is not a conventional philosophy book with a concise, tightly woven argument. It is a wonderful wander through her life's work as Marjorie Grene sought to clarify her own convictions about what a person is. Perhaps this effort comes close to Polanyi's definition of philosophical reflection in *Personal Knowledge*:

> I believe that the function of philosophic reflection consists in bringing to light, and affirming as my own, the beliefs implied in such of my thoughts and practices as I believe to be valid; that I must aim at discovering what I truly believe in and at formulating the convictions which I find myself holding; that I must conquer my self-doubt, so as to retain a firm hold on this programme of self-identification.[116]

PHIL MULLINS

MISSOURI WESTERN STATE COLLEGE
AUGUST 2001

NOTES

1. Michael Polanyi, *Personal Knowledge: Towards a Post-Critical Philosophy* (New York: Harper Torchbook Edition, 1964), p. xv.

2. Marjorie Grene, *A Philosophical Testament* (Chicago and La Salle, Ill.: Open Court, 1995), p. 5. The details on Grene's early professional life that are summarized in the next paragraph come from *A Philosophical Testament*, pp. 5–6.

3. Grene does provide more details as *A Philosophical Testament* unfolds; some of these and small remarks in other writing are illuminating and are drawn on in this section.

4. Grene, *A Philosophical Testament*, p. 5.

5. Ibid.

6. This and a number of succeeding details noted in paragraphs below about Polanyi's life and his interface with Grene are gleaned from a draft chapter "Manchester 1933–1959" of a forthcoming Polanyi biography by the late physicist and friend of Polanyi, William T. Scott, and Martin X. Moleski, S.J. Scott began this biography shortly after Polanyi's 1976 death, and he generated an enormous body of material on Polanyi's life and his scientific and philosophical work. Included were interviews with Grene and 127 other Polanyi contemporaries. Scott's last several years of work on this biography, before his death, were years in which his capacities were diminished by Parkinson's disease. Moleski, with the help of Monika Tobin, Scott's able assistant, and others, is presently completing this biography. For almost twenty years, I have been at least loosely connected with this biography project, hoping it will ultimately come to closure in a substantive publication. I have long been interested in Grene's connection with Polanyi. As the notes in this essay will show, I have scoured archival materials in the Papers of

Michael Polanyi and have noted many comments in Grene publications. But certainly my debts to Scott and Moleski (especially Moleski's 1999 version of the manuscript) in these reflections are large. The forthcoming biography is cited hereafter as simply Scott and Moleski.

7.   These details about Polanyi's life and his meeting Grene draw upon some discussions in Scott and Moleski, pp. 322–40.

8.   Scott and Moleski (p. 340) suggest that after meeting Grene, Polanyi later gave her some of his writing and solicited her criticism. Grene perhaps also is pointing to this early experience when she wrote the following in 1977: "In 1950, when I first read his work and discussed with him the project that was to issue in *Personal Knowledge*, Polanyi was wrestling with the problem, how to justify dubitable beliefs." See Marjorie Grene, "Tacit Knowing: Grounds for a Revolution in Philosophy," *Journal of the British Society for Phenomenology* 8, no. 3 (October 1977): 165.

9.   Grene, *A Philosophical Testament*, p. 91.

10.   Details in this paragraph summarize some of the relevant discussion in Scott and Moleski, pp. 341–51. There are all sorts of archival materials in the Papers of Michael Polanyi which also support elements of the account here. For example, there are many magazine and newspaper clippings telling of Polanyi's visa problems in the McCarthy era.

11.   Scott and Moleski, p. 356.

12.   The Scott-Moleski (pp. 351–78) discussion of the Manchester years after the Gifford Lectures indicates Grene was several times in Manchester. The fact that there is limited correspondence in the Papers of Michael Polanyi for the period after Grene moved to Ireland in 1952 until near the time of the publication of *Personal Knowledge* perhaps also implies Grene and Polanyi had a good deal of direct contact. The poet and literary figure Elizabeth Sewell who was friends with both Polanyi and Grene and living in Manchester from 1955 to 1957 suggests that Grene was in Manchester frequently and worked very closely and directly with Polanyi during these two years (see the quotation below). "Memoir of Michael Polanyi" by Elizabeth Sewell in Box 46, Folder 12, Papers of Michael Polanyi in the Department of Special Collections of the University of Chicago Library. Future references and quotations from materials in this archival collection of Polanyi materials will be shortened to a box and folder reference to the Papers of Michael Polanyi. Quotations from this archival Polanyi material are used with permission of the University of Chicago Library's Department of Special Collections.

13.   These activities are suggested by the comment by Sewell quoted below. Correspondence from the period after the publication of *Personal Knowledge* (some quoted below) makes clear that Grene's role should be viewed as much larger than that of a junior editorial assistant. Grene valued what Polanyi was interested in and was a valuable contributor to this enterprise.

14.   The acknowledgments (p. xv) of *Personal Knowledge* indicate that in addition to Grene, Elizabeth Sewell, Edward Shils, J. H. Oldham, and Irving Kristol read the whole manuscript. Polanyi seems particularly to have valued the comments of his friend, the Christian social activist Oldham. Kristol was asked late in the game to help revise the style of Polanyi's writing, due to some comments by Oldham. For a more general discussion of Oldham's influence on Polanyi, and particularly his role in shaping *Personal Knowledge*, see my essay "Michael Polanyi and J. H. Oldham: In Praise of Friendship," *Appraisal: A Journal of Constructive and Post-Critical Philosophy and Interdisciplinary Studies* 1, no. 4

(October 1997): 179–89. Elizabeth Sewell indicates that in the two years she lived in Manchester that Polanyi wrote chapter drafts and simply handed them out, one after another, to her and Grene for response. See "Memoir of Michael Polanyi" by Elizabeth Sewell in Box 46, Folder 12 (typescript p. 14), Papers of Michael Polanyi. Scott and Moleski (p. 360) indicate that Polanyi sent the draft of the "Articulation" chapter (chapter 5 of *Personal Knowledge*) to Grene in December, 1954. See also the Grene comment below on this chapter.

15. See her comments in "Tacit Knowing: Grounds for a Revolution in Philosophy," p. 167.

16. Scott and Moleski, p. 358.

17. As I suggest later in this essay, I believe that sometimes Grene, with her historical background and philosophical attunement, was better able than Polanyi to situate Polanyi's ideas in their connection with the philosophical tradition and to see his allies. For example, in *A Philosophical Testament*, Grene has much to say (in chapters 4, 6, and 7) about the way Polanyi and Merleau-Ponty's perspectives fit nicely together. Grene's correspondence with Polanyi also reflects her effort to get Polanyi to see this connection, but both the letters and Grene's 1977 article ("Tacit Knowing: Grounds for a Revolution in Philosophy," p. 164 footnote) on Polanyi reflect that "Polanyi himself would never quite admit this convergence." Polanyi does, however, in several essays and books suggest—although he never explores—a connection with Merleau-Ponty. I suspect that this suggestion is the influence of Grene.

18. Grene, "Tacit Knowing: Grounds for a Revolution in Philosophy," p. 168.

19. Ibid.

20. "Memoir of Michael Polanyi" by Elizabeth Sewell, Box 46, Folder 12, Papers of Michael Polanyi, (typescript p. 16).

21. Ibid., (typescript pp. 14–15).

22. *Knowing and Being: Essays by Michael Polanyi*, ed. Marjorie Grene (Chicago: University of Chicago Press, 1969).

23. Marjorie Grene, "The Logic of Biology," *The Logic of Personal Knowledge: Essays Presented to Michael Polanyi on His Seventieth Birthday* (Glencoe, Ill.: The Free Press, 1961), pp. 191–205. There are no editors listed for this festschrift, although the acknowledgments (vii) includes reference to "editors." I strongly suspect Grene was involved in putting this book together.

24. Scott and Moleski (p. 388) report that Grene and Polanyi's friend, the historian Veronica Wedgwood, organized a London celebration.

25. Marjorie Grene, "Tacit Knowing and the Pre-Reflective Cogito," *Intellect and Hope: Essays in the thought of Michael Polanyi*, Thomas A Langford and William H. Poteat (Durham: Duke University Press, 1968), pp. 19–57. Grene certainly knew Poteat, a philosopher-theologian who became interested in Polanyi in the period in which *Personal Knowledge* was written. Archival correspondence suggests that Poteat and Grene may have originally planned jointly to edit a Polanyi collection such as *Knowing and Being*, which Grene eventually did edit.

26. Grene provides most of the details used here about the Study Group in the two essay collections, mentioned below, which she put together for the Study Group: *The Anatomy of Knowledge: Papers Presented to the Study Group on Foundations of Cultural Unity, Bowdoin College, 1965 and 1966* (Amherst: University of Massachusetts Press, 1969), pp. vii–xiii. *Interpretations of Life and Mind: Essays Around the Problem of Reduction* (New York: Humanities Press, 1971), pp. viii–xvi.

27. *The Anatomy of Knowledge*, p. x.

28. Included in *The Anatomy of Knowledge* is Grene's essay "Hobbes and the Modern Mind" (pp. 1–28) and in *Interpretations of Life and Mind* is "Reducibility: Another Side Issue?" (pp. 14–37). The latter volume was a *festschrift* from the Study Group that was presented to Polanyi on his eightieth birthday in 1971.

29. Letter from Grene to Polanyi, June 20, 1963. Box 16, Folder 1, Papers of Michael Polanyi.

30. This is very likely Polanyi's "Logic and Psychology," *The American Psychologist* 23 (January 1968): 28–40.

31. Letter from Grene to Polanyi, Oct. 28, 1967. Box 16, Folder 1, Papers of Michael Polanyi.

32. Grene, "Tacit Knowing: Grounds for a Revolution in Philosophy," p. 169. A bit later in the same article, she puts matters this way: "Yet Polanyi never realized, or ceased to realize, the subtlety of his own anti-reductivist position; he was so much concerned to refute the 'denial of consciousness' by behaviourists that he failed to recognize how essential to his own philosophical position was the insistence on embodiment as the framework of mentality" (p. 170).

33. See, for example, the discussion in Grene's letter to Polanyi, Feb. 8, 1968. Box 16, Folder 1, Papers of Michael Polanyi.

34. Grene, ed., *Knowing and Being*, p. xiv. Polanyi makes this interesting comment about Grene's "Introduction" to *Knowing and Being* in a letter to Grene, 22 Nov., 1968, Box 16, Folder 3, Papers of Michael Polanyi: "I thank you also for your introduction, which I read with great interest. You do make me gradually familiar with a number of toes on which I have trodden. It is fascinating."

35. Letter from Polanyi to Grene, 4 September 1960. Box 16, Folder 1, Papers of Michael Polanyi.

36. See for example the following for a rich set of literature recommendations: letter from Grene to Polanyi, Jan. 19, 1963. Box 16 Folder 1, Papers of Michael Polanyi.

37. See especially his 1964 new introduction, "Background and Prospect" to the reprint of his 1946 book *Science, Faith and Society* (Chicago: University of Chicago Press, 1964), pp. 7–19.

38. See, for example, letter from Grene to Polanyi, Sept. 17, 1969. Box 16, Folder 4, Papers of Michael Polanyi. Here she questions Polanyi's developing account of symbols and the diagrams he was creating to express his views.

39. Grene, "Tacit Knowing: Grounds for a Revolution in Philosophy," p. 168.

40. Letter from Polanyi to Grene, 29 August 1971. Box 16, Folder 7, Papers of Michael Polanyi.

41. Letter from Polanyi to Grene, 20 April 1973. Box 16, Folder 7, Papers of Michael Polanyi.

42. Grene, *A Philosophical Testament*, p. 176.

43. See the syllabus of the Gifford Lectures, First Series; this language is used in the precis of Lecture 6. Box 33, Folder 1, Papers of Michael Polanyi. The term "post-critical" (i.e., Polanyi's alternative philosophical position) goes back at least to this First Series, as this syllabus reflects. See the discussion in my recent essay, "The 'Post-Critical' Symbol and the 'Post-Critical' Elements in Polanyi's Thought," in *Polanyiana* 10, no. 1–2 (2001): 77–90, also on the *Polanyiana* web site at http://www.kfki.hu/chemonet/polanyi/0112/tartalom.html.

44. See the syllabus of the Gifford Lectures, First Series; this language is used in the precis of Lecture 6. Box 33, Folder 1, Papers of Michael Polanyi.

45. Most of the elements of the account given here are reflected in the 1963 new introduction, "Background and Prospect" (pp. 7–19), to the University of Chicago reprint of *Science, Faith and Society.*

46. Grene, *A Philosophical Testament*, p. 63. Grene also suggests that Polanyi sometimes characterized some contemporary philosophers whose ideas were actually akin to his own as "positivists."

47. Grene, *A Philosophical Testament*, p. 63.

48. Marjorie Grene, "The Personal and the Subjective," *Tradition and Discovery: The Polanyi Society Periodical* 22, no. 3 (1995–96): 11. (This article, Grene's address at a Kent State centennial conference on Polanyi's thought, also appeared in *Polanyiana* 2, no. 4 and 3, no. 1 (1992 and 1993): 43–55) Grene is pointing to Polanyi's language in *Personal Knowledge*, p. 266. The "critical tradition" for Polanyi is in tension with "post-critical philosophy." In an unpublished November 1958 lecture titled "The Outlook of Science: Its Sickness and Cure" (Box 33, Folder 11, Papers of Michael Polanyi), Polanyi indicates "post-critical philosophy" is not "guided by the principle that doubt is the solvent of error which leaves behind truth." He implies that the "critical tradition" includes those who think otherwise, and he includes in his list Descartes, Hume, Kant, Mill, and Russell. But Polanyi does not seem to think primarily of Kant when he thinks of "critical" philosophy.

49. "The Personal and the Subjective," p. 11. Grene is pointing to Polanyi's language in *Personal Knowledge*, p. 265.

50. Polanyi, *Personal Knowledge,* p. xiv.

51. Polanyi, *Personal Knowledge*, p. ix.

52. Grene, "Tacit Knowing: Grounds for a Revolution in Philosophy," p. 167.

53. See the syllabus of the Gifford Lectures, First Series; this language is used in the precis of Lecture 6. Box 33, Folder 1, Papers of Michael Polanyi. There are indications Polanyi was already discussing "the fiduciary mode" in 1948 before he met Grene. See my discussion of Polanyi's correspondence with J. H. Oldham about his paper "Forms of Atheism" prepared for a December, 1948 Oldham gathering (Phil Mullins, "Michael Polanyi and J. H. Oldham: In Praise of Friendship," p. 184).

54. Grene, "Tacit Knowing: Grounds for a Revolution in Philosophy," p. 167.

55. Ibid., p. 167.

56. Grene, *A Philosophical Testament*, pp. 169–70.

57. In another essay ("The Personal and the Subjective," p. 10), Grene is quite clear about Polanyi's realism: "Polanyian personal knowledge, rooted in society and demanding active submission to a tradition, even if sometimes in partial rebellion against it, is nevertheless knowledge: a claim to be in touch with a reality beyond and independent of the claimant." There has recently been an extended discussion of Polanyi's realism in the Polanyi literature and Grene's view has sometimes been invoked; see *Tradition and Discovery:The Polanyi Society Periodical* 26, no. 3 (1999–2000).

58. Grene, "Tacit Knowing: Grounds for a Revolution in Philosophy," p. 165.

59. Ibid., p. 166.

60. Ibid., p. 168.

61. Ibid.

62. Ibid., p. 165.

63. Ibid. Working out the theory of tacit knowing ultimately, as Grene also points out in this essay, modifies the way in which the "fiduciary program" should

be understood: "The point is, I now see, that the fiduciary programme is supported, not so much by its expansion through analogical reasoning, as by the foundation common to all its instances, the foundation of tacit knowing"(p. 168).

64. Grene, "The Personal and the Subjective," p. 8.

65. Ibid. See also Grene's discussion in *A Philosophical Testament*, p. 122, where she summarizes Polanyi's view this way: "All knowledge has a 'from-to' structure: it is the groping *of* embodied beings *toward* the understanding of something in the world that surrounds them." In "Tacit Knowing: Grounds for a Revolution in Philosophy"(p. 169), Grene sharply criticizes (with good justification, in my view) Polanyi's effort, in a late essay, to modify his "from-to" structure of knowing by distinguishing "from-to" from "from-at."

66. Ibid.

67. In *A Philosophical Testament* (p. 108), Grene says: "I am myself given to remarking that all knowledge is orientation. Maybe orientation isn't just obeying orders, but knowing one's own way about. Again, it's perhaps a matter of accepting a less reductive version of Darwinism. Orientation in an environment can be a pretty subtle and complicated matter. And of course in the human case it is all sorts of social subworld, practical skills, games, sciences, in which we learn to find our way."

68. Grene, "The Personal and the Subjective," p. 6.

69. Ibid.

70. Ibid., p. 13.

71. Ibid., p. 14.

72. Grene, *A Philosophical Testament*, p. 171.

73. Ibid., p. 170.

74. Ibid.

75. Grene, "The Personal and the Subjective," p. 14.

76. Ibid.

77. I confess that I once tried, with only limited success, to sort out what Polanyi's account of religious meaning is in certain important sections of *Personal Knowledge*. See Phil Mullins, "Religious Meaning in Polanyi's *Personal Knowledge*," *Polanyiana* 2, no. 4 and 3, no. 1 (1992 and 1993): 75–83.

78. See my extended discussion of the influence of Oldham and his circle in "Michael Polanyi and J. H. Oldham: In Praise of Friendship."

79. Grene, "The Personal and the Subjective," p. 15.

80. Ibid.

81. Ibid., p. 14.

82. In 1977 in "Tacit Knowing: Grounds for a Revolution in Philosophy" (p. 168), Grene remarked, "And as I have learned a little more about evolutionary theory, both its subtleties and its limitations, I have grown more sceptical about cosmologies of emergence in any form." In her 1995 *A Philosophical Testament* (p. 171), she notes in passing "Polanyi's gross misunderstanding of evolutionary theory."

83. As Grene notes in *A Philosophical Testament* (p. 166), "there are diminishing degrees of tacit participation, and diminishing degrees of meta-phoricity. . . . " With Diotima, Grene goes on to affirm we are "makers, creators of a human world" and "people who live by symboling" (p. 167). However, Polanyi's efforts in this regard, in the last section of *Personal Knowledge*, for Grene seem to go beyond the pale.

84. Michael Polanyi, *The Tacit Dimension* (Garden City, N.Y.: Anchor Books,

1967), p. 52.
85. Ibid.
86. Grene, "The Personal and the Subjective," p. 14.
87. Grene, *A Philosophical Testament*, p. 3.
88. Ibid., pp. 4–5.
89. Ibid., p. 173.
90. Ibid., p. 9.
91. Ibid., p. 15.
92. Ibid., p. 27.
93. Ibid., p. 25.
94. Ibid., p. 42.
95. Ibid., p. 44.
96. Ibid., p. 26.
97. Ibid.
98. Ibid., pp. 63–64.
99. Ibid., p. 106.
100. Ibid., p. 94.
101. Ibid., p. 99.
102. Ibid., p. 107.
103. Ibid., p. 110.
104. Ibid., p. 47.
105. Ibid., p. 114.
106. Ibid., p. 173.
107. Ibid., p. 144.
108. Ibid., p. 164.
109. Ibid., p. 165.
110. Ibid., p. 167.
111. Ibid., p. 168.
112. Ibid., pp. 168–69.
113. Ibid., pp. 169–70.
114. Ibid., p. 181.
115. Ibid., p. 188.
116. Polanyi, *Personal Knowledge*, p. 267.

REPLY TO PHIL MULLINS

Phil Mullins has recalled a most significant period in my philosophical history, a half century ago. I am touched, once again, by the tribute he quotes from the preface to *Personal Knowledge.* Polanyi was wrong in saying that I had abandoned my own career to devote myself to his work; at the time I had no career. But it is certainly true that I was deeply committed to the development of the fiduciary program, and impressed, also, by the conception of tacit knowing that issued from it.

Mullins is also probably correct in believing that my years of working with Polanyi have continued to influence my thought, and writing, more than I have recently recognized. If I now call my view of knowledge "ecological," I am thinking not so much of the theory of tacit knowing as of the Gibsons' ecological psychology, which, of course, did not exist at the time. But Gibsonian perception is also tacit knowing; there is certainly a kinship between the two views. But I have also developed interests that were, so to speak, decidedly extra-Polanyian. Once I returned to teaching, I found myself fascinated by various figures, and periods, in the history of philosophy, subjects that held little interest for Polanyi. When I was working with him, I did indeed try to assist him with historical information when it was needed; but he thought of history from a scientist's point of view—as a source from which to cull tidbits, but no more. Further, when I looked more carefully than I had at that time into the literature of evolutionary biology, I found Polanyi's argument (of Part IV of *Personal Knowledge*) even more shocking than I had originally thought it; so that interest, too, took me away from his work. But I am grateful to Phil Mullins for recalling that long-ago collaboration.

Mullins is again correct in saying that I have understressed Polanyi's realism. It is certainly a feature of his argument that I still heartily subscribe to. And, despite my misgivings about Polanyi's treatment of evolutionary theory, I still appreciate his dubbing epistemology, or philosophy of science, "ultrabiology." When we reflect on the nature of epistemic claims, we are indeed studying the behavior of some peculiar animals, in this case, a subset of our own kind. On the other hand, I do still distrust that "treacherous footnote." "Post-critical" should not mean dogmatic, and it's in that direction that the classification of systems of belief in Part IV seems to me to be going. That does not mean that I never had, or do not have, some sympathy for Polanyi's Augustianism. I do believe that faith is prior to reason—only I don't believe it has to be faith held dogmatically, let alone faith in the supernatural. It's the difficult position described in the chapter on the critique of doubt that we ought to try to maintain.

M. G.

2

Jacquelyn Ann K. Kegley

THE CONTEXTUAL HUMAN PERSON: REFLECTIONS ON THE PHILOSOPHY OF MARJORIE GRENE

This reflection on the philosophical work of Marjorie Grene focuses on the concept, "the contextual human person." Providing an adequate explication of "person," in my judgment, is a necessity today for resolving a number of philosophical and practical questions. In fact, almost twenty-five years ago Grene insightfully identified this issue as a key one for Western philosophy.[1] It is ironic and puzzling that philosophers still have difficulties developing an adequate concept of "person," but this reexamination of Grene's philosophy may well provide a solid foundation for moving the question forward. Further, focusing on the concept of person in Grene's philosophy allows us to explore a number of other important themes in her work. These include her bold anti-Cartesian turn, her interpretation of Kant in a "new key," and her affirmation of an unwavering and unrepentant realism. Above all, the concept of an "embodied and contextual person" is central to Grene's sketch of an anti-reductionistic, philosophical anthropology, which stresses temporality, historicity, and a fundamental continuity with, yet difference from other members of the animal kingdom. I believe that these ideas, among others, are important to an adequate understanding of human person.[2]

THE PERSON AS BIOLOGICAL AND CULTURAL: A BEING IN AND WITH THE WORLD

Any exploration of Grene's concept of the human person or her philosophy in general must begin with her decidedly anti-Cartesian turn and all its implications. Again and again Grene asserts the need to start afresh on a more comprehensive, anti-dualistic foundation.[3] Rejecting the *cogito* as the starting point in philosophy, she argues that reflection must begin with "the rootedness of 'mind' in reality" and "the very structure of persons as being-in-a-world."[4] Grene's anti-Cartesian stance denies both sides of the Cartesian split, namely, the Cartesian mathematicizing mind *and* the Cartesian mathematicized matter.[5] In place of the dead end of dualism Grene asserts a marvelously fecund both/and position, one emphasizing that the human person has a place *within nature* and within that place *in culture.* This allows Grene, as she notes, to escape what so many recent philosophical expositions of self, mind, and person have done, that is, reduce these reflections to purely empirical explanations within a scientific discipline, for example, behaviorist psychology, neurophysiology, or evolutionary biology.[6] Grene eschews reductionist materialism, but she is also clear that human persons are physical/biological organisms and share many relationships and continuities with other living organisms. Grene also identifies important distinctions between humans and other animals, but she makes these distinctions without a dualistic framework and without any mysterious *élan vital* or focus on a narrow understanding of "mind" or a stress on "consciousness."[7]

In exploring the proper place of human persons within the whole of animal nature, Grene is clear that the Cartesian/Christian dichotomy between *animus* and *anima* is a superficial account of human nature and a flagrant misrepresentation of the remainder of the animal creation. She writes: "[N]o theory which makes human thought and feeling differ *toto coelo* from the thought and feeling of other creatures can ever be accepted by anyone who has had any ordinary experience of animals at all."[8] She also finds such a view contradicted by empirical facts and studies of certain species. The crucial question for Grene is this: "How can we retain a sense of [human] uniqueness . . . without resorting to the implausible and barren conception of a Christian-Cartesian soul split off from all natural kinship?"[9]

The first step in exploring this question, argues Grene, is to focus on the primary life world of humans and other animals and not on mathematicized nature, which is a construct of science and of Western culture. To develop a rich philosophy of "living things" Grene turns to the work of zoologist, Adolf Portmann.[10] Portmann studies the "primary life world," the whole range of perceived and perceptible phenomena available to the sense organs of living beings, and sees it as a level of reality based on the physical-chemical, but not exhausted by this level and with patterns and laws of its own. Further, Portmann asserts the inadequacy of any neo-Darwinian reduction of all organic phenomena to their functions. He does not believe that the whole detail of behavior and patterns of living organisms can be explained in selective and functional terms. Grene agrees with this view and states that it is wise "to restrict evolutionary theory to what it can cleanly and clearly handle: changes in relative gene frequencies."[11] Further, says Grene, life cannot be reduced to "'nothing but' statistical variations in the gene pools of populations."[12]

The theory of evolution is an important ingredient of Grene's philosophical anthropology, but unlike more recent versions, those of Dennett and Dawkins,[13] she denies that adaptation is the sole explanatory principle of all organic phenomena. Drawing on the work of Portmann, Grene points to two important characteristics of all living beings, including humans, namely, what he calls "display" and "centricity." All living beings have a way of being in the world: they are "centers of perceptions, drives and actions," of "doing and letting be." This does not mean, notes Grene, that consciousness or mind is being predicated of all animals. Rather, consciousness, as humans experience it, is only one form of centricity. "Centricity" expresses the "fact that organisms are centers of metabolism and development, of ordered reaching out toward an environment and taking in from it, of birth and death. It is this centered dynamic, dependent as it is on the existence of *individuals*, that *is* characteristic of all life and is *not* characteristic of inorganic phenomena."[14] It is this centricity of living beings, argues Grene, that gives lie to making adaptation the sole explanatory principle for living beings. A "use," says Grene is not only *for* something—in biological phenomena, for survival—but also to *someone*. The immense variety of biological mechanisms for self-maintenance, argues Grene, is "all . . . instrumental in relation to the intrinsic value of the entities so maintained."[15]

Grene finds other aspects of Portmann's work important to her view of the human person. Portmann, notes Grene, not only refuses to explain all living existence by the concepts of micromutation and selection, but he emphasizes the "rootedness of man's social life in his *biological* nature."[16] This is, in fact, Grene's own view, namely, that human beings are at home in the natural world and are "*biologically* formed to be *cultural* animals."[17] Crucial to her philosophical anthropology is Portmann's notion of *social gestation*. Portmann argues that only humans have a pattern of premature sociality and thus in addition to the development toward adult form which occurs in the uterus, there must be an additional twelve months of development in the "social uterus of maternal care."[18] Upright posture, speech, and rational action are developed in this period. There is, then, for the human species a long period of apprenticeship and the gradual assumption of responsible adulthood. Grene writes:

In short, the whole biological development of a typical mammal has been rewritten in our case in a new key: the whole structure of the embryo, the whole rhythm of growth, is directed, from first to last, to the emergence of a culture-dwelling animal—an animal not bound within a predetermined ecological niche like the tern or stag or the dragonfly or even the chimpanzee, but, in its very tissues and organs and aptitudes, born to be *open to its world,* to be able to accept responsibility, to make its own the traditions of a historical past and to remake them into an unforeseeable future.[19]

This notion of "social gestation" is a key aspect of Grene's own concept of the human person because it helps found her idea of humanity as an "achievement," the achievement of a natural being of an internalized cultural aspect. During the period of "social gestation," human young, in their utter dependency, assimilate the structure of their human community and its culture, which thus becomes internalized in the life history of each individual human person.[20] The concept of "social gestation" allows, I believe, a better handling of some of the problems of thwarted human development such as is displayed in antisocial and criminal behavior or in so-called "wolf children" without falling into genetic determinism. This notion will be discussed more shortly.

Drawing on the work of Helmuth Plessner,[21] a German philosophical anthropologist, Grene adds several other unique dimensions to human existence, in contrast with other animal life. The first of these is Plessner's concept of "positionality." Positionality has to do with the relationship of an organism to its internal and external environment. This relationship is one of independence from that environment and communication with it. Living beings, argues Plessner, are directed to their environments and yet also receive back from it. The rhythm of life is one of assimilation and dissimilation, adaptation and adaptability, passivity and activity. The degree of conformity to environment varies among living beings. Thus, the *open* form of plant life is unidirectional; the biological cycle flows in the same direction as the environment. Animal life, in contrast, is *closed form, in opposition to the environment*; the animal is always wanting, always essentially unfulfilled.[22]

Humans, however, argues Plessner, have *eccentric positionality.* Animals live *into* a center of experience and out *from* the center, but humans are also the center itself. Life out of the center has become reflexive. Humans are still bound by their animal nature and yet also detached from it. Plessner writes: "Positionally there is a threefold situation, the living thing is body, is in its body (as inner life . . .) and outside the body, as the point of view from which it is both (body and inner life). An individual, which is characterized positionally by this threefold structure, is called a *person*. It is the subject of experience, of its perceptions and its actions, of its initiative. It knows and wills."[23]

Plessner's notion of positionality helps Grene explicate her concept of the person as an "organized living body." This is because positionality is a boundary structure such that a living being both has its body and is its body. In the *open* form of plant life, this principle is relatively submerged, but with the *closed* form of animal life the distinction is sharpened. With a *closed* form, argues Grene, the body becomes a "lived body," a "*Leib*," possessed by a subject distinct from the physical body which it nevertheless is. Animals have a *subject-having* relation to their body, which gets stabilized through a central nervous system. This central nervous system, representing the center, the subject, mediates between the animal "*as* its body and the environment as external, as all that is *not* 'itself'."[24] Plessner argues that at this level of biological organization, "the animal achieves *self*hood. It becomes a *me*, though not an I. It *has* a body and *is* a self, but does not yet *have* a self, to which in turn it can take a stand in reflective awareness."[25] When it does this, it achieves a new level of existence called *personhood*.

However, only humans achieve this level of existence. Animal individuality is that of a me and not an I. Its center is wholly absorbed into the here and now. Nonhuman animals, argues Plessner, perceive *things*, not objects. Things are relative to drives and to uses, for example, they are lures, playthings, enemies, friends, and so on, and *not* entities understood in and for themselves.[26] Animals, in Plessner's view, lack a sense of *negativity*, a certain kind of distance between self and world. He also believes, however, that animals, unlike plants, do have insight and memory. Both are concrete and focused on the here and now. There is also learning and *spontaneity* in the animal kingdom. As against plants, Plessner believes that animals have a new dimension of freedom. In its here-and-now, as the body it has, the animal *acts* over against the environment, which both threatens it and presents to it opportunities for living. Animals have what Plessner calls "frontality." As an agent it confronts its world. "It takes not only a place, but a *stand*."[27] Grene finds Plessner's schema for animal life a significant alternative to the usual positions on animal intelligence. Grene believes that Plessner's account of the me-body structure of animal experience "brilliantly and with absolute cogency . . . sets off animal from plant life on the one hand, and on the other human from animal."[28]

I agree with Grene on this estimate and believe that the development of this kind of position on animal nature and intelligence would help philosophy of mind advance much more fruitfully than it has up to now. Credence is given to the validity of a concept of "animal mind" and to animal problem solving and thinking, without attributing too much cognitive ability to animals. In addition, the notion of human social gestation allows a further distinction between us and the rest of the animal kingdom while also explaining the somewhat human quality of some animals, like dogs and cats, who have experienced, in some manner, human cultural gestation. Finally, the stress on goal formation, desires, "frontality," and a subject-relation to body, provides a more solid foundation for explicating a notion of "animal rights." It allows an "intentional" stance toward certain animals without falling into Dennett's functionalism.

Only humans, then, in Grene's view, achieve the status of person, and their existence has an interesting threefold structure, that of outer world, an inner world, and a shared world. Humans live as animals do in an environment of which the body is center, yet, unlike other animals, the inner world of the human person has two aspects. There is the flow of experience, of sensations, of feelings, of mental events, which go on whether we are aware of them or not, and there is an I which can stand apart from this lived inner experience. This dual nature of the "inner world" of humans, accounts, argues Grene, for something both the empiricists and rationalists fail to explain, namely, the "vast range of unconscious mental life" that is part of human life. Such a distinction of the "inner world" of persons also makes sense, I believe, for a view of the "human self" not as a given, but as an achievement. The human ability to understand negativity and to gain distance from things experienced allows the development of a self "in contrast" to that which is around them, a "something other than." It allows a person to develop a narrative and a life story through interpretation of events. This notion of self has been developed most cogently, I believe, by the American philosopher Josiah Royce, who sees human self-consciousness arising out of a process of social contrast, *via* the contrast between what is and what is not mine, between the self and the not-self.[29] Royce also dismisses the argument from analogy as a basis for knowledge of other minds and sees the contrast process as the foundation for knowing that other minds exist. He defines another mind as "a system of ideas which is intelligible in itself but which certainly isn't mine."[30] Both Royce and Grene believe one must escape from the egocentric predicament engendered by a "perceptual" theory of mind.

Grene also believes that the notion of a dual human inner world explains why humans, as the existentialists insist, are both active and passive, free and bound.[31] This view of the human being helps us see why the freedom/determinism conflict is not a "pseudo-problem." It is, argues Grene, an insoluble problem, a both/and ambiguity of human existence as it is.[32] I believe this understanding of the free will problem an excellent and needed supplement to that espoused by Daniel Dennett in his book, *Elbow Room*.[33]

A third aspect of human existence, in addition to an outer world and a dual inner world, is a shared world, the *Mitwelt*. Human beings become fully human, fully persons, through human fellowship. Animals, we know, have social lives which serve to maintain and enrich their existence, but above and beyond this, human animals, as persons, are both I and we; they become an I through being a "we." With eccentric positionality, humans, unlike other animals, can stand against and detach from self, and thus they also have the power of putting self in place of any other person and even of any other living things. This ability is crucial to their "social gestation" and to establishing their social and cultural context. Humans can imitate and take on roles and this plays a key part in their self-development. Further, in taking on the role of others, they can learn to sympathize and, to a certain extent, "walk in the shoes of another." This is why humans, using Dennett's terminology, take an "intentional stance" toward other living beings. In Grene's terms, humans take "the first essential step beyond the positionality of animal life to see eccentricity, to see personhood, everywhere."[34] This ability also allows human beings to take and develop a "moral stance."

Indeed, the shared world aspect of human positionality establishes another key characteristic of human experience and mental activity, namely, the ability to grasp true universals. Grene writes:

> And, it is, Plessner argues, constitutive of a person to be both I and we, to be I through being we. Nor is the "we" entailed here any particular empirical we, not even that of mother and child or husband and wife. It is communion as such that constitutes the person: "as a member of the shared world, each man stands where the other stands." Only as the product of such sharing, moreover, is there *mind* (*Geist*), and its product, objectivity. The opposition of the I to it, the understanding that what confronts me is capable of being elsewhere or anywhere, in other words, the grasp of true universals which makes scientific knowledge possible: this understanding . . . is constituted . . . by the radical togetherness that is the very being of the person as such.[35]

The *Mitwelt* aspect of human positionality, argues Grene, is that which grounds the human ability to deal with true universals. It also sets the human person out as a being capable of submitting self to universal standards "whether for the objectification of perceptual experience that makes the external world knowable, or for the universalization of inner experience that generates moral law."[36] The human person described in Plessner's work, says Grene, is a person who unites all three Kantian questions: "he is the agent as such, whether of knowing, of doing or of hoping."[37] We will return to this assertion shortly when we discuss Grene's reinterpretation of Kant.

To flesh out further Grene's understanding of the proper place of human beings in the natural world, we turn to her essay, "People and Other Animals."[38] Grene develops a sketch of her philosophical anthropology in the context of a critical reflection on the modified dualistic position of Sir John Eccles who posits a three-world theory of reality.[39] Rather than a "Physical Object World," Grene identifies the "Natural World," in order to indicate that "the classes of living things, though included as subclasses in the class of physical systems, are nevertheless so organized as to differ from other physical systems in important ways."[40] Grene is clear that the difference has nothing to do with some "new stuff" added to physical systems. Rather, the key is "relational order," that is, "molecules so ordered as to generate systems that function in some new and interesting fashion, and these new and interesting fashions constitute higher levels of organization within the physical system in question."[41] Within the class of living things, Grene places two more distinct subclasses. The first is the class of learners which is the class of organisms "not wholly dependent throughout their lives on their packet of genetic information, but able to increase and alter information through experience."[42] Within the class of learners is yet another distinct subclass, that of *Homo sapiens.*

Grene now makes a radical break with any strictly hierarchical structure of natural reality by arguing that to talk about the unique organization of the world of *Homo sapiens* is already to talk about the "World of Persons" and the "Social World." Further, the "World of Persons" is not the world of merely subjective experience nor is "personhood" a special kind of "thing." Rather, as indicated earlier, it is something human organisms achieve in the period of social gestation, described by Grene as the "year of the social uterus." And the "Social World," the world of culture, is already implicated in the Natural World in its subclass of *Homo sapiens* because human infants become persons by *participation* in culture or the Social World in the year of the social uterus. And the Social World is *both* natural and *conventional.* This world, writes Grene, is

> *objective* in the sense that it is what the human beginner finds himself *in*; it surrounds him as surely and as necessarily as the natural environment surrounds any organisms. But it is also *conventional* in that it is man-made. . . . This social or cultural world then includes: first and most fundamentally languages, then other symbol systems—religions, art, cognitive systems, including theories, problems, arguments, systems of morality, as well as all the institutions, political, social, and economic, in which we live, move and have our being.[43]

Thus, Grene's world is not hierarchical, as it appears to be for Eccles and for Dennett, who speaks of a "Tower of Generation."[44] Rather the

World of Persons is a mediating world with interactive relations between both the Natural World and the Social World. The human person is in all three worlds at once. This fact also changes the nature of each of the three worlds. Thus, the Natural World becomes "personalized." Persons, like animals, are embodied and functioning physical systems; however, through their participation in culture, they personalize their bodily and physical nature. In Grene's words, a developed human being is "at one and the same time a *personalization* of nature and an *embodiment* of culture."[45] The key differentiation of human organisms from other animals is not, for Grene, the possession of some new entity called "soul" or "mind," but rather the power of detachment from the biological and physical which is the achievement of personhood through the *embodiment of a culture*. Grene writes:

> The achievement of the eccentric position of man, of *each man*, is dependent on the artifacts of culture through participation in which and in expression *of* which he achieves that position. In other words, just as much as a normally functioning central nervous system, an ongoing culture is a necessary, though not a sufficient condition, for the achievement of humanity. . . . [O]ver and above the novel and interrelated anatomico-physiological structures that make personhood possible, such as cerebralization, the capacity for upright posture, the eye-hand field and so on: what we have over and above this is *the ordered relation of an achievement—personhood—to an artifact—the social world of a culture.*[46]

In sum, humans have a unique characteristic which Grene calls "*natural artificiality*."[47] *Homo sapiens* achieve humanhood and personhood by relying on a complex network of artifacts: language and other symbolic systems, social conventions, tools, and so on, which are extensions of self, but which the self actualizes in a personal life. Further, human participation in the natural world is, to a larger degree, always mediated by the world of culture. The Social World, the man-made world through which humans develop as persons, permeates all experiences of the Natural World, all seeing, hearing, and so on.

This view of the human person's place in nature has profound implications for epistemology, and Grene has worked out a number of these. Indeed, she states the problem of knowledge in a unique manner when she writes: "Only *persons* can succeed in knowing anything. Therefore there can be no knowledge unless there are persons."[48] As already discussed above, the shared world aspect of human positionality allows human persons to grasp universals and to utilize standards in various areas of human endeavor. The very "objectivity" of human knowledge is founded in the fact that human persons are at once in all three worlds: the

Natural World, the World of Persons, and the Social World. Grene develops this notion in her reinterpretation of Kant in a "new key." Kant has made, argues Grene, an incontrovertible discovery, namely, the role of agency in knowledge. Human experience is only possible, argues Kant, through categorization. Yet, Kant's analysis fails, believes Grene, because for him the orderliness of nature rests on the Transcendental Unity of Apperception, which is a bare possibility that I could attach to any experience an "I think." Grene wishes to challenge the adequacy of the Transcendental Unity of Apperception to accomplish its work.

She proposes that one turn instead to a different unifying idea behind the categorization of experience, a real live, bodily-sentient, historical being, the human person who participates in all three worlds. If one does this, Grene argues, three important things are accomplished. First, "the *synthetic a priories* that make objective experience possible are historicized. Each society, each group of language-users, in a limited way each human being, has *its* categories and principles."[49] Secondly, the "I think" of the Transcendental Unity becomes the activity of a live, thinking, hoping, desiring being, and thus loses its septic isolation from human action, from *praxis*. Cognition becomes *one* kind of praxis among others having to do with "I feel," "I ought," and "I hope." Theoretical knowledge, morality, art, and religion are all praxes, all the same in that these are ways in which human persons, relying on self-imposed rules for working in symbol-systems, try to make sense of their surroundings.[50] A final consequence of Grene's transposition of the Kantian Transcendental Unity of Apperception is to break down the sharp barrier erected by Kant between appearances and things-in-themselves. A living, situated, historical person, argues Grene, finds "himself, bodily, within a real world of things themselves." Reality has been restored. Human persons do give order to nature, but it is not just our habit, but the essence of our rationality that we do so. Yet, Grene notes, "like Hume and unlike Kant, we never know for sure that we have done the job right." It is real things that human persons find themselves among, but one cannot claim apodicticity in our conceptions with respect to them. Yet Grene does not find this a fact to despair. She writes: "That's not tragic: it only means that being human is a precarious and never ending task. Who that thought well ever thought otherwise?"[51]

Grene's transposition of the Transcendental Unity of Apperception into activity by a live, historically situated human person intends to restore the reality of things, not as a network of phenomena only but as things in themselves which one tries to know. An important question, then, arises: does our hold on nature get lost when one brings the reading of nature into culture? "Remaining within the hermeneutical circle, can we found it on nature?"[52] Our exposition of Grene's view on the place of the human person in nature clearly allows us to say "yes" because the human person is "the personification of nature through participation in culture." Human beings are at home in the natural world and are biologically formed to be cultural animals.

Grene deals, in a number of her writings, with the notion of the hermeneutic circle and claims that all the disciplines, including the varying sciences, are interpretive activities operating within a hermeneutic circle.[53] Human persons, as we have seen, are always "beings-already-in-the world": they internalize a culture, a social world, in "the year of the social uterus." There is, for Grene, neither a view from nowhere nor a pure view from "in here." Every human person's world is already social, a fabric expressing the fundamental beliefs of a particular society, as these are internalized in the formative years of maturation. Further, there are various layers of social and cultural internalization as a human individual grows and matures in human relationships, individual, social, institutional, and so on. Thus, for example, a mathematician starts pondering problems given to him or her by and in a tradition. "S (he) is *somewhere* at the start and grows, whether in acceptance or dissent, from and within the circle established by that historic starting-place."[54] Thus, Grene agrees with the notion that all theory is "history-laden," laden with the belief structure of a particular community. She writes: "To recognize in some such way that interpretation stretches to all disciplines seems to me a necessary condition for the development of an adequate philosophy of science."[55] However, Grene remains a convinced realist and this is possible because her starting point is not a Cartesian split of a mathematicized, disembodied mind and a mathematicized, static, materialistic nature. Rather, she begins with the recognition that there is a living world of which human persons are part and out of which their cultural world arises.[56] Grene's assertion of a strong realistic stance along with an understanding of all searches for knowledge as taking place within a hermeneutic circle makes, I believe, excellent sense for a cogent philosophy of science.

IMPLICATIONS OF GRENE'S VIEW OF THE CONTEXTUAL HUMAN PERSON

In drawing to a close our very brief review of the work of Marjorie Grene, we turn to summarize some implications for future philosophical exploration and note with a degree of sadness Grene's failure so far to develop fully her own philosophical anthropology. However, Grene's sketch of a philosophical anthropology, although not fully developed, does, I believe, provide us a good foundation to move forward in a number of areas of philosophy. In the philosophy of mind, Grene allows us to focus on a philosophy of person and to escape the limitations of the various dominating frameworks of Cartesian dualism, reductive materialism, functionalism, and Darwinian evolutionary theory. Concerning the evolutionary context, we see that Grene sets limitations to any stress on selection and on function and develops a position on distinctions between the human world and animal world which provides a good foundation for a more reasonable view of animal minds and nature. Further, by embedding the world of culture in nature via the social gestation of the human infant, Grene overcomes the false dichotomy of organic and cultural evolution. Although these processes occur at very different rates, they become, in Grene's view, intertwined from very early on. To be a human animal is to be potentially a dweller *in* culture, *in* symbol systems, *in* language. The human person is *both* animal and responsible agent, as symbol maker and user.

Grene also helps us overcome the old tangles about teleology/mechanism. First, reducing human behavior to a "mechanical" level seems an absurdity. As Erwin Straus once noted, physics refutes physicalism.[57] If there is such activity as physicists exhibit in doing their research, then there is purposive behavior and teleology in the case of human beings.[58] Secondly, drawing on an argument by Polanyi, Grene dispels the confusion about the notion of "mechanism." Polanyi demonstrates that complete knowledge of physics and chemistry would not enable us to recognize a machine. To know that a machine is, for example, a clock, one must rely on operational principles analogous to engineering principles. Indeed, what is evident is two notions of "mechanics," namely, one explicable in terms of principles of physics and chemistry and the other explicable in terms of a functioning unit or device that works in terms of certain operating principles which constrain and so "direct" the working parts. As Polanyi aptly notes: *"The complete knowledge of a machine as an object tells us nothing about it as a machine."*[59] To overcome this kind of confusion would perhaps allow us to go beyond the strong functionalism still present in philosophy of mind and to deal more adequately with the notion of "machine intelligence."

Grene has also, in her writings, dealt extensively with problems of teleology in biology. Because of space constraints, I will not address these here, but merely note that her discussion of species, norms, and typology seems to me very insightful and also quite useful to a better understanding, for example, of "health," and "illness," as concepts based somehow on "normal human functioning."[60]

Turning again to philosophy of mind, Grene's sketch of a philosophical anthropology helps us get beyond the vexing problem of the "subjectivity" and "privacy" of human experience. Grene's adoption of Plessner's notion of the "natural artificiality," of the human being, namely, that "his nature is defined by, and necessitates, a dependence on artifacts, on the symbol systems that constitute culture"[61] gives us a basis to elude the problems of a "privileged access" notion of human self-knowledge and the "egological" predicament brought about by stressing the privacy of human mind. Symbol systems are fundamentally public, not private, and if "to have a mind" is, in some way, to acquire the capacity to use symbols in a certain way, then to have a mind is already to function as a member of the community of symbol users. Indeed, to see the mental in this way also allows us to see that what makes a person "is not the possession of feelings, but the structure of such feelings within the systems of symbols that constitute a human language or a human world."[62] Indeed, one of the truly dehumanizing aspects of "pain" is that it is often inexpressible in sharable language. It is very "private" and thus it is a true diminution of full personhood.

Indeed, Grene's view of the human person as a contextual being, biologically, historically, socially, culturally, provides an excellent foundation for dealing with a number of concrete problems in the area of bioethics and human health and illness. Thus, I have argued that to deal adequately with genetic information as well as other health decision-making, the following elements of a new framework are necessary.[63] First, persons, whether patients or other significant decision-makers, must be seen in a holistic manner in terms of complex relational networks, composed of a variety of physical and public aspects—bodily, neural, social, cultural, political, and economic—and a mix of inner aspects—sensual, emotional, mental, intentional. Secondly, "persons" must be seen as creatures of time who are capable of stagnation, development, growth, and able to take advantage of opportunities of the future, both short and long term. Grene's sketch of a philosophical anthropology provides a broadly holistic view of the human person and especially of the historical and temporal aspect of human existence.[64]

A crucial third aspect of an adequate framework for dealing with decisions in health care is that illness or disease must not be seen as located solely in a physically, malfunctioning body, though, as Grene makes clear, bodily existence is a crucial aspect of human persons. In addition to bodily malfunctioning, illness profoundly affects social, cultural, and personal life goal functioning. Grene's view of the human being as fundamentally cultural gives credence to such a view and could help provide a more refined explication of how illness affects persons in this manner. A fourth important element of the new framework is that a "person" must be seen as relational in a fundamental sense, namely, as a "being-with-others." Biological and social kinships, as Grene makes clear, are powerful aspects of human life and cannot be ignored in understanding human decision-making in any arena.

It is true that Marjorie Grene has not provided us with a fully developed philosophical anthropology nor has she given us any extensive writings in philosophy of man. However, she has broken new ground in mining the treasures of Continental philosophy and brought from this many new insights, still neglected today, which could set philosophy of mind and other philosophical discussions on new foundations and allow them to move forward in fruitful, innovative directions. Her excellent work in the philosophy of biology, combined with her explorations of philosophical anthropology, bequeaths to us a view of "a contextual human person" worth much future exploration.

JACQUELYN ANN K. KEGLEY
KEGLEY INSTITUTE OF ETHICS
CALIFORNIA STATE UNIVERSITY, BAKERSFIELD
JUNE 1999

NOTES

1. Marjorie Grene, "To Have a Mind," *Journal of Medicine and Philosophy* 1, no. 2 (1976): 178.
2. I also have addressed the issue of person. See Jacquelyn Ann K. Kegley, "Josiah Royce on Self and Community," *Rice University Studies* 66 (Fall, 1980): 33–53; "Peirce and Royce on Person," in *Peirce and Value Theory*, ed. Hermann Parrett (Amsterdam/Philadelphia: John Benjamin's, 1994); and *Genuine Individuals and Genuine Communities* (Nashville: Vanderbilt University Press, 1997).
3. Marjorie Grene, "People and Other Animals," in *The Understanding of Nature: Essays in the Philosophy of Biology*, vol. 23 of *Boston Studies in the Philosophy of Science* (Dordrecht/ Boston: D. Reidel, 1974), pp. 346–60. In this essay Grene considers four forms of reconciliation of the split that Descartes introduced between the "inner life of consciousness," and the "external material world." She opts for what she calls the "fourth possibility," namely, the one that entails "a radical rejection of dualism."
4. Marjorie Grene, *A Philosophical Testament* (Chicago and La Salle: Open Court, 1995), p. 14.
5. Marjorie Grene, "In and Out of Friendship," in *Human Nature and Natural Knowledge*, ed. A. Donagan, A. N. Perovich, Jr., and M. V. Wedin. (Dordrecht/ Boston: D. Reidel Publishing Company, 1986), pp. 358–59.
6. Ibid., p. 358.
7. Marjorie Grene, "The Character of Living Things III," in *The Understanding of Nature*, pp. 320–45.
8. "On Some Distinctions Between Men and Brutes," in *The Understanding of Nature*, p. 245.
9. Ibid., p. 251.

10. A. Portmann. *Animals as Social Beings*, trans. O. Coburn (London: Hutchinson, 1961), and *New Paths in Biology*, trans. A. Pomerans (New York: Harper & Row, 1964). Grene discusses Portmann's work in her essay, "The Character of Living Things I," in *The Understanding of Nature*, pp. 254–93.

11. Marjorie Grene, Preface, *The Understanding of Nature*, p. vii.

12. Marjorie Grene, "The Character of Living Things I," *The Understanding of Nature*, p. 269.

13. See Daniel Dennett, *Darwin's Dangerous Idea: Evolution and the Meanings of Life* (New York: Touchstone, 1996), and *Kinds of Minds: Towards an Understanding of Consciousness* (New York: Harper/Collins, 1997); and Richard Dawkins, *The Selfish Gene* (Oxford University Press, 1990), and *The Blind Watchmaker: Why the Evidence of Evolution Reveals a Universe Without Design* (New York: W. W. Norton, 1996).

14. Grene, "The Character of Living Things I," p. 274.

15. Ibid., p. 277.

16. Ibid., p. 285.

17. Ibid.

18. Ibid., p. 288.

19. Ibid.

20. Marjorie Grene, "The Paradoxes of Historicity," *Review of Metaphysics* 32, no. 1, issue 125 (September, 1978): 15.

21. Helmut Plessner, *Die Stufen des Organischen und der Mensch* (Berlin: de Gruyter, 1928 and 1965).

22. Marjorie Grene, "The Character of Living Things III," *The Understanding of Nature*, pp. 336–37.

23. Plessner, *Die Stufen des Organischen unde der Mensch*, p. 293.

24. Grene, "The Character of Living Things III," p. 337.

25. Ibid.

26. Ibid., p. 338.

27. Ibid.

28. Ibid., p. 340.

29. Josiah Royce, *The World and the Individual*, vol. II (New York: Dover Publications, 1959), pp. 171–72.

30. Josiah Royce, "Introduction: The 'Social Approach' to Metaphysics," in *Metaphysics (Josiah Royce)*, William Ernest Hocking, Initial Editor. Co-Edited by Richard Hocking and Frank Oppenheim (New York: SUNY Press, 1998), p. 16.

31. Grene, "The Character of Living Things III," pp. 340–41.

32. Ibid.

33. Daniel C. Dennett, *Elbow Room* (Cambridge, Mass.: MIT Press, 1997).

34. Grene, "The Character of Living Things III," p. 345, note 13.

35. Ibid., pp. 342–43.

36. Ibid., pp. 343–44.

37. Ibid., p. 343.

38. Grene, "People and Other Animals," pp. 346–60.

39. Grene is commenting on Eccles' essay, "The Brain and the Soul," in *Facing Reality* (New York: Springer, 1970), pp. 151–75.

40. Grene, "People and Other Animals," p. 352.

41. Ibid.

42. Ibid., p. 353.

43. Ibid., p. 354.

44. Dennett, *Kinds of Minds*.

45. Grene, "People and Other Animals," p. 354.

46. Ibid., p. 357.

47. Ibid., p. 358.

48. Marjorie Grene, *The Knower and the Known* (Berkeley: University of California Press), p. 202.

49. Grene, "The Paradoxes of Historicity," p. 20.

50. Ibid., p. 21.

51. Ibid., p. 22.

52. Ibid., p. 28.

53. Grene, *A Philosophical Testament*, p. 73.

54. Ibid.

55. Ibid.

56. Grene is, in my judgment, most perceptive in recognizing that Heidegger and Sartre remain Cartesian. Heidegger's human being is disembodied and Sartre pits the I against the total otherness of mere Being. "The For-Itself against the In-Itself against the For-Itself with No Exit," (*A Philosophical Testament*, p. 79).

57. Erwin Straus, *Vom Sinn der Sinne* (Berlin: Walter de Gruyter and Co., 1935). English Edition. *The Primary World of the Senses,* trans. Charles Taylor (New York: Free Press, 1963), p. 298.

58. See also Grene, "To Have a Mind," pp. 182–83.

59. Michael Polanyi, *Personal Knoweldge* (Chicago: University of Chicago Press, 1958), p. 330.

60. See Grene's discussion of these issues in "To Have a Mind," pp. 185–90; and "Is Genus to Species as Matter to Form? Aristotle and Taxonomy," in *Understanding Nature*, pp. 108–26; and "Biology and Teleology," in *Understanding Nature*, pp. 172–80.

61. Grene, "To Have a Mind," p. 190.

62. Ibid., p. 191.

63. Jacquelyn Ann K. Kegley, "A New Framework for the Use of Genetic Information," in *Genetic Information: Acquisition, Access, and Control*, ed Alison K. Thompson and Ruth F. Chadwick (New York, Boston, Dordrecht, London, Moscow: Kluwer Academic/Plenum Publishers, 1997), pp. 321–29.

64. Grene, "The Paradoxes of Historicity," p. 20.

REPLY TO JACQUELYN ANN K. KEGLEY

D r. Kegley's flattering estimate of the value of my work on persons makes it difficult to reply to her. At the same time, some of the passages she cites at length remind me of how much I have learned in the last few decades—or so it seems to me. So, with due respect and gratitude, I shall have to dissent from her report—and from my own earlier declarations—in some directions.

Ranging widely over my miscellaneous publications, Dr. Kegley has extracted what she considers a sketch of a philosophical anthropology, and she regrets that I have not developed that subject matter more systematically. Perhaps I should explain, to begin with, why I have not done so. I did think about it, thirty or more years ago. But I found much of the literature in this putative sub-discipline unsatisfactory, in ways that made me unwilling to spend my time assimilating and criticizing it. Writers like Gehlen—too close to Nazism—and Scheler—too close to theology—were unattractive subjects. True, as Dr. Kegley recognizes, I do believe that reflection on the problem of the person is alluring: much more so than what philosophers study in so-called philosophy of mind. As I have, I am sure, said more than once, I rather like Gilbert Ryle's suggestion that we speak of "minding" rather than of minds. Minding is something persons do. And in my *Philosophical Testament*, while I remarked that my chief interest has been in questions about knowledge, I have found such questions closely linked to the problem of the person. Only persons make knowledge claims, and it is an important aspect of their personhood that they are able to do so. So I suppose one could say that my Davis research lecture, "People and Other Animals," which I still do agree with, and some other similar pieces, including the *Testament*, offer something like an a-b-c of what might be called a philosophical anthropology. The name doesn't matter much. It's perhaps philosophizing that pays more attention than is usual to some empirical subject matters: biology or (recently, in my case) a certain brand of experimental psychology.

That I have taken a consistently—and persistently—anti-Cartesian stand is certainly correct, and so I discovered in writing the intellectual autobiography prefaced to this volume. What Helmuth Plessner called the Cartesian alternative is what we still need to overcome. Much of the twentieth century was spent by numerous thinkers in that effort, but apparently to no avail. Why is it so difficult to abandon such a plainly inadequate, incoherent, nonsensical alternative? I have no idea.

However, from my present point of view, some of the efforts I made in that direction now seem to me, in part at least, misguided. Dr. Kegley lingers over my essay on the work of the Swiss zoologist, Adolph Portmann. This was a chapter in a book I should not have written, *Approaches to a Philosophical Biology* (1969), reprinted in a collection of essays, *The Understanding of Nature*, in 1974. While I believe my account of Portmann's ideas is accurate enough, there is much in it to which I cannot now subscribe.

Portmann started as a marine biologist (as he remarked, that was rather like being admiral of the Swiss navy), and moved on to studies in comparative zoology. In particular, his study of the comparative development of human beings and other primates provided a valuable indication of the nature of human uniqueness. If our neonates appeared at the same stage of development as do chimpanzees, for example, we would need 21 months' pregnancy to get them that far. In other words, the first year of human life provides something like a "social uterus" (the phrase is Portmann's, I believe), in which our young look about and take an interest in their surroundings: from facial expressions to furniture. Our offspring are *secondarily patricial*. Unlike the young of other advanced mammals, they don't just get up and go, but unlike more "primitive" mammals—cats, dogs, rats—they are not born blind and inattentive. They take a year to assimilate their surroundings before they stand up, speak, and perform intelligible actions.

That's fine. It's an insight worth remembering. But the totality of Portmann's biological philosophy I cannot just swallow whole, as Dr. Kegley seems to want me to do. Even back then, I did not "turn to" Portmann as a cure for Cartesianism. I was asked to look up some bibliography in the philosophy of biology—I've forgotten by whom—and found some European writers I thought worth studying and expounding for English-speaking readers. I was wrong about the latter thought. In any case, what I must now disclaim in Portmann's approach as I then presented it—and, admittedly, also in my own view at the time—was a much too narrow conception of Darwinian evolution, against which, as a practicing zoologist, Portmann was reacting. That was the view of what Stephen Jay Gould has christened "the hardened synthesis," according to which evolution was just (allegedly) differential gene frequencies. One of the founders of the synthesis, G. Ledyard Stebbins, once referred to it in a lecture as "the synthesis of the mid-(twentieth) century." Fair enough. Some of the modifications needed in that narrow view were suggested, for example, in the book that I published with Niles Eldredge, *Interactions: The Biological Basis of Social Systems*. By now, in particular, excellent work is being done in the effort to assimilate development to evolutionary theory. A recent summary will be found in chapter 22 of the 2000 edition of Scott Gilbert's *Developmental Biology*. Admittedly, I am somewhat skeptical of some of what appears in the name of developmental systems theory, which is often more sermon than substance. But the greater richness of current evolutionary theory does, I'm afraid, make me ashamed of some of my pronouncements, not, indeed, in my callow youth, but in my naïve middle age. It is not only the first year of life in which we assimilate our culture: one does, or one can, keep revising one's beliefs. In this case, what I believed thirty years ago I want in part very emphatically to reject!

In fact, looking back in my autobiographical reflections on important lessons learned over the decades, I did not include Portmann's work among significant influences on my own thought. Even Plessner, whom Kegley also discusses at some length, and from whom I certainly borrowed more themes and concepts than I did from Portmann, I did not count among those who radically affected my own thinking. I'm not sure why not. Again, "People and Other Animals" is a very Plessnerian piece. Yet I still find, looking back, that it is successively Polanyi, Merleau-Ponty, and Gibson who mark the significant stages on my (intellectual) life's way. Plessner just seemed to fit in well, I suppose, with what I was already thinking. ("Natural artificiality," I should say in passing, is Plessner's expression, not mine, though I find it useful and revealing.)

It does surprise me a little, I must confess, to find Dr. Kegley alluding to Josiah Royce as someone to whose stance on human nature I should have referred. Elsewhere I have confessed to an allergy to idealism—acquired early in the study of Hegel under the tutelage of Karl Jaspers—and it has therefore never occurred to me to delve into Royce's arguments. I did encounter the "social contrast effect" in the writings of G. H. Mead, and found it less than satisfactory. It is being with others, and in a community— what Polanyi called "indwelling"—that is basic to our way of being. "Social contrast," to my ear, is too reminiscent of Sartre's being-for-itself *against* the other, or, if you prefer, of a Hobbesian, "war of all against all." Heaven knows, we have our conflicts, too; but it is being with, not against, we need to start from, or so it seems to me. I worry a little, also, about Kegley's allusion to my use of the term "inner world," since I want so much—again, as an anti-Cartesian—to avoid any systematic use of the concept of consciousness, let alone self-consciousness, in my reflections about our peculiar way of life. Also, my now twenty-year-long commitment to the principles of Gibsonian ecological psychology, makes me leery of such expressions. Again, I find some of what it appears I used to say somewhat suspect when it's quoted back at me now. This is probably, at least in part, because I talk and write too much too hastily and then regret what I've said too carelessly and too much off the cuff. But I hope it's also, to some extent, because I keep learning better. After all, as Merleau-Ponty and others have often stressed, it is the openness of our human world that we most cherish. We can always discover we were mistaken—well, about some things!

In conclusion, I should say again, as I did at the start, that I am flattered by the positive lessons Dr. Kegley has found in my work, even though I am not always sure I would now subscribe to everything she quotes me as having once said. It is gratifying that she finds my work of some importance for matters of practical ethical concern—matters to which I have myself paid little attention. Indeed, at a recent symposium of the Pacific Division of the American Philosophical Association, I publicly confessed some skepticism about the field of bioethics, admitting my ignorance of it, and, indeed, of ethics in general. If I have unwittingly been of some assistance in areas of urgent practical importance, I must again thank Dr. Kegley for finding that I have built better than I knew.

M. G.

NOTES

1. Eldredge and Grene, *Interactions: The Biological Basis of Social Systems* (New York: Columbia University Press, 1992).
2. Gilbert, *Developmental Biology*, 6th ed. (Sunderland, Mass.: Sinauer, 2000).

3

Helen E. Longino

MARJORIE GRENE'S PHILOSOPHICAL NATURALISM

R ecent philosophy has witnessed a resurgence of interest in naturalism, especially in epistemology. Many philosophers became impatient with a theory of knowledge that seemed increasingly preoccupied with apparently trivial matters such as papier-mâché barns. Others followed Quine's journey from rejection of the analytic-synthetic distinction to embrace of empirical science as provider of the answer to philosophical questions. This kind of naturalism, that replaces philosophical analysis with empirical data and generalization, has come upon hard times. But Marjorie Grene not only diagnosed the ills of this sort of replacement naturalism before it became popular; she also developed a more viable naturalism, if not under that name: an alternative to transcendentalism and crude or scientistic naturalism. Grene's ideas have found uptake in work in social epistemology and on pluralism in the sciences. In this essay I will sketch the problems with contemporary naturalism, revive Grene's criticism of an ancient form of it, and make salient the philosophical naturalism that is developed in her epistemological writings. I also want to show how certain philosophical ideas can sidetrack even the most wary.

THE STALEMATE IN CONTEMPORARY NATURALISM

Naturalism is not new in philosophy, nor is it a unified body of doctrine. The American pragmatists were naturalists; so were, according to Philip Kitcher, the British empiricists.[1] Quine, in "Epistemology Naturalized" announced the advent of the new naturalism, which not only treats cognition as causal, but turns explicitly to psychology. For example, in one of the more frequently quoted passages in that essay, Quine identifies the underdetermination problem in philosophy of science (perhaps the most pressing epistemological problem distinctive to the sciences) with a research problem of empirical psychology: how a human subject, "accorded a certain experimentally controlled input—certain patterns of irradiation in assorted frequencies, for instance—in the fullness of time . . . delivers as output a description of the three-dimensional external world and its history."[2] This problem holds interest for the psychologist for "the same reasons that always prompted epistemology; namely, in order to see how evidence relates to theory, and in what ways one's theory of nature transcends any available evidence."[3] Quine neatly equates the problems of evidence with the problem of providing a causal account of perception and perceptual cognition. Epistemology becomes another chapter of natural science. This consignment of epistemology to empirical science moots the classical problems of knowledge (do we know? what can we know?) by presupposing that we do know and transforms epistemology into an investigation of cognitive mechanisms.

This kind of naturalism is the kind that leads to a stalemate. While it shows that traditional normative epistemology in the analytic tradition imposes unrealistic constraints on *knowers*, naturalized epistemology fails to answer the most fundamental philosophical questions about *knowledge*. There are a number of strands of argument intended to establish the unreality or inapplicability of traditional epistemology.[4] Normative analytic epistemology is an a priori enterprise. As such, it must proceed in ignorance of the actual capacities of human subjects. Mark Kaplan notes that this licenses the complaint that normative epistemology is thereby incapable of determining what cognitive processes are apt to be reliable in actual agents.[5] (If one does not know what they are, then it is impossible to make discriminations among them.) I would make the additional point that if this principled ignorance is thorough, there is no guarantee that the methodological recommendations that issue will be relevant in any way to the practices and processes by which subjects form or come to hold beliefs. But this very agnosticism commits the traditional epistemologist to a characterization of knowers, that is, to the view that knowers are subjects with no subjectivity. Either human knowers (or aspirants to knowledge) have the capacity to transcend the conditions of their subjectivity (as Thomas Nagel suggests) or knowers are wholly ideal and knowledge unattainable. The first choice requires that humans become nonhuman. The second implies that to the extent the characterization of ideal cognitive agents can do no work in human contexts, it can't help answer fundamental questions that arise in those contexts, like what the difference is between knowledge and opinion. Epistemology becomes idle posturing.

Another complaint has to do with the object of or character of knowledge that we are given in a priori normative epistemology. Such epistemology must restrict itself to prescribing cognitive strategies that are optimal no matter what the world is like. This, Kaplan notes, is to abandon the aim of articulating strategies that will work well in the world we inhabit. But, one might go on to ask, is it not also to make some assumptions as to what the world is like? Certainly, to the extent that success conditions in definitions of "knowledge" require that the world be determinate in the ways indicated by our descriptive vocabulary, a priori epistemologies by default make assumptions about the world that can be known. With no guarantee that that world is our world, a priori epistemology can do no work in solving our ordinary puzzles about knowledge.

But familiar naturalizing moves will stand us in no better stead. If naturalizing epistemology means "letting the sciences tell us how we know" then it means studying how humans form beliefs, whether that involves studying the neurophysiology of perception and memory, the psychology of learning, or the sociology of learning and belief transmission. It means studying all episodes of belief formation, successful and unsuccessful alike. Now there is nothing wrong with knowing this, or should I say, nothing wrong about having some theories about such matters, but these enterprises either fail to address or presuppose answers to some of the central philosophical questions about knowledge. Given that we treat some episodes of belief formation as successful and other as unsuccessful, what does this distinction amount to? How are "successful" and "unsuccessful" defined? Or

What is knowledge?

What is the relation of knowledge to belief?

What is justified or reasonable belief? and what is the relation of that to knowledge?

What is the distinction between knowledge and opinion?

The empirical enterprises also foreclose investigation of the question "To what kind of view of reality (that is, to what metaphysics) does our conception of knowledge commit us?" These questions are not purely empirical questions that can be answered by the kinds of observational and experimental techniques employed in research from neurophysiology to sociology. They are questions about practices of ascription that, like any human practices, can only be fully understood in reference to the aims of those practices—the goods to be achieved by our engagement in them. So-called strong naturalism, what I would call neo-naturalism, achieves its strength at the cost of philosophical banality.

Marjorie Grene made exactly this point in her discussion of Plato and Aristotle in *The Knower and the Known*. Like that of many philosophical naturalists, her epistemological thought is closely bound up with her philosophy of science. Thus she is compelled by the problem articulated by Plato/Socrates in the *Meno*: how can we know what we don't already know? This is one way of expressing the conundrum of scientific discovery: how do we learn/discover new facts about the world? How do we know we have learned/discovered as distinct from merely conjecturing? Plato, notoriously, answered that learning was actually recollecting what was already known (by the soul prior to embodiment). Aristotle rejects Plato's theory of recollection, but his solution merely reinscribes Plato's theory, minus the recollection. Aristotle restates the problem as that of relating the general to the particular, relating, that is, our general knowledge that, say, the sum of the interior angles of a triangle is equal to two right angles to the properties of this triangle before us. What we learn are facts about particulars by apprehending the general in them. So we already know what for the epistemologist is the tricky part: the generalization. Grene says of this:

> [Aristotle] is saying: what we know in general, we may yet have to learn to apply in the particular case. And it is just this principle which makes Plato's solution not a solution of the problem of learning, but a denial that learning exists. Yet at least Plato did, in the confrontation of Socrates the seeker with Meno's dilemma, pose the *problem* as a genuine one. Aristotle's solution is just as spurious, but he does not seem so much as to have recognized that a problem exists. So, taking the question in its original Platonic context, his answer seems irrelevant. Plato proposes an absurd solution to a substantial problem; Aristotle proposes a trivial solution to a trivial problem.[6]

Grene goes on to say that for Aristotle, real puzzlement and real learning—advance from ignorance to understanding—have no place in science, because Aristotelian method concerns movement from the general (knowledge of which is assured by the identity of natural order and the intellectual order) to the particular. Contemporary neo-naturalism has the same character as Aristotle's epistemology: it rejects the transcendent as inapplicable to the human condition, but then it is constrained by presuppositions to which it is blind. But the philosophical work is in the presuppositions, after which any further analysis is trivial or simply spells out what is already implied in those presuppositions. Consider the Quinean picture again. This is a picture of an individual equipped with a capacity to reason in ways presupposed by first order logic (and perhaps a rule of induction) and a sensory system that detects disturbances at its periphery. The problem is that the "meager data" provided by those disturbances in combination with the rules of first order logic cannot select one among competing hypotheses as true or most plausible. But why is this the picture with which we must begin? The a priorist would start here presumably because these are elements of our cognitive equipment that can be affirmed independently of experience—the rules of logic are analytically true and the meager data—sense data, as it turns out—are what in the fashion of seventeenth- and eighteenth-century epistemology one cannot doubt. But notice how Quine simply transports (or recommends the transportation of) this analytically achieved stripped down cognizer into empirical psychology, whose job it will be to fill in the links between sense data and hypotheses by specifying mechanisms that effect the required transformation of input to output. Why, once we have turned away from the a priori realm, should we remain satisfied with this representation of the problem? Why, for example, should we accept the notion that the input is sense data, or, as Quine puts it, "patterns of irradiation"?

Richard Grandy emphasizes the arbitrariness of such a starting point, which he attributes to Quine's behaviorism, and recommends instead a cognitivist point of view which construes information more broadly. From this perspective, Grandy says, "the input is vast and the job of the perceptual system is to discard most of the information . . . "[7] Just as Grandy asks why when we naturalize we should remain loyal to a description of input achieved by a priori reflection, so we might also ask: why should we represent the epistemological starting point as that of a relatively mature human being cast adrift from social relations? Such a representation, it seems to me, implies that our cognitive apparatus must start afresh everyday as we arise from sleep and once again try to find order in the blooming buzzing confusion of our sense experience. But, of course, we don't have to do that unless we have, as some do, very serious brain damage.

A naturalist who takes a problem constructed by a priori analysis and, despairing of an analytic solution, tosses it to empirical science, may appear tough-minded, but cannot be considered a very serious naturalist. The contemporary naturalist is in the same boat with Grene's Aristotle: rejecting the transcendental solution but failing to interrogate the premises that seemed to make it so alluring.

Grene's discussion of Descartes makes this even clearer. Descartes's doctrine of ideas is the product of an intellect given over to abstraction, says Grene. The problem for Descartes is analogous to that of Quine: how to transform the subjective into the objective.[8] Grene, in a 1985 essay,[9] convincingly argues that, within Descartes's schema, only God's goodness and veracity permit the construction of objective knowledge from the subjective field of ideas. (One cannot get much more unnatural than that.) Granted Quine is not concerned to legitimate belief, but he has, as Aristotle did for Plato, transformed Descartes's quandary into a trivial sounding empirical problem, by rewriting the premise achieved by hyperbolic doubt as a self-evident empirical starting point. Grene suggests that "Descartes's neglect of the category of life" leads both to his improbable Godly solution and to "the dead end at which twentieth-century philosophy has consequently arrived."[10]

GRENE'S WAY

How does Grene propose we proceed? With characteristic modesty she attributes the insights to others, especially Maurice Merleau-Ponty and Michael Polanyi. Both of them start philosophy with embodied existence, rather than from the abstraction of Cartesian ideas or Quinean "patterns of irradiation." Grene, has, however constructed her own distinctive philosophical view using perspectives attributed to these philosophers and her own reading of the major thinkers of the Western philosophical tradition. One of the recurrent elements of this distinctive view is Grene's insistence on seeing human knowledge and human persons as features of the natural world. They demand naturalized analyses not because transcendent or normative ones have not worked, but because that is what they are. The natural world is where we begin, not just where we end up.

In *A Philosophical Testament*, Grene refines and crystallizes this view, which, had it been more widely taken up, might have saved twentieth-century Anglo-American epistemology from the sterility that has sometimes afflicted it. Here is her statement in the introduction to the volume:

> Seeing knowledge claims in historical context [which she will give us reason to do] means, further, seeing them as the activities of persons. This is an even harder row to hoe. To approach the question of knowledge claims in relation to the hopes, aspirations, defeats of those who claim, have claimed, will claim to know some aspect of reality appears to many . . . to mean asking about the causes of such claims, whether "internal" or "external," and abandoning the reasons. But that is to abandon the philosophical question at the core of my interest and it is also to abandon the very concept of "activity" or a "person." Knowledge claims are made, responsibly, by responsible agents, whom we call persons. . . . [11]

Grene was first a biologist, earning her bachelor's degree in zoology, and insists that we understand ourselves as animals and accept the limits such an understanding places on our philosophical reflection. At the same time, she is convinced that we have capacities that distinguish us from the other animals, at least so much as we know of them. The exercise of those capacities in a sequence of specific historical and social contexts in Europe and European influenced regions, like North America after 1500 or 1600, has given rise to what we identify as the Western philosophical tradition.

These twin convictions lead her to shun the transcendental, but equally to avoid the brute naturalism or materialism which says that there are only physical things obeying physical laws, so if we understand physical laws we understand everything there is to understand. The world is more complex than that. *A Philosophical Testament* is her effort to articulate a philosophical point of view that takes our propensity to philosophical reflection and our animality as equally central aspects of our being human.

This point of view is particularly evident in her treatment of perception. Here, Grene reverts primarily to the biological or biologically oriented thinkers for her account. Perception depends on but is not identical to sensation as the activity of individual organs of sense, but is rather the integration and coordination of sensory information (which, Grene insists, is not philosophical sense-data, but whatever it is that our sensory organs transmit to the brain for such coordination). Perception is, when things go right, knowledge, and knowledge in general is always grounded in perception.

> We are rooted through our senses in reality. . . . The artifactual devices we interiorize as we learn our way around a given discipline or acquire a given skill, however theoretical, are themselves alterations of, tinkerings with, perceptible, embodied things as much as we ourselves who do all this tinkering are animals finding our way through reliance on our integration of sensory inputs in a perceptible and therefore intelligible habitat. As there is no sharp cut between belief and knowledge, so there is no sharp cut between perception and belief. Perception is both primordial . . . and pervasive. . . . That is, I think, something like what Merleau-Ponty meant by "the primacy of perception." It is also the necessary foundation for Polanyi's doctrine of tacit knowing.[12]

And furthermore, both the justified belief account of knowledge and the thesis of the primacy (and pervasiveness throughout cognition) of perception must be understood realistically. "We dwell in human worlds, in cultures, but every such world is itself located in, and constitutes, a unique transformation of, some segment of the natural world, which provides the materials for, and sets the limits to, its constructs."[13]

If perception is the paradigmatic cognitive activity—what are we to make of philosophical views that seem to lead us from such an insight into pure subjectivism or idealism? Both her chapter on Kant's Transcendental Analytic in the *Critique of Pure Reason* and the following one on Wittgenstein are discussions of ways out of those directions of thought. They amplify the reflections and commitments of *Testament*'s first chapter.

In her treatment of Kant, Grene worries about the distinction between appearances and things in themselves. Accepting that Kant intended an unbridgeable gap, she wonders whether he must then be read as an idealist, denying the reality of anything but appearances, or whether he should/can be read as a realist. And if read as a realist, what is it that is real? Grene reports having been drawn to the notion of the Transcendental Object = X, which seems to be the answer in the first edition of the Analytic, but which disappears from the second.

The task of the Analytic is to answer the question, "how is our kind of experience possible?" where by that we mean sensory experience which is at the same time solid, objective, and of an ordered reality. Grene puts it this way:

> In Kant's view, transcendent truth is beyond us: that is, we have no insight whose content is wholly detached from our contingent, factual ways of experiencing things and events. . . . On the other hand, our solid, objective experience of an ordered reality rests on *some* principles; it is clearly not just Humean chaos, irrationally associated into a comfortable enough dwelling place by mere force of habit. As philosophers, we want to search, reflectively, for those principles: we want to seek out the necessary conditions indispensable to the kind of experience, the kind of well-ordered experience, the *objective* experience, we in fact have.[14]

What makes our kind of experience possible, what gives it unity, objectivity, and coherence is our ordering of it via those rules called the Categories. But the applicability of the categories presupposes an even deeper unity—namely that I can unite all my experience with an "I think." That is, underlying even the Categories is the Transcendental Unity of Apperception.

> The Transcendental Unity of Apperception is the final, unifying agent in the scene before me—not only in my "inner" apprehension of it, but in its very thereness: its objectivity as really before me, in the valley and the hill beyond my window. . . . We are in the world, willy-nilly; but the way we apprehend it is something we have imposed on it, indeed, cannot help imposing on it. And at bottom that means that the very fact of being able to give rules to experience, of being a unifier of experience, is the last, most fundamental necessary condition we find to make possible the experience we in fact have.[15]

But then, having tried unsuccessfully to locate the TUA via Transcendental Objects, necessary conditions, synthetic a priori judgments, even if only to lament their disappearance, Grene offers a reframing and rereading of the material whose exposition I have just summarized—a reading that loses some of the ponderous trappings, but attempts to render the spirit of Kant's argument in a naturalized setting. "Who," she asks, "is the TUA?" We know that answering "a self-knowing, thinking substance" in the manner of Descartes gets us into all sorts of trouble. What if we go a different route and say that the TUA is "a real, live, breathing, perceiving, exploring *animal*, destined to seek, and find, its way in a real, existent, challenging, but up to a point manageable environment"?[16] Three consequences are of note. One has to do with the knower: it is alive and thus historical. The second is that the target of our search for knowledge (what Grene terms her "beloved Transcendental Object = X") is no longer a "mere" appearance. The possible objects of experience become things in themselves. We cannot understand or know them to their core, but they are real things that we distinguish as we orient ourselves in our environments. "The order we give them is really their order, some aspect of their order, grasped in relation to us as knowers, but still theirs, not in any arbitrary way ours."[17] The third consequence is that the knower is part of the very nature it seeks to understand.

What remains of Kant in this are three points: (1) the active role of the knower in making experience objective (that is, making our experience an experience of objects); (2) the inexhaustibility of the known (though perhaps we should say of the knowable or of the objects of possible experience) and; (3) the indissoluble connection between knower and known. Gone are the twelve categories as universal and necessary principles of any understanding; gone is the synthetic a priori. What remains is a kind of historicized a priori—every knower, every community of knowers, has some starting points that it must take as given. These are what provide the distinctive character of different historically, geographically, and culturally bound cognitive practices and their products. But there is no one set of starting points that every knower must take as given.

The reference to things in themselves is puzzling. It seems out of place in this naturalized reading of the argument of the Analytic. That peskily seductive Transcendental Object = X is working its mischief here, I think. Kant did well to get rid of it in between the two editions, but like many philosophical concepts, once mentioned, it just won't go away. It is as though the mention of something unknowable prompts a philosophical reflex to find a way to make it knowable. I understood the point of Kant's invocation of things in themselves to be the contrast with the idea of things existing as objects of experience, things in themselves having properties or modes of being or something beyond our capacities of characterization. Those capacities are a function of the kind of cognitive beings we are, with the particular sensory systems common to all members of our species, and of the particular linguistic/conceptual apparatus which we share with our more local communities. But things having properties beyond our capacities of characterization, things whose essence, if you will, is having such properties, are things of which we cannot speak. As soon as we do, they are no longer things in themselves, but objects of possible experience. Objects of possible experience outrun our capacities to describe them. They are excessive in just the way what we think is real is excessive—never fully confined in or described by the particular descriptions we can give of them and characterized by an order not of our choosing, even when that order is meaningful to us. But as objects of experience they are (partially) graspable via our categories, our concepts. That's just what it is to be an object of experience.

Why, I want to ask Marjorie Grene, preserve the opposition between appearances and things in themselves, when that between appearances and objects of possible experience could do the job? And do so without invoking the kind of concept that gives rise to the forms of skepticism Grene has been put at such pains to avoid?[18] We might then make another distinction between things as objects of possible experience and things as they are in themselves. This would be a distinction between reality (all the reality we need) and a chimera of speculative metaphysics. The concern to preserve the notion of things as they are in themselves parallels her treatment of realism and the real in a later chapter. So I will return to this theme, but after picking up more tools from her continued discussion of knowledge.

PHILOSOPHICAL FLY-BOTTLES

I will make my case more pressing by summarizing, more briefly, Grene's uses of the later Wittgenstein and J. J. Gibson in rounding out her account of knowledge. In the chapter, "Beyond Empiricism?," Grene asks what about the philosophical tradition in the English-speaking world has made it so difficult to articulate a realistic epistemology.[19] It is, of course, that tradition's dominance by certain forms of empiricism; to put it telegraphically, forms of empiricism that we can find in Hume, in Berkeley, in A. J. Ayer (as England's exponent of logical positivism). The value of the late Wittgenstein's work is that he shows us a way out of the fly-bottle of that bad kind of empiricism. The argument against the possibility of a private language undermines the idea that foundations of knowledge can be found in private, sense-data like, experience. The concepts of language game and family resemblance free us from the idea of a one-to-one relationship between expressions and wholly explicit meanings or definitions. And, finally, the idea of a form of life and of a language game or collection of language games as a form of life makes of what is human—our use of language—something that neither transcends nature nor reduces to the merely verbal.

Even though we may reject the notion that anything like sense data could serve as foundations of knowledge (indeed reject the very idea of foundations) it has been hard to find accounts of perception that do without them. But if perception is our paradigm of knowledge, we are in trouble. This is why the work of ecological psychologists J. J. and Eleanor Gibson has been so important to Grene.

The traditional view of perception which Grene wants to reject holds that to see something—a desk or a pen or a tree—is "to receive visual data, meaningless in themselves, and to infer from these" that a something—a desk or tree—is over there. "The data themselves are simply *sensations*, pure givens private to me and in themselves indicative of nothing beyond themselves. *Perceptions*, in contrast, are the result of, if not identical with, judgments that I make on the inadequate evidence of my sensations combined with experience."[20] This notion has received reinforcement, perhaps merely through restatement and presupposition, from so many quarters that, as Grene remarks, "Indeed, the notion that perception has to be constructed, by devious and highly indirect means, from the extremely inadequate data of pure sensations: this notion has been assimilated over the centuries into the 'common sense' of all of us . . . "[21] This is why Quine can describe the central problem as explaining how from patterns of irradiation we construct a description of the three-dimensional world.

The Gibsons reject this assignment. For them sensation as classically understood is unimportant to perception. For ecological psychology "[w]hat is primary is not inner bits of sensation, but the grasp by an animal, through its perceptual systems, of what matters to it in its environment."[22] And "the information necessary to perception is conveyed in structures and deformations picked up by perceptual systems."[23] Grene quotes the Gibsons:

> In life, the sea of stimulus energy in which an observer is immersed is always an array and always a flow. The stimuli as such, the pin-pricks of light or sound or touch, do not carry information about their sources. *But the invariant properties of the flowing array of stimulation do carry information. They specify the objects of the world and the layout of its surfaces. They are invariants under transformation, non-change underlying change.* [Grene's italics][24]

What is important then are invariances, and the primary processes of perceptual activity are not the Humean associations of sense data into bundles, but discrimination and differentiation. Grene summarizes a recent exposition as follows:

> [A]ll perception involves three components: first, the things and events in the organism's environment; second, the available information for pickup by the

organism, usually in the form of invariants: constant mathematical ratios within
a flowing array; and third, *what* the organism uses its information pickup to
perceive: the *affordances* [i.e., features meaningful to the organism] that the
environment offers it. . . . To put it in Wittgensteinian terms, all seeing is
seeing-as, not through some trick of visual illusion, but because perception is
always the engagement of an active, exploring organism with the affordances
of things and events that are happening, within reach of its perceptual systems,
in its real ongoing world.[25]

Grene says, and I agree, that most of the interesting philosophical
questions about knowledge persist. But the ecological starting point
reinforces the naturalist point of view, and does so without risking banality.
This is evident when comparing Grene's endorsement of the Gibsonian
account of perception with her naturalization of the Kantian TUA. The
three consequences of making the TUA a living human animal are realized
here, but the surviving elements of the Kantian spirit are also realized.
Perceiver/knowers are active in making the world objective, (in Gibson's
language: contain the objects it contains for them), the world to be known
is inexhaustible (in Gibson's language: there are more affordances than I
or we ever encounter), and knowers and known are indissolubly connected
(in Gibson's language: the objects of our perception—those real objects of
experience—are "affordances" or those aspects of the environment we have
evolved to find significant).

Grene's embrace of Gibsonian theory of perception and her naturalized
reading of Kant's Analytic make the worry she expresses about realism and
the Real puzzling. She feels compelled to defend some form of commitment
to reality against realism's detractors among "a chorus of social
constructivists, deconstructionists, post-post-deconstructionists, pragmatists
and other nonsense mongers."[26] As an exemplar of anti-realism (though not
of nonsense mongering) she discusses Arthur Fine's Natural Ontological
Attitude (NOA). Fine argues, among other things, that arguments for
(scientific) realism cannot themselves have the same abductive structure
that arguments supporting the claims of particular theories have. The
argument that there is a material world that is the subject matter of science,
and that science gets it right, cannot have the same explanationist structure
as, say, an argument that the structure of DNA is double-helical (because
this best explains the patterns obtained by x-ray crystallography). Fine's
NOA is the view that no conclusion stronger than that is additionally
required to support our belief about the structure of DNA, and that such a
conclusion would, in any case, require a stronger form of argument. The
same kind of point holds for beliefs about the existence and function of
genes, the interiors of stars, the structure of atoms, and so forth. We are
justified in believing such things on the basis of ordinary empirical

arguments. Since these arguments are fallible, on further evidence we may have to revise our views about what there is and what it is like. Such a fallible argument will not do as an argument for realism. That there is a real world is not a provisional conclusion based on the best evidence to date, but must have some kind of necessity to it to be worth the trouble of its assertion.[27] Grene rejects Fine's approach, seeming to read in him the anti-realism of realism's detractors and a demand for total explicitness in the grounds of knowledge. Instead, Michael Polanyi's tacit knowledge provides the escape from the see-saw of realism vs. anti-realism.

In this discussion of realism, I think, Grene fails to acknowledge the power of her own naturalized epistemology. Hers, is, after all, a modest realism—a realism of genes and bones, of atoms and stones. Polanyi's tacit knowledge is an unnecessary postulate. The "from-to" structure she finds in it—"the groping *of* embodied beings *toward* the understanding of something in the world that surrounds them"[28] is already in the naturalized TUA account and the Gibsonian account and accompanies, but does not follow from, the assertion of a tacit dimension. I think it is just this kind of argument from conditions of knowledge to substantive claims about the world that Grene's reading of Kant and Wittgenstein *and* Fine's NOA proscribe. Our "object language" talk in ordinary and scientific contexts commits us to the existence of real things—from trees to genes. Fine claims that the scientific realist's argument to a global realist conclusion has the same structure as an ordinary empirical argument within a particular science, for example, an argument that proceeds from the description of the outcome of an experiment to a claim about the existence of a genetic sequence with a particular function. His point about the philosophical argument (which proceeds from a description of the overall success of science to a general claim about the reality of entities postulated in scientific theories) is that it either adds nothing to the conclusion of the ordinary argument (there is a genetic sequence of structure X with function Y) or adds too much, so that we end up ascribing existence with some degree of necessity to things whose existence is surely only contingent. Kantian, Wittgensteinian, Gibsonian reflections show us that the existence of real things is presupposed by the very character of our experience. To think there is some further problem of the real is to set the lessons of these reflections aside. It is a response to the siren call of the Transcendental Object, the naming of an unknowable, that sends the philosopher winging towards the fly-bottle.

The proper response to nonsense mongers is, instead, to point out the flawed premises which lead to the unfulfillable demand for a proof of the existence of the real. Grene might well have rejected the demand for proof by arguing that the basic presuppositions of knowledge and of our claims to know are so woven into the social relations that produce us as human beings, in our language and in our material and social interactions, as to be beyond articulation. Such a response would generalize a point about the acculturation of scientists she makes in a 1985 essay, [29] and might have made the link between her views and recent trends in philosophy toward scientific pluralism and social epistemology more evident.

CONCLUSION

Grene's naturalism, as I have been trying to suggest, consists in an insistence on our animality, an insistence which puts knower and known on the same plane of ordinary reality—in nature. Of course, there are differences between humans and other animals. While we err in one direction by overemphasizing the distinction, we err in another in overemphasizing the similarities. Her reflections on just what kind of animal we are can help us see why philosophical reflection continues to be necessary (inevitable) even from a naturalistic point of view.

So, what kind of animals are we? We are generalists, able to survive in many different kinds of environments from the tropics to the arctic to space and manifesting a diversity of behaviors representing solutions to a diversity of problems. As generalists we have evolved a nervous system and brain of which a much greater proportion is occupied by neocortex than is the case with other animals. The behaviors made possible by that cortex—language use and the panoply of institutions, rituals, and practices that language use makes possible—are what give rise to our philosophical conundrums, both as explicit subject matter and as cause. Consistently with her naturalist inclinations, Grene turns to social anthropology for an account of the significance of the human use of language. Through the symbolic medium of language we create the cultural realities we live in (the variety of our self-constituted forms of life). This is what I take to be the lesson from the social anthropologists. Not only promising, but storytelling, evaluation and normative judgment are ways of making real what is not materially before us. These and other behaviors are the building blocks of human ritual and institutions—the building blocks of forms of life.

Linguistic expressions, however, are multivalent, context-dependent, and their use always context-embedded. Philosophical problems arise in facing the incompatibility of things that it seems natural to say. To take the classical example: "every event has a cause" from the language game or form of life of natural science, and "human action is free" from the language game or form of life of moral judgment and deliberation. To the extent that philosophical reflection is about understanding and (possibly) reconciling conflicting language games or forms of life it is neither about transcendent reality, whether Forms or Noumena, nor about the material reality as studied by the empirical sciences. But in being about language or language use, philosophical reflection is not "merely verbal," but about humanly constructed realities.

Some philosophical problems are peculiar to the idiom of a particular historical and geographical context, some seem to recur or to persist. But even in their seeming permanence they are articulated in the vocabulary of a given context. Marjorie Grene's gift is to have translated the concerns of some key figures in the history of Western philosophy from their context into hers/ours: to have shown that the philosophical problems they worried over are not canceled by but rewritten in a naturalizing idiom. Her brand of philosophical naturalism biologizes and historicizes us, but it keeps intact the meaningfulness of our distinctively human capacities and aspirations.

HELEN E. LONGINO

UNIVERSITY OF MINNESOTA
JULY 2000

NOTES

1. Cf. Kitcher's "The Naturalists Return," *Philosophical Review* 101, no. 1 (January 1992): 53.

2. W. V. O. Quine, "Epistemology Naturalized," reprinted in Hilary Kornblith, ed., *Naturalizing Epistemology* (Cambridge, Mass.: MIT Press, 1994), p. 24.

3. Ibid.

4. Some of these are collected in Kornblith's *Naturalizing Epistemology.*

5. Mark Kaplan, "Epistemology Denatured," *Midwest Studies in Philosophy* 19 (1994): 350–65.

6. Marjorie Grene, *The Knower and the Known* (New York: Basic Books, 1966), p. 40.

7. See Richard Grandy, "Epistemology Naturalized," *Midwest Studies in Philosophy* 19 (1994): 341–49.

8. Their ways of expressing this are, admittedly, quite disanalogous.

9. Marjorie Grene, "Idea and Judgment in the Third Meditation: An Approach to the Reading of Cartesian Texts," chapter 1 in *Descartes* (Minneapolis: University of Minnesota Press, 1985); (Indianapolis and Cambridge: Hackett, 1998), pp. 3–22.

10. Ibid., p. 21.

11. Marjorie Grene, *A Philosophical Testament* (LaSalle, Ill.: Open Court, 1995), p. 4.

12. Ibid., p. 25.

13. Ibid., p. 26.

14. Ibid., p. 36.

15. Ibid., p. 41.

16. Ibid., p. 42.

17. Ibid., p. 43.

18. If things as they are in themselves are what is real, and genuine knowledge is knowledge of what is real, then the problem of knowledge is the problem of knowing things in themselves, which is by original definition impossible.

19. Chapter 3 of *A Philosophical Testament*, pp. 47–64.

20. Grene, *Testament*, pp. 131–32.

21. Ibid., pp. 132–33.

22. Ibid., p. 136.

23. Ibid., p. 138.

24. Ibid. From J. J. and Eleanor Gibson and Richard Gregory, "The Senses as Information-seeking Systems" and "Seeing as Thinking: An Active Theory and Perception," *Times Literary Supplement* (23 June 1972): 707–12. Also in Eleanor Gibson's, *Odyssey in Perception and Learning* (Cambridge, Mass.: MIT Press, 1991).

25. Ibid., pp. 142–43.

26. Ibid., p. 113.

27. I acknowledge that this latter point is not Fine's, but I believe it is in the spirit of his deflationist argument.

28. Grene, *Testament*, p. 122.

29. Marjorie Grene, "Perception, Interpretation and the Sciences" in *Evolution at a Crossroads*, ed. by David Depew and Bruce Weber. (Cambridge, Mass: Massachusetts Institute of Technology Press, 1985), pp. 1–20.

REPLY TO HELEN E. LONGINO

Helen Longino is one of the very few people who have actually made use of my forays into philosophy, as distinct from local problems in the history of philosophy or in the philosophy of biology, and I am grateful for her interest. Sympathetic though she is to my concerns, however, it is difficult for me to reply to her argument, partly because, bless her, she is much more tolerant than I am of main-line analytic philosophy. So, for example, I simply don't understand her report of Mark Kaplan. How are traditional epistemologists left with "knowers that are subjects with no subjectivity"? Nor, more generally, do I understand how it is that the same traditionalists are apriorists. C. I. Lewis translated Kantian synthetic a prioris into analytic ones, but his method in epistemology was not a priori: in the introduction to *Mind and the World Order* he gives what still seems to me a very reasonable account of how philosophizing grows out of our everyday experience. Never mind that; I have to plead ignorance. Let me try just to comment on some of the points Longino makes about my own presentations.

First, about Plato and Aristotle. *The Knower and the Known* was a deeply flawed book. I hadn't thought the first few chapters too bad, but what Longino quotes me as saying about Aristotle is downright silly. True, I still believe, with all due respect to my colleague Mark Gifford (who has spent years and covered reams of paper analyzing Aristotle's reply to the paradox of the *Meno*), that Aristotle didn't understand Plato's problem and was talking past it. But Aristotle had his own problem of knowledge, which he dealt with brilliantly in his own way. It's not our way, but we can learn from it, if chiefly in reflecting on how we differ from him. (That is, of course, if Frede and Patzig are mistaken and there are indeed this-suches, instances of forms of kinds, not (only) kinds of individuals. Otherwise the Aristotelian biology many of us admire could not exist. But it does.) I hope this is clear from the gist of the chapter, which was published three years after my crude, but still, I think, useful *Portrait of Aristotle*.

Again, I couldn't have said that Aristotelian knowledge moves from the general to the particular—and looking back at that long-ago text, I don't believe I did. It's just that for Aristotle the move from this to this-such, or from the particular to the "typical," is much easier than it is for us post-Humeans. Nor, I'm afraid, do I understand the parallel Longino is drawing between Aristotle and Quine.

Sorry about all that. Let me hazard a few remarks about Longino's report of, and comments on, my own views. First, she says I see "human knowledge and human persons as features of the natural world." Not quite. Responsible human beings, as I understand them, are natural entities who have achieved personhood through participation in a culture (or a spectrum of cultures) itself contained within nature. Longino does recognize this a little later in her text, but seems to take it apart again in her conclusion.

Second, about perception: Although Longino later stresses my reliance (in the last twenty years) on the Gibson's ecological perspective, her initial statement of my view of perception is both too neurological and too subjective. I'd rather stick here to Merleau-Pontyan or Gibsonian formulations.

Third, about the (admittedly very un-Kantian) rereading of Kant in my *Philosophical Testament,* I am afraid I must have expressed my suggestion very unclearly. In the first edition of the First Critique, Kant argued for a transcendental unity of apperception as the mere fact that all my experience could be united by an "I think" and, corresponding to this, he posited a transcendental object, not a "thing-in-itself," but, again, the mere fact that something is there to be thought of. That's the complement to the TUA that I want to rescue. In other words, I want to transform the TUA into a real, live person and, correspondingly, the TO, which is needed at the opposite pole of our experience, into real objects and events that we confront, interpret, and sometimes transform as we encounter them. These are *not* "unknowable" somethings-underneath-appearances, but just the very real things and happenings that we as real live beings meet in our daily lives. In other words, I am denying on principle the distinction between appearances and things in themselves, and putting us back, as real people, into the real world where we belong. I happened today to come across an eleven-month-old creeping among objects—something I'm sure the sage of Koenigsberg in his well-sheltered life never encountered. This was a real little person exploring the real world in which he was finding wonderful surprises and irritating obstacles; a transcendental apperceiver faced with transcendental (not transcendent!) objects. What's wrong with that picture? It's exactly the opposition between appearances and things in themselves I want to get rid of.

And I want, of course, at the same time, to abandon logical empiricists' arguments for "scientific realism": that is, arguments to some "theoretical entities" located somewhere behind a sea of phenomena on which the scientist is supposed to float. Maybe in that sense I am not as much in disagreement with Arthur Fine's NOA as I thought. But he does seem to me to want to get rid of the realistic starting point I find essential. It's a question of what Joe Pitt calls "Sicilian realism" or "realism with a vengeance." As against free-floating analysis on the one hand, or naively reductive "naturalism" on the other, this seems to me (when duly injected with a good dose of enculturation) the place, as Longino puts it, both to start and to finish. And this seems to me in that article what Fine seems to be wanting to deny. If I have misunderstood him, I offer my apologies.

Further, still in the context of the transcendental object, as Longino reads my argument: the from-to character of knowledge as Polanyi described it in *The Tacit Dimension*, does indeed supplement my TUA (and TO!) account as well as the Gibsonian approach to perception. It seems to me still extremely important as grounding the direction of knowledge away from the ghost of Cartesianism that still haunts much recent philosophizing, especially under the guise of cognitive science. There is the brain, and then we add consciousness. *No!* The normal direction of knowledge is just the other way around, from clues we rely on to reach out to a real world. This is not something that goes on in fly bottles; it's the way we live, from my recently encountered eleven-month-old (of course, in fact, from neonates or even late foetuses) all the way to Kant on his daily walk. Nobody's looking for something unknowable here, just trying to describe how things are.

In this situation, I am also a little uneasy, I'm afraid, about Longino's concluding resort to social relations on the one hand and language on the other. Once more, I seem to have put my case, in *Testament*, unclearly. I can't go from my experience to social relations, because I'm always, and always have been, already in them; and the "symboling" I tried to report from Peter Wilson's analysis is not solely linguistic: it underlies (transcendentally??) the very possibility of language. Sorry for my unclarities, both of understanding and of expression!

M. G.

4

Richard Schacht

THE FUTURE OF HUMAN NATURE: MARJORIE GRENE AND THE IDEA OF A PHILOSOPHICAL ANTHROPOLOGY

Among the most under-appreciated of Marjorie Grene's many contributions and services to the Anglophone philosophical community have been her persistent insistence upon the importance of the idea of the *human*, and her campaign for what is sometimes called a "philosophical anthropology," conceived as its philosophical exploration. Her campaign has been a rather lonely one; and her call for a refocusing of our philosophical self-interpretation upon the character and contours of "the human" (or "the person," as she sometimes also puts it), in place of or preference to such familiar alternatives as "mind," "soul," "spirit," "body," and "brain," has fallen on ears that have for the most part been unready to hear her.

I count myself an exception, and an ally of hers in this campaign; and, far from thinking that it is a hopelessly quixotic one (anachronistic at best and sophomoric at worst), I would contend that this is a good fight well worth fighting, and that we have the future on our side. In this we join the leading post-Hegelian champion of the idea of a philosophical "anthropology," Ludwig Feuerbach, of whose manifesto *Principles of a Philosophy of the Future* it was the centerpiece. By my lights we also join Nietzsche, of whose own *Prelude to a Philosophy of the Future* (as he subtitled *Beyond Good and Evil*) the same could be said—notwithstanding Foucault's invocation of him in the obituary of the very idea of "man" he presumed to write in *The Order of Things*. Grene and I think that reports of its demise are greatly exaggerated, and that what Foucault took to be its death throes were merely its birth pangs.

We thus link up with a significant but ill-starred philosophical-anthropological tradition in Europe in the early and mid-twentieth century. Its heralds and pioneers include one of Grene's own favorites, Helmuth

Plessner, whom she has sought—through both translation and commentary—to bring to the attention of Anglophone readers; Maurice Merleau-Ponty, whom she also favors; and Ernst Cassirer, with whom she likewise has a considerable kinship. They further include several others of whom she is less fond: in particular, Max Scheler and Arnold Gehlen, whose versions of a philosophical anthropology she respectively finds too spiritualistic and too biologistic for her taste. Heidegger was disdainfully dismissive of it, deeming it a superficial rival to his own ("phenomenological-ontological") kind of inquiry into our human manner of "existing"; but Sartre came around to his own quasi-Marxist brand of it in his late-existentialist phase, for which his "search" for an appropriate "method" in *Search for a Method* was explicitly conducted. It also was one of Habermas's points of departure.

With the honorable exception of Suzanne Langer (who represents a kind of synthesis of Cassirer and Gehlen), Grene was the primary visible North American advocate of the sort of philosophical project to which I am referring here when I first became aware of it (during a year at Tübingen in the mid-1960s). Grene may well be right in her conviction that, at least with respect to their contributions to it, Plessner is the best of the lot, followed by Merleau-Ponty (whose labelling as a "phenomenologist" does not do him justice). I do believe that she sells the others short; but I entirely share her high opinion of Plessner, who in a different sort of second quarter of the twentieth century (say, if the Weimar Republic had succeeded, and the Nazi nightmare had never been) might well have realized the promise he showed in the late 1920s of becoming a serious alternative to Heidegger. His day may yet come.

In any event, however she got there (perhaps beginning during her graduate studies at Freiburg and Heidelberg in 1931–33), Grene seems to me to have the extraordinary merit of having hit the bull's-eye philosophically—not only in her understanding of the need for and nature of a philosophical anthropology, but also in the general outlines of the matter itself. Or at any rate, she has the great virtue of seeing as close to eye-to-eye with me on the matter as anyone in the lists of whom I am aware, past or present. In what follows I shall begin by commenting on the strange fate of the idea of human nature during the past century, the efforts of Plessner and others (eventually including Grene) notwithstanding. I then shall make a case for it, and for a philosophical anthropology concerned with it, and shall offer a brief sketch of the way in which I propose to think about it. I believe this case and sketch to accord with Grene's thinking, and offer it as a kind of tribute to her; but, knowing her, I will not be surprised if she takes issue with me on at least some of what I say. I shall conclude by indicating and commenting upon the ways in which Grene makes and frames some of the main themes of her philosophical-anthropological writings.

I

Does "human nature" have a future? By this I don't mean to be asking whether our species will be around much longer. Rather: is there anything more than merely biological to the idea of "human nature"? Does it still make good philosophical sense to think so today? If Foucault and his kindred spirits are to be believed, the very idea of "man" is an idea whose time has come and gone. *We're* still here; but the idea that "we" have some sort of determinate nature, about which there is anything interesting to be studied and discovered and said, is purported by Foucault to be a nineteenth-century invention that we ought to drop. Nietzsche famously told us that God is dead; and according to Foucault, he ought to have said the same of "man." There is nothing *out there* that has a *divine* nature; and there likewise is nothing *around here* that has a *human* one. Or rather: there are human *natures* aplenty on this planet; but all of them are historically contingent affairs—and this supposedly makes nonsense of the idea that there is anything like a blueprint of humanity that we all either do or ought to exemplify.

This way of thinking has become quite popular in recent years. Time was, of course, when things were different, at least for a while. Descartes preferred to think of our nature in other terms; but Locke did not blush to publish his *magnum opus* under the title *Essay Concerning Human Understanding*, and Hume went so far as to entitle his *A Treatise of Human Nature*. Enlightenment *philosophes* in France, with Gallic zest, took up the idea that, whatever else we may be, we are first and foremost *human* beings. In German-speaking Europe Feuerbach rallied post-Hegelians to the banner of what he called the "anthropological reduction" of Hegelian speculative-philosophical talk of *Geist* (or "spirit") into naturalistic-philosophical talk of "man." *Geist* was out; *der Mensch* was in.

Marx, Kierkegaard, and Nietzsche, in their own quite different ways, and with plenty of other company, were also very much concerned with the problem of how to conceive of and understand human reality. Yet they also had deep and significant reservations with respect to ways of thinking about ourselves other than their own; and their philosophical fans for the most part have been more interested in their mentors' reservations than in their proffered alternatives. And during the past century hostility to the idea of "human nature" just might have been the closest thing we had to a philosophical common denominator. Positivists, linguistic-analytic philoso-phers, phenomenologists, existentialists, critical theorists, structuralists and post-structuralists, feminist theorists and analytical "philosophers of mind" might be able to agree on little else; but one thing they have had in common is the conviction that the idea of human nature has no place in philosophical discourse. They have supposed either that it is not the sort of thing philosophers have any business talking about, or that *all* talk about it is much ado about nothing—or worse. Thus as far as they have been concerned, *der Mensch* deserves to join *der Geist* in the philosophical attic, if not to be committed to Hume's flames.

What are we to make of this philosophical misanthropic turn? One possible answer is that the idea of the "human" must indeed be bankrupt if so many differently-minded philosophical clans all came to think so. Another possible answer is that fads and fashions change, in philosophy as in other walks of intellectual and cultural life (even in the two Cambridges and neighboring precincts); and that people just got tired of the idea of human nature, and decided to clean house. There probably is something to this analysis. But this cannot be the whole story either. A further part of it may well be that many of those who have talked about human nature—even about a philosophical anthropology—have given these notions a bad name in the philosophical community, either by what was said about them, or by how it was said, or by things with which they happened to be associated. Sociobiologists and others of even more dubious persuasions make much of it; but with such friends, the idea hardly needs enemies.

Kant and Hegel both offer versions of what they actually call "anthropology"—Kant in his *Anthropology from a Pragmatic Point of View* and Hegel, in the "Anthropology" section of the third volume of his *Encyclopedia*. But their "anthropologies" are only *parts* of their accounts of ourselves. And the dimensions of ourselves and our lives with which they deal in their "anthropologies" are at the bottom of their totem poles of our constitutions. Each in his own way reinforces the longstanding religious and philosophical prejudice that what is "human" about us is *all-too*-human; and that, while we obviously have *a kind* of human nature related to our animality and corporeality, *that* nature is what we were put in this world to *rise above*. It therefore is something to be made as little of as possible, and left to doctors and novelists. Moreover, anyone today who actually takes a look at the sorts of things these two giants of philosophy have to say in their writings on the matter is unlikely to be impressed, and might well conclude that, if this is the best that philosophy can do with it the idea of human nature, then to hell with it. And that may be exactly how the neo-Kantians and neo-Hegelians toward the end of the nineteenth century reacted.

The influence of Hegel—and also Marx, and subsequent thinkers such as Dilthey, Simmel, and Weber—has also made itself felt in another respect, of which the line taken by Foucault is a direct descendant. For them we have become what we most importantly are not by *nature* but by *nurture*—that is, in the course of history, and in the context of social, cultural, political, economic, and other such historically developing institutional circumstances.

Hegel called all of this by the name of *objektive Geist* ("objective spirit"), for which reason in German the disciplines concerned with them are called the *Geisteswissenschaften*. On our side of the English Channel they are sometimes called "the *human* sciences"; but to most people they are "the *social* sciences," because that is the dimension of human life upon which they largely focus. And if the "human" is resolved completely into the "social," the result is the dissolution of any more substantive notion of the "human" than can be extracted from the idea of "the social," which is not much. Hence the derision in which the idea of human nature is held by most social scientists; and hence also Foucault.

A century or so ago, when British and American neo-Hegelians were Anglicizing Hegel's terminology, the terms "spirit" and "spiritual" were deemed as infelicitous as the terms "man" and "human," though for opposite reasons. If "man" seemed too naturalistic, "spirit" seemed too *super*naturalistic. It therefore was decided to talk in terms of "mind" and the "mental" instead, and subsequently of "agents" and "action." And so we wound up with "the philosophy of mind" and "the philosophy of action." It was simply *bad form* to refer to ourselves in terms like "human." That fastidiousness eventually turned into the conviction that there is something hopelessly superficial, naïve, and just plain *unphilosophical* about all such talk. The human identity of those whose minds and actions were under consideration was one of the "unmentionables" in the laundry of the profession that was to be kept out of sight. *Who* was performing the actions? Why, "agents," of course! *Whose* minds? "Ours," obviously! To say more would be otiose and vulgar.

The ban on "man" deriving from this sensibility soon received powerful reinforcements from very different quarters. Phenomenologists objected to the naturalism implicated in the whole idea of taking our nature to be a fundamentally "human" one, to be understood at least in the first instance in terms of the sort of living creature we are. Existentialists seconded the motion, adding that in our case "existence precedes essence," and ruling out any meaningful conception of human nature beyond the idea of our "being" being an issue for each of us. In their book any such conception is a fiction by means of which we try to avoid having to face up to our *Angst*-laden freedom and responsibility for ourselves.

Marxists condemned the idea of human nature as a reactionary ideological invention, intended to thwart recognition of both the possibility of and the need for a profound transformation of the status quo. Structuralists followed suit, taking any and all forms of humanity to be functions of contingent arrangements having no significance beyond the specific contexts in which they are realized. Feminists condemned all talk of our kind in terms of "man" and "men" as sexist; and they sometimes even went on to discern sexism in the very idea of a human nature (sure to be male-modeled) that would apply across the board. And then along came Foucault and the other post-structuralists, for whom the very notion of a human nature is nothing more than the conceptual product of certain nineteenth-century disciplines in search of an object.

II

In the face of so much opposition, one might well conclude that the only future the idea of human nature is likely to have is that of whipping-boy for whatever else might come down the philosophical pike. If Foucault is to be believed, Nietzsche was one of the leaders of the pack of its detractors. As *I* read Nietzsche, on the other hand, he has precisely the opposite significance, giving *der Mensch* a new lease on life. In this respect, as in so many others, Nietzsche is truly one of Hume's heirs (as both of them are Aristotle's). Here are a few of the things Hume had to say in the Introduction to his *Treatise of Human Nature* (1739):

> 'Tis evident, that all the sciences have a relation, greater or less, to human nature; and that however wide any of them may seem to run from it, they still return back [to it] by one passage or another.

> There is no question of importance, whose decision is not compriz'd in the science of man; and there is none, which can be decided with any certainty, before we become acquainted with that science. In [purporting] therefore to explain the principles of human nature, we in effect propose a compleat system of the sciences, built on a foundation almost entirely new, and the only one upon which they can stand with any security. And as the science of man is the only solid foundation for the other sciences, so the only solid foundation we can give to this science itself must be laid on experience and observation.

> We must therefore glean up our experiments in this science from a cautious observation of human life, and take them as they appear in the common course of the world, by men's behavior in company, in affairs, and in their pleasures. Where experiments of this kind are judiciously collected and compared, we may hope to establish on them a science, which will not be inferior in certainty, and will be much superior in utility to any other of human comprehension.[1]

Nietzsche in effect undertook to practice what Hume here preaches, in his own inquiries into what makes human beings tick, with the advantage of a century and a half of developments in both the physical and biological sciences and the *Geisteswissenschaften*. After announcing (in *The Gay Science*) that "God is dead" but observing that the interpretive "shadows" cast by the God-gambit linger on,[2] Nietzsche then goes on to ask: "When will all these shadows of God cease to darken our minds? When will we complete our de-deification of nature? When may we begin to *naturalize* ourselves [literally "us humans," *uns Menschen*] in terms of a pure, newly discovered, newly redeemed nature?"[3] He explicitly proclaims this to be one of the main tasks of the "philosophy of the future" heralded and launched in *Beyond Good and Evil*—even if a rather daunting one, owing to the doubts about many of our most cherished ideas about ourselves to which it may give rise. "To translate man back into nature," he writes, "to see to it that man henceforth stands before man as even today, hardened in the discipline of science, he stands before the rest of nature . . . —that may be a strange and crazy task, but it is a task—who would deny that?"[4]

Like Hume, however, Nietzsche is far from taking our humanity to amount to nothing more than a variation on the general theme of animality. The common view of his general conception of our nature imputes to him strongly reductionist and biologistic tendencies. This view, however, distorts quite seriously his actual approach to and understanding of human nature. We began as animals, and animals we remain; and, as Nietzsche has Zarathustra say, "'soul' is only a word for something about the body."[5] But he also considers human life to have been fundamentally, pervasively and fatefully transformed—and to have become *human* life in the first place—with the advent of *society*. So it is that he devotes most of his attention, from *The Birth of Tragedy* onward, to phenomena associated with human social and cultural life.

Thanks to this revolution in our evolution, we are (as Nietzsche puts it) "the no-longer-merely-animal animal." Nietzsche does contend that what he calls "the entire evolution of the spirit" is ultimately to be referred back to "the body" and our physiological constitution. However, he places equal emphasis upon the ways in which human life has come to be reconstituted and shaped in the course of its development. And in this connection he makes much of the social and cultural phenomena associated with its transformation, in which its emergent nature is manifested, and through which the conditions of the possibility of its further enhancement have been established. The decisive development, he suggests, was the "fundamental change" that "occurred when [man] found himself finally enclosed within the walls of society," and that transformed the "semi-animals" we once were into the human beings we now are.[6] The earth now featured a novel sort of creature, with a novel sort of nature. We are that creature, and its nature is our human one.

Nietzsche repudiated the notion of human nature as a kind of "eternal truth," with an immutable blueprint. "Lack of historical sense is the [hereditary] failing of all philosophers," he writes. "They do not want to learn that man has become, that [even] the faculty of cognition has become."[7] Rather than abandoning the notion of the "human," however, he chose to recast it, and to make much use of it thus reconceived. He clearly supposed that it can and should be *rehabilitated,* and made the focus of enlightened philosophical inquiry of the sort he commended to his "new philosophers," and sought himself to undertake. It is no objection or fatal obstacle to the enterprise of a philosophical anthropology, for Nietzsche, that our humanity has a history and a genealogy, and that it remains capable of further transformation. In both cases, the moral he draws is not that the idea of human nature is ruled out, or that things human are matters with which philosophy is incapable of dealing. Rather, it is that philosophy must and can adapt itself to the character of these objects of inquiry, in aspiration and method, as it proceeds to deal with them—and that such inquiry is every bit as important and central to it as Hume had suggested.

III

Nietzsche thus joins Hume—as Grene and I join them—in advocating and exemplifying what might be called an *anthropological shift* in philosophy. By this I mean a general reorientation of philosophical thinking, involving the attainment of an "anthropological optic" and sensibility in thinking about ourselves, and also in thinking about most other items on the philosophical agenda. It thus involves the replacement of epistemology—as epistemology once replaced metaphysics—by a kind of philosophical anthropology as the central philosophical project. And it is as attuned to the respects in which human reality is a heterogeneous, historical, mutable array as it is to its fundamental general character as a distinct piece of evolved animate nature.

It is this kind of thinking about our human reality that Grene and I believe can and should have a future, philosophically and humanly. Human life, to our way of thinking, is undeniably both a biological and a sociocultural affair. Its sociocultural dimensions are obviously anchored in certain of its biological underpinnings, and clearly are importantly conditioned by them. But its biology is equally clearly engineered precisely for *plasticity.* The social and cultural diversity of human existence past and present is undeniable, and stands in striking contrast to the relative constancy and uniformity of our biological constitution. Moreover, the open-endedness of human life with respect to the possibility of the emergence of new sociocultural forms must at least be presumed. These are among our reasons for supposing that at least a good deal of what goes on in human life, at and beyond the level of sociocultural phenomena, is not explicable in merely biological terms—even though we readily grant that it is an open question in what respects and to what extent this is so, and have no metaphysical investment in the idea of free-floating, free-wheeling "free wills" frolicking about behind the scenes.

This sociocultural supervenience, to my way of thinking, is a profoundly important feature of human reality, and might be called our "true supernaturalism." It is not that we started out supernatural, or are so by metaphysical birthright, but rather that we have wound up that way. We are creatures of nature *and then some*, having bootstrapped our way beyond our original merely natural animality. With the transformation of our proto-human nature that both made possible and was required by our socialization and the invention of culture, human life broke the mold in which it had first been cast. A dialectic of nature and nurture has been going on ever since, to the point that the very impossibility of disentangling them is one of the hallmarks of our humanity. Hence also the fundamentally *historical* character of human life, which likewise is no less real than its inescapable animality, and indeed is intimately bound up with its socioculturality.

Our kind of animality thus is only a part of the story where our human nature is concerned. The nature-nurture dialectic and our historicality are others. Another is what might be called our *psychosomaticity.* There is little if anything that we experience and do as human beings that is not psychosomatic, in the sense of having both psychological and physiological dimensions that are deeply interconnected. Our senses, our emotions, and our sexualities are all cases in point—and so are our arts, sports, uses of language, interpersonal interactions, and even our religions and sciences, insofar as they are ongoing pieces of human life, having to do with forms of human activity and experience. Nor do they take shape and go on in a vacuum; the dynamics of the interrelations between the psychosomatic and the sociocultural are the heartbeat of the human.

A number of the features of our nature converge upon and frame the problem of human *mentality.* We obviously have brains. But we also obviously have "brains," in the figurative sense in which it is beyond dispute both that we are talking about something other than sheer quantities of grey matter inside our skulls, and that we are not all comparably endowed. How are we to understand what goes on in our "brain-processes" in relation to what goes on "in our minds," even if—and indeed particularly if—we recognize both expressions to be more than a bit metaphorical? And how are we to understand both sorts of goings-on in relation to what goes on in our lives? We may not have a monopoly on this sort of thing in the universe; but there can be no doubt that much about the way it all goes in our case is inextricably bound up with the genealogy of our humanity.

Human mental life goes on only when and where the appropriate sorts of neuro-physiological events are occurring; but that is not the whole story. The warp of its infrastructure may be neuro-physiological, but its woof is social and cultural. Its setting is not only the brain, but also human societies and institutions and their associated objectivities—from the languages spoken in them to the customs, practices, rules, laws, and institutions established in them, to the artifacts fashioned and products produced and exchanged within them. Indeed, human mentality *is* not only some subset of brain-states, but also is social, cultural, political, economic, religious, artistic, scientific, linguistic, and other such phenomena, in their living reality as intersubjective *forms of human life*. Mentality has to do at once with their objectifications and with the varieties of experience made possible and structured by these objectifications. Our mental life can no more be adequately understood simply in terms of something going on inside our heads, abstracted from this context, than organic life can be adequately understood in terms of something going on within the individual organism, abstracted from its relations to its environing world.

By the same token, human mental life also cannot be adequately understood in terms of the various sorts of "sensory inputs" our senses are biologically configured to be capable of receiving. And it is not enough to make further reference to the chemical and physical processes that occur from the moment our sensory receptors are impinged upon until the resulting neural ripplings subside. I take what goes on in our minds and lives to have a good deal more to do with the *significant content* that piggy-backs on these processes than with their nuts and bolts. What we "take in," beyond the media of the messages, may be broadly characterized as *information,* which at least for the most part is conceptually schematized, and bound up with the interpretive and evaluative contexts within which its meaning is constituted. Information may be coded, expressed, conveyed, and received in certain types of sensory images; but what is significant about these images is *the meanings they convey*, by virtue of the significance with which they have come to be endowed, as elements of conceptual, interpretive, evaluative *symbol-systems*.

We "take in" both these systems themselves (as we learn them and continue to learn modifications and refinements of them), and also the rich variety of particular things they are used to convey. What goes on inside our heads and in our human lives is to a great extent a function of *the symbol-systems we internalize* and the interactions, transactions, and other actions they make possible. We relate to each other by means of them; and our experience of environments and happenings is laden with them. It would seem to be in our nature to operate at least for the most part by means of *representations*. And to whatever degree this is so, the representations by means of which we operate owe at least as much to the symbol-systems we internalize as to the sensory and neural apparatus with which we are endowed. Our neural system is the place in which such representations become effective; but it is the meaning-content of the representations that is of paramount importance in human life. And that content requires an entirely different sort of analysis, in terms reflecting its symbolic elaboration and its sociocultural objectification.

It is not unreasonable to suppose that the human senses and brain have evolved in concert with the emergence and development in human social life of the phenomenon of symbolism—that is, in concert with the capacity to use, generate, teach, and learn symbols, and to establish systems or orders of this composition. Indeed, it would seem that one of the primary evolved functions of our senses and brain is precisely to enable us to internalize, enter into, and participate in whatever social symbolic order might be at hand—the content of which then comes to loom large in what we go on to do.

The significance of the brain in all of this is *not* that, of its own nature and in accordance with its own processes, it determines what forms these social and symbolic structures will take, and what courses of events will unfold within the contexts they set. Its significance rather is that it makes this remarkable manner of existence possible. Other animals have brains, and senses, and may (like our pets) live in the same environments we do; and yet they are quite oblivious to most of what is going on in the world in which we live and move and have our being. There is an important difference; but what is it? To ask what they lack, and to answer that they lack "minds," is only to offer a word where an account is needed. A better question is: what is it that occurs in our case that does not occur in theirs?

A clue to the answer may be found by asking what might be *needed to mediate* between symbol systems, on the one hand, and neural processes capable of engaging our organs of action and expression, on the other. Hand in hand with the elaboration of such systems, there must develop a way of internalizing them and representing their contents. In short, something on the order of *mental events* would seem to be required as an *intermediary* between an objectified symbolic order and the neural order. A long period of evolutionary development may have been required, during which this constellation of elements was increasingly strengthened, refined, and elaborated, before human life as we know and live it emerged; but it could well have occurred, and very probably did.

This view of the matter opens the door to a conception of human *agency* that also makes conceivable the human possibility of a limited but nonetheless significant measure of individual *autonomy*, sufficient to enable us to make sense of those human phenomena seeming to require it. Our expressions and conduct may always be strongly *conditioned* by a combination of the way our senses and brain operate, and by our history of exposure to and interaction with our multi-dimensional and diverse social-symbolic as well as natural environing world. One does not have to buy into some robust version of free-will metaphysics, however, to salvage the idea that everything in our lives is not invariably and completely dictated by the details of this combination.

To rehabilitate this idea without having to venture beyond the naturalistic parameters of the conception of our human nature I am sketching, little more is necessary than, *first*, to acknowledge the relative autonomy of the elaboration of the contents of socially engendered symbolic orders in relation to neurological and all other merely natural processes; *second*, to take seriously the notion of individual mental life as provisioned through the internalization of these contents; *and*, on the other hand, *third*, to observe that we also have an affective nature that is not strictly social, in which other forces are at work within us, and impinge upon what we internalize. It is this third consideration that may be the key to the possibility of a significant sort of human-personal autonomy transcending the effects of socialization and acculturation, even though by itself our affective nature is less than human.

What our minds have to work with, in all human cases, is derived from what might be called our social-symbolic education, and from the register-ing of the multitude of particular episodes of the kinds they make possible, in a manner conditioned by the deliverances of our senses and by the general character of our neural apparatus and its functioning. But a human mind is a *dynamic* ensemble rather than a mere inert result. Internalized elements and registering episodes are not merely recorded. They are drawn into interplay and interaction *both* by the meanings they carry in relation to each other *and* by the more fundamental psychological and physiological processes at work within us.

Now suppose some distinctive and relatively persisting configuration of symbolically-informed and meaning-textured dispositions emerges, under the sway of which particular impulses can be mastered, responses controlled, and objectives formed and pursued through strategies devised. The result can be a human being to whom as much autonomy is attributable as the champions of choice, responsibility, and creativity could reasonably desire and require. At the same time, this way of thinking of our nature also enables one to make good and important sense of the seemingly undeniable fact that human beings turn out very differently, and very frequently do not wind up attaining to anything like this sort of humanity, in any of its humanly possible realizations. What more could one want from such an account?

IV

In dealing with our nature, there is a good deal of difference between truth and the *whole* truth. It is of the greatest importance to avoid making too much of certain things that may be true enough as far as they go—for example, that we are featherless bipeds, or naked apes—but that fall well short of doing justice to their purported object. Accounts of human nature, both philosophical and otherwise, have long been vulnerable to criticism along these lines. But that vulnerability is hardly fatal to the enterprise. We just have to keep on applying our intellectual consciences and making our best efforts.

That is just what Grene has sought to do. A part of her contribution has been to guard against what might be called the "over-biologization" of our post-metaphysical and de-deified reinterpretation of our humanity, of which sociobiology has been and remains a particularly salient and popular example, and with which an intellectually responsible philosophical anthropology is all too easily confused. So, for example, in "Darwin and Philosophy,"[8] she argues that while the Darwinian revolution does have some significant consequences for our self-understanding, they are limited. On the one hand, it has shown beyond all reasonable doubt that there are no fixed species, and therefore no fixed species-essences; and that consequently we human beings cannot be supposed to have any timeless and immutable sort of "essential" human nature. It further has taught us that the various features of any given species are fundamentally contingent, ours included; and that our status, like that of any other species, is ultimately that of a type of living creature of nature, however different from other such types of creature we may have become along the way.

On the other hand, Grene warns against exaggerations of the implications of Darwin's revolution. The idea of an "evolutionary ethics," for example, is deeply misguided, because no normative questions are settled by evolutionary theory. For while the latter may shed light upon how human beings came to be capable of responsible choices and moral judgment, it cannot determine what standards are appropriate when we do so. The idea of an evolutionary critical social theory is also hopeless, because even if evolutionary theory were to be able to come up with convincing accounts of how various social structures and practices originated, it still would not settle the questions of what is to be made of them and done about them, once we become aware of them and subject them to critical assessment. And while an "evolutionary epistemology" might help us to understand how certain ways of thinking may have taken root in human life, it follows neither that we cannot arrive at other standards of validity, confirmation, and plausibility, nor that we cannot commit ourselves effectively to them.

In short, Grene very sensibly and importantly separates the wheat from the chaff here. The basic tenets of Darwinian theory not only should be beyond dispute, but also have a number of significant implications for our self-understanding. The soundness of Darwinian principles as far as they go, however, does not establish that they are decisive in all areas of social, cultural, intellectual, and interpersonal life. It leaves the door fairly far open to accounts of what does or may transpire in them in quite different terms. Evolutionary processes undoubtedly set the stage for all of human life, and condition and constrain it in various ways; but there are good reasons for supposing that much of it can and does go on in ways these processes and their outcomes do not specifically dictate and determine.

Grene thus is intent upon distinguishing good naturalistic sense from pseudo-naturalistic nonsense. This is a battle she has long fought; and it is a battle well worth fighting. On the one hand, she readily admits—and indeed insists—that "we are not as simply unique, even as animals, as we used to think." On the other, she observes—and also insists—that we have come to be markedly and importantly different: "it is still true that we live more massively than other animals *in* artifacts, *in* culture, *in language*." Consequently we live "within our own norms," which we have made and can, do, and must continue making and remaking. And she contends that we "forget . . . the *human* nature of human nature" if we "confuse their organization, their axiology, with the biological and psychological roots of their origin."[9]

Thus in "People and Other Animals"[10] Grene contends that it has become all the more important, in our time, "to think through anew the basic principles of our view of nature and of man and especially of the relation between nature and man."[11] She proposes to do so "primarily in terms of the category of the 'person' rather than of either body or mind."[12] "To be a person," for Grene, is not to be "a kind of *thing*," but rather "is something human organisms can *do*." But they cannot do it by themselves; for it requires *"participation* in a culture or a social world," which includes "first and most fundamentally languages, then other symbol-systems." In short, she contends, "a developed human being is at one and the same time a *personalisation* of nature and an *embodiment* of culture."[13] Moreover, while agreeing with Plessner that "every human person has at one and the same time an inner world, an outer world and a social world," she maintains that "the inner and outer worlds are dependent in their human character on the structure of the social world."[14]

It is this Cassirerian emphasis on the crucial role played by the sociocultural symbolic order in the genesis and constitution of human personhood that distinguishes Grene's account of the "human" from that of Plessner (and also from that of Gehlen). Indeed, she invokes it even to make sense of one of Plessner's central concepts, "the *eccentric position* of man," which she paraphrases as the ability a human being can and usually does come to have to "stand apart, to one side, 'eccentrically,' from his biological and physical being and consider himself in relation to them."[15]

For what makes this possible, as she puts it, is nothing other than "the *achievement* of personhood as the *embodiment* of a culture"; and such "eccentricity" is made possible and mediated by "the artifacts of culture through participation in which and in expression *of* which he achieves that position." Working this out, she suggests, would yield "a completed philosophical anthropology."[16]

One of Grene's best and most succinct presentations of her approach and thinking on this whole matter is to be found in her essay "'To Have a Mind . . . '."[17] Here again she contends that "we urgently need a new, or renewed, conception of what it is to be human," and that this issue is best cast in terms of the question "What is it to be the kind of animal that is capable of living a *human* life?"[18] And once again she explicates and alternately frames this question in terms of "the concept of the person."[19] A central theme of her discussion, here as elsewhere, is "the strange, ambiguous, psychophysical, as well as sociopsychological, character of human agents,"[20] and thus "the relation between the biological and cultural aspects of human nature."[21] The two basic strands of her understanding of our human nature are our "bodily being," revealing "humanity as one, if a very special, sort of animality," and "the symbol-based and therefore artifactual character of humanity."[22] Or, as she puts it, combining these strands: "even being a human *animal* is already to be, potentially, but necessarily for the achievement of humanity in each individual case, already a dweller *in* culture, *in* symbol systems, *in* language."[23]

Grene is firmly committed to a grounding of philosophical anthropology in the best biological theory available, updated as continuing inquiry may warrant; but she also vigilantly opposes any simple-minded and overly reductionistic biologism that is neither philosophically tenable nor even biologically warranted. Indeed, she argues that, properly understood, biology itself sets the stage for an emergentist interpretation of human reality. For "in biology, even in molecular biology," she asserts, "one is dealing with a functioning, hierarchically organized system, in which the higher levels form operational principles controlling the lower"; and such a system "is therefore describable and explicable on more than one level and . . . works as it does only because it is so organized."[24]

What makes us so distinctive in relation to other forms of animal life, according to Grene, is that in our case a "higher level" has come into existence that has radically transformed this already complex dynamic, opening it to a whole new dimension of further diversifications and metamorphoses. That "higher level" is what we comprehensively call *culture.* Our human nature, she contends, "is defined by, and necessitates, a dependence on artifacts, on the symbol systems that constitute culture"; and it is "reflected even in our anatomy and physiology as evolution has produced us."[25] Thus "the evolution of the human body and of human culture are inseparable, and so are human biology and culture as they have come to be today."[26]

Thus a human being may rightly be said "to have a mind" as well as a body; but for Grene it is a mistake to construe what this means in a dualistic manner. Rather: "to have a mind is to have the capacity to acquire the ability to use symbols"—and thus it is "already to function as a member of a community of symbol users."[27] We likewise have "feelings"; but what makes them human, and makes us human for having them, is "the structure of such feelings within the systems of symbols that constitute a human language or a human world."[28] Human life further involves human *action*, which may reasonably be held to involve *choice*; but all human choice has "cultural presuppositions," which are not merely antecedent "conditions," but rather "*structures within which* a choice can be made. And these structures are symbolic."[29]

Thus on Grene's account "a human being achieves personhood *within* the artifacts of culture" and by means of them, in a manner mediated by them and made possible only by them.[30] And the whole of *human* life—along with the nature of human nature—is to be understood in terms of this interweaving of our biology and our socially sustained and symbolically structured cultural existence. The human sciences have much to contribute to its comprehension, but by themselves are not adequate to it. They need supplementing by Grene's kind of philosophical anthropology. It has long been one of her philosophical passions; and it has become one of mine as well, owing in no small measure to her. There is no task to which the philosophy of the future might more appropriately dedicate itself. After all, this would only be to rededicate ourselves to the principle with which it all began among the Greeks: "Know thyself!"

V

Grene seems to me to have all of this exactly right—or rather, almost exactly. I do have one reservation about a piece of it that may be owing only to terminological considerations, but that seems to me to have problematic consequences. I refer to her readiness to gloss "the human" in terms of "the person" and "personhood," and to gloss "philosophical anthropology" as "philosophy of the person." She does have her reasons: both to indicate its difference of optic from "philosophy of mind" and to avoid the unacceptable "philosophy of man." Before we all became sensitive to the appearance (or more) of sexism in speaking of "man" in this context, Grene—along with most of the rest of us of a certain age—often used that term in this context, as the equivalent of "*der Mensch*" in German, to mean the kind of creature all of us humans are. As that has come to be frowned upon, however, alternatives have had to be sought. I prefer to replace talk of "man" with language that sticks where possible to "human" terms, such as "humans" or "human beings" and "humankind," supplemented by "human life," "human reality," and "humanity." This avoids inadvertantly prejudicing the direction and outcome of our inquiry into the emergent nature or character of "the human," as it has come to be configured in the course of human events, and so of what it is or means (at this juncture of our collective career on this planet at any rate) "to be a human being."

I am sure that Grene does not mean to be begging that question; but I do believe that the use of the language of "the person" tends or at least seems to do so. To be sure, there is one use of the term "person" that is basically synonymous with "human being." But the term has other meanings and uses that are by no means neutral with respect to the manner in which "the human" is to be understood. And I believe that Grene sometimes is inadvertently influenced and guided by them and their appeal, even if she does not actually trade upon them (as Heidegger does in the mileage he gets out of his choice of *"Dasein"* to designate our kind of reality, and *"Sorge,"* "care," to express the "meaning" of our general manner of "being").

The meaning of the term "person," as Hegel observed, and as I understand it, has evolved along with the historically engendered human phenomenon it has come to designate. There is nothing about either our genetic package or the human condition that guarantees the realization of this human possibility, with its strong cultural and developmental presuppositions; nor is "personhood" self-evidently the entire upshot or main point of being a human being. Our idea of a "person," like our idea of "freedom," is a very rich one, owing something to Greek, Roman, Jewish, Christian, and possibly even Germanic traditions, as well as to subsequent Renaissance, Reformation, Enlightenment, and Romantic influences, not to mention a variety of economic, social, and political developments past and recent. It goes beyond conveying simply that creatures to which it applies must be conceived in cultural as well as biological terms. For it further connotes (or is at least suggestive of) the possession of a certain kind and degree of personal identity and personality, individuation and individuality, autonomy and responsible agency, and status and worth. (Hence its invocation by Kant, for whom the term already was a very usefully loaded one along these lines.)

Like the idea of freedom, this idea is undeniably a very important one. Indeed, these ideas and the human possibilities they signify may be among the West's signal achievements. Hegel's famous contention that "freedom" is the very nature of the human spirit, however, and that its realization is what human-spiritual life is basically all about, is clearly problematic, at least unless and until it can be supported by some pretty substantial argument. And the same would seem to me to apply to glossing human reality in terms of "personhood." It builds a certain *norm* of humanity into its very designation and conception.

Grene evidently embraces this human norm, and thinks that one who is a truly human being will embody it. She recognizes and indeed insists upon the fact that "personhood" is an "achievement"; but she would appear to be thinking only individually (rather than culturally) when she does so, and thus does not confront the question of its more general status. I am well disposed to this norm myself; but I am not so sure that it can legitimately be built into the basic conception or very specification of "the human." And I likewise am not convinced that it can appropriately be conceived as the "natural" developmental outcome of the constituent elements of our humanity, even though I would certainly grant that it has come (however contingently, unevenly, and perhaps temporarily) to be a very real, important and even precious human possibility, in the absence of the realization of which a human life is the poorer.

In short, it would seem to me that one can be a full-fledged human being and yet not be a full-blown "person." Moreover, I also am inclined to think that one can be a full-fledged human being *and* "a person" in a quite full-blown sense and yet miss out on various other very significant human possibilities that have come to be on the palette of our humanity along with "personhood." Among them are the capacities for the cultivation of various forms of rationality and knowledge, creativity and sensibility, physical and social activity, and interpersonal relationships. All of them may of course be infused with and transformed by "personhood" (and vice versa); but none of them is identical with or sufficient for attaining it, and few if any are even necessary conditions of attaining it or necessarily conjoined with it.

I thus take Hegel to have been importantly right about the notion of being "a person": it is a historically (culturally as well as biologically and socially) contingent human possibility, bound up in its forms and expressions with the kinds of institutions, practices, norms, and values that set the stage for it (when they do so). It further seems to me that Nietzsche was right to emphasize the uneven attainment of "personhood" among human beings—"One should not in general assume that most human beings are 'persons.' Some are *several* persons, most are *none.*"[31] The achievement of anything along these lines amounting to much more than a jumble of fragments held together by a biological endoskeleton and a social exoskeleton is difficult and relatively rare. And I take both Hegel and Nietzsche to have been importantly right in their contention that, remarkable though the achievement of personhood may be, there is or can be a good deal else to our emergent and attainable humanity.

One could of course take the position that this is not the whole story, and that being "a person" in some significant sense of the term—perhaps in conjunction with some of the other capacities noted above—actually is a part of what it really does or should mean to be *genuinely* (if not *generally*) human. But that, it seems to me, is a substantive point requiring an argument. In any event, it obviously is not settled by the availability of "person" as a gender-neutral alternative to the term "man," together with the connotations it has come to have. Even if Grene herself were to be rigorously minimalistic in her own use of the term, availing herself of none of its richer meaning, the temptation to read more into it owing to these connotations is strong, and can easily result in misunderstanding. It also is all too likely to inspire the unwelcome embrace of some (for example, those eager to have their "personalist" leanings vindicated) while needlessly putting off others (such as those who have learned to be alert to and wary of covert essentialisms). Both reactions endanger the prospects of the very kind of inquiry that Grene herself is so concerned to foster, which can ill afford either outcome. To my way of thinking, therefore, this language is best left to later stages of the game, in which it can then very appropriately be employed to do some important work, for which its particular richness renders it well suited.

VI

But this reservation does not touch Grene's project, and leaves the general outlines of her conception of human reality standing. And indeed, for me, it actually is a kind of virtue of her use of the term "person" in this connection that it spotlights the very question with which the above comments are concerned, and (as is obvious in my case, at any rate) prompts reflection upon it. This is one of the provocations with which she has enlivened her forays into this territory. She may only have given us her general sense of the lay of the land; but to encounter her on the subject is to be both tantalized by its prospect and challenged to join, joust, and jest with her in its further exploration.

In 1927, in what turned out to be his swansong, Max Scheler sought to launch a philosophical anthropology with his manifesto and preliminary sketch *Man's Place in Nature*.[32] Grene has sought to relaunch it on our side of the water, with considerable improvements. I do wish that she had long ago given us at least something akin to Scheler's monograph (if not her counterpart to Hume's masterful *Treatise of Human Nature*), that could have been serving the same sort of purpose during the past quarter-century—and could be doing so today. But even without it, thanks in no small measure to her examples both in print and in person, I am convinced that the idea of human nature does indeed have a future, and a philosophical one at that; and that a philosophical consideration of it not only is quite possible, even after we have done our intellectual house-cleaning, but moreover belongs at the top of philosophy's agenda.

RICHARD SCHACHT

DEPARTMENT OF PHILOSOPHY
UNIVERSITY OF ILLINOIS AT URBANA-CHAMPAIGN
MARCH 2001

NOTES

Portions of this essay are adapted from two of my previously published papers: "Philosophical Anthropology: What, Why and How," *Philosophy and Phenomenological Research* 50, Supplement, pp. 155–76; and "Whither Determinism? On Humean Beings, Human Beings, and Originators," *Inquiry* 32, no. 3, pp. 55–77.

1. Hume, *Treatise of Human Nature* (Oxford: Clarendon Press, 1888, reprinted 1960), pp. xix, xx, xxiii.
2. Nietzsche, *The Gay Science*, trans. Walter Kaufmann (New York: Vintage, 1974), section 108.
3. Ibid., section 109.
4. Nietzsche, *Beyond Good and Evil*, trans. Walter Kaufmann (New York: Vintage, 1966), section 230.
5. Nietzsche, "Thus Spoke Zarathustra," in *The Portable Nietzsche*, ed. and trans. Walter Kaufmann (New York: Viking, 1954) I:4.
6. Nietzsche, *On the Genealogy of Morals*, trans. Walter Kaufmann and R. J. Hollingdale (New York: Vintage, 1967) II:16.
7. Nietzsche, *Human, All Too Human*, trans. R. J. Hollingdale, intro. Richard Schacht (Cambridge: Cambridge University Press, 1996) I:2.
8. Grene, "Darwin and Philosophy," *Academie Royale de Belgique: Connaissance Scientifique et Philosophie*, Colloque Orginiseac 1973. Reprinted in *The Understanding of Nature: Essays in Philosophy of Biology* (Dordrecht: Reidel, 1974). Page numbers cited in this essay are from the latter.
9. Ibid., p. 200.
10. Grene, "People and Other Animals," *Philosophical Forum* (1972): 157–72. Reprinted in *The Understanding of Nature*. Page numbers cited in this essay are from the latter.
11. Ibid., p. 346.
12. Ibid., p. 347.
13. Ibid., p. 354.

14. Ibid., p. 356.
15. Ibid.
16. Ibid., p. 357.
17. Grene, "'To Have a Mind' . . . ," *Journal of Medicine and Philosophy* 1 (1976): 177–99.
18. Ibid., p. 178.
19. Ibid.
20. Ibid., p. 179.
21. Ibid., p. 180.
22. Ibid.
23. Ibid., p. 181.
24. Ibid., pp. 186–87.
25. Ibid., p. 190.
26. Ibid.
27. Ibid., p. 191.
28. Ibid.
29. Ibid., p. 194.
30. Ibid., p. 192.
31. Nietzsche, *The Will to Power*, ed. Walter Kaufmann, trans. Walter Kaufmann and R. J. Hollingdale (New York: Vintage, 1967), p. 886.
32. Max Scheler, *Man's Place in Nature*, trans. Hans Meyerhoff (New York: Noonday Press, 1961).

REFERENCES

Selected publications of Marjorie Grene relevant to this essay include:

Approaches to a Philosophical Biology (New York: Basic Books, 1969).
The Understanding of Nature: Essays in Philosophy of Biology (Dordrecht: Reidel, 1974).
Interactions: The Biological Context of Social Systems (with Niles Eldredge) (New York: Columbia University Press. 1992).
"On Some Distinctions Between Men and Brutes," *Ethics* 57 (1947): 121–27.
"The Faith of Darwinism," *Encounter* 13 (1959): 48–65.
"Beyond Darwinism: Portmann's Thought," *Commentary* 40 (1965): 31–38.
"Positionality in the Philosophy of Helmuth Plessner," *Review of Metaphysics* 21 (1967): 250–77.
"Biology and the Problem of Levels of Reality," *New Scholasticism* 41 (1967): 427–49.
"Philosophical Anthropology," *Philosophy 1955–65*, ed. R. Klibansky, International Institute of Philosophy (Paris, 1969).
"People and Other Animals," *Philosophical Forum* (1972): 157–72. Reprinted in *The Understanding of Nature*.

"Darwin and Philosophy," *Academie Royale de Belgique: Connaissance Scientifique et Philosophie*, Colloque Orginiseac 1973. Reprinted in *The Understanding of Nature*.

"Mind and Brain: The Embodied Person," *Philosophical Dimensions of the Neuro-Medical Sciences*, ed. Spicker and Englehardt (Dordrecht: Reidel, 1976), pp. 113–29.

"'To Have a Mind' . . . ," *Journal of Medicine and Philosophy* 1 (1976): 177–99.

"Sociobiology and the Human Mind," *Sociobiology and Human Nature*, ed. Gregory, Silvers, Sutch (San Francisco: Jossey-Boss, 1978).

"Changing Concepts of Darwinian Evolution," *The Monist* (April 1981): 195–213.

"*Die Einheit des Menschen*," *Dialectica* 40 (1986): 309–22.

"The Objects of Hume's *Treatise*," *Hume Studies* 20 (1994): 163–77.

REPLY TO RICHARD SCHACHT

Richard Schacht's commentary on my rather patchy work in what is sometimes called philosophical anthropology is extremely flattering, indeed, excessively so. I thank him for his kind words. But he is, of course, correct in predicting that I will find some small bones to pick with his account.

First, I don't think I was ever concerned with the future of human nature—though perhaps I should have been. I was concerned, rather, with reflecting on what being human amounts to here and now. At the same time, Professor Schacht seems to think that it is the future *exegesis* of human nature that we are both concerned with. In that respect, he is much more optimistic than I am. As I see it—and I have remarked on this situation at the close of my autobiographical remarks, as well as elsewhere in my various comments on my critics—as I see it, mainstream philosophy becomes more and more trivial or irrelevant with every passing year. Philosophy of mind, as it calls itself, used to preach something called functionalism; now, an even more *outré* concoction called "the representational theory of mind" appears to have taken its place. Even a thinker as able as Kim Sterelny talks in these terms. This seems to me the sheerest nonsense. (Schacht himself mentions representation at one point, but he doesn't seem to make it quite as central as it is to other expositions—at least, I hope not.) But, please, my conception, say, of philosophical anthropology is not a representation. Neither is my idea of what Descartes was after in the *Meditations*, or of what Aristotle meant by final cause. Nor is my present perception of the tree outside my window. Representations, as J. J. Gibson made clear in his *Ecological Approach to Visual Perception*, are rather special and unusual phenomena in our experience. To make "philosophy of mind" do duty for reflection on what it is that makes us the funny kind of animals we are seems to me unfortunate to begin with; and to base the conception of mind entirely on the strange notion of a representation only increases that misfortune. Of course, there is an alternative:

cognitive science, of which the less said the better. No, I don't see our colleagues working in the direction Schacht envisages.

As to his special heroes, there I have problems, too. I don't know Feuerbach, I'm afraid, and apologize for my ignorance; but I must resist being thrown back on Nietzsche as an authority, even though some of the passages Schacht cites sound sensible enough (though we don't "stand before the rest of nature"; we are in it). True, when I was a student in Germany in my callow youth, I was filled with *Schwärmerei* for that over-eloquent writer, as we all were. When I came home in 1933, however, filled with misgivings about German *tiefere Bedeutungen,* I decided he was more a rhetorician than a thinker, and abandoned interest in his musings. I never had gotten much out of *Beyond Good and Evil* or *The Gay Science*, and surely it's obvious that *Zarathustra* is filled with bombastic nonsense. Besides, can one forget Nietzsche's remark: "Gehst Du zu Frauen? Vergiss' die Peitsche nicht!" I'm not a professional feminist, but all the same, that's more than I can take. And how one can pair Nietzsche with Hume I'm afraid passes my understanding.

As to my objections to Scheler and Gehlen, Schacht is correct about my reason for mistrusting Scheler. In the case of Gehlen, however, I thought it was a whiff of Nazism that I objected to; but it was all long ago, and perhaps I've forgotten. Nor do I quite see that Sartre was doing "our" kind of thing in *Search for a Method*—which was, after all, but the introduction to that overloaded, would-be Marxist *Dialectic of Practical Reason*, where it turns out, predictably, that it was only on July 14, 1789, and only in the parish of St. Antoine, that there was human society at all. And human nature without human society is—well, it's what *Being and Nothingness* says it is: a useless passion. Not much comfort there.

At the same time, I'm not at all sure that philosophers in general think they are rejecting the study of human nature. When David Hull gave his presidential address to the Philosophy of Science Association, arguing that there was no human nature, he certainly thought himself to be saying something quite novel, and, he thought we would think, close to outrageous. It's just that they see questions in that area in their peculiar analytical, nit-picking light.

Professor Schacht has sought far and wide to find contributions on my part to the "anthropological" philosophy that has interested us both—although I confess to having abandoned many years ago any effort to treat it as a discipline in its own right. Most of the literature seemed to me somehow a bit too hastily systematic—perhaps even just teutonically stuffy. That holds even for Plessner, from whom I did learn a great deal. When it comes to my own very fragmentary efforts, I think the best I have done is in chapter 8 of my *Philosophical Testament*. I mention it here, because I there modified, and I believe, improved on, the formulation by A.J.P. Kenny that I had relied on (with due acknowledgment) in the essay "To Have a Mind . . .". Kenny himself, as I pointed out in that chapter, later changed his definition (about our use of symbol systems), making it so complicated as to be nearly useless. And in any case, I prefer the notion introduced by Peter Wilson of "symboling" to designate the kind of activity that distinguishes us as, in his terms, "promising primates": primates who can develop in surprising new ways, hence promising; but also, and most fundamentally, who can make promises. Perhaps I may take the liberty of referring Professor Schacht to that text.

His final question, about my use of "person" as a central concept, I'm afraid I just don't understand. There are, of course, ethical questions about when a human foetus becomes a person, or whether a brain-dead patient on life support still is one. But surely that is not a question for philosophical anthropology. We just want to know what sort of strange animals we everyday, functioning human beings are. I have indeed sometimes used "person" as equivalent to "responsible agent," and that's too narrow, since infants are surely persons, but not yet exactly fully responsible agents. But, except in those borderline bio-ethical cases (which I confess have never interested me), who are the human beings who are not persons? I have no idea.

In conclusion, however, let me thank Richard Schacht again for his very generous estimate of my contributions to a field that has interested us both.

M. G.

5

Peter Machamer and Lisa Osbeck

PERCEPTION, CONCEPTION, AND THE LIMITS OF THE DIRECT THEORY

In this paper we take up a challenge laid down by Marjorie Grene in response to J. J. Gibson's provocative claim: "To perceive the environment and to conceive it are different in degree but not in kind. One is continuous with the other. . . . [P]erceptual seeing is an awareness of persisting structure. . . . Knowing is an *extension* of perceiving" (1979, p. 258). Grene, a longstanding admirer of J. J. Gibson's theory of direct perception, noted the lack of an adequate theory of knowledge consistent with this claim:

> Once we have shed this albatross [the distinction between perception and thought], we can acknowledge that, again in Gibson's words "knowing is an *extension* of perceiving." No one, so far as I know, has yet articulated adequately the philosophical implications of that acknowledgment. To do so would be to present a fully elaborated ecological epistemology. . . . any more abrupt distinction between "thought" and "perception" becomes inadmissible, nor is there a distinction of kind between tacit and explicit knowledge." (Grene 1993, pp. 115–16)

Our goal is to explore how far we can take this claim. The claim rests on an assumption that perception just is knowledge. Its epistemic status is equivalent to that of conception in that perception is not an impoverished relation requiring conceptual elaboration before it attains a superior status of "knowledge." However, the path of perception, and thus knowledge, may be direct or indirect. Too often, we think, the tendency has been to characterize all perception as either entirely indirect or entirely direct (for example, Fodor and Pylyshyn 1981 vs. Turvey et. al. 1981). Those models that do attempt to make room for both direct and indirect perception seem to do so by proposing separate but parallel cognitive modes or systems. We believe that this type of theory is unnecessary, often redundant, and is inconsistent with Gibson's aims (for example, Neisser 1976; Baron and Misovich 1999; Rochat 1998). The very notion of direct perception as a representational cognitive "process" is antithetical to Gibson's claims, particularly in his later work. How far a Gibson-type theory can go in avoiding recourse to representational structures will be considered here. Our task then, in short, amounts to finding a principled way of drawing lines about what is direct knowledge, and what is not. It is also to find out when a theorist must have recourse to internal processes. To restate, our major aim is to find a way of describing direct perception in a manner that shows how it relates to conception, and at what point it is necessary to bring in the additional notion of representation in order to account for judgment making and problem solving of certain kinds. In so doing we also argue that it is not appropriate to equate "representation" with "inference," for inference involves a further step beyond representation. It is inference that is associated with the elaboration and internal processing that Gibson and followers (ought to) eschew.

In order to evaluate Gibson's claim of perception/conception continuity, and to lay down a foundation for an ecological theory of knowledge, we need first to establish what we take to be the important aspects of Gibson's theory of direct perception with regard to both the environment and the perceiver. In doing so we highlight two conditions necessary for any direct theory which serve as adequacy conditions for any direct theory of perception. We then turn to a discussion, using examples provided by Gibson as well as some of our own, of perception that is mediated or indirect. We conclude by offering some guidelines for distinguishing between direct and indirect perception and relating these to a suggestive distinction arising in neuroscience.

DIRECT PERCEPTION

Even Gibson supporters often claim that direct perception draws its sense from the contrast with indirect perception. Shaw and Bransford (1977), for example, cite Austin's claim: "it is essential to realize that here the notion of perceiving indirectly wears the trousers—'directly' takes whatever sense it has from the contrast with its opposite" (1962, p. 15). Yet, we believe that there is a positive characterization of direct perception given by Gibson and adhered to by his most robust disciples. This theory rests on two key points that together enable us to call some perception direct. The first point concerns the nature of stimulation for perception, while the second concerns the activity and nature of the perceivers. These two aspects of perception are discussed separately only for convenience. Gibson's later (1979) definition of perception as an act that always includes co-perception of the self recasts perceiver and environment as two sides of the ecological system, noting "the reciprocity of observer and environment" (1979, p. 164).

1. The effective stimulus in Gibson's later work is always portrayed in terms of a continuous "flux" or "array" related to an environment. This contrasts with the behaviorist notion of the stimulus as a discrete, isolated unit to which an organism makes a discrete response. Information (about specific features of the environment) is contained in energy flux produced from the interaction of the environment and the ambient media. This information is extracted from the structure of the ambient media as an organism makes a continuous series of adjustments and explorations. Perception is not a passive "response." The organism's extracting of information about the environment and its using that information in its action is the knowledge the organism gains during its perceiving. Knowledge is not to be conceived as a static state produced in the organism by the perception, viz. a belief state.

Gibson's innovation was to see that the physical variables that are effective in perception are complex and relational. (Julien Hochberg [1974] calls them higher order complex variables.) For example, in the case of vision the effective variable is defined over spatial layouts and over time, and in relation to the perceiver. The effective stimuli are not just shapes and colors. They are complex relations such as changes of texture gradients, symmetrical or asymmetrical increase of size (in the field of vision),[1] motions of objects[2] (Cutting 1986), or regular changes over time of the jaw lines of human faces[3] (Shaw 1977). These are the classic cases that display by precise example the strength of the Gibson direct theory.[4]

Notice that all these cases involve features of the environment that are clearly and unequivocally physically described by mathematical relations among elements (one element being the perceiver). All the relata are defined over time and so are dynamic in character. That change over time is crucial surprises no one who thinks of auditory perception, for hearing a call or a tune requires time. But an important innovation of Gibson's was to show that visual perception takes place over time also. The elements and their relations must be describable by precise variables that refer to them. In the clearest cases the higher order variables are described mathematically. This was recognized in Cutting's 1986 characterization of an invariant, "I suggest that a perceptual invariant must be mathematically specifiable in one of two forms—as a real number or as an ordered relation among reals" (p. 75). Information is carried through the unique correspondence between the complex properties of the environment and the structure of the effective energy flux produced by those properties acting on a medium. So in the case of visual perception, the layout of objects among themselves (edges, occlusions, and so on) and their relation to grounds (for example, texture gradients) cause patterns in the reflected ambient optical array. These ambient light patterns are specific to the ecological situations that cause them, and by this specificity carry information about those causing situations. (This is all more detailed and carefully laid out in Machamer 1978; it fits with program that is outlined in Turvey, Shaw, Mace, and Reed 1981).

In the direct ecological theory of perception, however, information is always information for a perceiver. Many of the multitudinous relations in the environment structure ambient light. But only some of the structured patterns of ambient light are in a form that may serve as effective stimuli for or are able to be extracted by certain types of organisms. In fact, which patterns are effective depends crucially upon the type of organism, that is, upon the nature of the perceptual systems of that type of perceiving organism.

In Gibson's terms, this is a theory of information "pickup." An organism picks up or extracts information from the effective stimulus flux, information that is *about* the environment. Organisms, through evolution, development, and learning, become able to pick up determinate kinds of information. The information they pick up is information that is somehow serviceable for them, or, in more Gibsonian terms, affords them possibilities for action or behavior. In the direct theory, information is always information for action or behavior. The theory applies to nonhuman as well as human organisms. It is direct in the sense that it is not mediated by cognition, for the claim is that humans as well as birds, rats, and spiders perceive by picking up information. The assumption seems to be that certainly these "lower" animals do not have cognitive processes that augment their perceiving.[5] More precisely, the information the organism picks up is direct because that information, without augmentation or mediation, is used by the organism to guide or control its action. No other information than that specified by the effective stimulus flux is needed by the organism in order to act in a way appropriate to how it has evolved, developed, or learned. It should be noted, and is of great import, that this pickup of information is itself one type of action. This dynamic, active feature of perceiving is the reason Gibson often calls this process "extraction."

The opposing perspective to a direct theory of perception is one that characterizes perception as inevitably mediated by cognitive (inferential) processing. One aspect of the constructivist, opposing, theory, often called the "establishment theory" (for example, Fodor and Pylyshyn 1981), is worth noting here. Constructivists often refer to many of the same physical variables that the direct theorists do. Rock's work on distance perception is one example (Rock 1975). Thus, one way of talking about the distinction between direct and indirect perception theorists is to say that the former claim that the relations defining higher order variables among such physical properties occur in the environment (and in the interaction between perceiver and environment), while constructivists claim that such relations must be put together "in the head." What has yet to be resolved is whether there is a principled way to tell whether in any given type of case, the complexity is a product of the environment or the mind. One suggestion that we shall follow up later is that mental construction seems a warranted supposition only when the complex relation, that is the perception, may be decomposed mentally, and its elements used in subsequent imaginings or reasonings. Put another way, if the perception, for example, of looming, consists of picking up a higher order variable or calculating, albeit unconsciously, a higher order function, the result in either case is the information contained in the perception. Now, if in the head, the calculation must be performed on basic informational inputs. So may this perception later be broken apart by the perceiver, and the informational elements recombined into a new imaging, reasoning or some such product? If so, information about the elements must persist in the cognitive system in a form that allows for the subsequent deconstruction into elements. That is, the higher order relation is preserved as a set of ordered elements, such that because the elements and relations among them retain some independence, they can be isolated and retrieved at a later point in time. If they come holistically, presumably there is no way to recover the elemental data that went into their construction (either external or internal).

2. Now it becomes important to describe precisely the use of information extracted. In order to claim that perception is direct in this Gibsonian sense, there must be a description of the organism's use of information in performing some action that is causally correlative to the information the organism extracts. This is where activity and the functions of the organism enter into the direct perception. In the example of the time-to-collision informational variable, the correlative behavior is avoidance, moving to get out of the way of the soon-to-collide object (see Schiff 1965). Both the variability of the temporal parameter, when to move, and the appropriateness of the behavior, move to avoid collisions, provide the correlation. The perception is direct because the action needs no other, additional information for its execution. The information in the effective stimulus flow is sufficient for the skilled performance of the action. (Of course, motor skills, perceptual systems, and so on, must have developed in order for the organism to act on the basis of the information.) The action is appropriate

because the action is understood as relating to a problem in the environment to be solved. The information in the effective array is sufficient to provide the information the organism needs in order to solve the problem.

As we shall discuss below, another added element used to justify the appropriateness claim often comes from an appeal to evolutionary theory. For example, it is assumed that avoiding collision relates to survival, and survival is a trait that is selected for. Survival is an environmental problem set by the organism's environment. Besides evolutionary natural selection, similar appropriateness-strengthening moves may come from development or learning. This correlation of appropriate behavior to environmental problems is crucial.

A further element of direct perception becomes evident when one considers proprioception. At the same time the organism is moving around, extracting information about the environment, it is also picking up information about itself, which Gibson (1966) calls "proprioception." He states this more strongly in later work: "The continuous act of perceiving involves the coperceiving of the self . . . the very term perception must be redefined to allow for this fact" (1979, p. 240). The extraction of information from the environment is also always the extracting of information about the self, the body, in relation to the environment; which is just a way of saying that information about the environment is always information about the organism's relation to the environment. This mutuality is what Grene and others have remarked as being close to Maurice Merleau-Ponty's claim that perception (and perceptual knowledge) always includes a point of view in the world. More specifically, Merleau-Ponty adds, "through this situation I have become part of all action and all knowledge that can be meaningful for me" (1951, p. 501). Gibson calls, in fact, the distinction between observer and environment one of attitude (p. 116).[6]

Despite its departure from traditional behaviorist models of stimulus-response relationships and its reliance on evolutionary theory, Gibson's theory requires that learning play an important role in perception (and by extension conception). One important reason why perceptual theory needs a theory of learning is to avoid the excesses of bad evolutionary theory or, as Grene so rightly puts it, to avoid "the fatuity of the so-called evolutionary alternative " to traditional epistemology (Grene 1993, p. 116). The best way to see this is to note that the second requirement for direct perception calls for establishing a relation between the effective informational variable present in the energy flux and some appropriate behavior on the part of the organism. In Turvey et al. (1981), this is only indirectly acknowledged when they speak of an "affordance" being related to an "activity." They recognize that one needs correlatives between environmental objects, properties of the organism and the activities an organism does; so they design a table (see Table 1, p. 261) that relates affordances with effectivity and activity. What is of note is that active verbs and nominalizations from those active verbs describe all the examples in this table. It is this connection that we have labeled "appropriate," but it is the semantic connection among the tabular descriptors that legitimates the connection. So that a thing which is described by "affords climbing" is semantically related to "activity of climbing"; an organism needs a climbable thing in order to climb.[7] But this would almost be analytic, so something else is needed. What ultimately legitimates this connection of activity to environment, in the eyes of the direct theorists, is evolution, or "ecological evolution" as they often call it. For example: "the non-ultimacy of the requisite non-dispositional occurrent properties is consistent with the view that evolution engaged in a good deal of practical engineering, making use of ad hoc regularities in the animal's world and settling for specialized success" (Turvey et al. 1981, p. 267).

This widespread, uncritical use of evolution as engineering theory in the explanation of appropriate behavior is illegitimate. The attempt is to ground the appropriateness of behavior in natural selection (not evolution *tout court*). Natural selection "selects" an adaptive behavior, so therefore the behavior is appropriate to the animal's niche, which is why it was selected.[8] But natural selection *per se* may only be claimed justifiably when there are differential reproductive results that are directly tied to the trait being selected. Very, very few behaviors can be so tied. Even if we expand our natural selection criteria to include more broadly based goals or selective principles (survival for the sake of reproduction, sexual selection, or even inclusive fitness, as some might wish), there still are very few traits that can even be plausibly argued to be naturally selected. Reverse engineering criteria, and even worse, the completely *ad hoc*, "if it's there, it must have been selected for" principle, are inadmissible as general principles. They are just bad science. What this means is that any theory that is going to have a basis in appropriate behavior, needs theories of development and learning to justify the appropriateness of all those behaviors that cannot be tied to natural selection.

Gibson, to his credit, and to the discredit of many of his followers, recognized the need for a theory of learning. For Gibson, the emphasis in learning is on differentiation, a theoretical move that dates back to Gibson and Gibson 1955. The basic idea is that learning consists in a "tuning" or "educating" of the perceptual system so that it responds to new, more finely differentiated determinate higher order variables. Experience enables the organism to attend to features of the environment of which it was before unaware. Learning consists in coming to be able to attend to, pick up, or extract these variables; it is the increased ability to attend to finer and finer discriminations among the information carrying variables.

Many examples could be given to illustrate this conception of learning as enhanced discrimination. We mention only a few. (1) Pediatric nurses report an ability, based of experience with the infants, to make increasingly fine discriminations among infant cries, indicating hunger, fear, discomfort, etc. (King and Appleton 1997). (2) Art history students may learn to distinguish Ionic from Doric and Corinthian where they might have previously distinguished only columns. (3) For novices to analyze wines by tasting, they need to learn to detect physical aspects of the wine that have heretofore gone unnoticed, for example, tannin content. Tannin is present in most wines, but in varying degrees. It has a slightly bitter taste, but a quite noticeable tactile astringent quality. In addition to providing this information, one also directs the students' attention by mouth location and analogy: "Pay attention to the back third of your tongue, and try to recall the taste of cold tea." Most students quickly learn to identify tannin's presence in wine, and very quickly are able to estimate fairly reliably the amount of tannin present in a sample. Once learned, the procedure used to detect tannin very seldom has to be retaught. The students have learned how to attend to the tannin content of the wine, or, in other words, how to extract the physical properties that signal the presence and quantity of tannin. This seems a paradigmatic case of learning to perceive something directly.[9]

Note that one problem for all these learning cases is providing a reason why the organism first attends to the new property. Sheer repetition or exposure can never provide a sufficient answer to this question. Similarly, to invoke experience as a cause is to give a highly noninformative answer. Some motivational or directive attentional factor needs to be introduced to explain why the organism shifts from being nonattending to the higher order variable into a condition in which it attends to it for the first time, and then on subsequent occasions. Even chance would not be sufficient as an explanation because the question is why it learns to attend in future cases to this variable, and this must mean the variable is given some importance for the organism. In some cases, the behavior or activity that the variable affords the organism justifies the importance. (The organism need not be self-consciously aware of this, of course.) Trial and error could be the start of a sufficient answer, since by trial and error the organism determines for itself what is important. But even here, something must explain why the detection is important. In the cases above, for the novice tannin detector, the budding art critic, and the nurse, the motivations and importance are social (and/or economic). As the examples suggest, ostensive teaching and particular uses of language often serve as tools for educating attention and improving discrimination.

INDIRECT PERCEPTION

Talk of language and teaching reminds us of the important point that perception is not always direct. Gibson himself maintains that sometimes perception is mediated. The mediation may occur either through a representation and mental act or through a feature of the environment. Mediating mental representation and inferential activity are well-known features of contemporary cognitivism. We will discuss cognitivism only to the extent that it bears upon our criterion for direct perception. Gibson's position on when, where, and how cognitive activity occurs is not well developed. On one hand he makes reference to constructive activities such as imagining and guessing. But, by contrast, as we noted, he maintains that conception is but an extension of perception, and so denies any inferential mediation. So where and how cognition, and intra-organism mediation, fits into the direct picture is a project waiting.

However, Gibson does pay considerable attention to the other source of mediation, that is, mediation through "things" in the environment. In the case of humans, the environment includes a "very special class of artificial objects," such as pictures, images, words, and signs that permit the accumulation and storage of information, that Gibson equates with civilization (1979, p. 42). These afford "a special kind of knowledge" that he calls "mediated or indirect," in that it is "knowledge at second hand" (p. 42). As clarified by Reed (1987), Gibson offers a new definition of indirect cognition, not mediated as involving internal representation but as perceived through external, shared mediators, for example, pictures, language, symbols.

As Gibson later states (and Grene quotes):

> The child becomes aware of the world by looking around and looking at, by listening, feeling, smelling, and tasting, but then she begins to be *made* aware of the world as well. She is shown things, and told things, and given models and pictures of things, and then instruments and tools and books, and finally rules and short cuts for finding out more things. Toys, pictures, and words are aids to perceiving, provided by parents and teachers. . . . The extracting and abstracting of the invariants that specify the environment are made vastly easier with these [new] aids to comprehension. But they are not in themselves knowledge. . . . These extended or aided modes of apprehension are all cases of information pickup from the stimulus flux. The learner has to hear the speech in order to pick up the message; to see the model, the picture, or the writing; to manipulate the instrument in order to extract the information. But the information itself is largely independent of the stimulus flux. (Gibson 1979, p. 258)

Indirect, mediated objects include, as Gibson notes, representations (pictures) of all kinds and words. "All sorts of instruments have been devised for mediating apprehension" (1979, p. 260). Words, like toys and pictures, are aids to perceiving and serve to transmit information across generations, aiding in the extracting and abstracting of invariants that specify the environment. In the terms we have used above, the child learns to attend to an object, for example, the picture, which causes its own effective stimulus flux. These effective stimuli are themselves "tied" to the mediating object that is efficacious in producing them, that is, the child sees the picture. But they are as well tied to environmental objects and events represented in the mediating object, for this is what the object mediates. The information in these cases is originally and crucially in the environment and only representatively in the mediator that the child is attending to. But for mediating stimuli to work in the way Gibson wishes, for them be to only tools used for gathering information, there must be a very tight and determinate connection between the stimulus flux caused by the mediator, the mediated, and the environment. What kind of tie to the environment must the mediator have for the information picked up to counted as direct knowledge?

Let us create an example of socially mediated perception and see where it leads according to our criteria for a direct theory. Our example is chosen because it is clearly mediated externally and may be nonverbal. Most countries with roadways and automobiles have adopted a traffic system that includes green and red lights. The rules regarding traffic lights for drivers and pedestrians are well known, and despite local variations (for example, the disregard of traffic lights in southern Italy or jaywalking in Pittsburgh), there is a certain worldwide stability to them. Car drivers are supposed to drive through green lights and stop at red lights. Pedestrians are supposed to cross the street on green and stay at the curb when the light is red. Even preverbal young children can be taught the walking rules, and can learn to distinguish and attend to red and green lights. The greenness of light is not the meaning of the light; that meaning is given only by the social code of traffic and pedestrian laws and customs within which it is functions. Red lights do not function like cliffs, where the sharp drop-off is perceived as danger (see Gibson and Walk 1960).

On a standard cognitivist view one would see the red light as a stop signal, and therefore stop. This would mean categorizing the seen red light (maybe the percept or sensation) according to a remembered categorical social scheme of rules that had been learned. Again it is of note that the rules could have been learned nonverbally, so this conceptualization, even on the standard account, need not be verbal.

By contrast, on the direct theory, a person sees the red light and has learned a set of appropriate walking or driving behaviors in connection with it. (In behaviorist talk these seem much like discriminatory behaviors, but they are a much more specific set, that is, behaviors that show discrimination in accord with the social meaning as behaviorally specified by the learning of specific actions.) We might say the green light affords walking across the street. But the affordance here is not specified by the physical layout of the environment, but by the social rules codified into law that must be learned by the perceiver. But just as the rules need not be verbally stated in any given case of learning, the rules need not be learned explicitly, in the sense that the perceiver need not be able to make them explicit if asked or even indicate in any way, except through appropriate action, that she knows the rules. Here then would seem to be a case of mediated social perception.

The red traffic light is related nomically (though it's a man-made social law, not a natural law) to a unique social state of affairs, and the appropriate behavior is nomically specified by those social rules as to what behaviors are allowable and which are not. We can think of no reason why this should not count as a case of direct perception even though it is socially mediated and the meaning of what is perceived is given by something external to the perceiver and not part of "ecological semantics." A pigeon could learn socially appropriate behavior with regard to traffic lights.

But let us consider the instructive case of a seeing-eye dog. These guide dogs are trained to lead blind people across busy streets. The dogs, being color blind, do not attend to the light, but they do attend to the traffic noises. The dog is trained to attend to the command of the blind person, who listens to the directionality and amount of the noise, and then commands the dog to lead the way. But what happens to a guide dog, in the middle of crossing, when the light changes from green to red and the traffic starts?

An early account of guide dog instruction by the founder of The Seeing Eye Organization refers to "education" of these dogs, a word that is properly used instead of "training": "A trained animal can be counted on as long as its trainer is present and is in a position to enforce his will; an educated animal prepared for its calling by systematic instruction will cooperate with its instructor and draw proper conclusions by itself" (Eustis 1929). Judith Core, a public relations official with the Seeing Eye Organization recently confirmed by telephone that crossing at a traffic light is the one case in which a guide dog is encouraged to go against the verbal command of the blind person, when the dog "judges" the command to be inappropriate for the present traffic conditions. The dog must, as she put it, "use its intelligence." That is, even if the blind person commands the dog to go forward, the dog is expected to refuse the command if it judges conditions to be unsafe and, therefore, inappropriate for acting. The dog, too, makes judgments based on traffic noise. The training proceeds by putting the dog in a variety of practice situations. There is no "rule" it is expected to obey. It is rewarded with praise if the decision is a good one and punished if the decision is a not a good one.

On our earlier supposition about when cognitive construction may be invoked, this case seems to qualify. Recall, construction or cognitive activity seems a warranted supposition when the complex relation, that is the perception, may be decomposed mentally, and its elements used in subsequent or additional imaginings, decisions, or reasonings, or when the experience itself can be isolated by the organism experiencing and the experience itself used in some further mental action. The dog, the child, and the adult human, in the changed traffic condition, must make a decision, or fail to make one. The alternative would seem to try to account for the dog's subsequent action in terms of operant conditioning, but there is no "rule" to which to condition them. A Gibsonian explanation in terms of too little or too much information does not seem to work here because the information available in that precarious situation is all that is ever available, namely, the sounds of the traffic. It is the conflict in the information of the previous traffic sounds in one direction being replaced by traffic sounds from another direction. The conflict brings the halt in the action, and a need for a decision, and for a new action.

Let us consider another more complex mediate case that Gibson often talked about, picture perception. The cases that Gibson and his followers usually discuss are pictures that, through their optical relations to an environment, convey some of the information that the environmental scene would convey if it had been seen directly. It is in this sense that Gibson says the optical invariants present in the picture are already abstracted or extracted. A clear way to envision this is to recall Durer's (1525) perspective apparatus. The picture carries some of the information, usually about shape, size, and color, that the scene carries, and so could be used by the perceiver to behave in some ways that would be appropriate to the scene. Actually, however, there are very few such behaviors. The mediator represents, in ways yet to be specified, the environment. The picture, thus, mediates between the perceiver and the environmental scene of which it is a picture. This relation of information specificity is more complex (cf. Hagen 1986), but for our purposes this link will do as described.

What we want to note now is that while some pictures may be used by some perceivers sometimes as sources of information about the environment, they are not always, or even usually, so utilized. It has been said that one could use Dickens's novels as a guide to the streets of London. This is a possible use, but it is not why most people read Dickens. In the case of most paintings, many photographs, and some illustrations, this manner of use is not normal. It hardly seems to need argument that a painting by John Constable of a cow is not meant primarily to provide information about cows. In this way it differs dramatically from a butcher's diagram of a cow, or even the picture of a cow in an illustrated dictionary. Both of the latter are meant primarily to provide information about cows, though of different sorts for different purposes. Further, people use paintings in many different ways. An historian might look at a Constable painting in order to glean information about farm life of the period.

Pictures often become objects of perception and contemplation in their own right. When one perceives the painting as an art object, and scrutinizes its composition, one is not using it as a mediating source of information about its subject matter. One is, in such cases, doing something quite internal: attending to and reflecting upon the lines and shapes, and their relations as elements in one's conceivings about composition. Of course, a perceiver need not do this, but with paintings one often does.

Such cases of internal cognizing do not negate Gibson's point about perception and conception being along a continuum; they are meant to show when the continuum must go "inside the head." Recall our seeing-eye dog. It is not a difficult extension, except for species chauvinist humans, to say that the trained dog, in some sense, has the concept that traffic sounds mean "stop." This seems no more or less the case than the child and the green light, or the wine taster having come to learn to detect tannin, or the nurse recognizing hunger cries. But there is a point in each of these cases, including the dog, where the concept becomes more than just training with regard to, or having a law-like connection hold among, object, environment, and appropriate behavior. The information, or some of the variables used as elements in the specification of the information, come to be themselves represented internally. They may become explicit as internal information representations, and then may be used as elements in internal processing or cognizing. This is not to say the perceiver in such cases is able to make the information explicit, for instance, in the sense being able to verbalize it. The claim is merely that the information is represented internally in an explicit fashion that allows for decomposition and use by internal processing. The other sense of "explicit," when it means "accessible to consciousness" or even "verbalizable," relates to a different point.

One possible line to follow here, which would be an interesting characterization of the direct perception and a place to draw the line for explicit internal representation, though Gibson and his followers would abhor this suggestion, would be to borrow a distinction from the neuro-scientists, Cohen and Eichenbaum (1993). They distinguish between procedural and declarative memory. They discuss memory, but we could just as well talk about learning. So, for example, when Gibson talks about learning to differentiate and attend, they would talk about establishing a type of memory, the idea being that what is established in either procedural or declarative memory just is a knowledge representation, and therefore something learned. Cohen and Eichenbaum also use talk of representations to characterize the different types of memory as different forms of representation. But this is not necessary either (as we shall see). Direct theorists and Marjorie Grene herself, who would prefer to eschew any talk of representation, or even of neuroscience, may translate what is said below into an acceptable vocabulary. But it is never clear why they must so trans-late or ought to do so. The point is not to let the vocabulary get in the way of considering the idea. So from here on we will put their idea in our terms.

Procedural learning, on this Cohen and Eichenbaum–type view, comes through the creation of a specific neurological pathway for detection, which, when established, becomes part of the wiring of the system of the organism and which functions as a holistic unit (one might almost say a transducer). The examples Cohen and Eichenbaum give for such memories or learning are quite reminiscent of the examples found in the discussions of tacit or implicit learning, for instance, perception and motor skills. In this way procedural learning seems to coincide well with Gibson's direct (and externally mediated) perception. Differentiation as "learning to perceive" is learning an attentional procedure that then becomes part of the organ-ism's knowledge, so that it may be used to detect that newly learned variable or information again. Gibson might say one learns a skill or activity by which one may attend to a dimension of the environment. This is like our examples above of learning to detect tannin, or learning to differentiate babies' hunger cries from pain cries. Something about the organism has changed, and this change makes it possible now to attend to and detect what it could not before. In many such cases a theorist is happy to say the organism learned a concept.

The contrast with procedural learning (or memory) is declarative. Declarative memory (or learning) is characterized by its being made up of individual elements, somewhat independent of each other, so that each element may be combined in different ways during different subsequent tasks or activities. This combinatorial availability is why Cohen and Eichenbaum call these individual representations "promiscuous." This corresponds with our criterion for when a concept becomes internally represented and explicit. Each element in declarative memory, or in declarative learning, has its own internal representation, such that it may be used by different processing systems or operated upon by different rules to accomplish different goals.

Let us think about one more case, this time of word use. A child learns the word "cookie," and learns to use it to refer to a certain type of edible object. The word "cookie" is tied by social conventions of reference to this reasonably specific class of objects. This is a nomological connection. When the child is presented with a cookie visually or in an olfactory way, she has learned to say the word "cookie" as way of indicating desire for the object. The child later learns to utter "cookie" to ask for one, even when there are no cookies present. The word "cookie" in these cases is not playing a "cognitive" or inferential role. The word has become an integral part of the procedure to obtain this type of foodstuff, and is a way to focus the attention of herself and others on a type of object.

But contrast this use with the use of a child, probably somewhat older, who says, "Cookies are good for me." Here there is cognition, and the word "cookie" has to have an internal representation that allows for its use in numerous sentences that the child may create. Knowing "cookie" in this way also allows it to imagine eating cookies even when they are not present. The first child may demand a cookie when not present, but cannot, due to the lack of an internal cookie representation, use cookie as an element in her fantasies. Again the differences in this case might be easily described in terms of procedural and declarative knowledge. In the latter case the word is a discrete element that may be mentally recombined in different ways with many other different elements.

It needs to be noted here that internal representations, as we have been discussing them, need not be equated with mediating inferences that construct percepts into concepts. That is, to claim that an object, concept or word is represented and available for internal processing is not equivalent to saying that perception is inferential, or that it is constructive. In these representational cases there is another step which causes a representation to be formed. But this is not perceptual elaboration or construction of any kind, and it says nothing about perception in general.

So here is the test: Does the organism possess, by natural selection, development, or learning, an ability such that performing the right activity in the right environment picks up a specific, higher order informational variable? The organism in such cases has a dedicated procedure (the activity and the channel by which it is effected) that it uses to extract a specific kind of information from its environment. This procedure is dedicated in that it functions without access to any of its intermediate stages, and without the normal possibility of interruption or the possibility of "conceptual" interference. It is not decomposable. (Of course, malfunction or some such may interrupt it.) The procedure and information extraction is also tied to an appropriate behavior that the organism exhibits. If these conditions are satisfied, then the procedure is direct. If not, not. Most perception, on this view, is direct, and so is much cognition or thought. But not all.

PETER MACHAMER   AND   LISA OSBECK
UNIVERSITY OF PITTSBURGH   STATE UNIVERSITY OF WEST GEORGIA
JUNE 2000   JUNE 2000

NOTES

1. For a review of these studies see the text by Richard R. Rosinski, *The Development of Visual Perception* (Santa Monica, Calif.: Goodyear, 1977).

2. Here is an example of Cutting's (1986) results: "there is a different set of nested testoids for every fixated object at every instant around the line of sight, when the viewer is not looking in the direction of movement. This is simply a different way of stating there is a different set of parallaxes associated with every object that the viewer may chose to look at as he or she moves." (pp. 194–95)

3. For example, "The cardiodal transformations used in our studies can be stated most elegantly in polar coordinates as

(1) $r' = r'(1-k \sin \Theta)$
         $\Theta' = \Theta$

See Shaw and Pittinger 1977, p. 122.

4. For a more recent example of this mathematical line, see M. T. Turvey and Claudia Carello (1995).

5. However, historical arguments to the contrary are evident, e.g., Tolman, 1932.

6. Several authors note that the notion of continuous interactive adjustment when applied to the case of the social domain invites parallels to Vygotsky (1978) in particular (Rogoff, Gauvain and Ellis 1991; Baron and Misovich 1993a).

7. This actually relates too to the intentional character of laws that they discuss later, but we shall not discuss this aspect.

8. For the structure of such justifications, see Machamer 1976.

9. Once, many years back, Machamer described this training procedure to Jackie Gibson, who agreed it was an exemplary case. This should not be surprising since one of the early Gibson studies was on wine detection, see Dean Owen and Peter Machamer 1979.

REFERENCES

Austin, J. L. 1962. *Sense and Sensibilia*. New York: Oxford University Press.
Baron, R., and S. Misovich. 1993. "An Integration of Gibsonian and Vygotskian Perspectives on Changing Attitudes in Group Contexts." *British Journal of Social Psychology* 32: 53–70.
———. 1999. "On the Relationship Between Social and Cognitive Modes of Organization." In S. Chaiken and Y. Trope, eds., *Dual-process Theories in Social Psychology*. New York, N.Y.: The Guilford Press, pp. 586–605.
Cohen, N. J., and H. Eichenbaum. 1993. *Memory, Amnesia, and the Hippocampal System*. Cambridge, Mass.: MIT Press.
Cutting, James E. 1986. *Perception with an Eye for Motion*. Cambridge, Mass.: MIT Press.
Durer, A. 1977. *The Painter's Manual*. Translated with Commentary by Walter L. Strauss. New York: Abaris Books. Originally published 1525.
Eustis, Dorothy Harrison. 1929. "Dogs as Guides for the Blind." Available on website: www.seingeye.org/deustis.html.
Fodor, J. A., and Z. W. Pylyshyn. 1981. "How Direct is Visual Perception? Some Reflections on Gibson's 'Ecological Approach.'" *Cognition* 9, no. 2: 139–96.
Gibson, E. J., and R. D. Walk. 1960. "The Visual Cliff." *Scientific American* 202: 64–71.
Gibson, J. J. 1966. *The Senses Considered as Perceptual Systems*. Boston: Houghton-Mifflin.
———. 1979. *The Ecological Approach to Visual Perception*. Boston: Houghton-Mifflin.
Gibson, J. J., and E. J. Gibson. 1955. "Perceptual Learning: Differentiation or Enrichment." *Psychological Review* 62: 32–41.
Grene, M. 1993. "The Primacy of the Ecological Self." In Ulrich Neisser, ed., *The Perceived Self*. Cambridge: Cambridge University Press.
Hagen, Margret A. 1986. *Varieties of Realism: Geometries of Representational Art*. Cambridge: Cambridge University Press.
Hochberg, J. 1974. "Higher-order Stimuli and Inter-response Coupling in the Perception of the Visual World." In H. Pick and R. MacLeod, *Perception: Essays in Honor of J. J. Gibson*. Ithaca, N.Y.: Cornell University Press, pp. 17–39.
King, L., and J. Appleton. 1997. "Intuition: A Critical Review of the Research and Rhetoric." *Journal of Advanced Nursing* 26: 194–202.
Machamer, Peter K. 1978. "Gibson and the Conditions of Perception." In Peter K. Machamer and Robert G. Turnbull, eds., *Studies in Perception*. Columbus, Ohio: Ohio Studies University Press.
Merleau-Ponty, M. 1951. "The Philosopher and Sociology." In M. Natanson, ed., *Philosophy of the Social Sciences: A Reader*. New York: Random House, pp. 487–505.
Neisser, U. 1976. *Cognition and Reality*. New York: Freeman & Co.
Owen, Dean, and Peter Machamer. 1979. "Improvement in Wine Discrimination." *Perception* 8: 199–209.

Reed, E. S. 1987. "James Gibson's Ecological Approach to Cognition." In A. Costall and A. Still, eds., *Cognitive Psychology in Question*. Sussex: Harvester Press.

Rochat, P. 1999. "Direct Perception and Representation in Infancy." In Fivush Winograd and Hirst, eds., *Ecological Approaches to Cognition: Essays in Honor of Ulric Neisser*. Mahwah, N.J.: Lawrence Erlbaum Associates, pp. 3–30.

Rock, I. 1975. *An Introduction to Perception*. New York: Macmillan.

Rogoff, B., M. Gauvain, and S. Ellis. 1991. "Development Viewed in its Cultural Context." In P. Light, S. Sheldon, and M. Woodhead, eds., *Learning to Think*. London: Routledge.

Rosinski, Richard R. 1977. *The Development of Visual Perception*. Santa Monica, Calif.: Goodyear.

Schiff, William. 1965. "Perception of Impending Collision: A Study of Visually Directed Avoidant Behavior." *Psychological Monographs* 79 (11), no. 604.

Shaw, R., and J. Bransford. 1977. *Perceiving, Acting, and Knowing*. Hillsdale, N.J.: Lawrence Erlbaum Associates.

Shaw, Robert, and Pittinger. 1977. "Perceiving the Face of Change in Changing Faces: Implications for a Theory of Object Perception." In Shaw and Bransford (1977), pp. 103–32

Tolman, E. C. 1932. *Purposive Behavior in Animals and Men*. New York: Century Co.

Turvey, M. T., R. E. Shaw, E. S. Reed, and W. M. Mace. 1981. "Ecological Laws of Perceiving and Acting: In Reply to Fodor and Pylshyn." *Cognition* 9, no. 3: 237–304.

Turvey, M. T., and Claudia Carello. 1995. "Some Dynamic Themes in Perception and Action." In Robert F. Port and Timothy van Gelder, eds., *Mind as Motion: Explorations in the Dynamics of Cognition*. Cambridge, Mass.: MIT Press, 1995, pp. 373–401.

Vygoysky, L. S. 1978. *Mind in Society: The Development of Higher Psychological Processes*. Cambridge, Mass.: Harvard University Press.

REPLY TO PETER MACHAMER
AND LISA OSBECK

Machamer and Osbeck announce at the start of their essay that they are taking up a "challenge" laid down by me with respect to the epistemological implications of J. J. Gibson's theory of perception. According to Gibson, knowing is an extension of perceiving—which, in his view (and in fact, as I believe) is a primordial form of knowing and at the same time the foundation of all knowledge. The present authors tell us that I have "noted the lack of an adequate theory of knowledge consistent with this claim," and they quote a brief statement of mine from a paper on the primacy of the ecological self. That paper was prepared for a meeting organized by Ulric Neisser, in which I criticized his undertaking to distinguish, I believe it was five, different selves. In particular, I was at that point (at the conclusion of the essay) contesting a distinction of kind between what Neisser had called a perceived and a conceptual self, and I noted that to deal properly with the continuity I found here one would need to develop a full ecological epistemology. I was not suggesting such a "lack" as in any way indicating its impossibility. The point, made there in passing, and in the context of a quite different argument, is made more clearly, I believe, in the chapter of my *Philosophical Testament* in which I try to set out some of the philosophical implications of the Gibsons' theory. There I have asked: "where knowledge goes beyond the perceptual, is it nevertheless analogous to perception in its structure?" (p. 146). In other words, does it involve the triad, things or events in the world, invariants (that is, constancies through change that contain information), and, through the pick-up of that information, awareness of affordances offered to the perceiver (or more generally, the knower) by something in that environment? My answer was, "Yes." So I was not laying down a challenge in the sense of a dare, or even a challenge to a duel, as Machamer and Osbeck seem to think. I was suggesting that philosophical reflection about knowledge might, and should be enriched by reliance on the Gibsonian model of the way we orient ourselves, cognitively, in our environments, whether in everyday perception or in more sophisticated, if you like, more intellectual situations. As I put it, in part, in my "ecological" chapter:

> There is something in the real world that the scientist wants to understand; in his highly disciplined, artefactual environment, which includes not only his laboratory and its equipment, but the language of his discipline, the experimental techniques developed by his own group and by others he has met or read of: in that environment he has learned to pick up the information that allows him(her) to "see" what is going on: to pick up the evidence for something previously suspected perhaps, but not before substantiated. (p. 147)

Gibson called perception mediated by language, tools, or pictures "indirect," and Machamer and Osbeck make a great deal of that distinction. I think that is unfortunate: the cultural institutions within which we have our being are our home, and what we perceive there is as perception no more indirect than any other awareness of affordances. As I have noted elsewhere, Gibson's own sketch, in his last book, of the observer, clad and shod, beside a window and, if my memory serves me, even with a T.V. set in view, is highly enculturated. And, heaven help me, slave of technology that I am, when I look at my computer screen I am indeed looking, as much so as when I look at a young cardinal trying to fly from tree to tree. Thus there is no more a break between "direct" and "indirect" perception than there is between more and less perceptually grounded knowledge.

Machamer and Osbeck, however, want to make a great deal of that distinction. Indeed, they want, at one point (when "concepts" come into it, I guess) to turn from psychology to a neurological distinction. Of course there is nothing wrong with neurological explanations: it's a great and necessary science. But why start part way up the cognitive hierarchy? All perception could be studied at a neurological level, fine; without a working nervous system there would be no knowledge, perceptual or otherwise, and the more is understood about it the better. But it is also possible to study perception, or more generally our ways of becoming aware of things and events around us, behaviorally, rather than neurologically, all the way up. And further, philosophical reflection on our powers of knowledge, on the question, what it means to make a knowledge claim, is neither psychological nor neurological. Personally, I find the ecological approach illuminating for such reflection. But it's not the same thing. In any case, I must confess, I do not find the neurological distinction introduced by the present authors enlightening: I don't see that conceptual knowledge can always be taken to pieces, as they seem to be suggesting. Nor do I know what they mean by going "into the head." In fact, I was under the impression that at least four of our five perceptual systems were already conspicuously in the head; and maybe there is some central control of touch as well, I don't know.

When I have thought, as I confess I have done only spottily, about my hope of developing a Gibson-like ecological epistemology, I have usually thought, as the above passage indicates, about the cognitive activities of scientists. But let me try an illustration from history, a discipline in general far removed from everyday perception. Here, too, I think, the ecological trio applies. Mordechai Feingold is engaged in writing an exhaustive, and, he hopes, definitive history of the Royal Society of Great Britain. I have been interested in his claim that there was a longstanding debate in the Society between naturalists and mathematicians concerning the scientific standing of their respective disciplines, and I have before me a paper in which he has recently told this story under the title "Mathematicians and Naturalists: Sir Isaac Newton and the Royal Society."[1] What is Feingold doing here? He's a long way from ordinary perception. But I think the ever-present triad still applies. There are things and events that he wants to understand. They are past events, and past people, to be sure; he can't speak with his chief protagonists, or watch their body language. Without getting into the tricky—and usually rather silly—question about the reality of the past, we can surely say that there has been a Royal Society since the seventeenth century and certain figures were specially active in it, say between 1680 and 1720. Feingold, as a trained historian, reads, not only the *Philosophical Transactions* of the Society, but its participants' letters to one another and to others—which he knows how to find. These materials offer him sufficient constancies—invariants—so that he becomes aware of a persistent rivalry between two camps: naturalists like Sloan or Lister and mathematicians like Newton and his devoted followers. This is a long way from looking out my window at the dogwood blossoms and the cardinal, but it's still a case of approaching some aspect of the real world and finding in it persistent patterns that allow me to "see" what is going on.

Incidentally, of course, the same structure holds for Machamer and Osbeck's educated dog. It seems to me they have invented a problem, and they have certainly misread my 1993 suggestion, which expressed rather a hope than a challenge. I thank them for taking the trouble to develop their argument, but, alas, it leaves me unmoved.

M. G.

NOTES

1. In *Isaac Newton's Natural Philosophy*, ed. Jed Z. Buchwald and I. Bernard Cohen (Cambridge, Mass.: M.I.T. Press, 2000), pp. 78–102.

6

Michael Luntley

AGENCY AND OUR TACIT SENSE
OF THINGS

I

A standard view of the relationship between perception, thought, and action goes like this: Our perceptual apparatus comprises an assemblage of delivery systems that deliver packages of content to a cognitive center. These contents represent how things are. The cognitive center performs operations upon content. These are the operations of thought. (They may also include operations that operate at a level lower than that of conceptual thought.) Another delivery system comprising the passions and imagination provides the center with contents that represent not how things are, but how we desire them to be. When the cognitive center is in receipt of both kinds of content, the upshot of its operations upon them is the set of instructions for motor control that constitutes the beginning of action. Agency turns out to be something that is ascribable to things that exemplify this standard model.

It is not, however, easy to capture our ordinary concept of agency within the standard model. Our ordinary practices of agency ascription require a continuous self to bear responsibility for its doings. Following Locke, the smartest move still at play within the standard model is to attempt to define the identity of the agent in terms of a continuity of contents within the cognitive center. Such reductionism about the self renders problematic (if not unintelligible) some of our basic ideas, such as our concern to survive. More often than not this has been taken as an excuse for further philosophical industry rather than a signal that something is seriously amiss with the standard model.[1] No matter, for the standard model is false.

There is a growing body of work that makes it plain that, even disregarding its problematic consequences for agency, the very first move that treats perception as the delivery of information is simply unworkable. Anyone attracted to the idea of tacit knowledge or to the phenomenological tradition that sees perception as a "dwelling with things" will find the standard model deeply suspect. Perception is not so much the *delivery* of something as the *enabling* of our sense of things, where our "sense of things" is understood relationally. In the absence of an argument why the standard model *has* to be wrong, it is, however, open for its proponents to respond that such claims are the results of an undue reliance upon a common-sense and familiar description of how we take ourselves to be in the world. The fact that we do not ordinarily take the point of perception to be a delivery of information to us, but rather take it to be a direct engagement with things, may be, for all that, a consequence of a false view we have of ourselves. I do not believe that it is a false view of ourselves to see ourselves as fundamentally in touch with things, but we need an argument here. We need an argument that shows why the idea of a tacit and direct sense of things is essential to our self-conception.

I want to explore the idea that the concept of agency is central to the argument we need. Rather than being thought of as something to work on after a theory of content is in place, agency is central to the theory of content. Furthermore, I want to suggest that our basic orientation to the world is one that exhibits a fundamental restlessness of agency. We are, by nature, restless creatures and this restlessness is a primitive feature of our sense of things. This may sound obscure. From the perspective of the standard model, "restlessness" sounds like a label for something waiting to be understood, regimented, and tied down, rather than a primitive. The concept of restlessness that I want to articulate is not, however, the concept of something that marks a gap in the otherwise seamless transfer from perceptual input, through processing, to motor output and behavior. It is not an interruption, or a dithering, in the cognitive center. Restlessness is an essential characteristic of creatures that operate with concepts, whose sense of things is conceptually organized. Possession of concepts not only brings us directly in touch with things, but it provides us with a creativity of thought and action that lies at the heart of what I am calling the "restlessness of agency."

On the standard model, possession of concepts concerns the structures of the information packages delivered to the cognitive center by perception. It is this basic conception of conceptual content that is wrong with the standard model. The response that I want to explore arises from a reconfiguration of the notion of conceptual content. It is from an account of content that we see the inescapable attachment that we have to things. It is by possession of content that we are in touch with things, rather than imitations of things delivered by the perceptual inputs. And the way that concepts put us in direct touch with things makes the restless creativity of agency a core characteristic of our sense of things, not an aberration.

II

Professor Grene speaks of the precariousness of our sense of things. Her account draws upon and illuminates the sense of things of the artist:

> human dwelling through the body out there with things is . . . precarious. It is never total spectatorhood but neither is it quite total being-in. It has the doubleness experienced precisely in the painter's task: to achieve perception, achieve communion with the world by making something that expresses, but *is* not quite, the world itself.[2]

It is this "doubleness" that I want to get in focus. In her essay, Grene uses Merleau-Ponty's phenomenology to articulate the intimacy of our sense of things. Merleau-Ponty sees our sense of things in terms of *existence*, a mode of being that is "neither sensation nor thought, but bodily being-in."[3] I think the contrast with thought here is an overreaction to the dominant intellectualist and detached conception of thought found in the standard model. If we get right the account of thought, we will not need to see our engagement with the world requiring a grounding in something lower than the level of thought. Grene follows Merleau-Ponty and endorses the idea that our rationality "emerges on the ground of nonhuman nature."[4] This is offered as the "sensible world" as opposed to a Heideggerian conception of the "worked up world." But this notion of existence as bodily being-in "in the setting of a society, a language, a past and a present that endow it, intrinsically with sense"[5] itself has a precarious position in Grene's account. It is, for example, unclear how "bodily being-in" can be both endowed with sense by being in a language, time, and so on, and also have sense intrinsically.

My hunch is that the difference between Grene's account and the account I want to offer is, however, merely terminological. On my account, the precarious restlessness of agency is revealed from within an account of conceptual thought. It does not require a lower level and more animal account of our sense of things for conceptual thought to emerge. I do not deny the existence and importance of nonconceptual levels of experience. They are simply not required for the job at hand. The job at hand is that of articulating the basic restlessness of agency. In this essay I want to use contemporary philosophy of thought to draw out the character of agency in our sense of things.

Whatever else we need a notion of content for, our concept of content is fundamentally the concept of that which figures in rationalizing explanations of behavior. Folk may place all sorts of conditions of adequacy on rationalizing explanations of behavior—whether they are identifiable with, reducible to, supervene upon causal explanations, and so on—but the idea that content is needed in order to make sense of what we do is a common starting point. Frege's principle of content individuation makes this starting point constitutive of sense. It used to be thought that Frege's principle of content individuation, when applied to context-sensitive expressions such as perceptual demonstratives, ran into insuperable difficulties, for the sense of sentences containing such expressions could not be identified with anything that figures in the standard model of content.[6] The treatment of such cases as problematic is, however, unnecessary. These cases are only problematic if one assumes that content is individuated by sentences that can then be delivered to the subject in perception. The neo-Fregean application of sense to context-sensitive expressions rejects this assumption, for it reveals that the individuation of content is driven by the attention of an agent. An agent is something with the capacity to alter its perceptual inputs at will, for example, by turning its head. Attention is something we do; it is not something that happens to us. It requires a notion of the self as will. The perceiving subject is intrinsically active.

The role of will and activity here needs careful placing. I am not making the obvious point that we need to attend to what perception delivers to us, that we need actively to select from amongst the data that perception grants us. That point is compatible with the standard model in which perception is still the delivery of things, albeit things to which we have to attend and from among which we need to select. The place of the concept of will is more radical than that. I am not saying that we need to attend to contents (things delivered in perception), but that possession of content is an attending to the world. Content is not what is delivered in perception; rather, content is individuated by the direct attending to the world that is enabled by perception. The self as will is implicated not as a surveyor and selector of contents; it is implicated in the very individuation of content.

I shall speak of the "self as will," but this should not be taken to introduce an obscure metaphysical posit. This is not a queer entity lurking in the metaphysical shadows behind the ordinary person. Rather, the ordinary concept of a person, the concept of the subject in possession of content, is necessarily the concept of a subject with will. It is an agent. These claims are not speculative metaphysical theses; they are conceptual claims constitutive of the theory of content. The central role of the agent, the self as will, is a semantic role, not a metaphysical posit.

III

There are two aspects to the notion of tacit knowledge that the neo-Fregean theory of content can help explicate. The first is the direct unmediated character of our sense of things. The second concerns the idea of restlessness, the idea that the flow of experience is a flow of our active engagement with things. It is an engagement in which we attend to things and pass judgment on them, rather than an engagement in which we passively receive copies of them in data bundles. The first aspect is the more familiar and need not detain us long.

Frege's test says that we should count the thoughts expressed by two sentences different just in case it is rationally possible to assent to one and dissent to the other. With sentences containing, for instance, perceptual demonstratives, there is no purchase on the notion of the rational possibility of assent/dissent independently of how the thinking subject is placed perceptually in the environment. The conditions of rational assent/dissent to a sentence such as, "this is tasty" cannot be characterized independently of the thinking subject's perceptual engagement with the demonstrated object. Once such a sentence is assented to, assent remains rationally compelling just so long as the subject perceptually tracks the object, even if in so doing the subject moves away from the object and expresses its thought differently as, "that is tasty." Under such conditions these sentences would count as expressing a single dynamic thought retained over time and through relative movement between subject and object. The individuation of the thought is independent of the individuation of its vehicles of expression, for the real work is done not by the sentences, but by the account of the conditions under which the subject assents/dissents to the sentences. The conditions involve the subject's perceptual engagement in the environment.[7]

The account of the subject's perceptual engagement with the environment has to be understood relationally. The demonstrative mode of presentation is a thought constituent that is answerable to two constraints. First, it has to pick out the "this-ness" of the thinking—the way that the object is there-for-me. Second, it has to pick out an object—something that provides a conception of genuine truth-conditions for the thought. The first constraint ensures that the demonstrative mode of presentation really is a contribution to a theory of thought, an account of how things are for the subject—the subject's *take* on the world. The second constraint ensures that it is really the world that thought is measured against, the thought gets truth-conditions.[8] When we think demonstratively of an object we are not merely dwelling on our subjective impressions, we are thinking of something such that we can make sense of what it would be for that thing to satisfy predicates other than those immediately to mind. We know what it would be for other things to be true of this object. In understanding such things we manifest our grasp of objective truth conditions for thought.

This neo-Fregean account of thought is a radically externalist account of content individuation. The sense in which it is externalist picks out the first element of the concept of tacit knowledge that Marjorie Grene, following Polanyi, has advocated. The neo-Fregean externalism about content captures the idea of tacit knowledge insofar as the neo-Fregean view shows that key contents of belief, knowledge, and judgment are not capable of individuation independently or apart from the thinking subject's engagement with the world. The relational characterization of sense gives an account of content that cannot be fully individuated explicitly, for the idea of the subject's direct engagement with the world, the subject's orientation, never drops out of the picture. If we stick with the Fregean principles of content individuation, then rather than think that their application to sentences with context sensitive expressions is problematic for the standard model, an alternative response is available. The alternative is to reject the standard model. If we do this, the key Fregean concept of a mode of presentation is better labeled an "orientation" in order to mark the divergence from the standard model. So much, by now, should be familiar.[9]

The externalism of singular senses (our orientations to things) does not, however, take us to the heart of the matter that I want to explore. Singular senses are not explicitly codifiable. The subject's orientation to the environment cannot be fully stated; it must, in part, be shown by how the subject behaves in the environment. Thus far, one might think that such externalism does no more than provide a more expansive account of content than the standard model. Singular contents, as it were, take up more room, for the subject's psychology expands to include an engagement with things in its orientations to objects.[10] But there is a second aspect of Polanyi's notion of tacit knowledge that can be uncovered within the neo-Fregean project and it is this that I want to focus on.

Polanyi thought that tacit knowledge was foundational and although the formalization of tacit knowledge "opens up new paths to intuition," he also says that "any attempt to gain complete control of thought by explicit rules is self-contradictory . . . [t]he pursuit of formalization will find its true place in a tacit framework."[11] There is then a sort of spontaneity to tacit knowledge. The foundation that it provides for explicit knowledge and scientific theorizing is something that cannot be explicitly defined. It is not possible, Polanyi thinks, to formulate the rules that govern tacit knowing.

A first stab at explaining this spontaneity of tacit knowledge is to say that tacit knowledge is a result of something we *do* rather than something we merely receive. Tacit knowledge is essentially the knowledge of an agent, a subject that is in control of its knowledge gathering. This is because knowledge gathering exploits the role of judgment, it is not merely the application of technique. It has long been tempting to theorize knowledge gathering systematically, as the operation of techniques, something that could be made fully explicit and, as it were, left running without supervision. Tacit knowledge, on the other hand, is always an active interest in and attending to the world, the attending of an agent. The idea of knowledge gathering that is driven by the attention of an agent is problematic for the standard model.

The reason why the standard model has a problem with the concept of agency is that throughout the sequence of transactions, from perception through cognition to motor control, there is no point at which to locate the self that acts. Contents are delivered by the perceptual systems and manipulated by the cognitive center. The center's outputs begin the sequence that concludes with behavior. The self does not even fare as a node in this sequencing of transactions; it tends to disappear altogether. Now, merely to note the externalism of singular senses and the way that it gives us an account of our direct sense of things in perception does not, of itself, challenge the disappearance of the self as agent in the standard model. One might think that the issue about orientations, as elements in our psychology in which we enjoy a direct sense of things, merely throws more expansive, if slightly exotic, items into the sequences of states that the standard model describes. If that were so, we would still stand to lose the self as agent. There would be no place for it within the sequence of transactions that could, in principle, be plotted as the history of perceiving, thinking and acting. This would still be a history of transactions that instantiate general techniques or patterns; cognition would still be the unfolding of technique rather than the exercise of judgment. But to think that the account of singular senses merely serves to inflate the contents of inner space is to miss the central metaphysical reconfiguration that occurs when Frege's principles are strictly observed. One thing at issue in all this concerns the distinction between technique and judgment. On the standard model, action, including linguistic action, is a culmination of a technique. Regular patterns of stimuli and processing issue in behavior, including linguistic behavior. Just as the self as actor is invisible in all this, so too is the self as judge—the self that exercises judgment in its assertions, rather than being merely the mouthpiece of a technique. But this misdescribes us. Assertion, as with other forms of behavior, is something we do; it is not something that happens to us, or through us. To see how the neo-Fregean theory of content helps gain a purchase on this aspect of tacit knowledge, it is best to return first to the contrasting standard model.

IV

Why does perception matter? On the standard model perception delivers content, but why does that matter? Why is it important to have a belief content delivered to the cognitive center? The official answer will be that, on its own, delivery of a belief content does not matter at all. Beliefs are rationally inert. It always takes a desire to fire up the motivation to act. But that response misses the point for, on the standard model, desires have content too—how else do they integrate with beliefs? The question then is more general: How does content motivate?

It is a curious feature of the standard model that content as such does not motivate. Content under the attitude of desire, when held in tandem with content under the attitude of belief, motivates, but content as such is motivationally inert. Our engagement with the world, in the form of receipt of deliveries of contents, is motivationally inert. The fundamental attitude of content possession on the standard model is one of a detached gaze. We inspect and possess contents, but possession of content is not, for the standard model, possession of something that matters. Whether it matters is extrinsic to the possession of information. What I want to suggest is that the externalism of sense gives us an account of content that not only puts us in direct contact with the world, but that the attitude to the world in possession of content is fundamentally the attitude of an agent, a subject for whom the world matters. It matters because the subject is the self as will presented, in perception, with that which is independent of will. Perception is not the passive receipt of information. It is the active tussle between the will and world. This is the basic orientation in perception. Perception intrinsically matters. Its "mattering" is not a later add-on. What is given to us in perception matters not because it integrates with things under the attitude of desire, but because our fundamental orientation to the world is one that is intrinsically interested and active. The given in perception is an orientation in which the will is confronted with that which is independent of will.

On the standard model, perception delivers contents to the cognitive center where perceptual contents get manipulated along with contents under the attitude of desire. A lot of processing takes place and an action ensues. There are two problems with this standard model. The obvious one is that the attitude of desire has to bear all the weight of explaining the source of motivation for action, since beliefs as such are standardly thought to be motivationally inert. The standard model embodies a detached conception of the cognitive processes. Cognition is something that happens in between perception and action. Perception gives it data but, to cognition in itself, data do not matter. They are mere grist for the information processing mill. The data only get to matter by supplying this mill with further data under the attitude of desire. Without this, the cognitive center would, presumably, merely content itself with endless processing.

But that problem is not, to my mind, the really interesting issue. Of more concern is the point that, in a sense, under the standard model no-*thing* ever gets motivated, no *one* is ever moved by a reason. What we have is a complicated information processing system which, in the light of various inputs (beliefs delivered by perception) and given standing conditions (the system's desires and previously acquired beliefs) produces behavior. This is not a model of action, but of behavior production, for it is not a model in which there is a ready place for the agent.

This should not be surprising for, under the standard model, the concept of agency is problematic anyway. It is unclear that the standard model can give an account of the agent who is motivated by, amongst other things, what that agent finds out in perception. On the standard model, contents are delivered by perception and then processed by the cognitive center. That processing may include integration with desire contents, but none of this is really directed at an agent. There is a sequence of transitions at play, but nothing of this sort is really presented to an actor that, in the light of the transitions, is motivated to act. The action, should it occur, is simply the final move in a sequence that carries on regardless of whether an agent is motivated. Perception does not fundamentally matter, for there is, within the standard model, no thing to be moved. Contents shunt into other contents. They move one another in causal sequences. But they do not motivate.

An advocate of the standard model might respond by saying that I am confusing two separate levels of explanation. The account of perception, cognition, and action that I am attributing to the standard model is only an account of the "mechanisms" that underlie action. Such a sequencing within these sub-personal mechanisms simply *is* an account of what it is for something to be an agent. The response does not work. It is, of course, important to observe a distinction between personal and sub-personal levels of explanation and description. I have no quarrel with the provision of sub-personal levels of description of the cognitive architecture employed in human perception and cognition. But that is beside the point, for it is the ordinary, personal level, concept of "belief" that appears in the standard model as something that can be factored out of the subject's engagement with the world. It is the ordinary concept of belief that figures as an internal state in the sorts of patterns of sequencing that I have attributed to the standard model. And, in contrast, it is the ordinary, personal level, concept of belief that I want to insist finds its home in an account of perception as a direct and restless sense of things.

The standard model connects input to motor control via the sequence of transitions occurring in the cognitive center. This gives no purchase on the idea that the resulting motor control is the beginning of something an agent does for a reason, rather than something that merely happens for a cause. It does not even treat these happenings as things that happen to us, for the concept of the subject, whether active or passive, is problematic for the standard model. That is the point of the post-Lockean debate about personal identity. Defining personal identity over sets of contents over time does not define an agent. At best, such a definition picks out a temporary focal point in the sequence of transitions between contents. The agent gets no supervisory role over these sequences. The contents in the sequence stand in causal relations to one another and to the body to which they causally belong. The notion of personal identity amounts to no more than a temporary stability in the causal relations that obtain between these contents. (That it is a temporary stability is, of course, why Parfit is able to claim that survival is a matter of degree and that identity does not matter.) Certainly the stability of causal relations that connect these contents with a particular body is no passing accident. But then, no one seriously believes that the body and its causal connectedness can be used to define personhood. The strategy of the standard model is to give an impersonal description of the unity relation for persons. But such an account needs to pick out the right kind of causal relations between contents, and it is simply unclear that sense can be made of the "right kind" here without slipping back into the concept of a person.

Part of the problem is that when agents act for a reason, the patterns they follow are normative patterns. They act thus-and-so because they feel that is how they should behave given their interests, desires, beliefs, and so forth. The only patterns at play in the standard model are, however, causal ones. But all of this still misses the heart of the problem. The potential mis-identification of the nature of the patterns that matter when action is involved is symptomatic rather than constitutive of the real problem. The real problem is that normative patterns are patterns that agents find themselves in. Agents are more than nodes in causal sequences, they are the items that get motivated by reasons and the items that, in response, act.

Just as the post-Lockean debate has a problem in giving an impersonal description of the unity relation for persons over time, so too does the standard model have a problem in accounting for the motivational impact of content. The problem is, at heart, the same. The source of the problem is the need to give an account of how contents form a unity, a unity that makes sense of the pretheoretical idea of content mattering for someone. A core element of the idea that content matters for us is that content impinges on a unified point of view or perspective. The idea of a point of view is unavoidable if content is to matter.

The idea that contents form a unity, and that this makes sense of the pretheoretical idea of content mattering for someone, is a very basic idea about content. So far, I have presented the question "Why does content matter?" with the focus on rationalizing action, but the question bites at an earlier point. In order for action to be rationalized, our beliefs and desires must be capable of integration, they must bear upon one another in familiar systematic ways. Now, on the standard model, the attitude of desire seems to bear the brunt of making everything work, for otherwise, as I remarked, beliefs would carry on being processed without action ever occurring. But even this gives away too much to the standard model, for it presupposes a primitive notion of the unity of content in order to capture the idea that beliefs get processed. The very idea of beliefs being capable of integration with one another already presupposes a notion of the unity of content. Why should beliefs be integrated at all? Perhaps the answer is that they integrate in order to produce true beliefs. But why should the pressure to have true beliefs account for inferential integration? The reply that beliefs must integrate in order to satisfy a higher order desire for truth ducks the issue, for why not just aim for true beliefs held in isolation of one another rather than inferentially connected? I want to suggest that the primitive notion of beliefs being capable of integrating and forming a unity already presupposes a basic notion of agency, an idea of the self as will. It is the very idea of content forming a unity, something that enjoys familiar ideas of rational connectedness that shows the basic place for the concept of agency in the theory of content.

V

Whatever else content does, it exhibits a systematic connectedness and, in virtue of this, comes to bear upon the thinking subject rationally. In order for content to exhibit this connectedness, it needs, as it were, a site at which these connections are made. The bald, unowned belief that a bus is approaching cannot, by itself, integrate with the bald, unowned belief that buses are red, let alone integrate with the desire not to be hit by buses. Intuitively, beliefs and desires need to inhabit the same "location," they need to be had by a single subject. The point is obvious, but from within the confines of the standard model it is not easy to give it due credit. Within the resources available to the standard model there is no way of articulating the appropriate togetherness of contents that permits inferential connections to obtain between them.[12]

The point is an old one. Consider Lichtenberg's challenge to Descartes's use of the first person pronoun in his formulation of the *cogito*. Is Descartes entitled to the "I think" rather than merely "There is thought going on"? As Williams points out, the impersonal formulation gives no purchase on the connectedness of thought.[13] From the fact that "The thought that P is going on" and the fact that "The thought that Q is going on," we have no purchase on whether the thought that "P & Q" should be going on. In contrast, if a subject thinks P and thinks Q then the subject is normatively required to think P and Q, other things being equal. It is, however, difficult to see how such normative requirements can belong to thought without the thoughts being had by a person. We might try to get an account of the connectivity of thoughts by defining their togetherness spatially. We might say that the thought that P and the thought that Q are held in one place—*here*. But as Williams observes, the use of the spatial indexical is merely figurative.[14] He says that "further reflection suggests very strongly that . . . there could be no better candidate . . . than the Cartesian 'I'" to provide the appropriate togetherness of thoughts.[15] It is worth exploring a bit further the reflections that suggest that nothing less than "I" will do here.

The standard model has, at best, a spatial metaphor for the togetherness of contents that underpins their inferential connectivity. The standard model might say that the thought that P and the thought that Q are in the same system, but why should this make thought answerable to the norms of inferential connectivity? Suppose the thought that P and the thought that Q are in the same system. As it stands, it is unclear why this should be any better than saying that the thoughts are written as sentences on the same sheet of paper! Perhaps, everything hangs on the word "system," but if so, that puts all the weight of the connectivity of thought on what is built into the hardware of the system. The hardware will have to reflect just the right degree of rationality if it is to be plausible as a model that explains our inferential behavior. Should the hardware encode an ideal notion of rational integration of beliefs, such that the input of a belief that conflicts with those already present always has to be resolved, or would a more limited construal of the norms of rationality be acceptable?

The temptation for the standard model has to be to try to define various systemic constraints on belief in virtue of which perception comes to matter. The norms of rationality that govern what happens with a perceptual input will be seen as a top-down imposition upon the system. This is a familiar idea, but it is one that once again leaves the agent out of the picture. If the system of belief acquisition and management is driven by top-down constraints, then it is a system that runs on its own without a subject reviewing the process. Of course, the objection will be that such a model just is a model of what it is for a subject to review its own activities of belief acquisition and management. But the model, in being fundamentally a reductionist model, replaces the idea of an agent governed by norms with that of a system operating according to general principles. This model still fails to come to grips with the problem about the unity of thought; it gives no answer to the question of what defines the togetherness of thoughts so that they can enjoy inferential connectedness.

The question I raised was, "Why does perception matter?" The obvious response from within the standard model is that perception matters because beliefs received through perception are subject to constraints, defined by general principles that drive the rationality of the belief system. But none of this begins to answer the question posed. The general principles that drive the rationality of the system do not account for why perception matters, for such principles (for example, accept no contradictions) can only come into force once beliefs have fallen within their purview. But the question I posed was precisely that of what it means to say that a belief falls within the purview of rational constraints. Such general principles can only drive belief management once the beliefs are, as it were, in a location accessed by the principles. But that means that the notion of the location—not the general principles—does the work in accounting for why perception matters.

As already noted, the idea of location does not, of itself, give the appropriate sense of connectedness. The belief that P and the belief that not-P can be represented by sentences in the same location, on a page, without infringing any rationality constraint. Writing them down on a single sheet of paper affronts nothing and no one. It is only when that single sheet is taken into the unifying perspective relative to a reader, or a potential reader, that it matters that P and not-P figure together. Otherwise, there is no interesting sense in which they are together so that they can bear upon one another. Indeed, the beliefs as such plainly do not bear on one another. That is the point. Beliefs only bear on one another when held from a common point of view, when held within a common perspective. The unity of beliefs depends on the unity of the subject's point of view. The idea of a point of view is inescapable for an account of the unity of thought.

In order for general principles of rationality to take effect, the beliefs in question have to be brought into a single point of view. Only then can the general principles operate. But that means that the general principles play no role in accounting for the unity of thought. Beliefs do not belong to the same unity because they are subject to some general principle; rather, beliefs submit to the same token of a general principle because they belong to the same unity of thought.

The difficulty here is to see any way of explaining the unity of thought in anything more basic than the unity of the thinking subject. We have here an analogue of Kant's thesis of the "I" that accompanies all experience. The thesis we are exploring is that of the "I" that accompanies all inference. The inferential connectedness of thought is required for thought to meet its most basic constraint—that it figures in rationalizing explanations of behavior. But this connectedness only comes about when thoughts are had by the "I" that provides the point of view. To try to capture the idea of the point of view with, for example, a location, whether indexically picked out or not, fails to deliver the connectedness required.

We have become accustomed to think that the question of whether an inference is valid is a purely syntactic matter. This is right, but there is a danger here of agreeing to an obscure Platonism about inference. The sense in which it is right that validity is a syntactic matter is that schemata for valid inferences can be defined syntactically. Such schemata pick out some of the general principles that govern belief revision. Instances of such schemata are not, however, definable syntactically. The following is a schema for valid inferences:

$$\frac{\begin{array}{c} A \to B \\ A \end{array}}{B}$$

But to say that is not to say that any set of three propositions of this form—conditional + antecedent + consequent—makes a valid inference. Only a set satisfying this formal requirement and comprising an appropriate unity forms a valid inference. Belief contents do not, all of themselves, constitute valid inferences. If three people, in separate locations, were to assert in sequence,

   If George Bush wins California, he will win the presidency

followed by,

   George Bush wins California

followed by,

   George Bush wins the presidency

their assertions would not amount to a valid inference. It would take a peculiarly Platonic conception of inference to think that such a scenario amounts to an inference. It does not amount to an inference because the beliefs have not, as it were, "got it together." What forces the beliefs together? What makes them party to a common unity? The Platonist answer is to think that the driving force of inference flows from the general structure of Platonic beliefs. The above sequence is a valid inference insofar as it exemplifies the platonic forms of belief revision. For the Platonist conception, belief revision is a technique; it is something that occurs through the application of general top-down principles. There are rules that define this technique. The standard model is a variant on this view; it replaces Platonic heaven with a statement of natural laws. Both models are top-down accounts of the source of inference.

The alternative model is to see the driving force of belief revision, what gives beliefs their unity, as arising from the perspective of the will in perceptual contact with the world. Beliefs are integrated and conclusions get drawn when, other things being equal, the will moves to reduce a tension between itself and the world. The source of the requirement to revise a belief, or to draw a conclusion, is not the attempt to get beliefs in harmony with the abstract Platonic structure; it is to get a particular tension resolved between the self as will and world. This activity is not the application of a technique, a set of general principles, it is the application of judgment; it requires the attention and judgment of the self as will.

The Platonic account displaces the source of inference and lays itself open to a regress problem familiar from Wittgenstein's writings, for this account sees the source of inference in a requirement to match an abstract pattern. The standard model varies this requirement by replacing the abstract pattern with a natural law. Regarding any specification of the pattern, it is always possible to ask how it should be taken. The Platonist may respond that the pattern is specified once we know the meaning of the connectives. But that is the response that, as Wittgenstein has taught us, is worthless.[16] There is no independent fix on the meaning of symbols other than that provided by what we do with them. We cannot first fix the meaning, place it like an icon in Platonic heaven, and then follow in obeisance of the Platonic meaning structure. The meaning is fixed in terms of what we do with symbols. We are the ones in charge here, not the meanings! That is the point of the agentual turn in an account of content. We do not provide a theory of content, structures and items that get manipulated by the cognitive center and then look around for an account of the agent, defined over some collection of contents. Rather, we acknowledge that content resides in what we, as agents, do with symbols. The Platonist has meaning come first, judgment second, for judgment is something we do with meanings. The standard model has natural patterns first, while agency and judgment is something that instantiates these patterns. For both of these options, we select from amongst the meanings on offer to find the collection that is appropriate to the perceptual situation we are in. But the selection process amounts only to the application of techniques, as the cognitive center weighs and measures the contents delivered by perception against the contents already stored and those held under the attitudes of desire and intention. On the account that I am recommending, if anything, judgment comes first and meaning second. Perception provides a challenge to the will as it delivers a sense of things that does not fit the will's aims. In passing judgment how to proceed, a pattern is sustained and, sometimes, established.

In the beginning, the self pays attention to the world. The self adjusts its orientations in order to resolve conflict between the will and that which is independent of will. The self does not need general principles in order to draw conclusions from its inputs and standing beliefs; it needs only to pay attention. The idea that there are basic inferences our entitlement to which is founded on our attending to objects is not new. The inference from

This is F

and,

This is G

to

This is both F and G

needs no suppressed premise stating the identity of the object picked out by the two uses of the demonstrative "this." If we have kept track of the object in perception, the identity is something we can legitimately trade on. The point applies also to dynamic thoughts when the expression of the mode of presentation changes from "this" to "that" as we move away from the object. What we trade on is the fact that we have an orientation to the object that holds it steady for us in thought. The orientation has us engaged with the object so that its identity across the premises is guaranteed. When our identification of properties is also demonstrative, the need to see inference trading on a tracking of objects in perception becomes acute.

I will write "dF" for a demonstratively expressed predicate, such as, "that wet," "this sticky." Consider the invalid inference from

x is dF

to

x is dG.

The orientation to the properties picked out by these predicates is too contextualized and short-lived to make appeal to the universal

All dFs, dG

a plausible premise to render the move valid. Instead, our tracking of the properties and the inferences we make with them trades on a tracking of objects. We draw the conclusion because we have attended to, and are engaged with, the fact that

These dFs, dG.

It will be objected that we have no entitlement to the belief that the "these" covers the items picked out in the minor premise and conclusion, for perhaps x is not one of these? The matter deserves extended treatment. I will make two brief observations on it now.

First, our entitlement to "These dFs, dG" as major premise is no weaker than our entitlement to the universal "All dFs, dG." The objection that we are not entitled to take the "These" to quantify over the particular x can also be made against the more familiar candidate, for how do we know that the "All" covers anything more than "All observed items to date . . . "? The difference is that on the latter issue we can look only to Platonic heaven, or for a final and complete account of general laws, in order to ground our inference. On the option I am recommending we ground the inference by paying attention to what is before us! When we are working with demonstratively expressed predicates there is no reason to expect general laws or principles whatsoever, so the particular "These dFs, dG" is the only viable candidate.

Second, the demonstrative identification of properties is common in our basic inferences about the environment and how we behave in it. Anyone who has ever done home decorating will recognize the thought that when, for example, handling plaster or wall-filler, much of our understanding never gets beyond demonstrative expression. One can acquire a moderately sophisticated grasp of the plasticity of the material that has all sorts of consequences for how one handles it—its "gloopiness" on the trowel, its adhesiveness on the wall, when it requires certain sort of flicks of the trowel to catch it and apply it and when not. These are often short-lived abilities to track properties that are lost once the home-decorating job is complete. It is because one attends to and tracks these demonstratively expressed properties that one's handling of the material is rationalizable in the light of the beliefs one's perception makes available. But one only attends to and tracks these properties by attending to and tracking the objects (samples of plaster) that instantiate them. The properties in question are not candidates for properties that figure in universal laws.

The agentual account not only avoids Platonism, it fits the ordinary phenomena of belief revision. It locates the source of inference in the attention of a subject, a will looking to reduce tension between itself and the world as delivered in perception. The primitive force of inference comes from our attention to things, our sense of things in perception. So it is attention that matters. The central notion of a point of view—the shape of our orientations—is dynamic. That is to say, the agentual view is not driven top down by rules and general principles; it is driven by our attention to things. This sense of things is particular. Inference is driven from the bottom up, from our attention to things delivered to us in perception, where this delivery gives us things that matter, not inert contents. Inference is something we do. It does not just "happen," not here, nor in Platonic heaven. It is this bottom-up account of the source of inference that lies behind what I called the spontaneity in Polanyi's concept of tacit knowledge. Polanyi's concept captures the idea that our tacit sense of things is not explicitly codifiable, for it depends on the state of our attentional field. From such a reversal of the traditional perspective, the following fact is unremarkable.

It is not only possible, but commonplace for it to be true of a subject both that it knows that P and that it comes to believe something that entails not-P without this producing any rational response by the subject. All that is required is that the subject temporarily forget that it knows that P. Alternatively, it might be that the entailment of not-P by a new belief is too complicated for the contradiction to become apparent to the subject. It might take many years of work for a subject to realize that there is a conflict in its beliefs. Coming to realize this is moving beyond the stage of spatial togetherness of thoughts, of having the two beliefs in the same system; it is a matter of coming to realize, or to attend to, the beliefs in question. We do not form a whole system, for the primitive notion of subject is given by the attentional field of the self as will. Mere availability within a system is not enough. The notion of system can only work if defined as something accessed by the narrative autobiography of memory, a memory directed by the attentional field telling its stories. This is not the memory of bare repositories, it is the memory accessed and accommodated within the inferential structures of our ongoing attention. And the same has to be true in perception too, if perception is to deliver something that matters, something that bears rationally upon our beliefs and desires.

To take perception as the delivery of data merely postpones the point at which we have to have a subject that attends to things and passes judgment on the contents delivered by perception. Nothing is gained by this delay and much is lost. Why not resist the postponement and acknowledge that in perception we pass judgment on the world and accept that it is the world, as directly present to us in perception, that matters?

VI

Singular modes of presentation are answerable to two constraints: they must capture the way things are for the subject and they must pick out an object, something that provides the thought with objective truth-conditions. These two constraints are not, from the Fregean perspective, capable of being satisfied independently of each other. The mode of presentation is understood relationally, it is an orientation that relates the self to an object.

The first constraint is that the mode of presentation must capture the way things are for the subject, the perspectival character of thought. The point is clearest with demonstrative modes of presentation. The demonstrative mode of presentation, in addition to picking out an object, must pick it out in a way that captures the "this-ness" or "that-ness" of the act of thinking. The "this-ness" is the way that the object is picked-out-for-me. A demonstrative mode of presentation is something that is intrinsically a mode of presentation for a thinking subject. The self, that which stands to the object in an orientation of "this-ness," never drops out of the picture. This is the "I" that accompanies all inference. The "I" might be thought an anomaly, a metaphysical extravagance, but its role here should have been anticipated from the start. The Fregean approach takes the rationalizing role of content as constitutive of the principles of content individuation, and it takes the role content plays in rationalizing explanations of behavior for granted. But rationalizing explanations of behavior just are explanations of how subjects behave. It really should be no surprise that the subject never disappears in the account of content.

On the standard model, insofar as it has credible account of the subject, information is something that gets delivered to the subject. On the neo-Fregean account, the sense of a singular term cannot be thought of as something that gets delivered to the subject; rather, the sense is an orientation of the subject to the object. It has been much remarked that the neo-Fregean account of singular senses leaves sense "object-involving" or, better, "world-involving." That is correct and that is why it helps illustrate the first aspect of tacit knowledge I noted above. The world-involving nature of singular senses has been thought problematic, for it has been thought to render false thoughts impossible. This is a mistake. What has not been so frequently remarked is that singular senses are not just world-involving, but "self-involving" too. Satisfying the two constraints on singular senses does not produce a something that connects two separate things—the thinking subject and the world about which it thinks. Satisfying the two constraints on singular senses produces a single item, a singular thought in which the subject is orientated to the world. To say that the sense has to be understood relationally means that this is an account of content quite unlike the standard model and most traditional metaphysics of the mind.

Most theories start with a metaphysics that provides an account of the world, perhaps also of information packages and, if we are lucky, an account of the subject. Perception, thought, and all the rest are then elements in a story about how the world stands in information-carrying relations to the subject, although the subject is forever threatened with disappearance under the reductionist explanations this model offers. In contrast, the model I have been recommending starts with the inferential connectedness of thought. This is to start with the "I" that accompanies all inference, but one need not make any substantive claims about this "I." What the "I" is, and what the world is that it is confronted with in thought, is something that gets uncovered by tracing the distinctive patterns of inference in which the "I" engages. Tracing those patterns of inference cannot be done independently of a conception of both the "I" and the world. Doing this fills out the substantive things that turn out to be true of us and our world. What is, however, vital in all this, is that in giving such a central role to the self we need some basic purchase on it and that with which it is confronted in perception—the world. By starting with the inferential connectedness of thought, we have no license to start with substantive metaphysical claims about the nature of the world. We cannot simply avail ourselves of the notion of objects presented in perception. Neither, however, can we rest content with a mere coherentist conception of the inferential connectedness of thought. The danger here is obvious. On a relational account of singular senses, the self and its world turn out not to be understandable independently of one another. This seems to be problematic whichever way one looks at it.[17]

From the point of view of the realist about the mind, how can the subject's thoughts be world-involving? The externalism about singular senses seems to gain us the world only at the expense of losing our minds. How can such an approach deliver the notion of detachment from the world that seems intrinsic to conceptual thought? The short answer is, "Quite easily, as it happens!"[18] From the point of view of the realist about the world, the worry is reversed; we seem to gain our minds and lose the world: How can an account of the inferential connectedness of thought provide a robust enough conception of the world and its objects when all it starts from is a pattern of thoughts? The only way out of this double-sided problematic is for the accounts of the self and its world to be mutually definable in a way that captures both a genuine sense of the independence of the world and a genuine sense of selfhood.

The key lies in the notion of independence. If independence is defined causally, we are back to the standard model, for it becomes unclear at what point in the causal chain relating self and world we should draw the boundary between the two. The familiar demarcation point at the site of "surface irritations" is, considered as a point in a causal sequence, arbitrary and unprincipled. If the patterns of inferential connectedness are our starting point, the principled account of the differentiation between self and world must come from the semantic concept central to an account of inference—truth. And the core mark of the concept of truth is the idea that if a belief is true it is so independently of its being taken to be true, hoped to be true, wished to be true, and so on. In short, if it is true, a belief is true independent of will.[19] Truth is not something we can will into being; this has to be, for the inferentialist, the core to the concept of that with which we are presented in perception—that which is independent of will—namely, the world. But such a move immediately gives us purchase on the self and its contents too. For what makes my perceptions mine is precisely the fact that I can alter them at will, for example, by turning my head, closing my eyes, blocking my ears. In short, my perceptions are mine insofar as they fall within the single field of attention that I have. The fact that my perceptions are those that I can alter at will connects with the basic concept of an agent, something that can alter its perceptual inputs at will. There is, then, no problem in characterizing the boundary between self and world in a way that leaves them mutually definable but with a sharp point of contact, just so long as we are prepared to take the turn of treating the thinking subject as fundamentally an agent, something with an attentional field. This is a field of opportunities for action, of changing our perceptual inputs.

The attentional field is not, like the visual field of traditional empiricism, something to allow our gaze to wander over. It is not the field of spectatorship; it is the field of agency. In our simplest thoughts we are already actors. And we do not work to a predetermined script, for in our capacity to attend and pass judgment lies the seeds of our ability to create the patterns of our behavior as we go along.

MICHAEL LUNTLEY

DEPARTMENT OF PHILOSOPHY
UNIVERSITY OF WARWICK
COVENTRY, U.K.
MAY 2000

NOTES

1. A notable exception is J. Campbell, *Past, Space and Self* (Cambridge, Mass.: MIT Press, 1994), esp. chapter 5.
2. Marjorie Grene, "The Sense of Things," *Journal of Aesthetics and Art Criticism* 38 (1979–80): 377–89.
3. Ibid., p. 381.
4. Ibid., p. 378.
5. Ibid., p. 381.
6. For the *locus classicus*, see J. Perry 1979.
7. The idea of dynamic thoughts was first noted in G. Evans, *The Varieties of*

Reference (Oxford: Clarendon Press, 1982). For further development see M. Luntley, "Dynamic Thoughts and Empty Minds," in *European Review in Philosophy*, vol. 2, *Cognitive Dynamics*, ed. J. Dokic (Stanford, Calif.: CSLI, 1997), pp. 77–103, and the other essays in that volume.

8. In Evans's treatment these two constraints correspond to his requirement that a demonstrative idea of an object provides both an egocentric location of the object and an objective location. The former shows that the demonstrative idea is a component to *thought*, the latter that the thought has objective truth-conditions. See Evans, *The Varieties of Reference*, chapter 6.

9. For an overview, see Michael Luntley, *Contemporary Philosophy of Thought: Truth, World, Content* (Oxford: Blackwell, 1999), esp. chapters 11 and 12.

10. This is the point emphasized in J. McDowell, "Singular Thoughts and the Extent of Inner Space," in *Subject, Thought, and Context*, ed. J. McDowell and P. Pettit (Oxford: Clarendon Press, 1986), pp. 137–68. The extent of inner space is "far out."

11. M. Polanyi, *Knowing and Being*, ed. M. Grene (Chicago: University of Chicago Press, 1969; London: Routledge & K. Paul, 1969), p. 156.

12. The present argument is a more general version of the argument I gave in Luntley, "Dynamic Thoughts and Empty Minds," op. cit. (1997). There, I argued that the standard model lacked the resources to capture the rationalizing notion of content expressed in dynamic thoughts, for it lacked the resources to capture the correct inferential connectedness of dynamic thoughts. The present point is a generalization of this: the standard model cannot capture the inferential connectedness of the notion of content that rationalizes behavior, for it lacks the concept of the self as will.

13. B. Williams, *Descartes, the Project of Pure Enquiry* (London: Penguin Books, 1978).

14. Ibid., p. 97.

15. Ibid.

16. My reading of Wittgenstein is developed in a work in progress, *Wittgenstein: The Conditions of the Possibility of Judgment.*

17. See R. Brandom, *Making It Explicit: Reasoning, Representing, and Discursive Commitment* (Cambridge, Mass.: Harvard University Press, 1994) for an account of inferentialism that makes this problem compelling.

18. The easy bit is accounting for error, see Luntley, *Contemporary Philosophy of Thought: Truth, World, Content*, op. cit., chapter 12 for details. The harder bit is accounting for, or at least not altogether losing, the distinctive character and authority of self-knowledge. On this see the papers in *Self-Knowledge*, ed. Q. Cassam (Oxford: Oxford University Press, 1994).

19. I take this from D. Wiggins, "The Truth as Predicated of Moral Judgments," in *Needs, Values, Truth: Essays in the Philosophy of Value* (Oxford: Blackwell, 1987), pp. 139–84. See my *Contemporary Philosophy of Thought: Truth, World, Content*, op. cit., chapter 5 for details.

REPLY TO MICHAEL LUNTLEY

Some years ago, Michael Luntley published in the *Times Higher Educational Supplement* (Oct. 13, 1995) a charming review of my *Philosophical Testament*. It was one of the few reviews that ill-fated book received; I was duly grateful for it, and thank Dr. Luntley again now for his attention to my work. On that occasion he remarked that my readers would find "glimpses of important philosophical ideas that are more in tune with the fashions of professional academic philosophy than Grene perhaps realizes or would care to admit."[1] Puzzled by this allusion, I inquired of Dr. Luntley what those fashions were that I ought to welcome. He replied with some titles, adding that I probably would not understand them. I did look up at least one of them, I've forgotten what or by whom, and he was right: I didn't understand. Now do I fare any better in the present context? With due apologies, I must confess first, that I understand very little indeed of what Dr. Luntley is saying, secondly, that where I seem to understand it, I disagree with it, and thirdly, I don't see, on the evidence, what it has to do with anything I've ever said or thought.

First, then, let's look at some of the (to me!) obscurities. To start with, I really can't make out what that "standard model" (of what?) is, or who is supposed to have espoused it. After Locke, I presume it's the problem of personal identity, but that's only part of the model, or so it seems. Its first move, we are told, and its first error, is to treat "perception as the delivery of information." That sounds like a common *mis*reading of J. J. Gibson's ecological approach, which is itself surely far from standard. I would have thought the traditional view was rather Helmholzian (or what I take to be Helmholzian): that is, the view that sensation delivers to us meaningless data which we interpret in some way to yield perception. Further, it turns out that the "standard model" is a variant of some kind of Platonism. Sorry; I'm lost. It's one thing to flog a dead horse, but a horse one can't even locate is scarcely floggable. So I don't know what's being attacked.

Nor is it clear to me what Luntley himself is substituting for it. He makes a great deal of the will, which to me is an obscure, and even unnecessary, concept. He says "[t]he central role of the agent, the self as will" is not "a metaphysical posit," but a "semantic role." What does that mean? And what on earth (or off it) is a "theory of content," of which this semantic role playing will is said to be constitutive? Luntley's theory, moreover, is said to be neo-Fregean, again, a mystery, except of course for the fact that to refer deferentially to Frege is always a *good thing*. Somehow starting with the meanings (*Sinne*) of isolated predicates we are supposed to arrive at an integration of—the person?—in ways that we otherwise could not do. (When he started talking about "singular senses," I thought he meant senses like touch, vision, and so on, but presumably he means the sense of this particular predicate, in Frege's sense of sense. Why orient our orientation to things in this atomistic starting point? Again, I don't know.)

Enough of that. Suffice it to say that the essay is written in a language wholly unfamiliar to me. Wittgenstein argued against the possibility of private languages, but if there are no tongues intelligible to only a single individual, there are certainly languages encoded by groups of speakers destined, or even intended, to keep mystified those uninitiated into their vocabulary and their syntax.

Secondly, when Dr. Luntley does say something I believe I ought to understand, I have to demur. For example, he makes two points about Michael Polanyi's concept of tacit knowing. First, it puts us into direct contact with things. Okay. Second, it is ineliminable: thus, as Polanyi puts it, "[t]he pursuit of formalization will find its true place in a tacit framework." The second point, Luntley says, shows that there is a "sort of spontaneity to tacit knowledge." This leaps out at me as having nothing to do with the matter. Again, I just don't know what it means, but this time in a context where I thought I ought to understand.

Back to perception: yes, of course, it entails an active ingredient. But do we really just perceive what we *want* to? Yes, I can close my eyes, but I'd better not do so when I'm driving. And when my neighbors (not my immediate neighbors, I should say) have late night to early morning sessions of loud noises they call music, even closing the window doesn't shut out the clamor. Do I really hear just what I want to?

Thirdly, and finally, although I know he has read at least one book of mine, Dr. Luntley here draws only on a couple of sentences from a (rather strange) essay in which I explicitly announced that I was trying to give an intelligible account of Merleau-Ponty's view of the special significance of the painter's task in relation to our human situation. Although I am happy to acknowledge the influence of my reading of Merleau-Ponty on my own reflections, I was not in this case thinking or speaking in my own persona.

Thus, when I remarked that Merleau-Ponty placed our existence between sensation and thought (a contrast in which Luntley finds an "over-reaction" to his mysterious standard view), I was echoing Merleau-Ponty's habit of contrasting, over and over, both in philosophy and psychology, a reductive or mechanistic with an over-intellectual stance. I suspect that in the latter case he was expressing his own reaction against the idealist lectures his generation of *Normaliens* had been exposed to.

Luntley says his hunch is that the difference in our accounts is merely terminological. Terminology can run deep. Again, I thank him for taking the trouble to contribute to this volume. Perhaps some reader will understand what he is saying, and possibly even find that in some way it has some connection with some views or arguments of mine. If I live so long, oh percipient reader, please tell me! I'm sure I don't know.

M. G.

NOTE

1. M. Luntley, review of Grene's *Philosophical Testament* in the London *Times Higher Educational Supplement* (Oct. 1995), p. 32.

7

Anthony N. Perovich Jr.

PERSONS, MINDS, AND "THE SPECTER OF CONSCIOUSNESS"

Advocating a middle path has its disadvantages. To be sure, there are often the sympathy and encouragement extended from one extreme as one attacks the positions of another, but there are also the criticisms that can come from all sides once one's own position is offered. Moreover, since philosophical fashions frequently tend to the extremes, a moderate position can at times seem less electrifying than some competitors. Nevertheless, Marjorie Grene, hardly someone to be overly concerned about criticism or suiting her positions to philosophical fashion in any case, has aimed at a middle path in the area known (quaintly and misleadingly, from her point of view) as the philosophy of mind. Since the seventeenth century, she thinks, theorizing about mind has veered, on the one hand, into "incoherence" and, on the other, into "absurdity": the incoherence of Cartesian dualism and the absurdity of reductionism.[1] We all, of course, want to avoid incoherence and absurdity, if only we can figure out how. The way to escape these past errors, Grene suggests, is through the introduction of a new category, the category of "the person." By replacing discussions of mind with an attempt to conceive ourselves as persons, philosophy can understand what it is to be a human being in ways that neither set us over against matter nor reduce us to nothing but our most basic material components. To see in any detail how the concept of a person is supposed to help us evade such misguided alternatives, we need to describe what that concept amounts to. We shall then see how thinking in terms of the person not only is intended to help us avoid incoherence and absurdity but also aims to exorcize "the specter of consciousness"[2] quite generally and not merely in the shape of the *cogito* and dualism by which Descartes misled the philosophical tradition.

The exorcism, however, does not seem to me to be effective: although thinking in terms of the person helps to keep before us many of the philosophically significant ways in which we are situated in our natural and cultural environment, a focus on consciousness and what it makes possible is precisely what is needed to guard against some of the reductionist dangers about which Grene wants to warn us. It may or may not be possible to find a middle path between Cartesian dualism and reductive materialism; if it is possible, the "person" may be a useful concept for thinking our way along it. But I do not see that it will usurp "consciousness" as the locus of philosophical interest: Grene's own arguments point to the difficulty of viewing consciousness as a part of nature, and I do not think there is any way of explaining what is distinctive about the person except through appealing to consciousness. Consciousness, then, will remain central, even after granting that speaking of the person succeeds in calling our attention to the embeddedness in our environment that the philosophical tradition has too often overlooked.

I. THE CATEGORY OF THE PERSON

"If there is one thing that is clear about the philosophical foundations of our Western tradition, it is that we urgently need a new, or renewed, conception of what it is to be human, and that this innovation, or renewal, entails as a fundamental category not 'mind' (at least not mind as distinct from body), certainly not 'consciousness,' but the concept of the person."[3] A new conception of the human being is needed because the ways of conceiving human beings that have occupied the philosophical foreground since the seventeenth century have, in Grene's view, hampered us from integrating what we know about ourselves with what we have discovered about the world. We need a conception that will avoid the problems of each of its predecessors without falling into the problems of the others, and it is the category of the person that holds out the promise of doing justice to what we have learned about ourselves from the natural and social sciences over the last three centuries without forfeiting a humane understanding of ourselves to various sorts of scientistic shallowness. Three aspects of the person as Grene describes it seem to me intended collectively to accomplish this task of philosophical rejuvenation and to capture what is distinctive about this way of understanding what human beings are: the person is a part of *nature*, the expression of a *culture*, and a locus of *responsibility*.

A central reason why the category of mind needs to be replaced with the category of the person is that the former has Cartesian associations that lead us to think of the mind as an "alien excrescence," as something over against nature rather than part of it.[4] On the contrary, the person is most fundamentally an embodied being and, more specifically, an animal: one properly understands the human being not, as Descartes did, in terms of a mind superadded to our animal nature, but rather as a particular form of animal nature, the human form.[5] If Grene is willing in some contexts to speak of persons as "mind-possessing bodies," it is only because "having a mind" can be defined in a metaphysically harmless fashion in terms of the ability to operate with symbols (or, more accurately, in terms of the capacity to develop such an ability), an ability that can be acquired only by being part of a society of symbol users, that is, by being part of a culture; indeed, human minds are simply the uses to which brains are put in cultural contexts.[6] Thus, one must be careful, in the current philosophical climate, in speaking of Grene's account of the person as "naturalistic." It is so in a perfectly proper sense of the term, but it needs to be emphasized, first, that its focus is on our animal nature rather than more narrowly on the nature of our nervous system, and, second, that it makes culture a part of nature ("Culture for us is not unnatural"[7]) and crucial to the understanding of what it is to be a person.

Persons are made, not born, and participation in a culture is indispensable for the transformation of a human organism into a person. The human genetic endowment (or at least, one would presume, a genetic endowment that supplies its owner with the same sorts of capacities as ours gives us) is a necessary but not a sufficient condition for becoming a person. Being a person is an achievement which our genetic endowment makes possible, and what that endowment makes possible is our participation in a culture. Perhaps it would be better to say that persons are neither born nor made, if the latter expression suggests that becoming a person is simply something that is done to us; while it is true that Grene speaks of us as "life transformed through culture," the language of achievement and participation suggests that becoming a person is something that we ourselves do, at least in part.[8] By participating in a culture we become more than merely human organisms, we become "personalized" human organisms, each one of us a unique expression of our culture; the uniqueness of the person thus comes about through the intersection of the human organism with the culture in which it develops, so that *personal* identity necessarily becomes a matter, neither of a merely subjective unity of feelings nor of a merely objective physical unity, but of "the historical span of this lived body-in-its-world."[9] We have already noted the connection between participating in a culture and being part of a society of symbol users. The near synonymy of these two expressions is due to the fact that using symbols is not to be construed narrowly; it involves sharing in the use not only of languages, but also of "other symbol-systems—religions, art, cognitive systems, including theories, problems, arguments, systems of morality, as well as all the institutions, political, social and economic, in which we live, move and have our being."[10] Thus, to say that we are "mind-possessing bodies" (minds being interpreted in terms of symbol use) is to say that we are culture-inhabiting bodies.

What results from the participation of the human organism in its culture is a responsible agent.[11] We have our practical and our theoretical side, and persons are responsible, above all, for their actions and for their knowledge claims. Persons act freely who are "centers of responsible choice," whose commitments arise out of that centeredness, and who take control over the means to those ends to which they are committed.[12] Making responsible knowledge claims is something that only persons do, a fact that plays a central role in Grene's attempt to escape the absurdities of reductionist accounts of the human being.

From this overview of the person let us now turn to the ways in which the introduction of this category is supposed to help us avoid the pitfalls that have plagued the philosophical attempts up till now to get clear about who we are.

II. BETWEEN INCOHERENCE AND ABSURDITY

The incoherence of Cartesian dualism is something Grene, at least in certain contexts, seeks not so much to establish as to avoid. Even the first time she read the *Meditations* she "wondered how anyone could ever have taken the *cogito* seriously,"[13] and in the course of advocating her own views she can find that she "need not stop to enumerate" the "incoherencies of Cartesian dualism."[14] However, the heart of the problem lies in the Cartesian conception of the mind as over against the world: "There is no such thing as a mind by itself; there is no such thing in the living world as a body by itself. It is from this cardinal metaphysical error of Descartes that his epistemological errors, with all their misleading consequences, flow."[15] As we have seen, the person is not a mind by itself, over against the world; rather, it is in nature and is a part of nature. By conceiving of ourselves this way we are able to avoid the dead end of a Cartesianism that would seek to separate us from the living world of which we are a part. We are also able to avoid the inward-looking, subjective tendencies of various philosophical approaches to ourselves that focus, like Descartes, on consciousness. Neither trying to build up the self, as the empiricists did, solely out of discrete sensations, nor introducing as well a Kantian unity of apperception to which all the bits of conscious experience are related as "mine," does justice to the human being. Our perceptions are typically organized to begin with, and the exceptions, insofar as they exist, are philosophically inconsequential: the view "that there are sensations, isolable, identifiable, single 'bits of consciousness' out of which experience gets built is just plumb *wrong*."[16] To add to these sensations a bare point of apperception may represent a move in the right direction, for Kant at least points to the need to acknowledge the organized character of our experience. However, it is too thin to do the job assigned to it: "The Kantian agent, however, the I of the transcendental unity, is an agent with no identity, no individuality, no destiny. It is *I* in my concrete historical situation who aspires to know."[17] Such an "I" in its concrete historical situation, in the physical and cultural environment in which it has developed as a living organism—this "I" is the (or a) person.

So much, for the moment, for the incoherencies of dualism and other mistaken accounts of the human being that are related to it by their too exclusive focus on consciousness. A reductionist physicalism errs in the opposite direction: if Cartesian dualism seeks to constitute human beings out of more than is encountered in nature, the reductionist seeks to do the same out of less. On more than one occasion, Grene has quoted with approval Erwin Straus's epigram, "physics refutes physicalism."[18] The refutation starts from the existence of physicists, "people able responsibly to investigate and make knowledge claims about the physical world," and argues to the conclusion that there must be more in the world "than the subject matter of molecular science."

The argument is directed in the first place against any attempt to suggest that all there is to know are "material particles in motion," "molecules—or their constituent particles," the particles alleged by "classical, so-called mechanism": in short, any claim that maintains that the basic constituents of nature, whether conceived as the corpuscles of the seventeenth century or the atoms and molecules of the contemporary natural sciences, exhaust the subject matter of science, and thus of all knowledge. This cannot be all there is to know, because the knower—a responsible, symbol-using agent, a real existent who can "make a competent, if not a veridical claim" about the physical world—makes claims to truth. "But molecules can make no claim to truth, any more than they can err. So if there is any knowledge, even 'molecular science,' there is *something* more than the subject matter of molecular science. There are at least molecular scientists."[19] The situation is no better for those who would reduce us to computers rather than molecules. Artificial intelligence experts, while they may succeed in aping human behavior with their machinery, have only, through their own purposive, intentional activity, achieved "the hardware imitation of personhood in some of its aspects," not persons; the above argument, according to Grene, is equally effective in both cases. The attempt to reduce purposive, or intentional, behavior to computer processes or to physiology or to the ultimate constituents of matter and the sciences that treat them is, in her words, an "absurdity."[20]

Arguments of this sort of course can be and have been challenged, but perhaps the success of the argument is as threatening to Grene as its failure. One reason for this is that some have thought that arguments of this sort establish rather more than Grene does. Thus, rather than turn to possible criticisms of it I should like to discuss an argument put forward by Alan Donagan. I choose an argument from Donagan for three reasons: first, Grene says of him that he was "one of the few thoroughly academic philosophers whom I deeply admired and respected"; second, he was, in Grene's words, "an unrepentant dualist,"[21] and he thought the argument about to be described made a good case for dualism; and, third, the argument is essentially the same as Grene's. The fact that Donagan thinks the argument supports dualism makes us look more closely at Grene's use of it to establish the existence of persons, that is, those agents who make responsible claims to knowledge, for the introduction of persons was supposed to free us from the incoherence of dualism.

Just as Grene argues that physics requires physicists, that physicists make truth claims, and that a reductive physicalism cannot account for beings who made truth claims, Donagan similarly argues that the scientific research that treats nature in terms of fundamental physics is not itself intelligible in terms of fundamental physics at all. Donagan's argument starts from the notion of truth itself rather than truth claims[22] and maintains that we can neither abandon that notion (without abandoning natural science as well) nor account for it in physicalistic terms. Therefore, we should not be physicalists, and we should not be physicalists for basically the same reason that Grene urges: the activity of science cannot itself be understood in terms of a reductive physicalism. For Donagan, however, these are grounds for dualism. The reasoning he attributes to Spinoza but believes it should be ours as well:

> Spinoza found himself following in the footsteps of Descartes, for reasons which have not lost their strength. On one hand, he found persuasive reasons for treating nature, conceived as an object of scientific research (as *ideatum*), despite the hierarchy of beings it contains from simple minerals to complex animals, as a unity, in which the highest biological processes are intelligible in terms of fundamental physics. On the other, he found that the scientific research (*idea*) that so treated nature was not intelligible in terms of fundamental physics at all. The unity of nature, the very thought of which we owe to science, appears to include everything there is—except scientific research itself and the thinking of which science is one of the highest manifestations. It is

therefore, in Spinoza's terms, necessary to follow Descartes in recognizing that infinite substance has two attributes, and that those attributes are *realiter distincta*. There seems to be no reason to recognize more than two.[23]

Our situation, then, is this: Donagan, uses a version of the "physics refutes physicalism" argument in support of the existence of minds, dualistically understood. Grene uses the same argument in support of the existence of persons. The category of the person is, however, intended, among other things, to help us escape from thinking dualistically about the mind. We need to look more closely at the reasons that make Donagan think this argument should lead us to be dualists, for even if it does not succeed in pushing us down the Cartesian path, it leads us to attend to consciousness and the indispensable role it plays in making arguments like this work. I turn to consciousness not because I find Donagan's interpretation of the argument uncompelling, but because I find the consideration of consciousness has an intermediate role to play in any arguments of this form. This allows us to make some intermediate points about what the argument establishes that concern consciousness and that are relevant to evaluating the claim that philosophy of the person should replace philosophy of mind. These points seem to me to hold whether or not we ultimately conclude that the phenomena made possible by consciousness offer evidence for dualism.

III. THE SPECTER OF CONSCIOUSNESS

a. Consciousness and Levels of Reality

We characterized the person above by saying, first, that the person is to be situated in nature. In this section I shall try to develop the reason why Donagan's version of the "physics refutes physicalism" argument suggests that consciousness is more difficult to locate in nature than are other aspects of the natural hierarchy that also need explaining. This does not mean that it is impossible to do, but it does mean that an attention to consciousness and its relation to nature—a central concern of the philosophy of mind, traditionally understood—will remain a dominant philosophical topic for the foreseeable future, and I will suggest in the following section that this will be so even if we choose to make the category of the person central to our understanding of ourselves.

Grene insists that philosophically we need to acknowledge a many-leveled metaphysics. For in the first place a "one-level ontology contradicts itself,"[24] and although this can be seen in a number of ways, one way she offers is to use the "physics refutes physicalism" argument to show that a metaphysics that has place only for, say, molecules has no room for molecular scientists. However, there is one many-leveled metaphysics Grene wants to be sure to avoid, namely, the Cartesian. She wants to avoid it both because she thinks it is incoherent (presumably as a result of getting off on the wrong foot in its account of the mind's interaction with "dead matter," rather than working from living matter to begin with), but more significantly from the biological point of view because it simplifies the natural world by robbing it of its own levels and consequently encouraging us to see mind as something over against a simplified natural world: "To move straight from *res extensa* to something called the mind is to miss the myriad styles of life cast up by the processes of evolution, of which the human style of life is one—with a difference."[25] Now Donagan has offered essentially Grene's argument for essentially Grene's first point, the inadequacy of a one-level metaphysics. But he also uses it to argue for precisely what Grene wants to reject in her second point, a many-leveled metaphysics that is dualistic. So it is worthwhile to take a moment to reflect on Donagan's comments to see what sort of case he makes for the two-leveled ontology. What we find, I think, is one of the reasons that keeps consciousness at the center of the philosophical stage and that also prevents us, perhaps, from being willing to grant that Grene's ontological levels are the only ones that matter to us.

Donagan, like Grene, recognizes a hierarchy of beings in nature, ranging from inorganic nature to an organic nature distinguished by different levels of complexity. In spite of this, he conceives of the totality of this nature as being "intelligible in terms of fundamental physics." And this means that he thinks that mind is not so intelligible. Why not? We can of course make reference to semantic notions, such as "truth," or speak of "intentionality," and expect that Grene will agree to the irreducibility of these to physics or physiology. But what undergirds these notions and makes these ideas seem so peculiar is their relation to and dependence on consciousness. Meaning and truth (as well, of course, as affirmations of truth), insofar as they enter into human life, enter it through consciousness as the semantic contents of minds. And consciousness seems to be a very peculiar phenomenon indeed. One way in which consciousness seems to be peculiar is that its relation to ontological levels below it does not seem to be the same as the relation of other ontological levels to the levels below them. David Chalmers writes:

> And almost all the high-level phenomena that we need to explain ultimately come down to structure or function: think of the explanation of waterfalls, planets, digestion, reproduction, language. But the explanation of conscious-ness is not just a matter of explaining structure and function. Once we have explained all the physical structure in the vicinity of the brain, and we have

explained how all the various brain functions are performed, there is a further sort of explanandum: consciousness itself. Why should all this structure and function give rise to experience? The story about the physical process does not say.[26]

Chalmers's claim is that many so-called "higher level" phenomena can be explained in terms of their structure and function, but consciousness does not seem to be able to be so explained. The point is that consciousness seems to be a level unlike other levels.

Grene offers one hierarchy that can be taken as an example of a many-leveled ontology when she distinguishes, within the natural world, physical systems, living things, learners, and human organisms.[27] When she undertakes to distinguish, for example, living systems from physical systems, she remarks that the difference between them "consists, not of course in any new 'stuff' or 'entity' superadded to . . . [the physical systems]: living things, like any other things, are made of molecules. But they are made of molecules so ordered as to generate systems that function in some new and interesting fashion, and these new and interesting fashions constitute higher levels of organization within the physical system in question."[28] That is to say, what distinguishes living from nonliving things is the order or organization of the molecules in the living system (structure) and the new ways in which this order of molecules permits the living thing to operate or behave (function). In a multileveled ontology, one question to be asked concerns either mind (or consciousness) or its Grenean replacement, the person: is the mind or the person "just one more level"? Can all the earlier levels that one wants to recognize be explained, as Grene explains the transition from nonliving physical systems to living ones, in terms of structure and function, and, if so, can the level of mind or the person also be understood in this way? Donagan's answers here are clear enough: the hierarchy of beings, from the most basic of nonliving systems to the highest biological processes, can all be understood in terms of fundamental physics; the mental, however, cannot. Grene, as we noted, wants a different kind of hierarchy: physical systems, living things, learners, and human organisms, the last of which are able to achieve personhood. Unlike Donagan's, the mental is not distinguished as a separate level in Grene's hierarchy, and this is seen by her as an advantage by enabling us to talk about what it is to be human without bringing in "the specter of consciousness."

In the next section I discuss whether the focus on the person really frees us from a focus on consciousness, but here I want to suggest that one reason why a philosopher like Donagan inclines toward a two-leveled metaphysics is that he thinks that all the hierarchies in nature can be explained in terms of fundamental physics, presumably employing explanations that appeal to structure and function in the way that Grene characterized the transition from physical systems to living things. Consciousness does not seem to be the sort of thing that is readily explained in this way. This may not lead us to Cartesian dualism, though that is of course where someone sympathetic to Donagan's argument may think it points. But it does suggest that consciousness is a particularly puzzling phenomenon wherever it is encountered, in human beings and, presumably, in non-humans.[29] And the way in which it seems to resist being understood in terms of structures and functions constituted from lower levels, the perplexity with which we confront, to use McGinn's colorful metaphor, the prospect of understanding how "the water of the brain is turned into the wine of consciousness,"[30] seems to face us with an irresistible philosophical puzzle, and the puzzle seems to be precisely one that Grene's argument above sets before us.

If our task is to understand ourselves as in nature and part of it, then it would seem that figuring out how consciousness can be understood as a natural phenomenon is a prime philosophical task, and the amount of philosophical work currently being devoted to this project would seem to acknowledge the problem. But if it is fair to say that understanding consciousness as a natural phenomenon faces special difficulties that understanding other levels of the natural hierarchy does not, then any philosophical position that seeks to understand the conscious human being in nature and as a part of nature is called upon to offer special solutions in the effort to locate such beings in that natural world. And, as I now wish to suggest, rather than permitting us to dispense with the search for such solutions, the very characteristics that distinguish the person in fact call attention to the need for them.

b. Consciousness and Persons

We characterized the person above in two further ways, by saying, second, that the person was a participant in culture and, third, that the person was a responsible agent. In this section I want to suggest that consciousness is crucial to giving a nonreductive account of these characteristics and thus to explaining why the person introduces a new category, and that this is apparent from Grene's own account. What this suggests is that consciousness is conceptually prior to the person, so we cannot choose to focus on the person rather than to focus on consciousness: there is no focusing on the person *without* focusing on consciousness, there is no understanding the person *without* understanding consciousness.

Grene, however, thinks that we can get at what we are by leaving consciousness aside and focusing on our status as animals whose way of living in a world, particularly a cultural world, makes them distinctive:

> For what Heidegger is doing in his depiction of human being as being-in-the-world is to renounce radically and once for all the attempt to get at our natures through the concept of consciousness. It is a radical move against the *cogito* as the starting point of philosophy. We have to ask who we are, not in terms of "what it feels like to be a person," or of some secret inner something, to echo once more Wittgenstein's way of putting it, but in terms of where we find ourselves and of what we seek to make of ourselves. . . . From this perspective . . . the very notion of a "philosophy of mind" is an anachronism. There isn't stuff spread out there and mind in here; there is what it is to be human, which needs to be looked at straight, without the spectre of "consciousness" that has till now dominated our thought.[31]

Looking at what it is to be human "straight" is looking at ourselves as participants in culture ("where we find ourselves") and as responsible agents ("what we make of ourselves"). (Not that these two expressions point only to our cultural participation and our responsible agenthood, but surely they serve to indicate at least these.) The problem is, there is no way to look at ourselves in these ways (that is, "straight") without bringing consciousness into the picture. Let me enlarge on this for a moment before discussing whether this really results in any difficulties for Grene's attempt to rethink what it is to be human.

First, let us examine cultural participation. Persons become persons through their participation in symbol-systems, understood in the broad sense in which this is largely synonymous with participation in a culture. But to describe that participation in terms of structure and function—at least if we understand that in terms of the physical structure of our environment and the physiological structure of ourselves, and the interactions between the two—is certainly not going to generate the meaningful use of symbols. It is this sort of approach that leads, if not to holding that thermostats have beliefs, then to maintaining that the difference between us and the thermostat is just one of degree, not of kind, at least when it comes to ascriptions of intentionality.[32] Presumably, Grene wants no part of this. But it is the route one is going to be forced to take if one wants to understand human beings as natural beings, as symbol-users and cultural participants, while in any strict and serious way avoiding the "specter of consciousness." What makes the use of symbols genuinely meaningful, what makes various activities authentic participation in a culture, are the mental contents present in the symbol-users', in the cultural participants' minds. Thus to understand persons as participants in a culture is to understand them first of all as conscious beings, and one cannot look at their participation "straight" without highlighting their conscious nature.

Second, let us look at responsible agenthood. Responsible agents—persons—in the guise of physical scientists make truth claims about molecules, but molecules themselves do not. We attribute propositional attitudes such as ". . . affirms that 'P' is true" to responsible agents—persons—and not to, say, computers that have been programmed to make the same sounds as persons, and do so in appropriate circumstances. (Such statements, of course, are not offered as noncontroversial but rather as generally acceptable to those who, like Grene, think that computers merely ape human behavior without displaying genuine purposiveness or intentionality; they are thus being presented merely as common ground among those who, like Grene, believe that "the attempt to reduce human purposive, or 'intentional,' action to physiology and ultimately to physics and chemistry is an absurdity."[33]) What is it that makes the scientist a genuine symbol user and the molecule (or the *mere* system of molecules, understood solely in terms of their structure and function) or the computer not one? One might expect Grene to be sympathetic to what Searle famously suggests in his Chinese room example: computers—and a comparable point can be made in terms of brain activity described purely physically, at the level of molecules or systems of molecules—deal only in syntax, not in semantic content, and that semantic content is precisely what is encountered in the making of truth claims. But if one asks what it is that leads us to speak of semantic content in the case of the person but not the computer, I think the only plausible answer is that the person is a conscious being and that the computer is not. As Searle says, "Minds have mental contents; specifically, they have semantic contents."[34] There just is no meaningful use of symbols, no responsible (or irresponsible) use of propositional attitudes apart from conscious minds.[35] Thus to understand persons as responsible agents is to understand them first of all as conscious beings, and one cannot look at their responsible actions "straight" without highlighting their conscious nature.

Now perhaps it would seem that there is nothing in such an admission that is immediately troublesome for Grene. She certainly does not deny that persons are conscious; rather, at least part of the point seems to be to indict particular positions that get at who we are by focusing on consciousness: neither Cartesian "consciousness as a separate substance," nor the "bits of consciousness" of Hume and the other empiricists, nor the pin-point "unity of consciousness" of Kant offers the appropriate starting point for understanding what it is to be human. Nor is it clear that all forms of dualism are anathema to her, in that her criticisms of dualism seem invariably directed against substance dualism rather than what is usually called property dualism. Still, I think there are problems for her here. The point above is not simply that persons happen to be conscious beings; it is that one can only understand what persons do that makes them count as persons by reference to their conscious nature. Looking at ourselves "straight" is to look at ourselves as persons; to understand ourselves as persons is to understand ourselves as participants in culture and as responsible agents; and to understand ourselves as participants in culture and as responsible agents is to understand ourselves as conscious beings, for there is no way to explain what it is to be a participant in culture or a responsible agent without making reference to consciousness. Thus it is hard to see how the person offers us a philosophical fresh start that will "get at our natures" independently of "the concept of consciousness." The category of the person gets at our natures only by drawing attention to certain aspects of human life that cannot become intelligible except through the concept of consciousness.

Moreover, this point combined with what was said in the preceding section explains why locating the person in nature seems to me to be more of a project that a starting point. Suppose the following to be true. First, persons are ontologically irreducible, real existents because they participate in symbol systems and make meaningful and responsible statements intended to express truths about the world. Second, what permits persons to participate in such systems and to make such statements is the fact that they are conscious. Third, consciousness cannot be explained in terms of structure and function (whereas, leaving consciousness aside, all the other characteristics that serve to pick out a hierarchical station among "the myriad styles of life cast up by the processes of evolution" and among physical systems generally can be explained in terms of structure and function). It seems to me that one reasonable conclusion to draw from these statements is that consciousness, and not personhood, lies at the philosophical center of our being, because it looks like personhood is explained in terms of distinctive and irreducible characteristics, and the fact that those characteristics are distinctive and irreducible is explained by reference to the character of our consciousness. And it seems to me that a second reasonable conclusion to draw is that insofar as we do not have a satisfactory philosophical account of how consciousness is to be viewed as a part of nature, we do not know how to locate the person in nature either. It seems that consciousness is bound to lie at the philosophical center of attention because of the challenge it poses to typical naturalist explanations. Of course that challenge may be met, but the fact that there is a challenge at all guarantees a philosophically central place for the study of consciousness and for the place of consciousness in describing who we are. Until that challenge is met, it is difficult to see how the idea of the person as a part of nature is more than a promise.

What an emphasis on personhood does is to emphasize the natural context within which our consciousness finds itself and develops. And it is doubtless a justified charge against Descartes that the contribution of this context is underplayed. It is true, for example, to say of language that it "must be spoken or written, heard or seen (or touched if one is blind). It is a form of gesturing sustained and generalized by the development of natural languages. It exists, as we do, bodily or not at all." The purely physical aspect of language use, of course, can be mechanically imitated without generating genuine linguistic utterances. This leads Grene to add, "'Bodily' here, of course, does not mean 'explicable in terms of the laws of physics,' but existing as a living center of action and passion, coming to ourselves, in our case, in a human as well as a natural world."[36] Identification of the physical and cultural conditions for language is useful, but it still needs to be noted that it is in consciousness that semantic content is present. Consequently, the crucial feature of ourselves that talk of our being a "living center" needs to include is our conscious nature, and if this is so then looking at ourselves "straight," while it will involve a discussion of our natural (including our cultural) environment, will not involve any "radical renunciation" of the concept of consciousness as the central focus of what it is to be human. And this would be true even if we should ever succeed, *pace* Donagan, in viewing consciousness as a natural, biological phenomenon.

Even those of us who are tempted to subscribe to one of the positions that Grene labels as absurd or incoherent have reason to be grateful for her attempt to identify a category of the person. For the person, as she describes it, reminds us simultaneously about what makes us human and about how that humanity is related to, and develops within, a natural (including a cultural) world. Unfortunately, instead of showing us (at least the incorrigible among us) how to make a new start metaphysically, it rather also reminds us (again, at least the incorrigible among us) just how central consciousness is in coming to an understanding of what it is to be human, and just how philosophically perplexing it is as well. The category of the person reminds us of the centrality of consciousness by explicating the person through characteristics whose distinctiveness can be understood only by reference to consciousness and the forms it takes in human beings. And the category of the person reminds us of just how perplexing the phenomenon of consciousness is by calling attention to the difficulty of understanding it and the activities it underwrites in terms of the natural sciences. For the fact that not all of these are the lessons that she would have us learn from her discussion of the person, we can only beg her indulgence.

ANTHONY N. PEROVICH JR.

HOPE COLLEGE
APRIL 2001

NOTES

1. Reference to the "incoherencies of Cartesian dualism" may, for example, be found in Marjorie Grene, "Biology and the Problem of Levels of Reality," in *The Understanding of Nature: Essays in the Philosophy of Biology* (Dordrecht/Boston: D. Reidel Publishing Co., 1974), p. 44; cf. her remark that "despite the ingenuity of some of his remarks about the interaction of mind and body, the radical disconnection of these two kinds of finite substances made a coherent understanding of the world in terms of them impossible," in Marjorie Grene, "People and Other Animals," in *The Understanding of Nature: Essays in the Philosophy of Biology* (Dordrecht/Boston: D. Reidel Publishing Co., 1974), p. 346. In Marjorie Grene, "To Have a Mind . . . ," in *The Journal of Medicine and Philosophy* (1976), vol. 1, no. 2, p. 183, she insists that "the attempt to reduce human purposive, or 'intentional,' action to physiology and ultimately to physics and chemistry is an absurdity rather than simply a confusion." For an argument that in fact the only options available concerning the mind-body problem are dualism, reductionism, and eliminativism, see Jaegwon Kim's "The Myth of Nonreductive Materialism," his 1989 presidential address at the Central Division Meetings of the American Philosophical Association, in *Proceedings and Addresses of the American Philosophical Association* 63, no. 3, pp. 31–47.

2. The expression can be found in Marjorie Grene, *A Philosophical Testament* (Chicago and La Salle: Open Court Publishing Company, 1995), p. 71, as well as in the "Intellectual Autobiography" included in this volume.

3. Marjorie Grene, "To Have a Mind . . . ," p. 178; cf. "People and Other Animals," p. 347.

4. For the rejection of the Cartesian associations of the term "mind" as "misleading and irrelevant," see Marjorie Grene, *A Philosophical Testament*, p. 158; the phrase "alien excrescence" comes from Marjorie Grene, "Qualified Freedom," in *Perspectives in Philosophy*, ed. Michael Boylan (Fort Worth: Harcourt Brace Jovanovich, Inc., 1993), p. 282; for the idea that we are in nature and a part of it, not over against it, see *A Philosophical Testament*, p. 44.

5. On our embodied nature see "People and Other Animals," pp. 355–56; on the person as a special form of animality, not an animal with a mind added on, see "To Have a Mind . . . ," p. 190.

6. For the phrase "mind-possessing bodies," see "To Have a Mind . . . ," p. 196; in that article "mind" is defined in terms of the capacity for symbol use on p. 180, and she points out that such a capacity can be developed only among other symbol users and in a culture on p. 191; for minds as the uses made of brains, see Marjorie Grene, "Mind and Brain: The Embodied Person," in *Philosophical Dimensions of the Neuro-Medical Sciences*, ed. S. F. Spicker and H. T. Engelhardt, Jr. (Dordrecht: D. Reidel Publishing Co., 1976), p. 118.

7. "Qualified Freedom," p. 285.

8. For the role of our genetic endowments in becoming persons, see "People and Other Animals," p. 354; the expression "life transformed through culture" comes from "Qualified Freedom," p. 282; for personhood as an achievement, see "People and Other Animals," pp. 354, 357; for culture as something in which we participate, see "People and Other Animals," p. 354, *A Philosophical Testament*, p. 107, and "To Have a Mind . . . ," p. 191.

9. "Personalized" human organisms are discussed in "People and Other Animals," p. 354; for the person as a unique expression of a culture, see "To Have a Mind . . . ," p. 191; personal identity is discussed in "Mind and Brain," pp. 120–21.

10. "People and Other Animals," p. 354.

11. It is true that Grene not only speaks of "responsible agents, whom we call persons," *A Philosophical Testament*, p. 4, but also of "agency, or responsible personhood," *A Philosophical Testament*, p. 178. I am going to emphasize the former, because it seems to me that the overall thrust of her account of the generation of a person is to describe a process that, when successful, leads to an individual responsible for his or her actions and claims.

12. For the account of free action in more detail, see *A Philosophical Testament*, pp. 181–87 and "Qualified Freedom," p. 286.

13. *A Philosophical Testament*, p. 26.

14. "Biology and the Problem of Levels of Reality," p. 44.

15. Marjorie Grene, *The Knower and the Known* (New York: Basic Books, Inc., 1966), p. 88.

16. "Mind and Brain," p. 117. For the organized character of perception, see pp. 118 and 121. For the philosophical insignificance of unintegrated perceptions, see pp. 124–25.

17. *The Knower and the Known*, p. 143. For the "bare" nature of the transcendental unity of apperception, see p. 151. For an interesting passage on how to expand the transcendental unity of apperception into a person, see *A Philosophical Testament*, pp. 42–43.

18. "Biology and the Problem of Levels of Reality," p. 42; "To Have a Mind," p. 182.

19. "Biology and the Problem of Levels of Reality," p. 42.

20. "To Have a Mind," p. 183.

21. *A Philosophical Testament*, p. 177. A fourth reason is personal: it was Marjorie Grene's advice, more than any other factor, that led me to proceed from undergraduate work at the University of California at Davis, where I had been her student, to graduate study at the University of Chicago, where I was Donagan's.

22. He notes, however, that comparable arguments can be generated from sources that include Grene's case: "Quite obviously a related argument can be constructed from any thoroughgoing philosophy of history, or from any reasonably humanistic philosophical psychology, in which interest would focus not on truth, but on the propositional attitudes and the concept of intentionality" (Alan Donagan, "Realism and Freethinking in Metaphysics," in *Theoria* 42 [1976], p. 15).

23. Ibid., p. 18. It should be noted that Donagan highlights what he calls Spinoza's dualism. See ibid., p. 18, n. 7, and his *Spinoza* (Chicago: University of Chicago Press, 1988), pp. 116–19.

24. "Biology and the Problem of Levels of Reality," p. 44.

25. "People and Other Animals," p. 352.

26. David J. Chalmers, *The Conscious Mind: In Search of a Fundamental Theory* (New York and Oxford: Oxford University Press, 1996), p. 107.

27. "People and Other Animals," pp. 352–53.

28. Ibid., p. 352.

29. See Alan Donagan, "The Worst Excess of Cartesian Dualism," in *Human Nature and Natural Knowledge: Essays Presented to Marjorie Grene on the Occasion of Her Seventy-Fifth Birthday*, ed. Alan Donagan, Anthony N. Perovich Jr., and Michael Wedin, Boston Studies in the Philosophy of Science, vol. 89 (Dordrecht/Boston/Lancaster: D. Reidel Publishing Company, 1986), pp. 321–23.

30. Colin McGinn, *The Problem of Consciousness* (Oxford and Cambridge, MA: Blackwell Publishers, 1991), p. 1. It perhaps should be said that I quote various philosophers here whose remarks point to the difficulties of viewing consciousness as a part of nature without intending to suggest that they do not themselves want to locate it there.

31. *A Philosophical Testament*, p. 71.

32. John McCarthy has maintained that his thermostat has beliefs. Searle writes, "I once asked him: 'What beliefs does your thermostat have?' And he said: 'My thermostat has three beliefs—it's too hot in here, it's too cold in here, and it's just right in here'" (John Searle, *Minds, Brains and Science* [Cambridge, Mass.: Harvard University Press, 1984], p. 30). Daniel Dennett stresses that there is no real difference in kind between the thermostat and us: "There is no magic moment in the transition from a single thermostat to a system that *really* has an internal representation of the world around it. The thermostat has a minimally demanding representation of the world, fancier thermostats have more demanding representations of the world, fancier robots for helping around the house would have still more demanding representations of the world. Finally you reach us," Daniel C. Dennett, *The Intentional Stance* (Cambridge, Mass.: MIT Press, 1987), p. 32.

33. "To Have a Mind . . . ," p. 183.

34. John Searle, *Minds, Brains and Science*, p. 39.

35. See John Foster, "A Defense of Dualism," in *The Case for Dualism*, ed. John R. Smythies and John Beloff (Charlottesville: University Press of Virginia, 1989), pp. 9–11, for an account of how not only propositional *acts* are essentially conscious but how propositional attitudes, while not themselves essentially conscious, are "essentially linked with states of consciousness."

36. *A Philosophical Testament*, pp. 82–83.

REPLY TO ANTHONY N. PEROVICH JR.

Nick Perovich has composed an eloquent challenge to my neglect of consciousness as a central concept in the explication of what it is to be human. As an undergraduate at Davis, he was a student of mine, indeed, one of the two best students I ever had. It is sad that he fails to understand what I am trying to say. But of course, the other way around, I plainly fail to understand the case he is making for that wretched consciousness.

Obviously, I admit that if I were not conscious—if I were asleep or dead—I would not be writing this response—or this evasion, depending on how you see it. And if the family dog were asleep or dead, he would not bark loudly at every canine passing by the window. What explanatory work does such an insight do? On the one hand, there are lots of organisms that exhibit consciousness; so, on its own, consciousness tells us nothing about a unique human condition, if such there be. On the other hand, if we specify some special human form of consciousness, like self-consciousness, or, in David Rosenthal's formulation, "the consciousness of the unity of consciousness," what has that further specification accomplished? I don't see how anything purely subjective or inward can tell me who I am, what kind of life it is that marks mine out as human. Nor, unfortunately, do I see any way to mediate this reciprocal lack of understanding between me and the consciousmongers, who are certainly many and eminent, while I find myself a lone voice crying in the wilderness.

Not that I invented my concept of the person; I am far from claiming to be an original thinker. But most of those who have influenced my thinking on this matter, or have helped me to formulate my view, are dead: Michael Polanyi, Helmuth Plessner, Maurice Merleau-Ponty—writers unread, in any case, by contemporary analytic philosophers. More recently, as I indicated in my *Philosophical Testament*, I found Peter Wilson's *Man: the Promising Primate* an illuminating account of our strange place in a generally Darwinian nature. Earlier, I had also drawn insights from Marshall Sahlins's

Use and Abuse of Biology. Those are sources, I suppose, even more alien to the philosophic mind.

In these circumstances, what can I say? For one thing, I am not, as Perovich suggests, "aiming at a middle path" between two extremes. Instead, I am trying to take a new path, suggested in a number of ways by the writers I have mentioned, a path that avoids what Plessner called "the Cartesian alternative," not by finding a course half-way between them, but by setting off from a different starting point, one which takes seriously our *location*, not just geographically, of course, but within a tradition, or a cluster of traditions, in which we find ourselves and which we may in turn to some extent modify by the way we interiorize or, to some extent, reject, its ways of symboling. Merleau-Ponty's version of being-in-the-world, Plessner's account of the differences in positionality between plants, animals, and human persons, or Polanyi's concept of indwelling can all be useful, it seems to me, in helping to develop such a view.

As far as the proponents of the primacy of consciousness go, I can only remark that as I see the situation—very much from the outside, since I find it impossible to read all that consciousness literature—the appeal to consciousness stems from two sources. On one side are the mind-equals-brain people—so-called cognitive scientists, or at least a large heap of them—who find, surprise, surprise, that there is something more than just neurons firing. So, they exclaim, here is this consciousness, inside my head; what can I say about it? Their reasoning is like that of Tom Nagel's famous argument on what it feels like to be a bat. You want total, utter objectivity; you don't find it, so you fall back on a secret, inner something to fill this uncomfortable gap. Indeed, I could have a horrible toothache that was screamingly conscious: it would fill up my whole existence, for the duration. But what would it tell me about what it is to be a human being, to live a human life? Not much, I think. In this form, the craze for consciousness strikes me as just another philosophical fashion, a way of going round in circles, getting nowhere (unless getting tenure, so that one can do more of the same).

However, that is not the only form of consciousness-touting. There are those, like Alan Donagan and Perovich himself and, if I remember rightly, John Beloff, too, who argue for a more radical view. There is, they claim, a real, extra, nonbodily entity, a mind, a Cartesian thinking substance, that somehow inhabits a human frame. Perovich quotes me as calling this view "incoherent." I suppose it is; but I should rather have said that, for me at least, it is not so much incoherent as inconceivable. What could a disembodied mind be? Not only can I not imagine; I can find no reason to posit such an entity. I was born, have grown old, and will die. What is this "mind" that is supposed somehow to be attached to me? I have sometimes suggested that a good turn of phrase is Gilbert Ryle's "minding." There are indeed activities of which we are capable that we call mental. And I agree that it is inadequate to identify them as simply neural. But is there some kind of immaterial *thing* involved as the ground for their existence? I'm afraid I just don't know what it could be. In Donagan's case, and I presume also Perovich's, the reason for such a belief is religious. One can only respect other peoples' faith, and say, "*credunt quia absurdum.*" But I have not yet met any convincing philosophical arguments for such a view.

When it comes to our mental activities (our capacity for minding), what is characteristic, it seems to me, is our capacity for *intensionality*, for what Polanyi called intellectual passions. Perovich refers to John Searle's concept of "semantic content." This, he says, must be "in some one's mind." Yes and no. If I am now actually thinking about the Pythagorean theorem, it is "in my mind." But as something I could be thinking about, because I understand it, it is the target of my knowledge, more like a first than a second Aristotelian actuality. That's why the content is *semantic*: it's about something, usually something other than myself. To quote Polanyi again, knowledge is typically from-to. And the "to" can be amazingly detached from any given material basis. There was once a Greek who thought up that proof about right triangles; at some point it was "in his mind." But that is not what the Pythagorean theorem is. It is a demonstrable relation among angles, evident anytime anywhere to anyone who takes the trouble to learn about it. Beethoven's Ninth Symphony was created, miraculously, by a deaf composer, who had it "in his mind" before it was ever performed. Is that what the Ninth *is*? It is not only not just that; it is not even all the performances that ever have been or ever will be, each of which somehow instantiates or expresses it without being identical with it. Although I have in general little or no patience with the phenomenological tradition, I do think it is useful, with Husserl, to acknowledge the significance of *noemata* as distinct from the actual act of thinking. Indeed, that is the profound wisdom behind the much maligned "Platonic theory of ideas."

This, you may say, is a strange kind of dualism on my part: no separable minds, but objects of thought that are neither on land or sea. Yes, once you recognize that as members of a species evolved so as to depend on, to live in and through, the ways of symboling characteristic of a given cultural tradition, we have acquired a strange kind of detachment, of negativity, even, that allows interest in, and devotion to, entities or events or causes larger than ourselves. It is what Plessner called our "natural artificiality" that permits this. I have tried to give some account of what I mean by this, for example, in "People and Other Animals" and in my *Philosophical Testament*, both of which Perovich has read, and which he cites. But, alas, he has not grasped the first step, as exemplified, for example, in Merleau-Ponty's dictum that we are in a human world, itself in a natural world, which in turn is contained in the physical world. I don't want, as Perovich seems to think, to give physical explanations up to some point, then physiological ones, and then wait for something else. He complains that I deal only with "structure" and "function," whatever that is supposed to mean. Plessner's philosophical anthropology, for example, which I find illuminating, seems to be simply descriptive; I don't see where structure or function specially come into it. And what would be the matter with them if they did? Alas, I am lost.

One small point, though: Perovich refers to an essay of mine called "Mind and Brain: the Embodied Person." I was surprised to find myself employing the kind of "brain-mind" talk that I usually eschew. In fact, that paper was given as a response to an address which was heavily based on some remarks of Lashley's on mind and brain; so that was where I had to start. In retrospect, I believe that was misleading. But since more straightforward statements of my own views are so unconvincing, I suppose it doesn't matter. Alas, we simply have to agree to disagree.

M. G.

8

David M. Rosenthal

PERSONS, MINDS, AND CONSCIOUSNESS

There is a recurring tension in philosophical thinking having to do with the relations between wholes and their parts. Should we seek to understand things in terms of combinations of constituent parts from which they are, or might be, constructed? Or must we, instead, explicate those parts in terms of the wholes to which they belong? Both strategies have long histories and strong advocates.

This tension is especially vivid in cases in which we describe some phenomenon by reference to some distinctive unity or unifying function. An example of this is the problem of saying what it is for something to be a person. One difficulty in thinking about what it is to be a person stems from Descartes's famous argument in Meditation VI that, because the self is an unextended, thinking substance, it is distinct from anything bodily.[1] Persons are beings with mental capabilities, and that mental functioning is essential to their nature. But, as Marjorie Grene has forcefully and eloquently insisted, we cannot understand what it is to be a person as long as we see its mental functioning as that of a distinct Cartesian substance. We can understand the nature of persons only if we see that mental functioning as firmly rooted in the rest of reality.[2] It is not just that we must see persons as having both mental and bodily natures, as P. F. Strawson and others have argued.[3] As Grene rightly argues, we must represent these mental and bodily natures as functionally and inextricably unified.

Grene goes farther, however, in also arguing that we cannot capture the distinctive functional unity of persons in terms of the independent categories of mind and body. We must, she urges, rethink the issues "in terms of new categories, primarily in terms of the category of the 'person' rather than of either body or mind." We must try to "go between the horns of the traditional dilemma and to espouse neither matter nor mind, nor both of them, as [our] fundamental concepts."[4]

Here I am less certain. I believe that we need not start with the concept of a person, but can instead explain what it is for a creature to be a person by reference to various distinctive aspects of that creature's mental functioning. The issue here is not the ontological question of whether persons have distinct mental and physical parts; few today would maintain any such view. The issue, rather, is the methodological question about how to understand what it is for something to be a person. Can we understand what it is to be a person in terms of various aspects of the mental and bodily functioning of persons? Or must we posit a basic category of persons, which cannot in turn be fully understood in terms of the kinds of mental and bodily functioning that go into being a person?

In what follows, I sketch my reasons for believing that we can understand the concept of person in terms of the mental and bodily functioning characteristic of persons. In section I, I argue that we can understand mental functioning only as inextricably bound up with the interactions the relevant body has with its environment. This is not just because mental states are special cases of bodily states; it would be so in any case. But not all creatures that function mentally qualify as persons. So section II takes up the question of what it is that distinguishes persons from other creatures with mental endowments. It turns out that these distinguishing features all have to do with the special way in which persons are conscious of their thoughts, feelings, desires, and perceptions. Since we must understand consciousness to understand personhood, section III briefly sketches an account of what it is for mental states to be conscious, an account that avoids the Cartesian gulf between mind and matter. Section IV explains the special way in which persons are conscious of their mental states, which involve our sense of the unity of consciousness and the self, and section V considers several objections that explanation.

I. MIND, BODY, AND ENVIRONMENT

One reason for the continuing appeal of Cartesian approaches to understanding the mind is the difference between what it's like for one to feel, perceive, desire, or think something and how we think about somebody else's being in such mental states. It seems obvious to many that the mental properties in virtue of which one knows of oneself that one is in pain, for example, are of a wholly different kind from the properties in virtue of which one knows that somebody else is in pain. And similarly for perceiving, believing, desiring, and all other mental states.

Not all mental states occur consciously. It is now widely recognized that thoughts and desires occur without being conscious; people believe and desire many things without being in any way at all conscious of their having those beliefs and desires. There is also compelling reason to hold that even bodily sensations, such as pains and aches, and perceptual sensations, such as visual sensations of red, can occur without being conscious. In subliminal perception and peripheral vision, and in experimental results such as those involving masked priming,[5] perceptual sensations occur without the subject's being at all conscious of them. It even sometimes happens that we can tell from somebody's behavior, say, from a slight limp, that the person is in pain, even though the person may have been wholly unaware of it. And no mental state is conscious if the subject is in no way whatever aware of being in that state.

The recognition that mental states occur without being conscious causes us to rethink the apparent disparity between first- and third-person points of view about what it is for somebody to be in a mental state. The first-person point of view about mental states operates only when those states are conscious. That first-person point of view is cast in terms of what it's like for one to be in a mental state, and when a mental state is not conscious there is nothing at all that it's like for one to be in it. When the mental state one is in is not conscious, one has access to that state in just the way others might have access to it, by inferring from one's behavior and from the occurrence of environmental stimuli.

Any particular mental state, however, can be conscious at one time and not at another. Even when a belief or desire occurs without being conscious or a perception occurs subliminally, one can come to be conscious, in the way characteristic of our conscious states, of that belief, desire, or perception. But we can have a first-person point of view only about those of our mental states which are currently conscious. Since the very same states can be at one time conscious but not at another time, one must adopt a third-person point of view toward many of one's own mental states. Whatever disparity obtains between first- and third-person points of view is equally a difference between one's own conscious and nonconscious mental states. This underscores the need to dissolve the appearance of a gulf between first- and third-person approaches. We must find some way to explain how it is the very same mental phenomena to which we have access in the two ways.

Pressure to reconcile first- and third-person points of view about mental states makes so-called functionalist accounts of such states especially appealing. Such accounts define mental states in terms of the characteristic causal connections each type of state has with behavior, stimuli, and other mental states. On the version of this approach developed by David Lewis, the relevant connections are those we can extract from the folk-psychological platitudes that constitute our shared knowledge and assumptions about all the various types of mental state. These commonsense platitudes encapsulate general background knowledge not only about causal ties, but also about how the various mental states get grouped into types and other matters that help define them. Because the general background information defines each type of state in part by reference to the connections states of that type have with other types of state, we cannot define any state solely in terms of the behavior and stimuli that is relevant to it. Rather, we will cast the definition of each type of state in terms of ties that state has not only with behavior and stimuli, but with mental states of many other types.[6]

Since these functional definitions of mental states rely on the platitudes that constitute our shared folk-psychological knowledge, they will include shared knowledge about our first-person access to mental states. What it's like for one to be in conscious states of each type will include information about how the various mental states seem to resemble and differ from one another and how we taxonomize them from a first-person point of view. All of this will figure in the resulting functional descriptions of mental states. Lewis argues, moreover, that these functional descriptions define our concepts of each type of mental state. So our very concepts of the different types of mental state characterize not only those states in terms of environment and behavioral factors, but in terms of both first-person considerations as well. They represent all our mental states both from a first-person point of view and as inextricably embedded within nonmental reality.

Lewis develops his functionalist characterization of mental phenomena in the context of an argument for mind-body materialism. The discovery that certain bodily states realize the functional description our folk-psychological platitudes generate would sustain mind-body materialism. But the functional characterization of mental phenomena, by itself, is wholly independent of both dualism and materialism. It is a theory, rather, of the nature of mental states. And, since the theory relies on nothing but our shared folk-psychological knowledge, none of our commonsense intuitions about the mental can undermine it.

Not everybody writing today would accept Lewis's functional characterization of the mental states. Some theorists, indeed, would characterize at least some types of mental state in terms free of any essential ties with nonmental reality. Such characterizations of mental states, especially common for qualitative states, also make the reconciliation of first- and third-person points of view about mental states difficult, if not impossible.

But the persistence of such quasi-Cartesian approaches should not encourage us to think that we can overcome the Cartesian gulf between matter and mind and between first- and third-person only by adopting a basic category, such as that of a person. Lewis's functionalism shows that we can put those Cartesian oppositions to rest even if we operate with relatively traditional notions of mind and body.

Indeed, even for those who reject Lewis's functionalist approach, the dominant theoretical approaches today tend to characterize mental states in ways that minimize the Cartesian gulf. Many contemporary explanations of what it is for an intentional state to have content, for example, appeal in some ineliminable way to environmental factors.[7] Since content is essential to a state's being intentional, such externalist theories of mental content characterize intentional states in terms of such environmental considerations. Such characterizations are again independent of issues about dualism and materialism.

II. PERSONS AND THE MENTAL

Functionalism in the style of Lewis shows that we can characterize mental functioning in ways that reconcile first- and third-person descriptions and locate mental functioning inextricably within nonmental reality. But, by itself, that does not obviate the need for adopting a basic category of a person independent of the traditional categories of mind and body. For that, we must also show that we can understand what it is to be a person by appeal only to those traditional notions, without any primitive category of a person.

As Harry G. Frankfurt noted some years ago, traditional discussions often overlook the difference between what it is to be a person and what it is simply to be a creature with mental capabilities.[8] But there is more to being a person than just having a mental life. Many nonhuman animals that have relatively little in common with persons nonetheless have mental capabilities; indeed, psychologists continue to discover that the mental capacities of such nonhuman animals are astonishingly elaborate. Nor is the concept of a person simply the concept of a human being; though it is doubtful that any other terrestrial animals are persons, we all recognize the possibility of encountering nonterrestrial creatures that do count as persons.

Frankfurt's own account of what is special about persons appeals to an individual's ability to have second-order desires, desires that one have or not have some first-order desire. Forming such higher-order desires, he urges, involves identifying oneself with one, rather than another, of one's first-order desires. And he sees the ability to identify oneself in this way with one's first-order desires both as essential to the process of deciding and also as what is distinctive of being a person.

Doubtless the ability to identify oneself as an individual with certain desires is a crucial aspect of what it is to be a person. But self-identification by way of first-order desires is hardly the only way in which we identify ourselves by reference to our mental states. We also identify ourselves as individuals who think certain things, have various memories, and have characteristic feelings. All these self-identifications, moreover, play an important role in what it is for a creature to be a person. It would at best be an oddly limited person whose self-identification by way of its mental states was limited to being an individual that had certain desires.

Frankfurt's appeal to second-order desires does, however, point toward a more satisfactory account of what it is to be a person. Second-order desires presumably influence what first-order desires an individual will have, and thereby impose a measure of order and unity on that individual's mental life. Such order and unity in one's mental life are an important aspect of what it is to be a person. In influencing what first-order desires one will have, moreover, one's second-order desires will often lead one to reflect on one's desires and on what desires one wishes to have. In part this is because one's second-order desires will influence one's first-order desires when one desires not to have some first-order desire that one actually has or to have some first-order desire that one lacks. Such conflict between first- and second-order desires will often prompt one to reflect on both desires and the tension between them. And the ability for such reflectiveness is also central to what it is for a creature to be a person.

Second-order desires, however, are not the only sources for the mental unity and order and the self-reflectiveness that are characteristic of persons. One may come to reflect on one's mental states because one is puzzled about a practical problem or an intellectual issue, and one may reflect on one's perceptual experiences because of one's enjoyment of a situation or an aesthetic experience. Whenever one thinks seriously about something or attends to one's past or present experiences, one is likely to enhance the sense of unity and order in one's mental life.

Many creatures that do not qualify as persons have mental states and processes that exhibit an impressively high degree of integration and coherence. Integration and coherence of mental function is necessary to get around in the world successfully, and especially to interact with one's conspecifics. So it cannot simply be such integration and coherence that distinguishes persons from other creatures. What sets persons apart is rather that they are conscious of their mental functioning as being coherent and they are conscious of it as all belonging to a single individual. It is not mental unity and coherence that distinguishes persons, but consciousness of mental unity and coherence. Both the self-reflectiveness and the mental unity characteristic of persons are matters of how persons are conscious of their thoughts, feelings, and perceptions.

More must be said about these special ways of being conscious of one's mental states. As noted earlier, no mental state counts as being conscious if the individual who is in that state is in no way conscious of the state. But the routine way we are ordinarily conscious of our conscious states falls well short of the self-reflective, unified consciousness that is distinctive of persons. Section IV takes up the question of what this special self-reflective, unified consciousness consists in. First, however, we must address a Cartesian challenge about the consciousness of mental states generally.

Consciousness is the mark Descartes appeals to as distinctive of mental functioning. Thus he defines thoughts in the Geometrical Exposition of the *Second Replies* by saying that "the word 'thought' applies to all that exists in us in such a way that we are immediately conscious of it" (AT 7, 160). "[N]o thought," he reiterates in the *Fourth Replies*, "can exist in us of which we are not conscious at the very moment it exists in us" (AT 7, 246). Indeed, consciousness very likely underlies Descartes's very distinction between mind and body; it is presumably the unity of consciousness that underlies the Meditation VI claim that mind is indivisible, in contrast with the indefinite divisibility of body. Consciousness, it seems, is the fundamental property of mental reality which sets it apart from body.

This suggests a difficulty in explicating what is distinctive of persons in terms of the way persons are conscious of their thoughts, feelings, and perceptions. If we explain mind in terms of consciousness, there is nothing left by appeal to which we could, in turn, explain consciousness; consciousness will lie outside the net of naturalist explanation. And, if consciousness sets mind apart from all physical reality, the appeal to consciousness in constructing an understanding of personhood will bring the Cartesian gulf between mind and body along with it. The only way to avoid that gulf then would be, as Grene urges, to "go between the horns of the traditional dilemma and to espouse neither matter nor mind, nor both of them, as [our] fundamental concepts."

We need not follow Descartes, however, in defining mind in terms of consciousness; we can, instead, go in the opposite direction, and explain consciousness in terms of mental states that are not themselves conscious. That will allow us to operate with a concept of consciousness that implies no Cartesian gulf, so we can appeal to it in constructing our understanding of personhood without commitment to such a gulf. If we then also adopt a functionalist account of mind, we can explain both consciousness and personhood in a way that locates mental states firmly in the context of nonmental, physical reality. The following section, therefore, develops an account of consciousness in terms of which this can all be done.

III. CONSCIOUSNESS AND THE MENTAL

No mental state is conscious if the individual who is in that state is in no way whatever conscious of being in that state. This means that whenever a state is conscious, we are in some way or other conscious of that state;

being in some way conscious of a mental state is a necessary condition for that state's being conscious. Indeed, it is notable that Descartes never writes of a thought's being conscious, but only of our being immediately conscious of a thought, though it is plain that he means by this exactly what we mean by saying of a mental state that it is conscious.

Although we are in some way or other conscious of every conscious state, not every way of being conscious of a mental state results in that state's being conscious. Suppose, for example, that I am conscious of thinking or feeling something solely because I infer that I do, or solely because you tell me and I believe you. Being conscious of a thought or feeling solely in those ways does not result in its being conscious. So we need to specify just how one must be conscious of a mental state if that state is to be conscious. If we succeed in specifying that, we will have conditions for a state's being conscious that are not only necessary, but sufficient as well.

It might seem that explicating what it is for a state to be conscious in terms of one's being conscious of the state is unavoidably and viciously circular, since it seeks to explain consciousness in terms of itself. But the phenomenon of consciousness being explained here is not the phenomenon that the explanation appeals to. A mental state's being conscious is, intuitively, a property of that state in virtue of which it figures as part of one's stream of conscious. Conscious states are those which one can report on; one can tell others when they occur and what it's like for one to be in them. One can, moreover, deliberately shift one's attention to them. When a mental state is not conscious, one can do none of those things.

A mental state will exhibit none of these marks of its being a conscious state unless one is in some suitable way conscious of the state. But we understand independently of all this what it is for one to be conscious *of* something. One is conscious of something when one has some mental reaction to it that enables one to respond to its presence. There are, accordingly, two broad ways in which we are conscious of things: by sensing them and by having thoughts about them as being present. Having a sensation of something or a thought about it as being present, moreover, makes one conscious of that thing even when that sensation or thought is not, itself, a conscious sensation or thought. If I subliminally see something, my visual sensation is not a conscious state, but having that sensation makes me conscious of the thing I subliminally see. Though I am not conscious of seeing it, my seeing it still makes me conscious of it.

More important, we understand what it is for somebody to have a thought or a sensation of something independently of understanding what it is for that thought or sensation to be conscious. So we understand what it is to be conscious *of* something independently of understanding what it is for mental states to be conscious. There is no circularity in explaining what it is for a mental state to be conscious by reference to our being conscious of that state.

Corresponding to the two ways of being conscious of things, there are two models for how it is that we are conscious of those of our mental states which are conscious states: by sensing those states or by having thoughts about them. The first model, which posits an "inner sense"[9] by which we are aware of our conscious states, has been by far the dominant theoretical approach to the question of how we are aware of those states. And, since the access we have to things by sensing them seems unmediated, a model on which we sense our conscious states would readily explain why our awareness of our conscious states also seems to be direct and unmediated.

Despite its traditional popularity, however, the inner-sense model faces grave difficulties. Perhaps the most damaging is that sensing always involves some qualitative character, but there is no distinctive qualitative character associated with the way we are conscious of our conscious mental states. No qualitative properties figure at all in connection with our conscious intentional states, such as beliefs, doubts, desires, expectations, and the like. And, although conscious perceptions, sensations, and emotions do have qualitative character, the qualities are always those of the states we are aware of, not the higher-order states in virtue of which we are aware of them. Since some qualitative character always occurs in sensing, it cannot be that we are conscious of our conscious states by sensing them.

The only alternative is that we are conscious of our conscious mental states by having thoughts about those states as being present. Because these thoughts are about other mental states, I refer to them as *higher-order thoughts* (HOTs). A mental state is conscious if one is conscious of it by having a HOT about it, a HOT to the effect that one is in that state.[10]

The inner-sense model seemed to explain why the way we are conscious of our conscious states seems unmediated and direct, since sensing in general makes us aware of things that way. But HOTs can handle this as well. The only reason we have to think that we are directly aware of our conscious states is, after all, that it seems that way to us; it is just that nothing seems to mediate between those states and our awareness of them. And that often happens with the thoughts we have about things. When a thought relies on no observation and on no inference of which we are aware, nothing seems to us to mediate between the thought and what it is about. And we can stipulate that the HOTs in virtue of which we are aware of conscious mental states do not result from any inference of which we are aware.[11]

As noted earlier, the self-reflective, unified consciousness that distinguishes persons from other creatures goes well beyond the unreflective, seemingly automatic way in which we are ordinarily conscious of our everyday conscious states. It is plain, in the case of most conscious states, that we are aware of being in them; we can, if asked, say whether we are in them. Still, our awareness of our mental states in these cases is neither focused nor deliberate, nor, in these cases, do we not even notice that we are aware of those states. We are aware of them without noticing that we are. In the case of the self-reflective, unified consciousness that distinguishes persons, by contrast, the way we are conscious of our conscious states is deliberate and focused. We are not merely conscious of these states; we are actually conscious that we are. We are, in these cases, *introspectively* conscious of our conscious states.

The HOT model offers a compelling explanation of the difference between such introspective consciousness of our mental states and the way we are conscious of those states in the ordinary, unreflective cases. A mental state is conscious if it is accompanied by a HOT to the effect that one is in that state, a HOT based on no conscious inference. But that HOT is, itself, a mental state, and it will not be conscious unless it is accompanied, in turn, by a yet higher-order thought about it. In ordinary, unreflective cases, our HOTs are not conscious; they occur, but we are not aware of them. Introspective consciousness is the special case in which we are conscious not only of our first-order mental state, but conscious also of the HOT in virtue of which we are conscious of the target first-order state.[12]

This explanation of the difference between introspective and nonintrospective consciousness fits well with the intuitive data about both kinds of case. When a mental state is conscious in the ordinary, nonintrospective way, we are conscious of the state but not of being conscious of it. That is why we are unaware, in these ordinary cases, of having any HOTs; our HOTs are not, in these cases, conscious. When we are reflectively conscious of a mental state, and so conscious of it as being part of a unified fabric of conscious states, we are also aware of the way we are conscious of the state. We are aware not only that we are focusing on the state attentively and deliberately, but also that the way we are conscious of the state represents it as part of that unified mental fabric. We not only have HOTs about the state; the HOTs we have about it are conscious thoughts.[13]

This account of self-reflective consciousness we sometimes have of our mental states builds entirely on mental states that are not, in themselves, conscious states. A mental state's being conscious, on this account, is the relational property a mental state has of being accompanied by a HOT in virtue of which one is aware of being in that target state. And our being reflectively conscious of a state, and of ourselves as being in that state, consists in our also being aware of that HOT, itself. Having a HOT makes one conscious of oneself as being in the target state; so when a HOT is conscious, we are also aware of this way of being conscious of ourselves.

On this account, no mental state is intrinsically or essentially a conscious state. We do not explain mentality in terms of consciousness, but the other way around; consciousness is a special case of mentality. Since we can develop an informative explanation of consciousness, there can be no serious temptation to regard it as something apart from the rest of reality, and hence as nonphysical. We can thus appeal to reflective consciousness in explaining what distinguishes persons from other mental beings and still avoid commitment to the Cartesian gulf between mind and body.

The foregoing account of consciousness also fits comfortably with Lewis's functionalist theory about the nature of mental states generally. It is part of our folk-psychological understanding of a mental state's being conscious that one is conscious of that state. So a functionalist account that extracts defining causal relations from our folk-psychological platitudes will characterize a state's being conscious in that way. The result is a fully naturalist model for reflective consciousness that anchors it firmly in the context of the interactions between a creature's mental functioning, its bodily constitution, and its physical environment.

As noted earlier, many who reject such functionalism still characterize intentional states by reference to nonmental factors. That is because they hold that intentional content is determined in part in terms of those things in the physical environment to which intentional states refer. But this account may seem to raise a problem for the HOT model of consciousness. On such an externalist account of content, the content of a thought is a function of what environmental objects or substances the thought is connected to. Whether that content is about water or the macroscopically indistinguishable twin water of Hilary Putnam's famous twin-earth thought experiment would then depend on which of the two substances the actual environment contains.[14]

But the content of the HOT in virtue of which a first-order thought is conscious is only about that first-order thought. So its content would be a function not of what substance occurs in the environment, but just what mental state it is about. But the way HOTs characterize their target states determines the way we are conscious of them; we are conscious of being in the type of state a HOT describes. So how, if the content of our thoughts is in part a function of what they are about, could one be conscious of one's first-order thought *as* a thought about water, and not a thought about twin water?[15]

One possibility is that the HOT gets its content, insofar as that pertains to environmental objects and substances, from its target. But there is another possibility as well. An intentional state's actual content need not be the same as the content we are conscious of that state as having. The way we are conscious of our conscious states is a function of the way

HOTs characterize them; so when an intentional state is conscious, we are conscious of being in a state with the content the HOT represents its target as having.

Suppose, then, that one has a conscious thought about water; its being about water is a function of some connection the thought has with actual water in the environment. But the HOT one has about that thought, in virtue of which it is conscious, may well represent the thought in a way that is neutral with respect to the distinction between water and twin water. One would not be conscious of the thought *as* a thought specifically about water, as against twin water, but as a thought that is about some substance that could, for all one knows, be either. Indeed, it is likely that that is how we are actually conscious of many of the thoughts we have about water, at least those not cast, directly or not, in terms of chemistry.[16] Conscious states are seldom, if ever, conscious in respect of all their mental properties. So intentional states need not be conscious in respect of content that is as fine grained as the content they actually have.

IV. SELVES AND THE UNITY OF CONSCIOUSNESS

Descartes saw mind as nonphysical because the physical, being spatial in nature, is indefinitely divisible, whereas mind is indivisible. Even if there were, contrary to Descartes's own view, physically indivisible atoms, the atoms would be conceptually divisible. But mind might seem to be no less divisible, not spatially, but into mental parts. At any given moment, a person is in many mental states; why not, then, regard a person's mind as constituted by those states, and hence divisible into them? If the mind is, as Hume held, "nothing but a mere heap or collection of different percep-tions," each perception can, as he observed, "be consider'd as separately existent."[17]

But persons do not seem to be mere heaps or collections of mental states. The conscious states of persons seem, rather, to be unified somehow into a single consciousness. But it may also seem as though the HOT model of consciousness just sketched embraces a mental atomism like that of Hume. If each conscious state owes its consciousness to a single accompa-nying HOT, how can any sense arise of the unity of consciousness? Why would all our conscious states seem to belong to a single, unifying self?[18]

One unifying force in our mental lives is the way sensory experiences occur in relation one to another. Consider visual experience; we can locate each visual sensation in relation to every other, each appearing to be to the right or to the left or above or below every other such sensation. Similarly with all the other sensory modalities. And we calibrate this apparent spatial location from one sensory modality to another, so that a sound, for example, may appear to occur at the same place as a sight. Such cross-modal calibration appears to bind the various sensory fields together into a single modality-neutral field.

But the problem about the unity of consciousness is not to explain how the qualitative contents of experience are unified, but rather why we are *conscious of* those qualitative contents as being unified in a single consciousness. If a mental state's being conscious were an intrinsic property of that state, perhaps the unity of qualitative contents would carry along with it the unity of consciousness. But on the HOT model, a state's being conscious is not an intrinsic property of that state, but the relational property of being accompanied by a HOT. And we want to know why mental states that are conscious solely because each is accompanied by an individual HOT should seem to be unified in a single consciousness.

Part of the answer is that a HOT need not be just about a single target state, but can be about a number of states at once. Indeed, introspection itself suggests that we are conscious of our conscious mental states in this way. When something attracts our attention visually, we may be conscious of a small area of our visual field in considerable detail, but usually we are conscious of many different visual inputs, none in much detail, as a kind of overview. So it is reasonable to suppose many target qualitative states will be conscious in virtue of a single HOT that is about all of them, and about all of them as occurring in some suitable spatial array. Something similar happens with hearing, and even to some degree with tactile awareness. Doubtless a single HOT often has as its targets qualitative states from distinct modalities, as when we at once consciously see and hear a particular event. And our often being conscious of many sensory inputs as a group helps engender in us a sense that our qualitative states are unified, in that they belong to a single consciousness. The HOT model can readily explain this by supposing that, with many HOTs, each makes us conscious of large clusters of qualitative states.

HOTs operate in another way to produce in us a sense of the unity of consciousness. A HOT is a thought to the effect that one is in a particular mental state or cluster of such states. Such reference to oneself is required because a thought makes one conscious of things only when it represents them as being present, and the only way for a mental state to be present is for it to be a state of oneself. So the content of each HOT must make reference to a self that is in the state or states in question.

But this requirement cannot, by itself, give rise to a sense of the unity of consciousness, since the self to which each HOT refers might, for all we have shown so far, be different from one HOT to the next. And no sense of unity will result from each HOT's referring to a self unless it also seems that the self each HOT refers to is the same for all HOTs. And it may well seem that individual HOTs cannot achieve this sense of sameness.

We identify ourselves as individuals in a broad variety of ways that have little systematic connection. Some of these ways appeal to memories of personal history, while others rely on contingent facts about one's current location and situation. There is no magic bullet in virtue of which we identify ourselves, just a vast but loose collection of considerations, each of which, taken individually, is relatively unimpressive. But the combination is enough to identify oneself in any case in which the question may arise; any time one has a first-person thought, that is, a thought about oneself, one can, if pressed, specify the individual that thought is about.

Such self-identification operates in the first instance with the mundane first-person thoughts each of us has about ourselves, about what one's name is and where one lives, what one's personal history is, what one likes and dislikes, and so forth. Whenever one has a new first-person thought, one secures the reference to oneself that occurs in that thought by appeal to the referent of these other, self-identifying first-person thoughts. And this sometimes adds to the stock of self-identifying thoughts one uses to secure reference to oneself.

HOTs are also first-person thoughts, and the same process extends to them. We appeal to this broad, heterogeneous collection of contingent considerations to specify the individual each HOT represents its target state as belonging to. We take this heterogeneous collection to pick out the same individual from one case to another. And because that applies to our HOTs, it forms the basis for the sense we have that our conscious mental states are unified as belonging to a single individual. Our sense of the unity of consciousness does not result from something special about the way we are conscious of our conscious mental states. Rather, it is an extension of the everyday assumption we operate with that, for each of us, the heterogeneous collection of ways in which we identify ourselves go together to pick out a single individual.

The everyday assumption that our first-person thoughts all refer to one individual may suffice for some sense that our conscious states occur in a single consciousness. But that sense of unity will not, itself, be conscious unless some of one's HOTs are themselves conscious thoughts. And this is just what happens in the reflective consciousness distinctive of persons. When one is introspectively conscious of one's mental states, one is conscious not only of those states, but also of being conscious of them.

On the HOT model, that means becoming conscious of one's HOTs, each of which represents its target state or states as belonging to some individual. Since one secures the reference to that individual by way of one's heterogeneous collection of self-identifying thoughts, one identifies the individual to which each HOT assigns its target as being the same for all HOTs. So, when one is conscious of one's HOTs, one becomes conscious of them as assigning their targets to some single individual. One thereby becomes conscious of oneself as a center of consciousness.[19] We need not posit an indivisible Cartesian soul or any special kind of consciousness to explain traditional intuitions about self-consciousness and our sense of the unity of consciousness.

There are two main characteristics that distinguish persons: the ability persons have to be reflectively conscious of their mental states, and the sense they have that their mental states are unified by belonging to a single center of consciousness. The foregoing considerations explain why these two characteristics go together. Being reflectively conscious of one's mental life consists in being not just conscious of one's conscious states, but conscious, in addition, that one is conscious of them. On the HOT model, one not only has HOTs, in virtue of which one's mental states are conscious; one's HOTs are, themselves, sometimes conscious. And being conscious of one's HOTs enables one to become aware of one's conscious states as belonging to a single self.[20]

V. PROBLEMS ABOUT THE SELF

It might be objected that the appeal to a heterogeneous collection of contingent properties cannot do justice to the way one's first-person thoughts, including HOTs, refer to oneself. Mistakes are always possible in identifying oneself; one might, for example, think that one is Napoleon. As I have argued elsewhere, such error is even possible in the case of HOTs; one can be conscious of oneself as being in mental states that one is not actually in.[21]

But despite the possibility of these kinds of error, it has been argued that there is another way in which none of one's first-person thoughts can be mistaken. Though I can be mistaken in thinking I am Napoleon, it seems that I cannot in such a case be mistaken about who it is that I think is Napoleon. And if I think that I am in pain or that I believe a certain thing, I cannot be mistaken about who it is that I think is in pain or has that belief. One's first-person thoughts are, in Sydney Shoemaker's phrase, "immune to error through misidentification," misidentification, that is, with respect to reference to oneself.[22]

Such immunity seems to conflict, however, with the foregoing account of self-identification. Identifying the individual a first-person thought refers to by appeal to some heterogeneous collection of contingent properties plainly leaves open the possibility of error through misidentification. If I identify actually myself by reference to a heterogeneous collection of properties, I might do so erroneously. This holds for the HOTs in virtue of which we are conscious of our conscious states no less than for our other first-person thoughts.

When I have a conscious pain, I cannot erroneously think that the individual that has that pain is somebody distinct from me, though I can of course be wrong about just who I am. How can we capture this elusive distinction? When I have a conscious pain, I am both in pain and conscious of being in pain. The error I cannot make is to think that the individual who is conscious of the pain is distinct from the individual that has the pain of which some individual is conscious.

The HOT model allows for a natural explanation of this immunity from error. HOTs represent their targets as being states of the same individual that thinks the HOT. The HOT I have about a conscious pain represents that pain as belonging to the very same individual as the individual that thinks the HOT, itself. Thinking of the conscious pain as belonging to an individual distinct from me would mean thinking that the individual that has that HOT is distinct from the individual that HOT represents as being in pain. And that would conflict with the way the HOT represents things.[23]

The respect in which I cannot represent my conscious pain as belonging to somebody distinct from me consists in my being unable to represent the pain as belonging to somebody other than the individual who is conscious of the pain. The idea that some special immunity to error is involved here results from an illicit assimilation of mental states to one's consciousness of them.

Although I cannot think that the individual that has that pain is somebody distinct from me, I can be mistaken about just who it is that I am. Being mistaken about that is simply going wrong in how I identify the individual who is conscious of the pain. And that is possible because such identification consists in my identifying the individual who has the HOT in virtue of which my pain is conscious as the individual picked out by some heterogeneous collection of contingent properties. And I can be wrong about whether the individual who has the HOT about the pain is the same as the individual, if any, that has all those properties.

These considerations help also with another quandary about the self. It has often been noted that I can think that I, myself, have a particular property without thereby thinking that some individual has that property, even when I am the individual the first thought is about. Consider John Perry's vivid example, in which I see a trail of spilled sugar from somebody's grocery cart. My thought that somebody's grocery cart is spilling sugar does not imply the thought that my grocery cart is spilling sugar, even if it happens to be my cart.[24] This disparity between the two types of thought is sometimes taken to show that contingent properties cannot underwrite the reference to oneself that occurs in one's first-person thoughts. Whatever contingent properties one appeals to, a thought that identifies an individual as having those properties will still not be a thought about oneself, as such.[25]

But it is unclear what it actually is for a thought to be about one, as such. One natural possibility is that a thought's being about me is just its being about the individual identified by reference to the huge collection of contingent properties in terms of which I think about myself. If there is something more to a thought's being about me, as such, it needs independent explication, not just insistence on the difference.

There is, of course, a strong sense we have that a thought's being about me, as such, is something more than its being about an individual identified by reference to some collection of contingent properties. But we can explain that sense without crediting the intuition.[26] First-person thoughts are conscious, when they are, in virtue of their being accompanied by HOTs, and each HOT represents its target as belonging to the individual who also thinks the HOT in question. Something similar happens with my thoughts that are about me, as such. Suppose I think that I have some property, P. That thought's being about me, as such, consists in its representing the individual that has property P as being the very individual who thinks that thought. And no collection of properties figures in securing that co-reference. If I think that an individual that has some collection of properties also has property P, my thought will not automatically represent the property as belonging to the very individual who thinks that thought.

The present approach to personhood and the self also suggests a natural account for the puzzling phenomenon of Multiple Personality Disorder.[27] Consider a highly simplified, artificial case. An individual seems to have two selves, each with different thoughts, desires, and experiences. The first self, moreover, seems to know nothing of the second, though the second seems to know about all the thoughts, desires, and experiences of the first.

In part, such cases must involve an individual's having two partially disjoint series of thoughts, desires, feelings, and experiences. These collections will partially overlap when it comes to beliefs about a lot of shared background information, as well as matters pertaining to location and the environment; and they will overlap in other ways, as well. But they will diverge about many other things. The states in each collection fit with one another in a reasonably coherent way, though those in one group often do not fit comfortably, if at all, with those in the other.

But that is not, by itself, enough to explain the sense we have of two selves' being present in the individual. For that, we must posit two disjoint sets of HOTs the individual has about the various first-order states. In the first condition, the individual has HOTs about thoughts, experiences, and desires that occur in only one of the two partially disjoint collections. In the second condition, the individual's HOTs are about the states in the other partially disjoint collection.

We identify all our first-person thoughts, HOTs included, by reference to some heterogeneous collection of contingent properties. In the imagined case of an individual that appears to have two selves, that individual will use two, partially disjoint collections of contingent properties to identify the individual that its first-person thoughts are about. That applies equally to how the individual identifies who it is that is conscious of its current conscious states. The individual appeals, in the two conditions, to different self-descriptions in identifying who it is that is conscious of its conscious states.

This explains how the second apparent self can have access to the first self's states without those states being conscious, for the second self. In the second condition, the individual has many conscious thoughts about the desires, feelings, and experiences that occur in the first condition. It may even be that these conscious thoughts rely on no inference of which the individual is then aware. Still, the individual assigns all the states those thoughts are about to somebody identified as distinct from the individual that has those conscious thoughts.

There is a feature of persons so far not discussed which is often thought to be central to what it is to be a person. Persons not only do things; they have a sense of themselves as being in some important way free in performing many, at least, of their actions. Their actions seem, from a first-person point of view, not to be causally determined in the way other events are. Whether or not such actions actually have causal antecedents that determine their occurrence, we experience many of the actions we perform as being, in some significant way, free.

Even when we experience our actions as free, however, we also experience them as resulting from conscious desires and intentions we have. But, although we are conscious of desires and intentions that seem to cause our actions, we typically are not also conscious of anything as causing those desires and intentions.[28] Because we are typically conscious of our desires and intentions as being spontaneous and uncaused, we experience the resulting actions as also being free and uncaused.

Sometimes we are conscious of a desire or intention as resulting from other, earlier mental states; when we consciously deliberate, for example, we are aware of our desire as being due to that process of deliberation. But the conscious chain does not continue indefinitely. There is always an antecedent intentional state we are conscious of but for which we are not conscious of any cause, and we will accordingly be conscious of it as being spontaneous and uncaused.

None of this shows that any of our desires and intentions are actually uncaused. We are conscious of only relatively few of our mental states; so there will always be some mental antecedent of which we fail to be conscious. Still, the result is that we are always conscious of our desires and intentions and, indeed, our intentional states generally as being up to us. If we experience them as being caused at all, we experience them as resulting from a causal sequence of intentional states whose initial member we are conscious of as being uncaused. The sense we have of free agency results from the way we are conscious of our conscious desires and intentions. Here, again, what is distinctive of persons is a matter of the way they are conscious of their mental lives.

DAVID M. ROSENTHAL

CITY UNIVERSITY OF NEW YORK,
GRADUATE CENTER
NOVEMBER 2000

NOTES

1. *Oeuvres de Descartes*, ed. Charles Adam and Paul Tannery, Paris: J. Vrin, 1964–75, vol. 7, pp. 71–90, esp. pp. 78–86; see *The Philosophical Writings of Descartes*, by René Descartes, translated by John Cottingham, Robert Stoothoff, Dugald Murdoch, and Anthony Kenny, 3 volumes (Cambridge: Cambridge University Press, 1984–91), vol. 2, which includes page numbers for Adam and Tannery. Quotations are from this translation, cited hereafter as "AT."

2. For example, Marjorie Grene, "Knowledge, Belief, and Perception," in Grene, *A Philosophical Testament* (Chicago: Open Court, 1995), pp. 9–27, p. 14, and "People and Other Animals," in Grene, *The Understanding of Nature: Essays in the Philosophy Of Biology* (Dordrecht: D. Reidel Publishing Company, 1974), pp. 346–60.

3. P. F. Strawson, "Persons," in *Minnesota Studies in the Philosophy of Science* 2, ed. Herbert Feigl, Michael Scriven, and Grover Maxwell (Minneapolis: University of Minnesota Press, 1958), pp. 330–53; reprinted with slight changes as ch. 3 of P. F. Strawson, *Individuals: An Essay in Descriptive Metaphysics* (London: Methuen & Co., Ltd., 1959), pp. 87–116; and "Self, Mind and Body," *Common Factor* 4 (Autumn 1966): 5–13, reprinted in David M. Rosenthal, *The Nature of Mind* (New York: Oxford University Press, 1991), pp, 58–62.

4. Grene, "People and Other Animals," 347.

5. For early work on masked priming, see Anthony J. Marcel, "Conscious and Unconscious Perception: Experiments on Visual Masking and Word Recognition," *Cognitive Psychology* 15 (1983): 197–237, and "Conscious and Unconscious Perception: An Approach to the Relations between Phenomenal Experience and Perceptual Processes," *Cognitive Psychology* 15 (1983): 238–300.

6. David Lewis, "An Argument for the Identity Thesis," *The Journal of Philosophy* 63, no. 1 (January 6, 1966): 17–25; reprinted with additions in Lewis, *Philosophical Papers*, vol. 1 (New York: Oxford University Press, 1983), pp. 99–107; "Psychophysical and Theoretical Identifications," *Australasian Journal of Philosophy* 50, no. 3 (December 1972): 249–58; "Mad Pain and Martian Pain," in *Readings in Philosophy of Psychology*, ed. Ned Block, vol. 1 (Cambridge, Massachusetts: Harvard University Press, 1980), pp. 216–22; reprinted in Lewis,

Philosophical Papers, vol. 1, pp. 122–30, with postscript, "Knowing What It's Like," pp. 130–32.

Lewis's functionalist approach has been usefully developed in a number of writings by Sydney Shoemaker; see especially "Functionalism and Qualia," *Philosophical Studies* 27, no. 5 (May 1975): 292–315; reprinted, slightly revised, in *Readings in the Philosophy of Psychology*, vol. 1, ed. Ned Block (Cambridge, Massachusetts: Harvard University Press, 1980), pp. 251–67; and other articles in Shoemaker, *Identity, Cause, and Mind: Philosophical Essays* (Cambridge: Cambridge University Press, 1984), and in Shoemaker, *The First-Person Perspective and Other Essays* (Cambridge: Cambridge University Press, 1996).

7. For a sample, see Tyler Burge, "Individualism and the Mental," *Midwest Studies in Philosophy* 4 (1979): 73–121; "Individualism and Psychology," *The Philosophical Review* 95, no. 1 (January 1986): 3–45; Fred Dretske, *Explaining Behavior: Reasons in a World of Causes* (Cambridge, Massachusetts: MIT Press/Bradford Books, 1988); and Jerry A. Fodor, "A Theory of Content," in Fodor, *A Theory of Content and Other Essays* (Cambridge, Massachusetts: MIT Press/ Bradford Books, 1990).

8. Harry G. Frankfurt, "Freedom of the Will and the Concept of a Person," *The Journal of Philosophy* 68, no. 1 (January 14, 1971): 5–20.

9. In Kant's useful phrase: *Critique of Pure Reason*, trans. and ed. Paul Guyer and Allen W. Wood (Cambridge: Cambridge University Press, 1998), p. 174, A22/B37. Locke uses the phrase "internal sense" (*An Essay Concerning Human Understanding*, edited from the fourth [1700] edition by Peter H. Nidditch [Oxford: Oxford University Press, 1975], II, i, 4, p. 105). See also D. M. Armstrong, "What is Consciousness?" in Armstrong, *The Nature of Mind* (St. Lucia, Queensland: University of Queensland Press, 1980), pp. 55–67, p. 61; and William G. Lycan, *Consciousness and Experience* (Cambridge, Massachusetts: MIT Press/Bradford Books, 1996), ch. 2, pp. 13–43.

10. I have developed this HOT model in "Two Concepts of Consciousness," *Philosophical Studies* 49, no. 3 (May 1986): 329–59; "The Independence of Consciousness and Sensory Quality," in *Consciousness: Philosophical Issues, 1, Consciousness*, ed. Enrique Villanueva (Atascadero, California: Ridgeview Publishing Company, 1991), pp. 15–36; "Thinking that One Thinks," in *Consciousness: Psychological and Philosophical Essays*, ed. Martin Davies and Glyn W. Humphreys (Oxford: Basil Blackwell, 1993), pp. 197–223; "A Theory of Consciousness," in *The Nature of Consciousness: Philosophical Debates*, ed. Ned Block, Owen Flanagan, and Güven Güzeldere (Cambridge, Massachusetts: MIT Press, 1997), pp. 729–53; and "Consciousness and its Expression," *Midwest Studies in Philosophy* 22 (1998): 294–309.

11. We need not include the provision about observation, since an observation would figure in one's being aware of a mental state one is in only if one inferred one's being in that state from the observation.

12. For more on introspective consciousness, see my "Introspection and Self-Interpretation," *Philosophical Topics* 28, no. 2 (Fall 2000): 201–33 and "Unity of Consciousness and the Self," *Proceedings of the Aristotelian Society* 103, no. 3 (April 2003), forthcoming.

13. I argued earlier that sensing always involves mental qualities and no

higher-order qualities occur when we are conscious of our conscious states. So we are not aware of our conscious states by inner sense. An advocate of inner sense could reply that, since we are not in ordinary cases conscious of how we are aware of our conscious states, higher-order qualities could occur without our knowing it. But in introspecting we do become aware of the way we are conscious of our conscious states, and even then we are aware of no higher-order mental qualities.

14. Barring refinement about individuals' switching worlds, and the like. See Hilary Putnam, "The Meaning of 'Meaning'," *Minnesota Studies in the Philosophy of Science* 7, ed. Keith Gunderson (Minneapolis: University of Minnesota Press, 1975), pp. 131–93, and "Meaning and Reference," *The Journal of Philosophy* 70, no. 19 (November 8, 1973): 699–711.

15. This type of worry has been raised independently of the HOT model, as a problem for reliability of first-person access to our intentional states on an externalist theory of content. See Donald Davidson, "Knowing One's Own Mind," *Proceedings and Addresses of the American Philosophical Association* 60, no. 3 (January 1987): 441–58, and Tyler Burge, "Individualism and Self-Knowledge," *The Journal of Philosophy* 85, no. 11 (November 1988): 649–63; both reprinted in *Self-knowledge*, ed. Quassim Cassam (Oxford: Oxford University Press, 1994), pp. 43–64 and 65–79, respectively.

16. Davidson and Robert Stalnaker, "On What's in the Head," *Philosophical Perspectives: Philosophy of Mind* 3 (1989): 287–316, suggest in effect that intentional content in general is often neutral in this way. The present suggestion is that, whatever is so about the intentional content of thoughts in general, such neutrality typical holds for the intentional content of HOTs.

17. *A Treatise of Human Nature* [1939], ed. L. A. Selby-Bigge (Oxford: Clarendon Press, 1888), I, IV, ii, p. 207. Cf. Appendix, p. 634. For the famous "bundle" statement, see I, IV, vi, p. 252.

18. I am grateful to Sydney Shoemaker for pressing this question, in a paper entitled "Consciousness and Co-consciousness," delivered at the Fourth Annual Meeting of the Association for the Scientific Study of Consciousness, Brussels, July 2000.

19. This provides an answer, which Hume despaired of giving, to his challenge "to explain the principles, that unite our successive perceptions in our thought or consciousness" (*Treatise*, Appendix, p. 636).

20. For more on the apparent unity of consciousness, see "Introspection and Self-Interpretation," sec. VII.

21. See, for example, my "Consciousness and Metacognition," in *Metarepresentation: A Multidisciplinary Perspective*, Proceedings of the Tenth Vancouver Cognitive Science Conference, ed. Daniel Sperber (New York: Oxford University Press, 2000), pp. 265–95, sec. 5; "Consciousness, Content, and Metacognitive Judgments," *Consciousness and Cognition* 9, no. 2, Part 1 (June 2000): 203–14, sec. 5; and "Metacognition and Higher-Order Thoughts," *Consciousness and Cognition* 9, no. 2, Part 1 (June 2000): 231–42, sec. 4.

22. Shoemaker, Sydney, "Self-Reference and Self-Awareness," *The Journal of Philosophy* 65, no. 19 (October 3, 1968): 555–67; reprinted with slight revisions in Shoemaker, *Identity, Cause, and Mind: Philosophical Essays* (Cambridge: Cambridge University Press, 1984), pp. 6–18, p. 8. See also Gareth Evans,

"Demonstrative Identification," in *Evans, Varieties of Reference*, ed. John McDowell (Oxford: Clarendon Press, 1982), pp. 142–204, esp. 179–91.

23. In "Two Concepts of Consciousness," I wrongly suggested that we could construe the very content of HOTs along these lines, as being thoughts that whoever thinks this very thought is also in the target mental state. As Thomas Natsoulas pointed out, such content seems to imply that HOTs would always be conscious, since every HOT would be, in part, about itself ("What is Wrong with the Appendage Theory of Consciousness," *Philosophical Psychology* 6, no. 2 [1993]: 137–54, p. 23, and "An Examination of Four Objections to Self-Intimating States of Consciousness," *The Journal of Mind and Behavior* 10, no. 1 [Winter 1989]: 63–116, pp. 70–72). But HOTs can still represent their targets as belonging to the same individual that thinks the HOT, since the mental word 'I', in a HOT, would refer to whatever individual thinks that very thought.

24. John Perry, "The Problem of the Essential Indexical," *Noûs* 13, 1 [March 1979]: 3–21. See also Roderick M. Chisholm, *The First Person* (Minneapolis: University of Minnesota Press, 1981), chs. 3 and 4; and David Lewis, "Attitudes *De Dicto* and *De Se*," *The Philosophical Review* 88, no. 4 [October 1979]: 513–43.

25. For an argument that this conflicts with the HOT model, see Dan Zahavi and Josef Parnas, "Phenomenal Consciousness and Self-Awareness: A Phenomeno-logical Critique of Representational Theory," *Journal of Consciousness Studies* 5, no. 5/6 (1998): 687–705, sec. iii.

26. A satisfactory theory must explain the intuitions we have that pertain to the self, but may well not credit them all as being accurate. For a probing discussion of many aspects of the sense we have of the self, see Galen Strawson, "The Self," *Journal of Consciousness Studies* 4, no. 5/6 (1997): 405–28.

27. More recently this has also been called Dissociative Identity Disorder. The theoretical issues behind the terminology are irrelevant for present purposes.

28. As always, it is crucial to distinguish the mental state one is conscious of from the event of being conscious of it, in this case, to distinguish the event of deciding from our consciousness of that event. Robust experimental findings confirm that our subjective awareness of decisions to perform basic actions occurs measurably later than the events of deciding of which we are conscious. See Benjamin Libet, Curtis A. Gleason, Elwood W. Wright, and Dennis K. Pearl, "Time of Conscious Intention to Act in Relation to Onset of Cerebral Activity (Readiness Potential)," *Brain* 106, Part III (September 1983): 623–42; and Benjamin Libet, "Unconscious Cerebral Initiative and the Role of Conscious Will in Voluntary Action," *The Behavioral and Brain Sciences* 8, no. 4 (December 1985): 529–39. This work has been replicated and extended by Patrick Haggard, Chris Newman, and Edna Magno, "On the Perceived Time of Voluntary Actions," *British Journal of Psychology* 90, Part 2 (May 1999): 291–303; Patrick Haggard, "Perceived Timing of Self-initiated Actions," in *Cognitive Contributions to the Perception of Spatial and Temporal Events*, ed. Gisa Aschersleben, Talis Bachmann, and Jochen Musseler (Amsterdam: Elsevier, 1999), pp. 215–31; and Patrick Haggard and Martin Eimer, "On the Relation between Brain Potentials and Awareness of Voluntary Movements," *Experimental Brain Research* 126, no. 1 (1999): 128–33.

REPLY TO DAVID M. ROSENTHAL

David Rosenthal belongs to the prestigious, and proliferating, population of philosophers who spend their lives thinking about consciousness. Since he was doing this before it became as fashionable as it is now, I have to believe he really means it. Nevertheless, I find it difficult, indeed, impossible, to believe that grown-up people make a profession of this kind of to-ing and fro-ing. My reaction, I'm afraid, is rather like that of an old-fashioned logical positivist to metaphysics. So I really don't know how to begin to comment on Rosenthal's essay. He doesn't seem to me to argue for his position, he just takes it for granted, and he thinks the same of me. I want to think about persons rather than minds—certainly about persons rather than bits of consciousness—and Rosenthal seems to believe I want to take "person" as a primitive, unanalyzable term. So we can only talk at, not with, one another. In these circumstances, perhaps I may just mention some points in his presentation that I find puzzling, and attempt some response to them where I can.

Rosenthal states quite correctly that few of us any longer believe in two Cartesian finite substances. So, he seems to think, the "Cartesian alternative," as Plessner called it, is now disposed of. Far from it, in my view: as many philosophers hold, there is either brain or little "secret inner somethings," to borrow Wittgenstein's term (or an English rendering of it). That is Cartesianism pushed nearly to a *Nullpunkt* extreme. I have nothing against thinking about "mental functioning," or what Gilbert Ryle called "minding." It is one of the activities characteristic of persons that we want to reflect on and try to understand. "Mental functioning" for Rosenthal and Company, however, seems to boil down to "mental states," little subjective atoms which add up together to make the "unity of consciousness" that characterizes a person.

Section I is encouragingly called "Mind, Body, and Environment." This is a topic that cries out for ecological treatment, seeing animals, whether human or otherwise, as I have tried to say, for example, in the last chapter of my *Descartes*, or in chapter 7 of my *Philosophical Testament,* not as isolated entities impinged on by things out there, but as expressions of their unique ways of being *in* the particular *Umwelt* in relation to which, in the course of evolution, they have become the kinds of perceivers and actors that they are. True, I do not believe that scientific advances, as such, solve philosophical problems; but sometimes they can make a very great difference. And the philosophical implications of the Gibsons' ecological psychology—in particular, of the theory of affordances—are, or should be, tremendous. But nobody notices—or hardly anybody (there were once three promising young contenders; one betrayed the cause, one left philosophy, and one died). So Rosenthal is still talking about sensations as the foundation of our awareness of the outside world. Secret inner somethings again! There is a discussion of the tired old first- versus third-person point of view, and a lot about mental states that aren't conscious—without their being part of any Freudian "unconscious" or anything like that. I'm afraid I just don't understand.

Then we are to get a great deal of illumination out of David Lewis's functionalism. Now I always enjoyed listening to David Lewis, because he was so immensely clever. But it was quite clear that this was clever magic, in which what was pulled out of the hat, in fact, was only virtual rabbits. I'm reminded again of the philosopher's room I described in *Philosophical Testament*, where the door is firmly shut against reality—now, however, allowing in some new journals, devoted wholly to consciousness, or even what they call the "science of consciousness."

There are also, it seems, "externalist" theories of consciousness, which speak of environmental impact. Again, there is no sense of the intimate relation of being within one's dwelling place (in our case, both natural and cultural) that makes any organism what it is.

Section II, on "Persons and the Mental," is even more bewildering. Rosenthal refers to Harry Frankfurt's famous paper about second-order desires, as bearing importantly on his theme. In fact, when that article appeared (or when I read it, which I think was not long after), I was so impressed that I specially trudged along to Rockefeller University to meet the author. But I certainly had no idea its subject matter was "mental states." Surely desires, beliefs, whatever long-term attitudes shape our lives, are not to be numbered among mental states. Well, yes, if I feel I really *must* have some tidbit tasting of chocolate—that's a mental state. On the other hand, my desire to understand what it is to be human, or even just my desire to reply somehow reasonably to David Rosenthal's challenge—that's not a mental state. Admittedly, my impatience with him and his ilk (when I have to think about them) is a mental state. However, except for the obvious fact (which all my friends and relations are well aware of) that I am an impatient person, that momentary condition tells very little about the story that amounts to being me.

"It is not mental unity and coherence," Rosenthal tells us, that distinguishes persons, but "consciousness of mental unity and coherence." That is absolute nonsense. (The old nonsense, I suppose, about conscious-ness versus self-consciousness.) What distinguishes human beings from other animals with mental lives is our enculturation. As I have put it elsewhere, a developed human being is "a personification of nature through participation in a culture." Each of us is a history, starting, to be sure, with the genetic endowments, and limitations, laid down for us at our concep-tion, but nevertheless a history. And there is no history without a context. Ours, as Merleau-Ponty pointed out in that otherwise rather dreary book, *The Structure of Behavior* (and as I mentioned in my reply to Nick Perovich), is triple. We come to be within the living world, itself contained in the physical world, and within that living world, we are again confined within a cultural world into which we are born and within which we live our lives. That human world, paradoxically, however, both confines and liberates us. I must not go off here on a long sermon. Within the present volume, David Depew's account of my general position (qualified as I have suggested in my comments on it) gives a very fair description of my view of where we are in nature (perhaps without enough credit to the Gibsons, from whom I have been learning only in my old age—since 1980).

Since I have let myself be drawn into an attempted restatement of my own starting point, I should perhaps stop trying to answer particular difficulties I encountered in David Rosenthal's account. Two small matters I must mention, though, one still in Section II, and another in Section III (and finally, though only skimpily, two more substantive ones). First: the notion that Descartes might have thought up the indivisibility of mind because he recognized a kind of Lockean unity of consciousness hardly bears comment. Second: in the next section we hear about water and twin water. This, and all possible-world talk, is, in my universe of discourse, *strengstens verboten*—the next thing to brains in vats, which were, I believe, also Hilary Putnam's brainstorm. People who so patently talk nonsense just don't merit one's attention—especially when one has at most a few more years to live, and little time to waste. Sorry for being rude to my distinguished colleagues; I confess to yet another state of mind!

On more significant issues: Rosenthal deals with both the question of the self and the problem of freedom, still in terms of his bits of conscious-ness and consciousnesses of consciousness. Here (as he has referred his readers to other works of his) let me refer to places in which I have dealt,

I thought not too badly, with those questions, not in the consciousness context. On the self see "The Primacy of the Ecological Self" in a volume published by Dick Neisser, and on freedom, a lecture called "Qualified Freedom" which saw the light only in a textbook, where it appeared, as I recall, as a keynote essay on freedom and on dualism. Perhaps I may also just remark to my critic, respectfully and even affectionately, that I do not remotely have the hots for HOTS—this time an absent state of mind, to be ranked perhaps with those (in)famous Blockian absent qualia. The fact of the matter is that I deplore the state of philosophy, and Rosenthal celebrates it. So we differ fundamentally, thoroughly, irreversibly.

M. G.

9

Phillip R. Sloan

REFLECTIONS ON THE SPECIES PROBLEM: WHAT MARJORIE GRENE CAN TEACH US ABOUT A PERENNIAL ISSUE

Introduction

In this contribution to a volume dedicated to one of the great living philosophers, I have chosen to engage a problem to which Marjorie Grene has, in my view, made a major contribution.* This follows from her unusual ability to bridge the well-known divide between "analytical" and "Continental" approaches to philosophy. Only a few individuals have displayed some ability to move between these traditions with ease, and when the issue is restricted to the philosophy of the life sciences, there are almost no others. Marjorie Grene's remarkable education in the historical tradition of Western philosophy, in both its Continental and analytic manifestations, and her career as a philosopher, reflected in important studies on existentialism, Heidegger, Aristotle, Descartes, Sartre, and Spinoza, has enabled her to develop a penetrating set of insights that range over many areas of inquiry.

This remarkable range defies easy characterization of unifying thematics, and this essay will not attempt to give this. The insight I take as most important in her philosophy of biology has been her ability to approach the "problem" of biology from a deeply informed historical and philosophical perspective. It is this depth—not simply an "historical" approach, but an approach to the problems of the living world that is informed by the history of philosophy and by insights from several philosophical traditions—that seems most in need of recovery in our contemporary context. The remarkable success of high-technology molecular biology, the completion of the first phase of the Human Genome Project, the "consilience" of evolutionary biology, molecular genetics, and cognitive neuroscience, the power of physicalism and reductive explanations, in their combined effect threaten to annihilate a host of traditional humanistic concerns, not by directly answering the questions the humanities have posed, but simply by overpowering them with technology and reductionism.

The degree to which there is a "problem" to be solved here of course depends on one's more general philosophical concerns. For those within the tradition of logical empiricism, there are no problems for philosophy to solve beyond the analysis of arguments, the clarification of language, and the elucidation of scientific discourse, and for this reason the philosophy of science has no "critical" role to play that questions reigning scientific orthodoxies, theories, and research agendas. By self-admission, Marjorie Grene has been a dissenter from this aspect of the logical empiricist program almost from its beginnings.

The important clarification and specialization of inquiry the empiricist tradition has produced in the philosophy of science is undeniable. As its heritage was first extended into the foundations of analytic philosophy of biology through the efforts of individuals like J. H. Woodger, John Gregg, Morton Beckner, and Felix Mainx, the goal was to develop a philosophy of biology in touch with analytic philosophy of physical science and actual scientific research. This also implied the dismissal of an admittedly uneven body of reflection on the living world that drew on existentialist, personalist, neo-Aristotelian, phenomenological, and neo-vitalist traditions loosely forming a "Continental" tradition in the philosophy of biology.[1] The new analytic philosophy of biology that emerged placed it in close dialogue with the widely developed logical empiricist philosophy of physics, while still carving out a domain of inquiry that was in some measure autonomous from the philosophy of physical science.

The questions defined by analytic philosophy of biology have become in a substantial degree standardized in the English-speaking world, setting out domains of specialized research that have now been pursued in micro-detail: explanation and laws in the life sciences; the logical analysis of evolutionary theory and the status of historical explanations; analysis of the units of selection and the theory of natural kinds; reductionism and molecular biology; the analysis of taxonomic theory; and the analytic interpretation of teleology and developmental process.

The question is fairly posed whether any other approach to the philosophy of biology needs any longer to be considered. The textbooks, journals, and instructional programs in the field, at least those in the English-speaking world, have created a vital field of philosophy that young philosophers even from traditional bastions of Continental thought have been eager to join. Hegel, Schelling, Heidegger, Driesch, and Portmann, or Bachelard, Foucault, and Canguilhem, do not seem to have been able to create anything like the disciplinary following generated by David Hull, Philip Kitcher, Alex Rosenberg, Elliot Sober, Bill Wimsatt, and the larger community of biological scientists who have found these general empiricist perspectives the most congenial to their research agendas.

Marjorie Grene's relation to these developments has been a complex one, and without trying to detail either her larger intellectual project, or her complex intellectual formation, which she has done for us herself in her autobiography, her engagement with the philosophy of biology has from the beginning been that of a critic of orthodoxies as well as a clarifier of issues. Beginning dramatically with her "Two Evolutionary Theories" paper and amplified in many additional essays and journal articles,[2] it has been evident, for example, that standard Anglo-American neo-selectionist evolutionary theory has not been something she has lightly accepted.

In at least three ways her approach to the philosophical issues of biology has distinguished itself from typical analytic approaches. First, her work has been deeply informed historically, and by this I mean that she has concerned herself both with the history of science and the history of philosophy, including the direct reading and analysis of historical texts. Second, history also plays a deeper role in her work, reflecting what Joseph Kocklemans characterized as the "phenomenological perspective," namely the recognition of the "historical character of philosophical thinking," a recognition that "our philosophical thinking inevitably begins in a given situation that is explicitly or implicitly determined by the history of philosophy."[3] To this Grene would certainly add that it also implies the recognition of the social contextuality of thought.[4] Finally, her relational conception of epistemology interprets the act of knowing as a dynamic interaction of knower and known, rejecting the sense-datum empiricism of positivist philosophy of science. Operative in her work is a fundamental Heideggerian insight, refracted in many respects through Michael Polanyi, to whom her work has been continually indebted,[5] that knowing is a dynamic "indwelling" of the knower in the known, rather than a physiological processing of sensory information. This has substantial implications both for her ability to weave between "objectivism" and "relativism," and her ability to see science as a truth-seeking enterprise that is not willing to succumb to the historicism of Thomas Kuhn and his successors, even while acknowledging the importance of the historical and sociological turn in the philosophy of science largely inspired by Kuhn's work. This has also given her some interesting perspectives on the scientific realism question to which we will turn later in the essay.

Since this is not intended as an essay on Marjorie Grene's own philosophy, my goal is simply to draw upon some of the insights I have gained personally from her work in ways that I do not claim she endorses, in order to revisit a nagging issue in the philosophy of biology, the concept of species. By this I aim to display the way in which a historical and philosophical approach to this question, combined with aspects of Marjorie Grene's epistemological project, can be used to illuminate and clarify a complex problem in the philosophy of life science generally known as the "species" problem.

I shall approach this in the following way. First I set out the main issues underlying a large literature on the "species problem." Second, I situate these discussions within a larger historical perspective that illuminates some of the issues being debated at the moment; finally, I indicate the way in which Marjorie Grene's conception of "historical" realism provides a way of moving between "monistic" and "pluralistic" resolutions of this issue.

I. THE SPECIES PROBLEM

The difficulty within post-Darwinian, and as we will see, within pre-Darwinian biology, in settling on a universally satisfactory notion of species in the biological domain, has formed one of the recurrent problem areas in contemporary philosophical analysis of biology to the point that it has now generated a veritable "industry" around the topic.[6] Briefly stated, the issue concerns the inability to settle on a satisfactory conception of species that can deal on one hand with the practical issues presented by paleontology, field ecology, genetics, and the complexities encountered in the taxonomy of procaryotes and eucaryotes. On the other hand, it concerns the theoretical issues surrounding the role of species in evolutionary theory in its various formulations, and the importance of this concept in debates between evolutionary, phylogenetic, cladistic, and phenetic theorists. David Hull, for example, has delimited nine different species definitions, falling in three groups: similarity concepts; units of evolution concepts; and historical-phylogenetic concepts.[7] Other philosophers have subdivided these classifications into more than twenty different concepts.

The theoretical issues at stake in this debate are complex and not always, to my mind, completely clear. On one level, the debates can be read as a refined modern version of the classical medieval problem of universals: do universals, in this case species proper names, such as, *Perca fluviatilis*, denote real essences, forms, structures, or populations *in res*, or are they only arbitrary names applied for convenience to collections of dissimilar individuals? On a related plane it is a debate about the real reference of theoretical entities referred to in evolutionary theory, forming a special case of the realism-antirealism debate. A third cutting-up of the conceptual pie takes the "species problem" to be a debate about criteria: are organic species to be defined by relational biological properties such as fertile interbreeding, by lineage splitting events, or by similarity and difference relations such that the set-theoretical principles that can be used to classify books and buttons can also be applied to organisms? A fourth issue concerns the relation of historical process to the relative stability in limited time horizons of organic groups. Does this relative chronological stability of biological groups warrant a definition of natural kinds by necessary and sufficient properties in fairly traditional ways, an argument Grene herself has made,[8] or do species, in spite of this relative stability, nonetheless present issues different in kind from the definitional questions in other sciences? Fifth, does the importance of "variation" in evolutionary theory imply that natural kinds in biology are to be conceived as family-resemblance groups or cluster concepts rather than as clearly definable entities? A sixth issue relates directly to the complexity of living forms: spatio-temporal individuals within recognizable species of birds and mammals, for example, do not relate to one another in the same way as "individuals" within colonial invertebrates, plants, and bacteria. Does this imply something about the ontology of the units of selection? These complexities surrounding the "species" problem have both theoretical and practical implications for the development of a workable system of stable and standardized nomenclature according to international rules that is also informed by evolutionary principles.

At the forefront of discussion since Ernst Mayr's classic analyses of the "species problem" that commenced in the 1940s,[9] has been the debate over whether one, or at least a small number of these possible species concepts, such as the fertile interbreeding or "biological" species concept (BSC), should be privileged over the other options. Several philosophers of science have rejected such monistic solutions, either in the form of Mayr's BSC, Hennig's phylogenetic lineages, Ghiselin-Hull individualism, or the "operational" concept promoted by phenetic taxonomy that flourished for a brief period in the 1960s. A "pluralism" of concepts, related to different theoretical contexts, for many has been seen as the only workable solution.[10]

The problems presented by this complex set of issues on some levels resemble, but are considerably more complex than, those surrounding debates over the gene concept that also must deal with theoretical distinctions between "structural," "developmental," "populational," and Mendelian-transmission conceptions that only loosely map on to one another. Added to these issues is the general problem of the relation of empirical individuals to group concepts.

The position I defend in this essay is generally pluralist in its conclusion, and I consider it fruitless to try to defend an abstract definition of species divorced from its connection to specific theoretical, micro-social and even disciplinary contexts. At the same time, I do not embrace a "neo-pragmatist" solution that retreats from a realist position in science. To develop these arguments, I draw upon insights I have gained from Grene's own analyses of some more general issues in her essay "Historical Realism and Contextual Objectivity," that sets out some novel approaches to the realism-antirealism debate.[11] I also acknowledge my debt to Richard Burian who has made a similar application of some of these insights to gene concept, and to my colleague Lenny Moss's forthcoming study on the gene concept.[12] I begin by situating this discussion historically, amplifying some issues I have discussed briefly in a forthcoming article.[13] This will provide the background for some clarifications I believe can be gained from Grene's philosophical positions.

II. GETTING THE HISTORY RIGHT

Just as the complexity of the gene concept has been considerably clarified by a return to the history of the concept,[14] historical analysis can illuminate several otherwise puzzling features of the "species problem." In this case, however, the existing historical discussions have created as many problems as they have resolved. Through his impressive grip on the primary sources of biology, Ernst Mayr offered a historical framework for early discussions of the "species problem" to which I myself owe a considerable debt. Nonetheless, his historical discussions also created some unfortunate characterizations of the past that have been allowed to persist in the literature as unquestioned truisms that have affected much of the understanding of the issue among analytic philosophers of biology. Most fundamental has been the reliance on a historiography that makes Darwin the great watershed in reflection on the species question, distinguishing modern evolutionary conceptions of "populational" species from "essentialist," "typological," and "creationist" concepts that are assumed to have governed biological discussion before the *Origin*. This historical framework of analysis needs to be revisited in depth, and a host of misconceptions needs to be removed. Space will allow only a selective discussion of issues here.

I commence by returning to the mid-Enlightenment debates between George-Louis LeClerc (Buffon) (1707–1788) and his contemporary Carolus Linnaeus (1707–1778) that in important respects set the stage for subsequent developments in the conception of species. Behind this debate was a controversy that had already confronted Renaissance commentators who utilized Aristotle as the great classical authority on the arrangement of the biological world. The difficulty with which these early systematizers had to contend was a problem that has also been recognized more recently by Aristotle scholars.[15] This was the problem of reconciling the logical principles set out by Aristotle in the *Categories*, *Posterior Analytics*, and *Topics* with the empirical experience of natural kinds, explored by Aristotle in his biological treatises. To the reader of the *Categories* and *Posterior Analytics*, it would seem that the ordering of natural kinds should present no novel issues. Organic beings, as primary instances of sensible substance, are to be defined by genus and specific difference, and the logical principles of definition by division supplied the means to do this.[16] The goal of such "essential definition" was to arrive at a true definition of the indivisible species (*atomos eidos*). The use of true essential differentia was to be the key to a "natural" as opposed to a purely "nominal" or arbitrary system of arrangement. This search for essential definition, what later became the inquiry into a "natural" classification, meant the search for a definition of the presumably eternal, or in a later era created, natural kinds by a set of necessary and sufficient properties. The problem posed for this tradition, however, was that Aristotle himself in his biological treatises seems to have recognized that this method could not in fact be applied to empirical experience of the living world. This became a severe problem in the early modern period when Renaissance systematizers attempted to apply Aristotle's logic to the arrangement of animals and plants, and extended the known body of organisms to include those revealed by the Columbian encounters.

Aristotle's explicit critique of the method of division at *De Partibus animalium* I.2-4 suggested that any attempt to apply the logic of the *Analytics* to naturally occurring plants and animals inevitably resulted in the splitting or lumping of intuitively perceived natural groups.[17] In a passage that had considerable importance for some of the eighteenth-century debates we will examine, he commented:

> The proper course is to endeavour to take the animals according to their groups [*gene*], following the lead of the bulk of mankind [*hoi polloi*], who have

marked off the group [*genos*] of Birds and the group of Fishes. Each of these groups is marked off by *many differentiae* [*diaphora*] not by means of dichotomy.[18]

In other words, the starting point for *biological* classification was from the common intuitions and the usages established by tradition, which revealed groups defined by *complexes* of differentiae, rather than by a single distinguishing essential property. Furthermore, this definition of natural groups by a complex of properties, rather than by the hierarchical division of a sequence of genera by essential differences, prevented sharp lines from being drawn between groups. The notion of the graded scale of forms set forth in *Historia animalium* VIII, 588b, running from the simplest plants to the most complex birds and mammals, directly followed from this notion of groups as defined by many properties that overlapped between groups.

A further complexity for early modern reflections, with specific bearing on the notion of species, was contained in the Aristotelian meaning of *eidos*, translated into Latin as either *species* or *forma*. On one hand it stood for the universal in thought, secondary substance in the sense of *Categories* V.5. To define a "species" by genus and essential difference is to define a universal, not an individual organism. In contemporary terminology, this would roughly, if not exactly, map on to the notion of the definition of a species as a class or set of individuals sharing certain universal defining properties.[19] This is the sense of "species" employed in sixteenth- and seventeenth-century works of systematic arrangement of plants and animals into species and genera, such as those of Edward Wotton, John Ray, August Rivinus, Joseph Tournefort, and others, and it is the fundamental meaning of "species" encountered later in the Linnaean treatises and in the standard reference works of the early eighteenth century.[20]

On the other hand, *eidos* denoted the dynamic form in the individual living being, closely allied with soul or *psyche*, perpetuated in time by an eternal lineage of like producing like in the sense of *De Generatione animalium* II.1.[21] Aristotle's use of the same Greek term to designate both the form-in-things and the universal-in-thought was not accidental. It was intimately related to the fact that Aristotle's epistemology is realist in the sense that genuine knowledge is considered to be possible through an intimate connection between the individualized dynamic *eidos* in things and the abstract universal *eidos* in thought.[22]

These brief background reflections enable us to position the fundamental revisions of the concept of "species" of the mid-Enlightenment that were to have considerable impact on subsequent discussions. Linnaean systematics, commencing with the *Systema naturae* of 1735, introduced a fundamental innovation into the systematic ordering of forms by establishing six major levels of the Linnaean system: Kingdom, Class, Order, Genus, Species, Variety. These replaced the flexible ordering of genera that had characterized prior classificational systems. Except for this innovation, the intent of Linnaean systematics, like that of the prior tradition of early modern systematizers, was to arrive at essential definitions of the species as essence or form, a goal that was most clearly evident in the retention of the polynomial definition of species in Linnaeus's works until the tenth edition of the *Systema* of 1758.[23]

The mid-century debate between Linnaeus and Buffon, pitting the two great formulators of Enlightenment natural history in an often bitter personal dispute that had institutional and theoretical implications, in one important dimension revolved around some of the unresolved tensions in this Aristotelian heritage as it had been refracted through the reflections of early modern systematizers. These issues were brought to the fore by Buffon's attack on Linnaean systematics that commenced dramatically with the publication of the first volumes of his *Histoire naturelle, générale et particulière* in 1749, a critique elaborated in various ways through the main volumes of this work into the 1770s.[24]

It is clear from several lines of textual evidence that Buffon drew inspiration for these attacks both from Locke's distinction of the real and nominal essence, and also from Aristotle's own critique of the application of the method of division to biology.[25] This supplied him with a line of argument with which to attack his rival Linnaeus, and to do this precisely on the issue of biological species. As I have developed this point in more detail elsewhere,[26] the fundamental innovation Buffon introduced into the reflections on biological species involved an opposition he explicitly inserted between the meaning of species-as-universal and that of species-as-individuated-form, driving apart two notions that had been intimately linked within Aristotelian epistemology. Locke had initiated this divorce by distinguishing the unknowability of real essences, meaning in his parlance the specific arrangement of atomic particles in material bodies,[27] from the nominal essences or universals constructed in thought from atomized sense data. But Buffon carried this split between universal in thought and form in things to a new level and applied this distinction directly to the classificatory controversies of his age. In his polemic against Linnaean systematics, he explicitly *opposed* the concept of species-as-form perpetuated in reproduction of like by like, defined in fairly close resemblance to Aristotle's meaning at *Generatione animalium* II.1 to the notion of species-as-universal in the sense employed by his contemporary Linnaeus and the other systematizers of nature. Species as universals were relegated by

Buffon to the status of arbitrary "abstractions," divorced from the concrete reality of nature.

It is instructive to read closely Buffon's most explicit statement of this redefinition of the species concept presented in the fourth volume of the *Histoire naturelle* in 1753. His discussion commenced by summarizing the common "classificatory" meaning:

> An individual is a creature by itself, isolated and detached, which has nothing in common with other beings, except in that which it resembles or differs from them. All the similar individuals which exist on the surface of the globe are regarded as composing the species of these individuals.[28]

This "Linnaean" or "classificatory" conception of species (hereafter 'species$_c$') was based on similarity relations and presumed some kind of property identity as the basis of the species. But this concept Buffon explicitly contrasted with his new definition:

> However, it is neither the number nor the collection of similar individuals which forms the species. It is the constant succession and uninterrupted renewal of these individuals which comprises it. Because a being which would last forever would not be a species, no more than would a thousand similar beings which would last forever. The species is thus an abstract and general term, for which the thing exists only in considering Nature in the succession of time, and in the constant destruction and renewal of creatures. . . .
>
> It is thus in the characteristic diversity of species that the intervals in the gradations of nature are most sensible and best marked. . . . The species being nothing else than a constant succession of similar individuals that reproduce themselves, it is clear that this denomination must be applied only to animals and plants, and that it is an abuse of terms or ideas that the classifiers [*nomenclateurs*] have used it to designate different kinds of minerals.[29]

This definition of a species as a "succession" of recurrent individuals formed of reproductively generating individuals, added to the Aristotelian notion of the serial perpetuation of form via generation a stronger sense of material connectedness, and as Buffon's writings developed, it also connected this to historical and environmental changes. Buffon for this reason granted this "natural-historical" meaning of species (hereafter 'species$_h$') a metaphysical "reality, " with a privileged theoretical status in the life sciences.

Such "physical and real" species, as he termed them, were typically recognized by fertile interbreeding, although the conception of species as historical successions of interconnected individuals trumped the interbreeding criterion when conflicts arose. Consequently, in his later works, Buffon could speak of natural or "physical" species, comprised of groups of *genres* and *familles* descending from primordial stocks that radiated under the action of altering geographical and climatic conditions to produce distinct "races," as distinguished from Linnaean "varieties."[30] As he developed this notion in his writings of the 1750s and 60s, forms as distinct as wolves and dogs, cougars and jaguars, horses and zebras, and other groups of similar forms that might be quite unable to reproduce even infertile offspring, were nonetheless lumped in Buffon's later writings into a limited number of "physical" genera and families (*familles*) united by common descent.[31] Buffonian species, unlike those of Linnaeus, acquired an explicit ontology as the kinds of things that can migrate, disappear, racialize, degenerate in time, and for later authors embracing this concept of natural-historical species, also develop into new species over time.

The importance of these historical details is that from this mid-Enlightenment polemic between Buffon and Linnaeus onward we can follow a complex history of the species concept that was the heir to this splitting of species-as-universals (species$_c$) from species-as-immanent-forms (species$_h$) perpetuated by biological reproduction. Furthermore, the open conflict of the two giants of Enlightenment natural history, in an extended polemic on this point, heightened awareness by contemporaries of the issues involved.

The first evidence of the impact of this conflict in the literature is in the new level of attention given to the species concept in the writings of zoologists and botanists of the period. Beginning with a 1755 article in Diderot's *Encyclopédie*, one finds for the first time in the literature an explicit discussion of a "natural history" conception of species, attributed to Buffon, placed in contrast to the "abstract" meaning of species.[32]

The result of this shift in meaning was a substantial conceptual confusion displayed by a broad pluralism that developed over the concept of species in works of natural history of the late eighteenth and early nineteenth century. For those holding to species as class-concepts presumably referring to real divisions in nature (species$_c$), Buffon was viewed as an epistemological skeptic who denied all universals and consequently undermined all science and all knowledge.[33] Those adopting Buffon's novel definition saw this as granting some kind of new "reality" to biological species that now privileged species$_h$ over species$_c$ in the discussions of natural history.

A sampling of explicit species "definitions" from works on natural history in the post-Buffonian period displays some of the growing conceptual confusion. For example, the influential Parisian botanist, Antoine Laurent de Jussieu, essentially repeated Buffon's meaning, terming a species an "enduring succession of similar individuals made continuous by the generation of offspring."[34]

In contrast, Jussieu's contemporary, also affiliated with the Jardin du Roi, the Parisian botanist Michel Adanson, concluded after an examination of the competing definitions of species current in his own time that a "natural" definition of species must depend on consideration of "all the properties," and thus

> that it will consist not only in the constant or inconstant succession [of individuals], either by generation or not, but also in the comparison of the number, resemblance, and the duration of the individuals; and finally, in all the other properties whatever, such as size, color, and more or less enduring properties, and more or less essential in certain Families rather than others.[35]

Turning to German expressions, where Buffon's "natural-historical" species$_h$ seems to have been taken up and developed most deeply, Kant's reflections on these issues, beginning with his anthropology lectures in 1775, made some important distinctions relevant to the discussion, but also reinforced some of these confusions in the writings of his less philosophically astute successors.[36] In his efforts to clarify the distinction between the notion of "race" and the Linnaean conception of "Variety" within human populations, Kant made explicit the distinction between those concepts appropriate to the "description" of nature (*Naturbeschreibung*), and those relevant to the genetic history of nature (*Naturgeschichte*). The Linnaean concept was appropriate to the first notion, and the Buffonian to the second.

The impact of Kant's distinctions, and the failure to develop them coherently, can be seen in the subsequent German discussions. Species$_h$ as this had been defined by Kant, was explicitly adopted by some German naturalists to constitute the fundamental meaning of species in natural history. This was then placed in opposition to species$_c$. For example, the ornithologist Johann Karl Illiger, developing explicitly on Kant's notion of "natural historical" species, regards species as,

> The totality [*Inbegriff*] of all individuals which generate fertile young with one other. We can determine the species only from the experience of generation, and it is false if one assumes, as is the common assumption to be seen, that the species consists of the abstraction from several individuals of common characters [*Merkmale*].[37]

But a more common pattern in the literature of the period is a common tendency to *combine* species$_c$ with species$_h$ without necessary clarifying distinctions. For example, Buffon's understudy, Bernard de Lacépède, interweaves Buffonian historical meanings and group-character meanings in a long discourse on the historical duration of the species a decade after Buffon's death.[38] Similarly Jean Baptiste Lamarck, also clearly drawing both upon Buffon and the Linnaean tradition in his writings, terms a species "the whole collection of individuals which, during a long period, resemble one another such that by all their parts compared among themselves, the individuals only present small accidental differences that in plants, by the reproduction by seeds, will disappear."[39] The Swiss botanist Augustin Pyrame de Candolle similarly defines a species as,

> the collection of all the individuals which are more similar among themselves than they are to others, and which can, by a reciprocal fertilization produce fertile individuals, and which reproduce themselves by generation such that they can, by analogy, all be assumed to arise originally from a single individual or a single couple.[40]

Likewise, in his influential zoological works, Georges Cuvier terms a species "the collection of individuals descended from one another or from common parents, and of those who resemble them as much as they resemble one another."[41]

The extended survey of the species concept in 1838 by the botanist and member of the Imperial Society of Botany in Regensburg, Anton F. Spring, displays some of the conceptual unclarity that was prevalent in the literature by this date. Spring attempts to attain some satisfactory understanding of the issues by a survey of a welter of competing meanings, and settled as a solution on a modification of the Linnaean concept that also employed the notion of common descent.[42] Similarly, in a discussion that was important for Darwin's later presentations of the issue, Alphonse de Candolle, son of Augustin, summarized the issue in 1855, discriminating eleven different definitions of species.[43] On the eve of the publication of the *Origin*, the French botanist Alexandre Godron discriminated eleven different species concepts to display the existence of two main groups of naturalists, those who accepted the "reality" of species, and those who denied it.[44]

British and Scottish discussions by contrast, more deeply affected by Linnaean systematics than developments in French and German literature, display a greater tendency to preserve the meaning of species primarily in the sense of a class of individuals defined by essential common properties. In Charles Lyell's influential discussions of the species concept in the second volume of the *Principles of Geology* of 1831, for example, Lyell regards the "majority of naturalists" to "agree with Linnaeus in supposing that all the individuals propagated from one stock have certain distinguishing characters in common which will never vary, and which have remained the same since the creation of each species."[45] Against this meaning of the "reality" of species, Lyell contrasted Lamarck's notion of species imperma- nence, interpreting this as a claim about the "unreality" of species in nature.

This concept is then subjected to a long critique with the conclusion that the evidence indicates that there are indeed permanent and enduring characters of species, and hence real species in nature.

This brief sampling of the literature should illustrate the historical complexity of the post-Buffonian discussion of biological species evident in the literature considerably before Darwin's own engagement with this question. There is also clearly a recognition in the pre-Darwinian literature that there is some kind of fundamental "species problem" whose outlines are not clearly understood.[46] Disagreements over what is meant by a "species" display important national divisions, and interweave issues of criteria, historical existence, logic, and metaphysics.

These brief historical remarks should display how thin is the historical warrant for assuming that Darwin's views were developed against a uniform, or even majority, background of "special creationist," "typological," or "essentialist" conceptions of species unless we confine our attention to a narrow band of primarily British discussions against which Darwin was only in part responding.[47]

III. DARWIN ON SPECIES

Darwin's uses of the term "species" are widely diverse and reflect several historical strands that can be separated in his writings. To determine this, I have reviewed the 658 occurrences of the term "species" in the combined *Notebooks* and the 1,489 occasions of use in the first edition of the *Origin*.[48] This review displays the conflicting ways in which the concept is employed in his works. This also helps us understand the confusions of many of his successors and contemporaries in sorting out his meanings.

This survey of usages reveals that Darwin most frequently employed the term 'species' as a "class-concept" or "classificatory" term in the sense of species$_c$, as when he speaks of individuals within a species, or species within genera, or discusses the defining properties of individuals within a species. But alongside these usages we also find from his earliest notebooks onward usages that incorporate the tradition of "Buffonian" species$_h$, derived in part from his sources, and also from his own creative reflection on these issues in relation to empirical problems in invertebrates and plants. In these instances, species are analogized to individuals; they can "migrate" and "intercross"; they are born and die; they are governed by laws; and they emerge in time from varieties and races. Furthermore, they display the complexity evident to one whose expertise was most developed in the invertebrate groups. In an important passage from his early *Red Notebook* covering the late *Beagle* and early London period, Darwin for the first time brought together his empirical studies on regenerating flatworms and self-propagating plants, coral reefs and other colonial invertebrates with the notion of species, drawing an analogy between the complex individuality exemplified by these forms and the concept of a species as a material lineage formed by historical descent:

> Propagation. whether ordinary. hermaphrodite. or by cutting an animal in two. (gemmiparous. by nature or accident). we see an individual divided either at one moment or through lapse of ages.—Therefore we are not so much surprised at seeing Zoophite producing distinct animals. still partly united. & eggs which become quite separate.—Considering all individuals of all species. as <<each>> one individual <<divided>> by different methods, associated life only adds one other method where division is not perfect[. . . .] There is no more wonder in extinction of species than of individuals.—[49]

Darwin also frequently speaks from the *Notebooks* period onward of species as "real," "good," "natural," and "true," as when in the "B" notebook he defines a "good" species as "one that remains <<at large>> with constant characters, together with other <animals> beings of very near structure."[50] This also seems to be his meaning in the *Origin* where he comments that "I believe that species come to be tolerably well-defined objects, and do not at any one period present an inextricable chaos of varying and intermediate links."[51] At other times, his reference to "good" species applied to the external partitioning of groups by conditions of life into definable ecological niches or "stations in the economy of nature" in contemporary parlance, implying an ecological definition of species.

Darwin's efforts to "define" species explicitly in his published writings against the historical background I have sketched only served to confuse the issues more deeply for his contemporaries and successors, particularly since the *Origin* claimed to be a book about the origin of such entities. The primary discussion of the issue in the published *Origin* simply states that "I look at the term species, as one arbitrarily given for the sake of convenience to a set of individuals closely resembling each other, and that it does not essentially differ from the term variety, which is given to less distinct and more fluctuating forms."[52] This failed to keep in any way clear the complex interweaving of classificatory, geographical, lineage, ecological, reproductive, and fossil meanings of species that a review of Darwin's usages reveals. Louis Agassiz's query that "[i]f species do not exist at all, as the supporters of the transmutation theory maintain, how can they vary?"[53] is understandable in this context, if it was to miss Darwin's larger point, confusing his specific linguistic formulations with the substance of his argument that in primary respects was a novel thesis about the stability over time of species$_h$.

IV. Post-Darwinian Species Concepts

The standard story assumes a linear progressivist history of post-Darwinian developments that moves from Darwin's proclaimed anti-essentialism to a "populational" notion of species as real entities. A deeper historical understanding of the history of the species concept in the post-Darwinian period complicates this picture with at least two important developments.

The first is that which emerged within the German biological tradition that developed in transformist directions the pre-existent species$_h$ concept. In this framework, the historical lineage concept was transformed into a thesis that such entities could now be conceived to change gradually into new species and even into higher groups over time under the action of natural selection, while still retaining their ontological reality. These lines of development seem quite clear from a review of the relevant literature. I will illustrate this by attention to the work of the influential University of Munich botanist Karl Nägeli. As an early disciple of the philosophy of Schelling and Hegel, Nägeli had already in the pre-Darwinian period imported some of the holism of this tradition into the natural-historical conception of species. Commenting in a lecture delivered in 1853, for example, he remarked:

> Individual plants do not occur purely as independent Beings by themselves. They are at the same time also parts of a higher Totality, elements of a general motion [*Bewegung*]. Because they generate new individuals, because these propagate in their turn and the procreation process is repeated continually in their progeny, there arises from this an undetermined sum of plants, which is not to be considered a loose aggregate, but forms the species, an undivided whole, which is held together by a common Idea.[54]

Following his conversion to Darwin's theory, this concept was simply transformed into the conception of species as dynamic holistic entities that could now transmute in time: species "actually die like individuals [and] new species are developed once again like an individual."[55] Furthermore,

> varieties . . . become races . . . [and] by constant divergence of the movement [*Bewegung*] pass from Species into Genera, and these into Orders and Classes. Between the designated categories there is no absolute difference. . . . The Genera and the higher concepts are not abstractions, but concrete things, complexes of connected forms.[56]

Nägeli's discussion of the "evolutionary" natural-historical species then became one of the sources cited subsequently by Hugo DeVries as support for DeVries claim that "the fundamental conception from which almost all investigators start, is that species are the only real entities,"[57] meaning by "real" not simply that a species defines a coherent natural group possessing necessary and sufficient characters, but real in an ontological sense, referring to organismic entities that display internal biological cohesion and act like individuals. DeVries's mutation theory was explicitly based on the assumption of discontinuities between such species produced by mutations in the pangenes as the primary means of evolutionary development, rejecting the role of Darwinian natural selection. For those following this tradition, a "species" is constituted by biological relations and the sharing of genes, giving it a privileged ontological status. To quote a more extreme version of this development:

> There is no doubt that the species is something objective, material, that it is constituted by a substance incorporated in a mass. The existence of many such specific substances has been abundantly revealed by genetic studies. Each one of the specific substances is made up of essential sets of genes. . . . The distinctiveness of the individuals does not destroy the reality of the mass, since the individuals are not independent but are all interrelated.[58]

This genetic, holistic tradition in less extreme forms constitutes one strand of historical tradition within evolutionary biology that extends into subsequent discussions of the "biological" species concept and underlies the "individualist" concept of species.[59]

A second tradition developing from Darwin is the biostatistical interpretation of the species concept that created the tradition of modern populational and biostatistical analyses of evolution. This tradition developed the species$_c$ concept. As articulated particularly by Karl Pearson and W. F. R. Weldon in the 1890s and early 1900s, these workers developed the first genuinely "anti-essentialist" interpretations of Darwinian evolution by exploring the implications of Darwinian natural selection theory in a form that made no commitment to underlying material causation in the form of germ plasms, pangenes, stirps, or ids. A natural group was defined purely on the basis of the statistical properties of populations, utilizing such parameters as ranges, means, medians, and the variation and standard deviation displayed in measurements on morphological characters whose variations were then analyzed statistically for evolutionary differentiation. In their landmark studies on evolution in natural populations, particularly those on the common shore crab *Carcinus moenas*, Weldon and Pearson measured thousands of specimens, utilizing twenty-five different defining characters, which were then analyzed for quantitative variation. These measurements were partitioned statistically in order to discriminate those characters that varied independently of growth. By use of these techniques, Weldon and Pearson were able to make the first demonstration of micro-evolution of two distinct populations of crabs under slightly different environmental conditions.[60]

Pearson explicitly characterized his statistical approach to species definition as "typological," and it is exactly this. At the same time it is "anti-essentialist" in the most radical sense. A "type," as Pearson defined it, is simply a "modal value" at the intersection of the variation of a "great variety of characters," and distributed around this modal value are individuals displaying a range of *variations in* defining properties. "Here in variety, the various deviations from the racial type, we find the material for selection."[61] Pearson's populational definition of a species defined it as a group of individuals showing a set of defining characters. At the same time each of these varied statistically. This populational type was subject to the selective pressures of environmental conditions, without implying any stable essence over time.

To summarize the point of this historical review, I have given evidence for the continuity of at least two distinguishable traditions of species concepts in the post-Darwinian period. The difficulty facing any clarification of the contemporary "species problem" is that these competing traditions of interpretation must be sorted out more clearly. Museum taxonomists continue to utilize methods established by the biometricians in defining new species. On the other hand, there is a strong tradition, due in part to the importation of German ideas into Anglo-American biology by Ernst Mayr, that has emphasized an evolutionary interpretation of species$_h$ under the name of the "biological species concept." Consider the following quotation from an influential paper by Mayr:

> Species are not merely classes of objects but are composed of natural populations which are integrated by an internal organization. . . . This organization . . . gives the populations a structure which goes far beyond that of mere aggregates of bricks. . . . In a species an even greater supra-individualistic cohesion and organization is produced by a number of factors. Species are a reproductive community. . . . The species is an ecological unit which, regardless of the individuals of which it is composed, interacts as a unit with other species in the same environment. The species, finally, is a genetic unit consisting of a large, interconnecting gene pool whereas each individual is only a temporary vessel holding a small portion of this gene pool for a short period of time.[62]

It should be evident that to conceive of "species" in this sense is to understand species in the sense of species$_h$. Hence we read from a critic of Mayr, embracing species$_c$ the following response:

> All systematic categories (phylum . . . species) are universal concepts abstracted from individuals. As concepts, they exist only in the mind, but we find the basis for these concepts in nature. . . . The categories are, therefore, not

concrete things. . . . No more are they purely subjective fictions with no basis in reality as others . . . think. Nor is it correct to say with Mayr that the "species" are realities, but the higher categories are pure abstractions.[63]

The worry of opponents of conceptual pluralism as a solution to these difficulties is that they see pluralist solutions to be a threat to scientific objectivity, with attendant fears of subjectivism, or other consequences that would have negative implications for evolutionary theory.[64] Furthermore, neo-pragmatism and its tendency to reduce conceptual meaning to usages within Wittgensteinian "language games" threatens the "realist intent" of scientific inquiry.[65] We may now turn to insights that can be gained from Marjorie Grene, and behind her Michael Polanyi, in working through some of these complexities.

V. PERSPECTIVAL REALISM AND THE SPECIES PROBLEM

It has been Marjorie Grene's interest in allowing for pluralistic solutions to conceptual problems while avoiding the move into social constructivism or pragmatism that attracts me to her discussions of these issues. By her own admission, much of her approach is heavily indebted to Michael Polanyi, and I shall begin by elucidating some points of relevance first developed by Polanyi.

Polanyi's *Personal Knowledge*, published in the heyday of logical empiricism, and just before the "Kuhnian" revolution that in some important ways dethroned classical logical empiricism from its hegemony over the philosophy of science, was a work generally dismissed at the time, in part because of the idiosyncratic vocabulary employed by Polanyi. His use of the adjective "personal" seemed to place his philosophical reflections in the camp of subjectivism. With Kuhn, Polanyi was located among philosophers of science on the "irrationalist" side of philosophy, a position that was reinforced by his concept of "tacit" knowing. Subsequently, the "tacit" dimension of Polanyi's philosophy has become strongly imbedded in British-style social constructivism that is anathema to many philosophers of science. This history has unfortunately made it difficult to recover Polanyi's important insights in the epistemology of science that only Marjorie Grene has been willing to prosecute in a sustained way among Anglo-American philosophers of science.

The misunderstandings of Polanyi's positions, and often those of Marjorie Grene, are based on a misunderstanding of the ways in which they have attempted to articulate a philosophy of science that is at the same time (a) realist; (b) sensitive to history, to social epistemology, and to revolutionary scientific change; and (c) willing to embrace an "active" conception of the scientific knower. It seems that these important insights are being now "rediscovered" by a new generation of historians and sociologists of science, even if Michael Polanyi still remains largely unmentioned among the philosophers of science.

Polanyi's attempt to capture a synthetic a-priori in scientific reasoning, without the rigidity of Kant's formulations, is one way in which his meaning of "personal knowledge" can be reformulated. This rested upon his distinction of "tacit" and "explicit" knowledge, with the first supplied by language, social structure, and especially in the sciences, the educational and practical initiation into the skills of laboratory and empirical inquiry that Kuhn captured less dynamically in his original notion of paradigm-governed "normal" science. Because for Polanyi this was a thesis involving human intentionality, in the sense of Kuhn's paradigm-governed "seeing," the different formulations of some of the same basic points imply very different consequences for the truth-seeking dimensions of science.

Of further relevance is Polanyi's distinction of "focal" and "subsidiary" awareness and its application to epistemological questions. This latter insight, which he claimed was his most novel thesis,[66] threaded between the relativism of neo-pragmatism, and the hard objectivism of positivist reductionism. I will illustrate the application of Polanyi's distinctions with a concrete example of relevance, the proposal of a new species for scientific acceptance. To develop this in detail I have chosen the case of the recent proposal of the Madagascar freshwater bony fish of the family Bedotiidae, designated under the new name *Bedotia masoala*, to illustrate my point. I argue that this case can be generalized more broadly.

The genus *Bedotia*, first described in 1903, prior to 2001 contained five distinguishable species.[67] The proposed new species is based on the description of 69 specimens, one of which has been designated as the holotype, and the others as paratypes, taken from several collection sites from Madagascar. This new species is justified by a "diagnosis" that distinguishes it from the closely related *B. marojery*. The difference between these two species is not based on any one property, but on a conjunction of several differentiating characters—banding, total vertebral counts, lateral line scale counts, and palatine tooth patches. In each character there are displayed certain constant differences between *B. marojery* and *B. masoala*. The analysis of this new species is made in terms of a set of morphometric measurements carried out on many of these specimens, using 27 different characters, including scale counts, dorsal and other fin ray counts, gill-raker counts, body proportions, and total length. The specific characteristics found on the designated "type" specimen define that specimen, with the ranges in properties revealed by the morphometrics on the 68 paratypes. The ranges of variations in these properties define the range of variation in this species.

Remarkable about this form of description and the form of its proposal to the relevant scientific community for acceptance, is that very little has altered in this practice since Cuvier, and certainly little from the early work of the biometricians such as W. F. R. Weldon and others who pursued their biometrical means of species definition.[68] The new species is characterized by a collection of measurable properties whose metrical ranges necessarily include all the properties of the "type" specimen and the surrounding "paratypes."

There are some points that should be carefully noted in this common form of species definition encountered in taxonomic literature. First, this process of species definition is *not* accurately characterized by a Wittgensteinian "family resemblance" relation of properties that would imply a species is only defined "polytypically."[69] By this I mean that the description offered does not presume that this species is characterized by a set of interweaving *characters* of which only a large number are presumably possessed by any one specimen, such that only some specimens have gill rakers, only some have dorsal fins, scales, and so forth, on the analogy of Wittgenstein's family resemblance concept. Rather the "populational" notion rests on the *variation* within these universally possessed properties, not on their presence and absence. This populational notion implies that the species can indeed be defined by an "essential" set of properties that all members are assumed to possess.

Secondly, there is no warrant for concluding that the name *B. masoala* being proposed in this description is to be regarded as anything other than the proper name of an extensional class, denoting the set of individual fish on the island of Madagascar satisfying this definition. The use of the term "species" in this instance is fully in the sense of species$_c$ and makes an a-temporal, rational grouping of similar specimens a focal concept for a certain use—communicating and naming a new form of freshwater fish for a world-wide community. Further research might, in time, demonstrate that this is just a variant of *B. marojery* by discovery of an intermediate population, and the new species will "disappear" through synonymy. The proposer of this new species is, however, making a claim that is realist in intent. The extension of this proposed new species name is assumed to designate correctly, and not just arbitrarily for some pragmatic purpose, an existing group of organisms, distinct from those of other known species of this genus.

This use of such a "taxonomic" species concept is, however, but one interest of science. For the practicing taxonomist, species$_c$ is the object of "focal" attention in Polanyi's sense, while rendering subsidiary and background species$_h$. In turn species$_c$ can itself be rendered subsidiary to other theoretical interests. Constructing a cladogram or phylogenetic history of this group, and determining the historical relations of this new species to other related species in the evolutionary history of the group, means to understand "species" in a very different sense to satisfy different theoretical interests. Species$_h$, that is, a species as a historical lineage of materially interconnected organisms, is now the object of focal attention. This does not render species$_c$ "unreal," "subjective," or merely "abstract." It is simply making it subsidiary in Polanyi's sense. Without the prior recognition of the set-theoretical breakdown of genus *Bedotia* into now six discrete taxonomic species, the question of how these different species relate historically can scarcely even be posed. The taxonomic species$_c$ functions as an a-priori concept in subsequent evolutionary inquiry. In this case species$_h$ might indeed be considered to be an "individual" if we are to follow the language of Michael Ghiselin and other monists. In this different context, one that might be found for example in the discussions in the journals *Evolution* or *Systematic Zoology*, there are different scientific interests at play than those presumed in the journal *Copeia*. This recognition of the ability of scientific attention to shift between different contexts for different theoretical interests, making contrasting meanings of "species" the object of what Polanyi termed focal awareness, while other meanings are rendered tacit and subsidiary, seems to offer a dynamic way of dealing with the complexities of the relation between classificational and evolutionary perspectives.

Grene has explicitly utilized several of Polanyi's insights, while avoiding some of the difficulties in his formulations. The notion of "personal" knowledge seems more equivalent in her formulations to a notion of the active intentionality of consciousness, bringing this more into line with traditional phenomenology. She has also been in position to be able to respond to contemporary history, philosophy, and sociology of science in a form that has brought her arguments more into the community of discourse holding in Anglo-American discussions of science.

I illustrate these insights by displaying how they are at work in Grene's brief 1987 paper on scientific realism, "Historical Realism and Contextual Objectivity" and apply her suggestions in this paper to the issue of species pluralism. In this paper Grene develops two concepts. The first is the notion of "historical" realism, which she develops from David Annis's definition of "historical or methodological realism." Annis employs this concept to argue that knowledge claims can be justified without needing to give the kinds of reasons demanded by foundationalism. He claims that an understanding of science is productive of justified beliefs warranted by a "study of the actual practices [of science,] which have changed through time":

Science as *practiced* yields justified beliefs about the world. Thus the study of the actual practices, which have changed through time, cannot be neglected. . . . From the fact that justification is relative to the social practices and norms of a group, it does not follow that they cannot be criticized nor that justification is somehow subjective. . . . Just as there is no theory-neutral observation language in science so there is no standard-neutral epistemic position that one can adopt. But in neither case does it follow that objectivity and rational criticism are lost.[70]

To Annis's conception of contextualized realism, renamed "historical" realism by Grene, she has paired the notion of "contextual" objectivity, drawn particularly from biochemist-turned-philosopher Lee Rowen. By this she means that the justificatory warrant for truth claims must necessarily be made within a given linguistic and social context. But this does not reduce epistemic claims to social constructivism: "Contextual objectivity, then, is critical truth-seeking as practiced within a given social context."[71]

Following Polanyi, Grene accepts science to be a truth-seeking activity that posits claims about the world for universal acceptance, even if such claims may be in fact false, and even if all such claims must originate within and be inescapably connected to the historical and social situatedness of the knowing agent.

I just want to stress the *realism* in historical realism: the practices of critical truth seekers are truly the practices of *truth* seekers. Scientists are people really puzzled about how something in the real world really works. . . . Granted, their puzzles arise within a framework of beliefs and techniques that is highly acculturated, but after all labs—let alone gull's nests—are real places.[72]

This emphasis on the truth-seeking intentionality of science, in spite of its contextual situatedness, blunts the terror of Kuhnian relativism without abandoning the importance of Kuhn's insights. Grene terms her position "perspectivism," meaning a perspectivism that is deeply motivated by a truth-seeking drive to understand the world.

To apply these insights to the "species problem," there are two points I wish to make. First, as my historical review of issues has illustrated, there are many different species concepts currently available that are artefacts of a complex conceptual history. Teasing out these historical strands helps clarify some issues. But this only illuminates the different ways in which the concept of "species" is employed for different uses and situates these within different research traditions with different scientific interests. To this point, nothing implies the need to go beyond neo-pragmatist pluralism.

But the intentions of both the museum taxonomist carefully describing a new species, and the evolutionary theorist interested in working out phylogenetic history are realist and truth-seeking. Neither is satisfied with the conclusion that his or her reconstructions are simply conventions for convenient use within relativized language-games.

If we relocate these issues within a dynamic epistemological relation between knower and known, the position I see Marjorie Grene developing, we need not choose between a simplifying monistic solution and epistemic relativism:

> Once we assimilate the position articulated by Annis and exemplified in Rowen's account, we can start out by asserting confidently, as I have already done, that scientists are real live people concerned with real puzzles about how, and why, certain processes or events happen as they do in the real world.[73]

Although Grene terms her concept of historical and contextual realism "perspectivist," I would prefer, emphasizing Polanyi's notion of focal and subsidiary awareness, the concept of intentional human "interests" that can shift focus from one context to the other as interests of a dynamic human agent concerned with truth and seeking knowledge of universal validity. Such interests differ, and to some extent they may be exclusive of one another, similar to the exclusivity one finds in the fact that one cannot both perform a complex piece of music skillfully and also attend to the mechanics of finger motion while doing it. The shifting of interest from atemporal "classification" employing the species$_c$ concept, to evolutionary theorizing interested in species$_h$, simply means to background different things and make other issues focal without denying the realistic intent of either endeavor. Because this is a question of shifting and even mutually exclusive focal interests, we cannot expect in such a case to arrive at a single "monistic" conception of species. By acknowledging the important insight that a more dynamic theory of knowing can supply to scientific understanding, Grene and Polanyi have given some concrete ways to work through an otherwise insoluble conceptual impasse.

VI. CONCLUSION

The theses of this paper can be reduced to three claims. First, the "species problem" in biology manifests a history of conceptual confusion that dates back to the Enlightenment debates. This history has been largely unknown, and because of this historical ignorance, different concepts have come to underlie irreconcilable positions in confrontation with one another.

Second, the conceptual pluralism that has resulted from this history defines different usages within different scientific contexts. In many respects an analogy can be drawn here with the concept of the gene, which also displays competing structural, positional, populational, transmissional, and developmental meanings functioning within different research communities.

Third, by understanding these issues within the framework of Polanyi's conception of focal and subsidiary awareness, and Grene's notions of historical realism and contextual objectivity, it is possible to acknowledge this pluralism of uses, all bearing some connection to one another. Furthermore, all can lay claim to a realist interpretation in terms of contextualized theory that is in keeping with the truth-seeking goals of science.

Acceptance of these three theses allows for the following:

(a) It accords with, and recognizes the validity of, the actual practice of working taxonomists whose activities employ primarily set-theoretical meanings of species.

(b) It acknowledges the different theoretical interests of those concerned with evolutionary relationships and historical meanings of biological groups, captured in "individualist" and "cladistic" interpretations of group relationships.

(c) It acknowledges the realist, truth-seeking intentionality of science that claims to make true claims about the world, and opposes this to anti-realist, strong social constructivist, and neo-pragmatist conclusions.

(d) It reaffirms the importance of human intentionality in scientific inquiry without reducing science to subjectivity.

(e) It does not require settling on a single, monistic concept of species in order to satisfy the crucial claims of (a) through (c).

In pointing the way towards recovery of the deeply relational and intentional dimensions of human knowing, and breaking through the confines of the empiricism and behaviorist models of cognition that have fascinated too many philosophers of biology, Marjorie Grene has shown us that it is possible to make some interesting progress on a puzzling problem.

PHILLIP R. SLOAN

PROGRAM OF LIBERAL STUDIES/
PROGRAM IN HISTORY AND PHILOSOPHY OF SCIENCE
UNIVERSITY OF NOTRE DAME
MARCH 2002

NOTES

* I wish to acknowledge the very helpful comments of Rasmus Winther on an earlier version of this paper.

1. See for example, David L. Hull, "What the Philosophy of Biology is Not," *Journal of the History of Biology* 2 (1969): 241–68.

2. Marjorie Grene, "Two Evolutionary Theories," *British Journal for the Philosophy of Science* 9 (1958): 110–127; 185–93; idem., *The Knower and the Known* (Berkeley: University of California Press, 1974), esp. ch. 7; idem., "Evolution, 'Typology,' and 'Population Thinking'," *American Philosophical Quarterly* 27 (1990): 237–44; idem., "Introduction" to *Dimensions of Darwinism*, ed. Marjorie Grene (Cambridge: Cambridge University Press, 1983).

3. Joseph Kocklemans, *Phenomenology and Physical Science* (Pittsburgh: Marquette University Press, 1966), p. 16.

4. See Marjorie Grene, "Historical Realism and Contextual Objectivity: A Developing Perspective in the Philosophy of Science," in *Science and Philosophy: The Process of Science*, ed. N. J. Nersessian (Dordrecht: Nijhoff, 1987), pp. 69–81.

5. Michael Polanyi was generally very circumspect about his relation to Heidegger and existential phenomenology in his writings, and there is, for example, no mention of Heidegger, Husserl, or Merleau-Ponty in the body of his main work, *Personal Knowledge*. The most explicit effort to relate his project to that of existential phenomenology I have located in Polanyi's published writings appears briefly in the preface to the Harper Torchbook edition of *Personal Knowledge* (New York: Harper, 1964) where he seeks to clarify his often misunderstood meaning of "personal" knowledge by identifying his own notion of "indwelling" with Heidegger's being-in-the-world (p. x). Marjorie Grene's direct exposure to Heidegger's philosophy, and her years of collaboration with Polanyi make these associations more immediate. I do not claim she or Polanyi are in a clear way Heideggerians.

6. See for example the three recent collections: *The Units of Evolution: Essays on the Nature of Species*, ed. M. Ereshefsky (Boston: MIT Press, 1992); *Species: New Interdisciplinary Essays*, ed. R. A. Wilson (Boston: MIT Press, 1999); *Species Concepts and Phylogenetic Theory: A Debate*, ed. Q. D. Wheeler and R. Meier (New York: McGraw-Hill, 1999). This is just a sampling of the larger "units of selection" literature. For a review of this see E. Sober and D. Wilson, "A Critical Review of Philosophical Work on the Units of Selection Problem," *Philosophy of Science* 61 (1994): 534–55.

7. David L. Hull, "On the Plurality of Species: Questioning the Party Line," in Wilson, *Species: New Interdisciplinary Essays,* pp. 23–48.

8. Grene, "Evolution, 'Typology' and 'Population Thinking'" (note 2).

9. For an influential summary statement see Ernst Mayr "Species Concepts and Definitions," in *The Species Problem*, ed. E. Mayr (American Association for the Advancement of Science Publication No. 50; Washington, 1957), pp. 1–19.

10. See Philip Kitcher, "Species," *Philosophy of Science* 51 (1984): 308–33, reprinted in Ereshefsky, *Units*, pp. 317–41; and John Dupré, "Species," in Dupré, *The Disorder of Things* (Cambridge, Mass.: Harvard University Press, 1993), pp. 37–59; Dupré has moderated his broad pluralism in his more recent "On the Impossibility of a Monistic Account of Species," in Wilson, *Species*, pp. 3–22.

11. Grene, "Historical Realism," cited above (note 4).

12. Richard Burian, "'Historical Realism', 'Contextual Objectivity', and Changing Concepts of the Gene," (chap. 13 in the present volume); Lenny Moss, *What Genes Can't Do* (Boston: MIT Press, 2002).

13. P. R. Sloan, "Historical Analysis and the Species Controversies: How History is Relevant to the Philosophy of Biology," in *Proceedings of the 21st International Congress of the History and Philosophy of Science*, Mexico City, 2001 (in press).

14. See Petter Portin, "The Concept of the Gene: Short History and Present Status," *Quarterly Review of Biology* 68 (1993): 173–223.

15. See D. M. Balme, "Aristotle's Use of Differentia in Zoology," in *Aristotle et les problèmes de Méthode*, ed. Suzanne Mansion (Louvain: Publications universitaires, 1961), pp. 195–212; and idem., "Γενοσ and Ειδοσ in Aristotle's Biology," *Classical Quarterly* 12 (1962): 81–98.

16. *Posterior Analytics* XIII, 96b 20–97b30.

17. *Parts of Animals* I, 642b5–644a12.

18. Ibid., 643b 12–15, trans. A. L. Peck (Loeb Classical Library).

19. Although I am aware of dangers in drawing modern parallels, I consider the moderate "essentialism" advocated by Richard Boyd in his concept of "homeostatic property cluster kinds" to be reasonably close to capturing some of this basic Aristotelian insight. See his "Homeostasis, Species, and Higher Taxa," in Wilson, *Species*, pp. 141–85.

20. See for example, entries under "Species" in John Harris, *Lexicon Technicum or an Universal English Dictionary of Arts and Sciences*, vol. I (London, 1704); E. Chambers, *Cyclopedia: or an Universal Dictionary of Arts and Sciences*, rev. ed. (London: Rivington et al., 1783) vol. VI; Samuel Johnson, *Dictionary of the English Language* (London: 1765); and "Art" in J. C. Adelung, *Versuch eines vollständigen grammatisch-kritischen Wörterbuch* (Leipzig, 1774).

21. *Generation of Animals* II.1. 731b30–732a5.

22. For brief comments on this, see Marjorie Grene, "Individuals and their Kinds: Aristotelian Foundations of Biology," in *Organism, Medicine and Metaphysics*, ed. S. F. Spicker (Dordrecht: Reidel, 1978), pp. 121–36, esp. pp. 127–29. This epistemic connection means that this distinction cannot be simply characterized as that between "category" and "group" (later renamed "taxon") as set forth in the classic John Gregg paper, "Taxonomy, Language and Reality,"*American Naturalist* 74 (1950): 419–35. There are, nonetheless, important ways in which the universal-individuated form relationship bears on the category-taxon distinction

when translated into contemporary terminology.

23. Still useful in this regard is A. J. Cain's "Logic and Memory in Linnaeus's System of Taxonomy," *Proceedings of the Linnean Society of London* 169 (1958): 144–63.

24. See my "The Buffon-Linnaeus Controversy," *Isis* 67 (1976): 356–75.

25. This is implicit at several points in Buffon's critique of Linnaean taxonomy. His explicit awareness of the Aristotelian arguments against classification can be substantiated from the comments of his collaborator on the Natural History, Louis Daubenton: "Aristotle concludes that one must establish divisions only on positive and opposed characters, and not on partially positive and negative characters. . . . Aristotle enacted no plan of methodical distribution of animals; this sublime metaphysician who had been able to reduce the art of thinking into a system, and reasoning into a formula, outlines for us no series of classes, genera, and species for the divisions of animals. . . ." — L. Daubenton, "Exposition des distributions méthodiques des animaux quadrupèdes," in G. L. Buffon, *Histoire naturelle, générale et particuliere* vol. IV (Paris: Imprimerie royale, 1753), pp. 146–47. For some further remarks on this see my "Buffon-Linnaeus Controversy."

26. Phillip R. Sloan, "From Logical Universals to Historical Individuals: Buffon's Idea of Biological Species," in *Histoire du concept d'espèce dans les sciences de la vie*, ed. J. Roger and J. L. Fischer (Paris: Fondation Singer-Polignac, 1986), pp. 101–40.

27. John Locke, *Essay Concerning Human Understanding* III.iii.17 in A. C. Fraser edition (New York: Dover reprint, 1959), II, 27.

28. Buffon, "L'Asne," *Histoire naturelle* vol. IV (1753) in *Buffon: Oeuvres philosophiques*, ed. J. Piveteau (Paris: Presses universitaires de France, 1954), p. 355. This and other translations are my own unless otherwise noted.

29. Ibid., p. 356.

30. It should be carefully noted that for Buffon these *genres* and *familles* in this sense are *subordinate to* "physical" species.

31. Buffon, "De la dégénération des animaux," *Histoire naturelle* vol. XIII (1765) in Piveteau, *Oeuvres complètes*, esp. pp. 408–13.

32. Article "Espèce: histoire naturelle," *Encyclopédie ou dictionnaire raisonsée des arts et des métiers*, vol. V (1755), pp. 956–57.

33. See undated letter of Monboddo to Linnaeus in J. E. Smith, *A Selection of the Correspondence of Linnaeus and Other Naturalists* (London: Longmans et al., 1821), vol. II, p. 555.

34. Antoine Laurent de Jussieu, "Introductio,"*Genera plantarum secundum ordines naturales disposita* (Helvetorum, 1791), p. xxviii.

35. Michel Adanson, "Preface," *Famillies des Plantes* (Paris: Vincent, 1763), vol. I, p. clxviii.

36. See Kant, "Von den verschiedenen Racen der Menschen," (1775) in *Kants Werke*, Akademie Edition (Berlin: 1912), vol. II, 429–43. This has been recently translated by J. M. Mikkelsen in *The Idea of Race*, ed. R. Bernasconi and T. Lott

(Indianapolis: Hackett, 2000), pp. 8–22. See also my "Buffon, German Biology, and the Historical Interpretation of Biological Species," *British Journal for the History of Science* 12 (1979): 109–53, esp. 134 ff., and more recently R. Bernasconi, "Who Invented the Concept of Race? Kant's Role in Enlightenment Construction of Race," in *Race*, ed. R. Bernasconi (Oxford: Blackwell, 2001), pp. 10–36. Kant's distinction of concepts belonging to the "history" of nature from those utilized in the atemporal "description" of nature was immediately employed to clarify the race-variety distinction in the dispute with Georg Forster of 1785–1788. I have not found Kant's important distinctions clearly understood by his contemporaries.

37. Johann Karl Illiger, "Einige Gedanken über die Begriffe: Art und Gattung in der Naturgeschichte," in *Versuch einer Systematischen vollständingen Terminologie* (Helmstadt: C. G. Fleckeisen, 1800), p. xxvi. See also note 59 below on Ernst Mayr's appeal to this discussion as the origin of the "biological" species concept.

38. Bernard de Lacépède, "Discours sur la durée des espèces," *Histoire naturelle des poissons* (Paris, 1798), vol. II, pp. xxiii–lxiv.

39. Lamarck, "Appendice" to *Recherches sur l'organisation des corps vivants*, 1802 (Reprint edition, Paris: Fayard, 1986), pp. 100–101. See also his later article "Espèce," in *Nouveau dictionnaire d'histoire naturelle*, 2nd ed., ed. J. J. Virey (Paris: 1817–19), reprinted in *Articles d'histoire naturelle: Lamarck*, ed. J. Roger and G. Laurent (Paris: Belin, 1991), pp. 78–88.

40. Augustin Pyrame de Candolle, *Théorie élémentarie de la botanique, ou exposition des principles de la classification naturelle* (Paris, 1813), p. 157.

41. G. Cuvier, "Introduction," to *Le Règne animale, distribué d'après son organisation* (Paris: Deterville, 1817), vol. I, p. 19.

42. A. F. Spring, *Ueber die naturhistorischen Begriffe von Gattung, Art und Abart, und über die Ursachen der abartungen in den organischen Reichen* (Leipzig: Fleischer, 1838), p. 23.

43. Alphonse de Candolle, *Géographie botanique raisonée* (Paris, 1855), vol. III, pp. 1071–77.

44. D. A. Godron, *De l'espèce, et des races dans les êtres organisés et specialement de l'unité de l'espèce humaine* (Paris, 1859), vol. I, pp. 2–11.

45. Charles Lyell, *Principles of Geology*, 1st ed., (London: Murray, 1832), vol. II, p. 3.

46. See for example, M. Gérard, "l'Espèce," *Dictionnaire universel d'histoire naturelle*, ed. Charles d'Orbigny (Paris, 1849), vol. VI, pp. 428–52.

47. John Beatty ("Speaking of Species: Darwin's Strategy," in *The Darwinian Heritage*, ed. D. Kohn [Princeton: Princeton University Press, 1985], pp. 265–81) has shown how the discussions of Lyell, and particularly those of the botanist Hugh C. Watson formed the immediate backdrop against which many of Darwin's comments on species in the *Natural Selection* draft of 1856–58 were formulated. At the same time, Darwin's references and reading lists display a much wider

encounter with Continental discussions. Several of these sources draw upon the species$_h$ concept. For example, in the opening chapter of *Natural Selection* Darwin relies heavily on Alphonse de Candolle's morphological definition of species in his *Géographie Botanique*. Darwin then utilizes later in this same discussion the distinctions of races, varieties, and subspecies he seems to have drawn primarily from Johann Jacob Bernhardi's *Ueber den Begriff der Pflanzenart* of 1834 that employed the species$_h$ concept.

48. For this purpose I have used the word indexes in *A Concordance to Charles Darwin's Notebooks, 1836–1844*, ed. D. Weinshank, S. Ozminski, P. Ruhlen, and W. Barrett (Ithaca: Cornell University Press, 1990); and *A Concordance to Darwin's Origin of Species*, ed. P. Barrett, D. Weinshank, and T. Gottleber (Ithaca: Cornell University Press, 1981).

49. Charles Darwin, *Red Notebook*, ed. S. Herbert in *Charles Darwin's Notebooks, 1836–1844*, ed. P. H. Barrett et al. (Cambridge: Cambridge University Press, 1987), fol. 132, p. 63. For some of the background of this comment see the "Zoological Diary" entries, esp. entries for August 1834 and Feb. 10, 1836, in *Charles Darwin's Zoology Notes and Specimen Lists from the H.M.S. Beagle*, ed. R. Keynes (Cambridge: Cambridge University Press, 2000), pp. 251; 312–13.

50. Darwin, *Notebooks*, fol. 213, p. 224.

51. Charles Darwin, *Origin of Species*, 1st ed. (facsimile reprint; Cambridge Mass.: Harvard University Press, 1964), p. 177. All citations to the *Origin* to this edition.

52. Ibid., p. 52.

53. Louis Agassiz, *Contributions to the Natural History of the United States of America*, vol. III (Boston: Little, Brown, 1860), pp. 89–90 n. 1, quoted in Beatty, "Darwin's Strategy," in Kohn, *Darwinian Heritage*, p. 270.

54. Karl von Nägeli, "Systematische übersicht der Erscheinungen in Pflanzenreich," quoted in Hans Bachmann, "Der Speziesbegriff," *Verhandlungen der Schweizerischen Naturforschenden Gesellschaft* 87 (1905), p. 180.

55. Karl von Nägeli, *Entstehung und Begriff der Naturhistorischen Art* (Munich: Königliche Akademie, 1865), pp. 26–27.

56. Ibid., pp. 32–34.

57. Hugo De Vries, *The Mutation Theory*, trans. J. B. Farmer and A. Darbishire (Chicago: Open Court, 1910), vol. II, p. 589.

58. J. R. Beaudry, "The Species Concept: Its Evolution and Present Status," *Revue Canadienne de biologie* 39 (1960): 225.

59. Ernst Mayr implicitly recognized this historical heritage in his important historical discussion of the roots of the "biological" species concept, and traced this back explicitly to the post-Kantian statements of Johann Karl Illiger in 1800. See his "Illiger and the Biological Species Concept," *Journal of the History of Biology* 1 (1968): 163–78. See above, note 37.

60. A summary discussion of these experiments is given in W. F. R. Weldon, "Presidential Address to Section D," *Report of the British Association for the*

Advancement of Science (1898), 887–902. I have discussed aspects of this collaboration recently in my "Mach's Phenomenalism and the British Reception of Mendelism," *Comptes rendus de l'Académie des sciences: Sciences de la vie* 323 (2000): 1069–79.

61. Karl Pearson, *The Grammar of Science*, 2nd ed. (London: Black, 1900), pp. 381, 384. For simplicity I am not attempting to discriminate the relative contributions of Weldon and Pearson to these issues emerging from their intense collaboration in the period between 1894 and 1906 during which time Pearson wrote the important biological chapters for the second edition of the *Grammar*.

62. Ernst Mayr, "Species Concepts and Definitions," in Mayr, *The Species Problem*, pp. 13–14.

63. T. B. Borgmeier, "The Basic Questions of Systematics," *Systematic Zoology* 6, no. 2 (1957): 56–57.

64. For example, Michael Ghiselin, "Species Concepts," Hull, "Matter of Individuality," both in Ereshefsky, *Units*.

65. I would interpret John Dupré to represent this version of neo-pragmatist pluralism.

66. See "Preface," to the Harper Torchbook edition of *Personal Knowledge*, esp. p. x.

67. John S. Sparks, "*Bedotia masoala:* A New Species of Atherinoid Rainbowfish (Teleostei: Bedotiiade) from the Masoala Peninsula, Northeastern Madagascar," *Copiea*, no. 2 (2001): 482–89.

68. For a landmark paper on the application of these numerical techniques to vertebrate taxonomy see C. L. Hubbs and C. Hubbs, "An Improved Graphical Analysis and Comparison of Samples," *Systematic Zoology* 2 (1953): 49–56.

69. The "polytypic" interpretation of natural groups, interpreted as an implication of evolutionary theory, was first articulated by Morton Beckner and subsequently endorsed by George Gaylord Simpson and several philosophers of science as the basis for the claim that evolutionary definitions are anti-essentialist. See Beckner, *The Biological Way of Thought* (Berkeley: University of California Press, 1959), ch. iv, esp. pp. 63 ff. If it is possible to have, especially at higher group levels, some degree of presence and absence of properties, this is a restricted phenomenon. Defining major groups in the invertebrates can involve complex cases of this issue. But these are rare exceptions, and scarcely warrant an authentic "family resemblance" notion of natural groups as a general rule or as a presumed implication of Darwinian theory, as argued by some theorists.

70. David Annis, "A Contextualist Theory of Epistemic Justification," *American Philosophical Quarterly* 15 (1978): 216.

71. Grene, "Historical Realism," p. 75.

72. Ibid., pp. 72–73.

73. Ibid., p. 74.

REPLY TO PHILLIP R. SLOAN

For a series on the evolution of modern philosophy, David Depew and I have been writing a book on relations between biology and philosophy at various times and places in our tradition. At several junctures, we have acknowledged our debt to Phillip Sloan's distinguished work in this field. Can the debt really go the other way? If my approach to conceptual questions has in fact contributed to Sloan's preeminent scholarship and insight, as he kindly says it has, I am deeply gratified, and grateful. Certainly, Sloan's magisterial historical study of the species problem puts to shame the sketch I have written on recent species concepts in one of our chapters, and I can only hope the little I have said does not contradict his fascinating and carefully attested account. For the most part, there is little I can say about it except, "Hear, hear!"

One minor question only: Sloan speaks of the debate between Buffon and Linnaeus. That Buffon bitterly disputed the foundations of Linnean taxonomy is clear; but I had thought of this as one-sided: an attack rather than a debate, which seems to entail attack and rebuttal. I'm sure this is a matter of ignorance on my part, and I would be grateful for further instruction.

In addition, there is a very small historical matter on which I venture to disagree with Sloan's account: not about the large question of species, but about the relatively trivial question of the influence, or otherwise, of Heidegger in my work and in that of Michael Polanyi. I spent two semesters with Heidegger and two with Jaspers. I listened in amazement to Heidegger, as everyone did, and read *Sein und Zeit*—with very little understanding. And I learned something about the history of philosophy from both those sources: chiefly about Plato from Heidegger's *Phaedrus* seminar, and about Kant and Hegel from Jaspers. But when I came home in 1933, at the time of the so-called *Nationale Erhebung*, I was thoroughly disgusted with all German *tiefere Bedeutungen*. Partly through C. I. Lewis, I became interested in the emerging Vienna circle, and read with enthusiasm the first volumes of *Erkenntnis*. Then, in 1937–38, when I managed to enroll in Carnap's research seminar at Chicago, I became, in turn, disillusioned with logical positivism. Twelve years later, when I first encountered Polanyi, I thought he was developing the refutation of positivism that I had failed to articulate. So I was two removes, by then, from any interest in Heidegger. Indeed, when I reprinted my first essay on Heidegger I subtitled it "Confessions of a Young Positivist." Nor did my rejection of positivism by any means return me to the Heideggerian fold. What interested me in Polanyi's work was his reflection on scientific discovery and scientific knowledge. Heidegger's *Dasein* has little to do with knowledge of any kind. And Polanyi's concept of indwelling was a late comer in his thought, conceived in a context far removed from Heideggerian "being-in-the-world."

Polanyi was a physical chemist who turned to philosophizing in order to clarify, first of all, what he called the unspecifiable component of scientific practice. He was wholly innocent of any knowledge of our philosophical tradition, whether past or recent. There is simply no connection here with Heidegger. And as for phenomenology—I'm sure Polanyi never read a word of Husserl. Nor were there more than a few words of the master of phenomenology that I had then read, or that I ever came to understand. To acknowledge the intentional character of human discourse, surely one does not need all that bracketing mumbo-jumbo. True, when I finally read Merleau-Ponty's *Phenomenology of Perception* (which is decidedly *not* phenomenology!) in 1960, two years after the publication of Polanyi's *Personal Knowledge*, like some other readers I found a kind of parallel between the two works. But that was a parallel, not an influence, and one that Polanyi resented and rejected.

Of course, beside the large and illuminating history that Sloan relates in his essay, my worry about Heideggerian connections seem positively petty. But it is my life, and I'd like to have the record straight. Otherwise, again, I can only thank Phillip Sloan for a tribute which I am far from feeling I deserve.

M. G.

10

David L. Hull

A PORTRAIT OF BIOLOGY

Marjorie Grene began her career in philosophy translating and commenting on such Continental philosophers as Heidegger, Kierkegaard, and Sartre, but rather rapidly she turned her attention to the philosophy of biology as well. She began as an outsider, finding herself opposed to the neo-Darwinian versions of evolutionary theory prevalent at the time. Forty years later Grene has become an established figure in the philosophy of biology, selected along with Ernst Mayr as the first honorary presidents of the International Society for the History, Philosophy and Social Studies of Biology. At each meeting of this society, an award named after Grene is offered for the best paper presented by a student. Both of these honors indicate the respect and affection that the members of this society have for this early philosopher of biology. The juxtaposition of Mayr, a quintessential neo-Darwinian, with Grene, a philosopher who was for some time highly critical of neo-Darwinism, epitomizes the tension that has characterized Grene's work.

In this essay I will discuss Grene's contributions to the philosophy of biology, especially with respect to evolutionary theory, but also including her work on Aristotle's biology. She began in the late 1950s as a critic of evolutionary theory. By the early 1970s Grene came to appreciate evolutionary biology. However, just when Grene was making her peace with the biology of her day, new issues arose that required further rethinking—the punctuated equilibrium model of speciation, cladistics, the role of embryology in evolution, species as individuals, levels of selection, hierarchies in nature, population thinking, and the continuing problem of forms. Thus Darwinian theory has changed considerably during the past forty years. So have Grene's views. However, Grene continues to insist that some notion of species as types is necessary for us to be able to understand the living world. Each individual species must exhibit its own unique "form," and these forms are universals. How about conceptual systems such as those of Aristotle, Darwin, and Grene? In order for us to understand them, must they also be characterized by certain unchanging tenets? Must they have essences? Or are they better interpreted as historical entities, changing through time?

I conclude with the anachronistic exercise of contrasting Grene's positions through the years with present-day views. How prescient was she? Have those parts of evolutionary biology that she found most deficient been abandoned or modified in ways that bring them more closely in accord with the positions that she favors? In commenting positively on my distinction between replication and environmental interaction, Grene (1989a:67) begins by warning the reader that, "about philosophy of science, and perhaps philosophy as such, he and I could hardly disagree more." We shall see.

EVOLUTIONARY THEORY AND ITS SHORTCOMINGS

Grene arrived on the emerging scene of philosophy of biology with a flourish, publishing three papers in rapid succession. In her "Two Evolutionary Theories" (1958), she compared two closed interpretive systems—G. G. Simpson's neo-Darwinian version of evolutionary theory and O. H. Schindewolf's morphological theory. Both men were paleontologists, but Simpson viewed the fossil record in Darwinian terms—descent with modification, chance variation, and natural selection—while Schindewolf viewed it from the perspective of novel types arising in the course of embryological development. For Simpson, the historical perspective is fundamental. Species are lineages changing through time. For Schindewolf, morphology is basic. A family is a family because it exhibits a familial trait, a genus is a genus because it exhibits a generic trait, and so on.

In its simplest terms the disagreement between Simpson and Schindewolf turned on the relative priority that they placed on phylogeny and morphology respectively. For Simpson phylogeny is prior to morphology, and for Schindewolf morphology is prior to phylogeny. One of the problems in contrasting the work of Simpson and Schindewolf is the sort of priority that is being claimed. Is it logical, metaphysical, epistemological, temporal, what? Grene herself is interested primarily in the necessary role of types in knowledge acquisition. As she saw it, the chief difference between Simpson and Schindewolf was that Schindewolf openly and explicitly made use of biological types while Simpson, though he officially rejected treating biological taxa as types, actually did so surreptitiously.

This difference in perspective between Simpson and Schindewolf can be seen in the way that they interpret the evolution of higher taxa such as

Aves. Assume that *Archeopteryx* was the first feathered reptile. What if it had given rise to no additional species? According to Simpson, it would be just a peculiar feathered reptile, while for Schindewolf it would form a new class, Aves. In addition, Simpson viewed most evolutionary transitions as gradual, taking thousands of years and involving millions of organisms, while for Schindewolf, speciation is always discrete. Feathers did not come into existence gradually, becoming a little more like feathers with each generation, but in the course of a single birth event. A full-fledged bird hatched from a reptile's egg.

For Simpson, speciation is a populational affair; for Schindewolf it was part of embryological development. In this connection, Grene (1959:52) asks: "What of the mechanisms of development? Why not look at phylogeny as an ontogeny writ large, at the history of groups as expressing a fundamental rhythm still, in its intimacy, unknown to us, but analogous to the rhythm of individual development?" Given complex sequences of embryological development, different species branch off at different times. "For Schindewolf, evolutionary change occurs when a youthful animal takes a new turning on its ontogenetic course" (Grene 1958:123). One thing that is noticeably absent from Grene's description of Schindewolf's views is how these embryological sequences evolved in the first place. Once an embryological sequence is in place, an organism can take a "new turning" (that is, in neotony), but how did these embryological sequences develop in the first place? For her part, Grene (1963a:154) never claimed that "Schindewolf's theory gave an adequate explanation, but only that *it is epistemologically consistent with one*, which neo-Darwinism is not."[1]

In an essay that appeared a year later, "The Faith of Darwinism," Grene (1959) again chastised evolutionary biologists for the religious fervor with which they pursued their subject matter. In this essay she joined forces with Gertrude Himmelfarb (1959) in criticizing evolutionary theory. Just as Himmelfarb laid bare all the confusions and inconsistencies of Darwin and his nineteenth-century followers, Grene would do the same for more recent neo-Darwinians. Evolutionists ignored development. They insisted that not only was natural selection the "only mechanism we observe in present-day nature" (Grene 1959:52), but also that it was the "only conceivable alternative" (Grene 1959:50). Even worse was the ease with which neo-Darwinians could subsume conflicting views to their own theory transforming either the phenomena or their more inclusive theory. Grene complained that whatever "might at first sight appear as evidence against the theory is assimilated by redefinition into the theory" (1959: 53).

Here Grene is not reiterating the tired old objection that the principle of the survival of the fittest is a tautology, though she does periodically

introduce it into her critiques of neo-Darwinism. Instead, she complains that
the trio of concepts—descent with modification, chance variation, and
natural selection—are woven into too tight a circle. Data that do not fit
within this circle are rejected on this account as mistaken or assimilated to
it with hardly a skip in the beat. But unlike other critics of neo-Darwinism,
Grene acknowledges that all comprehensive theories are circular in the
same way. Her only complaint with respect to neo-Darwinism is that the
"circle seems so narrow, and the detours taken to maintain it in the teeth of
the evidence so circuitous and so many" (1959:52). This circular structure
that "seems so oddly illogical" to the outsider from the perspective of the
insider "most firmly supports the theory" (1959:51). Other critics of
Darwinism (that is, Himmelfarb 1959) discovered similar modes of
inference but thought that they were peculiar to evolutionary theory. Grene
acknowledges that they are common throughout science—common, though
objectionable.

In 1961 Grene again attacked the pretensions of the synthetic theory of
evolution, in this instance Fisher's mathematical version of the synthetic
theory. Grene (1961a) distinguishes between the actual content of this
formalism and the more general theory of evolution in which it is embedded. The problem is familiar: how to test fitness. If fitness is measured by
representation in future generations, then the survival of the fittest is the
survival of the fittest, but this tautology can be converted into a synthetic
claim by producing ways of deciding fitness that are at least partially
independent of survival to reproduce. Evolutionary theory in a more
inclusive sense adds causal factors to the equations. These additions explain
what *caused* the perceived changes in gene frequencies. For Grene that is
all well and good, but adding such contingencies to Fisher's genetic theory
robs it of its appearance of pristine mathematical formulation and smuggles
in several senses of "improvement" that his mathematical formulation does
not warrant.

In 1974 Grene published *The Understanding of Nature*, a collection of
her essays on philosophy of biology stretching from 1946 to 1974. In the
preface she announced a change in her "reflections on the conceptual
structure of evolutionary theory" (Grene 1974:vii) as a result of discussions
with her colleagues and students at the Davis campus of the University of
California. She details these changes in "Darwin and Philosophy." In this
paper she sets out the theory of evolution then current without criticizing it
and then turns to the implications of this version of evolutionary theory for
various philosophical issues. According to Grene, Darwinism has "forced
us to recognize mutability, the omnipresence of change. . . . The acceptance
of organic evolution eliminates an Aristotelian theory of nature, dependent
as such a theory must be on the existence of permanent natural kinds"

(Grene 1974:193). In addition to abandoning the permanence of Aristotelian nature, "we have also abandoned metaphysical necessity in favor of a recognition of fundamental contingency—and here too evolution, along with historiography as well as history itself, has played a role" (Grene 1974:194). However, she finds other implications questionable (that is, evolution being progressive) and others downright mistaken (evolutionary ethics). What is remarkable in this essay is that it contains no criticism of evolutionary theory, no hint of animosity! Grene came to appreciate evolutionary theory (at least certain versions of it) just in time for new issues to arise. How would she handle these new versions of evolutionary theory? Before jumping ahead to this fascinating turn of events, I must interpose Grene's work on Aristotle, especially his biology.

A PORTRAIT OF ARISTOTLE

Right in the midst of the controversy that Grene engendered over neo-Darwinian evolution, she published *A Portrait of Aristotle* (1963b), a work that has proven to be extremely durable as an introduction to Aristotle's philosophy (it was reissued in 1967, 1979, and 1998). With respect to evolutionary theory, Grene is blunt. Aristotle rejected the notion of species evolving, as he must given his philosophy, and, like it or not, species do evolve. The part of this book that has the greatest relevance to Grene's philosophy of biology is her insistence that Aristotle's experience as a biologist informed his entire world view. "D'Arcy Thompson was amply justified in his remark that Aristotle's biology may have provided the cornerstone for his metaphysics and his logic—for all his philosophy, in fact" (Grene 1963b:32). But if Aristotle's biology informed his philosophy and Aristotle held that species are permanent and stable (Grene 1963b:24), then his philosophy was informed by a view that turned out to be mistaken. Might not this cause problems? However, the biology that informed Aristotle's entire corpus was not his belief in permanent and stable species but a "certain kind of field naturalist's passion for the minute observation of the structures and life histories of living things" (Grene 1963b:34).

One of the recurrent problems in philosophy is the relation between the individual and the universal. Here is where Aristotle's experience as a practicing field naturalist comes in. In his investigations Aristotle is "too much preoccupied with the panorama of life before him to turn his eyes upward to the Platonic heaven of Forms. . . . He is observing both the individuals, which, as he well knows, are the only things that *are*, and the universals *in* them" (Grene 1963b:37). For Aristotle biological species were one sort of biological universal. "Aristotelian biology itself is founded on the conception of the being-what-it-is of fixed kinds of things in an eternally existing universe, a conception which our acceptance of evolutionary principles compels us to reject" (Grene 1963b:227). For Aristotle "change is always change from one form to another, or from the want of form to its presence, *in a subject*" (Grene 1963b:115). Change requires something that does not change (the forms) and something that does change (the individuals).

But how about biological species? Creationists to one side, anyone today who is moderately well educated knows that species evolve. That species evolve is an "incontrovertible fact" (Grene 1963b:230). As Grene (1963b:231) sees it, nothing "separates us more fundamentally from Aristotle than does this principle, based on the massive fact of organic evolution." For Aristotle, forms are permanent and stable. For evolutionists *forms themselves change.* Species are not themselves forms but only "potencies for other forms." Nothing could be more anti-Aristotelian than that. If species evolve, then:

> there is no being-what-it-is of each kind of thing, no ultimate and final definition of each natural class of substances, from which, with the necessary definiteness and precision, an Aristotelian science could take its start. We live for better or worse in an evolutionary universe, and, in the last analysis, evolution and Aristotelian science will not mix. (Grene 1963b:232)

Grene argues that evolutionary biologists as professional biologists have their species concept, but other biologists, ordinary people, and even philosophers have their species concepts as well. All of these species concepts are equally legitimate, serving as they do very different ends from the evolutionary species concept. Species as the things that evolve do not have any of the traditional characteristics of kinds or types. These other species concepts do. Most importantly, as Grene argues, we need a species concept that allows us as sentient beings to comprehend the world in which we live.

In her work on Aristotle, Grene is primarily concerned to argue that we need universals for knowledge, and I do not want to contest this claim. I agree totally. What these universals actually *are* is quite another matter. So too is the claim that some universals are more basic to human understanding than others. People do conceive of species of living creatures as Aristotelian kinds. Is this particular form of perception and conception *necessary* for knowledge of the living world? I do not have an answer to this question, but I do have strong doubts about such claims of necessity. One lesson that I have learned from my study of evolutionary biology is that time and again, chance variation and natural selection can actually do what seems impossible. From the perspective of functional anatomy, certain workers claim that certain forms of life simply could not possibly exist. X could not have evolved into Z because this transition would require an intermediate state Y that is functionally impossible. Then we find an organism actually doing the impossible. Could we have come to comprehend the world in which we live by some means other than perceiving species as Aristotelian natural kinds? I am betting that we could. I doubt that all human beings throughout all time have been able to perceive species of living organisms in one and only one way. I am inclined toward monism, but this is monism run amuck.

THE ESSENCE OF ARISTOTLE, DARWIN, AND GRENE

Grene provides an Aristotelian analysis of "species" and to some extent sides with Aristotle. The species recognized by evolutionary biologists certainly evolve, but we also need species concepts that treat species as kinds or universals. How about Aristotle's corpus? Is it a kind, a historical entity, or both? Should we construct two versions of Aristotle's views—one in which Aristotle holds fundamentally the same positions throughout his life and one in which he changes his mind through time, perhaps so much so that no single conceptual strand ties his philosophical system together?

One problem that any Aristotle scholar must face is that our records of Aristotle's philosophy are spotty and in places questionable. Some of the writings may be by Aristotle's students. Some may actually be from Aristotle's own hand, but we don't know for sure. Another problem is that Aristotle may have changed his mind over time—hardly a sin for which he must be punished. What look like apparent contradictions may actually be a maturing of his ideas. When Grene was doing the research for her book on Aristotle, the genetic school of Werner Jaeger was still in power. Although Grene concedes that the genetic method solves quite a few puzzles about Aristotle's corpus, it has one drawback: it denies that Aristotle's philosophy has an essence, a being-what-it-is. It is not permanent and stable but changeable and temporary:

> True, even the greatest philosopher may contradict himself; and where he does so, we may well suppose, as a working hypothesis, that he has changed his mind. But there must be some coherence, some unity rich enough to be meaningful and illuminating, in some one stage of his thought, if he is to come through to us as a great philosopher at all. There must be some richness and coherence in any one work which *is* one; and there must even be, it seems to me, one theme running through the philosopher's development, one predominating line of thought, one sovereign intellectual passion, of sufficient bearing on the persistent problems of philosophy to make him the philosopher he is. (Grene 1963b:29)

In short, Aristotle's philosophy not only has an essence, it *must* have an essence. Of course, this essence of Aristotle is not a *totally* fixed being-what-it-is. After all, Aristotle allowed that:

> *Within* the bounds of the nature of each kind of thing, there is a certain field of free play for mere "necessity"; but without those bounds and the ends or forms that eternally delimit them, there would be neither things to know nor minds to know them. (Grene 1963b:145)

Grene wants us to approach Aristotle's corpus as if it is a kind, because if it is not a kind, it is not knowable. We have access to the universal only through the individual, but only the universal is truly knowable. Thus, Grene is consistent in how she treats both species and Aristotle's corpus. For both she distinguishes between historical and nonhistorical perspectives and argues that both perspectives are necessary.

How about Darwinian theory, not to mention neo-Darwinian theory? Does it have an essence as well? Elsewhere I have argued at some length that evolutionary theory is best conceived of as an historical entity, not a kind (Hull 1983, 1985). No matter which tenet one selects to play the role of the essence of evolutionary theory, the resulting conception is gerrymandered beyond all recognition. If all it takes to be a Darwinian is that you believe that species evolve, then several of Darwin's fiercest critics become Darwinians. If you add a belief that natural selection is the primary cause of evolutionary change, then several of Darwin's most forceful defenders cease to be Darwinians. In fact, almost no one was a Darwinian until this century. Even so, numerous evolutionary biologists insist that Darwinism has an essence (Lewontin 1977, Gould 1980, Huxley 1981, Stebbins and Ayala 1981, Mayr 1983). They just can't agree about what this essence is. For these biologists, species evolve but scientific theories do not.

This same spectrum of opinion about the essence of Darwinism can be found among those of us who study science. Some of us insist that scientific theories change so radically through time that they do not have essences. Others view scientific change essentialistically but disagree about what these essences are. How about Grene? In "Changing Concepts of Darwinian Evolution," Grene (1981:195) addresses this very question. She acknowledges that Darwinian evolutionary theory seems "both remarkably simple and persistent in its basic principles, and yet remarkably flexible, not to say ambiguous, in some of its fundamental concepts," but in this essay she is interested in diachronic, not synchronic ambiguities. As a case study in the nature of change and stability in scientific theories, she investigates the ways in which current versions of Darwinian evolutionary theory relate to Darwin's versions of this very same theory.

Grene's (1981:209) conclusion is that the sequence of Darwinian, neo-Darwinian and the synthetic theory of evolution "appears to be one of the great success stories of twentieth-century science, or better of nineteenth-century science expanded, confirmed and vindicated in the twentieth." At this stage in her development, Grene conceives of Darwinism and Aristotelianism once properly understood as unified, coherent systems of thought. Each can be characterized by a carefully chosen list of principles that remain fundamentally unchanged. Later, however, Grene (1990a:75) changes her mind with respect to scientific theories. Although she would not go so far as to say that scientific theories like Darwinism have no essence or have only a genealogical essence, they are historical entities in the same way that organisms are. Theories are "congeries of human practices: actions, beliefs, and conformity to, as well as creation of, norms or values. Far from being fixed once for all, so that any anomaly suffices to defeat them, they are, when fruitful, capable of alteration and growth— and this in no epicyclic, but in a coherent, if by no means predictable, fashion."

From the halting prose of the preceding sentences, I cannot tell how far Grene is willing to go in treating scientific theories as historical entities. She compares scientific theories to organisms, but organisms can undergo complete change during their life cycle, exchanging all of their matter, totally modifying their structure (sometimes quite abruptly), and exhibiting radically different appearances. Just follow a parasite through the numerous stages in its life cycle, each stage radically different from the next.

In 1990 Grene took on the task of deciding whether recent advances in science are leading to the replacement of Darwinian theory with some new theory or only an expansion of Darwinian theory. Is evolutionary biology at a crossroads? With respect to genetics, systematics, paleontology, and embryology, Grene opts for expansion. Of all the scientists who claim to be revolutionizing evolutionary biology, only such idealists as Goodwin (1988) actually differ so markedly from Darwinism that their views would be a genuine replacement. Transformed cladists in biogeography also "constitute an anomaly for my attempt to minimize the significance of the crossroads metaphor" (Grene 1990a:71). Ecology remains so distinct from evolutionary biology that the issue cannot even be posed. Hence, Grene views evolutionary theory as expanding through the years but not as changing its fundamental principles all that much.

The next obvious question is how I propose to treat Grene's philosophical system, as a historical entity that can change indefinitely through time or as having some unity rich enough to be meaningful and illuminating. In doing the research for this essay, I read all of Grene's works on the philosophy of biology in chronological order and in this essay present the results of this research in this same order. My assumption in structuring both my research and my presentation was that Grene did not set out a grand system in her early years and spend the rest of her career developing it. She changed her mind on several issues. Most noticeably she came to appreciate Darwinian versions of evolutionary theory more than she had early in her career, but many of her views remained unchanged to the present. She held them early in her intellectual development. She holds them today. For example, she still insists on the epistemological necessity of types, even at the risk of being termed a "typologist." Whether or not certain themes run through Aristotle to make him the philosopher that he was, certain themes run through Grene's work to make her the philosopher that she is.

REDUCTIONISM AND OTHER THEMES

Most of the preceding discussion concerns Grene's early discontent with the views of neo-Darwinians. Neo-Darwinians railed against types even though they themselves surreptitiously used them. Schindewolf, as Aristotle before him, recognized the necessity of types in human understanding. In this section I turn to an issue that is at least as fundamental to Grene's philosophy as is the notion of types—her anti-reductionism. At the outset, she decries the tendency of both sides to pick the most extreme examples to discuss. No one in 1971 can be interpreted as a vitalist. Both sides of this debate agree that living and nonliving systems are made of the same kind of matter and obey the same physical laws (Grene 1971:16). For their part, anti-reductionists should also avoid the easy targets, that is, Crick in his *Of Molecules and Men* (1966). Instead, they should take issue with more sophisticated reductionists, such as Nagel in his *The Structure of Science* (1961).

Grene's anti-reductionism is part of her larger philosophy which she views as being heterodox in contrast to the more orthodox views of most philosophers and nearly all scientists (Grene 1969:61). Part of reductionism is the belief that a single-level, particulate ontology is adequate for understanding all of nature. Grene (1987), to the contrary, opts for a hierarchical view of nature. A hierarchy is made up of levels. At each of these levels, entities exist that are subject to laws peculiar to their level, but they also are related to each other in ways that produce patterns that impose restraints on these very elements. And here Grene uses her old bugbear neo-Darwinian theory to illustrate hierarchical organization. Only by conceiving of evolution in terms of populations can the evolutionary process be understood, and populations are more than mere collections of organisms (but see her later comments on populations as "heaps").

On this topic I find myself in agreement with Grene, albeit reluctantly (Hull 1972). I am a reluctant anti-reductionist, not because I have any in-principle objections to the program, but because thus far it has been largely a matter of hand waving—and I do not much care for hand waving. For example, in some sense Mendelian genetics has been reduced to molecular biology. When I was in college, I took an entire course in Mendelian genetics. At Northwestern University, at least, no one teaches an entire course on Mendelian genetics anymore. Biology majors get one week of Mendelian genetics in a three-quarter sequence. Phosphorous pumps get three weeks all on their own. But here all "reduction" means is "muscled aside." It is equally true that in the thirty years since Grene objected to reductionism, molecular biologists have made massive contributions to our understanding of the natural world, but reductionism involves more than just relative success. According to Nagel (1961), if Mendelian genetics is reducible to molecular biology, then the basic principles of Mendelian genetics must be derivable from those of molecular biology. Thus far, no such derivations have been provided. They were not available in 1971. They are not available today. Hence, in this case, either reduction is not doable or it is not worth doing. As far as I can see, either conclusion counts against the reductionist program.[2]

In her early writings, Grene (1959, 1961a) complained that reasoning about selection and adaptation can degenerate too easily into tautolo-gies—what survives to reproduce survives to reproduce. She does not claim that reasoning about such issues is inherently tautological, only that too often this is precisely what happens. In her later work, Grene (1981:207) reiterates the uneasiness she feels with the ease that Darwinians can make data fit their theory or ignore data that apparently do not fit. Robson and Richards (1936) collected all the evidence that they could find at the time both for and against the theory of natural selection. Although they found some evidence to support natural selection, most of it was either indeterminate or negative. Yet, when later Darwinians cited this work, it was for the support it gave their views, all the negative evidence notwithstanding (for more recent work on this topic, see Endler 1986). Grene has stumbled upon an important truth about how scientists reason. They are not dispassionate, disinterested, objective logic machines, especially when their own views are at stake. Would science proceed better if they were? Implicit in so many of the criticisms that Grene as a philosopher raises against Darwinian scientists is the conviction that it would. However, given her early work with Michael Polanyi, one would expect her to reject the logistic form of evaluations so characteristic of positivists.[3]

During the period in question, Michael Ghiselin (1974) and the author of the present essay (Hull 1976) began to champion the view that species, as the things that evolve, are better construed as individuals (or historical entities) than as kinds (natural or otherwise). Socrates is not a member of the class *Homo sapiens* but one strand in the genealogical nexus produced by the evolutionary process. As strange as it may sound, Socrates is "part" of *Homo sapiens*. The reason why Mayr put such emphasis on population thinking is that species are not classes at all, but individuals. As individuals they cannot be literally *defined* typologically or any other way. Individuals are the sort of thing that can have locations and geographic distributions. Classes defined in terms of predicates cannot have such locations and distributions because they are universals. Classes can have boundaries in abstract character space, but not *real* boundaries in *actual* space. My terminology reveals my own views on this subject. Thus, typologists are not wrong in defining class terms essentialistically, but in treating species as the sort of thing that can be defined. Perhaps they can be defined ostensively, but here "define" is being used ambiguously.

When it comes to the relative merits of typology, population thinking, and species as individuals, Grene (Eldredge and Grene 1992; see also Grene 1989b) cannot help but let her exasperation show. First off, she finds discussions such as the preceding way too crude. They "grossly misrepresent the history of philosophy." To attribute any beliefs to all philosophers or even most philosophers is simplistic. No two philosophers ever held precisely the same views on any topic. The only level of discussion acceptable in philosophy is the most detailed and precise. Second, she thinks that biologists are not being fair when they dismiss typologists as being the same sort of evil demons as philosophers such as Grene take positivists to be. In both cases, typologists and positivists are being used as all-purpose whipping boys. I agree with Grene that the biologists who joined in these controversies were not trained professionally as metaphysicians. They did not always express their views in ways that Grene would have liked. Even though officially I am a philosopher, Grene is even more unhappy with my level of exposition. But both Grene and I are engaged in an interdisciplinary activity. In such occasions both sides have to give a little. If I had set out the preceding distinctions in the detail that Grene would accept as adequate, very few biologists would have read my papers, or would have understood them if they had. Grene is loathe to compromise philosophy in the service of biology. I am more willing to do so.

In my reading of Grene in connection with these issues, she seems to attribute overly extreme positions to her opponents, in this case me. For example, Grene (1990b:238) remarks that, contrary to what Tennyson may have said, nature is not "careful of the type," nature "ignores types. Indeed there *are* no types, only minutely differing individuals aggregating to populations." Aristotle would term such aggregates "heaps." Grene is correct in claiming that I think that species are not kinds, but it does not follow that I think that there are *no* kinds. Lots of kinds exist in biology, not to mention all the rest of science; that is, herbivore, carnivore, peripheral isolate, ancestral group, homology, nucleotide, amino acid, gold, inert gas, electron, and so on. Nor do I (or Mayr) think that population thinking requires us to treat species as "heaps." One of the main reasons for treating species as individuals is that they are *not* heaps. They exhibit structure— population structure. Nor does anyone who claims that species are indi- viduals believe that species are organisms, contrary to Grene (1990b:239).

Grene (1990b:239) lodges an even stronger objection to population thinking. Population thinking "taken strictly turns out to be not only methodologically, but ontologically, impossible. Types, kinds, sorts are bound to crop up somewhere, else we not only could not speak about nature; there would not be a nature to speak about." And again, "There is nothing 'essentialistic' in the scholastic sense in the acknowledgment of such identities [of form]. Indeed, without them there would be no discourse, no science, no nature, no evolution" (Grene 1989a:70). In claiming that biological species as the things that evolve are not kinds, no one is committed to the view that no kinds whatsoever exist or that predicates are anything but universals. Lots of kinds exist, and many of them are definable in the traditional way. For example, one commonly reads that in any locale predators always outnumber prey. Here everything is as general as Grene would like. There are normal predators and normal prey, and they are distributed in a particular way. "There are no mammoths nowadays, but surely we can say something about the *kind* of ungulates mammoths *were*" (Grene 1990b:239). Of course, we can. For one thing, they were herbivores.

We can make two sorts of claims about mammoths, one concerns the taxa to which they belong, the other concerns the universal predicates that apply to them. The distinction is between homologies (in the sense used by present-day evolutionary biologists) and homoplasies. Homologies carve out chunks of the phylogenetic tree and as such are spatiotemporally localized. Homoplasies carve out chunks of abstract character space and as such are spatiotemporally unrestricted. Unfortunately, in the midst of highly involved discussion, this distinction can get blurred, especially when terms that look very similar to each other are used to mark this distinction. For example, "Carnivora" refers to a chunk of phylogeny. "Carnivorous" refers to all meat eaters. As it turns out, a couple of the species included in Carnivora do not eat meat very often, and millions of organisms that eat meat do not belong to this chunk of the phylogenetic tree; that is, lots of fish, insects, reptiles, and so on.

Quite a few biologists and philosophers of biology have argued that species are spatiotemporal individuals. It does not follow from this claim that we think *everything* is an individual. The scientific literature is full of references to kinds, relations, predicates, and so on. In addition, if we construe species as being individuals, then the issue of typology never arises because typology concerns the definition of general terms, and we insist that terms like "*Bos bos*" and "Mammalia" are not general terms. The issue of typology arose back in the old days when we were arguing whether taxa names can be defined in terms of necessary and sufficient conditions or in terms of clusters. In those days, lots of us said nasty things about typology, but for my part I was not rejecting typology as such but only typology applied to taxa names. Now I see more clearly what the problem was: we were trying to define the indefinable. Spatiotemporal individuals are not the sort of thing that one defines whether essentialistically or in terms of statistically covarying properties.

Two sorts of language permeate discussions of the evolutionary process. Both exhibit the superficial appearance of predicates. Claiming that pandas belong to Carnivora may appear to be the same sort of claim as pandas are not carnivorous. Carnivora, however, is not a universal, any more than the Baja peninsula is. Contrary to common usage, pandas are not members of the taxon Carnivora, they are parts of it, just as the Baja peninsula is part of North America. In general, Grene favors pluralism. For example, she maintains that we need at least two species concepts—one referring to the things that evolve and another referring to the natural kinds which seem so right to just about everyone. But implicit in this distinction is the contrast between the evolutionary homologies that characterize (but do not define) biological taxa and homoplasies that both characterize and define species as natural kinds.

RETROSPECTIVE EVALUATION

Are Grene's ideas today as heterodox as they once seemed? Grene liked three things about Schindewolf's version of biological evolution: speciation occurred quite abruptly, the mechanism was embryological, and types played a central role. Almost thirty years ago, Niles Eldredge and Steve Gould (1972) floated a theory of evolution as an alternative to phyletic gradualism—punctuated equilibria. When it was first introduced, it caused quite a stir. All speciation is punctuational? This theory was radically at variance with the orthodox neo-Darwinian theory and replacing it? All this excitement to one side, punctuational speciation has become part of orthodox Darwinian theory. It characterizes one mode of speciation, possibly the most common mode of speciation. In one respect it is quite similar to Schindewolf's views. By and large, the gaps in the fossil record are real. Some may be due to incomplete fossilization, but many, possibly most, are due to how rapid speciation happens to be. However, the mechanisms at the heart of these two theories differ: for Eldredge and Gould speciation is a populational affair, for Schindewolf it is individual—one organism giving rise to another organism that belongs to a different higher taxon.

In the nineteenth century, embryology was the paradigm of hard science in biology. Generation after generation, embryologists thought that it exhibited considerable promise. Any day now, it was going to give birth to a powerful new theory of some sort. Although massive amounts of empirical work was done, no such theoretical inflorescence occurred. As historians have noted, embryology played almost no role in the development of evolutionary theory from Darwin to the present. Is this state of affairs due to the bigotry of evolutionary biologists? I don't think so. If the embryologists had produced a body of knowledge that evolutionists could use, they would have used it. In the past few years a new developmentalist school of thought has arisen, starting with publications by Oyama (1985), Goodwin (1988), Griffiths and Gray (1994), Griesemer (1998), and Jablonka and Lambe (1998). As is usually the case, the preceding authors see their theory as totally replacing evil neo-Darwinian theory, but if the past is any indication of the future, the most that they can hope for is incorporation into the received view. Although Grene was one of the earliest authors urging that the synthetic theory of evolution become even more "synthetic" by adding a developmental perspective, she is not much impressed by the work of these new developmentalists (Grene 1990a).

Throughout its history, methodologists found evolutionary theory to be seriously wanting, whether it was the criticisms of John Herschel, William Whewell or (less obviously) John Stuart Mill in Darwin's own day, or Himmelfarb and Grene a century later. Because these same methodological criticisms are being raised today by religious creationists, more responsible philosophers have tended to tone down their criticisms, lest they be used in this recent skirmish between science and religion. One feature of these continuing disputes that has received insufficient attention is that these criticisms tend to be raised in the context of very unrealistic views of science. Everyone nowadays knows that positivism is dead, but the only way that evolutionary theory could come up to snuff methodologically is to exhibit all the characteristics that positivists attribute to science. With respect to Grene's criticisms, most have more than a kernel of truth to them. The problem is that these "weaknesses" are not peculiar to evolutionary biology but are common to all science, a point on which Grene, unlike other investigators, is clear. Enough detailed attention has been paid to evolutionary biology that its actual character has become well known. As comparable attention is paid to other branches of science, an equally complex picture of the methodology actually used is materializing.

In Grene's early methodological evaluations of Darwinian theory, I discern too many remnants of positivist philosophy, as she found in my own overly conservative view on laws of nature (see also, Grene 1997:263). When Grene and I began working in philosophy of science, positivism and its conceptual progeny, logical empiricism, were on their way out, but as always we both were imbued with the basic principles of this way of doing philosophy more than either of us realized at the time. Both of us looked at science as needing conceptual clarification and rational reconstruction. We looked for inconsistencies and invalid arguments. "Logic" was what mattered. Her contribution to *The Logic of Personal Knowledge* was "The Logic of Biology" (Grene 1961b), and the title of my dissertation was *The Logic of Phylogenetic Taxonomy* (Hull 1964). But in her more recent publications, Grene (1997:271) indicates that she has freed herself even further from these overly formalist concerns than I have. She now evaluates biology from a much more realistic point of view.

From the start Grene opposed reductionism, and she has not weakened her opposition in the interim. In this connection Grene's view is no longer heterodox, at least among philosophers of biology. Grene (1997:272) remarks that, on the whole, "reducibility is no longer an issue in philosophical debates." Nagel-type reductions have not taken place in biology and probably cannot take place. "Reduction" in other senses may have taken place, but the general tone of this literature is rather negative toward reduction. Biologists themselves fall into two camps with respect to reductionism: molecular biologists versus whole-organism biologists. This dispute has many dimensions, some of them as crass as money. So the story goes molecular biologists are getting way more than their share of research funds. Others raise issues of the sort that philosophers find worth investigating.

Grene rejects Dawkins's (1976) single-level gene selectionist view of evolution and opts for a hierarchical view of evolution—in fact two hierarchies, one genealogical, one ecological:

> Genealogical systems (local demes and, more stably, species and monophyletic taxa) are historical entities of packaged genetic information. They are (among) the results of the evolutionary process. In contrast, economic biotic entities (such as ecosystems) result from moment-to-moment economic interactions among component parts. (Eldredge and Grene 1992:3)

All along Grene has been sympathetic to my view that selection is not a single process but two subprocesses—replication and environmental interaction. Replication is concentrated at the lowest levels of the organizational hierarchy, while environmental interaction wanders up and down this hierarchy. What Eldredge and Grene (1992) have done is to dismantle the single organizational hierarchy and restructure it in terms of two hierarchies. This restructuring is consonant with Grene's emphasis on two species concepts—one genealogical and one "typological." The genealogical concept clearly belongs in the genealogical hierarchy, but the placement of the typological species concept is more problematic. It does not seem to fit so easily into the ecological hierarchy. However, the question remains whether or not a second typological concept is necessary for knowledge of the living world. People do stereotype, but is stereotyping necessary for knowledge?

If Grene is right about the need for stereotyping, then those of us who try to teach evolutionary theory are in real trouble. Our students will come into class viewing species typologically, and on the basis of this typological concept, we must teach them evolutionary theory, trying to get our students to understand species as the things that evolve. This is a tall order. But if the stereotyping implicit in the typological species concept really is necessary for us to become aware of the living world (it's in our genes), then we will have to fill this tall order year after year into the indefinite future. I find this prospect depressing.

Although Grene (1961b:195) was aware that in insisting upon "trueness to type" as necessary for our understanding the living world put her at odds with the "authority of the biological profession," she was unwavering in her support of this principle. In a recent essay concerning the history of science studies as applied to biology, I (Hull 2000) warn my fellow workers that getting involved intimately in biology is highly desirable but that it carries with it the danger of becoming little more than a biology groupie or camp follower. From the first, Grene was willing to stand up to some of the most powerful biologists of her day, criticizing the weaknesses that she found in their work. In her later publications, Grene actually joined in the ongoing process of biology, but she need not worry about ever being characterized as a groupie or camp follower. Her independence of intellect and spirit prohibit such a possibility (for a brief history of Grene's life, see Hull 1997).

DAVID L. HULL

DEPARTMENT OF PHILOSOPHY
NORTHWESTERN UNIVERSITY
AUGUST 2000

NOTES

1. In one place, Grene (1958:123) asserts that the appearance of a new type momentarily withdraws the new taxon from the confining influence of selection. Several of her critics are more than puzzled by this claim (Bock and von Wahlert 1963, Van Valen 1963). However, nothing much rides on this issue.

2. One objection that Grene (1971:18, 1987:506) raises to reductionism is the inability to reduce information to its constituent elements alone. Here I find myself in agreement with Grene. Information is absolutely central to our understanding the living world, and yet to date no analysis of information can distinguish between structure as such (that is, the structure of the paper that this article is printed on) and a narrower notion of structure (that is, the meaning incorporated in the little black squiggles on the paper).

3. Throughout her career, Grene has selected a series of scholars, mostly European, whose work she has tried to make more widely understood in the English-speaking world with mixed results; that is, M. Merleau-Ponty, H. Plessner, M. Polanyi, and A. Portmann.

REFERENCES

Bock, W. J., and G. von Wahlert. 1963. "Two Evolutionary Theories: A Discussion." *British Journal for the Philosophy of Science* 13:140–46.

Crick, F. 1966. *Of Molecules and Men*. Seattle: University of Washington Press.

Dawkins, R. 1976. *The Selfish Gene*. Oxford: Oxford University Press.

Eldredge, N., and S. J. Gould. 1972. "Punctuated Equilibria: An Alternative to Phyletic Gradualism." In *Models in Paleobiology*, ed. T. J. M. Schopf, pp. 82–115. San Francisco: Freeman, Cooper and Company.

Eldredge, N., and M. Grene. 1992. *Interactions: The Biological Context of Social Systems*. New York: Columbia University Press.

Endler, J. A. 1986. *Natural Selection in the Wild*. Princeton: Princeton University Press.

Ghiselin, M. 1974. "A Radical Solution to the Species Problem." *Systematic Zoology* 23:536–544.

Goodwin, B. C. 1988. "Morphogenesis and Heredity." In *Evolutionary Processes and Metaphors*, ed. M. W. Ho and S. W. Fox, pp. 145–62. New York: Wiley.

Gould, S. J. 1980. "Is a New and General Theory of Evolution Emerging?" *Paleobiology* 6:119–30.

Grene, M. 1958. "Two Evolutionary Theories." *British Journal for the Philosophy of Science* 9:110–27 and 185–93.

———. 1959. "The Faith of Darwinism." *Encounter* 13:48–56.

———. 1961a. "Statistics and Selection." *British Journal for the Philosophy of Science* 12:25–42.

———. 1961b. "The Logic of Biology." In *The Logic of Personal Knowledge: Essays Presented to Michael Polanyi on His Seventieth Birthday, 11 March 1961*, pp. 191–205. London: Routledge and Kegan Paul.

———. 1963a. "Two Evolutionary Theories: A Reply." *British Journal for the Philosophy of Science* 14:152–54.

———. 1963b. *A Portrait of Aristotle*. London: Faber and Faber Ltd.

———. 1969. "Bohm's Metaphysics and Biology." In *Towards a Theoretical Biology*, vol. II, ed. C. D. Waddington, pp. 61–71. Edinburgh: Edinburgh University Press.

———. 1971. "Reducibility: Another Side Issue?" In *Interpretations of Life and Mind: Essays Around the Problem of Reduction*, ed. M. Grene, pp. 14–37. New York: Humanities Press.

———. 1974. *The Understanding of Nature: Essays in the Philosophy of Biology*. Dordrecht, Holland: D. Reidel.

———. 1981. "Changing Concepts of Darwinian Evolution." *The Monist* 64:195–213.

———. 1987. "Hierarchies in Biology." *American Scientist* 74:504–10.

———. 1989a. "Interaction and Evolution." In *What Philosophy of Biology Is: Essays Dedicated to David Hull*, ed. M. Ruse, pp. 67–73. Dordrecht: Kluwer Academic Press.

———. 1989b. "A Defense of David Kitts." *Biology and Philosophy* 4:69–72.

———. 1990a. "Is Evolution at a Crossroads?" *Evolutionary Biology* 24:51–82.

———. 1990b. "Evolution, Typology and Population Thinking." *American Philosophical Quarterly* 27:237–44.

———. 1997. "Current Issues in the Philosophy of Biology." *Perspectives on Science* 5:255–81.

Griesemer, J. 1998. "The Case for Epigenetic Inheritance in Evolution." *Journal of Evolutionary Biology* 11:193–200.

Griffiths, P. E., and R. D. Gray. 1994. "Developmental Systems and Evolutionary Explanations." *Journal of Philosophy* 91:277–304.

Himmelfarb, G. 1959. *Darwin and the Darwinian Revolution*. Garden City: Doubleday.

Hull, D. L. 1964. "The Logic of Phylogenetic Taxonomy." Unpublished dissertation, Indiana University.

———. 1972. "Reduction in Genetics—Biology or Philosophy?" *Philosophy of Science* 39:491–99.

———. 1976. "Are Species Really Individuals?" *Systematic Zoology* 25:174–91.

———. 1983. "Exemplars and Scientific Change." *Philosophy of Science Association 1982*, vol. 2, ed. P. D. Asquith and T. Nickles, pp. 479–503. East Lansing, Mich.: Philosophy of Science Association.

———. 1985. "Darwinism as an Historical Entity: A Historiographic Proposal." In *The Darwinian Heritage*, ed. D. Kohn, pp. 773–812. Princeton: Princeton University Press.

———. 1997. "Review of M. Grene, A Philosophical Testament (1995)." *Philosophy of Science* 64:187–88.

———. 2000. "The Professionalization of Science Studies: Cutting Some Slack." *Biology and Philosophy* 15: 61–91.

Huxley, A. 1981. "Anniversary Address of the President." Supplement to *Royal Society News*, no. 12 (November 1981): i–vii.

Jablonka, E., and M. Lambe. 1995. *Epigenetic Inheritance and Evolution*. Oxford:

Oxford University Press.

Lewontin, R. 1977. "Sociobiology: A Caricature of Darwinism." In *Philosophy of Science Association 1976*, ed. P. Suppe and P. Asquith, vol. 2, pp. 22–31. East Lansing, Mich.: Philosophy of Science Association.

Mayr, E. 1983. "Comments on David Hull's Paper on Exemplars and Type Specimens." In *Philosophy of Science Association 1982*, ed. P. Asquith and T. Nickles, vol. 1, pp. 504–11. East Lansing, Mich.: Philosophy of Science Association.

Nagel, E. 1961. *The Structure of Science*. New York: Harcourt, Brace and World.

Oyama, S. 1985. *The Ontogeny of Information*. Cambridge: Cambridge University Press.

Robson, G. C., and O. W. Richards. 1936. *The Variations of Animals in Nature*. London: Longmans Green.

Stebbins, G. L., and F. J. Ayala. 1981. "Is a New Evolutionary Synthesis Necessary?" *Science* 213:967–71.

Van Valen, L. 1963. "On Evolutionary Theories." *British Journal for the Philosophy of Science* 13:146–52.

REPLY TO DAVID L. HULL

David Hull has read very carefully through a great deal of the—partly very bad—work I have published in the philosophy of biology over the past more than forty years. As his account makes clear, I write too much too hastily: a remark that can probably be applied to what I am writing at this moment. So be it; at ninety-one, although I hope I can still keep learning, I am unlikely to undergo a thorough change of character.

In terms of Hull's favorite conceptual distinction, as a matter of fact, however, I don't know what that would mean. He appears to see the world as divided into "universals" or "essences" that exhibit no change over time, but are eternally one and the same, and "historical entities" that come into being, change over time and pass away, but can be characterized only in terms of their temporal sequence—just one darned thing after another. Everything is either a class, a "universal" with an unchanging "essence," or an individual, a particular, natureless this. Hull has championed this ontological dichotomy ever since he adopted Michael Ghiselin's "radical solution to the species problem," which forbids us to say that organism A is a member of species S, but insists instead that A is part of S.[1] S is not, as we have foolishly thought, a natural kind, but simply a link in the sequence of evolutionary history, not even full of sound and fury, just signifying nothing. The same holds for ourselves, of course: among other things there aren't, according to Hull, there is no human nature, any more than there is my nature or yours.[2] There is only the individual *Homo sapiens*, of which I am one piece and you are another, just as this is my left hand and this is my right. Of course, Hull agrees, there are universals: for instance, there are predators and there are other things that are prey. So although there is no species, Lion, whose members chase antelopes, and no species Antelope (or Eland, or whatever), whose members run away from lions, there is Lion, pieces of which are running after pieces of Antelope which are trying hard to get away, the former being characterized by the universal predator, and the latter by the universal prey. Hull has published a collection of his essays—without which the philosophy of biology would certainly be gravely impoverished—under the title *The Metaphysics of Evolution*.[3] At bottom, I'm afraid, his metaphysics, not only of evolution, is utterly beyond my understanding. So, although in the present essay, he is treating my views with courtesy and something even close to tolerance, for which I am duly grateful, we are nevertheless talking at cross-purposes. Whatever I say in reply, he will find perversely essentialistic and whatever he says I am bound to find naïve and irrelevant.

This is no new misunderstanding. As I remarked in the autobiographical essay that opens the present volume, I have duly wrestled with this problem, and had difficulties with it in my work with Niles Eldredge, whom Hull had firmly convinced of the new gospel. But why? There are a great many classes that develop. Think of the central character in H. G. Wells's *Tono Bungay*, whose truthfulness is doubted by his mother's employers because he belongs to the servant class. Such a class surely does not exist nowadays, even in England, but it did. It had originated and it had its history and, we hope, it no long exists. Every regiment, every club is, while it exists, a class with members, but begins and changes (its membership and even its rules) and some time stops existing. There is no reason in logic, metaphysics, epistemology, or evolutionary theory why that should not be the case. Hull says we should change our intuitions—sure; we know the sun doesn't really set behind the horizon. But in this case, what do we gain by really believing (if we could), there's a piece of dog chasing a piece of cat?

In a rich and thought-provoking collection of essays edited by Robert Wilson, David Hull himself surveys the bewildering range of current "solutions" to the species problem, and concludes by recording his confidence that the Ghiselin-Hull "species are individuals" thesis will ultimately prevail.[4] Clearly, my hope is that it will not. A number of the essays in the Wilson collection support that hope, notably, for example, those of Richard Boyd, of Paul Griffiths, and of Wilson himself.[5] De Queiroz's "general lineage" position seems to offer an "individuality" view less radical than Hull's, accommodating within its scope most of the other phylogenetic or evolutionary conceptions currently available.[6] This is not the place to go into these debates; I may just remark that the discussions I have mentioned lend support to my skepticism.

Despite our reciprocal misunderstanding, however, I shall try to comment on some passages in Hull's essay. But first I must make one point about his dichotomy as applied to its original target: the nature (only it isn't a nature!) of species. If species are simply links in a genealogical chain, and if, as many biologists believe, life is monophyletic, then there is really only one species, life itself, or life on this planet. Cuts in the chain are wholly arbitrary. Hull has admitted this to me in conversation. So with all the paradoxes his basic distinction raises, I really don't see what good it does. Again, I refer the reader to Wilson's collection, and to the extensive literature there itemized, for ample indication that the "radical solution" is not yet final.

Let me try now, at last, to respond to some of the particular remarks in Hull's essay.

"By the early 1970s," he says, "Grene came to appreciate evolutionary biology." I would have said "came to appreciate the then current evolutionary biology." I have confessed to having been abysmally ignorant of the details of the synthesis when I began commenting on some of its classic texts, and I have since recognized that what I was objecting to was some features of what Gould has called the "hardened synthesis"—though I still believe my criticisms of Fisher were valid; perhaps he was "hardened" at the start, or better, self-deceptive and deceptively ambiguous. But, as I have noted elsewhere, I was brought up on a belief in evolution, and was educated via an old-fashioned version of evolutionary theory.

It seems I believe each species has a unique "form" and these forms are "universals." That is just one expression of the dichotomy I don't find myself accepting. The same problem arises in the question with which Hull closes that paragraph: "How about conceptual systems such as those of Aristotle, Darwin, and Grene? In order for us to understand them, must they also be characterized by certain unchanging tenets? Must they have essences? Or are they better interpreted as historical entities, changing through time?" I don't find myself with a "conceptual system," and it is difficult with the evidence available to know how Aristotle's system developed, though I believe the best scholars currently believe it did. Darwin's views certainly developed, as did those of his adherents, and here Hull has applied his own "conceptual system" rigorously enough to argue that for that very reason there is no Darwinian view, no "Darwinism," just a word (mis)applied to a series of statements by a series of people.[7] Despite this, he did contribute to *The Darwinian Heritage*, in effect denying its existence, even more radically than Peter Bowler has done in such works as his *Non-Darwinian Revolution*.[8] How can a historian as careful as Hull hold such an extreme, even self-contradictory position?

When it comes to my earliest paper in the field, "Two Evolutionary Theories," it is certainly not the case that I was "primarily interested in the role of types in knowledge acquisition." I was interested in the various kinds of sources of scientific disagreement, for example, at a visual as distinct from a conceptual level. I don't see what this has to do with types. And although I found dishonesty in Simpson's acceptance of "adaptive types" despite his denial of the existence of any types, I do not believe I supported Schindewolf's saltationism; I was not, and am not, in the business of deciding scientists' controversies for them. I was only trying to analyze one.

As to "The Faith of Darwinism," as I admitted in my autobiographical essay in the present volume, it is a production of which I am thoroughly ashamed. Alas, I included it in my book *The Knower and the Known*, and along with the teleology chapter, I wish I could disclaim it. Himmelfarb was a bad historian and I was a fool to take her seriously. I have no excuse, but perhaps a partial explanation is that I was following Michael Polanyi's request that I pursue heresies in evolutionary theory, and I knew too little about current orthodoxy to criticize it intelligently.

What Hull says about my work on Aristotle takes us back to our basic disagreement. He seems to think that because I believe a philosopher's work has to have enough coherence to make it intelligible, I think it has one of those immutable "essences." And then he quotes my description of Aristotle's view of natural kinds as if I accepted it. In the collection Hull refers to, *The Understanding of Nature*, I included an essay, "Aristotle and Modern Biology," in which I tried to make clear what I thought Aristotle could, and could not, teach us when we reflect on the character of the biological sciences. I thought I had made it quite plain that I am not an Aristotelian and, indeed, could not understand how anyone nowadays could be so. (I have also quoted this essay in my autobiographical sketch in this volume.) Incidentally, anyone who studies later Aristotelians knows there is no "essence" of being one, although there are recognizable differences between those who are and are not.

Further, in Hull's account of our confrontation, I don't see that I am trying to keep philosophy pure. It seems to me it is the practice of biology that is compromised by Hull's over-simple dichotomy. I am especially puzzled by his insistence that population thinking demands the stress on species as individuals. It is important for modern evolutionary biology to understand that it is not individuals that evolve, but populations. For Hull, then, populations too must be individuals: they have, he says, "population structure." In the history of evolutionary biology, however—I would even venture to say, in the history of Darwinism, or in the Darwinian tradition— there is a very significant shift from Darwin's exclusive attention to slight changes in the characters of individual organisms to a statistical approach to population structure: first with Galton, then the biometricians, and finally with the synthesis with Mendelism and the rise of population genetics.[9] It is precisely the fact that they are not individuals that makes populations so important. It is historically important, if ironic, to recognize that Darwin himself was not, strictly speaking, a population thinker. And please, David, I am not saying there is an "essence" of population thinking, only that there has been an interesting change in the conceptual structure of what is still recognizable as a Darwinian tradition.

In the light of his universal dichotomy, Hull has to hold that I accept two different species concepts, one typological and one historical. This is not the case. Not that I hope to tell taxonomists what species concept they should adopt, but insofar as I have my own inclinations, as I have already said, I sympathize with some of the suggestions described in Robert Wilson's collection, as well as with some features of some of the phylogenetic or evolutionary concepts that have been put forward. I don't see why I have to be caught between eternal non-entities on the one hand and a meaningless this-after-that on the other.

Finally, Hull considers that, despite my work with Polanyi (which was hardly "early"), I remained in my approach to philosophy of science under the spell of logical positivism. As, again, I have mentioned elsewhere, I became disillusioned with that philosophy in 1938, and my interest in Polanyi's work (starting in 1950) grew partly out of that disillusionment. If I called a 1961 paper "The Logic of Biology," this happened because, as Dr. Crowley of the Belfast Scholastic Philosophy Department pointed out to me, I was using the term "logic" in an unsuitably sloppy way. I have tried since then to avoid that usage. I did, as I have also confessed elsewhere, still have to teach in "logical empiricist" terms, because that was what one did in those days. But if my early assessments of Darwinian theory were ignorant and misguided, they were anything but positivistic. So as usual, David, we agree to disagree. It has been a friendly disagreement and I trust will continue to be so.

M. G.

NOTES

1. David L. Hull, "Are Species Really Individuals?" *Systematic Zoology* 25 (1976): 174–91.

2. David L. Hull, "On Human Nature," in *The Philosophy of Biology*, ed. David L. Hull and Michael Ruse (Oxford and New York: Oxford University Press, 1998), pp. 383–97. First published in *Philosophy of Science Association* 1986: ii. 3–13.

3. David L. Hull, *The Metaphysics of Evolution* (Albany: State University of New York Press, 1989).

4. David L. Hull, "On the Plurality of Species: Questioning the Party Line," in *Species: New Interdisciplinary Essays*, ed. R. A. Wilson (Cambridge, Mass.: M.I.T. Press, 1999), pp. 23–48.

5. R. Boyd, "Homeostasis, Species, and Higher Taxa," in Wilson, *Species*, pp. 141–85. R. A. Wilson, "Realism, Essence, and Kind: Resuscitating Species Essentialism," in Wilson, *Species*, pp. 187–208.

6. K. De Quieroz, "The General Lineage Concept of Species and the Defining Properties of the Species Category," in Wilson, *Species*, pp. 49–89.

7. David L. Hull, "Darwinism as an Historical Entity: A Historiographic Proposal," in *The Darwinian Heritage*, ed. David Kohn (Princeton, N. J.: Princeton University Press, 1985), pp. 773–812.

8. Peter J. Bowler, *The Non-Darwinian Revolution: Reinterpreting a Historical Myth* (Baltimore: Johns Hopkins University Press, 1988).

9. See J. Gayon, *Darwinism's Struggle for Survival: Heredity and the Hypothesis of Natural Selection* (Cambridge: Cambridge University Press, 1998).

11

David J. Depew

PHILOSOPHICAL NATURALISM WITHOUT NATURALIZED PHILOSOPHY: ARISTOTELIAN AND DARWINIAN THEMES IN MARJORIE GRENE'S PHILOSOPHY OF BIOLOGY

I. INTRODUCTION

Among the pioneers of the now flourishing field of philosophy of biology, Marjorie Grene has always occupied a place of honor. She was, I believe, the first philosopher to attempt to unravel the conceptual structure of Darwinian theory, publishing papers on this tangled, and still contested, subject as early as 1958. In this connection, Grene was among the earliest champions of the view that evolutionary biology cannot be reduced either substantively or methodologically to more basic sciences. About other issues her stance has been even more iconoclastic. She has, for example, consistently and unequivocally denied that philosophy's own problems—metaphysical, epistemological, ethical—have been or ever will be solved or dissolved by what evolutionary biology, or any other science, can tell us. She denies, that is to say, that selection fully explains our cognitive abilities and achievements ("evolutionary philosophy of mind"), or the structure and content of our knowledge ("evolutionary epistemology"), or our sense of responsibility ("evolutionary ethics"). Since not every philosopher of biology, perhaps not even the majority, agrees with this refusal to deploy evolutionary biology in the service of "naturalized" philosophy (according to which its questions are continuous with, and open to resolution by, empirical science) it seems useful to try to set out at least some of her reasons for remaining so confident about this important matter. The topic is especially inviting because Grene's views depend as much on how she interprets evolutionary biology itself as on what she takes philosophical thinking to require.

To be permitted to frame this issue is for me a distinct honor. My first encounter with Marjorie was as a graduate student at the University of California at San Diego. Having read *A Portrait of Aristotle* and a few of her other works, I had been mulling over the idea of transferring to the University of California at Davis to study philosophy of biology with her. That I did not follow through on this idea was due to personal consider-ations. I was not unaffected, however, by the fact that sometime during this period Marjorie descended upon UCSD to give a lecture (on Sartre, as I recall). In discussion, she made such mincemeat of my teachers that, once the *Schadenfreude* every graduate student must feel on such an occasion had worn off, I got a case of cold feet. If she could so reduce them, surely I would fare no better.

Nonetheless, my desire to study with Marjorie remained alive. Luckily, a few years later I got a chance to do so. In 1982, I was admitted to a Summer Institute for Philosophy of Biology which, under the auspices of the NEH and the Council for Philosophical Studies, had been organized by Marjorie and Richard Burian. Marjorie and Dick were able to assemble an accomplished array of philosophers and biologists, both as lecturers and participants, and to do so just when debate was intensifying about whether the Modern Evolutionary Synthesis (of genetics and natural selection) itself, as well as philosophical frameworks for analyzing it, stood in need of revision or replacement. Accordingly, this Institute became something of a catalyst in the constitution of philosophy of biology as a field. Whatever mentoring I have had since then has largely been due to Marjorie. It has been done with such a light, yet persistent touch (despite a few bawlings out) that I find myself considerably in her debt. Her thinking well enough of me to educate me has been just about the best professional compliment I've ever been paid.

II. NATURALISMS WORTH HAVING AND NOT WORTH HAVING

It is certainly possible to resist naturalizing philosophical questions while at the same time professing to be a philosophical naturalist. That is, in fact, Grene's stance. In order to put her qualms about naturalized philosophy in their proper light, accordingly, it will help first to clarify the sense in which she is a philosophical naturalist.

To be sure, Grene wholeheartedly approves of naturalists in the original sense of "natural historians." She gives us to understand, for example, that Aristotle's experiences as a "muddy boots" biologist helped shape his distinctive stance toward epistemological and ontological questions.[1] She also suggests that contemporary philosophy can benefit from biocentrism of this sort. In contrast to physicists, for whom the stretch between data and theory is a long one indeed, practicing biologists are immersed by the very nature of their work in the natural world in a way that supercharges their perceptions, elicits good habits of judgment about the relation between general and particular, and makes it psychologically difficult for them to be anything other than realists in interpreting what they study.

Many of Grene's salient themes come into focus in this connection. There is, in the first place, her stress on "the primacy of perception," discerned clearly in Aristotle, then in Darwin and other naturalists, and articulated into an account of knowledge by Grene herself under inspiration from writers as diverse as Michael Polanyi, Maurice Merleau-Ponty, and J. J. and Eleanor Gibson. Second, there is her positing of a sort of direct scientific realism founded in perceptual experience, which obviates the need to ground theories in reality by way of inferences to the best explanation (usually mediated by mathematics) from disaggregated data points.[2] Finally, there is the sense that, while Heidegger may have been right to insist that humans have a world, he was wrong (and regressively Cartesian in spite of himself) to deprive animals of theirs. Indeed, we humans have our world precisely in virtue of the fact that we are animals of a certain sort—animals whose ecological niche, and hence nature, is cultural, and whose way of life, in consequence, lies at one end of a spectrum between "rigidly programmed" behavior and "qualified freedom."[3]

As these themes suggest, Grene is a naturalistic philosopher not only in the sense of respecting the standpoint of practicing natural historians, but also in the sense that rules out supernatural, or vitalistic, explanations of natural facts. "The brief flurries of religiosity I have gone through, and come out of, in my long life," she writes in *A Philosophical Testament*, "were very thin and metaphorical. Certainly no creation story ever competed for a moment, in my mind, with the infinitely more plausible story of evolution."[4] Creationists are better dismissed out of hand than argued with.

Grene is decidedly not naturalistic, however, in a third sense that has become widespread among American philosophers since W. V. O. Quine spoke of "epistemology naturalized."[5] On this view, philosophy's issues are treated as continuous with, because potentially resolvable by, scientific theories (by reduction, replacement, elimination, or something else). Many professional philosophers of biology, as I have said, subscribe to naturalism in this sense. Marjorie Grene does not.

Grene's spurning of naturalized philosophy does not spring from a conviction that conceptual issues can be cleanly distinguished from empirical ones. Philosophical problems are not *merely* conceptual, and *a fortiori* not merely linguistic, puzzles.[6] Nor does her resistance rest on disputing Quine's characteristic claim that theories are underdetermined by facts. Theories may well be underdetermined by aggregates of data. But answers to philosophical problems are not hostages to theories in this sense. In saying this, Grene does not mean to imply that philosophy can go its merry way without paying attention to developments in science. For one thing, this view is impossible and, insofar as it encourages self-deception, unphilosophical. "[P]hilosophical reflection," she writes, "since it is situated, like every human activity, within the human world, is also influenced by the outcome of scientific research."[7] Grene grants that the fact of evolution is a necessary, though it is far from a sufficient, condition for grounding and assessing the scope of our cognitive powers and achievements. By telling us, for example, that live creatures must, on pain of extinction, orient themselves to a real environment by responding to arrays of information that are features of that environment itself, rather than of our minds only, evolutionary biology can free us from the Cartesian and Lockian distortions that have made it so difficult, during the entire period of modern philosophy, to answer philosophy's questions. Nonetheless, for Grene philosophy's questions are *philosophy's* questions. "Scientists can't tell us how to solve our [philosophers'] problems—which are always (almost always?) meta-problems"[8]—problems that may well be raised to a pitch by scientific knowledge, and are most certainly constrained by it, but are not reducible to it. Accordingly, in asserting that "[e]pistemology has not been naturalized, whether by physics or psychology; the mind-body problem has not been solved, whether by neurophysiology or by linguistics," Grene is expressing her conviction that they never will be.[9] Similarly, she asserts that, while evolutionary knowledge can "set conditions for our ethical speculations, . . . in itself [evolution] neither raises nor answers ethical questions."[10]

We arrive, then, at a picture like the following: Informed by the robust notions of perception and knowledge that good natural history both requires and fosters, we accede smoothly, almost intuitively, and without much sense of existential loss, to naturalism in the sense that rules out explanatory appeal to transcendent entities. We can and should do so, moreover, in a way that avoids modeling epistemological and other philosophical questions on scientific ones, and *a fortiori* avoids reducing these questions to fit scientific theories.

We may well ask what Grene's reasons are for declining to move, by way of philosophical naturalism, from natural history to naturalized philosophy. Her answer, roughly put, is that the stance of natural history and naturalism in the sense that rules out explanation of natural facts in terms of transcendent entities is sufficient for resolving basic philosophical problems. It does not depend, therefore, on scientific theories or models in the strict, methodological, mathematized sense. Philosophical issues will undoubtedly be taken up anew in each generation in the light of new scientific knowledge and shifts in cultural presumptions. But that fact casts no skeptical shadow over the possibility of philosophy itself. Nor does it allow that philosophical questions are in any way liable to being eliminated by scientific knowledge.

These are large, interesting, and even reassuring doctrines. To spell them out in any detail, however, as well as to assess them, requires working critically through Grene's interpretations of particular thinkers, especially Aristotle and Darwin. For Grene's stress on the embeddedness of organisms within the cultural environments to which they are adapted suggests to her that human animals think best when they acknowledge (as Descartes did not) their own embeddedness in an historically conditioned intellectual milieu. Present thinkers try to assess where they are and where to go next by engaging in dialogue with thinkers who were, in their own time, adept in doing precisely that.[11]

III. THE LEGACY OF ARISTOTLE

To me, the first pillar of Grene's philosophy is her conviction that the *very idea of an organism* requires a close bond between agency and embeddedness in a natural environment that demands metabolic, perceptual, and cognitive responsiveness. Grene claims that beings that can do this *must* be constituted in such a way that a higher level of organization, at which interactions with the environment are exerted, is *necessarily* served by lower-level processes in which materials are worked up and broken down.[12] The fact that organisms are, and are known to be, two-level affairs is both fundamental and, for Grene, grounded in perception itself. One need not be a rocket scientist, or even a biologist, to *observe* it. (If you are the former, you might not observe it at all.)

Grene's conception of organisms as necessarily structured into multiple levels, and her confidence that perception itself tells us so, is to some extent a legacy of her close encounter with Aristotle, which by her own account began about 1960.[13] With its three levels of metabolism, sensation, and (problematically) cognition, Aristotle's functional theory of soul (*psyche*) underlies his insistence that organisms cannot be experienced except as substances whose formal patterning remains the same over a great many material changes, changes in which the organism itself is the primary causal agent. Accordingly, Aristotle's theory of matter and form, particularly when it is viewed as a diachronic relation of potency (*dynamis*) to act (*energeia*), reveals a thinker for whom "*living* nature is made the focal point of philosophical reflection" (for the first, and for centuries the only, time).[14] Remove the empirical grounding in reflective observation of life-processes from conceptual distinctions such as form-matter and potency-act and one gets mere metaphysical wheel-spinning.[15] Remove the tie between development and differentiation, for example, and the potency-act distinction becomes vulnerable to quibblings about "dormitive virtue." Similarly, the concept of teleological explanation, which was designed to explain the acquisition of biological form by embryos,[16] is cut loose from its moorings when its biological background is forsaken. The consequences of the separation of philosophical categories from their biological roots are, moreover, of the utmost importance. It was by removing soul from its functional role in organic formation, growth, and maintenance that Descartes was encouraged to envision his "beast machine." In consequence, even Kant, for all his greatness, was prone to take far too seriously the possibility that organisms might in principle be reduced to the working of physical laws, even if we mere mortals cannot do it.[17] Needless to say, the problem of reductionism has haunted biology ever since.

Marjorie Grene is not, of course, the first historian of philosophy to point to the biocentric nature of Aristotle's philosophizing as the source of what is most insightful about his epistemology and metaphysics. Naturalistic Aristotelianism was common, in fact, among American philosophers in the decades before she started writing (though much of this earlier work seems not to have had much influence on her). What divided philosophers such as John Dewey from his Columbia colleague Frederick A. Woodbridge, for example, was not Aristotle's biocentrism, but whether following Aristotle's lead in treating biological questions as propaedeutic to philosophizing results in pragmatism or realism. The issue was not, in my view, happily resolved. Woodbridge affirmed realism, but only by disconnecting Aristotle's metaphysics and epistemology from anything stronger than mere respect for biology. By contrast, Dewey's pragmatized Aristotelianism (which is on display in John Herman Randall's *Aristotle*) affirmed the functional role of mind in guiding organic behavior. Dewey concluded, however, that in consequence of this fact philosophical questions must themselves be pragmatized and, to that extent, naturalized in the sense taken up by Quine. (There is, by Quine's own account, a more or less direct line from classical pragmatism to naturalized epistemology.[18])

As she remarks in her "Intellectual Autobiography" (and I have found out at my peril), Grene strongly resists pragmatism—as she resists anything that comes down the Hegelian pike.[19] This does not mean, however, that she retreats to a position like Woodbridge's. Rather, *A Portrait of Aristotle* demonstrates that taking Aristotle's biocentrism seriously results in the formulation of concepts and categories that can lead (as Aristotle himself thought they did) to the proper formulation and resolution of philosophical questions, instead of their mere evaporation, and can do so within a framework that is genuinely realistic. This possibility constantly pulls me back from following my pragmatic impulses.

Aristotle's philosophy of biology is closely associated not only with the notion that organisms are two-level affairs, but with at least three other related claims. One is that organisms are what Grene calls "this-suches," that is, individuals which are essentially instances (or perhaps members) of natural kinds, namely species. Another is that species-form (*eidos*)—the universal that is the same in all humans, for example—is what forms the matter of an individual into a member of that natural kind. Finally, there is the suggestion that species-forms themselves fall within genera in something approaching the modern taxonomic sense.

Since *A Portrait of Aristotle* first appeared, a good deal of first-rate scholarship has been done on Aristotle's biological works and their implications for his philosophy of mind, epistemology, and metaphysics.[20] Much of this work sustains Grene's views about Aristotle's commitment to the first two of the interpretive claims just mentioned. Aristotle does indeed think that organisms are two-level, form-matter set-ups, and that the formal patterns in question, once acquired, perpetuate themselves not only throughout an individual "this-such's" own life-time, but are passed on reproductively to descendent members of the relevant "such." On the other hand, much of this scholarship calls into question whether Aristotle himself—as distinct from a long tradition of scholarship and interpretation which from the start has been compromised by neo-Platonizing inclinations—ever asserted that *species* form is what confers substantial identity on individual organisms, or that terms like *eidos* ("species") or *genos* ("genus") mark off taxonomic ranks. It is worth asking whether Grene ascribes either of these two claims to Aristotle, and, if she does, whether, in the end, she is right to do so.

It is certainly the case that Aristotle does not hold a taxonomic view of the *eidos-genos* ("species-genus") distinction. Nor does Grene ever say he does. Even before David Balme's close study of Aristotle's *History of Animals* had shown that Aristotle does not use the *eidos-genos* pair to mark off species and genera as taxonomic ranks,[21] Grene had stated in *A Portrait of Aristotle*, "It is mistaken ... to interpret Aristotle as a hesitant and partial forerunner of Linnaeus or other great classifiers. ... [O]verall classification was not Aristotle's primary concern."[22] In subsequent writings, Grene has supported Balme's argument that Aristotle uses the *genos-eidos* distinction primarily to indicate diversity with respect to a given *characteristic* or trait at any number of what *we* would recognize as taxonomic levels. She was also aware from the outset that these great kinds (*gene*), such as bird, do not relate to lesser kinds, such as sparrows or swallows, in the way that systematic taxonomy requires. The properties Aristotle uses to define (in the sense of "mark off," *horizein*) each lesser *genos* (what we call "species") within a greater *genos* are, for one thing, multiple, not (as the later Plato hypothesized) single *differentiae*. More importantly, when Aristotle speaks of eight or nine great kinds he calmly allows some lesser kinds—the so-called "dualizers"—to fall within, or between, two greater genera, while others fail to fall within any. He nowhere exhibits any desire to fill in the taxonomic ranks, as it were, in order to place each species unambiguously within a given pigeon hole. This is simply not a taxonomic scheme in the Linnaean sense at all.

In the manner of taxonomy, then, Marjorie Grene has been on the side favored by scholarship. It is somewhat otherwise, however, when it comes to her attitude toward the issue of whether species-form forms matter into substantial individuals. She affirms it, while a formidable array of other scholars, including Balme, have denied it. Individual organisms are unquestionably paradigms of natural substances for Aristotle.[23] Balme and others have argued, however, that organisms are substantial "thises" for two reasons, one biological, the other metaphysical, and that these reasons conspire to call into question the traditional role of universal species-form as conferring substantiality on them.[24] The biological reason is that in *On the Generation of Animals* IV ontogeny is portrayed as a replication (more or less complete) of the entire structure of one's male parent rather than of a general species-form. This claim seems to be connected to a metaphysical view in which organisms, considered as substances, are more highly integrated, more individuated, more formal and less material, as it were, than mere matter-form compounds, or indeed than anything that could be constructed *de novo* by adding appropriate matter to a formal recipe. Artifacts, for example, are matter-form compounds, but are not substances. Their efficient and final causes lie outside themselves in their maker's purposes and technical actions; and their material element remains to some extent untransformed, as Antiphon's famous bed continued to sprout leaves. Organisms, however, are not like that. They are agents of their own making and more-making. Some of them, namely animals, are also agents in the sense that they use information detected in their environments to guide the satisfaction of their desires. In all animate substances, moreover, form penetrates matter so thoroughly that the proximate matter of living things is *organic* matter—matter that has been worked up by the growing organism itself precisely to realize, sustain, and pass on its form. Such beings cannot come into existence except as members of an endless chain of reproduction that at every point strives toward copying the male parent. In consequence, what is begotten is not made; what is *genitum* is *non factum*.

Recognizing this difference, some scholars, including Balme, have attempted to find sub-specific forms—individual (parental) forms—in Aristotle's ontology that can do the work of informing offspring. What happens to species-form as a consequence varies from author to author.[25] Nonetheless, virtually all interpreters who take this line are aware that in doing so they are making it difficult for Aristotle consistently to hold that we have scientific knowledge of organisms. For scientific knowledge, Aristotle plainly says, is of the universal, not the particular.[26]

Balme (though not every friend of individual forms) tries to get around this problem by asserting that our knowledge of universals (such as *anthropos*) is merely an empirical summary of similarities which arise inductively and *a posteriori* in virtue of the contingent, and seldom complete, success of males in passing along their individual forms to their male offspring. Universals, on this view, become reports of what is normal, rather than principles that enter into the substantial composition of organisms. Because of her respect for Balme's scholarship, Grene reports this interpretation as "unsettling," both for her own reading of Aristotle as well as for epistemological doctrines she commends in her own voice.[27] Nonetheless, she has steadfastly continued to buck the tide by reaffirming the interpretation of species-forms as conferring substantial identity on individual organisms that she sponsored in *A Portrait of Aristotle*. "An organism . . . is a this-such," she writes. "How could you study it, 'scientifically,' if it were not representative of its kind?"[28] And again, "If each kind or species of thing had not, once and for all, its being-what-it-is, if we could not define once and for all the peculiar substance of each kind of thing, we should have no stability, no knowledge."[29] If there is to be a contest between the requirements of biological knowledge and the ontology of individual organisms, it seems that Grene is clearly on the side of knowledge.

I think that Grene is right to resist having recourse to individual forms as conferring substantiality on organisms, and even more right to resist Balme's inductivism about our knowledge of universals. This sort of inductive process could not conceivably produce anything Aristotle would count as scientific knowledge (*episteme*). Merely empirical generalizations, no matter how accurate, fall well short of what Aristotle requires for science.[30] There is, moreover, a "normative ingredient" in Aristotle's theory of form that cannot be picked up having recourse to what is merely statistically "normal."[31]

One source of Grene's well-placed confidence on this point is her recognition that for Aristotle induction (*epagoge*) does not mean what it means for standard empiricism. The ascent from particular to universal can arise because universals are already implicit in informed perceptual judgments. "[S]ense perception," she writes, "already contains in rudimentary, or, as the *Physics* puts it, in a vague and general form, the universals which experience will develop and stabilize."[32] It is just this view of perception as progressive clarification and discrimination to which Grene has been led by way of her encounters with Polanyi and Merleau-Ponty. Knowledge is a matter of further articulating what is already there in rich, organically underwritten and action oriented perception itself. It is not a matter of aggregating and manipulating data points, as it is for Balme and many other modern "empiricist" interpreters of Aristotle.

Insisting that disputed points about Aristotle's ontology must be constrained by the need to preserve the possibility of scientific knowledge as Aristotle construed it is a *leitmotiv* of Grene's interpretation of that great biocentric thinker. Nonetheless, I wonder whether her knowledge-preserving conception of species-form as conferring substantial identity on organisms might have been articulated in a way that makes it easier to acknowledge points plausibly made by the friends of individual forms. It does not follow, for example, from the fact that substantial identity comes at the level of specific kinds that what goes on below that level is merely a matter of material indeterminacy or accident, as in the case of Antiphon's bed. On the contrary, just because genuine substantiality means that form goes "all the way down" we can expect further questions to arise about individual differences—about why, for example, offspring within a species variously resemble parents and ancestors. Answers to these questions may well involve appeals to the form of the male parent. Such questions, however, are subordinate to higher-level questions about substantial identity, not replacements for them. That is why Aristotle takes them up in *On the Generation of Animals* IV, a treatise that constitutes a different "inquiry" from what has been established about ontogeny more generally in earlier books.[33]

My way of posing this issue depends on distinguishing rather cleanly between matter-form compounds generally, which include artifacts, and those that are genuine substances. Aristotle says in *Metaphysics Z* that, among embodied beings, only substances are identical with their forms.[34] In the case of living or ensouled substances, this identity occurs at the culminating point in ontogeny, when organic material has been saturated by its species-specific essence. This is also the point at which the *atomon eidos* has been reached because generic matter has been most fully differentiated.[35] In the case of artifacts, which are mere matter-form compounds, this never happens at all. Although Grene does not say that artifacts are substances, we may ask whether it is enough to signal the distinction between substances and a wider class of matter-form compounds simply to report, as she seems at one point to do, that "[t]he thing *considered with respect to form* will be brought into proximity and even identity with its being-what-it-is despite its incarnation" (my italics).[36] Given such a perspectival interpretation, could not artifacts too be said to be identical with their forms? If so, perhaps a stronger interpretation of what it means for a substance to be identical with its form is required.

IV. AN ENCOUNTER WITH DARWIN

I have belabored these issues in Aristotle scholarship because Marjorie Grene's interpretation, as well as her appreciation, of Aristotelian nature has, I will be arguing, played a heuristic role in her interpretation of Darwinian nature. Getting Aristotle right is important in this connection. To defend Aristotle's relevance for contemporary philosophical reflection on living things on the basis of views that Aristotle himself never actually held would be fruitless indeed, if not obscurantist. In the face of the hostility many Darwinians have to all things Aristotelian, as well as of the resistance of some self-proclaimed Aristotelians to modern science, the significance of Aristotle to the central issues in the philosophy of biology is difficult enough to sustain even when it is confined to genuinely Aristotelian themes accurately interpreted.

This observation suggests a number of questions about Grene's interpretation of Darwin—questions made all the more interesting by the circumstance that there seems to have been a time when she did not think that Darwin himself was entirely on the side of the angels. In *Portrait of Aristotle*, Grene wrote:

> The authoritative position of "science" in our culture stems largely from the successes of the exact sciences. Others, be they biologists, sociologists, psychologists, hope to copy the rigour, the power of prediction of the sciences of inanimate nature, and so become more "scientific" in their turn. . . . What a deadly vision of the world. . . . Even evolutionary biology, founded on the kinship of men and animals, has gloried in reducing all alike to the single status of machinery-for-staying-alive. . . . The mysterious multifariousness of living

nature, formerly a massive obstacle to mechanistic thinking, was transformed by Darwin's genius into an indefinite aggregate of random changes mechanically maintained. Life itself became machinery, made by no one for no purpose except barely to survive.[37]

A brief inspection of Grene's subsequent work will show that it did not take long for her to abandon this view. Her ever-growing appreciation of Darwin as a natural historian seems never to have been accompanied, however, by any detectable weakening of her admiration of Aristotle, in spite of considerable differences between the two thinkers. This presents an interesting problem. When combined with her convictions about the keen perceptual judgments of good naturalists and their presumptive right to interpret their results realistically, Grene's approbation of both Aristotle and Darwin might seem to be on a collision course if she were not willing to suggest that both figures observe and correctly judge, if not quite the same things about living nature, then at least compatible or overlapping things. That, in any case, is just what Grene proceeds to claim.

One can effect such a *rapprochement* in either of two ways. One can picture Aristotle as more like Darwin than we have thought or, alternatively, fetch up a Darwin who is more like Aristotle than we had assumed. Balme, for his part, tilts in the first direction when he traces what he concedes is a regrettably "essentialist" element in Aristotle to a contingently incorrect empirical belief that the environment stays sufficiently constant to maintain species as descriptively "the same" in perpetuity.[38] The implication is that, *ceteris paribus*, Aristotle might have become a Darwinian if he had had reason to believe that species come into and go out of existence as individual organisms do.

Grene's reconciliationist impulse is more plausibly to move in the other direction. Her Darwin sees, or can be reconstructed as seeing, that organisms are inherently two-level affairs, in which variation at one level is shaped by adaptive utility working on individuals within populations over trans-generational time. Her Darwin even sees that organisms are "this-suches," even though they are also members of historical lineages. He sees too that these "suches" identify a pattern of activity, a life-style, that "between the origin and extinction of a species remains recognizably 'the same,'" and does so precisely because it uses lower-level processing to keep members of a particular species adaptively tuned, as it were, to a particular niche in the natural economy.[39] Aristotle's stress on a characteristic pattern of activity that helps each species maintain its place in nature is highlighted in this account of Darwin. Darwinian organisms do not remain adapted just because environments are constant, as Balme would have it. On the contrary, they evolve adaptations that allow them to retain their

species-specific life-style—Grene does not hesitate to say their "nature"[40]—by responding to changing environments. To be sure, Aristotle
missed the fact that species come into and drop out of the world. But why,
Grene asks, "just because something does not last forever, should it lack a
nature?"[41]

Grene recognizes, of course, that in Darwin's thinking individual
variation plays a quite different role than it does for Aristotle. For Aristotle,
variation represents either quirky, but adaptively neutral aspects of this or
that organism, such as blue or brown eyes, or material defects that are
inherently harmful to an individual's acquisition of eternal species-specific
forms and, accordingly, to their functioning and flourishing. For Darwin,
on the other hand, individual variations can play a positive role in better
adapting organisms within a given species to a changing environment, and
indeed in evolving new species from protracted bouts of this very process.
Accordingly, Darwin's organisms are, ontologically, more loosely integrated, as it were, than Aristotle's. In Aristotle, form penetrates matter to
such an extent that parts are defined (marked off, or differentiated, in and
through the process of ontogeny) by the precise assistance they lend to
substantial wholes in achieving their functions (*erga*). In Darwin's world,
we have instead what Grene sees as a productive "tension" between
material and formal aspects, efficient and final causes, and the whole and
its parts.[42]

What she means is that a balance is continuously being struck in
Darwinian nature between variation—the material element—and the
deterministic force of natural selection, which shapes, but does not call up,
this variation.[43] Natural selection exerts a pressure that bears down on
populations that contain an array of variant traits. But precisely because
variation plays a positive role in the process of adaptation, it results in
preserving, rather than eliminating, the teleological or finalistic element
that Aristotle had demanded. It does so by shifting end-directedness from
being a factor that does the explaining, an *explanans*, to an ontologically
deep property of organisms that is both explainable and explained, an
explanandum.[44] It is because adaptations are brought into existence by
natural selection working on very small, populationally distributed
variations that the ontogeny of each organism is oriented toward just the
traits that enable it to act in its environment in accord with a species-
specific pattern or nature. So construed, Darwinian organisms are as much
substantial wholes with functional parts as they are in Aristotle. Indeed, if
the tensions between matter and form, as well as between teleology and
what Grene calls "ordinary when-then" causality, were not maintained the
result would be regression either to unacceptable forms of essentialism, in

which wholes dominate parts to the point of vitalism, or to equally unacceptable reductionisms, in which parts are sundered from wholes in the interest of computing the organism from its least elements with the aid of mathematical models. The history of evolutionary theory is replete with mistakes of both kinds. Darwin's genius, according to Grene, was to have maintained the essential tension. To the extent that he did so, moreover, he preserved and advanced many, if not all, of Aristotle's philosophical insights into living things.

It is a considerable understatement to say that a *rapprochement* between Darwin and Aristotle, especially one drawn in this way, is not the conventional wisdom among philosophers of biology. Typically, they have insisted on a sharp contrast between Aristotle and Darwin. With his doctrine of the eternal identity of species, says Ernst Mayr, Aristotle was a "typological essentialist."[45] Darwin, by contrast, was a "population thinker," for whom there are no specimens at all, in the sense of normatively representative instances of a species kind. Aristotle's typological essentialism, writes David Hull, actually held up progress in biological science for two thousand years.[46] Until quite recently, Hulls asserts, it prevented biologists and biologically-knowledgable philosophers from recognizing that organisms are not instances of kinds at all, but parts of species considered as historical "individuals," bounded by an episode of phylogenetic splitting at both ends, and in the middle chock full of an indefinite number of descriptive changes. On this view, there is no reason to think that any particular combination of traits, even those regarding life-activity, must remain constant over the lifespan of a species, as Grene (working with an ecological rather than a purely phylogenetic species concept) insists they do. Even if they do remain constant, this is at best irrelevant to their ontological status; at worst it is an invitation to cling to the very essentialism that stands in the way of moving toward a fully Darwinian systematics. Darwin himself, the argument runs, provides a case in point. Ostensibly, he sought a "natural" classificatory system based on descent alone. But he was still too much under the influence of classificatory schemes that were infected by descriptive analogies (as opposed to real homologies) to achieve such a natural classification himself. His successors, Hull argues, will succeed only to the extent that they are willing to revise what looks like common sense ontology and epistemology in order to stay up with what evolutionary science suggests and requires. (This way of thinking is an example of naturalized philosophy.)

In responding to this account, Grene plausibly points out that the contrast between typological essentialism and population thinking is overdrawn.[47] Aristotle was not a typological essentialist. As we have seen, he was not interested in definition by unambiguous classification of types.

His species are species just because they maintain a descriptively continuous cycle of reproduction, development, and maturation. Aristotle's conception of that process certainly differs from an evolutionary one, in which species maintain a distinctive life-style only between their coming into being and their passing away. But the difference is not nearly as great as the one drawn by Hull on the basis of a discredited, even if ancient, interpretive tradition about Aristotle. That tradition, which goes back to Porphyry and is affected by his neo-Platonism, confuses the notion of essence with the unique "specific difference" that is supposed to place each plant or animal kind within a *scala naturae* conceived as a ramified classificatory scheme. If this interpretation were correct, Aristotle would indeed be held hostage to an incurably premodern world view, and so could not conceivably give any lessons to moderns.[48] Luckily, as we have seen, modern scholarship has shown that this portrait of Aristotle is almost entirely accumulated shellac.

More than a revised picture of Aristotle will be needed, however, if the contrast between typological essentialism and population thinking is to be diminished to its proper size. A more accurate, or at least more charitable picture, of Darwinism is also called for—a picture in which the Darwinian revolution does not require nearly as wholesale a revision of our common-sense ontology and epistemology as Hull, for example, is eager to imagine. In drawing such a picture, Grene denies that "population thinking," on which in some sense evolutionary processes are predicated, remains coherent if it refuses to let good natural historians, Darwin among them, use stereotypes to recognize and compare "specimens" of different species, and even allows them to incorporate such identificatory practices into the systematic classification of species.[49] In fact, Grene argues that "population thinking," when interpreted as excluding all "typological thinking," is itself incoherent. Population thinking, she writes,

> *taken strictly* turns out to be not only methodologically, but ontologically impossible (my italics). Types, kinds, sorts are bound to crop up somewhere, else we not only could not speak about nature; there would not be a nature to speak about.
> . . . Why, just because something does not last forever, should it lack a nature?
> . . . [T]o abandon talk of kinds or natures altogether gets us into very strange corners, and we need not after all go that way. . . . [A]n evolving universe can and does throw up things *of* kinds, *with* natures. . . . [50]

We see in this passage a theme we have already encountered in Marjorie Grene's discussion of the role of species form in Aristotle. In our philosophical interpretations of life and mind, we should not be too quick to jettison the presumption that natural historians can genuinely *know* things scientifically by using cognitive abilities, methods, and categories that are continuous with those of common sense. We cannot do without universals or with seeing particulars as instantiations or exemplars of them. Grene acknowledges that more radically reformist Darwinian philosophers of science and philosophizing biologists will respond to this assertion by claiming that sortal concepts are merely quirks of our linguistic and conceptual practices—products, perhaps, of our evolutionary history, but for that very reason no guide to the actual structure of things, about which philosophers must be willing to revise their accounts whenever the advance of science requires.[51] Grene rejects this view, however, as inconsistent with its own appeal to accumulated biological knowledge. Surely, what must be protected before any ontological or epistemological revision is undertaken is the reasonable conviction of practicing biologists that, in using classificatory categories and specimens, they are learning about the world *wie es eigentlich gewesen ist*. It is, moreover, a reasonable demand that evolutionary biologists should explain biological preconditions *of* our cognitive experiences rather than try to convince us that we do not actually *have* such experiences.

Still, it is important to bear in mind that, even as she narrows the gap between Aristotle and Darwin by pointing to their shared work as reflective natural historians, Grene does not deny that there is a very large gap indeed between a correctly interpreted Aristotle and *some strains* within Darwinism. As her appreciation of Darwin grew, the reductionistic and overly mechanistic proclivities that she glancingly ascribed to Darwin himself in the passage quoted at the beginning of this section are loaded instead exclusively onto the backs of those whom, writing with Niles Eldredge, she calls "ultra-Darwinians" (among whom rightly she does not include either Mayr or Hull):

> If the psychological least units of Hume have gone the way of sense data, and if logical manipulation has replaced resemblance as the alleged mechanism of scientific reasoning, the reliance on least particulars nevertheless persists: evolutionary biologists, though admitting that evolution works through phenotypes, find their "ultimate" explanations in changing relative gene frequencies, and genes are very satisfying, discrete, isolable bits.[52]

Ultra-Darwinians search for mathematically predictive models (ideally under universal laws of nature of the sort found in physics) of how natural selection achieves optimal adaptedness. To do so they must perforce sunder the organism into atomistically-construed traits, each of which is to be "coded for" by one or more genes. The organism is then interpreted as a reaggregation of these independently optimized traits. Not surprisingly,

Grene argues that this reductionistic and design-oriented account of evolution is simply inconsistent with the observable fact that organisms are multi-leveled wholes that maintain their place in nature's economy by adjustments distributed across the whole at both phenotypic and genotypic levels. Darwinian evolution is indeed adaptive evolution. But that does not require, or even tolerate, "looking in every nook and cranny, until organisms are reduced to an assembly of gadgets."[53]

Very early on, Grene roundly criticized R. A. Fisher, perhaps the most influential twentieth-century ultra-Darwinian, in ways that are still relevant to the issue of biological reductionism.[54] Her critique is worth recounting not only because Fisher was the acknowledged intellectual godfather of ultra-Darwinians still to come, but because in Grene's account of Fisher we observe the very opposite of the virtue she was soon to see in Darwin himself: an *inability* to maintain a balance between matter and form, mechanism and teleology, whole and part. Because he worked exclusively at the level of gene frequencies, and no less exclusively with physics-based mathematical models, Fisher viewed organisms merely as genes' ways of making more genes. In consequence, Grene argues that he could not help but fall into the pseudo-problem of evolutionary tautology (what survives survives).[55] To make matters worse, by neglecting the complex trade-offs required if organisms are to remain tuned to the real environments with which they interact Fisher smuggles in an illegitimate teleology that has each species severally, as well as all species taken together, moving in a linear way toward greater and greater perfection (in the interests, though Grene did not say so, of Fisher's eugenics program). This double fallacy, I suspect, can be expected to crop up *whenever* the essential tensions of which Grene speaks fail to be maintained (as it does in Richard Dawkins's *The Selfish Gene*).[56] The only cure for it is to move as quickly as possible back toward a hierarchical, and to that extent Aristotelian, view of the ontology of organisms, as Grene, Eldredge, Stephen Jay Gould, and many other Darwinian natural historians and their philosophical colleagues did not hesitate to do in response to the rise during the nineteen-eighties of reductive sociobiology and "selfish gene" talk—much of which was explicitly inspired by Fisher's gene-centered, physics-envying example.[57] In this connection, Grene's suspicion, first expressed in a paper published in 1971, that "reductionism" is "a side issue" has proven to be both prophetic and useful to later critics of genic reductionism.[58]

In these matters, I have been Marjorie Grene's faithful scholar. My only qualification is that, in drawing a contrast between Darwin's Darwinism and overly theory-driven versions of Darwinism such as those of Fisher and Dawkins, Grene may sometimes underestimate the role of mathematical theorizing in the brand of Darwinism she herself promotes.

This proclivity manifests itself, in the first instance, in a tendency to exaggerate the explanatory power of Darwin's own account:

> New field techniques, improved statistical methods, and new technologies all contribute to the work; but the argument, *the theory*, and the problem, are Darwin's, simon-pure, after so many alleged revolutions: genetic, biochemical, molecular (my italics).[59]

Admittedly, in this passage Grene is referring to Darwin's account of sexual selection. The point, however, is meant to apply to the entire panoply of evolutionary mechanisms postulated by Darwin, with adaptive natural selection at their core. It is simply not true, however, that Darwin's own Darwinism, even if it were helped out by statistical and other methods, was capable of solving many of the most important problems that fell within its domain. Darwin's account of evolutionary branching, for example, does not explain speciation; no Darwinian today believes it can be described simply as the slow extrapolation over time of ongoing anagenetic change parsed into new ecological niches. Indeed, the false belief that Darwinians were stuck with just such a view was what led, in conjunction with the first stirrings of genetics, to the well-known decline and anticipated "death" of Darwinism at the turn of the twentieth century.[60] If Darwin's basic idea of natural selection, which taken by itself falls far short of a theory, had not been articulated by means of a *succession* of theories in which statistics played a role in conceptualizing the *objects* of evolutionary science, and not merely as a methodological tool, I doubt whether Darwin*ism* would have been able to solve many of the problems that fall within the province of any account of biological origins. It was statistical thinking, for example, that made it possible to combine natural selection with such factors as genetic drift and gene flow, and in consequence to formulate models of the speciation process that allowed a range of testable solutions to appear. This, it seems to me, rather than anything more metaphysically suspect, is the real thrust of the claim that Darwinism requires "population thinking." Without the shift to a populational conception of species Darwinism would probably have remained just another "philosophy of nature" of the sort that proliferated both before and after him without ever being articulated into productive empirical research programs—Schelling's, Spencer's, Bergson's, and so forth.

This is not to contest Grene's claim that we can talk about "natures" without ceasing to be Darwinians. It is merely to call attention to her tendency to associate "population thinking" with ultra-Darwinian genocentric reductionism, and so to restrict the role of mathematics merely to serving as a methodological auxiliary of a "theory" that is presumed to remain constant from the outset. As I have written extensively on this theme elsewhere, I will desist.[61] I cannot help but point out, however, that many of the claims that are central to Grene's own vision of Darwinism do not leap directly off the pages of *On the Origin of Species*, but reflect the conceptual and empirical work of a "wing" of the Modern Synthesis that was led by Grene's former colleague at the University of California at Davis, the great Theodosius Dobzhansky.

Unlike Fisher's reductionist approach, which stresses how natural selection uses up accumulated genetic variation, Dobzhansky's research program in evolutionary biology concentrates on explaining the capacity of populations to preserve genetic variation. It is preserved variation that allows populations to adapt to changing environments by developing adaptations that allow them to orient themselves to changing circumstances—including perceptual and behavioral abilities of the sort already noted by Aristotle in his account of the perceptual-affective-locomotive soul of animals. Such adaptations are almost never traceable to genes that optimize single traits. Dobzhansky's admirable combination of empirical field research, mathematical analysis, and laboratory experiment thus *proves* the inadequacies of "ultra-Darwinism"—something philosophers could not do by themselves, but which they can certainly learn from. The contrast is not, accordingly, between a common sense theory and one that mathematizes the logic of adaptation, as Grene sometimes suggests. Instead, it is between two kinds of mathematizing and theorizing about adaptation.[62]

V. CONCLUSION: NATURALIZED PHILOSOPHY REVISITED

With these reflections in mind, we may return to the problem from which we set out, namely Marjorie Grene's resistance to naturalized philosophy. It virtually follows from Grene's reading of Darwinism and its tradition that, in spite of continuous bombardments from both the scholarly and popular press, we should *not* think of ourselves as badly maladapted to the environments in which we find ourselves in today. Nor should we presume that our genes are tugging at us to regress to behaviors that were genetically fixed in our ancestors in the Pleistocene. It is important to notice that Grene's consequent dissent from sociobiology[63] (and presumably from its more recent cousin "evolutionary psychology"[64]) does not spring from any easy conviction that cultural selection has displaced, or repressed, natural selection. That view still leaves the opposition intact; every time some new discovery about links between genes and behavior appears, it is free to raise its ugly head again. No, natural selection, construed along Dobzhanskyan lines, has given us an evolved nature that is chock-full of genetically and developmentally underwritten capacities for just the sort of deliberative, responsible, and reflective life in which, at our best, we obviously engage. Cultural environments are *natural* to us because they define our evolved nature:

> That our capacities for knowledge evolved, like other capacities, makes a difference (an essential difference?) to our attitude toward them: we can't claim for them separateness from nature or exemption from change. At the same time, it seems to me, such an acknowledgment of our historicity should also increase, not diminish, our confidence in developing and using such capabilities.[65]

This eloquently expressed idea encourages Grene to believe that philosophy can and should continue to ask and answer its own questions. Once a reflective life has emerged in culture (and found political support for sustained free inquiry) there is no reason why it cannot and should not be able to sustain the kind of thinking that we find in the discipline of professional philosophy—so long as philosophical reflection stays closely enough in touch with contemporary scientific and other forms of inquiries to disabuse it of dead ends and to suggest new beginnings. There is no need, accordingly, for us to remodel our philosophical life, or our scientific life, or our cognitive life generally in a way that takes science to be systematically undercutting the deliberative and reflective activities by means of which inquiry itself, including philosophical inquiry, is conducted—by refashioning it, for example, as a process of selection in which theories, or ideas, or "memes" are *unreflectively* weeded out of or propelled through society by means of a process that mimics natural selection. It is just such notions, however, that motivate "evolutionary epistemology" and "evolutionary ethics." It is not difficult, accordingly, to see why Grene discounts them.

Grene's approach seems to me to maintain a judicious mean between the brands of reductionistic and eliminativist philosophy of mind that are currently fashionable and the vacuous sort of evolutionary naturalism that I ascribed earlier to Woodbridge, which I find persisting today among philosophers such as John Searle. Like Grene, Searle wants to preserve the possibility of philosophizing within a world in which our minds, with their full panoply of conscious, intentional, deliberative, and reflective capacities, evolved naturally. Unlike her, however, Searle declines to look to the details of evolutionary theorizing, and to the natural-historical practice that sustains it, to identify the necessary, though not sufficient, means by which our minds could have, and indeed did, evolve these capacities, citing as his reason the view that such information is philosophically irrelevant in any case, since our direct acquaintance with our abilities always trumps scientific accounts. A related criticism could be raised against professed philosophical naturalists like Jerry Fodor, who neglects to defend his computationalist view of mind on the grounds that the information necessary to answer questions about the evolution of brain and mind has been buried forever in the sands of time. To both reductionists and their religiously inspired opponents, stances like these will always fail to be persuasive. They say too little. Their purported naturalism reduces to mere gestures. Marjorie Grene, by contrast, acknowledges that if philosophy is to stay vital its practitioners must continuously familiarize themselves with up-to-date evolutionary and other scientific work so that they will be able to interpret its relevance to our experience as knowers. This seems to me a kind of naturalism worth having.

DAVID J. DEPEW

UNIVERSITY OF IOWA
MARCH 2000

NOTES

1. Marjorie Grene, *A Portrait of Aristotle* (Chicago: University of Chicago Press, 1963; reissued by Bristol: Thoemmes Press, 1998), p. 231. See also "Intellectual Autobiography," this volume.

2. Marjorie Grene, "Perception and Interpretation in the Sciences: Toward a New Philosophy of Science," in *Evolution at a Crossroads: The New Biology and the New Philosophy of Science*, ed. D. Depew and B. Weber (Cambridge, Mass.: MIT Press, 1985); and in *Philosophy in its Variety* (Belfast: Queen's College, 1987), pp. 107–29.

3. Marjorie Grene, *A Philosophical Testament* (Chicago: Open Court, 1995), pp. 98–99. See also, "Puzzled Notes on a Puzzling Profession," Invited Panel: The Future of Philosophy, Sixty-first Annual Pacific Division Meeting (San Francisco, 1987), p. 77; reprinted in *Through Time and Culture: Introductory Readings in Philosophy*, ed. A. Iannone (Englewood Cliffs, N.J.: Prentice Hall, 1994), pp. 462–65.

4. Grene, *A Philosophical Testament*, p. 90.

5. W. V. O. Quine, "Epistemology Naturalized," in *Ontological Relativity and Other Essays* (New York: Columbia University Press, 1969), pp. 69–90.

6. Marjorie Grene, "Biology and the Levels of Reality," in *The Understanding of Nature: Essays in the Philosophy of Biology* (Dordrecht: Reidel, 1974), p. 41.

7. Grene, "Preface," *The Understanding of Nature*, p. viii.

8. Ibid.

9. Grene, "Puzzled Notes on a Puzzling Profession," p. 75.

10. Grene, *A Philosophical Testament*, pp. 110–111.

11. Grene, "Puzzled Notes of a Puzzling Profession," p. 77.

306 DAVID J. DEPEW

12. For a clear statement of this claim in the context of a critique of Kant, see "Individuals and Their Kinds: Aristotelian Foundations of Philosophy," in *Organism, Medicine, and Metaphysics: Essays in Honor of Hans Jonas on his 75th Birthday*, ed. S. F. Spicker (Dordrecht, Holland; Boston: Reidel, 1978), p. 126.

13. Grene, "Intellectual Autobiography," this volume. In saying this, Grene explicitly distinguishes between Aristotle's own thought and the "pseudo-Aristotelianism" that she had encountered at the University of Chicago.

14. *A Portrait of Aristotle*, pp. 227–28; see also "Aristotelian Foundations of Biology," p. 135; "Intellectual Autobiography," this volume.

15. Niles Eldredge and Marjorie Glickman Grene, *Interactions: The Biological Context of Social Systems* (New York: Columbia University Press, 1992), p. 33.

16. Grene, "Aristotle and Modern Biology," in *The Understanding of Nature*, p. 77.

17. Grene, "Individuals and Their Kinds," p. 125

18. W. V. O. Quine, "Ontological Relativity," in *Ontological Relativity and Other Essays*, pp. 26–27. Richard Rorty's election of Dewey as an icon of pragmatism carries the same message for his naturalistic eliminativism.

19. Grene, "Intellectual Autobiography," this volume, for example.

20. Grene acknowledges and comments on this body of work in the preface to the 1998 reissue of *A Portrait of Aristotle*, pp. v–vii.

21. D. Balme, "*Genos* and *Eidos* in Aristotle's Biology," *Classical Quarterly* 12 (1962): 81–98. Grene acknowledges and deals with this body of work in the preface to the 1998 reissue of *A Portrait of Aristotle*.

22. Grene, *A Portrait of Aristotle*, pp. 86–87

23. Aristotle's criteria for something counting as a substance (*ousia*) are that it must be a definite "this" (*tode ti*); must be cut off from (*choristos*) or separate from other things (as accidents, for example, are not); and must be a subject (*hupokeimonon*) that undergoes accidental changes without losing its identity. See *Metaphysics* Z (VII) 3.1029a7–32.

24. D. Balme, "Aristotle's Biology Was Not Essentialist," in *Philosophical Issues in Aristotle's Biology*, ed. A. Gotthelf and J. Lennox (Cambridge: Cambridge University Press, 1987), pp. 291–306

25. Other advocates of individual forms include Michael Frede, Mary Louise Gill, and Terrence Irwin. Their accounts differ substantially from one another.

26. Aristotle, *Metaphysics* Z (VII).15.1039a30–1040a1.

27. Grene, *A Portrait of Aristotle*, preface to 1998 reissue, p. vii.

28. Ibid.

29. Ibid., pp. 231–32.

30. Grene, "Aristotle and Modern Biology," in *The Understanding of Nature*, pp. 98–99.

31. Grene, "Individuals and Their Kinds," p. 135.

32. Grene, *A Portrait of Aristotle*, p. 105; "Aristotle and Modern Biology," in *The Understanding of Nature*, p. 99.

33. This point has been made by Montgomery Furth, *Substance, Form and Psyche: An Aristotelian Metaphysics* (Cambridge: Cambridge University Press, 1988), pp. 127–29. In contrast to a scholarly consensus that he duly reports, Furth is also convinced that the account of inheritance and resemblance given in *Generation of Animals* IV.3 is inconsistent with Aristotle's canonical account of species-specific form (Furth, pp. 132–33).

34. The identity of form and substance in *Metaphysics* Z is mediated, as Grene

also notes, by the identity of form with essence (*to ti en einai*) (*Metaphysics* Z [VII] 3.1029a30–33; 17.1041b7–8). My question is about how to interpret that identity. I do not think form and essence mean the same thing. Essence (*to ti en einai*) is a constitutive principle that makes something into a substantial unity. An account of that essence (its *logos ousias*) can be used to explain why each kind has the traits it does. Form, by contrast, is an achievement term, as Furth contends in *Substance, Form and Psyche* (p. 123). It comes in degrees. Fully attained, form individuates a substance as a member of its kind, making it a "this" and so making it, rather than the material it is made of, a substance. The individuality of a substance is, therefore, its form-ed-ness. The conflation of form and essence is ancient. It was encouraged, long ago, by the incorrect, neo-Platonic assimilation of both form and essence to classificatory kind concepts, or secondary substances. The claim that each individual has its own form (rather than its being its own formedness in accord with a *logos ousias*) either relies tacitly on the notion that each substantial being has its own essence, which Aristotle clearly does not hold, or implies it.

35. Genus is not primarily a classificatory concept, but a notion about material under differentiation. Grene intervened in an important debate about this idea in a way that suggests that she does not agree with the notion of "matter as goo." In "Is Genus to Species as Matter to Form?," *The Understanding of Nature*, pp. 108–26, she points to a variety of texts in which the concept of genus is not fully reducible to the concept of material indeterminacy. She may be right about the texts, but the overall thrust of her argument seems to me to resist too strongly the full force of a biocentric conception of genus and to retain traces of the old, classificatory interpretation. I do not know her current views about this topic.

36. Grene, *A Portrait of Aristotle*, p. 201.

37. Ibid., p. 228.

38. Balme, "Aristotle's Biology Was Not Essentialist," pp. 300–301.

39. Grene, "Evolution, Typology, and Population Thinking," *American Philosophical Quarterly* 27 (1990): 243. The same doctrine about a pattern of life activities as identifying species forms can be found in *A Portrait of Aristotle*, p. 232.

40. Grene, "Evolution Typology, and Population Thinking," p. 243.

41. Ibid., p. 239.

42. Eldredge and Grene, *Interactions*, p. 46. It is perhaps because of this looser coupling between matter and form that, seen from the point of view of Aristotle's theory of substantial form, Darwin's organisms have always been so tangled up with talk about designed objects. Nowhere is it more tangled up than among those whom Grene and Eldredge call "ultra-Darwinians," according to whom, "Only analogues of engineering devices . . . are to be explained as adaptation, and therefore as produced by natural selection" (*Interactions*, p. 43). It is telling in this connection that the Continental tradition in morphology and embryology, about which Grene has also written a good deal, tends to preserve its substantial holism about organisms by rejecting Darwinian natural selection altogether. I suspect that Grene calls Darwin's work "mechanistic" only when she has this contrast in mind. I am unable in this essay to go into Grene's writing on Continental biologists.

43. What follows in this paragraph is a summary of Eldredge and Grene, *Interactions*, pp. 46–49.

44. Grene (personal communication) thinks that the first clear expression of this point can be found in Robert Brandon, "A Structural Description of Evolutionary Theory," in *PSA 1980*, ed. P. Asquith and T. Giere (East Lansing, Mich.: Philosophy of Science Association, 1981) Vol. II, pp. 427–39. The essay is

reprinted in R. Brandon, *Concepts and Methods in Evolutionary Biology* (Cambridge: Cambridge University Press, 1996), pp. 46–57.

45. Ernst Mayr, "Typological versus Population Thinking," in *Evolution and the Diversity of Life*, ed. E. Mayr (Cambridge, Mass.: Belknap Press, 1976), pp. 26–30. Mayr qualifies his account of Aristotle as a typological essentialist in later writings.

46. David Hull, "The Effect of Essentialism on Taxonomy: Two Thousand Years of Stasis," *British Journal for the Philosophy of Science* 15 (1965): 314–26; 16: 1–18.

47. Grene, "Evolution, "Typology, and "Population Thinking," p. 238.

48. Alasdair MacIntyre's work is illustrative of what happens when something like this Medieval interpretation of Aristotle is treated as continuous with Aristotle's own work. The lessons that moderns should learn from this sort of Aristotelianism are to resist modernity. For all its elegaic aesthetic power, this is a reactionary view that should be resisted from both a scholarly and a political perspective—from a scholarly point of view because it is not genuinely Aristotelian; from a political point of view because it licenses repression. See MacIntyre, *After Virtue* (Notre Dame: Notre Dame University Press, 1981) as well as his later *Whose Justice? Which Rationality?* (Notre Dame: Notre Dame University Press, 1991).

49. Grene, "Evolution, Typology and Population Thinking," p. 239.

50. Ibid., pp. 239–40.

51. Ibid., p. 239.

52. Grene, "Aristotelian Foundations of Biology," p. 127.

53. Grene, *A Philosophical Testament*, p. 105.

54. See Grene, "Statistics and Selection," *British Journal for the Philosophy of Science* 12 (1961): 25–42, reprinted in *The Understanding of Nature*, pp. 155–71; see also Grene, "Explanation and Evolution," in the same volume, pp. 207–27.

55. "Statistics and Selection," in *The Understanding of Nature*, p. 165.

56. Richard Dawkins, *The Selfish Gene* (Oxford: Oxford University Press, 1976).

57. Grene, "Hierarchies in Biology," *American Scientist* 75 (1987): 504–9; "Evolution, Typology, and Population Thinking;" *Interactions*.

58. Grene, "Reducibility: Another Side Issue?" in *Interpretations of Life and Mind*, 1971, 14–37; reprinted in *The Understanding of Nature*, pp. 53–73.

59. Eldredge and Grene, *Interactions*, p. 54. I note the same ambiguity in a book review that has recently come to hand. "The interesting question is how [Darwin] managed to be so resoundingly right overall despite being wrong about, or ignorant of, much of what underpins his theory" ("Data Guy," Andrew Berry, review of *Almost Like a Whale: The Origin of Species Updated* by Steve Jones in *London Review of Books*, February 3, 2000: 34). The obvious solution is to concede that the *idea* of natural selection is not a *theory* of natural selection.

60. The story has been told several times. See, for example, P. Bowler, *The Non-Darwinian Revolution* (Baltimore: Johns Hopkins University Press, 1988).

61. David J. Depew and Bruce H. Weber, *Darwinism Evolving: Systems Dynamics and the Genealogy of Natural Selection* (Cambridge, Mass.: MIT Press/Bradford Books, 1995).

62. Grene presumes that Fisher and Dobzhansky are both parties to the same theory, the theory that defines the Modern Evolutionary Synthesis. So construed, the Synthesis, by *defining* evolutionary change as change in gene frequencies, builds in, and so constantly regresses toward, the genocentrism and reductionism that one finds in Fisher. Bruce Weber and I have argued that the Synthesis is a treaty,

however, not a theory; and that its two wings—genocentrically and phenotypically oriented—are held together by very little. Thus we believe that Fisher's "fundamental theorem," which Grene rightly criticizes in "Statistics and Selection," plays almost no role in the wing founded by Wright and Dobzhansky.

63. Grene, *A Philosophical Testament*, p. 109.

64. Sociobiology was originally formulated by E. O. Wilson, who, in his *Of Human Nature* (Cambridge, Mass.: Harvard University Press, 1972), is also responsible for the notion that our genes "tug" at us to regress to behaviors that were adaptations for long vanished environments. For the program of "evolutionary psychology," see J. Barkow, L. Cosmides and J. Tooby, *The Adapted Mind* (New York: Oxford University Press, 1992).

65. Grene, *A Philosophical Testament*, pp. 108–9.

REPLY TO DAVID J. DEPEW

David Depew's opening remarks are immensely flattering, but also puzzling. My only recollection of that talk I gave in San Diego was that I had a rather amusing exchange with Herbert Marcuse, in which I may have made a fool of myself, but certainly did not make mincemeat of him. And I'm sorry if I frightened off a potential student. And as to any "mentoring" I've done since—except for a few rhetorical points about the Aristotle chapter Depew wrote for the book we're working on together, and some sterner remarks about a first version of his Kant chapter—I can't have done it very successfully. Apropos of a chapter I've just been trying to write, I looked back at some parts of *Darwinism Evolving*, which Depew wrote with his then colleague Bruce Weber, and I found the pages littered with my exclamation points, question marks, and cries of "Ugh" or "Nonsense"—that apart from my profound disagreement with the major thesis of that work, which claims to derive three stages in the evolution of Darwinism from three different kinds of dynamics in physics. True, Darwin modeled his "long argument" on Herschel's view of scientific explanation, and Herschel in turn depended on Newton; but that doesn't make Darwin in any way himself a physicist. Fisher may indeed have depended on Boltzmann; I don't know, but would credit him with any kind of over-abstract mathematicizing. Yet surely the evolutionary synthesis is not identical with Fisher: there was Wright, Dobzhansky, Mayr, Simpson, Stebbins, even Huxley. And their third stage is, I suspect, a flash in the pan. So I haven't done a very good job!

Seriously, though, Depew's statement of my general position is a very good one, and I'm grateful for it. Even here, however, I do have some problems along the way, which I'll try to formulate.

Section II. Depew says I "discerned" the primacy of perception, "clearly in Aristotle, then in Darwin and other naturalists." Now Aristotle did lean heavily on perception as the starting point of knowledge, but if I was once happy about that, I had a sneaking hunch all was not really well in that quarter, and my worries were confirmed by a seminar Myles Burnyeat gave at Cornell while I was living in Ithaca. In fact, Aristotle argued that perception was *infallible*, in which case he must have been thinking of sensation rather than full-bodied perception, and in that way we're already started on the road to the standard modern misconception of our perceptual experience. So I'm afraid that on the subject of "the primacy of perception," Aristotle is unclear, or at least his readers are unclear about him. And I see nothing of this in Darwin; it's just not to the point there; of course, he was a magnificent observer and delved into living—and stony!—nature in every possible direction, but to refer to the "primacy of perception" is to make an epistemological point which is irrelevant to Darwin's teaching. In any case, it's Merleau-Ponty's phrase, and not easily generalized except on the later ground of Gibsonian ecological psychology. It certainly does not apply to Polanyi, whose view of sensory experience was necessarily limited to what was available to him at the time. And his from-to model of knowledge stems from his reflections about science rather than being directed to everyday perceptual experience.

About what's necessary to "resolve philosophical problems," I thought we agreed that, in general, philosophical problems don't exactly get "resolved"; they are indeed "taken up anew in each generation. . . ."

Section III. My worry here and in the following section is more general. David Depew is a true devotee of Aristotelian biology, and I believe that, since we work well together, he is lending me the cloak of his knowledge and enthusiasm. It was, I'm pretty sure, my sense of the complex nature of biological organization that helped me write a fairly good introduction to Aristotle via his biology, but it wasn't Aristotle who taught me this. Nor do I see Aristotle as giving us a way "to the proper . . . resolution of philosophical questions"—to his own satisfaction, perhaps, not ours. If I have written on "Aristotle and modern biology," I have done so chiefly to point out— less wittily than Delbrück did in "Aristotle-totle-totle"—that the form-matter distinction bears some resemblance to the reliance on the concept of a code in recent genetics. On the other hand, as is clear in relation to Darwin and the Darwinian tradition, while for Aristotle it is fundamental that act is prior to potency, for us it is precisely the other way around.

About individual forms, I admit, especially in the light of recent literature, there are problems. I can only say, while there's life, there's hope. But if I am "on the side of knowledge" as against the ontology of individual organisms, that's for Aristotle, not for myself! For anyone raised on evolution, as I was, and since recurrently interested professionally in evolutionary, or meta-evolutionary, questions, that's the only way it can be.

But, back to Aristotle again: please, I never, never, ever thought artifacts were substances, and I just don't understand what it is about anything I ever said that makes Depew think I might have.

Again, in passing: there is nothing about perception as such to be learned from Polanyi. It's Merleau-Ponty and Gibson.

Section IV. Perhaps, once more, it is David Depew's own love of Aristotle—and his later study of Darwin?—that leads him to see my approach to Darwin as stemming in part from Aristotle. As he illustrates with a quotation I am ashamed to own, when I wrote my little Aristotle book forty years ago, my understanding of Darwin was extremely limited. As I mentioned in my reply to Hull, the passage he quotes refers in truth only to what Steve Gould dubbed "the hardened synthesis," not even to the synthesis in general and certainly not to Darwin. If I have learned better, it is not through Aristotle, but through colleagues at Davis like Ledyard Stebbins or Arthur Shapiro (with both of whom I have taught courses), and from reading and teaching. But I see no great rapprochement between Darwin and Aristotle, except for the fact that each, in his time, was a great biologist, but very differently. It is no superficial matter that Aristotle believed organisms did not evolve. As I said earlier, in the light of evolution, we have reversed radically his deepest principle of the priority of act to potency. Moreover, if his matter-form analysis appears analogous in some ways to modern hierarchical thinking in biology, such analysis was not, I believe, at all characteristic of Darwin. The latter did distinguish between the level of minute variation, which provides (through unknown laws) the material for natural selection to work on, and the organisms whose somewhat more favorable small variations permit them to survive and to reproduce (through unknown laws of generation). But that is nothing like an Aristotelian form-matter analysis.

Nor, in my view, does Darwinian explanation now retain an iota of Aristotelian teleology. Although Darwin was ambiguous about teleology, he was never an Aristotelian teleologist (that demands fixed endpoints, which evolution lacks). And now, since, as Depew admits, "the appearance of end," as Waddington called it, has been moved from the *explanans* in evolutionary theory to the *explanandum*, any teleology, however questionable, has simply gone from the explanation itself. (Incidentally, the remark quoted from my "Aristotle and Modern Biology," like the earlier one from *Portrait*, is sadly dated. Such genic reductionism was once fashionable, but, happily, is so no longer—or in odd places.)

Finally, what looks like a really serious disagreement, but is perhaps just a misunderstanding: The examples I gave in the book I wrote with Niles Eldredge of twentieth-century Darwinian techniques are not meant to suggest that Darwin's own theory and the later view based on population genetics were identical. Of course I know there are major differences between the structure of Darwin's theory and that of the leaders of the synthesis, and of course I know that the statistical underpinning of modern population genetics had a lot to do with that. But if there were not some common strain running through both these theories, how could Depew and Weber have found Darwinism evolving? They'd have to say with David Hull, there ain't no such animal.

In general, I believe philosophers talk much too much about theories in science. The widely differing practices that constitute the family of the sciences—with their family resemblances and family quarrels—are relatively seldom directly centered in considerations of theory as such. I have long thought that exceptions to this rule were, obviously, theoretical physics and evolutionary theory. In the light of Depew's comments, I'm no longer so sure about the second. Darwin's theory did indeed lack the sound statistical grounding that the synthesis with Mendelian genetics was to give it—witness the criticism of Fleeming Jenkin, which Jean Gayon has so beautifully analyzed. And I find it a lovely irony of history that Darwin was not himself a population thinker (that doesn't make him a "typologist"— a very ahistorical dichotomy!). But there is some feature of Darwin's procedure as a naturalist that made it possible for biologists like Endler or Ryan (the two cases I mentioned) to work along Darwinian lines. In Ryan's case, I found it striking that a student of animal behavior publishing in 1995 should quote as paradigmatic for his work statements by Darwin published in 1871. That doesn't happen often in scientific publishing. Seventeenth-century Aristotelians were very far from Aristotle—in some ways, I have learned recently, almost up to Descartes, though not quite. Twentieth-century Darwinians were still in some sense Darwinian.

That's enough complaining about what is indeed a very gracious and thought-provoking essay. Thank you, David—only I don't want to effect a rapprochement between Aristotle and Darwin, and I do know there's a difference between Darwin and Fisher or Wright (a different difference, of course, in the two cases!). O.K.?

M. G.

12

Niles Eldredge

HIERARCHY: THEORY AND PRAXIS IN EVOLUTIONARY BIOLOGY

All evolution must occur through the interaction of the economic with the genealogical hierarchy. It is the investigation of such causal relations that current hierarchy theory should help to initiate.

—Grene (1987, p. 509)

With these two sentences, Marjorie Grene concluded her pithy review of "Hierarchies in Biology." That paper served to sort out and classify the various meanings of the term "hierarchy" as used in biology—and served, as well, to link older uses and contexts with the various meanings and intents of hierarchy theory as it was being developed in various quarters of evolutionary biology in the 1980s. Grene herself was playing an active role in that process—as evidenced not only in this paper (i.e., Grene 1987), but perhaps especially in an effort we produced jointly (Eldredge and Grene 1992), focused on issues raised by sociobiological theory. Grene's efforts in evolutionary biology (see also Eldredge, 1992 on Grene's earlier efforts of analysis of evolutionary issues) always have seemed to transcend the "purely philosophical"[1]—as if the most important issue is the "work" that may be performed in developing a deeper, more accurate view of the nature of biological entities, their behaviors, and their interactions that, together, produce the fallout we call "evolutionary history."

In this essay I shall review and analyze the work that the rubric of hierarchy theory has enabled in the realm of evolutionary theory since 1987.

Following Grene's dictate cited at the top of the present essay, I shall focus especially on results that have emerged explicitly from the analysis of the interactions between the "economic" and "genealogical" hierarchies.[2] After a brief encapsulation of the elements of the economic and genealogical hierarchies, I shall examine four separate examples of such work, two of which were evident immediately and the subject of analysis by Grene and others in the late 1980s and early 1990s; the third is a surprising set of insights on the status of our own species, *Homo sapiens*, that could be articulated only with the dual hierarchy scheme of biological existence firmly in mind; and the fourth—and perhaps the most exciting of all—is the marriage of hierarchy theory with empirical patterns in the history of life that sheds light on the nature of the evolutionary process only dimly glimpsed when Grene penned her sentences, quoted above, in 1987.

THE ECONOMIC AND GENEALOGICAL HIERARCHIES

Physiologists long ago compiled a list of basic organismic functions. The list includes digestion, respiration, elimination, excretion, and other processes manifestly vital for each and every organism's survival.[3] Also on this list is one function generally conceded *not* to be vital for an organism's continued survival: reproduction. If it stops eating, breathing, absorbing water, excreting, and so on, an organism soon dies; these are the basic "economic" actions of life. If, on the other hand, it does not reproduce, that is neither here nor there as far as its continued physical existence is concerned; reproduction is concerned with the making of offspring and the propagation, thereby, of the underlying genetic information, the blueprint, from which such offspring are produced.

There are further consequences of these basic physiological functions. In their constant search for energy and nutrient resources, their anatomical, physiological, and behavioral defenses against climatic perils and the threats posed by predation and disease, organisms find themselves variously competing and cooperating with other members of their species[4] with which they are forming local populations. Such populations ("avatars"—Damuth 1985), moreover, play characteristic roles in their local region: the local fox population, for example, exerts predation pressure on the various rodent, insectivore, and rabbit populations in its environs.

The characteristic economic interplay—the flow of matter and energy —among all such local populations of organisms (from microbes to mammals) and between them and the physical environment, is what simultaneously defines and binds together local ecosystems. And the characteristic economic roles played by each avatar of every different species present is what is known as its "ecological niche." Further, because it is important to a later consideration, it must be noted that each such population is limited in size by the "carrying capacity" of its local ecosystem —meaning for the most part the amount of energy and nutrients available given the basic economic adaptations of the organisms within each of the different avatars. Both Darwin and Alfred Russell Wallace (co-discoverer of natural selection) realized that there are finite limits to population growth—a key ingredient in their independently conceived notions of "natural selection."

But all the world's local ecosystems are interconnected as energy flows among local ecosystems: as when, for example, an osprey passing by takes a fish from a lake. Thus, local ecosystems are connected into regional systems, and regional systems into still larger systems eventually continent- and ocean-wide in scope. And though biologists frequently wince at some of the fanciful notions associated with the term "Gaia" (Lovelock 1979), there is little doubt that all the ecosystems of the earth are interlocked—and together with the atmosphere, hydrosphere, and lithosphere, are part of a single global energetics, or simply "economic," system.

Thus, every organism is a part of a local population, cooperating or competing for energy resources with other individuals of its species; these local populations are parts, in turn, of a local ecosystem, and local ecosystems are parts of still larger systems. The key here is matter-energy flow: at any given level of the economic hierarchy, the components are engaged in matter-energy processes that bind them together to form the next larger entity of the hierarchy (figure 1, left side).

Similarly for reproduction: for sexually reproducing organisms, finding a mate entails interacting within a local population of potential mates—that is, members of the same species of opposite sex. The plexus of local mates, the local breeding population, is what geneticists generally mean by the term "deme."[5] Demes, in turn, are parts of species—those collectives of all demes whose members share the capacity to interbreed (see note 4). Demes variably form, go extinct, and merge with one another—events and processes with enormous implications for the fate of genetic information within species—as first made evident, perhaps, by Sewall Wright in his "shifting balance theory" (Wright 1932) and much more recently by Eldredge et al. (2003) in their analysis of the phenomenon of evolutionary stasis.

The Economic and Genealogical Hierarchies

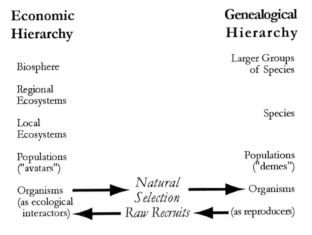

Figure 1. The economic ("ecological") and genealogical ("evolutionary") hierarchies. Organisms live economic lives and reproduce—functions that set up larger scale economic and genealogical systems. Each such system is a part of the next succeeding larger-scale system in its respective hierarchy. Natural selection is the effect that relative economic success has on an organism's reproductive success. It is the function of the entities in the genealogical hierarchy to supply organisms—"raw recruits" or "players"—to the economic systems. For full discussion, see text.

Further, as a key element of the evolutionary process, species make more species: they "speciate." One or more species arises, usually as a product of fission, from an ancestral species. Speciation, over time, produces skeins of ancestral/descendant species—clusters of related species themselves related to other clusters of species—and so on, into the familiar hierarchy of genera, families, orders, classes, and phyla. But, as Grene (1987) made so abundantly clear, this latter "Linnaean" hierarchy is not strictly speaking a continuation of the genealogical hierarchy of reproducing organisms/demes/species—as there is no equivalent reproductive process to the more-making of organisms, demes, and species underlying the production of, say, genera or families. Rather, the reproductive buck stops at species: the rest are simply higher taxa—clusters of related species linked together by propinquity of descent, the fallout of evolutionary history that stops at the level of speciation (though see below).

Thus "more-making" is the generic process underlying the construction of the genealogical hierarchy—just as "matter-energy" transfer among component parts defines and coheres the next larger unit in the economic hierarchy. Genes replicate, a process vital to both the continued production of new somatic cells in an organism's lifetime, as well as the production of sperm and eggs for reproduction; organisms mate and make more organisms—they make more "entities of like kind." Reproductive interaction among local conspecific organisms creates demes. Demes variably split and fuse, but arguably also "make more entities of like kind"; demes, in turn, are parts of species. At the upper limit, species produce descendant species—that is, they, too, produce more entities of like kind. That, in a nutshell, is the genealogical hierarchy (figure 1, right side); for far more detail on the nature and structure of the genealogical hierarchies, see Eldredge and Grene (1992) and references cited therein.

It remains now to see how these two very different hierarchies can interact as Grene (1987) avers they do to produce evolutionary history.

NATURAL SELECTION

Perusal of figure 1 reveals one obvious connection between the economic and genealogical hierarchies: each and every organism is a member, simultaneously, of both hierarchies.[6] This simple fact allows us to understand why Darwin's original definition of natural selection is preferable to more recent suggestions—and why, moreover, Darwin was right when he specified that *natural* and *sexual* selection are distinct processes. In *The Origin of Species,* Darwin (1859, p. 5) characterized natural selection as follows:

> As many more individuals of each species are born than can possibly survive, and as, consequently, there is a frequently recurring Struggle for Existence, it follows that any being, if it vary in any manner profitable to itself, under the complex and sometimes varying conditions of life, will have a better chance of surviving, and thus be *naturally selected.*

How beautifully Darwin's formulation of natural selection maps onto the lower rungs of the dual hierarchy scheme of figure 1! Darwin is in effect saying that competitive success in the economic arena of an organism's life

is bound to have an effect on its survival—and thus its chances for reproductive success. Comparative success in the economic game of life within
one's avatar has implications for reproductive success within the deme.

A further implication is that Darwin's later (1871, p. 256) amplification
and clarification of the notion of *sexual selection* (first mentioned in the
Origin) is entirely valid; sexual selection arises from "the advantage which
certain individuals have over other individuals of the same sex and species,
in exclusive relation to reproduction." In other words, certain organisms are
simply better at reproducing than others of their peers—thus also affecting
the genetic information passed along to the next generation, but without the
influence of relative economic success.

Thus Darwin himself had already teased apart the economic from the
reproductive aspects of organismic existence—a point long since lost sight
of as biologists habitually wrangled whether or not to accept sexual
selection as a mere subset of, or as a process quite legitimately distinct
from, natural selection. Hierarchy theory shows us that Darwin was right.

Moreover, beginning with the publication of Williams's (1966) *Adaptation and Natural Selection* and reaching its most explicit and strident
expression in Dawkins's (1976) *The Selfish Gene*, perhaps the dominant
strain of evolutionary biology has come to see natural selection strictly as
the outcome of a competitive struggle—among organisms, even among
genes—for representation in the next generation. An organism, in this view,
may eat to live—but it lives to reproduce. Evolution is literally driven by
the competition among genes (or at least among the organisms that carry
them) to leave relatively more copies of themselves behind—and in an
especially stark passage, Dawkins (1976, p. 90) says that someday this
insight will lead us to understand how ecosystems themselves are organized. In other words, this "ultradarwinian" (Eldredge and Grene 1992, p.
3) perspective sees the entire structural edifice of biological systems at the
level of organism and higher—entities as diverse in composition and
internal dynamics as ecosystems and species—as arising simply from
competition for reproductive success. In the ultradarwinian perspective,
reproductive competition literally drives the evolutionary process—a far cry
from Darwin's vision that relative reproductive success is a fall out, a side
effect, of relative economic success. The one vision sees natural selection
as nearly synonymous with "evolution,"—and, critically as an active
process[7]—while Darwin's vision, clarified through the dual hierarchy
scheme of figure 1, maintains the view that stability and change in genetic
composition of populations through time is simply a passive record of what
worked-better-than-what in previous generations. At the very least, the dual
hierarchy scheme of figure 1—where the component entities within the two
hierarchies are held to arise from very different kinds of interactive

processes, suggests that the "selfish gene" perspective cannot be construed as a wholly accurate account of either what drives evolution, or of the nature of larger-scale biological systems. More on this below.

SOCIAL SYSTEMS

Sociobiology (Wilson 1975) is the application of ultradarwinian principles to the nature and evolution of social systems.[8] In two seminal papers, Hamilton (1964a, 1964b) cut the Gordian knot—the paradox that troubled Darwin so much: if all is competition in the world of organisms, why is there so much cooperation? R. A. Fisher is popularly said to have suggested the solution to the problem posed by "altruism" when he showed mathematically (supposedly on an envelope in a British pub) that organisms can pass on their genes vicariously by aiding and abetting the reproductive activities of relatives. But it wasn't until Hamilton showed that degree of cooperation/altruism would be expected to be in direct proportion to degree of genetic similarity that the problem was formally considered solved. Sociobiology emerged shortly thereafter—arising from Hamilton's insights as well as the newly-minted gene's-eye perspective of the evolutionary process pioneered by Williams (1966) and, later, by Dawkins (1976).

Wilson (1975), an expert on ants, showed that ants and other hymenopterans (bees, wasps) have a peculiar form of inheritance ("haplo-diploidy"), wherein females of the colony/hive are more closely related to (i.e., share more genes with) each other than they are to the males. That is why workers —all of them female—in (often) several different castes are sterile: they work for the colony, performing economic and para-reproductive tasks (care of offspring), but leave the reproducing to the Queen—safe in the "knowledge" that their genes are being well looked after. This account is accurate as far as it goes; but as Eldredge and Grene (1992, ch. 6) point out, social systems of vertebrate organisms—*especially* humans—commonly do not consist strictly of relatives—nor are there any special genetic rules of inheritance as in the hymenopterans that would naturally tend towards the development of such a genetic (hence evolutionary) basis for the formation of social systems.

But for present purposes, the more important point is that, rather than being extended genetic cooperatives, social systems—*all* social systems, including ant colonies—are really hybrid fusions of the otherwise distinct avatar/demal division of the dual hierarchy system (Eldredge and Grene 1992). It is as if the economic and reproductive adaptations of organisms themselves have been brought together, so that a colony is simultaneously an economic entity, integrated as a part into the local ecosystem—and a reproductive entity, a special form of a deme (figure 2). To date, I regret to say, this particular insight on the dual economic and genealogic nature of social systems has yet to be absorbed by sociobiological theorists.

Social Systems

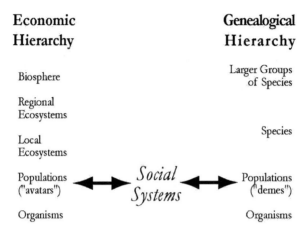

Figure 2. Social systems are amalgams—literally fusions, or "reintegrations" —of the normally distinct avataral and demal dichotomy within non-social species. For discussion, see text.

MALTHUS AND THE HUMAN ECOLOGICAL "NICHE"

As is evident from earlier discussion, and from figures 1 and 2, species are genealogical entities; they are parts of clusters of related species. Species are *not* economic entities—and with the exception of the special case of a species consisting of but a single local population,[9] species are not parts of specifiable economic systems (for more on this point, see Eldredge 1989). Rather, it is the local populations—avatars—of species that form parts of, and play distinct roles in, local ecosystems. Avatars have "ecological niches," while species do not.

The long list of anatomical and behavioral features setting humans apart from the rest of the biological world (despite sharing 98 percent of our genes with the common chimpanzee), includes such critical elements as language and other highly-honed cognitive capacities—related in some as yet dimly understood way to the increase in size of the neocortical region of the brain over 4 or 5 million years of evolution.

Hierarchy theory allows us to see how unique we have become in ecological terms. Cohen (1995) has reviewed previous estimates of human population size through time. Whereas there are over 6 billion humans currently on the planet, estimates of our numbers a scant 10,000 years ago vary between 1 and 10 million; let's arbitrarily call it 6 million—and then ask why, after 4 or 5 million years of hominid evolution with relatively scant growth, has there been a 1,000-fold increase in human population—literally an explosion of humanity in the past 10,000 years?

The answer patently lies in the invention of agriculture—beginning roughly 10,000 years ago. Conventional wisdom sees the advent of agriculture as having substantially modified the "human ecological niche." To the contrary, I have argued (e.g., Eldredge 1995) that agriculture did not so much as modify the human "niche" as to abolish it outright. Pre-agricultural peoples were all hunter-gatherers, meaning that all energetics and nutrient resources were gleaned from the local environment. As has been made abundantly clear in ethnographic studies, the relatively few remnant hunter-gathering peoples still on earth[10]—at least when first contacted by Western-world peoples—live in relatively small bands (usually no more than 70 people, frequently less), and bear the same relationship to the local ecosystem as do all species—namely, broken up into avatars and playing concerted, specifiable roles in the local ecosystem. In that sense, *Homo sapiens* per se—like all other species—had no "niche," but each of our component avatars certainly did, in the conventional sense. This was, of course, as true of all pre-agricultural peoples as it remains true of the few hunter-gathering groups still extant.

Clearly, agriculture (and the related animal husbandry) amounts to taking over direct control of food production (imperfect though it sometimes is—as famine has stalked humanity incessantly over the past 10,000 years). Clearing fields and creating monocultures where normally scores of different plant species naturally grow is, in effect, declaring war on the local ecosystem—rather than an attempt to continue living within it.

Thus, humanity has the distinction (if such it may be) of being the first species in the 3.8 billion year history of life *not* to exist as avataral parts of local ecosystems. The consequences have been many—including settled existence (with its myriad attendant implications for political control and cultural development) and population expansion. For once removed from the limitations of productivity—the "carrying capacity"—of local ecosystems, there no longer was any extrinsic, necessary control to human population numbers. And inasmuch as famine has been far offset by success in feeding ourselves, our numbers have, as a result, skyrocketed.

But there is more. Cohen (1995) has also reviewed the literature on expected upper limits on human population numbers—and though some estimates range into the several hundreds of billions, most converge on 11 to 15 billion—including, incredibly, the estimate of 13.4 billion given by Antoni van Leeuwenhoek, inventor of the microscope, as long ago as 1679 (Cohen 1995, p. 16). We must ask, why this expectation of limits—if the Malthusian lid has been removed, as it so patently has been, by the abandonment of local ecosystems with the coming of agriculture 10,000 years ago?

The answer is that demographers and ecologists (but not most economists!) think there is a finite carrying capacity for human life for the entire Earth. This implies that humans are still, after all, part of a large economic system—but this time, rather than as avatars integrated as parts of local ecosystems, it is one single, 6-billion member system acting in concert to exert an economic presence within the entire global energetics system. If so, that would make us *the first species to be an economic, as well as a genealogical, entity.* The idea gains credibility when we realize how interconnected the entire globe has become: we exchange over $1 trillion worth of goods and services globally among ourselves every day (Kennedy 1993). We are indeed economically integrated globally—unlike any other species now known, or likely to have existed in the past 3.8 billion years.

On the other hand, this second conclusion is less surprising when we realize that, having eliminated the avataral aspect of economic organization—having thus stepped outside of membership in local ecosystems, hence ecosystems generally—the human species has become in effect one enormous single population, at least in an economic sense. We are not (as yet, anyway) panmictic—but even genetic diversity is declining (along with cultural diversity: hundreds of languages have been lost in the past century) as globalization proceeds apace.

Thus, hierarchy thinking sheds light on our own ecological situation; human population growth and utilization of global resources underlie many of the problems faced not only by humanity itself, but by all the other species on the globe. But, though this has profound implications for the future of life on the planet—including its eventual evolution—it does not address per se the central issues of economic and genealogical hierarchies, and the interactions between them that lie at the heart of the evolutionary process. The final section, however, will do just that.

THE SLOSHING BUCKET

Evolutionary biologists have traditionally focused on genealogical matters—on entities such as genes, species, and monophyletic taxa. And for good reason: the original issue to be explained by the fundamental notion of evolution is the anatomical ("phenotypic") disparity among organisms on earth. Never mind that the disparity for the greatest part lies in features (e.g., "wings," "hair," etc.) that are economic in function: the information underlying these disparate features is ensconced in the genome, and we have all these different species, clustered together in arrays of progressively related species in "higher taxa" that are, by definition, the fallout of the evolutionary process. Whatever else it might be, evolution has always seemed profoundly genealogical—to the point of being nothing else.

The great discovery in the last two decades is that the history of life—the *evolutionary* history of life—is profoundly nongenealogical in one specific sense: evolution has been found to be linked with episodes of extinction—episodes, moreover, that commonly, even "routinely," affect more than one genealogical system (deme, if localized; entire species if regionalized; higher taxa if continental or global in extent) at the same time. In other words, if local foxes are affected, so are the local squirrels and chickadees. The root cause of these events[11] is invariably physical environmental change. And the nature—and the nature of the impact—of physical environmental change on biotic systems can only be understood with reference to the economic/ecological hierarchy.

Consider the elements of the ecological hierarchy. The effects of environmental change on ecological systems can best be summarized if we look at the end-member situations first: that of local avatars in local ecosystems near the lowest end of the spectrum—and then what happens when truly global events disrupt the entire biosphere—events that have occurred at least five times in the past .5-billion-year history of life.

At the lower end of the ecological hierarchy, we confront the phenomenon of "ecological succession." Ecologists still debate the intricacies of succession: how orderly is recovery when a local ecosystem is all but destroyed, for instance, by volcanic eruption, fire, or, these days, events like oil spills? Ralph Gordon Johnson (1972), for example, beautifully portrayed the slow but inexorable march of a sand bar across the bottom of a section of Tomales Bay in northern California. Everything in its path—all sedentary forms of marine life, such as tube worms, some of the clams, and so on, suffered death—while the luckier, more mobile organisms got out of the way. As the sand dune passed, bare seafloor was left exposed—but bare seafloor that soon became home to the familiar panoply of different organisms that had been there before.

Here is a low-key interplay between ecological and genealogical hierarchies: as each avatar was snuffed out, after the sandbar had done its destruction and vacated a segment of seafloor, neighboring demes (in this case simply adjacent populations) literally sent in recruits. For that is the main function of demes and species on the reproductive, genealogical side of life: to supply players to the game of life, a game which (save reproduction itself) is intrinsically economic and is played out in local ecosystems. Succession is the rebuilding of ecosystems—more or less in a form recognizable from pre-destruction times. And that involves recruits coming in from the outside.

Biologists are quick to aver that natural selection is *always* going on—during times of succession perhaps even more intensely than in times of "normalcy." Yet organisms invade unoccupied space because it seems a suitable habitat—they are, in other words, utilizing evolutionary economic adaptations already in place rather than developing new ones for the occasion. The essence of succession is the reconstitution of the status quo. Little, if any, evolutionary change is to be expected here—at least of the sort and magnitude that will show up as readily apparent anatomical transformations.

But that is at the lower end. It has by now become notorious that global mass extinctions greatly reset the evolutionary clock—and result in a complexion of life rather different from what had preceded the event. Yet a case can be made that even here—after lags typically in the 5 to 10 million year range—all is about the regaining of ecological "normalcy" as well, but that life rebuilds using only a subset of the genetic information that has managed to survive.

Perhaps the best example involves Paleozoic and Mesozoic corals: Both groups of Paleozoic corals became extinct in the great Permo-Triassic crisis some 245 million years ago.[12] Both groups had calcified (exo-)skeletons composed of the calcium carbonate mineral calcite; one of them had an interior quadripartite arrangement of partitions ("septa")—a fourfold pattern of internal symmetry.

Both groups became extinct in the Upper Permian—after hundreds of millions of years of both reef building and solitary existence. After a lag of millions of years, corals finally reappeared in the lower Triassic—but with a palpable difference: the new corals, like those alive today, were composed of the calcium carbonate mineral aragonite—and had a sixfold pattern of septal arrangement. Their closest relatives, it is now agreed, were not the forerunning Paleozoic corals, but rather the naked (i.e., skeleton-less) sea anemones—which also possess a sixfold symmetry. The presumption is that corals were in a very real sense "reinvented," using material that survived the extinction crisis—namely the naked anemones. Evidently, one branch of anemones acquired the ability to secrete calcium carbonate and *voilà*: corals once again graced the seas. But this was no evolutionary transformation from Ur-coral to modern coral: this was literally a co-opting of close relatives to, in a very real way, fill the void left by the demise of the Paleozoic corals. These were entire groups: Orders Rugosa and Tabulata replaced by Order Scleractinia. And this is just the coral story: many other groups of Paleozoic invertebrates died out at the same time—sometimes (though not always by any means) replaced by some sort of ecological equivalents.

By far the most familiar story, however, involves the dinosaurs (with collateral reptilian kin) and mammals. The moral is much the same, even if the details differ a bit from the coral story. Mammals and dinosaurs both arose in the Upper Triassic. For reasons unknown, it was the dinosaurs and other reptiles that proliferated into the great array of small, medium, and large herbivores, scavengers, and carnivores—while for 150 million years the mammals remained small and ecologically relatively undiversified. The dinosaurs suffered severe vicissitudes, but it wasn't until the famous Cretaceous extinction event (probably the result of the collision of one or more extraterrestrial objects with the Earth) that terrestrial dinosaurs became completely extinct. Mammals, however, survived—and, after a lag, for the first time proliferated into a diverse array of anatomical forms and, hence, ecological roles.

Mass extinctions, then, are like succession events—writ very large, and with the crucial distinction that "recruitment" from the genealogical side of the ledger means that ecosystems are rebuilt by those species from higher taxa that survive the event—and even more importantly, that evolution "kicks in" in a profound way, generating ultimately roughly as many new species as were lost to extinction. Global mass extinctions entail the demise of entire families, orders, and perhaps even classes of organisms—and it is the case that paleontologists often find themselves assigning equivalent ranks to the taxa that are generated by evolution, literally as replacements for the lost taxa. Or so, at least, it seems.

Avataral disruption-cum-ecological succession and global mass extinction-cum-evolutionary rebound are the two extremes—the end-members that box in the spectrum of environmental impacts on ecological systems and their evolutionary side effects. It is in the mid-range where it is apparent that most of the evolutionary action occurs. For it is when the ecological systems are sufficiently large to embrace the ranges of entire species that environmental perturbation leads to more than the destruction of isolated demes, yet not to the extinction of many closely related species (and thus the extinction of genera, families, and so on)—but rather the mid-range extinction of an assortment of species of different genealogical affinity—that the core of evolutionary action over life's entire history becomes apparent.

For example, in a paper published a scant two years before Grene's analysis of hierarchies in biology, Vrba (1985) coined the term "turnover pulse" as a category name for an event she studied in detail in eastern and southern Africa. Vrba noted that many species of antelope and other mammals (even hominids) disappeared at about the same time some 2.5 million years ago—replaced by many other species that appeared just as abruptly as the others disappeared. She attributed the "turnover" to a sharp decrease in temperature, one that took some 300 thousand years to occur, but one that was absorbed by the biota until, abruptly, the botanical species comprising the warm, wet woodlands were replaced by more open grasslands with species adapted to the cooler, drier climate. Some species migrated away, while others already adapted to cooler conditions and a grasslands setting migrated in—a process often called "habitat tracking." But still other species did in fact become extinct, while the disruption also seemed to trigger speciation events—in other words, true evolution.

The turnover pattern (also known as "coordinated stasis," Brett and Baird 1995), I submit, is *the* fundamental pattern of evolution in the fossil record,[13] at least from the Cambrian right up to the Recent. One of the original examples of "punctuated equilibria" (Eldredge and Gould 1972) came from the history of a group of Middle Devonian trilobites that spanned a 5 to 6 million year interval beginning some 380 million years ago. It turns out that not only these trilobites, but virtually *all* the other invertebrate fossils—virtually all the other clam, snail, brachiopod, bryozoan, and coral species present in the melange of ecosystems that made up this Middle Devonian North American biota—were present throughout that same interval of time, showing little or no evolutionary change throughout those 5 to 6 million years. But then all but 20 percent of them disappeared when the fauna was abruptly terminated (apparently by sea level changes) and replaced by successors of similar aspect—but for the most part different species membership. In other words, the pattern of "punctuated equilibria" pertains to individual, genealogically-pure species lineages; but the vast majority of all such species present in a region undergoes parallel histories of stasis, extinction and change in near-simultaneity. Turnover pulses, then, are many simultaneous and cross-genealogical examples of punctuated equilibria, all controlled by the same sets of environmental conditions and events.

Thus the middle ground: regional extinction events that take out a *pot pourri* of unrelated species trigger off an evolutionary response of speciation. If a threshold is not reached and species do not become extinct in large numbers, we observe instead much habitat tracking—where biotas move about as species seek and occupy "recognizable habitat." Regional habitat tracking is below the extinction/evolution threshold—and resembles, instead, a gigantic case of faunal succession—where little or no adaptive evolutionary change is likely to accrue.

This scalar spectrum of environmental events, localized vs. global, with a key threshold level in between, maps beautifully onto the ecological hierarchy—and further across the board to the genealogical hierarchy. I have called this the "sloshing bucket" notion of evolution (Eldredge 1999—figure 3).

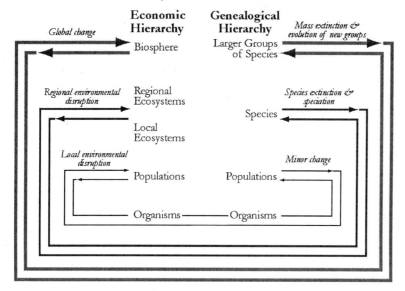

The "Sloshing Bucket" Theory of Evolution

Figure 3. The "sloshing bucket" theory of evolution—with reference to the economic and genealogical hierarchies. Environmental change is seen as the ultimate cause of evolution. Little environmental change means little evolutionary change through natural selection (thin dashed lines). Regional environmental change can lead to species extinction and evolution, with consequent larger-scale changes in ecosystems (thicker dashed lines). Mass extinction from global environmental change leads to extinction of large-scale evolutionary groups, and subsequent evolution of new large-scale groups and so to vast changes in the composition of ecosystems on Earth.

Low-level ecological disruption causes a low-level recruitment of new organisms to replenish depleted systems in ecological succession. Higher up the scale, regional perturbation triggers habitat tracking, with species survival largely intact, and with little or no perceptible evolutionary change. Natural selection at these lower levels is "stabilizing" rather than directional. Then, at the regional level, where environmental change in essence goes too far too fast, and habitat tracking is not possible for all species, extinction sets in—followed by an episode of speciation that includes true adaptive evolutionary change among a substantial subset of surviving species. At the higher, global level, extinction events may be so severe that entire groups of species—higher taxa—become extinct, and the evolutionary response is correspondingly intense, prolonged, and pronounced, so that entire skeins of related species evolve to form new "higher taxa."

All the way through this scalar series of environmental and reactive genealogical processes and events, it is the role of the genealogical systems to supply the players in the game of life. In a very real sense, only when those players—starting with organisms, but passing up through the crucial level of species and beyond—are eliminated do we start to see anything truly new appearing, and, indeed, it looks increasingly like entire species must fall before anything in the way of lasting evolutionary change is likely to take place. And species don't disappear in a vacuum: they do so in response to environmental events that are likely to take out many other species of the regional system at nearly the same time.

Hence the "sloshing bucket": causality begins with environmental disturbance at some entry level in the ecological hierarchy; it kills or dislodges organisms—and depending on the level, entire avatars, or entire local ecosystems, and the like. It is through the organism level that demes are affected—or, if the disturbance involves regional ecosystem complexes, entire species. But the effects always "slosh" back to the ecological side —as it is the genealogical entities that supply the players, at different levels, to the ecological systems, the arenas in which the economic game of life is played out on a moment-by-moment, day-by-day, year-by-year basis—up to and including the millions of years that are the lifetimes of stable regional and global biotic systems.

Thus it simply cannot be genes that, alone, are running the evolutionary show through their imagined competitive urges to leave relatively more copies of themselves to the next succeeding generation. Especially now that we understand that so much of evolutionary change is tied up with the appearance of new species; that so much of speciation is correlated with episodes of environmentally-induced species extinction; and that extinction, far from occurring in a vacuum, most often occurs near-simultaneously among a cadre of unrelated species living within the same regional biota, we see that evolution simply cannot be a purely genealogical process—still less one governed strictly by the machinations of genes.

Grene (1987), it turns out, was right when she remarked, "All evolution must occur through the interaction of the economic with the genealogical hierarchy." And she was also right in suggesting that the rather abstract formulations of biological hierarchy theory would, in a very real sense, pave the way for a deeper understanding of the nature of the evolutionary process.

NILES ELDREDGE

COMMITTEE ON EVOLUTIONARY PROCESSES,
   & DIVISION OF PALEONTOLOGY
THE AMERICAN MUSEUM OF NATURAL HISTORY
JANUARY 2002

NOTES

1. Whatever that may mean. Marjorie Grene once remarked to me that the difference between philosophy and biology is that biology "has a subject matter." It has always seemed to me that, whatever her "purely philosophical" interest in analyzing, say, the logical structure of a proposition in evolutionary biology might be, she has always been interested in seeing if that proposition could do real biological work. In other words, willy nilly Marjorie Grene has always been "doing" evolutionary biology whenever she has written on the subject—whatever purely philosophical issues might be addressed as well in the course of that work.

2. These are also sometimes known as the "ecological" and "evolutionary" hierarchies, respectively. Though I use both sets of terms in this paper, as the final section makes clear, it is perhaps misleading to call the "genealogical" hierarchy the "evolutionary" hierarchy—as evolution entails interactions between both hierarchies.

3. Clearly, the list is not identical for photosynthesizing plants and microbes, for fungi and for animals; plants, for example, do not have "digestion." For any particular kind of organism, however, there is a basic list of literally vital metabolic activities that have to do with obtaining and processing energy and nutrients so that the body may differentiate, grow, and remain alive.

4. I define species as the largest collective of organisms sharing a "mate recognition system" (Paterson 1985)—in other words, a group of organisms that shares the requisite features that allow reproduction to occur among component organisms, but not (at least as the overwhelming rule) with members of other such groups. Thus the lower levels of the "economic" hierarchy retain a flavor of the genealogical hierarchy.

5. Though similar in composition, a local deme and avatar of the same species typically do not consist of precisely the same set of individuals; for more on this point see Eldredge and Grene 1992.

6. This is so even if an organism does not reproduce: all organisms are products of the reproductive process and, unless diseased or malformed, carry the adaptations for reproduction of their species.

7. Viewing natural selection as an active process I have elsewhere observed (e.g. Eldredge 1999), I believe has had the psychological effect of "scientizing" evolution—pushing it into the realm of physics and chemistry rather than the seemingly less rigorously "scientific" so-called "historical sciences." This form of "physics envy" is wholly unnecessary—as analysis of repeated historical patterns in the history of life (as I discuss further below in this paper) in evolutionary biology is no different in logical structure than the activities of nuclear physicists analyzing the meaning of evanescent traces of subatomic particles in the cloud chambers of particle accelerators.

8. Similarly, "evolutionary psychology" is the application of sociobiological principles explicitly to human beings—an arena not discussed further in this essay.

9. Species can consist of single populations—as when reduced in numbers just prior to extinction, or when newly evolved and not yet expanded into a broad geographic range with many demal subsets.

10. All known hunter-gathering societies, for instance, San ("Bushmen"), BaAka, and BaMbuti ("pygmies"), are under threat of, at the very least, cultural extinction—and quite possibly genetic extinction as well.

11. Save the present mass extinction event—which is solely caused by one species—our own species *Homo sapiens* (see Eldredge 1998, for more on this so-called "sixth extinction").

12. The Permo-Triassic crisis is the most devastating of the mass extinctions yet to have occurred (at least since the advent of multicellular life over .5 billion years ago). Raup (1986), for example, has estimated that between 70 and 96 percent of all species became extinct at that time. The four other global mass extinctions were at the end of the Ordovician Period, within the Upper Devonian; end Triassic; and end Cretaceous Periods. The Cretaceous and Permian events divide the "Mesozoic" from the "Cenozoic," and the "Paleozoic" from the "Mesozoic" Eras (divisions of geological time), respectively—ample testimony to the changes in complexion of life on earth associated with these events.

13. Paleobiologists, of course, are not unanimous in embracing the importance (indeed, in some cases, even the reality) of turnover events in the history of life. Even Vrba's original "turnover pulse" example remains hotly debated (see, e.g., McKee 2001). More detailed studies will no doubt settle the matter—and I am betting that the results will parallel the earlier, related debate over stasis and punctuation in the fossil record (Eldredge and Gould 1972) in favor of the interpretation presented here.

REFERENCES

Brett, C. E., and G. Baird. 1995. "Coordinated Stasis and Evolutionary Ecology of Silurian to Middle Devonian Faunas in the Appalachian Basin." In *Speciation in the Fossil Record*, edited by R. Anstey and D. H. Erwin, pp. 285–315. New York: Columbia University Press.

Cohen, J. E. 1995. *How Many People Can the Earth Support?* New York and London: W. W. Norton.

Damuth, J. 1985. "Selection among 'Species': A Formulation in Terms of Natural Functional Units." *Evolution* 39:1132–46.

Darwin, C. 1859. *On the Origin of Species*. London: John Murray.

———.1871. *The Descent of Man, and Selection in Relation to Sex*. London: John Murray.

Dawkins, R. 1976. *The Selfish Gene*. New York and Oxford: Oxford University Press.

Eldredge, N. 1989. *Macroevolutionary Dynamics: Species, Niches and Adaptive Peaks*. New York: McGraw-Hill.

———. 1992. "Marjorie Grene, 'Two Evolutionary Theories' and Modern Evolutionary Theory." *Synthese* 92:135–49.

———. 1995c. *Dominion*. New York: Henry Holt and Co.

———. 1998. *Life in the Balance: Humanity and the Biodiversity Crisis*. Princeton: Princeton University Press.

———. 1999. *The Pattern of Evolution*. New York: W. H. Freeman.

Eldredge, N., and S. J. Gould. 1972. "Punctuated Equilibria: An Alternative to Phyletic Gradualism." In *Models in Paleobiology*, edited by T. J. M. Schopf, pp. 82–115. San Francisco: Freeman, Cooper.

Eldredge, N., and M. Grene. 1992. *Interactions: The Biological Context of Social Systems*. New York: Columbia University Press.

Eldredge, N. et al. 2003. "The Dynamics of Evolutionary Stasis." *Paleobiology*, submitted.

Grene, M. J. 1987. "Hierarchies in Biology." *American Scientist* 75: 504–10.

Hamilton, W. D. 1964a. "The Genetical Evolution of Social Behavior, I." *J. Theor. Biol.* 7: 1–16.

———. 1964b. "The Genetical Evolution of Social Behavior, II." *J. Theor. Biol.* 7: 17–52.

Johnson, R. G. 1972. "Conceptual Models of Benthic Marine Communities." In *Models in Paleobiology,* edited by T. J. M. Schopf, pp. 148–59. San Francisco: Freeman, Cooper.

Kennedy, P. 1993. *Preparing for the Twenty-first Century*. New York: Random House.

Lovelock, J. 1979. *Gaia*. Oxford: Oxford University Press.

McKee, J. K. 2001. "Faunal Turnover Rates and Mammalian Biodiversity of the Late Pliocene and Pleistocene of Eastern Africa." *Paleobiology* 27:500–11.

Paterson, H. E. H. 1985. "The Recognition Concept of Species." In *Species and Speciation. Transvaal Mus. Monogr.* 4:21–29, edited by E. S. Vrba.

Raup, D. M. 1986. "Biological Extinction in Earth History." *Science* 231:1528–33.

Vrba, E. S. 1985. "Environment and Evolution: Alternative Causes of the Temporal Distribution of Evolutionary Events." *S. Afr. J. Sci.* 81:229–36.

Williams, G. C. 1966. *Adaptation and Natural Selection: A Critique of Some Current Evolutionary Thought.* Princeton: Princeton University Press.

Wilson, E. O. 1975. *Sociobiology.* Cambridge, Mass.: Harvard University Press.

Wright, S. 1932. "The Roles of Mutation, Inbreeding, Crossbreeding, and Selection in Evolution." *Proc. Sixth Int. Congr. Genetics* 1:356–66.

REPLY TO NILES ELDREDGE

This is an exciting and innovative time in evolutionary theory. In 1959, the Darwin centenary was celebrated chiefly (if not altogether) as the triumph of the evolutionary synthesis, which successively united Mendelian genetics and the Darwinian theory of natural selection (Tax 1960). In their enthusiasm, many students of evolution envisaged the course of nature's history as a gradual alteration produced by the competition between genes directed by the power of natural selection. Niles Eldredge, together with Steve Gould, initiated a significant modification of the gradualism that characterized the synthesis, when they introduced their conception of punctuated equilibrium (Eldredge and Gould 1972; cf. Gould and Eldredge 1993). Some years later, a flurry of work in hierarchy theory seemed to be introducing further complications. The article of mine that Eldredge cites was written in response to those discussions. Hierarchy theory as such didn't come to much, but Eldredge has continued to make fruitful use of the concept of hierarchy, and, in particular, of his favorite distinction, that between two hierarchies, the genealogical and the ecological. In his 1999 book *The Pattern of Evolution* and in the present essay, he applies that distinction in particular to the problem of mass extinction. This seems appropriate. The stories of the corals and of the dinosaurs, for instance, are plausibly told in these terms (although I must confess to finding the "sloshing bucket" metaphor extremely unattractive!).

However, with all due respect, I venture to suggest two ways in which Eldredge's account needs to be supplemented.

First, there are other developments in recent evolutionary theory that deserve consideration. Eldredge wants to stress the importance of environmental factors at a number of levels of the genealogical hierarchy, and that's fair enough. But what he is opposing is what in the book we wrote together we called "ultradarwinism" (a name we should not have chosen, since it was already used a century ago to characterize the position of August Weismann—or at least of Weismannism (Griesemer and Wimsatt

1989). By this Eldredge meant (or we meant) what is perhaps better dubbed "genic selectionism": the view put forward by Williams (Williams 1966) and Dawkins (Dawkins 1976), which emphasizes the internecine war of gene against gene, and neglects the ecological agencies that undoubtedly figure in shaping the course of evolution, as well as the structure of demes or species, that is, entities higher up the genealogical hierarchy itself. Even if we look primarily at the genealogical side, however, the situation turns out to be more complicated than it once appeared. Genes come in modules, in organized clusters that remain constant throughout evolution, despite myriad changes in the phenotypes they initiate (see, for example, Raff 1996). And since constant configurations can give rise to novelty only through changes occurring during development, it turns out that developmental biology, which the older synthesis considered irrelevant, has a great deal to offer to its evolutionary sister. The new synthesis in process of formation is far richer in its conceptual structure than the single-minded genic selectionism Eldredge is opposing (Gilbert 2000, esp. pp. 703–5).

Nor, secondly, is the phenomenon of mass extinction, fascinating though it is for paleontologists—and especially, I suppose, for friends of punc eq!—the only feature of nature's history that needs explaining. Granted, the extinction of the dinosaurs gave the mammals, till then lurking somewhere inconspicuously in the undergrowth, an opportunity for their striking advance and radiation. But how did mammals originate in the first place? More radically, how did life originate? Or metazoa? For eukaryotes, we have the endosymbiotic theory (Margulis 1981), an account it would be difficult to twist to suit the Eldredge pattern. The origin of the vertebrate limb is another favorite question (Shubin, et al. 1997). In short, the question of evolutionary transitions has acquired a prominent place in the literature (Maynard Smith and Szathmáry 1995; Griesemer 2000). Of course, such problems demand external or ecological as well as internal factors for their resolution, but I suspect that they are not as neatly separable as Eldredge suggests. In short, what he is presenting is a model for mass extinction, rather than for evolutionary biology as such.

M. G.

REFERENCES

Dawkins, Richard. 1976. *The Selfish Gene*. New York and Oxford: Oxford University Press.

Eldredge, Niles. 1999. *The Pattern of Evolution*. New York: W. H. Freeman.

Eldredge, Niles, and Stephen Jay Gould. 1972. "Punctuated Equilibria: An Alternative to Phyletic Gradualism." In *Models in Paleobiology*, edited by T. J. M. Schopf, pp. 82–115. San Francisco: Freeman, Cooper.

Eldredge, Niles, and Marjorie Grene. 1992. *Interactions: The Biological Context of Social Systems*. New York: Columbia University Press.

Gilbert, Scott L. 2000. *Developmental Biology*. 6th ed. Sunderland, Mass.: Sinauer.

Griesemer, J. 2000. "The Units of Evolutionary Transition." *Selection* 1: 67–80.

Griesemer, J., and W. C. Wimsatt. 1989. "Picturing Weismannism: A Case Study of Conceptual Evolution." In *What the Philosophy of Biology Is: Essays for David Hull*, edited by Michael Ruse, pp. 75–137. Dordrecht: Kluwer.

Margulis, Lynn. 1981. *Symbiosis and Cell Evolution*. San Francisco: Freeman.

Maynard Smith, J., and E. Szathmáry. 1995. *The Major Transitions in Evolution*. Oxford: W. H. Freeman.

Raff, Rudolf A. 1966. *The Shape of Life*. Chicago: University of Chicago Press.

Shubin, N., C. Tabin and S. Carroll. 1997. *Nature* 388: 639–48.

Tax, Sol., ed. 1960. *Evolution after Darwin*. 3 vols. Chicago: University of Chicago Press.

Williams, George C. 1966. *Adaptation and Natural Selection: A Critique of Some Current Evolutionary Thought*. Princeton: Princeton University Press.

13

Richard M. Burian

"HISTORICAL REALISM," "CONTEXTUAL OBJECTIVITY," AND CHANGING CONCEPTS OF THE GENE

[W]e really must get over the absurdity of holding what is cultural to be unreal. After all, acid rain is real, smog is real, the bomb is real. And if ostrich-like we choose to ignore the evils that are our own doing, our ignorance is real.[1]

—Grene

INTRODUCTION

Marjorie Grene has long been fascinated by the history of genetics, changing concepts of the gene, and the ramifications of the complex conceptual changes in genetics for various domains of biology. She remains actively interested in the topic; recently, she participated in a course I taught on the topic, criticized a number of papers on the history of gene concepts, and instigated the formation of a reading group dealing with gene concepts in evolution and development. In thinking about how best to tackle an essay for this volume, I thought it appropriate to address gene concepts and an aspect of her work that influenced my approach to that topic. To start, I focus on some features of her general approach to the philosophy of science, turning thereafter to a discussion of how that approach plays out in thinking about the history of genetics and, more particularly, of gene concepts.

We will start with a consideration of historical realism and contextual objectivity, two aspects of Professor Grene's work that will be focal in this essay. These labels do not refer to rigid dogmas or formal doctrines; rather, they designate an approach that pays serious attention to the historical setting of scientific and philosophical work and seeks to understand what, in context, counts as epistemically responsible support for claims that something-or-other is true or justified. We then turn to a few aspects of the history of gene concepts that are of interest to philosophers—and not only for philosophers of biology. Finally, I will highlight the concordance of the work on gene concepts with the philosophical commitments taken, in good part, from Grene's work.

HISTORICAL REALISM AND CONTEXTUAL OBJECTIVITY

These terms come from the title of a short article that Marjorie Grene published in 1987 (Grene 1987) in which she took me to task in passing for taking "the problem of scientific realism" too seriously (Burian 1985). As she showed, I was already substantially committed to views that she and others had long advocated, views that should lead one to set aside the problem of scientific realism in its traditional forms. She argued, *inter alia*, that one's epistemic responsibility in science (and in much else) is *local*, that it depends on one's specific cultural location and that, nonetheless, the resulting historicism does not result in pernicious relativism or antirealism. This sort of historicism in no way removes us from the world, from contact with reality, or from having effective tools for getting below surface appearances to underlying realities. It does reveal, however, that we encounter multiple levels of phenomena in the world within which we, as knowing subjects, are embedded. Correspondingly, seemingly conflicting explanations often deploy levels of explanation complementary to, but not contradictory with, one another.[2] Witness the epigraph to this essay.

Against this background, Grene holds that the supposed *global* issue about scientific realism—couched, simplistically, as "are theoretical entities real?"—is a nonstarter. Rather, we face piecemeal problems about the reality and properties of quarks, genes, higher order control processes and the like, about the interconnections and interrelations among the ontological levels we find in things and the explanatory possibilities provided at different levels. As embodied beings, always in the middle of things in the world into which we are born and within which we are raised, the question should not be whether we have knowledge of the world around us, but how we gain—and correct—knowledge of the particular things, processes, and happenings in our world and what forms that knowledge takes. (There is, of course, much more than this involved in Grene's view, for scientific and epistemological issues touch only a small proportion of the problems we face in dealing with our multileveled reality.) The multileveled character of the world is something found, part of what we encounter as we explore our surroundings (Grene 1978). And, as many philosophers of science have argued of late, our knowledge is nothing like knowledge as characterized in empiricist fantasies of a foundation of knowledge in pure sensory knowledge. Grene argues, rightly, that our knowledge is produced by active interaction of embodied, knowing subjects with each other and with their surrounding world. As such beings, we must operate from within some particular perspective or other and must live within a culture or an overlapping group of cultures. Nonetheless, such knowledge is genuine knowledge of the world in which we find ourselves and which we modify by our deeds.

Given all of this, a core issue is how we can make our knowledge of our surroundings as good as possible, that is, in terminology she adopted in her article on historical realism and contextual objectivity, how to be *epistemically responsible*. In rough summary, the following claims characterize knowledge gained by beings in the middle of things in a multi-leveled world:

- Our embodiment limits us to certain perceptual connections to the world and, as of any period of time and span of places, limits the perspectives we can gain on it.
- The fact that each of us is raised in a particular culture (or cultures) and can participate in only a restricted range of cultures and sub-cultures limits our means of interacting with the surrounding world. Understanding this is crucial in delimiting what we can know and how.
- More specifically, within individual lifetimes we can access only limited technical and conceptual modalities by means of which to acquire contact with, and knowledge of, our surroundings and to work with in attempting to transcend the limitations of our conceptual schemes and perceptual apparatus. As far as we can tell,
- the limitations we face are not fixed; we can improve our technical and conceptual tools as we work on matters of interest to us or react to the many surprises we encounter. Thus,
- the principal way to assess knowledge claims properly is "locally" in terms of the available instrumental, theoretical, and conceptual tools available in the situation of interest. This applies, self-reflexively, when we think about ourselves and about what we can know in our own situations.

These limitations are not as constraining as they sound at first. Historically, we have managed changes in concepts, theories, and experimental technologies that provide ample evidence of our ability to improve scientific knowledge. What follows are some thoughts about how we break through the limitations imposed by the restricted access we have to the world. This will provide the starting point for a consideration of what happened to the concept of the gene in the last century, a task that will occupy the second part of this essay.

Understanding properly how we are embodied wholly undermines empiricist passivism and lands us in an activist theory of mind. As exceptional animals, we are trained and enculturated by interactions with our peers and by interacting with an environment. In order to do the things we do, we must learn to differentiate among environmentally salient objects and occurrences. We learn to do so both by being taught to categorize in particular ways and by doing things that alter our surroundings and our category structure. The historicity of human beings is crucial—by learning to do things, including to speak and think, we learn who and what we are and re-form our understandings of what we are, can be, and do. The historical processes by which we become the persons we are interact with the culture and the larger environment.

Grene's understanding of our interactions with the environment was greatly influenced by J. J. Gibson. She quotes him thus:

> The human environment is not a *new* environment—an artificial environment distinct from the natural—but the same old environment modified by man . . . It is a mistake to separate the natural from the artificial as if there were two environments: artifacts have to be manufactured from natural substances. It is also a mistake to separate the cultural environment from the natural environment, as if there were a world of mental products distinct from the world of material products. There is only one world, however diverse, and all animals live in it, although we human animals have altered it to suit ourselves. We have done so wastefully, thoughtlessly, and, if we do not mend our ways, fatally. (Gibson 1979; quoted in Grene 1987, p. 73)

To understand the changes we effect on the environment and our thought, we must attend, first and foremost, to the specific practices involved. Isolated anticipations of new theories, not taken up by others, do not count for much in the history of science; similarly, environmental change and transformations of thought do not affect us significantly unless they affect our practices. And this is markedly true in science, where specific instrumentation is usually required to embody new theories and practices. The instrumentation and the practices surrounding it are based on significant regularities and on interactions with the supposed entities with which scientists are concerned. This is how scientists gain feedback from, and well-grounded knowledge of, the entities they study. As Grene puts it, "Instead of logical reconstruction almost wholly detached from any contact with the life of science, [what we need is study of] . . . specific famil[ies] of practices . . ." (Grene 1987, p. 70). Again, modifying some phrases taken from David Annis (Annis 1978, p. 216),

> "science as practiced *has yielded* justified beliefs about the world." In any ongoing scientific discipline there is a body of truths (as we hope) already relied on, within the compass of which inquiry at the forefront of knowledge proceeds. What used to be problematic becomes accepted knowledge; what *was* theoretical comes to belong to the background of accepted "fact." Indeed, one of the intriguing questions in the new philosophy of science is the problem of how theories become facts—an inconceivable transition in the older tradition, but a fundamental one on this newer, more concretely realistic . . . style of thought. (Grene 1987, p. 72)

The practices of scientific communities are epistemic. They include norms for criticism, standards for evaluating the seriousness of criticism, and meta-norms that militate against shutting out potentially serious criticisms. Examples of such criticisms are those that come from neighboring disciplines with sharply different perspectives, but that nonetheless rest on well-grounded expectations about the behavior of the same objects or processes as are dealt with in a particular base discipline. But for such criticisms to take effect their impact must be primarily local rather than global. Serious objections have to alter commitments, practices, and the epistemic weight of specific background knowledge. We will see this last point play itself out importantly in my discussion of gene concepts.

One further way in which Grene has influenced my account of gene concepts is in fostering explanatory pluralism, which is required by the multiple explanatory and ontological levels that she has stressed. Many issues are bundled together here, among them the issue of reductionism and the roles of higher order organization in the causal order. Grene advocates, and to a considerable extent has converted me to, a position that she characterizes as "hopelessly pluralistic."

> [W]e recognize the rich and multi-dimensional organization of the natural world, such that the orderlinesses of parts of it not only may be studied in different ways and/or at different levels, but *exist* in different ways and/or at different levels. . . . [From this perspective,] the old over-abstract question [of reduction] is transformed into a more fruitful one: about particular *contexts* within which relations between different disciplines arise. The question is always: what needs explaining in the context of this particular problem, and what other concepts or principles or methods can appropriately be imported here and now from other disciplines, and whether at a more or less "micro" level of analysis. (Grene 1987, p. 77)

Let us see how this plays out in dealing with recent work on the history of gene concepts and the impact of the Grenean philosophical perspective on that work. To facilitate this project, I turn to a summary account of the different gene concepts in four genetic disciplines: transmission genetics, population genetics, molecular genetics, and developmental genetics.

DISCIPLINARY DIFFERENCES IN THE HISTORY OF CONCEPTS OF THE GENE

Transmission Genetics

Mendel's famous account of the constitution of his peas (Mendel 1865, 1966), which helped shape the discipline of genetics after it was "rediscovered" in 1900, was based entirely on his analysis of extraordinary paradigmatic experiments involving hybridization of carefully chosen strains. From these experiments, Mendel concluded that in the ovaries of the hybrids there are formed as many sorts of egg cells, and in the anthers as many sorts of pollen cells, as there are possible constant combination forms (subsequently interpreted as homozygotes with fixed traits) and that these egg and pollen cells agree in their internal compositions with those of the separate forms. (See Mendel 1966, p. 24.)[3] With the rediscovery of Mendel's work, there was an efflorescence of breeding work aimed at identifying the traits determined by the "elements" that determine the constitution of the egg and sperm cells and, with that, identifying the elements responsible for the constitution of the organism. The principal (and, for many workers, the only) tools available for testing Mendelian claims about the hereditary constitution of organisms were breeding, the use of pedigrees, and the study of patterns of inheritance of trait differences. This had the consequence that the sole means of identifying what later came to be called genes required the existence of detectably different versions of specific discrete traits inherited in definite patterns. Because of this concentration on the patterns in which traits—and especially trait differences—are transmitted from parents to offspring, the resultant discipline has come to be called *transmission genetics*. Initially, in the absence of stably inherited trait differences (by means of which alternative alleles of a single gene were identified) transmission genetics had no way to pick out specific genes. Thus, genes were identified only by means of the inheritance of specific phenotypic differences. In spite of considerable complications of detail, this remained true throughout the history of classical genetics: genes were identified by the detectable differences they caused or, more cautiously, with which they were correlated.[4]

These limitations of breeding experiments, joined to the need to establish specific differing traits that yield constant forms, led to one of the two attitudes that dominated classical genetics from roughly 1910 (by which time genetics was becoming established as a distinct discipline) until about World War II. This attitude was prominent in the work of such founding figures as William Bateson and Wilhelm Johannsen, who coined the term "gene" in 1909 (Johannsen 1909). They both held that the constitution of genes is unknown and that the concept of the gene should be emptied of theoretical commitments on this score. On this view, the gene concept provided means for summarizing breeding data and served as the key to a system of calculations for predicting distribution of traits in well characterized populations. The gene concept thus codified the claim that in certain conditions certain distinctive alternative states of the egg and sperm (the presence of particular alleles) could determine the presence, absence, or state of the traits correlated either with one allele, an alternative allele, or the pairing of the two alternative alleles. On this supposedly atheoretical operational account, genes are of unknown physical constitution. No gene is intrinsically characterized, but it is identified functionally by the effects that its variants have on form, color, size, weight, and so forth, of organisms, and on specific parts of the body, specific behaviors, or specific chemical constituents of plants and animals. One might hope to understand the physical constitutions of genes some day, but those constitutions might not be material. For example, genes might be harmonic resonances or some sort of stable equilibria in the cell as a whole.[5] The staying power of this anti-theoretical operationalist attitude, which can be found throughout the classical period, is evident from the fact that it was still strongly advocated in a famous valedictory paper on the gene by L. J. Stadler, an important plant geneticist, written on his deathbed (Stadler 1954). This attitude, however, was in dialectical tension with a second attitude from at least 1910 on.

An alternative attitude toward the classical gene was rooted in the developments of cytology and in the strong materialist commitments of many geneticists, including T. H. Morgan and H. J. Muller. Starting in 1910, Morgan and his disciples developed the chromosomal theory of the gene, already partially articulated in papers of Boveri and Sutton in 1902 (Boveri 1902; Sutton 1902; see also Sutton 1903). Famously, the Morgan group was able to demonstrate that particular alleles are located in particular regions of particular chromosomes and to develop a technology for locating genes at chromosomal regions by a mixture of breeding techniques and cytological tests and tricks.[6] Muller's and Stadler's discoveries of X-ray mutagenesis (Muller 1927; Stadler 1928) and Painter's discovery of the usefulness of giant salivary gland chromosomes for constructing physical maps of chromosomes (Painter 1934) greatly accelerated this work. X-rays made it possible to create new chromosomal aberrations and gene mutations, thus leading to the discovery and manipulation of many new genes.

Morgan and Muller became the leading theoreticians of the chromosomal theory of the (classical) gene, arguing that genes are material particles arrayed on chromosomes and that genetics should study their material constitution. Muller argued that genes would have to manifest unique properties to explain the transmission of traits across generations. As early as 1922,[7] he held that these physical properties included

- self replication (which he called "autocatalysis")
- ability to manufacture different products such as the pigments and the proteins that make up the bodies of plants and animals (which he called "heterocatalysis")
- the ability to mutate and continue to replicate, while making alternative or variant products.

Muller held that the physical constitution and properties of genes were the holy grail of his discipline. He hoped that ever-finer grained genetic and cytological experiments might yield the exact physical locations and structures of particular genes, but insisted that all means of physical and chemical analysis should be employed in the service of this task. Alas, before World War II the available tools were not sufficient even to identify the substance of which genes are made. Proteins were the most prominent candidate, with combinations of proteins and nucleic acids being second most likely. Nucleic acids—then thought to be boring, essentially invariant, molecules that form a structural scaffold on which proteins were stretched to maintain particular conformations—were quite implausible candidates to be genes. In the face of these difficulties, operationalists like Stadler treated the putative chromosomal locations of genes as aspects of the phenotype—they were *correlated* with genes rather than serving as a means of determining their physical constitutions. Thus, in 1954 Stadler, emphasizing his pessimism about geneticists' ability to determine the physical constitution of genes, denied that there was any prospect of validating Muller's or any other "theoretical gene" (Stadler's term) in the near future.

Population Genetics

The second discipline to be discussed is population genetics. This discipline uses mathematical models to trace out the fate of genes in populations, assuming that they behave in accordance with Mendelian rules (including various complications thereof) and, thus, seeks to describe the evolution of populations over a limited number of generations under various selective regimes and the like. Population genetics became, among other things, an important tool for reconciling transmission genetics with Darwinian evolutionary theory.[8] I will set aside enormously important issues about the

history of population genetics to adumbrate three aspects of the reconciliation between transmission genetics and evolutionary theory important
to the present discussion. These concern the compatibility of macroevolution with the mechanisms of microevolution as they were understood
by population geneticists, the fact that most population genetic models
relevant to evolution made no claims regarding the inner constitution of
genes, and the fact that most models bearing on long-term evolution did not
need to examine interactions between genes.

The reconciliation of microevolution and macroevolution in the
evolutionary synthesis rested on a compatibility argument. Population
genetics modeled the genetic evolution of populations under genetically
plausible scenarios in which selection, sampling error in small populations,
mutation, and interactions among genes all played a role. In the absence of
other, specific, evolutionary forces, and in light of R. A. Fisher's theorems
about the great power of selection to shape genetic evolution in large
populations, population geneticists grew confident that they had laid out
everything needed to understand macroevolution—that is, large-scale
evolutionary change. As Theodosius Dobzhansky put it in 1937 in one of
the formative documents of the evolutionary synthesis, his magisterial
Genetics and the Evolution of Species, "we are compelled at the present
level of knowledge reluctantly to put a sign of equality between the
mechanisms of macro- and micro-evolution . . ." (Dobzhansky 1937, p.
12).[9] Later, this position hardened considerably, into a dogmatic insistence
that the only mechanisms or sources of evolutionary change required to
explain macroevolution are those countenanced in microevolution thus
analyzed.[10] Even more important was the deployment of a technical notion
of heritability, more specifically, of so-called narrow heritability.[11]
Mathematical development of the theory of narrow heritability allowed
population geneticists to assimilate the effectiveness of both artificial and
natural selection to the replacement of single alleles by alternative alleles,
with genes considered one by one, in independence of each other. Models
constructed in this way could be fit to most microevolutionary change. In
consequence, it was often argued that the genome is generally so structured
that evolution can take place one gene at a time. This slightly tricky idea is
nicely expressed in a quotation from a review by John Maynard Smith, in
which he disagrees with Richard Lewontin about the importance of
interactions between genes in evolutionary contexts:

> [S]uppose we want to know whether one gene [i.e., allele] at a locus will
> replace another in evolution. The new gene will have an effect: in the first
> instance, it will cause the appearance of an altered protein, or perhaps of the
> same protein at a different time or place in development. But whether this will
> increase "fitness" depends on how its effects interact with everything else

going on in the organism, and on how the organism interacts with its environment.... [Lewontin argues] that genes at different loci ... will become preferentially linked together in co-operating units, and that it is these units, rather than individual genes, that are relevant in evolution. Now this *might* be true. ... However, observations . . . suggest that in actual populations it is rarely the case (technically, genes in natural populations tend to be in linkage equilibrium).

What this means is that, for most purposes, it is correct to think of evolution occurring "one gene at a time." ... [I]t seems that it is usually *not* the case that groups of co-operating genes are held together, so that they can collectively spread through a species, replacing an earlier group of genes. (Maynard Smith 1986; reprinted in Maynard Smith 1989, quotation at pp. 34–35)

Population genetics recognizes many important ways in which genes interact with one another, many complex breeding systems that can affect the course of evolution, and many difficult issues about the impact of small populations on speciation and on particular pathways in evolutionary history. Nonetheless, Maynard Smith's claim is that in much of population genetics the genome can be treated as if it were composed of independent genes whose variants are replaced, independently of one another, one gene at a time. Like the genes of classical transmission genetics, these genes are treated as unitary entities, with distinct variants, and the dominant models of the theory purport to show that, to a good first approximation, most evolution is driven by the replacement, gene by gene, of one variant with another under the influence of phenotypic selection.[12]

Molecular Genetics

The advent of molecular genetics, especially the molecular genetics of eucaryotes (organisms with nucleated cells, including all genuinely multi-cellular organisms and many microorganisms such as yeasts, molds, and protozoa, but not bacteria or green algae) has enormously complicated gene concepts. Because of space limitations I cannot portray these complications seriously. To illustrate the sorts of difficulties that must be faced, I will list a few of the dozens of points established in the last quarter century, all found in current college textbooks, that disrupt the classical concept of the gene.

- In some small viruses, genes overlap in such a way that adjacent nucleotides serve as the starting point for transcription. Thus, measured in terms of protein products, two or more different genes are interleaved in the exact same stretch of DNA, i.e., two genes for unrelated protein products may be encoded, inextricably, by one DNA sequence.
- Typical eucaryotic genes are not contiguous. The "coding regions" (or

"exons") that contain the nucleotide sequences that specify the amino acid sequence encoded by the gene in question are usually in linear order, but are separated by "intervening sequences" or "introns." The exons, which often correspond to functionally significant domains in the corresponding protein, can be "shuffled" in evolutionary time. This means that it is possible for functional units within genes to be recombined on an evolutionary time scale far more efficiently than if functional genes had to be built one nucleotide at a time. Many ordinary genes contain more than ten coding regions; some contain hundreds!

- The introns of a eucaryotic gene sometimes (though rarely) contain sequences of nucleotides that encode information employed in making another protein, distinct from that encoded by the gene within which the intron is embedded. Thus, sometimes, genes *cannot even be "read out" in linear order* as one proceeds along a chromosome. A maze of regulatory controls is required to ensure the "correct readout" of any eucaryotic gene. And the RNA transcribed from a eucaryotic chromosome must be processed to remove the segments corresponding to introns in order to yield a "mature" messenger RNA.

- During the lives of some multicellular organisms, the structure of some genes changes by a kind of nucleotide shuffling so that the protein structures produced by some cells of the adult are not encoded in the genome of the zygote. This device of (restricted) nucleotide shuffling is crucial to mammalian immune systems. It enables distinct lines of immune system cells to produce the approximately one million distinct proteins required for immune function.

- The product encoded by a given string of nucleotides depends on the cellular context in which those nucleotides are found. This context dependence takes many forms. For example:
  A. The genetic code is sometimes slightly different in the nucleus than it is in mitochondria and slightly different in some species than in others. Thus, to know what protein (i.e., what string of amino acids) a particular sequence of DNA nucleotides will yield, one needs to know its location within the cell and in what organism the DNA is located.
  B. Messenger RNA is often altered systematically in the cytoplasm ("post-transcriptional modification"), so that the product of a protein-encoding gene cannot be read off the sequence of nucleotides in the DNA or even the RNA transcript of the DNA when that transcript is still in the nucleus. Furthermore, in many cases, the precise way in which an RNA message is altered in the cytoplasm depends on the physiological state of the organism or the sort of cell (e.g., liver or kidney) in which the transcript is processed, so that even within a single cell or organism, the same nucleotide

sequence yields different products at different times or places.

C. In different cellular contexts, the same protein plays radically different functions. The same segment of DNA, regulated so as to produce its product in different times and places in the life cycle of the organism, may thus serve entirely different functions, and thus justifiably be counted as encoding different genes.

- A veritable zoo of distant elements in the genome serve as regulators, promoters, inhibitors, modulators, and so on, of gene action. Such regulatory elements affect the timing of gene expression, the quantity of product produced, the size of the molecule produced (i.e., at what point transcription is halted or RNA is cut), the parts of the body in which it is produced, and so forth.

These points yield some simple morals for present purposes. The protein produced by transcribing and translating a given sequence of nucleotides from a DNA molecule is context dependent. Even in "simple" cases, where the context-dependence is not critical, the protein that results is a function not only of the sequence of nucleotides but also of many other cellular factors. As best we can tell, there are no easy general rules as to precisely how much of the rest of the cell must be held fixed to ensure that the same product will result. Put differently, neither the quantity nor content of the biological information contained in a segment of a DNA molecule is specified simply by the sequence of nucleotides it contains. Both the quantity of information and its precise content can be—and often are—altered by changing other aspects of the cellular context, which means that it is enormously difficult to provide a univocal delimitation of molecular genes (Portin 1993; Burian 1995; Fogle 2000). In particular:

- The cellular context varies systematically with the general physiological condition of the organism. Alternative cellular states often feed back onto the apparatus for reading out DNA or on post-transcriptional processing of messenger RNAs in the cytoplasm. In well-delimited cases, such contextual changes alter the product of determinate sequences of nucleotides. Similarly, in different cells, the same protein product of a given gene may be used to perform drastically different functions. Therefore,
- the intrinsic characterization of a DNA molecule does not, by itself, specify how many genes it contains, what those genes do, or even (in the case of genes that code for proteins) what sequence of amino acids they will yield. The illusion that the nucleotide sequence of a DNA segment suffices to specify its product(s) arises from the fact that in many important cases when a DNA sequence of interest is transported

from one setting to another, the same product, serving essentially the same function, is produced. But this is far from universally true. Not only are there many exceptions, but the systematic differences involved in particular cases enforce the abstract point that it is DNA-in-a-specific-context that plays the role of a particular gene, not simply the DNA as such.

Developmental Genetics

Recent work on the control of development in higher organisms has produced a new concept of a *developmental gene*. Of particular interest are the ways in which developmental genes are tied together in evolutionarily conserved packages, sometimes referred to as "modules." These modules function as supragenic entities whose structure and function cannot be understood solely by analysis of the intrinsic structure of the DNA and the proteins of which they are composed.[13] Perhaps the most dramatic example to convey the extraordinary conservation of systems involved in the control of developmental processes is this: by using the new tools of biotechnology, one can transfer a gene called *Pax 6* from a mouse to selected cells in a drosophila (a fruit fly)—say the cells in a region set aside in the larva fated to make a wing, or a leg, or an antenna in the adult. By using the tricks for regulating genes that have been learned in recent years and applied with great precision to drosophila, one can turn on that mouse gene—or the homologous drosophila gene, called *eyeless*, named for the effect that results from having defective copies of that gene. It does not matter whether the gene that is expressed is the mouse's *Pax 6* or the drosophila's *eyeless*, the result of turning it on is to initiate the cascade of events that makes an eye—a histologically normal drosophila eye that grows nerves to the part of the brain that normally receives input from eyes. So we now can grow drosophila eyes on a drosophila wing, leg, or antenna by use of a mouse gene (Halder, Callaerts, and Gehring 1995; Burian 1997; Gehring 1998).

This dramatic case is exceptional in many ways, but it connects closely to a series of fundamental discoveries that show that modules that include so-called developmental genes specify division of the body into parts and the identities of various neighboring parts. Thus, for example, there are "signal transduction" modules that regulate DNA transcription and, in the process, specify where the divisions between segments of a drosophila thorax occur. These modules are composed of a small number of genes and associated activating proteins, some of which are produced by those very genes themselves. Tight feedback controls determine what the module as a whole does within a particular physiological setting. A second specific set of modules determines that each successive segment in the series of segments in the thorax (working from front to back) has the identity of one segment further to the rear than its predecessor. These modules and the mechanisms by which they work are now moderately well understood. They are laid out in sequence on the drosophila genome and the action of each is needed to activate its physical successor. As one proceeds down the body, once the cell divisions are laid down, the protein products involved in defining the boundaries between body compartments play a role in activating the successive segment-identifying modules, so that the interaction of these modules with those proteins is part of what sets up the controls that identify the segment.

Comparing mice and drosophila, it turns out that the same control modules employed in defining segment divisions (the divisions between vertebrae in the backbone) and segment identities (e.g., the identity of the third vs. fourth thoracic vertebrae) in mice are involved in parallel processes in drosophila. Although there are some specific molecular differences between the genes in the mouse and drosophila modules, they are relatively minor and irrelevant to the fact that the genes play precisely parallel roles in the functioning of the control system. Furthermore, some of the same modules that define anterior to posterior boundaries in drosophila, mice, humans, and many other organisms also are reused to define boundaries and segment identities from proximal to distal in legs and antennae in insects and arms and legs in mammals. Thus, the system of interrelated control modules has been evolutionarily conserved since before the separation of arthropod and vertebrate lineages—that is, for more than 500 million years. Unlike classical genes, the developmental genes found in these modules are properly identified by the invariant way in which they perform the same function in the context of their modules rather than by differences of the sort that were the key to identifying classical genes.

Thinking functionally, the reason that developmental genes were not discovered in the classical era is that there were no available variants, no differences that made a difference, with which to work in recognizing these genes. It was only when molecular similarities could be discovered that those genes were identified (and, arguably, only with tools that allowed analysis of similarities rather than differences that they were identif*iable*). Again, arguably, it is the tight integration of these modules that have kept them stable for over 500 million years. The product of one gene within the module interacts with some of the DNA within the module to regulate the expression of other genes within the module. This being so, it is the package of genes and gene products that constitute the control unit and an analysis of the disaggregated parts of the module, and the behavior of those parts taken singly, would not provide the information needed to understand the behavior of the integrated module.

These are large and controversial claims and our biological knowledge of this domain is evolving quite rapidly, but the general picture is one on which I think it safe to stand. If so, in spite of the fact that all genes are composed of sequences of nucleotides, there are major differences among genes that are recognized at different levels. Developmental genes, identified via the constancy of their roles in control modules, are very different entities than classical genes, which are identified by the different effects of their variant alleles, which are different in turn from molecular genes, which are identified in extremely context-specific ways. This is so because of the tight structural integration of developmental genes in modules that delimit segments and provide those segments with specific sequential identities, the relative independence of classical genes from each other, and the functional and content-dependence of molecular genes on the cellular context.[14]

CONCLUSION

To close, let us return to the relationship of this discussion of gene concepts to the earlier discussion of Marjorie Grene's views on historical realism and contextual objectivity. It is of particular interest to note the close correlation between the practices and questions of biologists who work in different disciplines and pursue different lines of work and the concepts that they use to characterize the entities and process with which they deal. Following Hans-Jörg Rheinberger (Rheinberger 2000; see also Keller 2000), I maintain that each of the genetic disciplines we have discussed (and others as well—e.g., biochemical genetics and physiological genetics) have distinct concepts of the gene.

The variation from discipline to discipline is rather extreme, as even my brief discussion shows. Because the practices of classical genetics were rooted in breeding experiments and chromosomal analyses, classical genes could be identified only in virtue of the existence of well-established allelic differences and well-established patterns of inheritance. Given the linkage to chromosomal locations and the yes/no identification of particular alleles, classical genes were taken to be wholes, linearly ordered on chromosomes. The contrast with molecular genes is nearly total. In the latter discipline, there are no adequate ways of establishing *the* boundaries between molecular genes, which are ill-bounded parts of a macromolecule. The genes of molecular biology need not be linearly ordered since multiple genes, in various topologies, may be found within a single stretch of nucleotides and since the criteria for identifying genes allow dispersed combinations of nucleotides to belong to a single gene. And depending on the specific function being investigated, entirely different boundaries will be established for the gene under investigation (Portin 1993; Burian 1995; Fogle 2000). In the case of population genetics, thanks to the nature of evolutionary processes and the means used to identify genes, many causally effective genetic units and allelic substitutions are effectively independent of one another, so, most of the time, the molecular complications do not need to be taken into account. In short, in this discipline, many (but by no means all) cases studied involve something very closely akin to classical allelic differences between independent genes. This means that the allelic substitutions studied in population genetics deal primarily with genes that are free of major interactions in the course of the short-term evolutionary histories under investigation and may well lead to serious underestimates of the extent of interaction between molecularly defined genes.[15] So, typically, but not always, the complications found on the molecular level do not enter the relevant causal interactions. Finally, in developmental genetics, modules composed of interacting genes and proteins with invariant control functions are repeatedly deployed in different contexts. The minor nucleotide substitutions that occur in the relevant genes do not alter the constancies that allow them to perform the same functions in organisms as widely separated as mice and drosophila. Thus, we can see that the cultures of the four disciplines we have discussed deal with different questions on different scales and identify genuinely effective causal units, all under the label "gene," that have different causal structures and, correspondingly, fall under different (though related) concepts.

The gene concepts just described appear on the surface to be incompatible. Yet in the cases we have examined, they are complementary rather than incompatible—something that, of course, is not always true with the concepts of neighboring disciplines and which may yet prove illusory in some of the cases discussed here. Still, all of the disciplines discussed here exemplify the general pattern of historical realism and contextual objectivity that Prof. Grene described and deploy gene concepts nicely correlated with the multidimensional agencies involved in inheritance, evolution, and ontogeny. Geneticists deal with a multileveled reality by use of a battery of historically and culturally conditioned concepts—concepts that (with all due cautions) provide objective descriptions of the world and that, in spite of apparent surface contradictions, match very well the strictures of local realism about theoretical entities.

ADDENDUM

In commenting on an earlier version of this essay, Marjorie Grene pointed out that it lacks—and requires—an account of error. This deficit is critical to a full defense of the historicist and objectivist thrust of the position taken above. A theory of error is needed to account for the long list of failed theories and now-abandoned theoretical entities. (Examples include phlogiston, various ethers, absolute space, metagons, and the like, to which one could add many more examples.) Such epistemological pessimists as Larry Laudan (Laudan 1977, 1981) cite these examples in arguing against scientific realism, and such arguments can be applied to local as well as global realism. One might even argue (as Evelyn Keller would like to, I believe) that genes belong on such a list.

This is a topic to which I hope to return in future work. The discussions of epistemic responsibility and explanatory pluralism earlier in this paper provide some hints about the sort of account I think likely to succeed. Epistemic responsibility requires serious norms for criticism, standards for evaluating the seriousness of criticism, and meta-norms that militate against shutting out criticisms that might be developed into serious criticisms. We may well not be able to mirror classical genes precisely within molecular genetics. Nonetheless, the sorts of criticisms that place them at risk within that domain do not eliminate their value—indeed, inescapability—in transmission genetics and their close analogues in population and evolutionary genetics. And the pluralist recognition that classical genes, *understood as occurring at the appropriate level and in the proper context*, are compatible with our molecular knowledge of the genetic material allows us to bypass the conundrum raised by Laudan. Indeed, the difficulty in delimiting molecular genes univocally is, in its way, a marker that the supposed conflict between molecular and classical genes is not as straightforward as has often been argued.

These comments are a far cry from providing a theory of error of the sort that is required to handle these matters. But that is genuinely a topic for another occasion.

RICHARD M. BURIAN

DEPARTMENT OF PHILOSOPHY AND
    CENTER FOR SCIENCE AND TECHNOLOGY STUDIES
VIRGINIA POLYTECHNIC INSTITUTE AND STATE UNIVERSITY
MAY 2001

NOTES

This paper was originally presented at a symposium in honor of Marjorie Grene's 90th birthday, organized by the Department of Philosophy at Virginia Tech. I thank my colleagues and the audience for helpful discussion and Marjorie Grene for her comments. More generally, I wish to acknowledge my debt to Prof. Grene for her longstanding friendship, intellectual companionship, and encouragement of my work, and for her guidance in seeking to reconcile the seemingly conflicting complementary concepts discussed in this paper.

See References for full bibliographic information.

1. Marjorie Grene, "Historical Realism and Contextual Objectivity: A Developing Perspective in the Philosophy of Science," *The Process of Science* (1987), p. 74.

2. This last sentence paraphrases part of a sentence at p. 30 of Grene (1978). That article is helpful as an introduction to the wider metaphysical development of some of Prof. Grene's views connected with the positions taken in this section.

3. See Burian (2000, p. 1129) for more about the interpretation of the passage paraphrased here. Mendel was primarily concerned with hybridization in ways that do not entirely match the genetic views later read into his paper. On this issue, see Olby (1979) and the dispute unleashed by this article.

4. For amplification and discussion of further consequences of this point, see Burian (2000, pp. 1131–34); Gifford (2000); Schwartz (2000). The best synopsis of the technical literature and theoretical positions during the era of classical genetics, with ample references to relevant sources for the positions described in this section, is Carlson (1966).

5. This was the private belief of Bateson (1913), expressed in a few published passages, some of which are cited in Burian (2000). See the accounts in Coleman (1970) and Cock (1983).

6. An enormous amount of material has been published by and on the Morgan group. The best biography of Morgan is Allen (1978). Carlson (1966) provides a detailed account of the Morgan school's experimental approach. Darden (1991) reconstructs helpfully the Morgan school's cross-disciplinary employment of cytological and genetic findings.

7. See Muller (1922). Muller's work in this connection is nicely described by Carlson (1966, 1981). See also the articles in Muller (1962).

8. There are many topical histories of aspects of population genetics, but the *locus classicus* for an account of the origins of this discipline and its early interactions with classical genetics remains Provine (1971). See also Provine (1978, 1981).

9. For more on this particular passage in Dobzhansky, see Burian (1994).

10. See Gould (1983). The sentence quoted from Dobzhansky represents a major step in a longstanding debate about whether extrapolation from micro-evolution to macroevolution could be justified.

11. This is a statistical formalism for measuring the extent of genetically

controlled change in a particular population exposed to a particular environment. The only changes that enter into narrow heritability are those that are due to the replacement of alleles by alternative alleles, each allele taken singly, in the absence of interaction effects between genes.

12. For an extended argument that genes are created in the course of evolutionary modification of the genetic material and that an evolutionary concept of the gene should be the proper and dominant gene concept, see Beurton (2000). It should be noted that Beurton does not endorse the "atomism," just described, that requires genes to be unitary entities in a strong sense.

13. The best single text covering the biological work sketched here is the sixth edition of Scott Gilbert's *Developmental Biology* Gilbert (2000). A number of Gilbert's historical essays touch on the points raised here, as do five chapters (by Keller, Gilbert, Morange, Rheinberger, and Griesemer) in Beurton, Falk, and Rheinberger (2000). For a technical review of the notion of modularity, which is employed far more widely than is indicated above, see Schlosser and Wagner (in press).

14. Evelyn Fox Keller's recent book (Keller 2000) offers a more radical critique of gene concepts, although she also argues that the ambiguities of gene concepts of the sorts discussed here are a major source of their usefulness. She emphasizes the difficulty of reconciling stability in development with the variability and redundancy of genes—even supposedly essential genes can be eliminated without damaging the development or functioning of the organism. On grounds like these she argues that the time has come for biologists to seek a replacement for gene concepts to provide a better conceptual basis for explaining the phenomena now known.

15. For stronger claims about evolutionary gene concepts, see Beurton (2000).

REFERENCES

Allen, Garland E. 1978. *Thomas Hunt Morgan: The Man and his Science.* Princeton, N. J.: Princeton University Press.

Annis, David. 1978. "A Contextualist Theory of Epistemic Justification." *American Philosophical Quarterly* 15:213–19.

Bateson, William. 1913. *Problems of Genetics.* New Haven, Conn.: Yale University Press.

Beurton, Peter. 2000. "A Unified View of the Gene, or How to Overcome Reductionism." In *The Concept of the Gene in Development and Evolution: Historical and Epistemological Perspectives,* edited by P. Beurton, R. Falk and H.-J. Rheinberger. Cambridge and New York: Cambridge University Press.

Beurton, Peter, Raphael Falk, and Hans-Jörg Rheinberger, eds. 2000. *The Concept of the Gene in Development and Evolution: Historical and Epistemological Perspectives.* Cambridge and New York: Cambridge University Press.

Boveri, Theodor. 1902. "Über mehrpolige Mitosen als Mittel zur Analyse des Zellkerns." *Verhandlungen der Physikalischen-medizinischen Gesellschaft zu Wuerzburg* 35:67–90.

Burian, Richard M. 1985. "On Conceptual Change in Biology: The Case of the

Gene." In *Evolution at a Crossroads*, edited by D. Depew and B. Weber. Cambridge, Mass.: MIT Press.

――――. 1994. "Dobzhansky on Evolutionary Dynamics." In *The Evolution of Theodosius Dobzhansky*, edited by M. Adams. Princeton, N.J.: Princeton University Press.

――――. 1995. "Too Many Kinds of Genes? Some Problems Posed by Discontinuities in Gene Concepts and the Continuity of the Genetic Material." In *Preprint 18: Gene Concepts and Evolution*. Berlin: Max Planck Institute for the History of Science.

――――. 1997. "On Conflicts Between Genetic and Developmental Viewpoints and their Resolution in Molecular Biology." In *Structure and Norms in Science. Proceedings of the 10th International Congress of Logic, Methodology, and Philosophy of Science*, edited by M. L. Dalla Chiara, K. Doets, D. Mundici and J. van Bentham. Dordrecht: Kluwer.

――――. 2000. "On the Internal Dynamics of Mendelian Genetics." *Comptes rendus de l'Académie des Sciences, Paris. Sciences de la vie / Life Sciences* 324:1127–37.

Carlson, Elof Axel. 1966. *The Gene: A Critical History*. Philadelphia and London: W. B. Saunders.

――――. 1981. *Genes, Radiation and Society: The Life and Work of H. J. Muller*. Ithaca, N. Y. and London: Cornell University Press.

Cock, Alan G. 1983. "William Bateson's Rejection and Eventual Acceptance of Chromosome Theory." *Annals of Science* 40:19–59.

Coleman, William. 1970. "Bateson and Chromosomes: Conservative Thought in Science." *Centaurus* 15:228–314.

Darden, Lindley. 1991. *Theory Change in Science: Strategies from Mendelian Genetics*. Edited by R. M. Burian, R. W. Burkhardt, Jr., R. C. Lewontin and J. Maynard Smith. *Monograph Series in the History and Philosophy of Biology*. New York: Oxford University Press.

Dobzhansky, Theodosius. 1937. *Genetics and the Origin of Species*. New York: Columbia University Press.

Fogle, Thomas. 2000. "The Dissolution of Protein Coding Genes in Molecular Biology." In *The Concept of the Gene in Development and Evolution: Historical and Epistemological Perspectives*, edited by P. Beurton, R. Falk and H.-J. Rheinberger. Cambridge and New York: Cambridge University Press.

Gehring, Walter J. 1998. *Master Control Genes in Development and Evolution: The Homeobox Story*. New Haven: Yale University Press.

Gibson, James J. 1966. *The Senses Considered as Perceptual Systems*. New York: Houghton-Mifflin.

――――. 1979. *The Ecological Approach to Visual Perception*. Boston: Houghton Mifflin.

Gifford, Fred. 2000. "Gene Concepts and Genetic Concepts." In *The Concept of the Gene in Development and Evolution: Historical and Epistemological Perspectives*, edited by P. Beurton, R. Falk and H.-J. Rheinberger. Cambridge and New York: Cambridge University Press.

Gilbert, Scott F. 2000. *Developmental Biology*. 6th ed. Sunderland, Mass.: Sinauer.

Gould, Stephen Jay. 1983. "The Hardening of the Modern Synthesis." In *Dimensions of Darwinism*, edited by M. Grene. Cambridge: Cambridge University

Press.

Grene, Marjorie. 1978. "The Paradoxes of Historicity." *Review of Metaphysics* 32:15–36.

———. 1987. "Historical Realism and Contextual Objectivity: A Developing Perspective in the Philosophy of Science." In *The Process of Science*, edited by N. Nersessian. Dordrecht: Nijhoff.

Halder, Georg, P. Callaerts, and Walter J. Gehring. 1995. "Induction of Ectopic Eyes by Targeted Expression of the Eyeless Gene in Drosophila." *Science* 267 (5205):1788–92.

Johannsen, Wilhelm. 1909. *Elemente der Exakten Erblichkeitslehre*. Jena: G. Fischer.

Keller, Evelyn Fox. 2000. *The Century of the Gene*. Cambridge, Mass.: Harvard University Press.

Laudan, Larry. 1977. *Progress and its Problems*. Berkeley, Calif.: University of California Press.

———. 1981. "A Confutation of Convergent Realism." *Philosophy of Science* 48:19–49.

Maynard Smith, John. 1986. "Molecules Are Not Enough." Review of Richard Levins and R. C. Lewontin, *The Dialectical Biologist. London Review of Books* (February, 1986).

———. 1989. *Did Darwin get it Right? Essays on Games, Sex and Evolution*. New York: Chapman and Hall. Original edition, in Great Britain, 1988.

Mendel, Gregor. 1865. Versuche über Pflanzen-Hybriden. *Verhandlungen des naturforschenden Vereines in Brünn* 4:3–47.

———. 1966. "Experiments on Plant Hybrids." In *The Origin of Genetics: A Mendel Sourcebook*, edited by C. Stern and E. Sherwood. San Francisco: W. H. Freeman and Co.

Muller, Hermann J. 1922. "Variation Due to Change in the Individual Gene." *American Naturalist* 56:32–50.

———. 1927. "Artificial Transmutation of the Gene." *Science* 66:84–87.

———. 1962. *Studies in Genetics*. Bloomington, Ind.: Indiana University Press.

Olby, Robert C. 1979. "Mendel no Mendelian?" *History of Science* 17:53–72.

Painter, Theophilus S. 1934. "A New Method for the Study of Chromosome Aberrations and the Plotting of Chromosome Maps in *Drosophila melanogaster*." *Genetics* 19:175–88.

Portin, Peter. 1993. "The Concept of the Gene: Short History and Present Status." *The Quarterly Review of Biology* 56:173–23.

Provine, William B. 1971. *The Origins of Theoretical Population Genetics*. Chicago: Chicago University Press.

———. 1978. "The Role of Mathematical Population Genetics in the Evolutionary Synthesis of the 1930s and 1940s." *Studies in the History of Biology* 2:167–92.

———. 1981. "Origins of the Genetics of Natural Populations Series." In *Dobzhansky's Genetics of Natural Populations, I-XLIII*, edited by R. C. Lewontin, J. A. Moore, W. B. Provine and B. Wallace. New York: Columbia University Press.

Rheinberger, Hans-Jörg. 2000. "Gene Concepts: Fragments from the Perspective of Molecular Biology." In *The Concept of the Gene in Development and Evolution: Historical and Epistemological Perspectives*, edited by P. Beurton,

R. Falk and H.-J. Rheinberger. Cambridge and New York: Cambridge University Press.

Schlosser, Gerhard, and Günter Wagner, eds. In press. *Modularity in Development and Evolution*. Chicago: Chicago University Press.

Schwartz, Sara. 2000. "The Differential Concept of the Gene: Past and Present." In *The Concept of the Gene in Development and Evolution: Historical and Epistemological Perspectives*, edited by P. Beurton, R. Falk and H.-J. Rheinberger. Cambridge and New York: Cambridge University Press.

Stadler, Lewis John. 1928. "Mutations in Barley Induced by X-rays and Radium." *Science* 68:186–87.

———. 1954. "The Gene." *Science* 120:811–19.

Sutton, Walter S. 1902. "On the Morphology of the Chromosome Group in *Brachystola magna*." *Biological Bulletin* 4:24–39.

———. 1903. "The Chromosomes in Heredity." *Biological Bulletin* 43:231–51.

REPLY TO RICHARD M. BURIAN

As Richard Burian notes, he presented this essay at a colloquium which some of my colleagues kindly held in celebration of my ninetieth birthday. On that occasion, I made only one remark: that plural conceptions of a given reality may not always be equally valid; sometimes one or more may prove to be mistaken. He has now replied to that point, and I shall reply to his reply. But I also find a misunderstanding earlier in his argument, which at that time I overlooked. So I have two points to make.

First, however, I must thank him for his very generous tribute to our friendship and, he says, to my influence on his thought. The latter I am sure must be exaggerated. When we first met, I had been teaching philosophy of biology for some time, and Burian was just turning to it. Since then, he has so far outdistanced me in his expertise that I really must take his statement as more a gesture of friendship than of truth—and I must certainly question his initial assertion about my long-time, deep interest in genetics. Anybody who does any work in the philosophy of biology must, of course, have some interest in that discipline, but I find myself very much an outsider in that field, as in so many others in which, at one time or another, I have found myself dabbling. I have to take Burian's case study as the report of someone who knows the subject matter very much better than I could claim to do.

So the two points I want to make are purely philosophical—whatever that means. And I think they are related.

First, Burian says I reproached him in the past for making too much of the so-called problem of scientific realism, which, he says, I found too "global." Not at all. The trouble with that alleged problem was that it was too limited. In the bad old times of the received view, science was supposed to float on a sea of phenomena subject to direct observation, and then the question was: were we entitled to claim that there were entities we couldn't observe, like atoms or genes or quarks or what you will? It was the very lack of global realism that occasioned the question. But, as I am tired of saying, scientists are real people trying to solve problems about how something in the real world really works. Between disciplines, each of which deals with some aspect of a complex reality, they may attempt this through differing techniques, differing vocabularies, differing thought styles. This may happen either because reality itself is complicated, or because our approaches to it are so, or both. As Helen Longino puts it in her recent *Fate of Knowledge*: "pluralism only has the bite it has in the context of realism. Various kinds of realism have been proposed to accommodate pluralism. . . .What these realisms have in common is a resistance to treating the susceptibility of our singular world to multiple adequate representations as grounds for metaphysical idealism or for epistemological skepticism."[1]

Now I am not suggesting that Burian would disagree with such a statement. But as I said, it is the very lack of global sweep in the traditional problem of scientific realism that I was objecting to. And I'm afraid that in the rather hasty and occasional piece of mine on which Burian was commenting, I may have misled my readers by adopting the phrase "historical reality." "Contextual objectivity" isn't so bad, although the two turns of phrase together do give an unfortunate relativistic impression. It is global, ecological realism we should acknowledge from the start: we find ourselves as real beings in a real world in which we are trying to find our way. That is exactly why the possibility of "multiple adequate representations" is interesting.

Secondly, at the close of his essay, Burian recalls that at our colloquium I pointed out that multiple interpretations are not always all equally correct. Indeed, in the case he is presenting, we have at the start Bateson, who coined the term "genetics" and was one of the leaders of the new discipline in its early years in Britain, refusing, until he was ultimately forced to, to acknowledge the location of genes on chromosomes. Well, though he contributed a great deal—including, for example, the discovery of homeosis—on that he was just wrong. Despite the more complicated siting of genes in molecular genetics, they do have some connection with the chromosomes! In these circumstances, Burian says, we need to take account of error. He even says we need a "theory of error"—why, and what could it be? The possibility of error, it seems to me, is written into the very possibility of knowledge as we understand it, or ought to understand it. As I put it in that paper: "The question is, how, within a given field of inquiry, a group of critical truth seekers move[s] forward to state justified beliefs, which they hope are true."[2] I have of course borrowed this formulation from Michael Polanyi's concept of personal knowledge. And what needs to be stressed, in particular, is, as he came to formulate it, the *from-to* structure of knowledge. From within the real world in which we find ourselves, we seek to reach out from clues given us by our initiation into the particular discipline in which we are working, to something in that same world, but beyond ourselves. We may succeed, often in complex and differing ways such as Burian has pointed out; but we may also fail. Our access to the way things are isn't too bad, but neither is it perfect. A pluralism grounded in realism needs no special account of error; it presupposes our fallibility. Reality is complicated and so are our ways of making contact with it—or aspects of it. In such a situation, we hope to succeed, but we can always go wrong. About that, I hope I am not mistaken!

M. G.

NOTES

1. Helen Longino, *The Fate of Knowledge* (Princeton, N.J.: Princeton University Press, 2001), p. 142.

2. Marjorie Grene, "Historical Realism and Contextual Objectivity: A Developing Perspective in the Philosophy of Science," in *The Process of Science*, ed. Nancy Nersessian (Dordrecht: Nijhoff, 1987), pp. 70–71.

14

Eugenie Gatens-Robinson

THE TELIC CHARACTER OF LIFE: MARJORIE GRENE ON THE ODDNESS OF LIVING THINGS

Living things are an oddity, and some odd people may show an interest in them, but they have no central place in our conception of the world around us.

—Grene and Eldredge

Nature is conceived to be wholly mechanical. The existence within nature and as part of it of a body possessed of life, manifesting thought and enjoying consciousness is a mystery.

—Dewey

The first quote above is from Majorie Grene's and Niles Eldredge's 1992 collaboration *Interaction: The Biological Context of Social Systems.*[1] Grene and Eldredge number themselves proudly among the *odd* people that have spent most of their lives interested in living things. They are clear that if living things have no central place in our conception of the physical world then it is time that we revise that view. They call for an enriched ontology for the biological sciences.[2]

The second quote comes from John Dewey's *Experience and Nature.*[3] It also represents a challenge to the mechanistic paradigm. Dewey goes on to argue that a way of conceptualizing life and mind in which qualitative experience is incomprehensible must be mistaken.

How is our view of living things to be revised? In what sense does the conceptualization of the natural world in terms of efficient causality and quantitative, but not qualitative categories, render the phenomenon of life in which we partake, literally *inconceivable?*

For at least the past four decades, Marjorie Grene has called on philosophers to take up this problematic tension between given scientific categories and the phenomenon of life. Writing in 1974, she puts it as the central challenge of philosophy. "To put finally to rest our Newtonian delusions, to renew our conception of nature as *living*, and so to see ourselves once more as living beings in a world of living beings, constitutes, it seems to me, the major task of philosophy in the twentieth century."[4]

I would claim that philosophy and the biological sciences have moved into the twenty-first century without meeting this challenge. Grene predicted that given the success of what she called the "'new mechanical philosophy,' founded on biochemistry and cybernetics" this task would become more difficult and more urgent.[5] Grene claimed that we will need "to complete a fundamental revision of our basic ways of thinking."[6] It seems to me that she was right about both the difficulty and the urgency of this task. The success of modern molecular genetics and its primary achievement, The Human Genome Project, has made the need for such a revision very difficult to articulate. We are told that the secret code of life has been broken! Yet the urgency to revise our vision of human knowledge and the place of humans in nature given global environmental deterioration seems even more pronounced.

Thus I would like to take up Grene's question. What is it that makes living things odd in relationship to the mechanistic paradigm of modern science? It seems that there are two central and probably related characteristics of living things that make them puzzling *vis-à-vis* mechanistic science. One is their telic character, to use Grene's phrase. Living things have functional form and precisely unfolding patterns of development. They are "self" directed in relationship to their needs and the feature of their environment. A ciliate protozoa moving toward something eatable within its surround is different in a significant sense from a magnet drawn to a lodestone. Living entities do not just move. They behave. Further, living entities do not just change. They develop, mature, senesce, and die. The pattern of change is at once quintessentially historical and temporally structured. Living things keep time, pulse, throb, beat, cycle. They are rhythmed.

The other characteristic of living things that remains at odds with purely mechanistic accounts is the qualitative aspect of life that is difficult if not impossible to give account in the quantitative language of the physical sciences. Sensation, perception, emotion are characteristic of living and not of inanimate nature. These qualitative capacities allow for discernments whereby affordances of the environment are experienced as meaningful, if only rudimentarily so. I am using "affordance" here, as Grene does, in the sense coined by J. J. Gibson,[7] as what the environment offers the organism as eatable, climbable, rest-on-top-able, fall-off-able, mate-able and so on. As Grene tells us in reviewing James and Eleanor Gibson's work,

> "Meaning" is not something superadded to the environment by human linguistic of other conventions; the worlds of animals are full of meanings which are perceived as such through the pickup of invariants. . . . Perception is always the engagement of an active, exploring organism with the affordances of things and events that are happening, within reach of its perceptual systems."[8]

Grene points out that at the very outset of modern physical science, Galileo proudly presented us with a world from which *"living creatures were removed."*[9] For him and for the scientific mechanistic paradigm in general, the real properties of things, their primary properties, are mind/life independent features of nature itself, a nature from which life is absent and thus so are qualities. Grene protests: "Yet we do have a world of color and taste and smell and sound which is not just part of our individual subjectivity but part of our biological environment, genetically determined as much as our more 'mechanical powers' are determined."[10]

It is the absence of life in the explanatory categories of science that Grene challenges. She points out that a teleological style of explanation in the biological sciences is a genuine part of the knowledge of living things. "If therefore teleological explanation is a genuine part of the knowledge of living things, it is so because living things are not only apparently, but genuinely telic. It is, again, the lingering authority of the machine analogy that prevents our admitting the truth of this statement."[11] Further she says, "The conclusion that there are telic phenomena is inescapable, but also so incredible to most scientists and to a public nourished in the mythology of purely one-level, purely 'mechanistic' science, that it is suppressed as a piece of lingering superstition or willful obscurantism."[12]

DEEPER NATURALISM

I take Grene to be calling for a deeper view of naturalism that includes life as the Galilean world could not. At the moment natualism is identified with a form of philosophizing about our scientific understanding that takes seriously the findings of our "best" science and which tends to be overwhelmingly reductionistic, explaining things in terms of least parts and basic physical mechanisms. This shallow naturalism is firmly centered in the mechanistic paradigm that Grene finds inadequate in certain areas of biology. Daniel Dennett, who sees anything but a purely mechanistic account of life as an illegimate reaching for what he calls "skyhooks,"[13] is a naturalist of this sort. This view claims that to bring teleological explanation of any sort into science introduces an element of the non-natural, perhaps even the supernatural. The genuinely "natural" is lifeless and mindless, on this view.

Given the centrality of this shallow naturalism to the paradigm of the science we have, it is very important that one lay out one's views clearly so that easy dismissal is not the result. Over the years, Grene has done careful work in laying out her position in this area. She says that neither she nor her admired Aristotle is using teleological concepts in the sense of positing conscious purposes as causes in nature. She claims that the choice between thinking of natural events as *"either* planned *or* wholly undirected"[14] is merely a legacy of the Cartesian split between matter and thought.

Most philosophers of science, taking the lead of the mechanistic paradigm, are comfortable construing teleological concepts as merely regulative or heuristic in biological thinking, with the hope that such concepts will be eliminated in time. The mechanistic paradigm allows for only one form of causal explanation, what might be called efficient causality, and thus allows only one form of genuine explanatory account. From this perspective, teleological accounts that give explanations in terms of the occurrence of some event as "for the sake of" some functional goal are not genuinely "explanatory." Such functional explanations are purely regulative of thinking in biology. This strategy for dealing with teleological judgment goes back at least to Kant and is reflected in the strategies of recent writers who analyze functional explanation in biology.

Indeed, Grene concurs that teleological concepts in biology do have what could be called a regulative function in that they are needed for the scientist to choose the data and problem that he or she is going to pursue. A teleological description of some aspects of organic processes is needed in order to get "the object of . . . investigation so to speak into focus."[15] "Only, . . . when the concept of germination is understood and its designatum assumed to exist, do the details 'fall into order and acquire a significance', such that detailed analysis of some parts of the process of germination can be undertaken."[16] Thus it is only when one sees germination as an orderly development "towards a normal end" can one begin to parse that process into its components and study them singly on a genetic or biochemical level.

Nonetheless, to those swept up in the Newtonian revolution and its powerful mechanistic paradigm, the realm of the animate with its clearly functional structures, wings, claws, eyes, and the like, and its apparently teleological developmental patterns is anomalous, in a literal sense, viz., beyond the realm of scientific laws. Kant settled for a biology that would carry on *as if* these processes were purposive. Teleological concepts were to be regulative ideals of biological thinking. But Kant warns us that "[i]n our empirical investigation of nature in its causal connection, we can and should endeavor to [proceed] in terms of nature's merely mechanical laws. . . . [f]or in these laws lie the true physical bases for [an] explanation [of nature . . .][17] Teleological judgments in terms of natural ends are not determinate, do not tell us about the necessity of things, since to make them so would be to "suggest causality that lies beyond the bounds of nature."[18] Thus, teleological judgments were to be made with a wink and a nod in the direction of the Newtonians, who seemed to have things well under way in the domains of physics and chemistry, and to God who seemed, in this case, to be lurking just out of sight in the wings. (Pun intended.)

Grene asks, "But is that all there is to it? A Kantian regulative idea . . . is a pure *as-if*. And many modern thinkers would be content with this, with 'the appearance of end'."[19] Grene contends that especially in the area of organic development Kant's view is less than satisfactory:

> To assert that a robin's egg hatches out a robin and not an oak tree is to state not a regulative idea but a fact of nature. . . . It locates in the real world an orderly process. . . . It selects certain segments of the orderly process *in* its orderliness as the locus of an inquiry. To this extent it locates real, not apparent, ends and suggests really, not seemingly or misguidedly, teleological questions.[20]

Grene allows that in ontogenesis of the organism the genuinely telic character of the phenomenon demands that we take our teleological conceptions and questions as more than mere *as-ifs*; in the domain of evolution, phylogensis she is much more cautious. Part of the core of the Darwinian theory of evolution is the rejection of cosmic teleology. She argues that teleological thinking in the domain of evolutionary theory is indeed merely regulative and not explanatory. Genuine explanations in evolution, Grene contends, as Kant would have preferred, "are . . . explicated on principle, in terms of natural, that is, physico-chemical laws."[21]

Thus Grene divides the domain concerned with teleological talk into two separate affairs. In the case of ontogenesis of individual organisms and the behavior of animals, she has in the past recognized teleological questions and perhaps explanations as having some legitimacy, a legitimacy that the mechanistic paradigm fails to accommodate. On the other hand in the case of phylogenesis, that is evolution, on which most of the conversation in philosophy of biology is now focused, she sides with the more standard view that explanations here are in terms of simple efficient causal mechanisms, albeit more complex ones than neo-Darwinians might allow. Living things are genuinely telic, but the process of evolution which they constitute is not. It seems to me that given her radical call for a revisionist metaphysics and epistemology, our understanding of the process of evolution must come under the same kind of revision. We need a richer ontology and epistemology in this area as well, especially in relationship to the connection between causality and explanation.

The literature on teleology in philosophy of biology is stranded in the area of functional explanation, where the view of teleological, here read functional explanation, is more easily rendered harmless by a Kantian reading. Since focus in recent years has been on evolution and the so-called modern synthesis between evolutionary theory and genetics, the literature centers on natural selection as the primary explanation of the adaptive structure of the organism. The literature on explanations in biology has tended to give functional explanations a regulative or heuristic interpretation and thus defuse any lingering worries about implied purposes as causes within the domain of the natural world. Grene praises the analysis of Richard Brandon who tackles apparently teleological explanations such as "birds have wings in order to fly" as being amenable to a mechanistic explanation. Here the existence of the wing is explained by the function it subserves. This kind of explanation is "teleological" because it is an answer to a what-for question. But the occurrence of a particular trait has a straight forwardly mechanistic explanation in terms of the history of its occurrence and the adaptiveness of the trait in question. Thus Brandon claims that there is a mechanistic explanation of a teleological phenomenon. "Thus the sort of teleology that survives in contemporary evolutionary biology is not only compatible with a mechanistic world view; I have explicated the sense in which what-for questions and their answers are teleological in purely mechanistic terms."[22]

Grene says approvingly of Brandon's analysis that "[t]he teleological language belongs to the phenomenon to be explained, not to its explanation."[23]

In a 1986 paper she says,

Again, this classic problem [teleology] has lost interest. There was a spate of work on it about a decade ago, including some excellent analyses of the relation between "functional" and "teleological" statements or explanations. Now it seems that the place of teleological (or teleonomic) discourse in evolutionary theory has been tidily located, and outside of evolution functional discourse, or even, in a limited fashion (as in ethology), teleological accounts are routine and harmless.[24]

Grene seems unworried that this "solution" to the problem of teleology in the domain of evolution is the fruit of the same tree that she and Eldredge call ultradarwinism.[25] They recognize that even in a Darwinian paradigm that is classically deterministic there lingers an essential teleological component. "Both the axiom of adaptivity—the fact that selection works only for useful traits—and the lure (or the snare) of evolutionary progress seem to infect this offshoot of classical determinism. . . ."[26] I would like to suggest that Grene in her legitimate criticism of ultradarwinian adaptionism, a false teleology, she is giving up too much. The division she has made between ontogenesis and phylogenesis in terms of their respective character I think is a problematic one.

This move is not radical enough to meet her initial challenge, to achieve "a fundamental revision of our ways of thinking." Let me suggest some things that might be necessary for such a revision to be possible, things some of which Grene herself has suggested or endorsed.

THE UNFINISHED SYNTHESIS

Part of the problem of revising our view of life, at the moment, is the structure of inquiry in the area of evolutionary theory. What has become known as "the modern synthesis," the synthesis between molecular genetics and evolutionary biology, is from Grene and Eldredge's point of view incomplete. They call for a "new new synthesis."[27] Evolutionary theory of what they have called an "ultradarwinian" form, more Darwinian than Darwin, has joined with a biochemical genetics as a powerful paradigm in contemporary evolutionary thought.

The place of development in evolutionary theory is not well worked out. Timing in development as an important causal factor in the evolutionary process beyond natural selection is only now beginning to be explored.[28] Furthermore, the idea that developmental constraints play an important causal role in evolution brings forward the idea that the organismic form itself functions in setting the trajectories of evolutionary change. There are researchers looking at this aspect of the evolutionary process but they are not part of the dominant main stream.[29]

Evolutionary thought especially in its contemporary, ultradarwinian form, seems to be tightly wedded to certain strategies of explanation and conceptualization that block a confrontation with the phenomenon of life in its full empirical richness. Population genetics looks not at organisms but at gene frequencies in populations and has even redefined evolution as changes in gene frequencies. Even those who argue that selection acts on the phenotype, not merely on genes, tend to look at the end products of ontogenies, adult morphologies, represented in the fossil record, as that which natural selection selects. Darwin himself was able to give us an evolutionary account that is powerful and continues to hold sway even as he held a radically mistaken view of genetics and development. It must still seem to many neo-Darwinians that they too can study and understand the mechanisms of evolution and the patterns of phylogeny while ignoring developmental process and morphogenesis. Nonetheless, it is not merely adult phenotypes that are selected for or against, but ontogenies.

Another science that has not been integrated into evolutionary theory is ecology. As Grene and Eldredge point out, Darwin himself was deeply ecological in his thinking.[30] Grene and Eldredge recognize the difficulties this mode of thinking brings to evolutionary thinking.

> Ecosystems are inherently cross-genealogical—hence their characteristic absence in all but peripheral evolutionary discourse. Evolutionary theory has traditionally focused almost completely on the genealogical products of evolution: species and monophyletic taxa of higher rank. In so restricting itself, evolutionary theory almost totally ignores large-scale biological entities that form as a direct consequence of the organismic adaptations devoted to economic processes.[31]

Eldredge's work on exploring the connections between genealogical and economic hierarchical systems in the living world has begun this integration of ecological thinking into evolutionary theory.

The mode of thinking that has become prevalent in evolutionary biology is one that Grene and others see as having fragmented the organism into separate traits, seeking to explain everything on the lowest organizational level possible and losing all notion of form as having a place in understanding living processes. Grene says, "Traits, the characters or behaviors of phenotypes, . . . do not come singly, and neither do genes. . . . [E]volutionary theory suffers from a neglect of form. Wholes are more than aggregates because they are structured."[32]

And finally, an area of biological study that has faded into the background of biological research is comparative morphology, the very field which funded evolutionary thought in the nineteenth century. The trained eye of the comparative morphologist is in danger of extinction. The knowledge of forms and their geographic distribution is part of the big picture of evolutionary change that seems essential, even primary. However it requires a slow pace of study and focus on natural history that is fast becoming *passé* in the world of big science. But if the overall connection among forms is to be understood, this kind of knowledge is vital. Patterns of mimicry, convergent and divergent evolution, and so on, will go unnoted. As Libby Hyman said in 1922, "The whole aim of comparative anatomy is to discover what structures are homologous."[33] That is, the task is to ascertain which structures are part of the same evolutionary line of descent and do not merely look alike. The wing of the bat and the wing of the bird are homologies; the wing of the butterfly and the wing of the bat are merely analogous.

Thus it seems that a genuine new, new synthesis powerful enough to fund Grene's "revisionary" metaphysics might require that evolutionary thinkers, both philosophers and scientists, take on the task of becoming much broader in their focus and take on new modes of thinking that are more integrated with knowledge of development, ecology and comparative morphology. This would require changes not only in the educational curricula of evolutionary biology but also in the culture of science as it is currently structured.

THE DICHOTOMIES THAT BIND

Philosophers might be of special help in making clear the conceptual *Bauplan* of our contemporary view of living things. I would like briefly to discuss a cluster of distinctions mightily at work in biological orthodoxy that seem to structure our thinking in this area. I cannot say exactly what our thinking would be like if we abandoned or modified these distinctions, but I feel that it would do some of the work that Grene claims we must do to bring life back into nature. The particular dualisms I have in mind are the germplasm/soma distinction, the phenotype/genotype distinction, and the organism/environment distinction.

The germplasm/somatoplasm distinction is attributed to August Weismann and has served as an underpinning for what has become known as the Central Dogma in molecular genetics. For Weismann the germplasm, as the genetic material was then called, determines the body cells, and not vice versa.[34] As with the Central Dogma, this view eventually underlined the primary causal role of the DNA. The direction of information flow is outward from the chromosomes. There was no mechanism of feedback from the soma or the environment to the genome. Thus changes in the genome are random and undirected mutations. Grene and Eldredge point out that this "asymmetrical vector of causality has strongly influenced much of the theoretical study of the origin of life ("Biogenesis")."[35] It has also under-pinned the mechanistic view of the evolutionary process. It follows from this view that the organism has no causal role *per se* in evolution. The organism is an artifact of its genes. Its unique history of interaction with its environment dies with it. As it seemed to bring cosmic teleology into evolutionary thought to attribute trends and directionality to organic evolution, so now it is considered "Lamarckian" to suggest that mutational changes can be the result of some feedback mechanism from the environment. This is a heresy that a number of biologists are beginning to risk, especially those working with invertebrates and plants, organisms notoriously impatient with one way of doing things.[36]

The distinction between the genotype and phenotype, which parallels the above distinction between germ and soma, has contributed to the fragmentation of the organism to which Grene objects. Organisms are seen as a collection of traits determined by various genetic combinations. Again, this view is based in a causal primacy of the genome whereby the genotype causes the phenotype. The genotype is a blueprint, a set of directions for building an organism and regulating its living processes. This model gives the impression that somehow the stable genotype stands apart from the organism in some mysterious manner as a cause and not a participant in the living system itself. But of course the chromosomes are actually a part of the phenotype and respond as organelles within the environment of the cell. The genotype is a very dynamic blueprint to say the least, since it has the capacity to rearrange itself and respond in various ways to changes in the environment of the cell. The realm of the genotype seems to be far more open and active than previously thought. As Brian Goodwin, a theoretical biologist, puts it "[t]he causal connections between the genotype and the phenotype are not simply atomic, Humean, cause and effect relations mediated by molecules. This duality, like the mind/body duality, generates confusion and mystification, and it has a similar origin."[37]

Finally, we come to the organism/environment distinction. As Grene and Elredge pointed out above, there is no "environment" in the Newtonian world. Organisms and environments co-create one another. There are no pre-existing niches to which organisms adapt or fail to adapt. As Goodwin puts it, "[o]rganisms both select and alter their environments, and their intrinsic dynamic organization limits the hereditary changes that are possible, so that the variety available for evolution is restricted."[38] Thus the organism is not passively in an environment that then selects the fittest. Rather Goodwin claims that "organisms themselves have the potential for appropriate response to the environment, so that much of the variation that is available for evolutionary change arises not from random mutation but from the intrinsically regulative and plastic responses of the organism. . . . "[39] Like Grene and Eldredge, Goodwin is claiming that the organism is an active participant in the process of evolution.

A NEW EPISTEMOLOGY

Finally Grene has called for a new epistemology. In her book, *The Knower and the Known*, Grene points out that we are still captive of an old epistemology that takes knowledge to be totally explicit. What is required if we are to have a new view of nature, especially living nature which includes ourselves, is a new concept of our own activity of knowing.[40] It might be said that on the Galilean-Newtonian view of nature, knowing is even odder than life. Grene makes some very important suggestion for how we might think differently about living things, including ourselves.

Drawing on Michael Polyani's view of tacit knowledge she claims,

> Knowing is essentially temporal activity, directed temporal activity, drawn by the future pull of what we seek to understand. Knowing . . . is essentially learning; and learning is a telic phenomenon, in which the end in sight, even only guessed at, *draws* us toward a solution.[41] [My emphasis.]

From this reflection on the character of our knowledge of the world Grene makes a further claim, linking her epistemological claim to her metaphysical view. On analogy with this complex living phenomenon, learning, she claims that living organisms as such exist within a temporal structure that is telic. That is, they exist as processes that are marked by achievements or failures, temporal categories, in relationship to a future to which they open, or as she says, towards which they are drawn.

"For living things, therefore, past and present depend on the *future* as primary." This is what she calls a "future-drawn" structure that is evident in "the developing embryo, the dance half-performed, the melody half-sung, the nesting behavior in course of enactment."[42]

I will end with a quote that seems like a call to do some of the philosophical and scientific work discussed above.

> we need to articulate an enriched ontology for the biological sciences, an ontology that not only "restores the organism to biology" but restores the environment as well to its pivotal place in evolutionary theory and, firmly putting aside an exclusive emphasis on least parts, recognizes the existence, and the causal roles in evolutionary history, of entities, not only beyond the gene, but beyond the organism as well.[43]

This is an invitation to participate in a revolution in thinking at least as important as the one that Galileo and Newton initiated. It is an invitation to move away from a science in which life is "odd" and of interest only to a few odd people, to one in which living processes are the basic categories by which we understand the natural world and our place in it.

EUGENIE GATENS-ROBINSON

SOUTHERN ILLINOIS UNIVERSITY CARBONDALE
MARCH 2002

NOTES

1. Niles Eldredge and Marjorie Grene, *Interactions: The Biological Context of Social Systems* (New York: Columbia University Press, 1992), p. 36.

2. Ibid., p. 58

3. John Dewey, *The Later Works of John Dewey*, vol. 1, *Experience and Nature*, ed. Jo Ann Boydston (Carbondale, Ill.: Southern Illinois University Press, 1981), p. 191.

4. Marjorie Grene, *The Understanding of Nature*. Boston Studies in the Philosophy of Science, vol. 23. Synthese Library, vol. 66 (Dordrecht: D. Reidel Publishing Company, 1974), p. 173.

5. Marjorie Grene, *The Knower and the Known* (New York: Basic Books, 1966), p. 228.

6. Grene, *The Understanding of Nature*, p. 179.

7. J. J. Gibson, *The Ecological Approach to Visual Perception* (Boston: Houghton Mifflin Company, 1979), p. 127.

8. Marjorie Grene, *A Philosophical Testament* (Chicago and La Salle, Ill.: Open Court, 1995), p. 143.

9. Grene, *The Understanding of Nature*, p. 262, n. 6. Quoted from Galileo, *Discoveries*, p. 272; *Il Saggiatore*, pp. 347–48.

10. Ibid., p. 263.

11. Ibid., pp. 178–79.

12. Grene, *The Knower and the Known*, p. 239.

13. Daniel C. Dennett, *Darwin's Dangerous Idea: Evolution and the Meanings of Life* (New York: Simon & Schuster, 1995).

14. Grene, *The Knower and the Known*, p. 228.

15. Grene, *The Understanding of Nature*, p. 176.

16. Marjorie Grene, "Aristotle and Modern Biology," *Topics in the Philosophy of Biology*, ed. Marjorie Grene and Everett Mendelsohn. Boston Studies in the Philosophy of Science, vol. 27; Synthese Library, vol. 84 (Dordrecht: D. Reidel Publishing Company, 1976), p. 7.

17. Kant, *Critique of Judgment*, trans. ed. Werner S. Pluhar (Indianapolis, Ind., 1987 [1790]), p. 424.

18. Ibid., p. 425.

19. Grene, "Aristotle and Modern Biology," p. 7.

20. Ibid., p. 8.

21. Ibid., p. 12.

22. Robert N. Brandon, *Adaptation and Environment* (Princeton, N.J.: Princeton University Press, 1990), p. 189.

23. Grene, *A Philosophical Testament*, p. 104.

24. Grene, " Philosophy of Biology 1983: Problems and Prospects." In *Logic, Methodology, and Philosophy of Science* VII, ed. Ruth Barcan Marcus, George J. W. Dorn, and Paul Weingartner (Elsevier Science Publishers B.V., 1986), p. 442.

25. Eldredge and Grene, *Interactions*, p. 54.

26. Ibid., pp. 46–47.

27. Ibid., p. 54.

28. Stephen J. Gould, *Ontogeny and Phylogeny* (Cambridge, Mass.: Belknap Press, 1977), p. 283.

29. See *Beyond Neo-Darwinism*, ed. Mae-Wan Ho and Peter Saunders (New York: Academic Press, 1984); *Theoretical Biology: Epigenetic and Evolutionary Order from Complex Systems*, ed. Brian Goodwin and Peter Saunders (Baltimore: The Johns Hopkins University Press, 1989).

30. Eldredge and Grene, *Interactions*, p. 56.

31. Ibid., p. 77.

32. Grene, *A Philosophical Testament*, p. 106.

33. Libby Hyman, *A Laboratory Manual for Comparative Vertebrate Anatomy* (Chicago: University of Chicago Press, 1922), p. 3. Quoted in "Morphology in the Evolutionary Synthesis," by William Coleman, in *The Evolutionary Synthesis: Perspective on the Unification of Biology*, ed. Ernst Mayr and William B. Provine (Cambridge, Mass.: Harvard University Press, 1980), p. 174.

34. August Weismann, "The Continuity of the Germ-Plasm as the Foundation of a Theory of Heredity" (1885). Reprinted in *Readings in Heredity and Development*, ed. J. A. Moore (New York: Oxford University Press, 1972).

35. Eldredge and Grene, *Interactions*, p. 67.

36. See *Evolutionary Processes and Metaphors*, ed. Mae-Wan Ho and Sidney Fox (New York: John Wiley & Sons, 1988).

37. Brian Goodwin, "The Causes of Biological Form," in *Causes of Development*, ed. George Butterworth and Peter Bryant (Hillsdale, N.J.: Lawrence Erlbaum Associates, 1990), p. 54.

38. Ibid., p. 55.

39. Ibid.

40. Grene, *The Knower and the Known*, p. 240.

41. Ibid., p. 244.

42. Ibid., p. 245.

43. Grene, "Darwin's Great Tree of Life: Roots and Ramifications," *Barnard Alumnae* (Fall 1987): 13.

REPLY TO EUGENIE GATENS-ROBINSON

Unfortunately, Dr. Gatens-Robinson's essay is a morass of confusion. Admittedly, this is in part my fault. Four decades ago, as she points out, I made some remarks about what I called the "telic" character of living things, in 1964 in a brief essay in the *Cambridge Review*, and in 1966 in a chapter of a deeply flawed book, *The Knower and the Known*—deeply flawed in view of the presence of that chapter, and of an appallingly bad chapter on Darwinism. Not long thereafter, I thought better of this foray into teleology. In my 1974 collection of essays, *The Understanding of Nature,* I (stupidly, it appears) included the '64 essay in order to have before the reader a text I would go on to renounce—and *de*nounce (in the essay "Explanation and Evolution"[1]). Dr. Gatens-Robinson, like at least a couple of other readers, has taken this to be my considered opinion. Clearly, I should have omitted the errant article from the collection; it has me branded forever as a teleologist.

Gatens-Robinson also singles out a second alleged characteristic of living things, which she calls "qualitative." I'm not sure what that means, and can't connect it easily with the reference to Gibsonian affordances to which she attaches it. Most of her argument, however, seems to concern that telic business and that's what I want to try to deal with here.

There are several problems. First, as I have already said emphatically enough, that characterization is something I have never returned to and have explicitly rejected. Second, Gatens-Robinson attaches teleological significance to statements of mine, and of others, where that inference is totally misplaced. Take Eldredge and Grene, for example.[2] We objected to what we called "ultradarwinism" (as I mentioned in my reply to Eldredge, this is an expression we should not have used, since it had been appropriated long ago by Weismann). What we were questioning was what is sometimes called "genic selectionism," and that for two reasons. Adopting David Hull's distinction between replicators and interactors, we argued, first that even on the replicator side, there is more than one particulate level involved, and second, that interaction must be considered as well as replication.[3] Organisms don't only reproduce; they have to make a living. So Eldredge has distinguished, both in our joint volume and elsewhere, between two hierarchies, a genealogical and an ecological hierarchy. *Neither one carries the least tincture of teleology.*

Similarly, Gatens-Robinson refers to a paper of mine on "Aristotle and Modern Biology" as if I were embracing with enthusiasm Aristotle's teleological naturalism. I thought what I had stressed in that essay was that what we can learn from Aristotle is the importance of form, or organization: formal cause, not final cause, is what can guide our reflections. Of course, given his own theory of reproduction, Aristotle can often identify three of his four causes: the father is the moving cause of the offspring, since he furnishes the seed; that seed must somehow contain the form that will eventuate in a new organism, and of course the final cause of the procedure is an adult male of the species in question, even though it sometimes partially fails and turns out a mere female, a monstrosity which nature manages to use, as matter, for her own ends. Thanks a lot! Outside that context, however, we can think about the relation of form to matter, of organizing principle to what it organizes. That's where, if anywhere, we can find a useful lesson. Recall Delbrück's paper, "Aristotle-totle-totle," in which he proposed (tongue-in-cheek, of course) that Aristotle should be posthumously awarded the Nobel prize for discovering DNA. It's a question of in*form*ation.[4] Again, when I speak, in a passage Gatens-Robinson quotes from my *Philosophical Testament,* of "wholes as more than aggregates because they are structured," this has obviously nothing whatsoever to do with teleology; it's levels of organization that are in question, not ends.

Gatens-Robinson also proposes that evolutionary theory be reformulated so as to include development. That is happening, but not at all in the sense she seems to have in mind. For one thing, she refers in this context to some very questionable sources, who do not, in any case, appear to be especially "developmental" in her sense, that is, "teleological" in their approach.[5] The sense in which evolution was itself developmental, that is, somehow directed or orthogenetic, is surely nowhere any longer current. More fruitful is the present prospect, and even actuality, of a synthesis between the older synthesis and recent work in developmental biology, a movement called by its friends "evo-devo." This is not a refutation of the mid-twentieth-century synthesis, but a completion, and in some respects, correction of it. To put it very crudely, the point is that evolution involves not only the replication (and replacement) of genes, and the activities of the organisms in which they are housed, but the development of those organisms. For the older synthesis, development was a black box. But it is in the main changes in development that provide the opportunities for natural selection to operate. Again, however, if you please, there is nothing in the least telic or teleological in the processes involved. It is a question of investigating what follows what and on what molecular and biochemical basis. In the most recent edition of his canonical *Developmental Biology*, Scott Gilbert enumerates some presuppositions of the older population genetic model of evolution which have had to be modified. They are: gradualism (thanks to punctuated equilibrium); extrapolation from micro-evolution to macroevolution; specificity of phenotype from genotype; lack of genetic similarity in disparate organisms. None of these revisions entails any introduction of teleological thinking in any respect whatsoever.[6]

What is Gatens-Robinson thinking of? She seems to have embraced an ontology somewhat like that of nineteenth-century natural theologians: either you have a simple, one level type of billiard-ball causality, or you have purposiveness: those are the only alternatives. I regret having misled her through my mistaken pronouncements of nearly forty years ago. There appears to me to be no conflict, such as she envisages, between a selectionist view of evolution and the study of individual development as the process that has both resulted from evolution and contributes to it.

M. G.

NOTES

1. Marjorie Grene, "Explanation and Evolution," *The Understanding of Nature* (Dordrecht/Boston: D. Reidel, 1974), p. 209. See also "Darwin and Philosophy," pp. 189–200.

2. Niles Eldredge and Marjorie Grene, *Interactions* (New York: Columbia University Press, 1992)

3. David L. Hull, "Individuality and Selection," *Ann. Ev. Ecol. Syst.* 11 (1980): 311–32.

4. Max Delbrück, "Aristotle-totle-totle," in *Of Microbes and Life*, ed. Jacques Monod and Ernest Bonek (New York: Columbia University Press, 1971), pp. 50–55.

5. See my essay "Is Evolution at a Crossroads," *Evolutionary Biology* 24 (1990): 56–81.

6. Scott F. Gilbert, *Developmental Biology*, 6th ed. (Sunderland, Mass.: Sinauer Associates, 2000), pp. 703–70. See also Scott F. Gilbert and Richard M. Burian, "Development, Evolution, and Evolutionary Developmental Biology," in *Keywords and Concepts in Evolutionary Developmental Biology*, ed. Brian K. Hall and Wendy M. Olson, forthcoming (Cambridge, Mass.: Harvard University Press, 2003).

15

Hans-Jörg Rheinberger

A NOTE ON TIME AND BIOLOGY

M arjorie Grene has written widely on the topics of species, evolution, and natural history, but somewhat less on the specific issue of time in general. I would like to use this opportunity to elicit her comments upon the relations among the various levels and senses that may be given to time in the physical, biological, and historical domains.

In section 89 of his *Philosophical Investigations*, Wittgenstein asks with Augustinus (*Confessiones* XI/14): "Quid est ergo tempus? Si nemo ex me quaerat scio; si quaerenti explicare velim, nescio." To be asked about time makes fade away all one intuitively knows about time. Wittgenstein comments: "Something that we know when no one asks us, but no longer know when we are supposed to give an account of it, is something that we need to remind ourselves of."[1] Wittgenstein underlines the word "besinnen" in the German version of the text. One has to remind oneself of something when the immediacy of knowledge has gone with the attempt of explaining. Time is both familiar and strange to us.[2]

In this essay I will sketch a few reflections on time from the perspective of biology. To do so I start with a short explication about what time means in physics, followed by an excursion into history. Having done that I will explore whether time structures, forms of time, and time patterns of organic beings can be linked to a concept of history and finally, how they are connected with our personal experience of time. The latter exercise forces entry into a circle which this short article cannot hope to exhaust.

TIME IN PHYSICS

In mechanics, time figures as the second fundamental term after the geometric parameter of length. It also plays the role of a kinematic parameter in classical dynamics where mass as a third dynamic term is added. The trajectories that are described by the system of dynamic equations are invariant upon time reversal. They do not have a privileged orientation in time. Therefore they are also called reversible or symmetric with respect to time. If a physical process described by these parameters is cyclical it can be used to measure time, that is, to measure the duration of time. Newton called such a measure "relative" time; that which it measures he termed "absolute" time. Absolute time, according to Newton, "in and of itself and of its own nature, without reference to anything external, flows uniformly and by another name is called duration."[3] Einstein's theory of relativity suspended the absolute character of time. But even there time retains its symmetry characteristics.

In thermodynamics we encounter a "processual time."[4] Energy dissipating processes in closed systems which are described by the second fundamental law of thermodynamics are not invariant towards time reversal. They have a privileged orientation. They irreversibly proceed toward a point of equilibrium. They have a favorite time direction which is characterized by a positive amount of entropy production per time unit and which becomes zero at equilibrium.

Material systems which we deem to be organisms are not reversible systems in the sense of classical dynamics. Neither are organisms material systems as described by the second fundamental law of thermodynamics, that is, they do not strive towards an equilibrium in which entropy production becomes zero and the total entropy has reached its maximum. At least it is not characteristic of the normal state of a living system to strive toward such a state. This is, of course, not to say that in organic life no entropic processes take place, but the system as a whole remains in a stationary state as long as life endures, thus a far cry from the thermodynamic equilibrium. We say, according to Ludwig Bertalanffy, that living systems are in a "dynamic" or "flow equilibrium," or in transition from one particular "steady state" to another.[5] From the point of view of the thermodynamics of open systems, steady states are characterized by minima of entropy production per time unit within defined boundary conditions. It is possible to regard living beings from the perspective of either *dynamic* or *processual* time—and indeed we have to do so, whenever the dynamic or entropic aspects of living beings are concerned, aspects which, as material systems, living beings share with other material systems. This, however, does not bring us any nearer to solving the problem as to what distinguishes the time structure of organic beings insofar as and to the extent that they are living.

A HISTORICAL EXCURSION

At this point, a historical digression may be useful. It shows that the problem of time has occupied the sciences concerned with the living since the eighteenth century. As an example, let us have a short look into the articulation of time, change, and process in Buffon's work.[6]

Both at the beginning and toward the end of his monumental *Histoire naturelle* Buffon wrote a geological tract: The *Histoire et théorie de la terre*[7] appeared in 1749 and the *Epoques de la nature*[8] was published in 1779. In his history and theory of the earth Buffon describes an essentially unchanging world in which constant forces cause multiple changes which, however, in the end balance each other out. Finally all local modifications that the earth undergoes are of a cyclic nature. As a theory of a physical system of forces balancing each other the theory of earth has an object which in its essence remains unchanged over time. For Buffon, material systems, if they are to be worthy of a theory, are generally characterized by not being subjected to the regime of time. In *De la nature, Deuxième vue*, published in 1765, Buffon makes the following general statement: "Insofar as the *relation of things* to each other remains the same, it appears to be exempted from the *order of time*."[9]

However it is our daily experience that particular, individual things —contrary to the timelessness of systems, that is, the relation of things to each other—are subject to the order of time. Mountains arise and disappear during the history of the earth, single organisms are born, grow, come of age, and die. "*Time itself*," according to Buffon's second vista on nature in 1765, "only concerns individuals."[10] For them time is not just a mere medium of existence, a steady stream which does not concern them because it is "absolute" in Newton's sense, a time "without reference to anything external," but time is at work in their production as well as in their degeneration. In this respect, Buffon characterizes time as a "real ingredient" of material objects, as a "substance,"[11] although not a material one, which over centuries, for instance, may cause the crystallization of diamonds. Hence, there is a time of coming into existence and passing away which is part of every individual being, living or nonliving, whose existence is not exempt from the stream of time but which is in a *substantial* sense time-bound, affected by time in its existence.

With respect to the organic world, this means, for Buffon, that single organisms cannot represent the biological equivalents of stable, physical systems independent of time.[12] And it is to such systems that Buffon turns his attention. His concern is with the following question: What in the organic world can represent the "relation of things to each other," a relation that is "exempted from the order of time?" In the fourth volume of his *Histoire naturelle,* in the article *De l'asne* (1753), Buffon addresses this question by discussing the notion of species. He comes to the following conclusion:

> Species . . . is an abstract and general word; the thing that it means only exists in so far as one regards nature in a *succession of times* and the steady destruction as well as the steady renewal of beings: while we compare nature of today with times gone by and today's individuals with those of the past, we get a clear idea of what one can call a species . . . [13]

Thus the actual *biological system equivalents*, the organic constants of nature, or so to speak the relations of things remaining untouched by the passing of time, are the species. They provide the theory of the organic with an object, equivalent to the one described by the theory of the earth which is not affected by time and thus appears to be exempted from the regime of time.

If one looks more carefully at Buffon's definition of the species, however, the dimension of time reveals itself to acquire yet another meaning. A species does not just exist as a collection of individuals in space and time but as a *genealogical continuum*. A species is a diachronic system of elements. One could say that a species as a system itself *contains time*. As a system of individual beings a species is, on the one hand, exempt from the rule of time in the sense that it remains stable and essentially unchanged over the generations. On the other hand, as a reproductive process, it is marked by an internal temporality. It does not keep itself going as a system of stable elements in motion like, for instance, the solar system, but through the reproduction of units that are themselves essentially time-limited.

The peculiar time structure of a biological species implies that its constancy as a biological system depends on the finiteness as well as the constancy of every single organism throughout its lifetime. In general, however, single organisms are not only finite, but also undergo changes. The logic of the system as such, that is, as a genealogical continuum, does not exclude a change of the species over time. From 1753 onwards Buffon keeps coming back to the idea of the variability of species, above all in connection with his interest in domestic animals and animals from the New World. In 1756 he writes: "The big workman of nature is time."[14] And even more sweepingly Buffon states in 1761: "Nature, I have to admit, is in a continually flowing movement."[15]

In Buffon's later work, this movement to which the units of organic nature are fundamentally subjected is embedded in an overriding process of geological change. In the *Epoques de la nature* the earth, as one could say in today's terminology, is subordinate to "processual" time, a fact that as far as organic systems are concerned manifests itself and results in their degeneration. The physical principle which lies at the heart of the planetary process is the "Law of Cooling."[16] The epochs of nature represent just so many stages of an orderly, forward-moving, irreversible process in the course of which, according to Buffon's calculation, organisms spontaneously appeared some 37,500 years ago, in the further course of which they gradually degenerate and sometime, according to his calculations, will disappear from the earth after another 93,000 years.

To conclude, Buffon's natural history tends to subvert the discourse of classical physics with respect to time, and in one and the same movement uses the precepts of classical physics to subvert traditional natural history. This double subversion manifests itself in his uses of the concept of time. Of course, Buffon can be seen as the founder neither of thermodynamics nor of the theory of evolution. Both sciences would come into being only in the following century. But Buffon does show us the place where *time* penetrates the sciences of living nature. I now want to proceed with a sketch of how the problem of time in biology can be formulated today, without continuing to follow the history of science as a guide.

TIME IN BIOLOGY

Which then are the aspects of time that can be helpful and have meaning in characterizing living beings? To answer this question it is useful to look first for the minimal prerequisites which are supposed to characterize a material system that we want to call a living being. With reference to Aleksandr Oparin[17] and Manfred Eigen,[18] one can formulate three such minimal prerequisites. (1) If living beings are seen as open systems in stationary states far from thermodynamic equilibrium, states which have to be kept stable if life is to be maintained, then all organisms require a metabolism. This means that they depend on a steady through-flow of energy and matter. (2) If material systems which we call living do not arise *de novo*, then they must be endowed with the capacity of self-replication. The basic feature of biological self-reference as a prerequisite for replication, according to molecular biology, is complementarity. It rests on the stereochemical configuration of a certain class of macromolecules, the nucleic acids. Reproduction, based on complementarity, is a cornerstone of any definition of life. (3) If living beings are not only to be maintained through reproduction, but should also be able to evolve over time, reproduction must be differential. Living beings as we know them are variable. Changes can be passed on. Beyond a certain degree of complexity, both in a living being's inner structure and in its environment, differentiation is the only possible way for living systems to survive. We call this differentiation *evolution*. At the basis of all difference lie the chance events of statistical fluctuation. Their distribution, however, is believed to be asymmetric, that is, governed by the course of evolution itself.[19]

We can now ask whether these three characteristics of living systems are linked in some way to certain forms of time. The assumption is that certain *time structures, forms of time*, or *time patterns* correspond to these characteristics of organic objects; moreover, that we experience them in equally characteristic ways. What is meant by time structures? Ilya Prigogine has suggested defining time not only as a parameter (t), but introducing an "operative time" into the theory of irreversible processes, that is, defining time as an operator (T).[20] Generally an operator is taken to be a mathematical instruction which, when applied to a specific function, reproduces this function, multiplied by a constant. For example, the operation of derivation transforms e^{3x} into $3e^{3x}$, that is, e^{3x} multiplied by a factor of 3. Functions which behave in this way toward an operation are also called the Eigenfunctions of the operator, the corresponding constants being its Eigenvalues. For instance, in quantum mechanics, the temporal development of a wave function is described by an operator. But what could it mean to treat time itself *operationally*, neither kinematically nor processually? I want to try to give an intuitive, nonformalized picture of an operational time, or, to express it differently, a picture of the forms of temporality of organic beings.

The first time structure charactistic for a living being is linked to *periods* of partial systems of its metabolism. We know them, for instance, as circadian rhythms, photoperiodisms, in short, as biological clocks. In an organism such as a human being there are more than a hundred physiological rhythms which are interconnected among each other, and which are partly responding to exterior influences and partly endogenous. Because of disturbances and inherent fluctuations in individual rhythms and their complex interaction, integrated super-periods always return only approximately to their initial state. The system oscillates around stationary states. Organic periods are marked by repetition *and* difference alike, by regularity *and* slight (but significant) derivations. These periods form the basis for the short-term scanning of organismal activity, for its short-term ordering and orientation in time.

The second time structure peculiar to an organism is based on the first and is tied to the general transformations which it undergoes as a stationary system from birth to death. The ensemble of the successive operations which the morphogenetic process performs on the developing organism defines its *life span*. The life span is fundamentally finite. Organisms have an age. It is neither kinematic, chronological time, that is, the measured duration of their existence, which tells us how old organisms are, nor is it processual time, in other words, their vicinity to or distance from the thermodynamic equilibrium. The age of an organism is determined in operational terms: it is an internal state which is essentially generated by the kind and the number of preceding changes that led to the actual state. The age of an organism depends therefore on the trajectory it has followed. We can call this its *ontogenetic age*. Here we can perhaps understand best in an intuitive fashion what operational time means in the realm of the living. It is an intrinsic property of a system: the system does not simply move along a time axis, it carries time along with it in a certain way. We say: somebody is old, or he or she is young, irrespective of how many years old he or she may be.

The third time structure peculiar to an organism is connected to the finiteness of its life span and based on the reproductive differences of individuals and the reproductive differentiation of collectives, that is, species. One can call this structure a *field*, or more precisely, to stress the phenomenon of differentiation, an "evolutionary field."[21] Unlike periods and life spans, the evolutionary field conveys a time structure to the life of species rather than to the life of individuals. Its operational character is linked to a special form of iteration: to autocatalytic replication, to reproduction through complementarity. Because of the subcritical, finite precision of replication, systems of species are in a position to evolve over long time lapses. When populations diverge, an original species can develop differently and bifurcate in the evolutionary field. In this sense, species as the actual units of evolution also have an age. We can call it the *phylogenetic age*. It can be adequately understood neither in chronological nor in processual terms; rather it is defined by the number of ramifications or nodes a unit has passed through in the field of evolution. We speak of primitive species or living fossils, although these species, if we suppose common origins, have passed the same chronologically measured time distance as, for instance, human beings. In the evolutionary field therefore slow-downs, differing time scales, and catch-ups all play a role as soon as one looks at its units—species and their ages—and asks how they are related to one other.

The evolutionary field has, unlike the closed periods and the finite life spans which constitute it, an open time horizon. Whereas periods and life spans run along trajectories, the field creates its own trajectory to a certain extent. All three time structures—forms of time, time patterns—rest, however, fundamentally on iteration with small differences, thus on differential repetition. All three time structures create a temporality which in their combination is peculiar to living systems. They can be subsumed under the concept of operational time. Periods and life spans as time structures mark the phenotype, they control the area of biological functions and characterize ontogenesis. The time structure of the evolutionary field marks the genotype, it rules the area of biological information and characterizes phylogenesis.

At this point, let us have a look back at Buffon's discussion of time. Buffon is thoroughly rooted in the Newtonian tradition. The point of departure in his theory of the earth was the reversible time of dynamics. In his late work on the epochs of nature Buffon anticipated, anachronistically speaking, the processual time of an irreversible dissipation of heat. In Buffon's discussion of living nature, we find only two of the three aforementioned organismal time structures. Organisms, of course, are subject to *periods*. And insofar as time operates on them as a "real ingredient," individual organisms have a *life span*. However, when it comes to the third time structure, the *field*, Buffon has recourse to the first, to periodicity. As a result the biological equivalents of a system, that is, the species as a genealogical continuum, are in a way laden with internal time. However, the time structure of the period excludes the organic world to assume a *history* in the emphatic sense of its contingent diversification in an open time horizon. Dominated by the processual time of a cooling earth, the cyclic time of the organic can, according to Buffon's framework of reasoning, only express itself as a *degeneration*.

HISTORY

I have avoided the term *history* up until now. Some might think it advisable to dispense with the term altogether in the context of physical, chemical, and even biological systems and to reserve it for time structures of *cultural systems*. Let us see whether we can come to an agreement about what is meant by history. In the realm of organic things, periods, from which life spans are made up and which in turn make up an evolutionary field, lead to a complex, hierarchical time structure. *Differential reproduction* appears to be the overarching characteristic of this structure. It is through differential reproduction that biological information is retained, changed, and extended. In order to produce *new* things—not just different ones—old things have to be perpetuated. Since reproduction takes place with only a finite exactitude (in the end because of stochastic, microscopic events which build up macroscopically), new things can emerge in the evolutionary field and old things eventually can disappear. In other words: evolution presupposes the appearance of *swarms*—multiplicities or collectives—and the existence of *filtering mechanisms*. Swarms are produced in the realm of organic things essentially through mutation and recombination, and filtering happens essentially through selection, which lends the process a direction even if this direction is never predictable.

If we look at the time structure of the evolutionary field from a formal point of view, it is not really important how the production and filtering mechanisms, used to produce and stabilize novelty, work in detail. What is decisive is that we are dealing with a transindividual procedure of reproduction with its built-in contingency. In this respect, for the evolution of organisms as well as for all areas of material and intellectual culture it holds, as George Kubler says, that "everything made now is either a replica or a variant of something made a little time ago and so on back without break."[22] In the history of technology, for example, we are concerned with swarms of replicas of tools whose innovative variants depend on an ever more complex filtering of needs and demands. In the swarms of experimental systems in science today, the differentiality of reproduction has itself become the filter of its replication. In the third chapter of her book on *Time*, "Kronos' Fear of New Time," Helga Nowotny describes vividly that movement, that "process of innovation" which is characterized exactly by the fact that the "creation of novelty" quasi-hypercyclically becomes fed back into a loop of repetition. Paradoxically enough, the "creation of novelty" itself becomes the paragon of replication.[23]

Of course, there can be no question of imposing the *particular* form of biological evolution on the history of human cultures, thus adding new misunderstandings to old ones rooted in social Darwinism or sociobiology in their various guises. The terminology should not mislead us in this point. What I seek and would like to make clear is that the time structures of organic things—periods, life spans, and fields—constitute a movement which, carried by the deeply contingent differential reproduction of the organismic genomes, eventually has led to the emergence of those material systems of reproduction to which the human species owes its *social* coherence as well as its historical cultural divergence. Each of the social and cultural replication systems finally is grounded in periodically re-occurring needs, is composed of entities with life spans, and produces the open time horizon of a field. But each of these systems also has its specific incontrovertible and irreducible mechanisms for the production of the swarms and their filtering through which the system is constituted and perpetuated. With that view, we have come further than ever away from the romantic illusion of history as an expressive totality obeying some kind of intrinsic unfolding principle. The contingent figure of differential replication produces another, but no less comprehensive coherence. This coherence no longer rests on the simultaneity of a totality of transformations in a single all-pervasive space, but on the co-existence of replicating systems which carry their own age along with them. Its overall structure is not that of a network of expressive relations but rather that of a tense ecological reticulum of precessions and delays, extinctions and amplifications, interferences and intercalations.

THE EXPERIENCE OF TIME

Do the time structures of organic beings determine our subjective experience of time, and in the end our perception of time? "Time is in us."[24] It is in us in the form of the cyclical order of our life, in the ontogenetic and phylogenetic form of our age, in the form of social cycles in which we participate, and also in the form of the age of things with which we deal. The transformations to which the time operator subjects all these different regimes define our own personal time as individuals, which is different both from the time of the other and also from the time of the things that surround us. Our own personal time experience has something hermetic about it. We live it in an eminently practical way; reflecting about it inevitably leads us into Augustinian difficulties of "reminding."

Our experience of time is linked to regular reoccurrences, to cycles, to periods, to those of our body, to those of the surrounding nature, and to those which are socially regulated and culturally sanctioned. Without periodicity we could not experience identity or nonidentity. The experience of identity and nonidentity is the basis of all reflection. Gotthard Günther has expressed this with the following statement: "The whole problem of reflection . . . has its roots in the elementary formal problem of repetition."[25] Without repetition there would be no experience of time for us. But there is difference in repetition and it is the abstraction from the difference in repetition which leads to the idea of a continuous, undisturbed flow of time.

Our experience of time is, however, also linked to the finiteness of our life span, to the sequence of our ontogenetic aging process. Through its passage we do not only experience our existence in time but the irreversible changes we go through. Likewise, abstracting from the differences in aging, that is, the transition from one configuration of periods to another, leads to the idea that time flows continuously in one direction, that there is a time arrow.

This is not to say that time and change can be grasped alone in terms of our subjective experience of biological rhythms and life spans. They are, however, my concern here, a concern which is deliberately limited to the question of time and biology. We are confronted with time and change just as much through the social rhythms and life spans which structure our cultural relations, as through the rhythms and life spans of things and tools with which we try to put the world around us at our disposal. Furthermore, through these things and tools, insofar as they act as objects of scientific research, we elaborate those abstractions of time which allow us in turn to handle and manipulate these very objects in terms of dynamic, processual, and operator time and allow us to explore the temporal characteristics which mark them out as material systems. From this circularity of experience and orientation there is no escape. Our behavior towards things as objects of scientific research constitutes that figure which, as Jacques Lacan once put it, makes "the subject . . . as it were, internally excluded from its object."[26] Our temporal experience of the world cannot be cut off from our temporal experience of ourselves. Inasmuch as we ourselves represent tools for the investigation of nature, we must, as it were, be able to interact with it, be *compatible* with it. As Grene once put it: "To know ourselves as knowers, we need to know we are alive."[27]

The third time structure we encounter in the realm of living, the evolutionary field, does not go together with an immediate experience of time. Our organically "experienced time," our "lived history" is embedded in the biological time structure of periods and life spans which possess their Eigenvalues. The evolutionary dimension of time becomes accessible to our experience only through the mediation of a *genuinely historical process*. Our historical time horizon is marked by various forms of extragenetic reproduction—by technological systems, language, writing, and the arts. André Leroi-Gourhan remarks in this respect:

> Analysis of techniques shows that their behavior over time resembles that of living species, as though driven by an apparently inherent evolutionary force that places them outside human control. . . . There is room for a real "biology" of technics in which the social body would be considered as an organism independent of the zoological one—an organism animated by humans but so full of unforeseeable effects that its intimate structure is completely beyond the means of inquiry applied to individuals."[28]

These processes take place in a horizon of medium time dimensions. But the transformations that cultural time effects upon these systems create time structures which extend beyond one individual's life thus embedding us in *traditions*. The biological reproduction of man takes place in these historical trajectories. However, since cultural evolutionary fields share one basic structure with biological fields, that is, the contingency of differential reproduction, they remain related to each other. It is only our historical time experience resulting from cultural evolution that enables us therefore to conceptualize the time structure of biological evolution. Thus, whereas we have a primary biological experience of the persistence of time and of irreversible change, our primary experience of history is necessarily *cultural*.

At that point, times begin to be woven into each other. My objective has been to explain how the time structures of *period*, *life span*, and *field* correspond to our ideas of *duration, change*, and *history*. At the end, I wanted at least to hint at the idea that things can have their times, too. Hopefully Professor Grene may provide her view of this along with a general assessment of the topic of the essay. With that, I close the loop by coming back to Wittgenstein once again who in the *Tractatus* enigmatically remarks that besides space and color, time, too, is a *"form of objects."*[29]

HANS-JÖRG RHEINBERGER

MAX PLANCK INSTITUTE FOR THE
    HISTORY OF SCIENCE
BERLIN, GERMANY
FEBRUARY 2000

NOTES

This essay is an English version, with revisions for the context of this volume, of "Zeit und Biologie," an article first published in Georg Christoph Tholen and Michael O. Scholl, eds., *Zeit-Zeichen. Aufschübe und Interferenzen zwischen Endzeit und Echtzeit* (Weinheim: 1990), pp. 127–36.

1. Ludwig Wittgenstein, *Philosophical Investigations* (Oxford: Basil Blackwell, 1953), p. 42[e].

2. John T. Fraser, *Time the Familiar Stranger* (Amherst: University of Massachusetts Press, 1987).

3. Isaac Newton, *The Principia: Mathematical Principles of Natural Philosophy*, trans. I. Bernard Cohen and Anne Whitman, preceded by "A Guide to Newton's *Principia*" by I. Bernard Cohen (Berkeley: University of California Press, 1999), p. 408.

4. Friedrich Cramer, *Chaos and Order: The Complex Structure of Living Systems* (New York: VCH, 1993), p. 189.

5. Ludwig Bertalanffy, *Perspectives on General System Theory,* esp. chapter 10 (New York: George Braziller, 1975).

6. For a more complete treatment of many of these same issues from a similar perspective see Grene's chapter "The Eighteenth Century: Buffon," forthcoming in *Philosophy of Biology*, by Marjorie Grene and David Depew (a volume in the series The Evolution of Modern Philosophy to be published by Cambridge University Press). Marjorie Grene has kindly provided me with a draft of this chapter.

7. Georges Buffon, *Oeuvres philosophiques*, ed. Jean Piveteau (Paris: Presses Universitaires de France, 1954), in the following abbreviated as: *OP*.

8. Georges Buffon, *Les Époques de la Nature*, ed. Jacques Roger (Paris: Editions du Muséum, 1988).

9. Buffon, *OP*, p. 35. Italics added.

10. Buffon, *OP*, p. 36. Italics added.

11. Georges Buffon, *Histoire naturelle des minéraux*, vol. 1 (Paris: Imprimerie royale, 1778), p. 13.

12. As Grene states it: "time is for [Buffon] the real relation between events: it is no more abstract than are the real entities whose interrelation it expresses." ("Buffon," section 3, forthcoming.)

13. Buffon, *OP*, p. 355–56. Italics added. For a fuller treatment of this, see Grene, "Buffon," section 3, forthcoming.

14. Buffon, *OP*, p. 362.

15. Buffon, *OP*, p. 382.

16. Buffon, *OP*, p. 186.

17. Aleksandr Ivanovich Oparin, *The Origin of Life* (Moscow: Foreign Languages Publishing House, 1955).

18. Manfred Eigen, *Laws of the Game: How the Principles of Nature Govern Chance* (New York: Knopf, 1981).

19. Manfred Eigen, *Steps Toward Life: A Perspective on Evolution* (Oxford: Oxford University Press, 1992).

20. Ilya Prigogine, *From Being to Becoming: Time and Complexity in the Physical Sciences* (San Francisco: W. H. Freeman, 1980).

21. Compare also Cramer, *Chaos and Order*, p. 173.

22. George Kubler, *The Shape of Time: Remarks on the History of Things* (New Haven: Yale University Press, 1962), p. 2.

23. Helga Nowotny, *Time: The Modern and Postmodern Experience* (Oxford: Polity Press, 1994), pp. 102–3.

24. Nowotny, *Time*, p. 7.

25. Gotthard Günther, *Logik, Zeit, Emanation und Evolution* (Köln-Opladen: Westdeutscher Verlag, 1967), p. 22.

26. Jacques Lacan, "Science and Truth," *Newsletter of the Freudian Field* 3 (1989): 4–29, p. 10.

27. Marjorie Grene, *A Philosophical Testament* (Chicago: Open Court, 1995), p. 67.

28. André Leroi-Gourhan, *Gesture and Speech* (Cambridge, Mass.: MIT Press, 1993), p. 146.

29. Ludwig Wittgenstein, *Tractatus logico-philosophicus* (London: Routledge & Kegan Paul, 1992), p. 13 (2.0251).

REPLY TO HANS-JÖRG RHEINBERGER

Hans-Jörg Rheinberger remarks correctly that I have not written much about time. When I come to think of it, in fact, I find the famous Augustinian tag puzzling. Is time so bewildering when one turns one's attention to it? I can think of it in Kantian terms, especially in terms of the way I believe it functions, in the First Critique, in the transcendental deduction of the principles, where, it seems to me, the separate time and space of the Aesthetic are transformed into the space-time of our objective experience. And when I was young, I also thought of time in existential terms, putting the future first: that is, putting first what the developmental psychologist Eleanor J. Gibson calls "prospectivity." Note, that is not thinking of time subjectively, either: it's the structure in terms of which we live our lives, not the way we feel it, that is being referred to. Later, when I was writing about the work of the Swiss zoologist Adolf Portmann, I quoted extensively from an essay of his on "Time in the Life of the Organism," in which he discusses what Rheinberger calls periodicity, the rhythms that govern the lives of various animals. In all these contexts, time is certainly of philosophical interest, but not, it seems, especially puzzling. Did Augustine think so because of his conversion, and the odd structure it gave his life, or because of his hope of immortality? And why did Wittgenstein quote him? I don't know.

That's all beside the point, however. Dr. Rheinberger asks me to comment on his reflections. I'll do so, if only patchily.

First, on time in physics: even before Einstein, surely, it was not necessary to accept Newton's absolute time as one's model. For Leibniz, time was the phenomenal expression of a relation: of the order holding among the sequential expressions of a monadic substance. Although dependent on a (nontemporal) absolute, it was not itself absolute. For Kant, time was a pure intuition transcendentally justified: falling, ontologically, he argued, between Newton's absolute time on the one hand and Leibnizian relations on the other. So even the reversible time of classical physics does not have to be understood as itself absolute.

My treatment of Buffon in the book Rheinberger refers to is in complete agreement with his account, although I ought perhaps to have put more emphasis on the earth-historical background of Buffon's view. On time in biology, although of course Rheinberger's distinctions are entirely appropriate, I do object to his concluding statement about life spans: "We say: somebody is old, or he or she is young, irrespective of how many years old he or she may be." I know: "You're as young as you feel." Nonsense! Take it from me—at ninety-one, I know!—when you're old, you're old. True, one can say, "You don't look your age," or something like that. But one *is* however old one is, there's no way around it; and at least in extreme old age—in my experience, which is all I have to go on—not only relative age, but the very calendar years that mark it, matter a lot. I remember when I was a small child, thinking, there are people who can remember twenty years back! Now that I can remember at least snippets from eighty-six or so, I find that very fact astonishing, even absurd. Just the number of decades is overwhelming. True, I can also feel myself wearing out: every day I find new things that are difficult or impossible to do (although, as the present text testifies, so far I do go on talking!). But it's not only the change in my capacities that strikes me, it's the sheer calendar length of the whole thing. Here we are in the twenty-first century, and I was born only ten years into the last one. The system *does* move along a time axis, darn it. If "time is in us," as Rheinberger remarks later, so are we in time. Just wait, Hans-Jörg, you'll find out!

That's all an outcry against one sentence. When it comes to the section on history, I have some more substantive problems. At first we are dealing with evolution, and that seems all right until we get to "swarms." I have taken the liberty of asking Dr. Rheinberger what these could be; he says they are something like aggregates of slightly differing organisms. He objects to "populations," because in the context of evolution at least that term suggests units that interbreed. In ordinary English, I don't think it does. In any case, in the next paragraph, in the context of technology, perhaps "collections" of replicas of tools would do. But then we come to the "swarms of experimental systems in science today." In what follows, even if I substitute for "swarms" some phrase that will carry what I believe Rheinberger is speaking of—to judge from his thought-provoking work on the structure (or nonstructure!) of experimental science—I am really wholly lost. Ms. Nowotny's ruminations, expressed, I presume, in the language of Hegel, are wholly beyond my English-bound mind to comprehend. I am reminded of a remark made long ago by an Italian political scientist who was in the States as a refugee from fascism. Coming from a country where late-nineteenth-century Hegelianism still lingered, and speaking of a colleague whose competence he questioned, he announced: "But X came to political theory through philosophy, and phil-o-soph-y is a faahc-to-ry of dark-ness." So it sometimes seems. And I'm afraid what follows about the relation of culture to evolution appears to me equally obscure. If we have escaped "the romantic illusion of history as an expressive totality" (a view which, again, I am inclined to credit to, or blame on, Hegel), I really have no idea what this creation-in-repetition is that we are supposed to have substituted for it.

My bewilderment at this juncture makes the rest of the argument also hard to follow. I seem to be able to make it, at least superficially, some of the way, but am brought up short by the statement, "The evolutionary dimension of time becomes accessible to our experience only through the mediation of a genuinely historical process." And again, I'm sorry; the rest of that paragraph as well simply eludes me. Is the point that animals lacking our form of enculturation probably don't have theories of evolution? They probably don't have theories of physics, either, or constitutional governments, or arts, or organized wars, or lots of other things that only our culture enables us to have. How does this amount to a different structure of time? I agree that cultural time, or tradition, differs from the three biological varieties of time that Rheinberger has distinguished. I believe the old distinction between "Umwelt" and "Welt" has sometimes been used to stress the openness, and hence flexibility, of our style of living. But tradition, on the other hand, suggests closure rather than openness. Somehow, as Merleau-Ponty tells us in the *Structure of Behavior*, the invention of culture both confines us further than our biological nature does *and* makes it possible for us, within those new limits, to change our world by our own agency, in a way unavailable to less enculturated organisms. And that does perhaps entail a double alteration in the patterns of time that mark our lives. Was something like that the point of the history section? Once more, I don't know.

I have learned a lot from Rheinberger's work on experimental systems, and I appreciate his generosity in submitting an essay to this volume. So I can only apologize for my inability to understand the latter part of his argument.

M. G.

16

John Beatty

"THE HISTORICITY OF NATURE?" "EVERYTHING THAT IS MIGHT HAVE BEEN DIFFERENT?"

INTRODUCTION

Marjorie Grene points proudly to significant changes in her views on evolutionary biology.[1] Compare, for example, her provocative essay, "Two Evolutionary Theories," published in 1958, with the equally provocative, but otherwise very different trio of essays published in 1974, "Darwin and Philosophy," "Explanation and Evolution," and "On the Nature of Natural Necessity."[2]

Despite the differences, though, there has been a recurring issue in her work, namely, the deeply *historical* character of Darwinian evolutionary thought. For example, in 1958, she recommended "an historical form of Kant's transcendental method" for evolutionary biology.[3] In 1961, she criticized R. A. Fisher for "think[ing] unhistorically about an historical subject matter."[4] In 1974, she credited the Darwinian revolution with bringing about a fundamental revision of ontology, which involved taking history much more seriously:

> [T]he Darwinian revolution undermined not only Aristotelian species, but the simple eternity of the Newtonian world itself. It put process before permanence, development before structure. True, this emphasis is not now, explicitly at least, current in philosophical discussion, at least in the English-speaking world. The slogan that we should "take time seriously" has now a quaintly old-fashioned ring. But if, without acknowledging it, we *have* a metaphysic (and we always do), it is a metaphysic of mutability.[5]

One of the most significant differences between Grene's earlier and later work on evolutionary biology has to do with the way in which she began, in the 1970s, to articulate the historical character of evolutionary reasoning (a manner of articulating it that she has emphasized fairly consistently ever since). That is, Darwinian evolutionary biologists, like historians and historiographers, take *contingency* very seriously. As she once put it (continuing from the passage above),

> with the permanence of Aristotelian nature we have also abandoned metaphysical necessity in favor of a recognition of fundamental contingency—and here too evolution, along with historiography as well as history itself, has played a role. Everything there is, we must acknowledge, might have been otherwise.[6]

I agree with Grene concerning the fundamentally historical character of evolutionary reasoning, and also concerning the extent to which contingency is key to that characterization.[7] Yet, however true it may be that Darwinism is a deeply historical science (with a heavy emphasis on contingency), it is nonetheless easy to overstate the point, especially in connection with the reception and development of Darwinism. In the first place, it is important to take into account the extent to which the distinction between "history" and "science" widened rather than narrowed in the wake of Darwin. Indeed, Darwinism figured prominently in late nineteenth- and early twentieth-century attempts to articulate the distinction between history as an "idiographic" discipline and science as a "nomothetic" enterprise. This insistence on the distinction raised problems for the favorable reception of Darwinism. In the second place, it is important to acknowledge that, for a Darwinian, the living world may be more or less historical in the sense of contingent. Darwin's Darwinian successors have argued that the world is far more contingent than Darwin ever dreamed.

DISTANCING SCIENCE FROM HISTORY

I will begin with the manner in which Darwinism was implicated in attempts to distinguish between science and history in the late nineteenth and early twentieth centuries.[8] These included attempts to distance *science from history*, and also attempts to distance *history from science*.

Attempts to distance science from history were part of a reaction against what was perceived to be the excessively "historical" and insufficiently "scientific" character of evolutionary biology in the late nineteenth century. This had a lot to do with the way Darwinism was portrayed by one particularly prominent Darwinian, Ernst Haeckel. Consider, for instance,

Haeckel's portrayal of Darwinism in his best-selling, ten-edition *Natural History of Creation*. First, Haeckel identified "Darwin's theory" with the doctrine that "all organisms are derived from one single, or from a few simple original forms, and that they have slowly developed from these by a course of gradual change."[9] Second—that is, much later in the book—he identified "Darwinism" with the role of natural selection as a mechanism of evolution.[10]

While Haeckel certainly considered natural selection to be an important mechanism of evolutionary change, it did not play much of a role in his elaborations of evolutionary thought. The real work, for Haeckel, was determining the actual course of evolutionary history, and that constituted by far the bulk of his bestsellers, like *Natural History of Creation*, *The Evolution of Man*, and *Riddle of the Universe*. The history of life had to be explored/uncovered/discovered. Evolution by natural selection, on the other hand was, for Haeckel, a "mathematical necessity." That is, given variation, inheritance, and scarce resources, evolution by natural selection follows quite simply. Darwinism in this sense "needs no further proof."[11] While this much is certain, however, the actual course of evolutionary history is not, and in this respect there is much work to be done.

Haeckel's main tool for reconstructing evolutionary relationships was the so-called "biogenetic law," according to which the pattern of ontogeny (the stages of development from egg to adult) characteristic of a species "recapitulated" or replayed the "phylogeny" (the evolutionary ancestry) of the species.[12] In other words, as an individual organism develops, it passes through stages that correspond, in order, to the sequence of species that gave rise to it. For example, early in its development a human embryo passes through a stage corresponding to an ancestor that we have in common with fish (characterized by gill folds), later through a stage corresponding to an ancestor that we have in common with other tailed mammals, and so on. Phylogeny can thus be "read" from ontogeny; Haeckel followed the morphologist Fritz Müller in referring to ontogeny as a "historical document."[13]

Critics of this position charged that (1) there was no general *law* connecting phylogeny with ontogeny, that is, that the biogenetic "law" was really no such thing, and (2) *scientific* accounts rely on laws.

Regarding the supposed lawlike status of the biogenetic law, Haeckel was well aware of the difficulties in defending it as such. For example, he was well aware that the truth of the "law" depended on a number of assumptions about the processes of heredity and evolution. Among other things, it assumed that new adaptations were always added onto the previous end of the developmental sequence. Only in this way would the sequence of developmental stages characteristic of a species reflect the sequence of evolutionary forms that gave rise to that species.[14] Haeckel was also well aware that the assumptions behind his law were often not realized. For example, new adaptations are sometimes acquired during juvenile periods of development. Over time, Haeckel tried to revise his formulation of the biogenetic law with qualifications to cover the exceptional cases.

But all the while, critics like Wilhelm His were outraged that Haeckel should refer to the biogenetic law not only as a "law," but as a "Grundgesetz!"[15] Somewhat more sympathetically, Wilhelm Roux argued that the supposed "Grundgesetz" relied on assumptions about heredity that might in the future, but could not at present be expressed in general lawlike terms.[16] (I will return shortly to the issue of laws of heredity.)

Perhaps the most ardent critic of Darwinism-à-la-Haeckel was Haeckel's former student, Hans Driesch. Driesch found incomprehensible his teacher's emphasis on phylogeny from a scientific point of view. It is simply too particularistic: "It is completely indifferent to us . . . whether exactly such and such forms existed and succeeded each other on the Earth. It is completely indifferent to general theoretical science, for which historical ideas limited by time and space are alien."[17]

At best, phylogenies themselves might be understood in terms of deeper laws of heredity. However, Driesch, like Roux, argued that we are not in possession of any such laws (again, a concern to which I will return shortly). So a phylogeny, even if correct, is worth about as much, and is just as boring, as a picture gallery of the ancestors of some prince![18]

Later, in his Gifford Lectures of 1907, Driesch drew a very distinct line between "science," which deals with general laws of nature, and "history," which deals with "particular events in space and time."[19] Phylogeny is much more like history than science, and in this sense is "second rank," "just as geology stands in second rank as compared with chemistry or physics."[20] In other words, the laws of physics and chemistry explain the particular history of the earth as one possible outcome of those laws. Similarly, phylogeny might be explained by deeper laws of heredity, if only such laws were available.

In response to critics like Driesch, Haeckel proudly accepted the characterization of his work as historical: "I am one of those scientists who believe in a real 'natural history' and who think as much of an historical knowledge of the past as of an exact investigation of the present. . . . Historical knowledge cannot be replaced by any other branch of science."[21] (This may not have endeared Haeckel to the historians of his generation any more than to the biologists, for reasons that I will consider in the next section.)

DISTANCING HISTORY FROM SCIENCE

Grene urges that the reception and impact of Darwinism be considered in the context of contemporaneous developments in history *per se*—in particular, developments in "historical method."[22] I agree, and in this section I want to consider the influence of historians and philosophers of history on the reception of Darwinism qua historical discipline.

The impact can be seen quite clearly in the case of Driesch, whose attempts to distance *science from history* were based on a contemporaneous distinction (between science and history) drawn by the historians and philosophers of history, Wilhelm Windelband and Heinrich Rickert. In order to make sense of their distinction, it is important to step back a bit and consider how and why they were concerned to distance *history from science*.

R. G. Collingwood, Ernst Cassirer, and many others have written about "the growing autonomy of historical thought" that occurred in the late nineteenth century.[23] This is generally understood to have occurred as a reaction against efforts to improve history by making it more like science. It is understood, more specifically, to have occurred as a reaction against "positivist" history, as championed in the abstract by Auguste Comte and John Stuart Mill, and as practiced, for example, by Henry Thomas Buckle in his extremely influential, *History of Civilization in England* (published at the same time as the *Origin*).[24] The ideal of historical science, thus conceived and exemplified, was the discovery of historical laws on a par with those of the natural sciences. For example, as Buckle reasoned about the place of marriage in English society (just to give you a taste of lawlike history),

> It is now known that marriages bear a fixed and definite relation to the price of corn; and in England the experience of a century has proved that, instead of having any connection with personal feelings, they [marriages] are simply regulated by the average earnings of the great mass of the people: so that this immense social and religious institution is not only swayed, but is completely controlled, by the price of food and by the rate of wages.[25]

So historians were supposed to investigate marriage regularities, not individual marriages.

The ideals of positivistic, scientific history were reinforced by Darwinism, and more especially by accounts of human evolution that made human history continuous with natural history. There were supposedly no longer ontological grounds for distinguishing natural history, which was subject to natural laws, from human history, which was not.

Haeckel was among the most outspoken proponents of the idea that human history could and should be reduced to natural history. While proudly accepting the label of "historical" for his own natural history (e.g., in the quotation above), Haeckel nonetheless condemned historians (in the sense of civil history) for not being sufficiently acquainted with the history of nature, and for not realizing that "man is, after all, only a most highly developed vertebrate animal, and all aspects of human life have their parallels, or more correctly their lower stages of development, in the animal kingdom."[26]

In reaction to this attempted incorporation of human history into science, a number of late nineteenth- and early twentieth-century historians and philosophers defended history as an autonomous discipline, distinct from natural science, with its own ideals and methods. For example, Heinrich Rickert found it quite objectionable that the philosophy of history had come to be dominated by evolutionary reasoning—Haeckel over Hegel, if you will:

> Around the middle of the nineteenth century the historical continuity of our intellectual life was interrupted [by Darwinism—most likely Haeckel's *Darwinismus*], and, as a consequence, precisely those elements of a German philosophy [Hegel] which are important for an understanding of history are still insufficiently known outside relatively narrow circles. Even where Hegel's categories are used, an awareness of their significance and import is lacking. If, for example, the question of "evolution" is at issue in the cultural sciences, this idea is, for all that, frequently associated with a man who was of no consequence as a philosopher [definitely Haeckel], though undoubtedly worthy of the highest admiration as a specialist in a particular field of the natural sciences; and "Darwinism" is quite seriously regarded as the "new" philosophy of history. The result of this and similar confusions is the demand that the cultural sciences should adopt the "method of the natural sciences."[27]

Rickert, following and elaborating on the work of Wilhelm Windelband, argued that history is an "idiographic" discipline, which deals with individual, unique events, while the natural sciences are "nomothetic" disciplines, which deal with abstract laws and with individual events only as instances of those laws.

Instead of conceding history to the natural sciences, Windelband and Rickert actually claimed part of the natural sciences—evolutionary biology—for history (although as we shall see, this was a temporary takeover). Insofar as the study of evolution concerns the history of life on earth, they argued, it concerns a unique phenomenon and is essentially a historical discipline. As Windelband put it,

> Consider . . . the subject matter of the biological sciences as evolutionary history in which the entire sequence of terrestrial organisms is represented as a gradually formative process of descent or transformation which develops over time. There is neither evidence nor even a likelihood that this same organic process has been repeated on some other planet.[28]

The origin of the vertebrates is no different from, say, the Reformation in this respect.

Rickert more carefully distinguished the generalizing aspects of evolutionary studies from hypotheses about evolutionary history.[29] The former fit better within the category of natural science. But the latter, phylogenetic biology, could be counted among the natural sciences only to the extent that its subject matter had more to do with natural than with human history. Nonetheless, Rickert argued, phylogeny was essentially an idiographic, historical enterprise.

All the while these late nineteenth- and early twentieth-century historians and philosophers of history were attempting to distance history from science, there were, as we have discussed, biologists attempting to distance science from history. Driesch's own efforts to demarcate science from history were informed in part by his reading of Windelband and Rickert, whom he cited.[30]

Ultimately Rickert, influenced by Roux and Driesch, whom he cited in turn,[31] had second thoughts about what to make of the historical nature of phylogenetic biology. Perhaps biology had temporarily benefited from "the irruption of historical ideas into the science of living creatures." But in the long run, the influence of history on biology seemed to produce an unhealthy identity complex:

> it looks as if biology . . . no longer sees its proper task to consist so much in the construction of "family trees" and "genealogical tables" according to historical principles as in the ascertainment of general relations within the organic world in terms of universal concepts and laws. The more it concentrates on these endeavors, the sooner will biology, after a kind of crisis which it has passed through, once again will become a generalizing science and thus a natural science in the formal and logical sense as well, just as it had always been before Darwin . . . .[32]

Rickert placed the blame for this crisis on Haeckel, for his gross boundary transgressions: "It was not so much Darwin himself as a few of his followers, Haeckel in particular, who were responsible for the fact that biology generally came to assume a character that seems incompatible with the antithesis we have drawn between the natural and cultural sciences."[33]

Unfortunately, Rickert continued, the debate about the value of phylogeny within science had extended to the value of history *per se*, and here the criticisms had gone too far. After all, "portrait galleries are not always boring, and the ancestry of humans has considerable [he adds "scientific" here, but not "naturwissenschaftlich"] interest. Why should we not want to know about the unique evolutionary history of life on earth?" He added, however, that this knowledge would not contribute to biology as a "science of laws." And Rickert emphasized again his conviction that historical and scientific biology would continue to grow apart.[34]

TAKING HISTORY MORE AND MORE SERIOUSLY

So, to summarize up to this point, while we may want to acknowledge the ultimate contributions of Darwin and Darwinism to "historical science," we should also be careful not to lose sight of the more immediate role that Darwinism had in polarizing science and history.

In discussing the impact of Darwin and Darwinism on the historicizing of nature and science, we must also be careful not to exaggerate by over-radicalizing Darwin and many Darwinians who followed. This is especially the case if we articulate the "historicizing" of nature and science in terms of an emphasis on contingency, as does Grene:

> Now, it is true, I believe, that part of the explanatory force of evolutionary theory rests in its emphasis on contingency. Everything there is *might* have been different: this belief in the historicity of nature is one of the metaphysical strengths of the Darwinian creed.[35]

Yes, but consider the range of Darwinian perspectives in this respect. Consider for instance Charles Sanders Peirce. Peirce, an admirer of Darwin, nonetheless admonished Darwin and other scientists for not taking history more seriously. Sure, the solar system, the earth, and life on earth had all received historical accounts. But, Peirce complained, the *laws of nature* were still treated as if they were simply given, when clearly they had to come from something, somewhere.[36] Not only nature, but the laws of nature, could have been otherwise. Perhaps such an idea crossed Darwin's mind, but he never elaborated on it.

It is, after all, a strange idea. Truth-for-all-time seems inherent in the notion of a scientific law. How could a law, true for all time, *come* to be true? And if it came to be true, then might it not also possibly come to be false? For Peirce, the evolution of laws indeed implied that "laws" of nature were laws in name only; the evolution of laws implied in his terms "a certain swerving of the facts from any definite formula."[37]

Darwin would have had nothing to do with this. He sought laws. There may have been change over time in Darwin's world, but it was law-governed change. Species may have had histories, but the laws governing species did not.[38]

Peirce's more radically historical conception of science was largely ignored in his time, which is not surprising given the extent to which the distinction between lawlike science and particularistic history was growing wider during this period. In this context, Darwinism would be judged successful to the extent that it was lawlike. And indeed, it initially failed in this respect. In the first place, there seemed (in the late nineteenth and early twentieth centuries) to be no generalizable mechanism of evolution. In the second place, some prominent Darwinians, like Haeckel, seemed to put all their effort into reconstructing the particular evolutionary history of life on earth. This really did seem to be just history, not science.

A more and more common feeling of the time was that evolutionary studies should be at least temporarily, if not permanently, excluded from biology qua science. There were other, more promising lines of research. A much better example of nomothetic (and experimental) biology in the early twentieth century was Mendelian genetics. Mendel's laws—successfully applied through breeding experiments to trait after trait in species after species—were cherished by biologists, in part for their comparability with the laws of physics, which helped put biology on a par with the best of the nomothetic (and experimental) sciences.

There was also the hope that Mendelian genetics would eventually illuminate the lawlike mechanisms of evolution (which was similar to the outlook of pre-Mendelians, like Roux and Driesch, that the laws of heredity, once discovered, would illuminate the principles of evolution). But many early Mendelians, like William Bateson, were cautious in this regard, and urged that inheritance be studied for the time being just for the sake of inheritance:

> Genetic experiment was first undertaken . . . in the hope that it would elucidate the problem of species [i.e., evolution]. The time has come when appeals for vigorous prosecution of this method should rather be based on other grounds. It is as directly contributing to the advancement of pure physiological science that genetics can present the strongest claim. We have an eye on the evolution-problem. We know that the facts we are collecting will help in its solution; but for a period we shall perhaps do well to direct our search more especially to the immediate problems of genetic physiology, the laws of heredity, the nature of variation, the significance of sex and other manifestations of dimorphism, willing to postpone the application of the results to wider problems as a task more suited to a maturer stage.[39]

With regard to the "evolution-problem," geneticists should for the time being remain "agnostic."[40]

After all, what did Mendelian geneticists have to gain from studying evolution? It was certainly not as though Darwinism, or any other evolutionary perspective, could shed light on Mendelian genetics! It is interesting that Bateson even considered the possibility—à la Peirce—that Mendel's laws evolved and that evolutionary reasoning might illuminate Mendelian genetics. Nonetheless, having briefly entertained the idea, he flatly rejected it. Mendel's laws apply too generally—inheritance is too "orderly"—to be the result of evolutionary happenstance. As Bateson put it, "[t]his order cannot by the nature of the case be dependent on Natural Selection for its existence, but must be a consequence of the fundamental chemical and physical nature of living things."[41] The implication is that if Mendelian genetics were the product of evolution, then there would be more exceptions (indeed! as we shall see!).

However, it was not long before the tables turned, and the light of evolution was thrown on genetics. The English geneticist, Ronald Fisher addressed the Sixth International Congress of Genetics in 1932:

> The title chosen for our discussion is "Contributions of genetics to the theory of evolution," and that these contributions are of two kinds, somewhat sharply contrasted, is well illustrated by comparing Haldane's subject, "Can evolution be explained in terms of present known genetical causes?" with the heading under which I chose to speak, "The evolutionary modification of genetic phenomena." . . . [On my approach,] genetics supplies the facts as to living things as they are now, facts which, like the living things in which they occur, have an evolutionary history and may be capable of an evolutionary explanation, facts which are not immutable laws of the workings of things but which might have been different had evolutionary history taken a different course.[42]

And as the English geneticist and cytologist Cyril Darlington added in his 1939 book, *The Evolution of Genetic Systems*, "there is not one system of heredity and variation, but many. . . . Since the properties of heredity and variation themselves show heredity and variation under experiment, they must, like other properties of the organism, be susceptible to selection and adaptation."[43]

Finally, by the 1960s (perhaps earlier, I am not sure, but see sources cited below), the turnabout was complete. Biologists had documented numerous exceptions to Mendel's "first law," which proclaims the universality of 50:50 ("fair") segregation of alleles into gametes during the process of meiosis. Having recognized that the meiotic mechanism, and segregation ratios in particular could vary, biologists also began to study the evolution of these mechanisms, thus acknowledging the very real sense in which Mendel's "first law" could be said to have evolved. This was surely Peirce's vision realized.

Or perhaps it was an even more radical outcome. For consider that if the mechanisms of Mendelian heredity, like 50:50 segregation, influence the way in which evolution occurs—as Bateson quite rightly assumed—and if the mechanisms of Mendelian heredity fail to hold, then evolution may not occur in the same way. And to the extent that the mechanisms of Mendelian heredity are the contingent outcomes of evolution, then so too are the causally derivative mechanisms of evolution. More precisely, since the fundamental principle of population genetics, the so-called Hardy-Weinberg "law," rests on the premise of 50:50 segregation, then to the extent that 50:50 segregation fails to be true, so too does the Hardy-Weinberg law, and to the extent that 50:50 segregation can be said to be an outcome of evolution, so too can the Hardy-Weinberg law. As the population geneticist Marcy Uyenoyama put it, "[j]ust as the meiotic mechanism [leading to 50:50 segregation] directs evolution through its effects on the pattern of inheritance, the process of genetic transmission itself evolves by natural selection."[44]

Darwinians today have acknowledged quite explicitly the extent to which the mechanisms of evolution are themselves only contingently true. As Brian Charlesworth and Daniel Hartl reflect:

> Finally, a word about the theoretical population genetics of non-Mendelian segregation is in order. Virtually all "general" principles of population dynamics are violated when segregation is non-Mendelian: average fitness is not maximized in random mating populations, even for a single locus (Hiraizumi, Sandler and Crow 1960); the fundamental theorem of natural selection does not hold (Hartl 1970); . . . . It makes one wonder whether there are *any* general principles of population genetics whose validity does not depend on the supposition of Mendelian heredity.[45]

Just as the principles of Mendelian genetics yielded to evolutionary historical analysis (and with them the principles of evolution themselves), so too the principles of molecular genetics have yielded to evolutionary historical analysis. To someone like Bateson, this would have sounded as counterintuitive, or possibly even more counterintuitive than the idea that Mendelian heredity would be understood evolutionarily. Recall Bateson's argument that the universality of Mendelian heredity could not possibly be due to evolutionary happenstance, and "must [instead] be a consequence of the fundamental chemical and physical nature of living things."[46] Clearly he did not consider that the chemical and physical nature of living things might itself have an evolutionary history!

The evolutionary history of the molecular basis of life was emphasized strongly by evolutionary biologists in the 1960s and early 1970s. The dazzling successes of molecular genetics, in the wake of Watson and Crick's discovery of the structure of DNA, had once again raised the possibility that genetics—now at the molecular level—might be the deepest of biological truths. In response, evolutionary biologists like Theodosius Dobzhansky, Ernst Mayr, George Simpson and others went to considerable effort to advance the argument that molecular genetics itself must be understood evolutionarily.[47] For example, a thirty-something Richard Lewontin made the point nicely in his review of Franklin Stahl's *The Mechanics of Inheritance*, one of the first textbooks of molecular genetics:

> Stahl does deserve our praise for his attempt to write about the mechanics of inheritance in a way that takes into account the recent advances in molecular genetics. . . . However, Stahl, in common with many enthusiasts, has mistaken the tail for the dog. . . . That is, except in a trivial sense, the laws of genetics are not the result of the structure of DNA, but rather DNA has been chosen by natural selection from among an immense variety of molecules precisely because it fits the requirements of an evolved genetic system. DNA is only the tactic adopted in the course of working out an evolutionary strategy. That is why some organisms can get on without it.[48]

The argument had a wide range of applications. For example, just as it is a matter of evolutionary history—not necessitated by physics and chemistry alone—that the hereditary material is (usually) DNA, so too it is a contingent outcome of evolution that there is a particular genetic "code"—that is, a particular set of nucleotide-sequence-to-amino-acid translation rules. Crick himself proposed an evolutionary account of the code. According to Crick, once the code had evolved in a primitive lineage, any change in the code would have resulted in changes in the amino acid sequences of many previously adaptive proteins. Such a cascading effect could not conceivably be beneficial overall. Thus the code became, in Crick's term, a "frozen accident" of evolution.[49]

Actually, Crick miscalculated somewhat. "The" genetic code is not universal after all; different codes have been found in different taxa. The code has been evolutionarily conserved in many but not all of the lineages that descended from the primitive lineage in which it first appeared. Evolutionary diversification of the code has also occurred. As a recent reviewer, S. Osawa, summarizes the current state of understanding, "the genetic code, formerly thought to be frozen, is, in fact, in a state of evolution."[50]

CONCLUSION

I tend to think that the "Darwinian revolution" is a long way from over. The term "revolution" is appropriate for the significance of the metaphysical and methodological implications involved. But the term perhaps inappropriately suggests *an* abrupt change—*an* "aha" moment—rather than the *ongoing* project of working-out what it all means.

The Darwinian Revolution is in no small part about the importance of history. But it was not immediately apparent how Darwinism could be historical and at the same time scientific. And Darwinism has become more deeply historical over time.

Marjorie Grene's assessment of the implications of the Darwinian revolution is far from just a report of "what happened." Rather, it points in a direction. Darwinism is *in the process* of historicizing nature and science. And we are *in the process* of understanding just how contingent are the past, present, and future states of nature.

JOHN BEATTY

DEPARTMENT OF ECOLOGY, EVOLUTION AND BEHAVIOR
UNIVERSITY OF MINNESOTA
MARCH 2002

NOTES

1. Marjorie Grene, *The Understanding of Nature* (Dordrecht: Reidel, 1974), p. vii.

2. Grene, "Two Evolutionary Theories," *British Journal for the Philosophy of Science* 9 (1958): 110–27, 185–93, reprinted in *Understanding of Nature*, pp. 127–53; "Darwin and Philosophy," *Proceedings of the Colloquium 'Connaisance Scientifique et Philosophie,'* Académie Royale des Sciences, des Lettres et des Beaux-Arts de Belgique, reprinted in *Understanding of Nature*, pp. 189–200; "Explanation and Evolution," *Understanding of Nature*, pp. 207–27; "On the Nature of Natural Necessity," *Understanding of Nature*, pp. 228–42.

3. Grene, "Two Evolutionary Theories," *Understanding of Nature*, p. 150.

4. Grene, "Statistics and Selection," *British Journal for the Philosophy of Science* 12 (1961): 25–42, reprinted in *Understanding of Nature*, p. 170.

5. Grene, "Darwin and Philosophy," *Understanding of Nature*, p. 194.

6. Ibid.

7. Or perhaps I have gone too far? See John Beatty, "The Evolutionary Contingency Thesis," *Concepts, Theories, and Rationality in the Biological Sciences*, The Second Pittsburgh-Konstanz Colloquium in the Philosophy of Science, ed. Gereon Wolters and James G. Lennox (Pittsburgh: University of Pittsburgh Press, 1995).

8. This section of the paper is indebted in a number of respects to the work and insights of Lynn Nyhart, *Biology Takes Form: Animal Morphology and the German Universities, 1800–1900* (Chicago: University of Chicago Press, 1995).

9. Ernst Haeckel, *The History of Creation: Or the Development of the Earth and Its Inhabitants by the Action of Natural Causes*, trans. E. Ray Lankester, 4th ed., 2 vols. (New York: Appleton, 1892): vol. 1, p. 4.

10. Haeckel, *History of Creation*, vol. 1, pp. 153–79.

11. Ibid., vol. 1, pp. 171–72.

12. Ibid., vol. 1, pp. 332–62, esp. 354–55.

13. Haeckel, *History of Creation*, vol. 1, p. 358.

14. See Stephen Jay Gould, *Ontogeny and Phylogeny* (Cambridge: Harvard University Press, 1977) for a nice discussion of Haeckel's reasoning in this regard, and also for a nice discussion of the reception of Haeckel's views.

15. Wilhelm His, *Unsere Körperform und das physiologische Problem ihrer Enstehung* (Leipzig: Vogel, 1874), p. 166.

16. Wilhelm Roux, "The Problems, Methods, and Scope of Developmental Mechanics" (1894), trans. William Morton Wheeler, *Defining Biology: Lectures from the 1890s*, ed. Jane Maienschein (Cambridge, Mass.: Harvard University Press, 1986), p. 175.

17. Hans Driesch, *Die Biologie als selbständige Grundwissenschaft: Eine kritische Studie* (Leipzig: Engelmann, 1893), p. 27.

18. Driesch, *Biologie als selbständige Grundwissenschaft*, pp. 29–30.

19. Driesch, *The Science and Philosophy of the Organism*. The Gifford Lectures Delivered before the University of Aberdeen in the Year 1907 (London: Black, 1908), pp. 13–14, 300–303.

20. Driesch, *Biologie als selbständige Grundwissenschaft*, pp. 26–31.

21. Haeckel, *The Evolution of Man*, 5th ed., trans. Joseph McCabe (New York: Truth Seeker, n.d.), p. 357.

22. Grene, "Darwin and Philosophy," in *Understanding Nature*, p. 193.

23. Collingwood, *Idea of History*, p. 131; Ernst Cassirer, *The Problem of Knowledge* (New Haven: Yale University Press, 1950).

24. Henry Thomas Buckle, *History of Civilization in England* (1856–1861), 2 vols. (New York: Appleton, 1910).

25. Ibid., pp. 23–24.

26. Haeckel, *History of Creation*, pp. 336–37, 175; see also 319ff.

27. Heinrich Rickert, *Science and History: A Critique of Positivist Epistemology* (1926), trans. George Reisman (Princeton, N.J.: Van Nostrand, 1962), pp. 8–9.

28. Wilhelm Windelband, "History and Natural Science" (1894), trans. Guy Oakes, *History and Theory* 19 (1980): p. 176.

29. Rickert, *Science and History*, pp. 104–8.

30. For example, Driesch, *Science and Philosophy of the Organism*, pp. 13–14, 315–16.

31. Heinrich Rickert, *Die Grenzen der Naturwissenschaftlichen Begriffsbildung*,

4th ed. (Tübingen: Mohr, 1921), p. 261.

32. Rickert, *Science and History*, pp. 108–9.

33. Ibid., p. 108.

34. Rickert, *Die Grenzen der Naturwissenschaftlichen Begriffsbildung*, p. 199.

35. Grene, "Nature of Natural Necessity," *Understanding of Nature*, p. 229.

36. Charles Sanders Peirce, "The Architecture of Theories" (1891), *The Essential Peirce: Selected Philosophical Writings*, Vol. 1 (Bloomington, Ind.: Indiana University Press, 1992), p. 288.

37. Ibid., p. 289.

38. Michael Ruse, *The Darwinian Revolution: Nature Red in Tooth and Claw* (Chicago: University of Chicago Press, 1979).

39. William Bateson, *Mendel's Principles of Heredity* (Cambridge: Cambridge University Press, 1909), p. 4.

40. Bateson, "Evolutionary Faith and Modern Doubts" (1922), *William Bateson, F.R.S., Naturalist: His Essays and Addresses*, ed. Beatrice Bateson (Cambridge: Cambridge University Press, 1928), 391, *et passim*.

41. Bateson, "Heredity and Variation in Modern Lights" (1909), *William Bateson, F.R.S.*, p. 223.

42. R. A. Fisher, "The Evolutionary Modification of Genetic Phenomena," *Proceedings of the Sixth International Congress of Genetics* 1 (1932): 165–72, reprinted in *Collected Papers of R. A. Fisher*, ed. J. H. Bennett (Adelaide: University of Adelaide, 1973), p. 165.

43. C. D. Darlington, *The Evolution of Genetic Systems* (Cambridge: Cambridge University Press, 1939), p. 123.

44. Marcy K. Uyenoyama, "Genetic Transmission and the Evolution of Reproduction: The Significance of Parent-Offspring Relatedness to the 'Cost of Meiosis," Meiosis, ed. Peter B. Moens (Orlando, Fla.: Academic Press, 1987), p. 21.

45. Brian Charlesworth and Daniel L. Hartl, "Population Dynamics of the Segregation Distorter Polymorphism of Drosophila melanogaster," *Genetics* 89 (1978): 171–92, page cited 188; quotation also includes references to Y. Hiraizumi, L. Sandler and J. Crow, "Meiotic Drive in Natural Populations of Drosophila melanogaster. III. Populational Implications of the Segregation-Distorter Locus," *Evolution* 14 (1960): 433–44; Hartl, "Population Consequences of Non-Mendelian Segregation among Multiple Alleles," *Evolution* 24 (1970): 538–45.

46. Bateson, "Heredity and Variation," p. 223.

47. See for example, Beatty, "Evolutionary Anti-Reductionism: Historical Considerations," *Biology and Philosophy* 5 (1990): 199–210; Beatty, "Ernst Mayr and the Proximate/Ultimate Distinction," *Biology and Philosophy* 9 (1994): 333–56.

48. Richard C. Lewontin, "A Molecular Messiah: The New Gospel in Genetics?" *Science* 145 (1964): 566–67, page cited 566.

49. Francis Crick, "The Origin of the Genetic Code," *Journal of Molecular Biology* 19 (1968): 367–97.

50. S. Osawa, *Evolution of the Genetic Code* (Oxford: Oxford University Press, 1995), pp. i, 73.

REPLY TO JOHN BEATTY

My first response to John Beatty's paper was just, "Amen," and "Thank you" for his illuminating account of variants in the stress on contingency in the Darwinian tradition, and especially of the different post-Darwinian oppositions between science and history, or history and science. And I was grateful as well for his recognition that I, too, have modified my own view of the Darwinian tradition. Although one hopes to become a little wiser as well as older as the years go by, some of my critics have held me to the follies of my callow middle age. So thank you, John.

On second thoughts, however, though without in any way dissenting from the story Beatty is telling, I do want to pose two questions, one rather abstract, the other bearing on some recent controversial literature in the philosophy of biology.

First, about contingency and history. It's true, of course, that a sense of contingency must underlie any post-Darwin metaphysic. Spinoza's grand intellectual vision fails us, superficially—or we fail it—because it is too difficult to understand what responsible agency could be in a world of total necessity. But at bottom it is the fact that things could have gone otherwise—the chanciness of Darwinian causality—that cuts us off from Spinoza's dream of God-or-Nature. Beatty welcomes that insight, which he himself has expressed, and which was recurrently conspicuous in Steve Gould's *Natural History* columns. Yet, come to think of it, does contingency—the fact that things might have happened differently—entail history in the sense of change? Couldn't things just happen—with a big bang, or whatever—and then just happen to stay that way? If nothing is necessary, why is change necessary? Why does Darwinism have to take different forms, and why do I have to change my perspective on it? That is a mere philosophical speculation; it has no effect on the truth or the interest of the history Beatty relates, but there it is, off on the sidelines, and I thought I'd better give it a nod.

My other question is more urgent. If contingency reaches all the way down to the evolution of the genes themselves or their encoded arrangement(s), it seems that all fundamental questions are historical and all biological questions evolutionary. Beatty's account of these developments is perspicuous. I remember reading Darlington's *Evolution of Genetic Systems* long ago, and finding it singularly refreshing in the atmosphere of dogmatism that seemed to surround the "central dogma." It is good to learn that such insights are now more widely established and accepted. But does that mean that the leading question must always be, how did it get that way? That sometimes seems to be a conclusion entailed by the stress on contingency, and history, all the way down.

Beatty refers, in particular, to the pleas put forward in the sixties and early seventies by the leaders of the evolutionary synthesis against the encroachment of an increasingly fashionable, and increasingly funded, molecular approach to biological problems. In this context, he cites his own fascinating paper on the role of the famous proximate/ultimate distinction at different stages of Ernst Mayr's career. The stress on contingency seems to demand, and to underwrite, that distinction. In the last analysis, it's always the evolutionary explanation—in effect, the explanation through appeal to natural selection—that tells you *why*, not just *what* or *how*. Mayr had been led to evolutionary explanation as "ultimate" in his study of bird migration. And in 1961, when he gave his famous lecture on "Cause and Effect in Biology," [1] he was clearly committed, as a leader in evolutionary biology and newly appointed director of the Museum of Comparative Zoology at Harvard, to the founding status of evolutionary explanation (against those molecular invaders). So the position he was taking is certainly intelligible and (historically) justified.

Still, taking that celebrated article just in its own terms, I must confess that, as an outsider studying the conceptual structure of biological practice, I have always had doubts about it. The zoologist Herman Spieth of the University of California, Davis, once remarked to me that all biologists, at least, I'm afraid one has to add, all *reasonable* biologists, accept evolution, and natural selection, in the background of their work, but relatively few are actually engaged in the search for evolutionary explanations. Spieth did not elaborate, but I have tried to do so a number of times. The explanation many biologists are after—for them, the "ultimate" explanation—is something about how some system or partial system works, how its parts are arranged (in such a way that it works), or even, without any sinister reductive intent, what it's made of. So, although thanks to Beatty's account, I understand why they were definitive for Mayr, "proximate" and "ultimate" seem to me somewhat unfortunate terms. As an irredeemable pluralist about scientific practices, I don't want my acceptance of contingency, or of the primacy of history, to lead to such a single-minded dichotomy. If Mayr's intent in the early sixties was to save biology from molecularization, the appeal to evolutionary explanation was not the only way to do it. Mayr himself concedes that biology is irreducible to the study of least parts in part because of the hierarchical organization of its subject matter, as well as in virtue of its history.[2] For him, of course, such physiological accounts are also merely proximate, but my point is that they justify the claim of autonomy for the biological sciences, short of the appeal to evolution. And again, they may constitute the "ultimate" explanation for workers in many areas.

Recently, in fact, my skepticism has been exacerbated, or, rather, moved to downright rejection, by the spate of philosophical literature about the concept of function in its biological use. This is not the place to plunge into that dismal swamp; I have tried to deal with its miseries in a book I have been writing with David Depew on the history of the philosophy of biology.[3] But I have to point to it briefly here, if only as a warning.

The debate, exemplified in a plethora of recent volumes, concerns two opposing accounts of biological function.[4] One, first put forward by Larry Wright in 1973 (and in book form in 1976), has come to be known as "Wright function," or selected effect function. According to this view "the function of X is Z" means: "Z is a consequence (result) of X's being there," and "X is there because it does (results in) Z."[5] This is said to be an "etiological" account. When we cash it out, it seems, we specify a process of selection, design in the human case and natural selection in the biological. This concept of function is now described by its proponents (though with in-house disagreements) as "teleosemantic"—despite the patent fact that explanations by natural selection are classically causal, with a statistical ingredient, but with no teleological component whatsoever (also despite the fact that such accounts, if we had them, would tell us nothing about how the thus produced process or organ works—nothing, in other words, about its function). But, alas, this conception has become more and more widespread, indeed, it has been declared "an example of real progress in philosophy."[6] I read those words and still can't believe them. To me it feels more like a slide downward into one of those egregious muddles in which our profession often indulges.

There is, however, another concept of function stemming first from Robert Cummins in 1975, and restated, with appropriate criticism of the SE view, in a forthcoming anthology. In his 1975 paper, Cummins defended what has been dubbed Causal Role (or CR) function. "To ascribe a function to something is to ascribe a capacity to it which is singled out by its role in an analysis of some capacity of a containing system."[7] This conception does not, like its more popular opponent (recently called by Cummins "neo-teleology"[8]), pretend to be teleological, and, again unlike its opponent, it does have to do with the functional question, how something works, or what it does in its place in some organ or organism—or perhaps, in ecological terms, in its place in a particular environment. This view seems to me to correspond much more closely to the practice of many biologists. In the chapter I have referred to, I cite statements that support this position from the ethologist Niko Tinbergen, the historian of paleontology Martin Rudwick, and from recent work in functional genomics. I will not repeat them here. But I do want to warn our readers (Beatty's as well as mine) not to carry the stress on contingency or on history so far as to confuse historical with functional explanation as the "teleosemanticists" do. If I worry a little about Mayr's thesis that it is always evolutionary causes that are "ultimate," what am I to say about the effort to reduce functional, or in Mayr's division, "proximate" investigations to searches for past selective histories? At the very least, it is thoroughly confused, I would even say, absurd.

As I remarked earlier, this is in no way to question the import of Beatty's rich and instructive essay, only to point out some extravagances that some philosophers have committed in some (perhaps remote) connection with his argument.

M. G.

NOTES

1. *Science* 134 (1961): 1501–6.

2. Ernst Mayr, *This is Biology* (Cambridge, Mass.: Harvard University Press, 1997), pp. 20, 22.

3. Marjorie Grene and David Depew, *The Philosophy of Biology,* in the Cambridge University Press series on "the evolution of modern philosophy," forthcoming, ch. 10.

4. See e.g. C. Allen, M. Bekoff and G. Lauder, eds., *Nature's Purposes: Analyses of Function and Design in Biology* (Cambridge, Mass.: M.I.T. Press, 1998); David L. Buller, ed., *Function, Selection and Design* (Albany: State University of New York Press, 1999); P. McLaughlin, *What Functions Explain: Functional Explanation and Self-Reproducing Systems* (Cambridge: Cambridge University Press, 2001); R. Cummins, M. Perlman and A. Ariew, eds., *Functions and Functional Analysis in the Philosophy of Biology and Psychology* (Oxford: Oxford University Press, 2002 [in press]).

5. Larry Wright, *Teleological Explanations* (Berkeley and Los Angeles: University of California Press, 1976), p. 81. See also L. Wright, "Functions," *Philosophical Revue* 82 (1973): 139–68, reprinted in Allen, Bekoff and Lauder, 1998 and Buller, 1999.

6. Godfrey-Smith in Buller, p. 185; also Buller, p. 20.

7. Robert Cummins, "Functional Analysis," *The Journal of Philosophy* 72, no. 20 (Nov. 20, 1975): 741–65; reprinted in Allen, Bekoff and Lauder, 1998 and Buller, 1999. The quoted passage is from Allen, Bekoff and Lauder, p. 193.

8. See Cummins, in press.

17

Richard Glauser

DESCARTES, SUAREZ, AND THE THEORY OF DISTINCTIONS

All of Descartes's thought rests precariously on an edge: on the edge of modernity, on the edge of disaster.[1]

—Grene

Few philosophers have equaled Marjorie Grene in combining a profound sense of historical perspective with acute critical insight. This is obvious in her publications and editorial work on Descartes, Spinoza, and other seventeenth-century philosophers. She has considerably developed our understanding of Descartes, not only in relation to other modern authors, major and minor, of that century, but also in relation to those forming his scholastic background. One of the central aspects of Descartes's philosophy she studies is his theory of substance. In the second chapter of her *Descartes*, she shows how he is led to an incoherent theory of the passions largely because of his real distinction between mind and body, which is itself incoherent, or so she claims.[2] In the fourth chapter she attacks Descartes's notion of substance. Both issues—the real distinction and the theory of substance—are pursued in the fifth chapter and in her Aquinas Lecture, *Descartes Among the Scholastics*.[3]

Several strands run through her discussion of both issues. First, Descartes's philosophy is plagued by an "anti-natural bent," stemming from his anti-empirical method, his intellectualist epistemology, his mathematical physics, and, last but not least, his sparse ontology, which divides substances into thinking and extended ones, and reduces the natural hierarchy of things to modes, finite substances, and God. All four aspects of his philosophy lead Descartes to a "neglect of the category of life,"[4] a disregard for what we and his Aristotelian predecessors and contemporaries take to be the biological organization of living individuals and the structure of the natural world. Aristotelianism attempted to keep its metaphysics of substance in line with the way in which nature is divided and hierarchically structured from a biological point of view. And it did not lose sight of the fact that a human being is a part of nature. This outlook was implemented (though not without some difficulty) in the hylomorphic theory of substantial form as a principle of life, a principle sustaining the natural organization of a body, whether the form be a nutritive, a sensitive, or a rational soul. Even a human being's rational soul was basically a biological principle, at least as long as it remained united to matter, since, apart from its intellectual and volitional powers, it had the further functions of a nutritive and a sensitive soul. Much of this is lost with Descartes. However, as Marjorie Grene correctly stresses, Descartes's philosophy—including his theory of substance—is deeply embedded in late-scholastic philosophy.

Hence, concerning substance, we must try to distinguish between what Descartes is taking over, what he is discarding, and what he is changing in order to find out what it is exactly that gives his theory of substance its specifically "anti-natural" aspect. The question is complicated, however, because, as Grene acknowledges, late-scholastic philosophy is sometimes at a far remove from Aristotle. Something entirely novel in Descartes with regard to Aristotle may not be so with regard to late-scholastic philosophy; or, it may be explained as a justifiable reaction to an aspect of late-scholastic philosophy. And it may also be that, on some points, Descartes's reaction actually makes him closer to Aristotle than was his late-scholastic context. I wish to show that such is the case with a few of Descartes's moves concerning substance. Although Grene rightly insists on the importance, for Descartes's thought, of the Jesuits in general and of the great Spanish Jesuit philosopher Francisco Suarez in particular,[5] she leaves him comparatively out of the picture when she sorts out the old from the new in Descartes's theory of substance and the real distinction.[6] I wish to pursue her analysis by attempting to understand how Descartes relates to Suarez on the topic of created substance.

A second strand running through Grene's work on Descartes consists of three interrelated points: Descartes's reform of metaphysics is undertaken *within* the context of scholastic metaphysics; the reform aims at securing a metaphysical foundation for his new physics and his faith; but he wants to reform scholastic metaphysics only just enough to fulfill these goals.[7] The reform consists largely in granting God a foundational role with regard to the status of necessary truths and certain knowledge and in building a novel theory of substance. I will consider only the latter aspect. Grene suggests that, inasmuch as Descartes's reform of the theory of substance is undertaken *within* traditional metaphysics, there is a background or framework he shares with some scholastic philosophers. What, then, is that framework? Part of the answer, I suggest, is the theory of distinctions.

Descartes explicitly works out such a theory for the first time in his *Principles of Philosophy* (1644), originally intended as a textbook to be used in the schools.[8] As Gilson showed long ago, it is quite remarkable that Descartes should make use of *only* the three distinctions accepted by Suarez.[9] Why is this remarkable? By the end of the sixteenth century a great number of different kinds of distinctions had been accumulated by various philosophers. The resulting complexity and apparent obscurity brought Suarez to attempt a systematic classification and critique of the current distinctions, whereby he whittled their number down to three—the real distinction, the modal distinction, and the distinction of reason—and attempted to show that besides these three, "there is no other [distinction] which is not common to these, or is not comprised in them."[10] He did this in the seventh of his *Disputationes Metaphysicae*, published in 1597, just forty years before Descartes's *Discourse on Method*. The three distinctions that Suarez accepts are precisely those that Descartes expounds in the first part of his *Principles of Philosophy* (§ 60–62) and subsequently applies in the following articles of the first and second parts. As Gilson notes, "among all the possible classifications of the distinctions, Descartes chooses precisely that of Suarez"; Suarez is the likely source of Descartes's doctrine of distinctions, as Julius Weinberg and Marleen Rozemond also confirm.[11] Also, it is significant to find Descartes taking it for granted that there are only three distinctions, and that there is a modal distinction, intermediate between the real distinction and the distinction of reason. Suarez had to argue at length for both points in his Disputation VII. Thus, Descartes accepts as established something that Suarez had to fight for against the whole scholastic tradition. Descartes hardly even raises the question of whether there might be other, or more, distinctions than these three.[12] This attitude may be seen as a further sign of how reliant on Suarez he is regarding this issue.

To return to Grene's idea of a common metaphysical framework, I suggest that a theory of distinctions is more or less *common* to Suarez and Descartes, and that it is a *framework* within which both authors develop their respective theories of substance. The connection between the theory of substance and the theory of distinctions is clearly indicated in Descartes by the fact that he sets them side by side in the first part of the *Principles* (§ 51–57 and § 60–62). Of course, Suarez's and Descartes's theories of substance are very different. But, the more or less common framework may serve as a theoretical background in order to help us discern what was novel and what was not in Descartes's conception of substance. True, Descartes never attempted a systematic classification of the distinctions before writing the *Principles*. It was quite natural for him to seek inspiration among the scholastics on this issue when writing this work, since it was intended as a textbook to be used in the schools. But he certainly had at least a rough idea of his theory of distinctions in mind long before writing the *Principles*, since much of it was implicit in the 1630s when he began to develop his theory of substance and to criticize real accidents, incomplete substances, and material substantial forms. In fact, it would be rather futile to wonder whether, from a historical point of view, Descartes adapted his theory of distinctions to his theory of substance, or vice versa. They go hand in hand; they are so dependent on one another that they have to be built up together.

A third feature of Grene's reading of Descartes is her analysis of his rejection of forms (except in the case of minds), incomplete substances, and real accidents. This is part of Descartes's reform of substance theory. Ultimately, the reform is intended to have the dual function of contributing to a metaphysical foundation of his mathematical physics and of clearing away what lies in the way of his physics. Although I agree with this reading, I also think that his rejection of real accidents has a different goal, independent of his mathematical physics, for Descartes rejects real accidents of all substances, whether thinking or extended. Given that mind and body are really distinct, it is hard to see how getting rid of purportedly real accidents of minds could have directly helped his project of founding—and clearing the way for—his mathematical physics. I hope the comparison with Suarez will shed light on another, strictly metaphysical, reason for criticizing real accidents, a reason directly linked to the problem of the real distinction. In talking about substances, I will be dealing only with created substances in Suarez and Descartes, setting aside God (and angels in Suarez). Also, I will not discuss their clearly related theories of the distinction of reason *ratiocinatae*, but will focus on their real and modal distinctions.

SUAREZ ON INDIVIDUATION

Suarez's theory of distinctions is developed in Disputation VII. Since his real and modal distinctions depend on what he calls *res* and modes, and since all *res* are individuals according to Suarez, it may be useful to begin by summarizing some points made in Disputation V concerning individuality.

For Suarez individuality is what he calls "individual unity"; it is a negative feature, that is, the indivisibility of a being (*ens*) into two or more things of the same sort as itself.[13] A further feature accompanies individual unity (indivisibility so defined), and that is a thing's distinction from all other things, whether they are of the same species as the original or not. However, although the feature of distinction is closely tied to individual unity, it is not conceptually identical with it. Indivisibility (individual unity) and distinction are conceptually different, and the second feature is in fact a consequence of the first.[14] Also, individual unity is the definition, or intension, of "individuality." But what the term "individuality" refers to in an individual is its individual difference, which Suarez conceives as bearing to an individual's common (specific) nature a relation somewhat similar to that of specific difference to genus.

In Disputation V Suarez argues a number of points. First, "all things that are actual beings (*entia actualia*) or that exist or can exist immediately, are singular and individual."[15] This Suarez shows to be a necessary truth, for "to be an entity and to be divisible into many entities such as itself implies a contradiction."[16] One can understand Suarez's reason for claiming this to be a necessary truth in the following way. For Suarez, as for many scholastic philosophers, *unum* is a transcendental term; as such it is coextensive with *ens*. One meaning of *unum* is "individual unity." So every being (*ens*) is *unum* (has individual unity). Also, every being or thing (*res*) is an entity (*entitas*). What is an entity? Suarez distinguishes between a broad and a strict sense of the term. In the broad sense an entity is "whatever is not nothing." In the strict sense "the entity of a thing [*entitas rei*] is nothing but its real essence as it exists outside its causes."[17] The expression "outside its causes" refers to actual existence, for Suarez defines existence as the being (*esse*) of a thing outside its causes.[18] Thus, an entity, properly so called, is an actually existing essence.[19] We see, then, that every being is an entity (an actually existing essence) and has individual unity. However, "unity adds no thing to entity, except for the negation [indivisibility] accompanying it."[20] Therefore, every entity is necessarily individual: "not even by [God's] absolute power can a real entity, as existing in reality, not be understood to be singular and individual."[21]

Second, there is neither a real nor a modal distinction, but rather a mere distinction of reason (albeit with a foundation in reality) between a substance's individuality (its individual difference) and its common nature.[22] True, a substance's individual difference is something in addition to its common nature, but the "addition" or composition of individual difference and common nature is metaphysical, as in the case of genus and specific difference, not physical as in the case of matter and form.[23] To say that the composition is metaphysical, as opposed to physical, is to imply that although the terms (common nature and individual difference) of the composition are both real, the "joining together" or "composition" of the terms is not; it is performed by the mind and is in the mind. Just as the distinction between a thing's common nature and its individual difference is a distinction of reason and, hence, is only in the mind, so is their (metaphysical) composition, which is the same operation in reverse.[24]

In the third place, the question arises as to what is the principle, or cause, of a substance's individuality. Here Suarez rejects several solutions proposed by other philosophers. First, he rejects the opinion of Aquinas, according to whom a substance's principle of individuality is designated matter. Next, he rejects the opinion that substantial form is a substance's principle of individuality. Finally, he objects to the idea that either existence or subsistence could be the principle of a substance's individuality.[25] His own position is that any substance, whether material or not, created or not, is individuated by its very own entity: "it needs no other principle of individuation in addition to its entity"; "in the individual substance the individual difference does not have some special principle or foundation which is distinct in reality from its entity; and, thus, in this sense . . . each entity is by itself the principle of its individuation."[26] This stems from the aforementioned thesis according to which "unity adds nothing to entity, except for the negation [indivisibility] accompanying it."

How does this general thesis apply to the individuality of a created substance, made of matter and form? According to Suarez, "just as the principles of its entity are matter, form, and their union, so [likewise] these same [principles], taken in the individual, are the principles of its individuation."[27] Hence, a created substance's individuality is merely the result of the individuality of the principles entering its physical composition, that is, the individuality of this form, the individuality of this matter, and their individual union, which, as we shall see, is a third term (a mode) super-added to them.

What, then, accounts for the individuality of this matter and of this form? Concerning matter, Suarez argues at length in order to eliminate several rival explanations: matter cannot be individuated by a substantial form, nor by a determinate relation to this substantial form, nor by quantity or any collection of accidents, nor by the action of some agent; hence, it must be individuated by its very entity. As to substantial form, it, too, is intrinsically an individual by its very entity. It cannot be individuated by one or more accidents, nor can it be individuated by this matter. Hence, a "form is not 'a this' because it is related to this matter but only insofar as it has a particular aptitude for informing [some] matter."[28] A substantial form has this aptitude in virtue of its intrinsic entity. In sum, this substantial form has an intrinsic aptitude to inform some matter, just as this matter has an intrinsic aptitude to be informed by some substantial form. This does not contradict the general thesis according to which both items are individuated by their respective intrinsic entities. Of course, matter and substantial form are not complete substances, but physical principles of substances, in other words, incomplete substances. Yet, even if this form is naturally united to this matter, the individuality of the one does not depend on the other. Each is an individual in its own right, independently of the other, in virtue of its own intrinsic entity. In the last sections of Disputation V, Suarez goes on to argue that accidents are also real things, and thus individuated by their intrinsic entities.

SUAREZ ON THE REAL DISTINCTION

Suarez recognizes two actual distinctions, or distinctions *ex natura rei*, that is, distinctions that are not made by the mind, but discovered in reality. One is the real distinction; the other is the modal distinction. A real distinction is defined as an actual distinction "between thing and thing [*rei a re*]."[29] Since *res*, in this definition, is used in its technical sense as a synonym for *ens*, the real distinction obtains only between items having entity, hence, individuality. Only individuals can be really distinct.[30] Among entities or *res*, Suarez counts not only complete substances, but accidents,[31] matter, and substantial forms. Hence, a real distinction obtains just as well between things that are naturally united (such as substance and accident, or matter and form) as between things that are naturally separated. This matter is really distinct from its substantial form, and this quantity is really distinct from its substance, because such items are individual entities or *res*.

Suarez is very cautious when he discusses, in great detail, the signs or criteria we might make use of to ascertain that a real distinction obtains between two given items. However, he holds that if two items are entities, and thus really distinct, they can exist separately, either naturally or at least through God's absolute power. God's absolute power does not violate the principle of non-contradiction. Thus, to say of any two entities that they can exist separately, even if only through God's absolute power, is to express a logically possible state of affairs. What is it for two entities to exist separately? Apart from some exceptions,[32] it means, first, that both can exist simultaneously and independently, that is, without any kind of union between them. It means, secondly, that one of them can exist while the other is annihilated, and vice versa.[33] Such is the case, for instance, with the matter and substantial form of a complete substance. This immaterial substantial form can naturally exist without being united to this matter, and this matter can naturally exist without being united to this form. But Suarez also raises the question whether this form can exist without being united to any matter; whether this matter can exist without being united to any form;

and whether, if such a radical separation is possible, it is possible naturally or only through God's absolute power. Suarez accepts that such a radical separation is always possible at least by God's absolute power.[34] Such entities are separable in both senses mentioned above. And the same goes for substance and quantity, or other accidents. According to Suarez: "such [really distinct] things can always be . . . separated by God's absolute power . . . *nor is any exception to be made in this matter*," for "if things are really distinct, they can also be really disjoined; and if they are really disjoined, no repugnance or contradiction is involved in the notion of one of them being preserved by God without the other."[35] If one wonders how this is possible (since matter depends causally on form, form on matter, and quantity and other accidents on substance), the reply is that God can supply for such causal dependence by his infinite power.[36] In sum, a real distinction between two entities implies mutual separability; even if the separation is not possible naturally, it remains possible by God's absolute power.

True, matter and substantial form, by their very entities, are naturally capable of being united in order to constitute a complete substance. But they do not contain actual union. *Mutatis mutandis*, the same goes for substance and quantity, or other accidents. Therefore, the actual union of matter and form, and the actual inherence of an accident in a substance, have to be something over and above the mere entities of these items. This is why Suarez holds that in a complete substance, there is not only this form and this matter, but a further item, a *tertium quid*, which is their mutual union. Similarly, inherence is a *tertium quid* between this accident and this substance. Substantial union and accidental inherence are modes of *res*. This brings us to Suarez's theory of modes and the modal distinction.

SUAREZ ON MODES AND THE MODAL DISTINCTION

Contrary to complete substances, matter, substantial forms, and accidents, which are all *res*, modes are not, strictly speaking, entities or *res*. Yet Suarez's ontology would be incomplete without modes, because they are determinations of entities or *res*.[37] Modes have a kind of being which is intermediate between nothingness and proper entity. They are real in the very broad sense that they are not nothing; they "are something positive and of themselves [they] modify the very entities by conferring on them something that is over and above the complete essence as individual and as existing in nature."[38] It is precisely for this reason that the distinction between a mode and the entity it modifies, that is, the modal distinction, is not a mere distinction of reason, but an actual distinction. For a distinction of reason is between an entity conceived through one incomplete concept and the same entity conceived through another, whereas a mode actually adds something to an entity. Hence, modal distinctions are not merely made by the mind, but discovered *ex natura rei.*

On the other hand, however, modes cannot be really distinct from the entities they modify. For they have an imperfect kind of being in comparison with entities or *res* properly so called. If modes were entities or *res* in the full-blooded sense in which complete substances, matters (bodies), substantial forms, and real accidents are, then modes would be really distinct from the entities they modify. And this would lead to an infinite regress. Suarez explains this clearly in the case of the mode of inherence, taking as an example the inherence of quantity in substance. If the inherence of this quantity in this substance were itself a *res* or proper entity, then it, too, would require a further item to unite it to this quantity, and another to unite it to this substance, and so on *ad infinitum.*[39] In order to avoid such a regress, the mode of inherence must not be a proper entity, but something essentially and directly dependent on the thing it modifies—dependent in a much stronger sense than that in which an accident depends on a substance, or in which matter and form depend on each other. Such an essential dependence is what makes a mode an imperfect kind of being. In a nutshell: "there are in created entities certain modes affecting these entities, and their nature seems to consist in this, that they do not of themselves suffice to constitute being or entity in the real order of things, but are intrinsically directed to the actual modification of some entity without which they are quite incapable of existing."[40]

In order to get a better understanding of a mode's imperfection and essential dependence, it is useful to compare the modal distinction (between a mode and the *res* it determines) and the real distinction (between two *res*). Whereas this form and this matter, or this accident and this substance, can be separated by God inasmuch as they are all really distinct from each other, he cannot—not even by his extraordinary power—maintain a mode in existence without the thing it modifies. Thus, he could not preserve this mode of union of this form and this matter if he separated the latter two or if he destroyed one of them. Nor could he preserve this mode of inherence of this accident in this substance if he separated the accident and the substance or destroyed one of them: "this mode so necessarily includes conjunction with the thing of which it is a mode that it is unable *by any power whatsoever* to exist apart from that thing"; "for *the very essence of a mode* demands that it cannot exist unless actually united to the thing it modifies, seeing that it is united by means of itself and not by some other mode of union."[41] Thus, whereas a real distinction between two entities implies mutual separability (at least by God's absolute power), a modal distinction implies nonmutual (in)separability in the sense that this mode cannot be preserved—not even by God's absolute power—if the entity it modifies is destroyed, or if the entity is separated from the mode.

Apart from matter-form union and accident-substance inherence, many other modes are to be found in Suarez, such as: subsistence, figure, local presence (*ubi*), the dependence of an effect on its active cause, and so on. I will dwell on only two of them, subsistence and figure, as these will be important in connection with Descartes.

According to Suarez, in any existing substance there is both the nature or essence of the item and its subsistence. But why add subsistence? Is it not enough to say that the essence is actual or exists? No, because existence is merely the fact that an essence is "outside its causes," that is, it is actual. Both substances and accidents exist, of course, but not in the same way: the first subsist, the second inhere. Subsistence and inherence are two distinct ways of existing; they are determinations or modes of existence.[42] Fine, but why not say that there is a mere distinction of reason between a substance's existence and its subsistence? For the following reason: According to Suarez, there is only a distinction of reason, *ratiocinatae*, between the (actual) essence of a being and its existence. Yet there certainly is an actual distinction between the essence or nature of a substance and its subsistence; likewise, there is an actual distinction between an accident's essence and its inherence in something else. Therefore, there must be some kind of distinction *ex natura rei* between a substance's existence and its subsistence: "in so far as subsistence is distinct from actual essence, it is necessarily distinct from the existence of that essence."[43] The actual distinction cannot be a real distinction, however, for, once again, this would lead to an infinite regress, so the distinction must be modal. Hence, in every created substance there is a modal distinction between the mode of subsistence and the nature or essence.

Up to here I have been speaking of the mode of subsistence as a mode added to the nature of a complete substance, a created primary substance. Suarez also deals with the question of what happens to a person after death. Obviously, when this immaterial substantial form, or rational soul, is separated from this body, their mode of union is destroyed. But given that the soul is immortal, the question arises as to whether it acquires its own mode of subsistence as soon as the matter-form union is dissolved, or whether it had its own mode of (partial) subsistence all along, even when it was united to this matter, so that after death the soul just goes on subsisting by the same mode of subsistence. Suarez takes the latter opinion to be the more probable. But this is the case only for rational souls; forms of purely material substances do not have their own mode of (partial) subsistence, and so do not *naturally* exist after the destruction of the matter-form union. However, since matter can naturally subsist after being separated from its substantial form (whether the form is a rational soul or not), matter, too, has its own mode of (partial) subsistence even when united to a form.[44] This is of crucial importance, as we shall see, with regard to Descartes. For what is implied in the case of a substance which is a person, according to Suarez, is that both substantial form and matter actually subsist by themselves *even when united*; each has its own mode of (partial) subsistence.

As to figure, it is a mode of the accident of quantity. Quantity is either plurality or magnitude. Plurality is numerable quantity, divisible into non-continuous parts; magnitude is measurable quantity, divisible into continuous parts. The kind of quantity that figure modifies is magnitude: "'figure' properly signifies a certain mode resulting in a body from the determination of magnitude."[45] It is relatively easy to see why Suarez thinks that figure is a mode and not a real accident. Something has to be added to continuous quantity (extension) in order to obtain a certain geometrical figure. What is added, however, is not an extra *res* or a new entity, but only a certain limitation.

DESCARTES ON THE REAL DISTINCTION

For all its originality, Descartes's metaphysics is deeply entrenched in the Suarezian difference between *res* and modes. This is clear from the opening sentence of the section of the *Principles* in which Descartes begins his theory of substance and his theory of distinctions: "In the case of those items which we regard as things [*res*] or modes of things [*rerum modos*], it is worthwhile examining each of them separately."[46] Also, in taking over Suarez's real and modal distinctions, he retains some of their most significant ontological implications. (Of course, Descartes and Suarez have very different theories of the signs or criteria for recognizing real distinctions. This is an epistemological matter of fundamental importance which I have no space to discuss here.)

Let us begin with the real distinction. For Descartes, just as for Suarez, "whatever is real [*reale*] can exist separately from any other subject."[47] Here, the expression *quicquid est reale* means "whatever is a *res*," for in this context Descartes wants to "explode" the "reality" of accidents, that is, to deny the status of *res* to the accidents that Suarez and other scholastics held to be really distinct from their substances. If we combine this with Descartes's discussion of the real distinction in *Principles* I, § 60, it appears that, for him, if A and B are both *res* (neither is a mode), they are really distinct, which is to say that they can be mutually separated, either in the sense that A and B can exist simultaneously and independently, or in the sense that one can be annihilated while the other continues to exist, and vice versa. For Suarez, a separation, in either of the two senses, is always possible at least by God's extraordinary power. Furthermore, Suarez claims that "there is no point to inquiring whether such separation can take place naturally or only through God's absolute power,"[48] because what counts in the real distinction is the logical possibility of separation.

Now, in contexts where Descartes sets aside the question of God's incomprehensible power as *causa sui* and creator of the eternal truths, and talks about what God can do given the eternal truths he has created, he closely follows Suarez on two crucial points. First, in the *Principles*, he explains, as did Suarez, that two really distinct items remain distinct even when they are naturally united: "For no matter how closely God may have united them, the power which he previously had of separating them, or keeping one in being without the other, is something he could not lay aside; and things which God has the power to separate, or to keep in being separately, are really distinct."[49] Second, Descartes makes it clear that "the ordinary power of God . . . in no way differs from his extraordinary power,"[50] so that "[o]ur knowledge that two things are really distinct is not affected by the nature of the power that separates them."[51] Why? Because, given the eternal truths God has created, both God's ordinary power and his extraordinary power conform to the principle of noncontradiction, and because what counts in the real distinction, for Descartes as for Suarez, is the logical possibility of separation.

To cast another light on this last point, consider Descartes's definition of substance in *Principles* I, § 51, to which I will return later: "a thing [*rem*] that exists in such a way as to depend on no other thing [*re*] for its existence."[52] He adds, of course, that the definition, strictly taken, applies only to God; it cannot be taken to apply univocally to God and to created substances. For "[i]n the case of all other [i.e., created] substances, we perceive that they can exist only with the help of God's concurrence."[53] The French translation makes it clear that Descartes is speaking of God's ordinary concurrence, which is continuous creation. Yet, in another context, when Descartes discusses God's incomprehensible power as creator of the eternal truths, he mentions the hypothesis that "God might have brought it about that his creatures were independent of him."[54] This would obviously contradict the idea of substance as applied to created substances, since they are defined as depending for their existence on nothing except God's ordinary concurrence. Descartes ranks the hypothesis among the "contradictions which are so evident that we cannot put them before our minds without judging them entirely impossible."[55] Yet, his point in this context is to claim that one cannot deny God the power to actualize the hypothesis. This shows us that Descartes's definition of created substance is itself a created truth, a truth we cannot deny that God could, or could have, contradicted. But both the hypothesis mentioned above and God's incomprehensible power are kept entirely out of the picture when Descartes is talking about the real distinction and the power, ordinary or extraordinary, God has of separating any two *res*.

Another point worthy of notice is that Descartes implicitly distinguishes, as Suarez did explicitly, between a real distinction and an essential difference. Suarez explains that a real distinction can obtain between two entities, whether their essences are the same (although numerically distinct, as in the case of two tulips), or whether their essences are different (as in the case of a tulip and a man).[56] Descartes accepts this general claim, adapting it to his own views on what the basic essences of created substances are, namely, thought and extension. For example, in the *Principles* (I, § 60) he holds that a real distinction obtains just as well between two minds, or between two bodies or parts of extension, as between a mind and a body. So, following Suarez, Descartes does not believe that for two substances to be really distinct it is necessary that they have dissimilar essences, still less incompatible ones. What is peculiar in Descartes's distinction between mind and body is that, in this case, to put it in the vocabulary of Suarez, Descartes *adds* dissimilarity of essence to the real distinction. But even this is done in a special way, for thought and extension are not only dissimilar essences, they are incompatible in one and the same substance, since thought is necessarily indivisible, and extension necessarily divisible.[57]

As Grene explains, Descartes's ontology is extremely sparse in comparison with those of the scholastics. Although Descartes continues to think in terms of *res* and modes, the items which come under the two headings are far fewer than with many scholastics, and with Suarez in particular. Suarez accepts among *res* not only primary substances, but substantial forms (immaterial and material), matter, and real accidents such as quantity; he also distinguishes accidents that are *res* from accidental modes. So how does Descartes perform his metaphysical reduction? Principally, but not exclusively, by two fundamental moves, both of which gain significance when understood against the background of Suarez. One of these consists in restricting the scope of the real distinction so that it applies principally to substances only.[58] Since, as we saw, he agrees with Suarez that a real distinction obtains only between one *res* and another, to say that the real distinction holds principally between substances is to imply that all (and only) *res* are substances. This move, I will suggest, is partly, though certainly not entirely, Aristotelian in character. It can be justified in Descartes's historical context quite apart from his project of giving a metaphysical foundation to his physics. Taken in itself, there is nothing specifically anti-natural about it.

Let us begin by returning to a well-known passage of the Replies to the

Sixth Set of Objections, where Descartes is discussing the impossibility of real accidents:

> Secondly, it is completely contradictory that there should be real accidents, *since whatever is real can exist separately from any other subject; yet anything that can exist separately in this way is a substance, not an accident.* The claim that real accidents cannot be separated from their subjects "naturally," but only by the power of God, is irrelevant. For to occur "naturally" is nothing other than to occur through the ordinary power of God, which in no way differs from his extraordinary power—the effect on the real world is exactly the same. Hence if everything which can naturally exist without a subject is a substance, anything that can exist without a substance even through the power of God, however extraordinary, should also be termed a substance.[59]

Descartes is apparently familiar with Suarez's distinction between accidents that are *res* and accidental modes, for in speaking of "real accidents," here, he clearly means "accidents that are *res*." This is borne out by the fact that he immediately adds, quite correctly for Suarez, that "whatever is real [i.e., a *res*] can exist separately from any other subject." In this passage Descartes is not denying the existence of any accidents that Suarez or other scholastics consider as *res*; he is merely denying them the status of *res*. Descartes knows that it remains to be seen, for Suarez, whether two really distinct *res* are separable naturally or only through God's (extraordinary) power. This is why he immediately forestalls the question by declaring it irrelevant. And in doing so, as we saw above, he comes close to Suarez. Not that Suarez rejects the distinction between God's ordinary and his extraordinary power, but he would grant that their difference can at least be set aside insofar as all really distinct items are separable, if not naturally, at least by God's (extraordinary) power. To return to the beginning of the text, it is clear that, for Descartes, the separability of two *res* is a sufficient condition of the substancehood of both: "anything that can exist separately in this way is a substance." Whereas Suarez held that only some really distinct items (*res*) are substances, Descartes adds that all (and only) really distinct items (*res*) are substances. Hence, for Descartes, contrary to Suarez, a real distinction holds principally between substances only: all *res* are substances.

Now, taken by itself, the claim that all (and only) really distinct entities (*res*) are substances is not foreign to Aristotle's way of thinking in the *Categories*. It distantly echoes Aristotle's focus on primary substances as the fundamental ingredients of the world, all other items, in the *Categories*, being either "said of a subject" or "in a subject." Also, there is a distant, but significant, similarity between, on the one hand, Aristotle's distinction between "what is said of a subject" and "what is in a subject," and, on the other hand, Descartes's distinction between attributes and modes. Up to now, we have not yet encountered an anti-natural bent in Descartes's metaphysical reduction. In fact, at this stage, what I have called the first important move of Descartes's reductionist program arguably takes him closer to Aristotle than was Suarez.

If Descartes is considered against the background of Suarez, the claim that all *res* are substances (or, if you prefer, that all really distinct entities are substances) can cut two ways, depending on which scholastic *res* he is prepared to accept as mutually separable (really distinct), and which he is not prepared to accept as such. This is important if we want to understand the significance of Descartes's reduction in his context. On the one hand, given that Descartes agrees with Suarez that whatever is not a *res* is a mode, then, if he agrees with Suarez and other scholastics that certain entities are really distinct *res*, he has to make arrangements for them to be substances. On the other hand, if he believes that certain other entities that Suarez considers as really distinct *res* are not so, then Descartes has to make arrangements for them either to be modes, or to be reducible to nominally different modes (such as motion and figure), or to be fictitious.

Suppose that one has good reasons for accepting as really distinct some of the items that Suarez considered to be so, then the items that one accepts as really distinct will have to be (complete) substances after all, even though fundamental adjustments will have to be made in order for them to be counted as such. Such is the case with the rational soul (immaterial substantial form) and body. Descartes agrees with Suarez that they are really distinct; hence, they both become Cartesian (complete) substances. Such is also the case with the scholastic real accident of continuous quantity, that is, extension; Descartes agrees that it is really distinct from other *res*, and so it becomes a substance or, rather, the essence of matter. The difference is slight, since Descartes holds that there is only a distinction of reason between extension and matter (*Principles* I, § 62–63).

Since he is prepared to count the rational soul and its body as really distinct *res*, he is willing to make them complete substances. Here, two questions arise. First, what is old and what is new in Descartes's conception of the relation between the rational soul (mind) and its body? Second, is there some justification for Descartes's decision to make them two complete substances given his context?

Let us begin with the first question. In Suarez, (1) a rational soul and its body are really distinct; (2) they are individuals in virtue of their very entities (it is not the case that one of them serves to individuate the other); (3) a rational soul subsists by means of its very entity; it has a mode of (partial) subsistence even when united to a body, so that, once separated, it goes on subsisting by means of the very mode of subsistence it had all along. All of this had been established before Descartes. Descartes accepts the first point in much the same sense as Suarez. Also, since he declares the rational soul and body to be two complete substances, he can hardly avoid accepting the third point, although he does not explain subsistence in terms of a Suarezian mode of subsistence. As to the second point, he certainly accepts it for the rational soul, since each rational soul is an "I" independently of the existence of matter. But it is doubtful whether he accepts it for the soul's body, for on one occasion he says that a human body is individuated by its form, which is the soul.[60] However, this must be taken with caution, for Descartes is notorious for having never worked out a proper theory of the individuation of material substance(s). For all that, inasmuch as he accepts all three points *mutatis mutandis*, he is not inventing anything new. So what is original? This can be brought out more clearly if we go into the second question I mentioned above: is there some justification for Descartes's decision to make the rational soul and body two complete substances?

I think there is. For Suarez's theory of the rational soul is the locus of a tension between two diverging theoretical forces, pulling at it from opposite directions. Given that the entity of a *res* is its actual essence, the entity of a rational soul is by itself sufficient to guarantee that the soul: (1) is really distinct from its body and from any other entity; (2) has its own individuality; and (3) has its own subsistence even when united to a body. Why, then, are the rational soul and its body incomplete, not complete, substances? Suarez's reply is that the rational soul is always "essentially a part" because, even when it is actually separated from its body, "it has an incomplete essence, which is by its own nature ordained to make another essence complete; hence it is always an incomplete substance."[61] Notice that the rational soul is not an incomplete substance because its essence *necessarily* or always makes another essence complete, for it does not do so necessarily, or always, since it is separated from its body after the death of the human being. Rather, it is an incomplete substance only because, even when it does not actually complete another essence, it remains "by its own nature ordained" or apt to complete another essence. So let us add this fourth point: (4) the rational soul does not necessarily or always complete another essence. Given these four points, it appears that the ontological independence of a rational soul is very great indeed. It is so great, in fact, that the soul cannot even be united to matter immediately and by itself. On the contrary, (5) in order to be united to matter, the entity of the form must be modified by an intermediate *tertium quid*, a mode of union.

This is where we can see the tension. On the one hand, given the five points mentioned above, the rational soul has quite an extraordinary ontological independence, an independence so great that, as a matter of fact, it will subsist incomparably longer than any created complete substance such as a human being. On the other hand, for all its independence, the rational soul is not a complete substance. There is no incoherence though, for Suarez does not make subsistence a sufficient condition of *complete* substancehood.

But, to feel the tension more clearly, consider things *sub speciei aeternitatis*, that is, by forming a more complete picture of the destiny of a rational soul, considering not only its life on earth, but also its immortality. This is something to which Descartes feels deeply committed, since as early as 1630 he hopes to "complete a little treatise of Metaphysics . . . in which I set out principally to prove *the existence of God* and *of our souls* when they are separate from the body, from which their immortality follows."[62] From this point of view, given that the very same actual essence, or entity, of the rational soul is such, according to Suarez, that it implies the five above mentioned points, then the reason given by him for calling it an incomplete substance seems of little significance. To be sure, the essence of a rational soul is naturally capable of completing another essence. But it will only do so during a human being's lifetime. And what is a human lifetime compared to the soul's eternal independent subsistence? Furthermore, once the rational soul is separated from matter after the human being's death, in all likelihood its essence will never again complete another essence. Of course, it remains capable of doing so. But if, once separated, it will never do so, and if it remains separated for eternity, then its mere capability of completing another essence seems a flimsy reason for calling it an incomplete substance. It should rather seem that a human being is the result of an extremely brief accidental union of two ontologically independent and subsisting entities, in other words, complete substances. This fits in well with what Descartes says in the *Synopsis* of the *Meditations*: "absolutely all substances, or things which must be created by God in order to exist, are by their nature incorruptible and cannot ever cease to exist unless they are reduced to nothingness by God's denying his concurrence to them."[63] It should also appear that to consider a human being this way—as a short-lived accidental union of two complete substances—is to take only one step further down a road Suarez had already followed to a considerable extent. Of course, once the step is taken, Aristotle's primary substances are definitely discarded. And at this point, Descartes's anti-naturalism becomes clear. However, although Suarez had not lost sight of Aristotle's primary substances, he had already stopped focusing on them. I suggest, first, that in this context Descartes's further step is not a very big one in comparison with the ontological independence Suarez already granted the rational soul, and, secondly, that Descartes has some justification in taking the step. This reading sustains Grene's claim that "[t]hrough his Jesuit education he shares certain important premises with his scholastic critics and is confident that he ought to be able to persuade them on points where they differ"; the Jesuits in particular, Descartes thinks, "given a chance, will surely come around to seeing things his way."[64]

But then, Descartes must accept that the subsistence of a *res* is a sufficient condition of its (complete) substancehood. And this is precisely what he does when he defines substance as "a thing [*rem*] which exists in such a way as to depend on no other thing [*re*] for its existence."[65] In order to grasp the full meaning of the definition as applied to created substances, it is important to keep in mind that Descartes assimilates ontological independence ("to depend on no other [created] thing for its existence"), existing *per se*, and subsistence.[66] So that, if a created *res* has ontological independence, existence *per se*, or subsistence, it is a complete substance. This should not come as a surprise, because it goes hand in hand with Descartes's sound, Aristotelian claim (I mean the Aristotle of the *Categories*) that real distinctions obtain principally between substances only.

Nevertheless, we see where Descartes's antinaturalism comes into the picture, in two ways. First, notice that the expression "to depend on no other thing [*re*] for its existence," when applied to a created substance, means that a created substance's existence depends on that of no other created *res*. As we saw before, "absolutely all substances . . . are by their nature incorruptible and cannot ever cease to exist unless they are reduced to nothingness by God's denying his concurrence to them"[67]; Descartes even acknowledges that he, *qua res cogitans*, was not produced by his parents.[68] This rules out natural generation and corruption in any strict sense from Descartes's world, even with regard to material substance(s).

As to the second antinatural feature, it follows from the peculiar way Descartes makes the two *res* complete substances. A Suarezian rational soul is an incomplete substance because of its essence: its essence is naturally capable of completing another essence. So, if one intends to make the rational soul a complete substance, one is bound to produce a novel theory of the respective essences of the rational soul and of body. Presumably, that could be performed in any number of ways. But, when discussing Descartes's way of doing it, it is important to keep in mind that, for him, as for the scholastics, it is not necessary for two really distinct *res* to have different essences. Descartes accepts a real distinction between two minds, which have the same essence, and between two bodies, which also have the same essence. But in the case of mind and body, as we saw before, Descartes adds to their real distinction what Suarez called an essential difference. For a series of reasons that I have no space to examine here, but which Grene explains in detail, the way Descartes chooses in order to make the rational soul and body complete substances is to construe their essences respectively as thought and extension. This is a second aspect of Descartes's antinatural bent. What I would like to say, though, is that it is also a highly original move, one that cannot be explained by Descartes's Suarezian context. Nor can it be explained by Descartes's own theory of the real distinction, precisely because it is not at all necessary for a real distinction. As far as Descartes's theory of the real distinction goes (*Principles* I, § 60), the claim that mind and body have incompatible essences—thought and extension—is only required as a criterion for the certain knowledge of their real distinction. Within Descartes's theory of the real distinction, the claim does not make their distinction any more real than that between two minds, or between two bodies. With regard to the real distinction, the essential difference plays only an epistemic role: the knowledge that the essence of a *res* (A) is thought, and that the essence of a *res* (B) is extension, has the epistemic function of enabling us to know that A and B cannot be one and the same *res*, hence that they are two substances. Yet, on the ontological level, the real distinction between A and B is not greater than that between two substances having similar essences. This is not to say that the essential difference between thought and extension plays no role on the ontological level. On the contrary, it guarantees that A and B are complete, not incomplete, substances. For, thought being necessarily indivisible, and extension necessarily divisible, they cannot complete each other in a higher essence. This is what breaks down the Suarezian claim that the rational soul and body are incomplete substances. If this reading is correct, it accounts for Descartes's own estimation of his originality: "I am the first to have regarded thought as the principal attribute of an incorporeal substance, and extension as the principal attribute of a corporeal substance."[69] Although mind and body are still naturally capable of being united, their essences are no longer capable of completing each other in a higher essence, an essence of one and the same complete substance.[70]

This should dispel the aura of mystery shrouding Descartes's claim that our primitive notion of the mind-body union is not a clear and distinct idea, contrary to our primitive notions of mind and of body.[71] The claim is not surprising, since, when mind and body are united, their essences do not complete each other in a higher essence. If Descartes could accept a further essence resulting from their union, he would be in a position to hold that our primitive notion of the union is based on a clear and distinct idea of that higher essence. But this has been ruled out.

Although Descartes will go on to speak of the soul as a form, and even as "informing" a body, it is nevertheless far from obvious what this means exactly. Why? Because the very notions of "form" and of "informing" cannot be used meaningfully outside a theory of formal and material causality typical of hylomorphism. Yet, when we turn to the *Passions of the Soul*, we find that the causal relations between mind and body are generally based on efficient causality, not on formal and material causality.

Nevertheless, we can see why Descartes has no need for the Suarezian substantial mode of matter-form union. Such a mode, in Suarez, modifies the entities (actual essences) of the *res* to be united. For Descartes, however, the mere fact that mind and body are united does not modify their essences. Something different happens when they are united: they causally interact in such a way as to acquire certain accidental features (Cartesian modes) they would not have otherwise. Therefore, Descartes can find no use for the Suarezian substantial mode of mind-body union; it must have appeared to him as a kind of theoretically vacuous metaphysical glue.[72] Instead, he gives a psycho-physical description of the union that is based on efficient causality. Surely this is an additional reason for which, as Grene reminds us, he considers his explanation of the union superior to rival accounts.[73]

DESCARTES ON MODES AND THE MODAL DISTINCTION

Descartes also retains many of the most significant ontological implications of Suarez's modal distinction. He distinguishes, as did Suarez, between the modal distinction strictly so-called, which is between a mode and the thing it modifies, and the distinction between two modes of one and the same modified thing (*Principles* I, § 61). We are concerned here with the first case, between mode and *res*, for it is the most important. According to Descartes and to Suarez, if this A is a mode of B, B is a *res*, and A and B are modally distinct. This means that they are non-mutually (in)separable: whereas B can exist without (being modified by) this A, this A cannot exist without (modifying) this B. For instance, says Descartes, "neither this shape nor this motion can exist without this body."[74] The same goes for a mode of thought, such as an idea, considered in its formal reality, and the mind that it modifies. Now, what does it mean to say that this mode *cannot* exist without (modifying) this *res*? Let us look at Descartes's definition of a mode: "the nature of a mode is such that it cannot be understood at all unless the concept of the thing [*rei*] of which it is a mode is implied in its own concept."[75] Descartes claims no originality in defining modes this way, for he explicitly refers to "what it is that philosophers term a 'mode.'" But, obviously, if the idea of a mode analytically contains the idea of the *res* it modifies, then it is not logically possible for this mode to exist without its *res*. As far as I can see, Suarez does not give this general definition of a mode, to which I will return later. But he certainly comes close to it when he says that "modes of their very concept lack sufficient entity to sustain them; they have entity only by reason of a certain identity with the things in which they exist"; and he makes the point that figure is a mode that "cannot be even conceived by the mind as separated from all quantity and from the thing of which it is the figure."[76] Hence, to say that a mode cannot be separated from the *res* it modifies is to say that even God cannot separate this mode from its *res*. This is a point on which Descartes (as long as he considers God as acting according to the eternal truths he has created) entirely agrees with Suarez.

I said above that Descartes performs his metaphysical reduction with two basic moves, both of which gain significance when understood against the background of Suarez's theory of distinctions. One of them, we saw, is to restrict the scope of the real distinction—and the extension of *res*—so that they apply to complete substances only. This has consequences concerning modes as well. First, since for Descartes all *res* are substances, then, contrary to Suarez, only complete substances can have modes. Second, if all *res* are substances, then no accidents are *res*; hence, no accidents are really distinct from substances. Consequently, all the accidental features of a Cartesian substance are afforded the ontological status Suarez granted to modes, and all Cartesian modes, in the strict sense, are accidental features.[77] (This is why Descartes prefers the term "mode" to "accident," even though Cartesian modes are accidental features.)

Therefore, one could say that Descartes both displaces the modal distinction and limits its scope. In Suarez the modal distinction between *res* and mode was somewhat ubiquitous, since there are all kinds of Suarezian *res* (not only complete and incomplete substances, but also accidents) and modes (substantial and accidental modes). In Descartes, given that all *res* are substances and all modes are accidental features, the modal distinction is restricted principally to the distinction between Cartesian accidental features and Cartesian substances.

Descartes's second fundamental move, I suggest, is his definition of a mode, which we encountered above: "the nature of a mode is such that it cannot be understood at all unless the concept of the thing [*rei*] of which it is a mode is implied in its own concept."[78] For Descartes, the concept of the essence of a kind of *res* is contained in the concept of each of its modes. Thus, Suarez gets things exactly right, from Descartes's point of view, when he claims that figure (shape) is a mode of continuous quantity (extension).[79] The example perfectly fits Descartes's definition of a mode, because the concept of figure includes that of extension. But his definition has the result of generalizing what was only a special case in Suarez.

What I take to be Descartes's second fundamental move is important, for it follows from the definition that every one of a thing's modes is conceptually dependent on its essence. And this affords a clear and distinct explanation of the ontological dependence of an accidental feature on its substance. Another implication is that the inherence of accident in substance, and the connection of mode to *res*, which were two very different kinds of connections in Suarez, are no longer different in Descartes; they are one and the same. Since all accidental features are modes in Descartes, the first connection is in fact reduced to the second.

There are at least two significant consequences of this reduction. First, it means that the connection of a Cartesian accidental feature with a substance is no longer mediated as it was in Suarez; it no longer requires a *tertium quid*—a Suarezian mode of inherence that modifies the entity of the accident. (One can hear Aristotle applauding.) For, if a Cartesian accidental feature of a substance is given the ontological status of a Suarezian mode, then its connection to the substance is direct, unmediated. Surely this is why Descartes never mentions Suarez's mode of accident-substance inherence. Second, since there is only a modal distinction between substance and accidental feature, it is no longer the case, as it was in Suarez, that an accidental feature can be maintained in existence without its substance. (Here again, Aristotle approves.) Suarez knew very well that, according to Aristotle, "the essential notion [*rationem*] of every accident consists in actual inherence in a subject," and that "no reason can be given for an accident to be preserved without a subject."[80] Suarez also knew that this could be held only if all accidents were modes, which he denies. Descartes, on the contrary, seems to follow Suarez's hint and declares all accidental features of substances to be modes, or to be reducible to modes.[81] Thus, he revives the common-sense, Aristotelian claims that accidental features are directly connected to their substances, and cannot be maintained in existence without them. This sustains Grene's claim that "by eliminating 'accidents' (which some might think real, hence quasi-substantial) and keeping only modes, we return, paradoxically, to a much purer Aristotelian conception, . . . but paradoxically also non-Aristotelian insofar as modes are all expressions of the essence of some substance, as most 'accidents' were not."[82] I agree with this reading, although I hope that the explanations I have given will remove the appearance of paradox.

Of course, the conceptual dependence of accidental feature on substance is thoroughly rationalist; it will be adopted by Spinoza. One may justly find it antinatural. Nevertheless, given Descartes's context, it was the price to pay in order to deny the separability of accidents. It was a price that he was quite willing to pay for other reasons as well. Although some of his reasons lie within his project of giving his physics a metaphysical foundation, it should be noted that the conceptual dependence typical of Descartes's modal distinction applies just as much in the case of the relation of mind to its modes as it does in the case of the relation of material substance to its modes. So the second important move by which I have attempted to explain Descartes's metaphysical reduction—his definition of a mode —cannot be entirely explained by his project of furnishing his physics with a metaphysical foundation. The move is partly made on purely metaphysical grounds.

I mentioned above that Descartes's denial of real accidents, taken by itself, does nothing to eliminate any of the scholastic real accidents and sensible qualities; it only denies them the status of *res*. Thus, Descartes complains that philosophers are mistaken "when in the same body they make a [real] distinction between the matter, the [material] form and the various accidents as if they were so many distinct things [*res*]."[83] Once that is said, it remains to be seen whether they are modes, or whether they are reducible to nominally different modes, or whether they are to be declared fictitious. Further arguments, independent of Descartes's denial of real accidents, are required for any one of these three alternatives. A somewhat similar point should be made concerning Descartes's definition of a mode with regard to sensible qualities. Taken by itself, the definition does little to eliminate sensible qualities from the class of modes, because qualities such as colors (and perhaps others as well) fit Descartes's definition of a mode: insofar as they can be conceived (however obscurely and con-fusedly), they are conceived as extended. This is why Descartes gives further, independent grounds for reducing them to nominally different modes such as figure and motion. Others, such as Grene, Stephen Menn, and Marleen Rozemond, have discussed Descartes's complex treatment of scholastic material substantial forms, real accidents and sensible qualities, so it is not necessary for me to go further into the question here.[84]

Suarez distinguished between accidental modes and substantial modes; the latter—such as the mode of subsistence and the mode of matter-form union—pertain *"ad constitutionem et complementum ipsius substantiae."*[85] Since Descartes considers all modes, in the strict sense, to be accidental features of substances, what happens to the Suarezian substantial modes? We saw above why Descartes has no need for the mode of matter-form union. But what of subsistence? It cannot become a Cartesian mode, for it is not an accidental feature. Descartes ranks subsistence among a sub-stance's attributes,[86] that is, as one of its invariable, permanent, or immuta-ble properties. Remember that for Suarez both a rational soul and the matter it informs have modes of (partial) subsistence. Descartes can easily accommodate this in his own way. For he accepts not only principal attributes, but also attributes which are common to minds and bodies.[87] Obviously, the kind of attribute subsistence becomes is a common attribute.

I have attempted to pursue Marjorie Grene's critical discussion of substance in Descartes by approaching Descartes's notion of substance from within the framework of the theory of the real and the modal distinctions he had more or less in common with Suarez. The changes he brings to the two kinds of distinctions go hand in hand with his reform of the theory of substance. I have left very much out of the picture, in particular the notorious problem of the individuation of Cartesian material substance(s). I suggest that a few of the moves Descartes makes in reforming the theory of substance arguably take him closer to the Aristotle of the *Categories* than was Suarez. Other moves, while not doing so, are nevertheless justifiable on purely metaphysical grounds, independently of his desire to give a foundation to his physics. And some of his moves consist in going a step or two further than Suarez had gone. Unsurprisingly, it appears that Descartes's really original and anti-natural move lies in his conception of the essences of mind and body. It is this conception that accomplishes the questionable feat of entirely eliminating Aristotelian primary substances, while paving the way for Descartes's radical dualism. It cannot be accounted for by Descartes's scholastic context. Although radical dualism is obviously quite compatible with Descartes's theory of distinctions, it cannot be entirely explained from within that framework. Nevertheless, it is good to keep in mind that the whole problem started with Aristotle himself, in his *Metaphysics*, where he began to wonder whether substantial forms might not be, in a sense, more substantial than primary substances. That is where the risk of losing sight of primary substances, with their biological richness and complexity, as the basic individuals of the natural world, was first taken. If we keep this in mind, Descartes's anti-natural dualism will appear as little more than an extreme position along a road opened by Aristotle himself, perhaps unfortunately.

Richard Glauser

Institut de Philosophie
Université de Neuchâtel
July 2000

NOTES

1. Marjorie Grene, *Descartes* (Brighton, U. K.: Harvester Press, 1985), p. 92. Hereafter: Grene 1985.

2. Grene 1985, pp. 22, 30–31 and 46–52.

3. Marjorie Grene, *Descartes Among the Scholastics* (Milwaukee: Marquette University Press, 1991). Hereafter: Grene 1991.

4. Grene 1985, p. 21. See pp. 38–39, 52, 80–81, 104, 108, 117, 131, 135, 137.

5. For instance, Grene 1991, pp. 6–14.

6. Although this is true in Grene 1985 and 1991, Suarez is prominent in Grene's "Epilogue," in *Descartes and His Contemporaries: Meditations, Objections, and Replies,* ed. R. Ariew and M. Grene (Chicago: University of Chicago Press, 1995), hereafter: Grene 1995.

7. Grene 1985, pp. 39, 88, 92–93, 95, 96, 107, 139, 144–46, 150–51; Grene 1991, p. 34.

8. AT III, p. 233. I refer to Descartes in the *Oeuvres de Descartes,* ed. Adam and Tannery (Paris: Vrin), hereafter: AT. When quoting, I use *The Philosophical Writings of Descartes,* vols. I–II, trans. Cottingham, Stoothoff & Murdoch (Cambridge: Cambridge University Press, 1985), hereafter: CSM; vol. III, the same with Kenny 1991, hereafter: CSMK.

9. E. Gilson, *Index scolastico-cartésien* (Paris: Felix Alcan, 1913), p. 87. Hereafter: Gilson 1913.

10. Disp. VII, sect. 1, § 21. I refer to Suarez's *Disputationes Metaphysicae* in *Opera Omnia* vols. 25 and 26, ed. C. Berton (Paris, 1866); reprinted by Olms, Hildesheim, 1965, 2 vols. Where possible I use available English translations: Disputation V *Suarez On Individuation,* trans. J. J. E. Gracia (Milwaukee: Marquette University Press, 1982); Disputation VII *On the Various Kinds of Distinctions,* trans. C. Vollert (Milwaukee: Marquette University Press, 1947, second printing 1976). Other translations are my own. [Editor's note: When Disp. V and VII are cited, Gracia's and Vollert's pagination will be included.]

11. Cf. Gilson 1913, p. 87; J. Weinberg, *Ockham, Descartes and Hume,* (Madison: University of Wisconsin Press, 1977), pp. 71–82; M. Rozemond, *Descartes's Dualism* (Cambridge: Harvard University Press, 1998), p. 6.

12. He does not entirely ignore the question though, for he mentions Scotus's formal distinction, equating it, first, with his modal distinction (AT VII, pp. 120–21), and later, with his distinction of reason (AT VIII-1, p. 30; IV, p. 349).

13. Disp. V, sect. 1, §§ 2–3 [pp. 30–32].

14. Disp. V, sect. 3, §§ 6, 12 [pp. 78–80, 84]. Cf. Gracia, *Suarez On Individuation,* p. 4 and p. 39, n. 23. Whereas a being's individual unity is intrinsic to it, its distinction from other things is an extrinsic, relational feature. Hence, a universe containing only one individual is logically possible. Such would not be the case if individuality essentially involved separation or distinction from other existing things.

15. Disp. V, sect. 1, § 4 [p. 32]. Suarez says "'immediately' in order to exclude the common natures (*rationes*) of beings, which, as such, cannot immediately exist or have actual entity, except in singular and individual entities" (*loc. cit.*).

16. Disp. V, sect. 1, § 5 [p. 32].

17. Disp. VII, sect. 1, §§ 19, 12. As we shall see, Suarezian modes are entities in the broad sense, not in the strict sense. Hereafter, when speaking of entity in Suarez, I will be using the strict sense unless otherwise indicated by the context.

18. Disp. XXXI, sect. 6, § 23.

19. However, one must not overlook the fact that, just as "entity" has a broad and a strict sense, so does "essence": "Essence can mean strictly a nature sufficient of itself to constitute an entity in the real order, or, more widely, any real principle that is constitutive of real being or mode. In this latter sense we concede that there are distinct essences in a thing and in a mode . . . " (Disp. VII, sect. 1, § 30). I will be using "essence" in the strict sense, i.e., that which constitutes an entity or *res* as distinguished from a mode, which is not, strictly speaking, an entity.

20. Disp. V, sect. 6, § 5 [p. 125].

21. Disp. V, sect. 1, §5 [p. 32].

22. Disp. V, sect. 2 [pp. 41–68].

23. Disp. V, sect. 3, § 2 [pp. 75–76].

24. "For just as the separation of the common nature from the individual difference is only conceptual, so, conversely too, the addition of the individual difference to the common nature is to be understood only conceptually. For there is not that proper addition in reality, but in each individual there is only one entity really having by itself both natures (*rationem*)" (Disp. V, sect. 2, § 16 [p. 52]). This point depends crucially on Suarez's theory of the (intrinsic) distinction of reason *ratiocinatae*, based on a foundation in reality. Such a distinction is not discovered by the mind, but made by the mind; it is entirely within the mind, even though the items distinguished are not in the mind (Disp. VII, sect. 1, §§ 6–7 [pp. 19–20]). In fact it is misleading to speak of "items" distinguished, in the plural, for the distinction of reason *ratiocinatae* is between one item conceived through one inadequate concept and the same item conceived through another inadequate concept (Disp. VII, sect. 1, § 5–8 [pp. 19–21]). The foundation in reality for this distinction of reason is not itself a distinction. In the same way, items that are "metaphysically" composed can be real, even though their composition is mental. Cf. J. J. E. Gracia, "What the Individual Adds to the Common Nature According to Suarez," *New Scholasticism* 53 (1979).

25. Disp. V, sect. 3, 4 and 5 [pp. 75–118].

26. Disp. V, sect. 6, § 1 [p. 122].

27. *Loc. cit.* Cf. sect. 6, §§ 14–16.

28. Disp. V, sect. 6, § 13 [p. 131].

29. Disp. VII, sect. 1, § 1 [p. 16].

30. Thus: "a real distinction between actual entities is not intelligible except insofar as they are individual and singular.". . . "[B]ecause a distinction between entities presupposes that each entity is constituted in itself and, consequently, [that it is] one and singular" (Disp. V, sect. 2, §§ 12, 11 [pp. 49, 48]). "For in general I think that it cannot be [the case] that a thing be really distinguished from another by [still] another [thing] distinct from itself, but [only] by its very entity, by which it is constituted into the being it is (*esse*), because, . . . a thing is distinguished by what constitutes it" (Ibid., § 13).

31. In Suarez, an accident is "a form having its own entity that of itself is really distinguishable and separable from every other entity" (Disp. VII, sect. 1, § 29 [p. 38]). This is what Descartes will call a "real accident," i.e., an accident that is a *res*.

32. Disp. VII, sect. 2, §§ 24–27 [pp. 58–59].

33. Disp. VII, sect 2, §§ 9, 22 [pp. 46–47, 56–57].

34. Disp. XV, sect. 9; VII, sect. 2, §§ 7–8 [pp. 44–46].

35. Disp. VII, sect. 2, §§ 22, 24 [pp. 56–57, 58]; my italics. Obviously, one important exception to this is the real distinction between God and any one of his creatures; a creature could not exist if God were annihilated, even though it is really distinct from him (cf. § 25). The same is the case in Descartes.

36. Disp. VII, sect. 2, §§ 7–8, 22 [pp. 44–46, 56–57].

37. The term "mode" was common long before Suarez gave it his own technical meaning; he cites Augustine and Aquinas as two of his predecessors and gives other sources as well (Disp. VII, sect. 1, §§ 17, 19 [pp. 28, 30–31]). The reason for which he needs modes, in his technical sense, in addition to entities is the following: "since creatures are imperfect, and hence either dependent or composite or limited or mutable according to various states of presence, union and termination, they

require these modes by which all those characteristics may be brought to realization" (Disp. VII, sect. 1, § 19 [p. 30]).

38. Disp. VII, sect 1, § 17 [p. 28]. Cf. XXXII, sect. 1, § 13.

39. Cf. Disp. VII, sect. 1, § 18 [pp. 29–30].

40. Disp. VII, sect. 1, § 18 [pp. 29–30].

41. Disp. VII, sect. 1, § 20 [p. 32] and sect. 2, § 9 [p. 46]; my italics. Also: "the inherence has a mode of being such that it cannot exist unless it is actually joined to the form [quantity or any real accident] of which it is the inherence, and . . . this particular inherence can modify or rather unite only this particular form to which it is, so to speak, affixed. Such a mode of affecting is never found in those forms or things which have proper entities of themselves" (sect. 1, § 18 [pp. 29–30]).

42. Cf. Disp. XXXIV, sect. 4, §§ 23–24. As to the meaning of the verb "to subsist," cf. Disp. XXXIII, sect. 1, § 1–3.

43. Disp. XXXIV, sect. 4, § 15.

44. Cf. Disp. XXXIV, sect. 5, § 33, 35–36 and 42.

45. Disp. XLII, sect. 3, § 15. Although figure modifies quantity, it must be classified under the category of quality, because "it affects and perfects a subject" in much the same way as other qualities do (Ibid.; cf. Disp. XXXII, sect. 1, § 14).

46. AT VIII-1, p. 24; CSM I, p. 210. This important sentence disappears in the French version.

47. AT VII, p. 434; CSM II, p. 293.

48. Disp. VII, sect. 2, § 10, [p. 47].

49. AT VIII-1, p. 29; CSM I, p. 213.

50. AT VII, p. 434; CSM II, p. 293. I take Descartes to mean that God's ordinary and extraordinary powers, inasmuch as there is any distinction between them, both lie *within* the field of what God can do without violating the eternal truths he has created. What Descartes adds, when compared to Suarez and all other major philosophers, is that over and above the distinction between God's ordinary and extraordinary powers, lies God's absolute and incomprehensible power, by which he is *causa sui* and creator of eternal truths. Hence, Descartes's distinction between God's ordinary and extraordinary powers, however insignificant it may be in comparison with his absolute power, is similar in one respect to that of Suarez: for both authors, God's ordinary and extraordinary powers cover whatever is logically possible and go no further than that. Although I have been speaking of "powers" in the plural, one must keep in mind that God has basically only one power which can be exercised in different ways: "the idea which we have of God teaches us that there is in him only a single activity, entirely simple and entirely pure" (AT IV, p. 119; CSMK III, p. 235).

51. AT VII, p. 170; CSM II, p. 120. This sentence comes just after another in which Descartes speaks of God's extraordinary power.

52. CSM I, p. 210.

53. Ibid.

54. AT IV, p. 119; CSM III, p. 235.

55. Ibid.

56. Disp. VII, sect. 1, § 22 [p. 33].

57. AT VII, p. 13; IV, p. 120.

58. There is also a real distinction between one substance and the mode of another substance, or between two modes belonging to different substances. But real distinctions such as these are secondary, for, as Descartes's examples show, any real distinction that is not between two substances necessarily depends on one

that is (AT VIII-1, pp. 29–30). I will discuss the second fundamental move in the next section.

59. AT VII, p. 434–435; CSM II, p. 293, my italics. Instead of "the effect on the real world is exactly the same," the French version has: "et laquelle [puissance extraordinaire], ne mettant rien de nouveau dans les choses, n'en change point aussi la nature" (AT IX-1, p. 235).

60. AT IV, p. 346.

61. Disp. XXXIII, sect 1, § 11; cf. Disp. VII, sect. 1, § 19 [pp. 30–31]. Descartes cannot be thinking of Suarez when he says: "if the reason for calling them [certain substances] incomplete is that they are unable to exist on their own [*per se solae esse*], then I confess I find it self-contradictory that they should be substances, that is, things which subsist *(per se subsistentes)* on their own, and at the same time incomplete, that is, not possessing the power to subsist on their own [*per se subsistere*]" (AT VII, p. 222; CSM II, pp. 156–57). Suarez does not hold that the rational soul and matter are incomplete substances because they cannot exist *per se*. On the contrary, they can exist separately. His reason is that the essence of the one is always capable of completing the essence of the other.

62. AT I, p. 182; CSMK III, p. 29.

63. AT VII, p. 14; CSM II, p. 10.

64. Grene 1985, pp. 117 and 137.

65. AT VIII, p. 24; CSM I, p. 210.

66. He uses "existing *per se*" and "subsisting" equivalently throughout the context of the phrase "substances, that is, things which subsist on their own *(per se subsistentes)*" (cf. AT VII, p. 222; CSM II, pp. 156–57). In the following passage he uses equivalently "existing *per se*" and "being independent" (not needing something else): "the notion of a substance is just this—that it can exist by itself *(per se)*, that is without the aid of any other substance" (AT VII, p. 226; CSM II, p. 159).

67. AT VII, p. 14; CSM II, p. 10.

68. AT V, p. 357.

69. AT VIII-2, p. 348; CSM I, p. 297.

70. Descartes grants that mind and body are incomplete substances in a purely relative sense. A mind, for instance, "although it has nothing incomplete about it *qua* substance, [ ] is incomplete in so far as it is referred to some other substance in conjunction with which it forms something which is a unity in its own right" (AT VII, p. 222; CSM II, p. 157). Notice that the higher unity, formed by the conjunction of mind and body, is not itself a new substance or essence.

71. AT III, p. 665 ff.

72. When he suggests that Regius say that mind and body are united by a true mode of union (*per verum modum unionis, qualem vulgo omnes admittunt*), he is not endorsing a mode of union in its technical, Suarezian sense (cf. AT III, p. 493).

73. Grene 1985, p. 102.

74. AT IV, p. 349; CSMK III, p. 280.

75. AT VIII-2, p. 355; CSM I, p. 301. The definition is clearly made use of implicitly in the *Principles* (AT VIII-1, pp. 25 and 29–30).

76. Disp. VII, sect. 2, § 10 [p. 47].

77. AT IV, pp. 348–49.

78. AT VIII-2, p. 355; CSM I, p. 301.

79. "Motion, and all the other modifications of substance which are called *qualities*, have no greater reality, in my view, than is commonly attributed by

philosophers to shape, which they call only a *mode* and not a *real quality*" (AT III, pp. 648–49; CSMK III, p. 216).

80. Disp. XXXVII, sect. 2, § 2.

81. Cf. AT III, pp. 648–50; CSMK III, pp. 216–17.

82. Grene 1995, p. 232.

83. AT III, p. 435; CSMK III, p. 197.

84. Special reference must be made to Stephen Menn's article, "The Greatest Stumbling Block: Descartes's Denial of Real Qualities" (in Grene 1995), which contains a detailed analysis of the relation of Descartes to Suarez and other scholastic philosophers on the question of real accidents and sensible qualities. Menn's analysis complements the general views I have expounded here.

85. Disp. XXXII, 1, § 15.

86. AT VIII-2, p. 348.

87. AT VIII-1, pp. 26–27, 30; AT IV, p. 349.

REPLY TO RICHARD GLAUSER

Richard Glauser's careful comparison of Descartes and Suarez on the theory of distinctions sheds interesting light on a prominent area of scholastic controversy and on Descartes's response to it in the first book of the *Principles*, where he was, as he himself more than once declared, trying to formulate his own philosophy in a style suitable for adoption in the schools. Glauser here joins a (happily) growing number of scholars who believe that philosophical works should be studied, not only within the four corners of the document, but in the context of the intellectual community within which they were conceived and to which they were addressed. As he points out, I have myself professed adherence to this creed, although I am surprised, and indeed embarrassed, to find my work taken as a signal example of its application. True, in my *Descartes* I did take seriously the Objections to the *Meditations*, and I did publish a lecture on "Descartes among the Scholastics," but those were only small excursions into what is fast becoming a field of scholarship far beyond my ken. The one relatively substantial piece I have published in this general area concerns, not Descartes's own background, but some of the ways in which his doctrines were more or less partially assimilated by later seventeenth century writers.[1] However, I hope I have learned enough in the past decade to be able to raise some questions about Glauser's argument. Without claiming any authority of my own in the matter, I am relying here on insights gleaned from such sources as Dan Garber's *Descartes' Metaphysical Physics*, Dennis Des Chene's *Physiologia*, and Roger Ariew's *Descartes and the Last Scholastics*, as well as innumerable conversations with Ariew on Cartesian and peri-Cartesian questions.[2]

There is one feature of this new style in the history of philosophy that is essential to what I want to say about Glauser, Suarez, and Descartes, to which I am a recent, and only partial, convert. The contexts investigated by contextual historians have, so to speak, a temporal as well as a spatial dimension: philosophers read this way not only respond to their contemporaries, they develop—they positively change their minds! Now as recently as in my Aquinas lecture (nine years ago at this writing), I stated in an appendix my unwillingness to adopt developmental hypotheses based solely on internal evidence.[3] Many decades ago I saw hideously misguided examples of this style (which, so far as it is based on such internal evidence, doesn't seem exactly "contextual" anyway), and I didn't want to give in to it in my old age. In fact, my respected friends Ariew and Garber have positively bullied me out of any gleam of interest I ever had in the works of Gottfried Wilhelm Leibniz. I have written very little about this puzzling philosopher, but I did have what I thought was a rather fruitful overall view of what he was after, and I used to like to teach him in those terms. Alas, I would not dare even to think along those lines today. It seems the wretched man changed his mind every year, every month, every week, every day—every hour? Heaven alone knows; but I certainly want no truck with a thinker as elusive as that. And now I have to admit Descartes's development! Come to think of it, I did so myself with respect to Descartes on the passions—since the incompatibility between his statements in say, 1632 or 1641 and 1648 seemed so glaring. All the same, I find it hard to swallow Garber's thesis that Descartes abandoned a concept of method. Descartes without method? Surely, Descartes himself didn't think so.

On the other hand, the developmental question that arises in the present context is not one that is elicited from the interior of a text, with no hint from its author. It is a question of Descartes's own pronouncements about his intentions in different works, and about his own intellectual activities at different times. In the light of this evidence, I have to ask two questions. Is it really the case, as Glauser contends, that the theory of distinctions was always as fundamental to Descartes's position as the concept of substance itself? And, when Descartes did turn his attention directly to his scholastic predecessors and contemporaries, was Suarez as prominent in those reflections as Glauser makes him out to be?

First, does the theory of distinctions play a leading role in Descartes's philosophizing in the *Meditations*, let alone in the *Discourse* or *Le Monde*? (Never mind the uncompleted *Rules*, which I used to find illuminating, but which developmentalists, if one may so call them, have taken to bits and so as good as trashed as a reliable source from which to infer Descartes's philosophical intentions. I still have a weakness for them, I'm afraid; older is not always wiser!) Following Gilson, I have always believed that Descartes should be read within a scholastic context; but I had only the vaguest idea of what that meant. Clearly, a substance metaphysic of some kind, some kind of reasoning in terms of degrees of reality, heavy reliance on the veracity and goodness of an infinite God, and so on. Although, if at very long intervals, I had worked my way several times through the Adam and Tannery edition, including the correspondence, I had not taken seriously Descartes's remark to Mersenne in September, 1640, that he had not read the scholastic literature for twenty years, and that now he intended to do so in order to prepare a more pedagogically useful text.[4] Now since before he embarked on the project that was to issue in the *Principles*, Descartes discussed the theory of distinctions only briefly in reply to Caterus's citing of Scotus in that connection, this does not seem to indicate that he had been studying such scholastic texts carefully in composing the statement of his first philosophy to which, indeed, he was still receiving, and answering, objections. What chiefly concerns him is the fact, as he believes, that there are only two kinds of finite substances, minds and bodies, which are radically different in their very natures from one another: thought is not extended and extension certainly doesn't think. He probably vaguely remembered something about a real distinction versus a "distinction of reason" or some such. But he had not thought out the matter as carefully as he did in writing the *Principles*; that is what he himself says in *Principles* I, 62:

> I am aware that elsewhere I did lump this type of distinction [i.e., conceptual, or "distinction of reason"] with the modal distinction, namely at the end of my Replies to the First Set of Objections to the *Meditations on First Philosophy*; but that was not a suitable place for making a careful distinction between the two types; it was enough for my purposes to distinguish both from the real distinction.[5]

Descartes cannot quite bring himself to admit he had been mistaken; but he does confess there was something he had overlooked. Now that he has been (re)reading the scholastic writers he had had only vaguely in his memory, he can give a more accurate account of their theory of distinctions.

Such a change also seems likely in view of the fact that in the *Meditations* Descartes had not yet distinguished between accidents and modes, as he began to do only as his replies to objectors, and his plans for a Cartesian textbook, developed. But that distinction seems to be essential to the theory as scholastic philosophers propounded it: accidents were indeed dependent on the substances they were "in," but they could be *res*, and so really distinct from one another, or from those substances they inhered in, while modes were radically dependent on the very essence of their bearers. As he thought his position through, it seems to me, Descartes came to see that in abolishing "real accidents," he was doing away with accidents altogether; the only kind of attachments permissible for his finite substances were what his teachers had called "modes." (I should confess that I myself did not appreciate this change in Descartes's discourse until I read Jean Baptiste DuHamel's comments on the new philosopher's usage. Nor did I understand it until I read Garber's discussion in his book of 1992.) In these circumstances, then, while I find it illuminating in connection with the

Principles, I cannot quite accept Glauser's thesis that from the beginning, the scholastic controversy about distinctions had been as central to Descartes's thought as was his concept of substance.

My second question concerns the place of Suarez in Descartes's reflections, whether early or late. Glauser treats the Spanish philosopher as extremely important for Descartes; indeed, he even identifies Suarez with "Descartes's context." Granted, it is true that in the Replies, Descartes's answer to Caterus's question does fit in with Suarez's classification of distinctions. At the same time, he referred explicitly to Suarez only in connection with the concept of material falsity in the Replies to the Fourth Objections, and here, it appears, not very accurately, since he declared his view of material falsity, which applied to ideas, to be identical with that of Suarez, which referred to propositions.[6] Moreover, when he asked Mersenne for advice about scholastics to read in connection with his new project, he listed as writers he recalled from his schooldays the Coimbrans, Rubius, and Toletus.[7] A little later, in search of philosophers he could cite as good scholastics, he says he will read Abra de Raconis,[8] and of course he toys with the idea of using the *Summa* of Eustace of Saint Paul (himself far from a Jesuit!) as a model scholastic against whom to pit his own new doctrines.[9] The name of Suarez is here conspicuous by its absence. Granted, when he put forward in the Third Meditation his famous distinction between objective and formal reality, he may have been recalling controversies he would have heard about in his schooldays in which Suarez had played a conspicuous part—against, not for, the distinction.[10] But that scarcely puts Suarez in as pivotal, let alone as pervasive, a position in Descartes's scholastic context as Glauser gives him.

One last brief comment: apparently I have not expressed clearly my thesis (which I believe, again, I learned from reading Gilson, very many years ago) that Descartes wanted to change in the scholastic tradition just enough to make possible his mathematical physics. Richard Glauser appears to think I am referring only to Descartes's reduction of the things in the world around us to pure geometrical objects. But Descartes's professed aim in the *Meditations*, to lead the mind away from the senses, also entailed the purification of mind (all that's left of soul) from a welter of confused ideas to the clear and distinct apprehension characteristic of the geometer. Though mind and matter may be two very different things, the meditator's program is intended to remake them both: mathematical physics needs its knower as well as what he knows.

M. G.

NOTES

1. Marjorie Grene, "Aristotelico-Cartesian Themes in Natural Philosophy: Some Seventeenth-Century Cases," *Perspectives on Science* (1993): 66–87. (I also co-authored two of the essays in Ariew's recent book; see note 2.)

2. Daniel Garber, *Descartes' Metaphysical Physics* (Chicago: University of Chicago Press, 1991); Dennis Des Chene, *Physiologia, Natural Philosophy in Late Aristotelian and Cartesian Thought* (Ithaca: Cornell University Press, 1996); Roger Ariew, *Descartes and the Last Scholastics* (Ithaca: Cornell University Press, 1999).

3. Marjorie Grene, *Descartes among the Scholastics* (Milwaukee: Marquette University Press, 1991).

4. AT III, 185.

5. CSM I, 215; AT VIII A 30.

6. Ariew, *Descartes and the Last Scholastics,* p. 32.

7. AT III, 185.

8. AT III, 234.

9. E.g., AT III, 232.

10. See Ariew, *Descartes and the Last Scholastics*, pp. 41–45.

18

John Cottingham

THE ULTIMATE INCOHERENCE?
DESCARTES AND THE PASSIONS

I. INTRODUCTION

Marjorie Grene's distinguished contributions to Cartesian scholarship illuminate many aspects of Descartes's thought. Among the areas in which she provides a philosophically invigorating take on the Cartesian system is the theory of the passions, where the prevailing tone of her work is sharply critical. The verdict, in the chapter of her full-length study on Descartes devoted to "Cartesian Passions," is that his theory is guilty of "ultimate" and "fundamental" incoherence.[1] Now the uncovering of alleged tensions and contradictions is, to be sure, the stock in trade of the philosophical critic, and there is no canonical philosopher, from Plato onwards, so exalted that he has not been accused of inconsistencies. But Grene's complaints about Descartes's account of the passions are expressed with a striking vehemence and commitment, almost as if she is determined to bring into proper focus the very passionate aspects of our human nature that she accuses the fastidious Frenchman of failing to accommodate. Descartes's views, as delineated by Grene, move in the course of a decade from "easy dogmatism" to "ambiguity" and "anomaly"; his position is at once "ridiculous" and "appalling."[2] And the whole chapter coruscates with an irritation bordering on contempt.

In one respect, Grene's tone here is in line with that of a great deal of philosophical writing in the last fifty years or more, which has tended to hold up Descartes as a kind of icon of error. So strong has been this tendency that the label "Cartesian" has almost become a term of abuse, designating a cluster of gross philosophical confusions and pitfalls: dead-end immaterialism in the philosophy of mind; outmoded foundationalism in epistemology; arrogant apriorism in the philosophy of science; untenable subjectivism in the theory of meaning.[3] But Grene's critique of Descartes on the passions comes, I think, from a rather different and in some ways more interesting quarter than these familiar lines of attack, and its negative assessment of Cartesianism has links with what might loosely be called the perspective of "feminist humanism." Writers such as Val Plumwood, in her *Feminism and the Mastery of Nature*, have recently charged Descartes's mind-body dualism with producing a "polarizing effect of radical exclusion" which "leads to an alienated account of human identity in which humans are essentially apart from or 'outside of' nature, having no true home in it, or allegiance to it."[4] The criticism is a powerful and disturbing one, which resonates with a certain discomfort many people feel on encountering Descartes's conception of the disembodied thinking subject; and it is interesting to see the Plumwood line strikingly anticipated, nearly a decade earlier, in the closing sentences of Grene's critique of Descartes:

> [T]he Cartesian enterprise, motivated by the hope for a new physics, reached the limit of its explanatory power: in the concrete life of feeling, which Descartes, mathematician, physicist, expatriate and would-be recluse, had done his best to avoid, and in the way in which attention to that embodied yet sentient aspect of our own experience confounds the attempt to cut ourselves off from the norm of animal existence in which, without the artifice of Cartesian method, we would find ourselves spontaneously at home.[5]

What finds eloquent expression here is a cluster of concerns, centering around the estranging implications for humanity of Descartes's metaphysics and his program for science. There is no space here to address all these concerns, but in what follows I would like to look at the possibility of defending Descartes against at least some of the charges brought. The aim is not to "refute" Grene's criticisms, for I believe they draw attention to something important and worrying about the Cartesian system— something we ignore at our peril. The goal, rather, is to see how far the problems raised are indeed inherent in the program which Descartes inaugurated, and to discern whether the language of Cartesianism may not in fact provide the resources for a more nuanced and sensitive account of the human condition, and our relationship with the rest of the natural world.

II. THE ALLEGED INCOHERENCE OF DUALISM

The starting point, and indeed leitmotiv, of Grene's exposé of the incoherence of Descartes's theory of the passions is a premise about the fundamental "untenability" of his dualist metaphysics.[6] There are many difficulties that beset mind-body dualism, though the most serious is, surprisingly, seldom if ever raised by its critics: the question of whether, even before we come to the question of interaction, the idea of an incorporeal thinking self may not be, in itself, incoherent. Descartes's claim that "this 'I'—that is, the soul by which I am what I am— . . . would not fail to be whatever it is, even if the body did not exist"[7] is by most modern lights strongly counter-intuitive; but curiously even its fiercest critics are often inclined to make the key concession that such an incorporeal *res cogitans* is at least a *logical* possibility. Yet suppose someone were to assert the "at least *logical*" possibility of a *res digerens*, a "digesting thing" that "would not fail to be what it is even if the stomach did not exist." Reflection shows that such a claim would not be just false but incoherent; for digestion logically implies the processing of nutrient materials, and there is no possible world in which nutrients could be processed without some organ (stomach or analogous to a stomach) to do the processing. By parity of reasoning, is it not equally clear that thinking implies the processing of information? And once this is conceded, a very strong onus falls on the defender of the "at least *logical*" possibility of an incorporeal thinker to explain how there could be such processing in the absence of any vehicle for carrying the relevant information—an organ (brain or analogous to a brain) to handle the relevant inputs and outputs.[8] To digress for a moment, there is a paradox here in that Descartes evidently believed that his notion of the incorporeal thinker supported the Christian faith, by bolstering the doctrine of the afterlife;[9] yet if the above argument is valid, it seems that a coherent notion of personal postmortem survival would require not the continuance of a Cartesian ghost, but rather the informing of new materials to carry the informational content associated with any given thinking person. The upshot is that Cartesianism ends up providing much less satisfying support for the after-life than the traditional notion of the resurrection of the *body*—though it should be added that this need not necessarily be this familiar carbon-and-water based body, but perhaps the *soma pneumatikon* or "spiritual body" contrasted by St. Paul with our *soma psychikon*, or "biological body."[10] In short, the intuitions of Aquinas were sound: a hylomorphic account of the soul fares better than a Platonic one when it comes to providing appropriate philosophical support for the Faith.[11]

It is, however, not an objection to the notion of the *res cogitans* as such that fuels Grene's dismissal of dualism, but rather the problem of how such a substance could interact with the body. The story about the pineal gland "acting immediately on the soul" to facilitate vision, or the animal spirits "exciting a movement in the pineal gland" to produce a passion, can, she observes, "only be taken as a joke."[12] Spinoza, it appears, took a similar view.[13] The wretched pineal gland has certainly taken its share of ridicule over the centuries, at least with respect to its Cartesian function as what Daniel Dennett has scathingly called a "fax machine to the Soul";[14] but in fact the idea of a specific corporeal organ to which the sensory information from the body is channeled so as to produce conscious reactions is pretty much what we all now accept (albeit we now, of course, give that role to the cerebral cortex). As for the idea of a causal transaction between bodily organ and incorporeal soul, once the notion of an incorporeal consciousness is granted, it would take a pretty hefty load of metaphysical assumptions about causality to show that such interaction is ruled out. On a Humean view of causality, for example, interactions turn out ultimately to be brute conjunctions, with no a priori constraints whatever on what can be conjoined with what. And though his own use of causal language is often not very perspicuous,[15] Descartes himself was clear that he did not acknowledge any a priori obstacles to transactions between heterogeneous items.[16] Even within the physical realm, causal transfers are not, for Descartes, "transparent," in the sense that we can somehow "see" how some movement of particle A must produce a certain movement in particle B. The effects are, it is true, deducible from the covering laws of Cartesian physics, but this derivative kind of "mustness" is no more than the most radical Humean would cheerfully allow. The fact remains that when we come to the covering laws themselves, we are dealing, in Cartesian physics, with mathematical equations laid down by God, whose will is inscrutable to us.[17] The causal opacity that obtains in the mind-body correlations, decreed by God, is no denser than the opacity which ultimately obtains with respect to all God's decrees.[18] Should God withdraw his concurrence, particle A could hit particle B without producing the typical movement we expect; and similarly pineal movement X could occur without the arising of conscious perception Y. God's constancy and immutability no doubt ensure that this kind of thing will not occur, but the latter case is, in itself, no more problematic than the former. The upshot, I believe, is that whatever problems may beset Descartes's strange scenario of messages between soul and pineal gland, specific problems about the concept of causality are not among them.[19]

III. THE HUMAN BEING

I turn now to the question of whether the Cartesian system can do justice to what Grene aptly calls the "embodied yet sentient aspect of our own experience"—in short, to the question of whether Descartes's approach to mind and body can really accommodate what it is like to be a human being. Since this is an issue which I have discussed elsewhere at length,[20] I will be brief. The key to understanding Descartes's much misunderstood position is, in my view, to see the importance of the distinction between what is true of me qua *res cogitans*—the thinking subject of metaphysical inquiry—and what is true of me qua *human being* (the subject of psychology and ethics).

To constitute a genuine human being—*un vrai homme*—it would not be enough, Descartes argues, for a soul merely to be lodged in a body.[21] If an angel were in a human body, "he would not have sensations as we do, but would simply perceive the motions which are caused by external objects, and in this way would differ from a real [man] *(a vero homine)*."[22] The genuine, sensing, human being is most emphatically not to be identified with the *res cogitans* that is the subject of pure thought, since Descartes says quite explicitly, in a crucial but insufficiently noticed passage in the Sixth Meditation, that "I [the *res cogitans*] could clearly and distinctly understand the complete 'me' without the faculty of sensation."[23] Now sensations, though not part of the defining essence of a "thinking being," are an inescapable part of our daily experience as human beings. The official dualistic model recognizes only two types of notion: the soul (the pilot, as it were) and the body (the ship). But our human sensory awareness, our having of experiences like those of "pain, hunger, thirst and so on" reveals, says Descartes, that we are not merely "lodged" in the body as a pilot in a ship, but are intimately united with the body. A pure *res cogitans* would be endowed only with intellection and volition, the two "modes of thinking."[24] A purely material creature, on the other hand, would operate without thought, as a mechanical automaton.[25] But when a thinking thing is "really and substantially" joined with a body so as to form a true unit, then there arises a distinct kind of phenomenon, sensory experience, which cannot be attributed to mind simpliciter, nor to the body, but which belongs to a third kind of being, a *human*.[26]

This "trialistic" classification (as I have elsewhere called it) implies that a complete list of the essential attributes of thinking things and of extended things would not include sensory experiences; and conversely, that human sensory experiences are not wholly reducible to, or fully analyzable in terms of, the properties of thinking and extended things.[27] This is expressed by Descartes in terms of the claim that human sensory experiences belong to the "third primitive notion" of which he spoke so emphatically to Princess Elizabeth.[28] The doctrine of the mind-body union as a "primitive" may seem inconsistent with the official Cartesian position that humans owe their existence to just two basic substances, thinking substance and extended substance. But this criticism can be obviated by construing the "primitive-ness" of the union as asserting that the mind-body complex is something which is the bearer of distinctive and irreducible *properties* in its own right; in this sense we might say that water is a "primitive" notion, meaning that it is not a mere mixture but a genuine compound, possessing attributes "in its own right" (distinctive "watery" characteristics that cannot be reduced to the properties of the hydrogen or oxygen which make it up).[29] Construed attributively, Descartes's trialism is not formally inconsistent with his ontological dualism; and, however construed, it does indeed accommodate (with a considerable degree of success, so it seems to me) the "sentient yet embodied" aspect of our human experience.

IV. PASSIONS AND THE ANIMALS

I now come to the final and most pressing part of Grene's attack on Descartes's theory of the passions, namely her critique of his treatment of animals. It is here, Grene argues, that the "anti-natural bent" of Cartesian thought is revealed in its full, and appalling, starkness:

> [T]he doctrine of the *bête machine*, which denies feeling of any kind to beasts . . . relegates the human as well as the animal body to the status of an automaton. "Nature" in the sense of the living scene made up of untold styles of life, nature in the naturalist's sense, is not only inferior to the geometer-mechanist's extended universe: it is illusory.[30]

The complaint here can be seen as part of a more general one that has surfaced in many forms as humankind has endeavored to come to terms with the harsh realities of the universe as disclosed by the modern scientific revolution. From Descartes onwards, the environment as conceived by science becomes increasingly inhuman: instead of inhabiting a "living scene," full of warmth and color, we confront a jangling maelstrom of particle-interactions, a "bleached out" universe, as Bernard Williams has called it,[31] in which our natural ways of perceiving the world are relegated to the status of "secondary" effects, or observer-projections, rather than primary features of reality. And with the arrival of Darwin, the "disenchant-ing" of the universe is complete: all traces of purpose and meaning vanish in a bleak concatenation of random mutation and blind "selection," in which the whole rich tapestry of human ingenuity and creativity turns out to be no more than a temporary blip, or "by-product" in a pointless march towards extinction.

Such is the world we seem obliged to inhabit. Yet even Darwin, the arch-destroyer of humankind's illusions, preserved (in one sense at least) our kinship with the natural world. The very fact that so shocked the Victorian clergy, namely our sharing a common ancestry with the apes (and indeed ultimately with all living things), at least locates us where we belong, in the biosphere. The benevolence and harmony of Paley's universe is eroded, but at least we escape the Cartesian threat of total alienation from nature.

But how far (to come back to Grene's case against Descartes's view of animals) is the Cartesian picture really as harshly antinatural as she and others make it out to be? Grene's powerful critique begins by focusing on Descartes's letter to Pollot of 1638, following the publication of the *Discourse*. Pollot, attacking the picture of animals presented in part five of that work, had suggested our experience shows that animals "function by a principle more excellent than the necessity stemming from the dispositions of their organs; that is, by an instinct, which will never be found in a machine, or in a clock, which have neither passion nor affection as animals have."[32] Descartes, in reply, invokes a thought-experiment. Imagine someone brought up in a mechanical workshop, accustomed to help in the manufacture of ingenious working models of animals, who later goes out into the real world and learns something of the wonderful intricacy of micro-structure which supports the observed functioning of plants. If such a person is "filled with the knowledge of God" (that is, understands how incomparably greater is the divine artifice than anything humans can devise), will he not easily conclude that real animals are "automata, made by nature, incomparably more accomplished that any of those he had previously made himself"?[33]

The argument plainly recapitulates the line taken in the *Discourse*: given "how many kinds of automatons, or moving machines, the skill of man can construct with the use of very few parts," is it not reasonable to regard the body as a machine "made by the hands of God"?[34] Machine, yes; mechanical structure, yes; automaton—that is, machine capable of movement without immediate external power source—yes. But does this much really cut humanity off from the animal world? Does it entail that animals (since they are "nothing but automata") lack any feeling or sensation? Grene, and many others, have so concluded; as Grene puts it, "the doctrine of the *bête machine* denies feeling of any kind to beasts." This is the ridiculous and offensive doctrine that Descartes promulgated in the 1630s; and as for the passages from his later writings where he talks as if the animals have passions, well, this just shows that his account of the animals and the natural world had "broken down."[35]

The first thing that we need to notice, in evaluating this interpretation, is that the master argument in the *Discourse*, the source and fountainhead of Descartes's notoriety over animals, is *an argument about thought and language, not about animal sensation*. Descartes is speaking primarily as a scientist: we do not need to posit a rational soul in animals in order to explain their behavior, since it can all be accounted for on mechanical principles; but we *do* need to posit a rational soul in man, since the infinite variety of human linguistic output could never be explained mechanically.[36]

So far from being an absurd or repugnant set of claims, this argument embodies a great deal that everyone today fully accepts. No modern biologist, so far as I know, thinks that the attribution of a soul is needed in order to provide a full explanation of animal behavior; and conversely, many (from Chomsky onwards) maintain that human linguistic abilities defy analysis in terms of stimulus-response mechanisms.[37]

So far so good; but does not the use of the word "automaton" imply that animals are zombies, lacking any passion or feeling? The short answer, it seems to me, is no, and that Grene's talk of the *relegation* of the animal "to the status of an automaton"[38] is misleading. All that the use of the term "automaton" properly implies is that the explanation of animal behavior is to be found entirely in terms of (environmental stimulus plus) the organization and functioning of the various intricate internal organs, without reference to any external puppeteer (or, in this case, any internal but incorporeal principle). And this again, surely, is something that pretty much everyone now believes.[39]

In evaluating Descartes's approach to animals, it cannot be stressed too strongly that a scientific explanation of a phenomenon in terms of underlying structures is not necessarily "relegatory" in the sense of eliminating the phenomenon to be explained or reducing it to the "mere" operation of the underlying structures. If I explain the anger of my dog or the fear of my cat by reference to movements of vapor through the nerves (as Descartes does), or the rather more sophisticated apparatus of electrical impulses and the secretion of hormones (as modern biologists do), *none of this denies the truth of the original statements, "Fido is angry" or "Felix is frightened."* There is no "relegation" of Fido or Felix involved in such an explanation, any more than in explaining the properties of a medicine by reference to its molecular structure I am denying its genuine healing function, or somehow "relegating" it to the status of a pseudo-medicine, a bunch of "mere" chemicals.

But while it may, perhaps, be conceded that neither (a) the use of the label "automaton" nor (b) the general Cartesian program for explaining animal behavior, necessarily commits Descartes to denying that animals have feeling and sensations, does not Descartes not in fact make that extra denial? Grene cites the letter to Pollot as damning evidence: the child brought up in the mechanical workshop, on first seeing real animals "would not judge that there was in them any real feeling or any real passion, as in us, but only that they were automata . . . made by nature . . ." (*ne jugerait pas qu'il y eût en eux aucun vrai sentiment, ni aucune vrai passion, comme en nous, mais seulement que ce seraient des automates . . . composés par la nature . . .*).[40] This is indeed a crucial text; but it all hinges on what Descartes means by the phrase "vrai sentiment . . . comme en nous."

Something, to be sure, is missing in animals; but what Descartes declares to be missing is not any feeling whatever (i.e., he does not assert that sentences like "Fido is angry" or "Felix is hungry" come out *false* on his interpretation); rather he points out that we should not attribute to them any real feeling or passion *as in us*.

We thus have to ask what it is, for Descartes, for us humans to have "true passions and feelings." His answer is tolerably clear: it is for us, in virtue of the mind-body union, to have "confused thoughts" about our bodily condition, and about what is beneficial or harmful to our nature as "combination of mind and body" (for example, a sensation of thirst is a kind of confused awareness that drink is necessary to our human health and survival).[41] There are many details in Descartes's account that can be debated, but the crucial feature is the reference to "aboutness": *Descartes construes human feelings and sensations as having intentional content.* Once the matter is put this way, it becomes both understandable and entirely appropriate that Descartes would wish to deny to animals "genuine feelings as in us." Whatever we may want to say about creatures who lack language, we cannot plausibly say that they are capable of "confused thoughts" in the sense now under discussion. And it seems to follow that the Cartesian perspective is in this sense accurate: in attributing feeling and passion to language-users we are ascribing something quite distinct from whatever can be ascribed to creatures devoid of reason and language.[42]

Does this cut us humans off from the rest of nature? Perhaps it does, but only in the sense that the ascription of feelings and passions in the case of beings endowed with rational thought and language belongs in a radically different category from the ascription of feelings and passions to those not so endowed. Notice, however, that ascriptions in the latter category are not thereby ruled out; indeed, in the several passages cited by Grene as proof of Descartes's "inconsistency" or the "breakdown" of his views, he does explicitly ascribe to animals *passions* such as "anger, fear, hunger," and, again, "fear, hope, and joy."[43] The radical difference from the human case in these kinds of ascriptions is linked to the Cartesian claims that the language of physics is not adequate to explain the propositional and intentional activities of human language users; whereas it *is* adequate to explain everything we need to explain in the case of other animals. Descartes is surely right about the first of these claims; the second is a more complex and contentious issue (still the subject of intense debate)—but at the very least it is not a matter on which Descartes can plausibly be accused of asserting something monstrous or obviously incoherent.

At this point it might be objected that this defense of Descartes skirts around the vital question of *what it is like* for an animal to have a passion. Does Descartes, or does he not, think there is "something that it is like" for

Fido to be in pain, when he has hurt his paw? And if not, then how can his account of animals be acquitted of the "appalling" implications of which Grene and others complain? The presuppositions of this type of objection depend on the importance of the "phenomenological" dimension of consciousness, powerfully evoked by Thomas Nagel in his celebrated discussion of what it is like to be a bat.[44] I have already indicated that the Cartesian approach to mental states focuses on the dimension of intentionality, rather than that of phenomenology, and, if I may venture to be dogmatic for a moment, this seems to me to be to his credit.[45] So obsessed has much current philosophy of mind become with so-called *qualia,* that it seems to me that in a certain sense we have become more "Cartesian"—more focused on the "inner"—than Descartes himself ever was. We take it that notions like "being in pain" stand for the occurrence of a mysterious private *quale,* accessible only to the subject. We then infer from Descartes's mechanistic explanation of animal reactions that he must be denying that animals "have" such in-principle-unknowable qualia, and swiftly proceed to accuse him of saying something monstrous and disgraceful.

Yet one does not have to be a devoted Wittgensteinian to acknowledge that the private language argument successfully disposes of the idea that the meaning of terms like "pain" and "hunger" can be given by reference to a private beetle in my mental box (a "beetle" of a kind I can never, even in principle, know is occurring in the mental box of you, my fellow human, let alone Fido, my dog). Ascriptions of pain, and other mentalistic terms, must be subject to public criteria. Clear and compelling though this argument is, however, it does not quite settle the matter at issue. For it seems very hard to deny that, when I have a toothache, the damage to my tooth is signaled to me in a distinctive and urgent way, a way not seemingly captured by even the most exhaustive scientific description of my behavior, or of what is going on in my brain—a way that appears to allow me to ask meaningfully whether something similar is mirrored in your experience when your tooth is damaged, or in that of my dog when the vet probes its diseased tooth. Since this issue remains one of the most vexed unsolved issues in contemporary philosophy, it would be rash indeed to broach it in the brief concluding stages of this paper. What may be said on Descartes's behalf is that in his role as a scientist he attempts to provide an explanation of all phenomena within the animal realm, including animal anger, fear, hope, pain and the like, without any reference to supposed qualia; but in that respect he does not differ from any other subsequent natural scientist. For since such qualia are, by their very nature, not accessible to scientific scrutiny, it can hardly be a complaint against the scientist that he does not accommodate them, let alone a complaint against Cartesian science in particular that it does not refer to them.

Could there be something that it is like to be a Cartesian *"bête machine"*—something that it is like to be a purely physical organism formed with such spectacular intricacy that it is able to produce a vast range of appropriate responses to changes in the environment and in the state of its internal organs? Descartes has no means of answering such a question[46] —but, in fairness, our modern Nagelian qualia-merchants should acknowledge that *neither do they*.

I hope I have said enough to show both how challenging is the critique which Marjorie Grene has provided of Descartes's views on human and animal passions, and also of some of the ways in which a defender of Descartes might wish to proceed. Let me end with a very short mention of one of the most fascinating issues she raises *en passant*: "what did Descartes think the pineal gland was doing in other [nonhuman] animals?"[47] The answer, I think, is that, not having a soul to fax to, the gland must be performing the same kind of function as it does in humans when (to use one of Descartes's examples) we are "walking, singing and the like, when these occur without the mind attending to them" [*animo non advertente*].[48] Even when the faculties of thought and reason are not involved, and even when seemingly conscious activities are in fact performed entirely by a semi-automatic subroutine, there still has to be a vast amount of information-processing, and this in turn requires a neural center where messages from the body are handled. The almost miraculously complex things we can do without conscious direction—and the point applies equally to our fellow-creatures in the animal kingdom—shows just how intricate a purely "mechanical" process in nature can be, and how far the resulting phenomena exceed the capacity of those lumbering machines constructed by human inventors. To have the status of a machine "made by the hand of God" is to be something worthy of awe and wonder. And respect? It would be nice to be able to add this to the list, but here at last (if I may end on a note with which I think Professor Grene would concur), we encounter something in the Cartesian system which is seriously deficient. Yet since the founders of the two most seminal moral philosophies of modernity, Kant and Bentham, signally failed our animal cousins in this regard, we might well show the affectionate owner of "Monsieur Grat" a little indulgence.[49]

JOHN COTTINGHAM

DEPARTMENT OF PHILOSOPHY
THE UNIVERSITY OF READING
JUNE 2000

NOTES

1. Marjorie Grene, *Descartes* (Brighton: Harvester Press, 1985), ch. 2, p. 23. Reissued (Indianapolis: Hackett Publishing, 1998).

2. The "easy dogmatism of the 1630s" with implications that are "appalling" (p. 47) and "ridiculous" (p. 38) is maintained until it "breaks down" through the introduction of "ambiguities" (pp. 46–47). The passions "hang there like a kind of anomaly" (p. 50).

3. For more on this, see my introduction to *Descartes' Meditations: Background Source Materials*, ed. Roger Ariew, John Cottingham and Tom Sorell (Cambridge: Cambridge University Press, 1998).

4. Val Plumwood, *Feminism and the Mastery of Nature* (London: Routledge, 1993), pp. 70–71.

5. Grene, *Descartes,* p. 52.

6. Ibid., p. 24.

7. *Discourse on the Method* [*Discours de la méthode*, 1637], part iv, AT VI 33: CSM I 127. In the present essay, 'AT' refers to the standard Franco-Latin edition of Descartes by C. Adam and P. Tannery, *Œuvres de Descartes*, 12 vols (revised edn., Paris: Vrin/CNRS, 1964–76); 'CSM' refers to the English translation by J. Cottingham, R. Stoothoff and D. Murdoch, *The Philosophical Writings of Descartes*, vols I and II (Cambridge: Cambridge University Press, 1985); and 'CSMK' to vol. III, *The Correspondence*, by the same translators plus A. Kenny (Cambridge: Cambridge University Press, 1991).

8. I should make it clear in passing, that this argument is not meant to disprove the possibility of an immaterial Deity: God, being eternal and immutable, is not subject to the changes implied by the notion of processing and throughput.

9. See the Dedicatory Letter to the Sorbonne, prefixed to the first edition of the Meditations (*Meditationes de prima philosophia*, 1641).

10. I Corinthians 16: 42–4: "So also is the resurrection of the dead. It is sown in corruption, yet raised in incorruption . . . It is sown a biological body [*soma psychikon*] and raised a spiritual body [*soma pneumatikon*]." See further J. Cottingham, "Cartesian Dualism: Theology, Metaphysics, and Science" in *The Cambridge Companion to Descartes*, ed. John Cottingham (Cambridge: Cambridge University Press, 1992), ch. 8.

11. For Aquinas, the soul needs to be united with the body in order to be a complete substance: *Summa theologiae* [1266–73], Ia 75.4 and Ia 118.2. Compare Francisco Suarez, *Metaphysical Disputations* [*Disputationes metaphysicae*, 1597] 33.i.11: "anima etiamsi sit separata est pars . . . essentialis, habetque incompletam esssentiam . . . et ideo semper est substantia incompleta."

12. Grene, *Descartes*, p. 48. The text being referred to is *The Passions of the Soul* [*Les passions de l'âme,* 1649], part i, arts 31–7 (AT XI 351ff: CSM I 340ff).

13. Spinoza, *Ethics* [*Ethica ordine geometrico demonstrata*, c. 1665], preface to part v.

14. David Dennett, *Consciousness Explained* (Harmondsworth: Allen Lane, 1992), p. 106.

15. Compare for example his use of the metaphor of "transfer" of quantity of motion from one body to another (*Principles* [*Principia philosophiae* 1644], part ii, art. 48). For further discussion of Descartes's causal language in physics, see J. Cottingham, "Force, Motion and Causality: More's Critique of Descartes," in *The Cambridge Platonists and the World: Philosophy, Ethics and Policy*, ed. G.A.J. Rogers, J. M. Vienne and Y. C. Zarka (Dordrecht: Kluwer, 1997), pp. 1–15; and D. Garber, *Descartes Metaphysical Physics* (Chicago and London: University of Chicago Press, 1992), chs. 6–9.

16. Letter to Clerselier of 12 January 1646 (AT IXA 213: CSM II 275). Compare R. C. Richardson, "The Scandal of Cartesian Interactionism" (*Mind*, 1982).

17. For the "arbitrariness" and (in a certain sense) contingency of the principles of Cartesian physics (at least from a human perspective), see J. Cottingham, "The Cartesian Legacy," *Proceedings of the Aristotelian Society*, sup. vol. 66 (1992): 1–21.

18. Indeed, in some respects it is *less* opaque, since we can clearly see how the divine institution of the mind-body correlations is designed to conduce to the welfare of the mind-body composite; see Meditation Six, AT VII 87–88: CSM II 60.

19. There is no space here to discuss the allegation made by some critics that the possibility of mind-body causation risks violating the Cartesian principle of the conservation of the motion in the physical world. For this, see D. Garber, "Descartes and Occasionalism," in *Causation in Early Modern Philosophy*, ed. S. Nadler (University Park, Pennsylvania: Pennsylvania State University Press, 1993), pp. 15–19.

20. See especially my *Philosophy and the Good Life* (Cambridge: Cambridge University Press, 1998), ch. 3, section 4.

21. *Discourse*, part v, AT VI 59: CSM I 141.

22. Letter to Regius of January 1642 (AT III 493: CSMK 206).

23. "Sine [facultate sentiendi] totum me possum clare et distincte intelligere" (Sixth Meditation, AT VII 78: CSM II 54).

24. *Principles of Philosophy* [*Principia philosophiae*, 1644], Part I, art. 32.

25. I shall come to nonhuman animals in the final section of this paper.

26. For an analysis of Descartes's theory of human nature that is more in line with Grene's critical stance, see S. Voss, "Descartes: The End of Anthropology," in *Reason, Will, and Sensation*, ed. John Cottingham (Oxford: Clarendon, 1994), pp. 273ff.

27. So far as I know, the use of the term "trialism" in this connection was first introduced in my "Cartesian Trialism" (1985); cf. John Cottingham, *Descartes* (Oxford: Blackwell, 1986) pp. 127ff. Notwithstanding some subsequent mis-understandings, I made it clear in the places cited that the threefold classification

was not meant by Descartes to be an *ontological* one; it relates, rather, to the irreducibility of our distinctively human *attributes* to the attributes either of pure thought on the one hand or of extension on the other. A more "realist" (and in my view mistaken) interpretation of the mind-body union is offered by Martial Gueroult, who construes it ontologically, as a *"substance psychophysique"*; see *Descartes selon l'ordre des raisons* (Aubier: Paris, 1968) vol. II, pp. 201ff.

28. Letter of 21 May 1642 (AT III 665: CSMK 218).

29. In virtue of our embodied state, as creatures of flesh and blood, human beings enjoy modes of awareness which (to use Descartes's own language) "must not be referred either to the mind alone or to the body alone." The list of items comprised in this category includes "first, appetites like hunger and thirst; second, emotions or passions which do not consist of thought alone, such as the emotions of anger, joy, sadness and love; and finally all sensations, such as those pain, pleasure [and the other manifold kinds of sensory awareness arising from the stimulation of the sense organs]" (*Principles*, Part I, art. 48). For a detailed discussion of how the "trialistic" schema applies in Descartes's account of passions such as love, see *Philosophy and the Good Life,* ch. 3, section 5.

30. Grene, *Descartes*, p. 38.

31. B. Williams, *Descartes: The Project of Pure Inquiry* (Harmonsdsworth: Penguin, 1978), ch. 8.

32. Letter from Pollot to Descartes of February 1638, AT I 514; cited in Grene, *Descartes*, p, 36.

33. Descartes to Reneri for Pollot, April or May 1638 (AT II 41: CSMK 100).

34. AT VI 56: CSM I 139.

35. Grene, *Descartes*, p. 51.

36. AT VI 57: CSM I 140.

37. See Noam Chomsky, *Language and Mind* (New York: Harcourt, Brace and World, 1986).

38. Grene, *Descartes*, p. 38.

39. For more on the meaning of "automaton," see John Cottingham, "A Brute to the Brutes? Descartes's Treatment of Animals," *Philosophy* 53 (1978): 551–59. Reprinted in *René Descartes, Critical Assessments,* ed. G. Moyal (London: Routledge, 1991), vol. IV, pp. 323ff., and in *Descartes.* Oxford Readings in Philosophy series, ed. John Cottingham (Oxford: Oxford University Press, 1998), pp. 225–33.

40. AT II 41: CSMK 100.

41. See Sixth Meditation, passim.

42. See further John Cottingham, "Phenomenology or Intentionality?: Descartes on the Objects of Thought," in *History of the Mind-Body Problem*, ed. Tim Crane and Sarah Patterson (London: Routledge, 2000).

43. Letter to Newcastle of 23 November 1646 (AT IV 574: CSMK 303); letter to More of 5 February 1649 (AT V 276: CSMK 365). Cf. Grene, *Descartes,* pp 50–51.

44. Thomas Nagel, "What Is It Like to Be a Bat?" in *Mortal Questions* (Cambridge: Cambridge University Press, 1979).

45. For this point, see my "Phenomenology or Intentionality?" cited above.

46. It may not be too farfetched to suppose that some perplexity along these lines might have been going through Descartes's mind when he wrote to More that his views on animals had to remain merely probable, "since the human mind does not reach into their hearts" (letter of 5 February 1649, AT V 277: CSMK 365). Cf. Grene, *Descartes*, p. 52.

47. Grene, *Descartes*, p. 48.

48. Fourth Replies, AT VII 230: CSM II 161.

49. The affection in which Descartes held his dog is clearly evidenced by its name, recorded by Baillet (*La Vie de Monsieur Des-Cartes* [1691]). The best Kant can do for animals is to argue that those who mistreat them are bad because they are likely to go on to mistreat humans (*Lectures on Ethics* [*Einer Vorlesung über Ethik*, 1775–80], Part B, section ix). Bentham's utilitarian calculus notoriously allows animals no rights whatever; in the chilling phrase of utilitarian champion Peter Singer, they are "replaceable"; see Peter Singer, *Practical Ethics* (Cambridge: Cambridge University Press, 1979; 2nd ed. 1993), ch. 5.

REPLY TO JOHN COTTINGHAM

John Cottingham's rich and thought-provoking criticism of my argument on the Cartesian passions deserves a more detailed reply than I give it here. Let me hop, skip, and jump through his text, commenting on some of his claims.

Section I. At the start Cottingham writes: "Grene's complaints about Descartes's account of the passions are expressed with a striking vehemence and commitment, almost as if she is determined to bring into proper focus the very passionate aspects of our human nature that she accuses the fastidious Frenchman of failing to accommodate." My critic has hit the nail on the head—if he omits the "almost." I do indeed believe that it is one of the great, even tragic, failures of our philosophical tradition, all the way back to Plato, that we set emotion over against reason as its archenemy. At least in the triad of the *Phaedrus* there is a good horse as well as a bad one, and in Spinoza there can be active as well as passive emotions. Although, in my view, the tradition of psychological atomism that Hume followed to its logical conclusion badly needs to be replaced, his famous one-liner is profoundly true: "reason is and ought to be the slave of the passions." Science, history, any developed and originative discipline can exist only if carried by what Michael Polanyi called "intellectual passions." Why did Descartes exile himself to the Netherlands, if not because he thought he would find there fewer obstacles to his single-minded, impassioned search for what he conceived to be the truth?

Cottingham regrets that in our time "the label 'Cartesian' has almost become a term of abuse." True; but the oddity of the situation is that it is a kind of last-ditch Cartesianism that appears nowadays to be in high fashion: the physical world and the brain on one side, and on the other something quaintly called "consciousness." Professor Cottingham himself confirms this when he speaks of Tom Nagel's famous bat, and the consequences of worrying about how it feels to be one. That is the Cartesian heritage, what Helmuth Plessner called "the Cartesian alternative," which still holds much contemporary philosophizing in its grip. (In the same paragraph, Cotting-ham identifies my position on all this with that of Val Plumwood. What he quotes from her I do indeed agree with, but I must confess my astonishment at being labeled a feminist of any sort whatsoever!)

Section II. Cottingham professes surprise that critics neglect the most serious difficulty in mind-body dualism, "the question of whether, . . . the idea of an incorporeal thinking self may not be, in itself, incoherent." He seems to think that I, along with others, am concerned chiefly by the problem of interaction, while allowing that an "incorporeal *res cogitans* is at least a *logical* possibility." I should have thought "incoherence" and "logical (im)possibility" were not quite the same; but the first claim, that the notion of an incorporeal thinking thing is incoherent, I have myself argued in the pages just preceding my Passions chapter—although I should rather have said (for me) inconceivable, rather than incoherent. If I may quote myself:

> There is, I submit, no such event as an experience of mind without some bodily resonance—"bodily," of course . . . in the sense of a live, breathing, organic body. . . . [M]y own awareness of myself is not a special, pure inner something set against the world. To be aware of myself is always and essentially to become sentient of my bodily existence, located here and now in this both biological and social place. . . . That ambiguous yet pervasive thinking-through-my-lived-body is the datum with which, as a philosopher, I have to begin. It is the notion of separate mind that is *un*intelligible. (*Descartes*, pp. 20–21)

I agree that the question of mind-body interaction is ancillary to the funda-mental question of the conceivability of a separate, or separable, thinking thing. Yes, thinking does entail "the processing of information," if one must put it that way. (For myself, I would prefer a less cybernetic formulation.)

The argument that follows rests on granting "the notion of an incorpo-real consciousness," a grant I have not made. However, I'm afraid our even deeper disagreement rests on my inability to accept the role of the deity in Descartes's universe. I acknowledge that Professor Cottingham's account of Descartes's position is entirely correct. However, we are here not arguing an historical point, but talking about our own beliefs, albeit in the context of studying Cartesian texts. And I'm afraid that if I find mind/body separation incoherent, but am not entirely certain that such incoherence amounts to a logical impossibility, I do believe, once more with Hume, that, given the existence of evil, the conception of an infinite all-good and all-powerful God is self-contradictory. Of course I respect others' faith, but can credit it philosophically only if it is *quia absurdum*. Cottingham writes: "The causal opacity that obtains in the mind-body correlations, decreed by

God, is no denser than the opacity which ultimately obtains with respect to all God's decrees." And in note 18 he adds: "Indeed, in some respects it is *less* opaque, since we can clearly see how the divine institution of the mind-body correlations is designed to conduce to the welfare of the mind-body composite." Yes, Descartes says so; but even supposing God existed, could we poor finite beings know his mind?

Section III. Here we come upon the very sticky problem of the third common notion. What is it to be a (Cartesian) human being, and how well can we know this? Cottingham says we must distinguish between myself as "the thinking subject of metaphysical inquiry" and myself as human being, "the subject of psychology and ethics." Since I have already confessed my nonunderstanding of the real distinction (when I am thinking for myself rather than trying to understand Descartes and his like-minded contemporaries), I cannot effectively follow Cottingham's analysis. But I hope I can, without disrespect, pin-point some of the remarks I find especially puzzling. For example: if it is the "substantial" union of mind and body that permits sensation, it seems clear that either animals exemplify a similar union, or else they have no sensations. (It is the latter position I believe Descartes took at least into the early 1640s.)

Further, I wonder what this third something *is*. According to Cottingham, Descartes was a trialist; but this third something, the human being, has no ontological standing (see note 27); it is a question of attributes without a substance to inhere in. For a thinker within the tradition of substance metaphysics, a tradition to which Descartes surely belonged, what is this? Descartes tells Princess Elizabeth that it is difficult to understand common notions one and two (mind and body) at the same time as common notion three (him or herself *qua* human being). Indeed, it appears that, in Cartesian terms, the apprehension of the third common notion is necessarily confused. Surely it makes more sense, in our time and place, to start with ourselves as human beings—that is, primates with distinctive gifts as well as distinctive fragilities, instead of haring off after pure minds and purely geometrical bodies, held together by a self-contradictory God. I'm afraid I still say, as I have been saying for some sixty-odd years, that the *cogito,* far from being the uniquely correct starting point for philosophy, was the starting point for a disastrous downhill slide toward the distressing *Nullpunktsexistenz* of much of today's professional discourse.

Section IV. The *bête machine.* The exchange with Pollot still seems to me to speak loud and clear, as does the reply to Arnauld, about the sheep running from the wolf. After all, sensation stems from the united mind-body. Automata, bodies without minds, cannot be said to sense. Descartes's world of God, minds and geometricized bodies suited him just fine. As I and many others have said many times, it is a world without life. (Incidentally, wearing my other hat—as a student of Darwin rather than Descartes, I must register a protest at the very bleak description of Darwin's transformation of our world view. But that's not what's in question here.) What happened, as I see it, was that Descartes was encouraged by Princess Elizabeth to think about the life of emotion. On his premises, he was unable to carry out a consistent account, and that difficulty is reflected in his later correspondence as well as in the treatise on the passions itself. Granted, in the course of evolution we have developed a kind (or a degree?) of intentionality that is, so far as we can tell, unique. I would put this down, as some anthropologists have done, to our power of "symboling"—an ability that includes language but also other cultural rites and artifacts. As Merleau-Ponty put it, there are three concentric worlds: the human world has developed within the living world, and the living world in turn is contained in the physical world, though not identical with it. Descartes's vision cancelled the world of life in favor of a highly attenuated matter, and, in terms of clear and distinct ideas, stripped down our embodied, human existence to an equally attenuated bare intellect. True, the third common notion is there, but only in confusion, and needing the assistance of God's goodness.

Finally, let me say: if I must disagree with John Cottingham, I do so regretfully, and in full awareness of the debt that all Descartes scholars owe him.

M. G.

19

Desmond M. Clarke

EXPLANATION, CONSCIOUSNESS, AND CARTESIAN DUALISM

Marjorie Grene has drawn attention in a number of places to what she calls the "fundamental incoherence" in Descartes's account of mind-body unity, and in the theories of the passions and of animal sentience which result from Cartesian dualism.[1] She also displays unwarranted impatience with the tardiness of the hapless French philosopher in recognizing the reality of the passions and with his apparently unsuccessful efforts to resolve what emerged as a major difficulty in his system. "We know there *are* passions of the soul, but they turn up in a rather dreary postscript to Descartes's published work and are in themselves an embarrassment to his pure dualistic doctrine."[2] Thus Cartesian dualism is a failed enterprise, and we ought to look elsewhere for enlightenment on the issues it was meant to address.

It would be difficult to find many philosophers today who disagree about the limitations of the substance dualism proposed by Descartes. But the merits of the theory today are hardly the criterion by which its contribution to seventeenth-century philosophy should be measured. I assume that Grene agrees with this latter comment; her objection is not that Descartes performs poorly by today's standards, but that he performed poorly by the standards of his own day. This, then, is the question at issue: To what extent was Cartesian dualism a doomed enterprise by the standards that prevailed in the early modern period and the insights that were available to the lapsed Aristotelian from La Haye?

I argue that Descartes made a very significant contribution to the modern concept of scientific explanation, and he did so partly by contrasting his proposals with the practices of his scholastic contemporaries. Despite his consistent objections to Aristotelian forms, faculties, or powers, however, the new ideal of scientific explanation did not preclude all use of such concepts; they reappeared at the limits of scientific explanation. Thus Descartes, like Newton, endorsed the theory that matter is endowed with some fundamental properties which are best described as powers or dispositions; hence such apparently scholastic properties survive a rigorously Cartesian application of Occam's razor. The human soul, as a substantial form, likewise appears at the limits of scientific explanation; but neither Descartes nor Grene has correctly diagnosed the reasons for its apparent unavoidability and irreducibility.

EXPLANATION

Descartes notoriously complained, very frequently, about scholastic explanations and he argued that the type of explanation that he was proposing was vastly superior. His objections to the scholastic style of explanation may be grouped under a number of subheadings: (a) they appeal to occult realities; (b) they are redundant; (c) they presuppose an obscure mechanism; and (d) they compromise the distinction between matter and spirit.

Scholastic explanations were described as "occult" because they allegedly were not understood even by those who proposed them. Thus, despite the irenic motivation involved in writing to Regius in 1642, and despite the toleration proposed there for scholastic philosophers, Descartes wrote that "their defenders [those who proposed substantial forms] admit that they are occult and that they do not understand them themselves. If they say that some action results from a substantial form, it is as if they said that it results from something they do not understand; which explains nothing" (AT III, 506: CSM III, 208).[3] Such explanations were said to explain the obscure by what is even more obscure, "*obscurum per obscurius.*"

The second reason for rejecting scholastic explanations was that they were redundant. This, of course, presupposes agreement on what it means to *explain* some phenomenon, or it assumes that Descartes's readers would agree that the type of mechanical explanations for which he searched would, if available, make it unnecessary to look for anything more. This is the point made so forcefully at the outset of his scientific work in *Le Monde*:

> Thus someone else may imagine, if they wish, the "form" of fire, the "quality" of heat, and the "action" which burns it, as things that are completely distinct in the wood. For my part . . . I am satisfied to conceive in it the movement of its parts. You may posit "fire" and "heat" in it, and make it burn as much as you wish; but if you do not also assume that some of its parts move and become detached from those which are next to them, I could not imagine that

the wood could undergo any change or alteration. On the other hand, take away the "fire" and the "heat" and prevent it from burning; on condition simply that you grant me that there is some power which violently moves its finer parts and separates them from the larger parts, I find that this alone could cause it to undergo all the same changes which are observed when it burns.[4]

In other words, a mechanical explanation in terms of the movement of unobservable particles would be sufficient to explain what is happening in the phenomenon we call burning, and any appeal to forms and qualities is therefore redundant.

The final two objections may be considered together and presuppose the sharp dualism of mind and matter for which Descartes argues throughout his work. The substantial forms proposed by scholastics should be rejected, he claims, because they compromise the distinction between matter and spirit. "Some people commonly mingle the two ideas of body and soul when they construct the ideas of real qualities and substantial forms . . ." (AT III, 420: CSM III, 188). And if the province of matter and spirit are so distinct, then it follows that scholastic explanations involve some kind of unintelligible interaction between realities that have little in common. "We cannot in any way understand how the same things [viz., size, shape, and motion] can produce something else of an entirely different nature from themselves, such as those substantial forms and real qualities that many [philosophers] suppose in things; nor indeed how, subsequently, these qualities or forms can have the power to excite local motion in other bodies" (AT VIII–1, 322: CSM I, 285).

This all amounts to a proposal in favor of exclusively mechanical explanations of natural phenomena; if we leave aside the details of what Descartes was willing to include in such explanations, it is at least clear what he wished to exclude. There seems to have been no room for forms, qualities, and so on; in the context of explaining natural phenomena, these are poorly understood, they compromise the distinction between matter and spirit and, if we already have mechanical explanations, they are redundant.

POWERS AS EXPLANATIONS

If Descartes was so rigorous in clearing out redundant explanatory entities, it remains something of an enigma why he not only tolerated substantial forms to explain human consciousness but even invoked the allegedly clear distinction between matter and spirit among the reasons why scholastic explanations are unacceptable. That left him open to the charge that he was making the same mistake with which he charged those whom he criticizes, admittedly in a narrower range of *explananda*, and that the objections he articulated so clearly against the school philosophy applied equally to the unique example of a substantial form, the soul, which survived in the Cartesian system. Hobbes put the point with characteristic bluntness, in his Third Objections to the *Meditations*:

> If Mr. Descartes is suggesting that he who understands is the same as the understanding, we shall be going back to the scholastic way of talking: the understanding understands, the sight sees, the will wills and, by a very close analogy, the walking . . . walks. All these expressions are obscure, improper, and quite unworthy of Mr. Descartes' usual clarity. (AT VII, 177: CSM II, 125)

In other words, Descartes explains our ability to think by postulating a "thinking faculty." This requires some account of why faculties, powers, forms, and similar postulated realities are acceptable to Cartesians in some cases and not in others.

Of course, the question about forms and faculties is not limited to one exceptional case—viz., the soul as the substantial form of a human being; for, despite the apparent implications of Descartes's general critique of forms and occult powers, there are very frequent references to faculties or powers in Cartesian philosophy. Descartes often uses the Latin terms *potentia, vis, virtus*, and *facultas* and the corresponding French terms, *puissance, force, vertu*, and *faculté* to characterize the explanatory realities which he postulates, as appropriate, either to specify something that requires an explanation or to take the first step in providing one. Thus, for example, he claims that the human soul has the following faculties: a *vis intelligendi* (a power of understanding); a *facultas cogitandi* (a faculty of thinking); a *facultas eligendi* or *vis volendi* (a power of choosing); and a *facultas locum movendi* or a *vis movendi corpus* (a power to change place or to move its body).[5] While this might seem already to be drifting in the direction of scholastic prodigality, Descartes is quick to acknowledge that not everything that we are capable of doing presupposes a distinct faculty or power; thus we are capable of making mistakes, but we do not need a corresponding mistake-making faculty, what he calls a *facultas errandi* (AT VII, 54).

All these faculties are predicated of the soul or mind, leading one to suspect, perhaps, that spiritual substances are exceptional and that they alone are the locus of Cartesian faculties. But this is not so. Evidently, God is a paradigm case where powers of an infinite kind are typically found, and here Descartes is very close to the style of argument found in Aquinas. But God and the soul are not the only substances of which powers are predicated. Even bodies have various powers, and the introduction of the latter is not a late development in response, for example, to otherwise insoluble problems in physics. As early as the incomplete *Rules* (c. 1628), Descartes discussed the role of what he called a "natural power" (*potentia naturalis*) in explaining a specific type of refraction.[6] He subsequently claimed in his mature physics that bodies have the power to resist motion and, once they are in motion, they have the power to continue to move indefinitely in a straight line. There is clearly a major problem in interpreting these suggestions in a manner consistent with Descartes's explicit mechanism, and many readers have been tempted to gloss such texts as if their author were a committed, if only implicit, occasionalist.[7] However, it is also consistent even with Descartes's mature physics to understand him as postulating certain distinctive powers in matter—on the assumption that none of them belongs essentially to matter, but that they all originate in some way from the creative action of God.

Thus Cartesian mechanism is consistent with predicating "active principles" of matter, on condition that they are not confused with the scholastic qualities to which he objects. Even in the letter to Regius already quoted above, in which he advised against recourse to scholastic forms, he wrote:

> It cannot be absurd to say this [i.e., that substantial forms are the immediate principles of action] if one does not regard such forms as distinct from active principles. Now we do not deny active qualities, but we say only that they should not be regarded as having any degree of reality greater than that of modes; . . . nor do we deny dispositions, but we divide them into two kinds. Some are purely material . . . others are immaterial or spiritual. (AT III, 503: CSM III, 208)

In the Sixth Meditation, Descartes argues that our ideas of physical realities originate in physical things; therefore, material substance must have a power of sending us the appropriate signals. "He [God] . . . gave me a strong tendency to believe that these ideas are emitted by physical things, and therefore I cannot see how he can be understood as not being a deceiver if they originated from anything except physical things [*si aliunde quam a rebus corporeis emitterentur*]."[8] The same thesis is repeated towards the conclusion of the *Principles*:

> [W]e know that the nature of our soul is such that different local motions are quite sufficient to produce all the sensations in the soul. . . . In view of all this we have every reason to conclude that the properties in external objects to which we apply the terms "light," "colour," . . . are . . . simply various dispositions [*dispositiones*] in those objects which make them capable of setting up various kinds of motions in our nerves. (AT VIII–1, 322: CSM I, 285)

Texts such as this, of which there are very many, suggest that there are dispositional powers even in physical things, and that such powers have a role in Cartesian explanation. Evidently, one could try to purify Descartes's language so that all such references are systematically translated into a mechanistic language with fewer ontological commitments. Or one could try, as I do below, to see whether they have a limited role in his explanatory enterprise.

The feasibility of being a mechanist with strong antischolastic objections to forms and properties, while retaining some role for dispositional explanatory entities, is taken up explicitly by Antoine Arnauld in *On True and False Ideas*, and his proposed solution seems to fit neatly with Cartesian practice. When Malebranche objected to explanations in terms of natures, faculties, and the like, Arnauld distinguished between correct and incorrect ways of using faculty language:

> [T]hese [i.e., "faculty," "nature," etc.] are words which can be used correctly or wrongly . . . the word "faculty" is used wrongly when one understands by it something distinct from the thing to which one attributes that faculty, . . . when one claims to have given an explanation of an effect that is known . . . by using the general term "faculty" to describe its cause, as when one says that the magnet attracts iron because it has this faculty . . . the abuse of the word in those cases consists principally in this: before knowing what is involved in iron being attracted to a magnet, . . . one is satisfied with saying that the magnet . . . [has an attractive faculty].[9]

Arnauld goes on to explain that if we already understand the mechanism involved in magnetic attraction—for example, by hypothesizing Descartes's screw-shaped pores—and if we wished to know why this mechanism works as it does, that is,

> how it comes about that the magnet has screw-shaped pores, then it would be perfectly all right to reply by saying that it is because such is the nature of the bodies that we call . . . magnets. . . . [I]f one asks in general terms why matter is able to move, it is perfectly proper to reply by saying that such is its nature, and that God, in creating it, has given to its parts this faculty by which one of them can be moved closer to, or further from, another.[10]

Arnauld is arguing here that explanation must come to a stop somewhere and that, when it does, it is appropriate to say: that is the way things are. But to say this too early is to short-circuit the explanation. Secondly, the scholastics gave the impression of having made progress in explaining phenomena by disguising their ignorance with the introduction of new, apparently technical terms, such as the "sympathy" and "antipathy" that were used widely by seventeenth-century scholastic natural philosophers.

The correct approach, according to Arnauld, is to identify the mechanisms by which various natural phenomena occur, and not to say simply and immediately that something occurs because that is the nature of things.

Given the Cartesian strategy of developing mechanical explanations, we should anticipate that all physical phenomena are explained in terms of the motions and interactions of unobservable parts of matter. This in turn presupposes some account of why pieces of matter move and interact as they do and it is precisely at this point, in describing the primary or unanalyzable properties of pieces of matter, that Descartes may legitimately attribute to matter the various powers or dispositions which feature in his explanations, without exposing his account to the charge of scholastic pseudo-explanation.

A similar justification for maintaining a limited role for powers or forces is offered by Newton, in the final query to the *Opticks*, in which he relies on motive and inertial forces despite explicit reservations about occult scholastic powers:

> [T]hese particles have not only a *Vis inertiae* . . . they are moved by certain active Principles, such as is that of Gravity, and that which causes Fermentation, and the Cohesion of Bodies. These Principles I consider not as occult Qualities, supposed to result from the specifick Forms of Things, but as general Laws of Nature, by which the Things themselves are form'd; their Truth appearing to us by Phenomena, though their Causes be not yet discover'd. For these are manifest Qualities, and their Causes only are occult. And the *Aristotelians* gave the Name of occult Qualities, not to manifest Qualities, but to such Qualities only as they supposed to lie hid in Bodies, and to be the unknown Causes of manifest Effects. . . . Such occult Qualities put a stop to the Improvement of natural Philosophy, and therefore of late Years have been rejected. To tell us that every Species of Things is endow'd with an occult specifick Quality by which it acts and produces manifest Effects, is to tell us nothing: But to derive two or three general Principles of Motion from Phenomena, and afterwards to tell us how the Properties and Actions of all corporeal Things follow from those manifest principles, would be a very great step in Philosophy, though the Causes of those Principles were not yet discover'd.[11]

Newton's progression from "occult qualities" to "manifest principles" may be forgiven as a rhetorical flourish; the difference between the theoretical entities (that he is willing to endorse) and those of the scholastics (which he rejects) is not a function of their being more or less manifest. For Newton, there is no objection in principle to a two-stage process, the first step of which involves a description of the relevant phenomena and their incorporation under general laws, such as Newton's laws of motion. The second step is to search for the cause of the regularity of such motions (for example, gravitational force). This may remain hidden, and in that sense is occult; it is manifested only in the patterns of observed motions. However, the fact that we have made little progress on the second part of this explanatory project should not deter us from taking the initial step of collecting a range of data which fit under a relatively small number of general laws.

Thus Arnauld and Newton both object to scholastic explanations for similar reasons, that is, they seem to involve an *unrestricted* use of specific occult qualities to explain every particular phenomenon. But they likewise defend the intelligibility of predicating, of matter, some fundamental properties which remain (at least for some time) described as powers or forces which cause a range of diverse effects at the level of observable phenomena. This option was also available to Descartes; he was not necessarily committed to the kind of reductionism involved in Malebranche's occasionalism.

Assuming, then, that Descartes may use powers and forms in a limited role in scientific explanation, it remains to be seen whether his espousal of substance dualism is consistent with his otherwise widespread criticism of scholastic practice. Before doing this, I need to draw attention to one other feature of his concept of explanation.

ABSTRACTION

As early as Rule xii of the *Rules for Guiding One's Intelligence in Searching for the Truth*, Descartes acknowledges the abstractness of explanations. Thus when he suggests that we think of all sensations as impressions made on our sensory organs by physical shapes, and that we understand this literally rather than analogically, he claims that:

> it is possible to demonstrate that this assumption has no more false consequences than any other. For example, you may imagine colour to be anything you wish, but you will not deny that it is extended and that it therefore has a shape. As long as we take care not to invent any new entity uselessly and foolishly, while not denying anything that others have preferred to claim about colour, what difficulty could result if we merely abstract from everything else apart from the fact that colour has the nature of shape and if we conceive the difference between white, blue, red, etc., as being like that between . . . [various shapes]? (AT X, 413: CSM I, 40–41)[12]

The reason he gave for choosing shape, rather than some other feature, was that "nothing is more accessible to the senses than shape, for it is both touched and seen." If we take Descartes's question literally and ask: who could object if we abstract from everything apart from shape, I suspect one answer is: Marjorie Grene. Why? Because by focusing exclusively on shapes, or by modelling variations in perceived colors onto variations in shape, Descartes omits something essential and irreducible about the phenomenological experience of seeing different colors.

The objection here may be that our perception (through touch and sight) of shapes is not remotely similar, from the point of view of the perceiver, to the perception of colors. Alternatively, it may be that the impact of shapes on our senses is an inadequate set of theoretical entities with which to explain our perception of colors. The assumptions implicit in these objections might be called, for easy reference, the Principle of Phenomenological Similarity (PPS) and the Principle of the Adequacy of Theoretical Entities (PATE). I have argued elsewhere that some of Descartes's explanations in physics fail to satisfy PATE.[13] But my attitude toward the deficiencies of Cartesian physics is more indulgent than Grene's. I sympathize with Descartes's strategy of using a principle of parsimony from the beginning of a scientific project, and of introducing supplementary theoretical entities only when we have tried, and failed, to manage with fewer. I suspect that Marjorie Grene agrees with this as a general principle, but she may wish to claim that it was patently obvious, from the very beginning of *Le Monde*, that Descartes had not provided himself with sufficient theoretical entities to make much progress on his stated objectives and that his stubbornness in resisting the addition of what was needed was due to other theoretical commitments that he should have, and could have, recognized as unwarranted. However, I shall not pursue this line of discussion here. I revert, instead, to the other principle, the PPS.

Before saying something more about it, it may be worthwhile to consider briefly Descartes's justification for breaching it, as presented in the *Rules*. The main reason is that there may be a significant disparity between the way in which we know things and the way in which such things exist objectively; "to view things from the perspective of our knowledge is different from speaking about them as they really are."[14] This means that we may conceive of things as composite even when, in reality, they are simple and singular and this applies even in the case of physical things. Thus "since we are discussing things here only insofar as they are understood by the intellect, we apply the term 'simple' only to those the knowledge of which is so clear and distinct that they cannot be divided by the mind into other things that are more clearly known."[15] Evidently, such a strategy leaves room for mistakes, when we forget that our knowledge may not match, in every respect, the realities we claim to explain. One of the objectives of Rule xii was to alert readers to this distinction between things as we know them and things as they are objectively, and to warn them of the consequent dangers of error.

There are reverberations of this point almost twenty years later, in correspondence with Princess Elizabeth about mind-body unity. Descartes's royal correspondent had requested, soon after publication of the *Meditations*, that he explain how a purely immaterial substance can interact with a physical substance: "how can the human soul, which is only a thinking substance, determine the movement of the animal spirits in order to perform a voluntary action?"[16] After a series of unsatisfactory and slightly condescending replies, Descartes eventually suggested that we cannot think of the mind and body, at one and the same time, as distinct and as united, because to do so would involve thinking contradictory thoughts: "the human mind is incapable of conceiving very distinctly, and simultaneously, both the distinction and union of body and soul. The reason is that, in order to do so, it would be necessary to conceive of them as one single thing and, at the same time, to conceive of them as two things —which is self-contradictory."[17] Thus despite the consistency with which Descartes analyzes human experiences by reference to substance dualism, he also suggests that the two substances must form a single substance, that this is something we know from our experience, but that there remains some kind of conceptual block to the possibility of being able to think, consistently, of the mind as distinct from and as united with the body. But our dualistic thinking need not compromise our experience of mind-body unity. Human beings therefore provide another example of the point made in the *Rules*, that things may be composite from the point of view of our knowledge even though, in reality, they are singular and unified.

CONSCIOUSNESS

Some recent discussions in philosophy of mind have identified consciousness as the stumbling block on which any form of materialism must founder. When Thomas Nagel asked what it is like to be a bat,[18] the implication was that even an inadequate description of what it is like shows that it is impossible, in principle, to explain the phenomenological uniqueness of this experience by reference to any form of materialism. The subjective feel of what it is like cannot be captured in any account of brain cells and their mysterious functioning.

Marjorie Grene has joined this side of the debate in arguing against the viability of reductive theories of the human mind.[19] Without rehearsing the details of the arguments in this case or claiming to report them adequately or accurately here, the underlying objection to contemporary materialist accounts of mental experiences is sufficiently similar to the PPS above to ask if there is a common source to both. I suggest that there is—the common link, for Marjorie Grene, is that she is an Aristotelian, in the relevant sense, and that her qualms about Descartes's explanatory enterprise result, not from well-known or widely accepted objections to its deficiencies, but to the very nature of the enterprise itself. Even if the project had been carried out with singular success, Grene would object to what Descartes was trying to do.[20] On this point, she has identified something very significant about Cartesian dualism but, I argue, has misunderstood its remedy. For substance dualism is the honest expression, in the language of the seventeenth century, of the theoretical limits to scientific explanation; and the proper response to recognizing those limits is to cease to demand of explanation something that it cannot deliver, rather than to lapse back into the more comprehensive but less explanatory descriptions of Aristotelianism.

The reason why what it is like to be conscious of something is not amenable to explanation depends on how we conceive of what allegedly needs to be explained. There is no suggestion here that we do not have the experiences that are typically described as conscious experiences. The question is whether such subjective conscious experiences can, without remainder, become the object of another act of consciousness and, as an object, be described in sufficient detail to appear as an *explanandum* in some account of what goes on in the mind. Wilfrid Sellars argued many years ago that the distinctive phenomenology of pain does not appear in an explanation of pain.[21] Similar arguments have been developed more recently for the failure, in principle, of materialism to provide an explanation of the phenomenology of any conscious experience.[22] The question with which I began above, about evaluating Descartes's position in the light of what might reasonably have been available to him in the seventeenth century, becomes relevant at this stage. It seems as if the problem with which he was trying to cope is still a highly contested issue in philosophy of mind, and one on which philosophers have not reached agreement.

The issue raised by Nagel, in discussing what it is like to be a bat, focuses attention on the subjective dimension found in all intentional acts and on the distinction between what we are aware of and the awareness in virtue of which we are aware of anything, that is, on the intentional object of awareness and the act of awareness which is directed towards it. Descartes alludes to this in the Sixth Meditation, in the famous passage about a pilot and a ship:

> Nature also teaches by means of the sensations of pain, hunger, thirst, etc., that I am not present to my body only in the way that a pilot is present to a ship, but that I am very closely joined to it and almost merged with it to such an extent that, together with it, I compose a single entity. Otherwise, when my body is injured I (who am nothing but a thinking thing) would not feel pain as a result;

instead I would perceive such an injury as a pilot perceives by sight if some part of the ship is damaged. . . . [T]hese sensations of thirst, hunger, pain, etc. are undoubtedly mere confused ways of thinking that result from the union and, as it were, the thorough mixing together of mind and body.[23]

In feeling pain, for example, the object of my act of awareness is the injury in my foot and I call this peculiar type of awareness a pain. By reflection, I can then make the act of awareness of pain the object of a different act of awareness and I can describe some of its properties, such as how long it lasted, whether or not it was very intense, and so forth. But it remains an open question whether what Nagel calls the "what it is like" to be in pain can be captured as the *object* of a reflective act of consciousness. If the "what it is like" is an irreducibly subjective experience—if it includes all the subjective phenomenology of being in pain—then the demand that theories of mind provide an explanation of subjective pain experiences is a demand to do the impossible, to capture without remainder in an objective description the subjective feel of what it is like to be in pain. In other words, it is a demand that we think of the subject as an object. In response to a similar misguided demand, Descartes argued that his critics "expect me to do the impossible, . . . they do not know what they are asking for, nor what they ought to ask for" (AT II, 141–44: CSM III, 103–4).[24] In this context, the recognition that the "what it is like" of acts of awareness cannot be explained by theories of mind is not an indication of a defect in such theories; it is a symptom, instead, of the unavoidable limits of any explanation of subjective experiences. The subjective feel of pain cannot be made the object of a description (or explanation) without remainder. In a strict sense, it is inexplicable. We have reached the limits of what any explanation can be expected to do, even if it availed of the full resources of substance dualism.

There is thus an interesting parallel between the two types of case in which Descartes, the consistent critic of scholasticism, resorts to forms, faculties, or powers. The ideal explanation of a natural phenomenon, for a Cartesian, is a mechanical one, in which we are provided with a mathematical description of the mechanism by which, hypothetically, such a phenomenon occurs. Explanation must come to a stop somewhere and, where it does, it acknowledges or postulates properties in matter which cannot be further analyzed or explained. They are simply there by nature; for a Christian like Descartes, they are there because that is the way God decided to create things. Since these properties cannot be explained further, it is appropriate to identify them as in-built, irreducible features of matter which have a tendency to cause the effects we attribute to them. They are called powers, faculties, forces, or whatever other dispositional term is appropriate in the context. When confronted with the experience of human consciousness, Descartes recognized the limits of the type of scientific explanations that he was proposing. Again here, once we meet up with the limits of our explanatory strategy, it is appropriate to postulate the powers that would be needed to give effect to the experience we unambiguously have. That leads to substance dualism, and that in turn leads to a theoretical impasse. There is enough evidence in Descartes's correspondence with Princess Elizabeth to indicate that he realized the impasse into which he was led by the logic of his arguments. From one perspective, that of the subject, we experience ourselves as a single, integrated substance which can experience directly the injuries we suffer, and we do not perceive them as events in a distinct object (like a pilot and his ship). From another perspective, that of scientific explanation, we are led to think of ourselves as dual, as including many features that can be the object of scientific description and explanation, and of others that cannot.

What does this imply for our assessment of Cartesian dualism, in comparison with the merits of his contemporary scholastic critics? It must be conceded that, by embarking on the novel path of constructing abstract, mechanical explanations, Descartes exposed the limitations both of his own conceptual resources and, more significantly, of any attempt to explain the subjective phenomenological or first-person experience of thinking, feeling, and the like. In retrospect, this fits coherently into an understanding of the history of science which takes in its stride the fits and starts of conjectures and, *contra* Popper, which does not concede that a hypothesis has been refuted until some better theory becomes available. In the case of Cartesian dualism, its limitations were quickly recognized, even by its principal proponent, but it was necessary to wait for a long time before some way out of the impasse became available.

In contrast, the theory of mind that one finds in medieval scholastics or their seventeenth-century equivalents is careful (usually) not to develop dualism to its logical conclusion. The theory of the soul as an immortal substance, or quasi-substance, that was a commonplace in the tradition that Descartes rejected offered a mere description of our mental life, in scholastic categories, as if it were an explanation. This was a much less risky undertaking than Descartes's. One became so impressed by the magnitude of the task involved in explaining the range of phenomena that are available to us through experience, including the phenomenology of our own experience, that one never embarked on the explanatory trail at all.

In a word, Descartes helped formulate a new concept of scientific explanation and, in the process of applying it, showed up its limits and helped focus attention on apparently irreducible and inexplicable features of human consciousness. The Aristotelians remained content with a redescription of what they needed to explain, insisting on the richness of the phenomena and the abstractness and inadequacy of explanations. In doing so, they camouflaged the extent to which they were already committed to substance dualism without making any progress in explaining human or animal consciousness.

DESMOND M. CLARKE
NATIONAL UNIVERSITY OF IRELAND
AUGUST 2000

NOTES

1. Marjorie Grene, *Descartes* (Minneapolis: University of Minnesota Press, 1985), pp. 23, 30. See also "Animal Mechanism and the Cartesian Vision of Nature," in *Physics, Philosophy, and the Scientific Community*, ed. K. Gavroglu et al. (Boston: Kluwer Academic, 1995), pp. 189–204.

2. Grene, *Descartes*, p. 26.

3. All references to Descartes are to the standard Adam and Tannery edition of his works, *Oeuvres de Descartes* (Paris: Vrin, 1964–74), and are identified as "AT" with volume and page number. I also include a reference to *The Philosophical Works of Descartes*, 3 vols., trans. J. Cottingham et al. (Cambridge University Press, 1985–91); these are identified as "CSM," with volume and page number. Finally, I have used my own translations, where available, and these are taken from *Meditations and other Metaphysical Writings* and *The Discourse on Method and Related Writings* (London: Penguin, 1998 and 1999).

4. AT XI, 7–8: CSM I, 83; *Discourse on Method and Related Writings*, pp. 87–88.

5. *Meditations*, AT VII, 26, 56, 58, 78, 219, 389.

6. AT X, 395: CSM I, 29.

7. For example, Daniel Garber reads references to forces and powers in Descartes's physics in this way; see Daniel Garber, *Descartes' Metaphysical Physics* (Chicago: University of Chicago Press, 1992).

8. AT VII, 79–80: CSM II, 55; *Meditations and Other Metaphysics Writings*, p. 63.

9. Antoine Arnauld, *On True and False Ideas*, trans. Stephen Gaukroger (Manchester: Manchester University Press, 1990), p. 153.

10. Ibid., p. 154.

11. Isaac Newton, *Opticks* (New York: Dover, 1952), pp. 401–2.

12. *Discourse on Method and Related Writings*, p. 153.

13. See Desmond Clarke, *Occult Powers and Hypotheses* (Oxford: Clarendon Press, 1989), chs. 3 and 4.

14. AT X, 418; CSM I, 44; *Discourse on Method and Related Writings*, p. 156.

15. Ibid.

16. Elizabeth to Descartes, 16 May 1643 (AT III, 661): *Meditations and Other Metaphysical Writings*, p. 148.

17. Descartes to Elizabeth, 28 June 1643 (AT III, 693): *Meditations and other Metaphysical Writings*, p. 153.

18. Thomas Nagel, "What Is It Like to Be a Bat?," *Philosophical Review* 83 (1974): 435–50.

19. See my "Teleology and Mechanism: M. Grene's Absurdity Argument," and Marjorie Grene's reply, "Comment on Desmond Clarke," in *Philosophy of Science*, 46 (1979): 321–27.

20. I might anticipate, in a note, that Marjorie Grene will not take offense at this; she will surely see this as a compliment, even if she disagrees completely with my characterization.

21. Wilfrid Sellars, *Science, Perception and Reality* (London: Routledge & Kegan Paul, 1963).

22. See Colin McGinn, *The Problem of Consciousness* (Cambridge, Mass.: Blackwell, 1991). Here, and in the next paragraph, I borrow with acknowledgment from the work of my colleague, Mark Rowlands.

23. *Meditations and Other Metaphysical Writings*, pp. 63–64.

24. *Discourse on Method and Related Writings*, pp. 73, 74.

REPLY TO DESMOND M. CLARKE

As in the cases of Perovich and Rosenthal, Desmond Clarke reproaches me for my insufficient homage to consciousness as a central philosophical concept, this time, however, in the context of Descartes's own intellectual situation in the seventeenth century, rather than in terms of our twentieth- or twenty-first-century concerns. I'm afraid I find his argument very difficult to follow, but I'll do my best to reply to some points in it.

First, I still do not find my impatience with Cartesian passions "unwarranted." Far from it. I have reread the relevant chapter in my book on Descartes, and I believe it stands up pretty well—though I should not have alluded, in general, to Cartesian dualism as such as incoherent. As I have said in earlier comments, from my perspective, it is inconceivable. Historically, however, I must admit that it was not so, and not necessarily incoherent, for Descartes's readers. What I tried to indicate in that chapter was that, so far as I can tell, Descartes was expressing a coherent position in his remarks about the sheep and the wolf in the reply to Arnauld's question. In terms of his own position, and in terms of reasonable approaches at his time, it is true that a mind-body substance dualism was not unexpected or inappropriate. Scholastics, as Christian thinkers, had somehow to allow for this possibility, and Descartes certainly believed he was clarifying and purifying the position they ought to hold. However, if we consider the two old-fashioned criteria for a metaphysics, we need not only coherence, but also adequacy. And when a strict mind-body dualism is applied to the concrete life of emotions —where, I believe, Descartes would never have bothered to apply it had it not been for Elizabeth's urging—it turns out to be inadequate. This inadequacy appears to me to become evident in the text of *The Passions* itself, and particularly in the letters Descartes wrote to the Marquis of Newcastle (probably) and to Henry More, in which his embarrassment on the subject of animal mechanism—the alleged foundation for his theory of the passions, as he tells Elizabeth—

becomes apparent. As mathematical physicist, and serene pursuer of truth, he had no problems; but thrust him into the mire of emotion and he doesn't come out so well. So I wasn't saying dualism was a doomed enterprise in the seventeenth century; it wasn't necessary—witness the philosophies of others, like Spinoza or Leibniz, who could deal with thought as against extension without admitting two kinds of substances. But it was a position one might well have taken—and Descartes took it, I believe, not only as a good Catholic with faith in immortality, but as a seeker after the truth about nature, which he believed could be achieved only by a mathematical mind freed from bodily entanglements to contemplate the truths of geometry and therewith of physics.

About Clarke's account of Cartesian explanation for the phenomena of extended nature, I have little to say. I do confess, however, to being persuaded by what seems to be the authoritative reading of Cartesian science by Daniel Garber in his *Descartes' Metaphysical Physics.* I don't believe Garber quite turns Descartes into an occasionalist, but he does show, as I believe the texts do, that Descartes can only introduce forces, or powers, into his extended universe by invoking the power of God.

Never mind that disagreement. What really astonishes me is the move Clarke makes to invoke mind, as consciousness, at, or beyond, the limit of explanation. Surely for Descartes mind is the *sine qua non* of explanation, its very ground, its unique foundation. What is the message of the *Meditations*? The aim of that document is, its author himself tells us, to lead the mind away from the senses, to liberate mind from subjective moments of consciousness, like being now in pain, or seeing something bright or dim, or feeling something hard or soft. As he will make plain in the *Principles*, sensation, this bit of consciousness here and now, has validity only insofar as I recognize its sheer subjectivity, its irrelevance to clear and distinct thought, to the kind of knowledge that the meditator, like Descartes himself, is seeking to achieve. True, the *cogito* is a momentary occurrence, but of what? Of the thought of myself as *res cogitans*, which in turn prepares me for the thought of God's existence, a thought I have in fact had from birth by my very God-given nature. It allows me, too, to recognize other ideas I have always had: that two and two are four, or that the three angles of a triangle equal two right angles. God's veridicity, once I recognize it, or recognize that I have always known it, will in turn allow me to know bodies in their geometrical nature—while the tastes and sights and smells and feels that belong to my everyday consciousness will be given the merely practical significance that is all they merit. The piece of wax, remember, is not known by my consciousness of its (changing) size or color or temperature or odor or taste, but by my intellectual grasp of what it is to be a flexible piece of extension. Even if there are no bodies to induce sensations in me, that is what I know. And without that kind of intellection I couldn't explain anything, other than in the muddled infantile, scholastic way that is, as Clarke points out, occult, redundant, and confused. What matters here is not some secret, inner, inexplicable consciousness, but ideation, thought, clear and distinct ideas applicable by the mathematicizing mind to a geometrical universe. Mind comes, not where explanation fails, but before it, making it possible.

True, what matters, as Clarke points out, is not just what we know, but the agency through which we know it. Cartesian clear and distinct ideas, like the intuitions of the *Rules*, are both thoughts and objects of thought. But those thoughts are *acts* of thinking, not little bits of feeling, like being in pain, that are passivities, almost bereft of meaning, certainly irrelevant for the great enterprise of building Cartesian science—not beyond explanation, but immaterial to it.

Clarke refers us to the famous dictum in the correspondence with Elizabeth, to the effect that it is difficult to know at one and the same time the substantial separateness of mind and body and their substantial union in this life. But Clarke seems to have the situation here just backwards: "things," he says, "may be composite from the point of view of our knowledge even though, in reality, they are singular and unified." But surely the situation for Descartes is that we know clearly and distinctly that mind and body are distinct, and, given God's unwillingness to deceive us (except when, for practical purposes, he finds he has to!), we can assert this is how it really is; while on the other hand we have a muddled sense of union, which has to guide us through our time in this vale of tears, but does not correspond to how things really are. Mind and body are really separate, but we live with them as a unity. In reality, they are not singular and unified; we are only constrained to feel that way. And once more, feeling is no guide to truth.

To justify his turn to consciousness at the limit of explanation, Clarke invokes that ever recurrent Nagelian bat. What it's like to be a bat, however, is surely a twentieth-, not a seventeenth-century, question—and it is presumably the seventeenth-century context Clarke has in mind. I don't know how this turn to subjectivity came about—perhaps starting from Fichte's reading of Hume. In its recent shape, it seems to me, as I have remarked elsewhere in the answers to my critics, to be a reaction against the search for an impossible pure objectivity, adding a secret inner something to the wholly, one-level, external, meaningless out-there-ness we believed science was looking for. I have never subscribed to this argument, and I don't know why Professor Clarke thinks I did. The irreducibility of mind to matter, or to brain, is not, in my view, to be found along this path.

Nor, about Clarke's principles of PPS and PATE, do I know how I am supposed to stand in respect to them. If I regret the implications for our understanding of ourselves and of nature of the primary/secondary quality distinction, it is not because I am dwelling on the "phenomenological" uniqueness of color, for example, but because (as I have tried to explain both in the last chapter of my *Descartes* and in my *Philosophical Testament*) I believe we need a new and truly revolutionary approach to perception, which sees that process as the result of an embodied being's location of itself in its environment, and also as the foundational form of knowledge, whose structure is mirrored in more sophisticated forms of cognition. That's quite a different story. And I have never (at least consciously!!) worried for a moment about a sufficiency or otherwise of theoretical entities.

To return for a moment from consciousness to dualism—which, as Perovich, for example, acknowledges, is a separate problem (most present-day consciousness-touters claim not to be dualists)—as I said earlier, I should not have called dualism in a seventeenth-century context incoherent. Again, in my own late twentieth-century or early twenty-first-century terms, I find it inconceivable. And defending the status of the human person against reductivist arguments of the mind-equals-brain type, it is not to subjectivity that I find it fruitful to appeal. I have said enough about that already, both in this volume and elsewhere. In this respect, I find myself, astonishingly, in agreement with Descartes: whatever is important about mind (or, as Ryle put it, minding), it is not bits of conscious feeling.

M. G.

20

Kathleen Blamey

PASCAL AND DESCARTES

In numerous works, Marjorie Grene has vividly presented both the allure of Descartes for the modern mind, intent on establishing a firm foundation for knowledge, and the dangers stemming from this very project, which has limited and divided the intellectual orientation of Western philosophy, in its Continental and Insular forms.[1] In "The Errors of Descartes" Grene offers a short list of principles evoked by Descartes in the early elaboration of his philosophy, which she considers to be fundamental to his enterprise, describing them more specifically as fundamental mistakes which misdirect our understanding of the nature of human knowledge, the character of scientific investigation, and even the grasp we have of our being. Such false starts in the arenas of epistemology and ontology cannot fail to entangle Descartes's successors in all sorts of unhappy, not to say unfruitful, undertakings. Although the starting point is crucial in all philosophical work, in the case of Descartes—preoccupied with discovering an absolutely firm Archimedean point and a criterion of indubitability—the starting point determines rigorously what is and what is not the province of investigation. This clear delineation of proper subject matter (what can be known to me clearly and self-evidently) and of the precise steps to be taken (the method—*methodos*, the path to be followed) in extracting this knowledge casts the philosopher in the role of disembodied mind and the results of her investigation in the guise of conceptual atoms of geometrical science, each idea luminously clear, self-contained, and universally self-evident.

The establishment of Cartesian philosophy, in its reliance on the model of geometrical clarity, is often explained on the basis of the historical conjunction in the seventeenth century of the development of the "new science," mathematical physics, and the rejection of Scholasticism and its Aristotelian models by philosopher-mathematicians, like Descartes and, later, Leibniz. Recognizing the power and rigorousness of mathematics, while lamenting the narrowness of its sphere of application, Descartes sets out in the *Discourse on Method* to extend its model of clarity and universality to the entire range of philosophical investigation. Or, looking at the matter the other way around, he limits the province of philosophy to that range of ideas that are presented to the attentive mind in accordance with these criteria. So, the story goes, seventeenth-century rationalism, defining itself in terms of the transparency and universality of mathematics, becomes the model for philosophical thought, the standard for scientific knowledge, and erects the framework for the, henceforth, irreparable split between mind and body.

Sketching the period in such broad strokes fails, of course, to describe the turmoil of activity, the leaps of discovery in physics and in mathematics, the fear of official rebuke and interdiction (works are hidden away, passed in secret from hand to hand), and the great controversies in every area of scientific and intellectual endeavor. We know that to avoid such distractions and to pursue his investigations along the path he has outlined, Descartes lived most of his adult life outside of France, away from the society of his compatriots. To this self-imposed exile, we owe the wealth of Descartes's correspondence from Germany and Holland, which helps us form a rich picture of the stages in Descartes's own work as he describes his efforts in these letters. That the seventeenth century was not all of a piece in its views of philosophy, science, religion, or politics is brought out in Grene's discussions of a number of Descartes's contemporaries in her book *Descartes*; dissenters include the scholastic philosophers, and especially the authors of certain objections raised in response to the *Meditations*—Hobbes, Gassendi, and Arnaud. The English materialist, the cleric who was both a Lucretian atomist and an experimental scientist, and the Port-Royal theologian and logician all address their concerns and critiques to Descartes, with responses on the part of the author of the *Meditations* varying from exasperation (with Hobbes) to respectful appreciation (directed to Arnaud). All this is to say that, even in Descartes's own time, there was no unanimity among his contemporaries in the sciences, in mathematics, and in philosophy, on many of the "fundamental" points on which his philosophical work rested.

Let us look at one of Descartes's contemporaries—a younger contemporary, if one likes—who was himself prominent as a mathematician, who practiced experimental science, and who, while reserving the term "philosopher" for the extreme forms of rationalism and skepticism, nevertheless, remains a thinker, a seeker after knowledge and truth, bestowing upon us his posthumous *Pensées*. Blaise Pascal's first encounter with Descartes, on the common terrain of mathematics, during Descartes's visit to Paris in 1647, produced little in the way of mutual sympathy. Instead, the publication the following year of Pascal's experiments on the vacuum, in which he verifies Torricelli's hypothesis, drove the two men farther apart. Pascal's claim that "Nature has no abhorrence for a vacuum" was not simply an experimental result that differed from the one predicted by Descartes. Rather, it pointed to a direct confrontation between their respective views of the nature of knowledge in the sciences and its metaphysical underpinnings. The first obvious difference lies in the fact that Pascal conducted these experiments himself, with the help of his father and the mathematician Pierre Petit, a friend of Gassendi, and later with his brother-in-law, Florian Périer; and these experiments were conducted repeatedly, in Rouen, at the Puy-de-Dôme, and at the Tour Saint-Jacques in Paris. Descartes, who was known to have worked on other experiments—and even to plead, in the *Discourse on Method*, for the help of assistants to aid him in his work[2]—was satisfied in the matter of the vacuum, however, to analyze and interpret the results of others. This was because, more significantly, while Pascal was searching for experimental confirmation or infirmation of Torricelli's hypothesis, Descartes's formulation of the object of scientific investigation had already, it can be argued, eliminated by definition the existence of a vacuum. The division into thinking and extended substance, into mind and body, identifies matter—as extended substance—with extension in space. In his *Principles of Philosophy*, Descartes provides the framework for the rejection of the notion of a vacuum by positing extension as the principal attribute of bodies:

> A substance may indeed be known through any attribute at all; but each substance has one principal property which constitutes its nature and essence, and to which all its other properties are referred. Thus extension in length, breadth and depth constitutes the nature of corporeal substance; and thought constitutes the nature of thinking substance.[3]

A vacuum, the void, is excluded, not on the basis of experimental results and their interpretation, but by the very foundation of Cartesian physics; it is not so much that Nature "abhors a vacuum" as that Nature *is* extended, corporeal substance, standing over and against thinking substance—unextended, incorporeal. There is no room in the natural world for "empty" space, extended and lacking bodies. This opposition between Descartes and Pascal, occurring on the level of experimental science, reflects a clear and pervasive philosophical difference between them. Pascal's own work can serve as a guide to illuminate and respond to the failings of Cartesian philosophy, enumerated in Grene's "Errors of Descartes."

The power and audacity of Cartesian philosophy is evident in the challenge it continues to present to those who would refute it, surpass it, or evade its oppositions (subject/object, mind/body). Nietzsche fragments, disperses the *cogito*; Heidegger dispenses with a starting point in subjectivity; Wittgenstein eclipses the dualisms of mind and body, self and world. It is in the history of French philosophy, however, that the influence of Descartes has been most strongly felt and most intensely resisted. While the work of Jean-Paul Sartre presented a twentieth-century Cartesianism in which the nothingness of consciousness erupts against the backdrop of being, thick and opaque, Maurice Merleau-Ponty challenged this dualism by demonstrating the intelligence of the lived body and the ineradicable corporeality of human thinking. Closer to our own time, a number of contemporary philosophers, recognizing the Cartesian framework which continues to structure modes of thinking, methods of analysis, and the very language of philosophical discourse, have turned to the work of Blaise Pascal, which points out the "errors of Descartes," and in confronting them sets philosophical inquiry along different, and likely more fruitful, paths. I am referring here in particular to recent works by Cathérine Chevalley, *Pascal: Contingence et probabilités*; Pierre Bourdieu, *Méditations pascaliennes*; and Louis Marin, *Pascal et Port-Royal*.[4]

In "The Errors of Descartes," Grene examines what she considers the "four theses, which, taken together, constitute the core of Descartes's theory of knowledge and method."[5] Grene follows the presentation of these theses in the *Rules for the Direction of the Mind*, but they are also the foundation of the philosophical method of the *Discourse*, of the first philosophy of the *Meditations*, and the enumeration of *The Principles of Philosophy*. They are: "the principles of (1) indubitability, (2) self-evidence or total explicitness, (3) the unity of science, (4) the duality of man. These four principles are not isolated; they form a structure."[6] The interconnectedness of these principles is, of course, apparent in the systematic nature of Cartesian philosophy, but it is also an important factor in the critique of any one of the four theses, which will have significant repercussions for the other three. I propose, then, to examine each of the four Cartesian theses presented by Grene and to show, in light of recent readings of the work of Pascal, that the "errors of Descartes" were already in conflict with the "Pascalian meditations" which provide a response in keeping with Grene's views of knowledge and the human person.

FIRST THESIS: INDUBITABILITY

The first principle, that of indubitability, is essential to the Cartesian enterprise because it allows a starting point for philosophy. The search for an initial certainty is described in *The Discourse on Method* and in the *Meditations on First Philosophy* in vivid, autobiographical terms. The systematic extension of doubt from sensory experience, to reasoning, and to our awareness of the distinction between sleeping and waking in the *Discourse*, is carried to what could be considered the extreme of skepticism in the *Meditations*, with the proposal of an evil genius, a Great Deceiver, complete with divine powers, against whom Descartes nonetheless remains resolute and steadfast in his power to withhold his assent. Descartes's search for an Archimedean point in *Meditation Two*, one firm and fixed point, "one thing, however slight, that is certain and unshakeable,"[7] is the pivot that will shift the philosopher from the furthest point of skepticism to the firm certainty of the dogmatist, whose philosophy is built upon unshakable first principles. Grene's dissatisfaction with the thesis of indubitability is that it fails to allow for the necessity of criticism, of revision and reworking, in the construction of all knowledge. Meeting the criterion of certainty provides, in the Cartesian view of science, a ground upon which to continue to build, with no need—ever—to look back upon what has been acquired, the only question being that of the next element of certainty, the next stage in the tower of knowledge. The images that proliferate in Descartes's writings concern razing the old, cluttered, jerry-rigged structures of the past and their replacement, from the foundation up, with rationally designed, securely anchored constructions, built through the efforts of a single, disciplined mind.

In the writings of Pascal, the search for knowledge is also central—whether in mathematics, the physical sciences, or the vastly more complex undertaking of the knowledge of the self and of others. If the Cartesian search is focused on establishing *certain* knowledge, the Pascalian quest is establishing the conditions and limits of *human* knowledge, knowledge compatible with our being, as social, historical, and biological creatures. Human knowledge is conditioned by our mediate status, described by Pascal in his *Pensées*, in the fragment on the disproportion of human beings in relation to the natural world.[8] This celebrated fragment places us between two infinites. On the one hand, we are placed against the vastness of the universe (in relation to which we can only acknowledge our insignificance or, more precisely, the absence of any determinant relation or proportion). On the other hand, we peer into the vertiginous hole of the "infinitely small," seeking some furthest point, some smallest unit that would be the stopping point in this regression to nothingness. This disproportion is not only that of physical size, of course, but also refers to the incapacity of the human mind to grasp the beginning and end of things, first principles or ultimate ends.

> For finally what is man in nature? A nothing in relation to the infinite, an all in relation to nothing, a mean between nothing and everything, infinitely removed from comprehending the extremes, the end of things and their principle are, for him, invincibly hidden in an impenetrable secret (*what then shall he be*

able to conceive?). He is equally incapable of seeing the nothingness out of which he was drawn and the infinite, which engulfs him.[9]

In a sense, it is our desire for knowledge that is directed toward these two extremes: to know all, the totality of things, and to pierce to the ultimate foundation of what is. Pascal considers this a form of *hubris* characteristic of philosophers:

> For having failed to contemplate these infinites, men have rashly pursued the investigation of nature, as if they had some proportion to it.
>   It is strange that they wanted to understand the principles of things, and from there to arrive at knowledge of the whole, with a presumption as infinite as their object.[10]

To read this passage as a reproach directed to Descartes is strengthened by the mention, in the same fragment, of *The Principles of Philosophy* as an example of the attempt of philosophers to arrive at an ultimate starting point. And Pascal recognizes that the claim of mastering the beginning is at the same time a pretension to knowledge of the whole:

> And it seems to me that whosoever is held to have understood the ultimate principles of things would also be able to arrive at a knowledge of the infinite. The one depends upon the other, and one leads to the other.[11]

However, the beginning and end of all things is not the province of human knowledge; they would be comprehended only in the mind of a supreme being. Instead, Pascal argues, let us accept our lot:

> Let us then know our reach: we are something and we are not everything. The being we possess hides from us knowledge of first principles, which are born out of nothing. And the slight being that we do have conceals from us the view of the infinite.
>   Our intellect holds the same rank in the order of intelligible things as our body in the extendedness of nature.[12]

Our inability to reach the terms of the two directions in which we are pulled does not mean that we occupy a *center*, either physically or intellectually. A center would provide a focus, a stable viewpoint from which to organize experience and knowledge. But, this stable point, according to Pascal, is not to be found in

> our true state. This is what makes us incapable of certain knowledge and of absolute ignorance. We are floating on a vast sea, always uncertain and drifting, blown from end to end. When we think to attach ourselves to some end and make it fast, it shakes loose and leaves us. And if we follow after it, it

escapes our grasp, slips away and flees for all time. Nothing stops for us, and this is our natural state, yet just the opposite of our inclination. We burn with a desire to find firm ground and an ultimate sure base upon which to construct a tower that rises to infinity, but our entire foundation cracks and the earth opens up to the abysses.

Let us therefore not look for certainty and stability.[13]

The situation described by Pascal cannot be set aside by means of abstraction or other intellectual strategies; it is the condition of our being ("C'est sortir de l'humanité que de sortir du milieu")[14] and, as Cathérine Chevalley emphasizes,[15] it is a condition of our knowledge as well. Pascal's conception of knowledge is rooted in two ideas, Chevalley argues: first, that human beings are "middle beings" (*êtres de milieu*), which leads Pascal "to recognize the impossibility of perfect knowledge," and second, that human beings are "composite beings" (*êtres composés*), by which he "recognizes the anthropological character of all human knowledge."[16] By the second point, Pascal at once underscores and refuses the dichotomy of mind and body, thought and extension (this aspect will be discussed further under the final thesis: *duality*). Let us simply state here, following Chevalley, that this composite nature, which permeates all aspects of human experience, is also not amenable to abstraction or to some sort of *epoché*. Unlike Descartes, for whom the pure knowledge of simple natures is not only possible but necessary if philosophy is to begin, Pascal affirms over and over "we are composed of spirit and of matter; we cannot know perfectly simple things whether spiritual or corporeal."[17] While certainty is not within our scope, this does not mean that Pascal despairs of human knowledge as such. Pascal's discussions of mathematical demonstration, the work of the physical experimental sciences, the practice that is the object of the human sciences, and the task of self-knowledge confirm his rejection of the second Cartesian thesis, concerning the luminous self-evidence of the content of intellectual vision.

Second Thesis: Self-evidence or Total Explicitness

The natural light by which the mind of Descartes sees the first truths, those things conceived "very clearly and very distinctly,"[18] is displayed to best advantage in the demonstrations of geometricians. Here, each step, simple and evident, can be displayed to the mind's eye, which perceives it fully and completely. According to the mathematical model represented in the method, the total explicitness of knowledge directly follows, there being "only one truth concerning any matter [so that] whoever discovers this truth knows as much about it as can be known."[19] The comprehensive character of knowledge—when we know, we know all there is to know and so can move on—may be best illustrated in the domain of mathematics,[20] but as a principle it will apply to the entire range of knowledge. Mathematics is not apart from but is the very substance of the physical world. In the *Fifth Meditation*, after securing the existence of God as the guarantor of the truth of every science, Descartes affirms that "now it is possible for me to achieve full and certain knowledge of countless matters, both concerning God himself and other things whose nature is intellectual, and also concerning the whole of corporeal nature which is the subject-matter of pure mathematics."[21]

Here Pascal and Descartes part ways. As was indicated briefly above, Pascal's experimentation on barometric pressure and his attempt to reproduce Torricelli's results confirm his distance from a deductive style of physics. In the passage from the *Meditations* cited above, Descartes links the certainty of my idea of myself with the certainty of God's existence, and following from that, the necessity of the truth of whatever I perceive clearly and distinctly, just as I perceive the object of pure mathematics. Pascal rejects this linkage and its use to provide a supposed theological foundation for the new mathematical physics. Pascal substitutes a three-phase analysis of the infinite for Descartes's ontological argument, which holds that I know that God exists because I know that the infinite exists (although I cannot comprehend its nature). In *Pensées*, Pascal maintains that our capacity to recognize the concept of infinity and even to manipulate it, for example in mathematics, does not imply in any way that we can know the existence or the nature of God. Our knowledge is not of first principles or final ends, knowledge that would be certain or pure. Instead we possess an understanding of those things with which we have some relation. This is why we cannot reason from our own condition to the existence of God, as the guarantor of the laws of nature and the truth of our apprehensions: "Let us speak now according to natural lights. If there is a God, he is infinitely incomprehensible, since having neither parts nor limits, he is without any relation to us."[22]

Descartes's metaphysical foundation allows a knowledge of essences, and the clear distinction between thinking substance and extended substance. For Pascal, as we have seen, our composite nature excludes knowledge of such separate essences. While Descartes places physics in the realm of pure mathematics, Pascal considers physics as a science based on proposing, confirming, and refuting hypotheses, an endeavor grounded in contingency and historicality. Chevalley presents an analysis of Pascal's physics of the void, as a "human science," that is a science that respects the general limitations of human knowledge, a science of experimentation and the generation of hypotheses, and one that makes no reference to the notion of universal or necessary law. Pascal's physical science dissociates geometrical concepts and methods from those of physics. If geometry is deductive, physics is "ostensive"; ostensive physics parts ways with Cartesianism as much as with Aristotelianism. In each of Pascal's four scientific treatises, *les Expériences nouvelles touchant le vide*, the *Récit de la grande expérience de l'équilibre des liqueurs*, and the two *Traités de l'équilibre des liqueurs et de la pesanteur de la masse de l'air*,

> the usual deductive exposition of the treatises of natural philosophy is replaced by a presentation based on visibility: it is a matter of showing the instruments used, of relating the experiments conducted, drawing a few "maxims" or "propositions" and of basing on these propositions . . . an hypothesis. It is not a question of defining space, light, or movement (but of carefully describing the equipment employed and the results obtained).[23]

Having separated physical properties from geometrical principles, Pascal is unencumbered by the seemingly contradictory concept of the void, of extension that contains no bodies. Chevalley shows that Pascal firmly responds to the objection of his correspondent, Etienne Noel, who argues that, as the empty space in the tube possesses length, width, and depth, it *must* thereby be a material body. This argument, Pascal insists, confuses "dimensions with matter . . . immateriality with nothingness."[24] The condition for the development of physics as an autonomous discipline is the recognition that it is not a province of pure mathematics but an experimental science, a science of hypotheses permitting multiple explanations, and requiring constant revision over time.

Just as the first thesis, indubitability, is closely tied to the second, self-evidence or total explicitness; so too the second thesis is bound up with the third, the unity of science. We have already seen that Pascal's challenge to a presumed self-evident starting point for knowledge also involves the renunciation of a single method of investigation and the claim to universality. The science of nature and the science of geometry require different approaches and refer to separate domains of experience, as Pascal makes clear in his division of the three orders. Although there is, Pascal recognizes, an *esprit de géométrie*, characterized by the philosopher-mathematician, this is an approach with strict limits on its effectiveness and usefulness—while beyond it lies *"Descartes inutile et incertain."*[25]

THIRD THESIS: UNITY OF SCIENCE

In Descartes's writings, the disciplined exercise of thinking, following the proper order of reason, provides the stable criterion for knowledge. The philosopher moves from the mathematical model of simplicity and clarity to the definition of the natural world as extended substance, which, as knowable, corresponds to the object of pure mathematics. The scope of knowledge is unlimited, to the extent that each step secures a further atom of evidence. Knowledge is one because reason, the activity of the intellect, is universal, the same for all who employ it but also the same in every area of investigation. Grene points out, in this regard, that the Cartesian distinction between the identity of cognitive activity and the diversity of physical or manual activities is the inevitable result of the claim that, in the search for truth, the mind is set apart, cut off from its association with a body.

> Science, he held, is everywhere simply the light of reason and as such is one, in contrast to the multiplicity of arts or skills. But again, analogously, we shall insist that just because it has a tacit core . . . , knowledge is, on the contrary, essentially skill-like, and, like skills, therefore necessarily diversified.[26]

Pascal's response to the question of the unity or diversity of knowledge falls plainly on the side of multiplicity. Human experience includes a number of different spheres which cannot be fruitfully explored from a single viewpoint or by means of a single instrument of analysis. This division appears most broadly in Pascal's distinction between the *esprit de géométrie* and the *esprit de finesse*. The *esprit de géométrie* characterizes Descartes's thinking substance; it is the mathematically adept mind that begins with definitions and first principles and proceeds in a rigorously deductive manner. In his treatise, *De l'esprit géométrique*, Pascal recognizes the power and methodical nature of geometrical demonstrations: this is the domain in which we can speak of certainty and can state rules that will allow us to avoid error. However, even here, the principles on which geometry is founded are not themselves demonstrated, nor are its primitive terms defined:

> if this science does not define and does not demonstrate everything, it is for the sole reason that this is impossible for us . . . its order of truth does not provide a superhuman perfection, but rather all that to which human beings can aspire.[27]

The principles on which the rational constructions of geometrical demonstrations are built are not themselves the products of reason. These principles, just as our starting points in all endeavors, result instead from our unreflective, contingent mode of being—what Pascal terms instinct or heart: "Our soul is thrown into the body, where it finds number, time, dimensions. It reasons upon this basis and calls this nature, necessity, and can believe nothing else."[28] The two passages quoted point to a number of important distinctions by which Pascal attempts better to understand the contradictions and contrarieties that make up the human person. In reasoning or understanding we find the opposition between the *esprit de géométrie*, the mathematical mind, which seeks univocal definitions for its terms and strict rules of method in order to proceed, and the *esprit de finesse*, the subtle, nuanced, intuitive mind, which follows a witty conversation or makes judicious choices in the complex situation of social and political life. The mathematical mind functions smoothly in its own area, but falters in a domain of experience in which all the elements cannot be rendered entirely explicit.

> [Mathematicians] accustomed to the precise and plain principles of geometry and not reasoning until they have well inspected and arranged their principles, are lost in things of *finesse*, where the principles do not permit being ordered in this way. . . . These principles are so fine and so numerous that a very delicate and clear sense is needed to perceive them and to judge rightly and justly when they are perceived, without for the most part being able to demonstrate them in order as in geometry . . . And thus it is rare that geometricians are *fins* (subtle, nuanced) . . . because geometricians want to treat matters of *finesse* mathematically, and make themselves ridiculous, wanting to begin with definitions and then with principles, which is not the way to proceed in this kind of reasoning. Not that the mind does not do so, but it does it tacitly, naturally, and artlessly for the expression of it surpasses all men and only a few are able to feel it.[29]

There are corresponding limitations on those proficient only in matters of *finesse*, for they lack the patience necessary to arrive at the first principles of things; used to taking things in at a single glance, they are "repelled and disheartened" by the processes of analysis that explain each step by means of definitions and axioms. These two kinds of reasoning do not overlap in some middle ground, nor can they, in human experience, be synthesized into some higher form.

The importance of distinguishing separate forms of reasoning, each appropriate in its own domain and inaccurate and purposeless when applied outside of it, is compounded by another Pascalian division: what he terms "the three orders." This threefold distinction refers not only to forms of knowledge or modes of apprehension, but to realms of experience. The three are named in a number of different ways: the first order is that of sense experience, termed body or flesh. It is the sphere of sensation, of both the pleasures and mortifications of the body, of worldly goods, and public glory. It is also the domain of the natural world and includes the natural sciences. The second order is that of the mind, the achievements and delusions of the intellect. It includes human intellectual creations and abstract sciences, such as mathematics, whose objects are not real entities, but conceptual constructs. The third order is the most elusive; it is the domain of the will, instinct, or feeling—sometimes termed "heart," and most frequently referred to as the order of charity.

The division into three orders separates regions of experience, to which different strategies of exploration apply, in which different measures of achievement or success are recognized and different kinds of error and delusion become apparent. Descartes, for example, recognized the errors of the senses but failed to see the errors associated with the claims of reason. His exaggeration of the one way, *methodos*, to follow, which alone will provide the useful and certain knowledge he seeks, appears from the perspective of Pascal's distinction to be a form of tyranny, the tyranny of the second order—the geometrical mind—"which seeks to attain by one path what one can only attain by another."[30] "Tyranny," Pascal writes in the section on human *Misery*, "consists in the desire for universal domination outside of one's order."[31]

In Pascal's own search for knowledge in the physical sciences, he relies upon this division between the orders. Cathérine Chevally's insightful study of Pascal's conception of science, as activity and form of knowing, emphasizes that in his work there is

> no all-embracing theory of knowledge in the strict sense, no single mode of knowledge sufficiently general to provide access to all of the regions of experience. Rather, to the idea of a science that is one in its method and necessary in its foundation, Pascal opposes a series of pragmatic attitudes in which method is determined by the kind of experience that is involved.[32]

In accordance with the division into the three orders, physics belongs to the first order, that of the natural world, while mathematics is placed in the second order, that of the intellect and its creations. Both of these are separate from the domain of charity, in which knowledge of God is possible because it stems from love of God. In this way, the supports for Descartes's unified system of knowledge are struck down: for Pascal, one can move to God neither starting from nature nor starting from mathematics. In the same manner, the distinction of the three orders makes it just as impossible to move from mathematics, or from God, to the corporeal world.[33] It is this separation that allowed Pascal to proceed with his experiments in physics without relying on the notion of universal and necessary laws. The natural sciences proceed on the basis of confirming and refuting hypotheses. As such the natural sciences are contingent and historical. They belong to the first order, while mathematics, dealing with things abstract and immaterial, belongs to the second. Finally, the type of knowledge obtained through these investigations is not knowledge of the essence or nature of things, but knowledge of relations. For example, what changes occur in the materials used in the experiments on barometric pressure, when we move them from one altitude to another? A further consequence of Pascal's distrust of the extreme or absolute positions that characterize the tyranny of the second order is his practice of composing contraries—what we are in the habit of placing at opposite poles: knowledge and ignorance, glory and misery, matter and nothingness. Since, for Pascal, we can only know that with which we have some relation, a shift in that relation, a change of perspective, will provide a different view, making new relations emerge. This does not imply, Chevalley insists, that all perspectives, in theory, converge on some underlying essence or confirm an immutable truth regarding a proposition or the nature of a thing.[34] Instead, in Pascal's investigations, the opposition between something and nothing gives way to the notion of empty space, the existence of the void. So, too, will chance and necessity lend themselves to the play of *pour au contre*, to the composition of contraries, in Pascal's work in the geometry of chance, what will come to be called the theory of probability, in which the uncertainty of chance combines with the demonstrative power of mathematics.

FOURTH THESIS: MIND-BODY DUALISM

The appeal of Pascal for many contemporary philosophers lies, precisely, in his dismantling and supersession of Cartesian dualism. It is indeed the fourth thesis, the mind-body dualism which, Grene states, underlies all the others, since "were the mind not cleanly and essentially separate from the body in nature and function, the whole programme would collapse."[35] The opposition of mind and body, subject and object, continues to provide the framework for much frustrating and unproductive debate. Pascal, in fact, characterizes philosophical discussion as a sort of battlefield where the opposing sides attack each other's weaknesses, resulting in the general destruction of both camps: "one establishing certainty, the other doubt; one the greatness of man, the other his weakness, each destroys the truths as well as the falsehoods of the other."[36] Competing viewpoints are lodged in different perspectives on the human condition, on the powers of our cognitive faculties, and on the origin of our conceptions of science and objectivity. How can we escape these confrontations, in which "neither side can remain standing because of its errors, nor unite with the other because of their oppositions, so that they break one another up and are mutually annihilated"?[37]

These are the issues that Pierre Bourdieu deals with in his *Méditations pascaliennes*, where he takes the author of *Les Pensées* as his guide in navigating between the Scylla and Charybdis of traditional polar opposites. Bourdieu heeds Pascal's warning of the two dangers, two temptations to be avoided: we tend toward "two excesses: excluding reason, admitting only reason."[38] The second alternative leads to establishing reason as the self-grounding principle of knowledge. It posits a fixed and universal standpoint for an observer who is separate, detached from the object of investigation. This sovereign viewpoint Bourdieu identifies with Cartesian rationalism. The former excess, equally to be avoided, is the turn toward irrationalism, with its surreptitious link to dogmatic rationalism and the fear that if knowledge is not grounded in certainty and universality, then we can know nothing at all. Pascal's description of our position in the physical universe—"we are something, but we are not everything"—applies as well to the situation of human knowledge—we can know some things well, with clarity, and even with varying degrees of assurance, but we cannot know everything, nor can the knowledge we acquire simply be filed away as the unassailable product of natural light. The knowledge we do construct must be capable of revision, re-examination; and the philosopher should be in the forefront, reflecting on the conditions and limits of thought and its powers. Pascal, according to Bourdieu, challenges the fixed and universal viewpoint of Cartesian reason, by which "the philosopher . . . freely considers himself to be *atopos*, unsituated, uncategorizable," whereas he is "just like everyone, included within the space he claims to comprehend."[39] When Descartes proclaims the real distinction of mind and body, he places the thinking subject outside spatial and temporal relations.

In place of the detachment and sovereign viewpoint of the *ego cogito*, Pascal provides us not with a new dualism, but with what Bourdieu in his chapter, "Knowledge Through the Body," terms a "double inclusion." Bourdieu cites

> a very beautiful Pascalian formulation that leads us directly beyond the alternative of objectivism and subjectivism: " . . . by space, the universe encompasses me (*me comprend*) and swallows me up as a point; by thought, I comprehend it." The world encompasses me (*me comprend*), includes me as a thing among things; but as a thing for which there are things, a world, I encompass (*je comprends*) this world . . . The "I" which practically comprehends physical and social space (subject of the verb to comprehend, it is not necessarily a "subject" in the sense of philosophies of consciousness, but rather a *habitus*, a system of dispositions) is comprehended, in an entirely different sense, that is to say, encompassed, inscribed, implicated in this space.[40]

This relation of "double inclusion" is at work in all of the seeming paradoxes presented by Pascal in his reflections on human misery and greatness, on the complex structure of the social order (the nobles and the people), and the constant reversal of traditional oppositions such as nature and custom.[41]

In his *Méditations pascaliennes*, Bourdieu recognizes the impasse of these traditional oppositions, which he views as complementary errors: subjectivism and objectivism, mechanism and finalism. Knowledge through the body does not take as its locus an isolated intentional consciousness; it is a form of practical knowledge through which the subject of action, including cognitive activities, appears as the result of a biological, historical, social process of individualization. Referring to Pascal's "double inclusion," Bourdieu ties this practical knowledge of the world to the reciprocal play of comprehension, encompassing and being encompassed:

> if the agent has an immediate understanding of the familiar world, it is because the cognitive structures employed are the product of the incorporation of the structures of the world in which he acts, because the tools of construction he uses to know the world are constructed by the world. These practical principles of organization of the given are constructed on the basis of the experience of situations frequently encountered and are capable of being revised and rejected in the event of repeated failure.[42]

The relation of double inclusion is credited with placing us beyond the alternative of thing and consciousness, mechanistic materialism and constructivist idealism. It allows us to avoid both errors:

> on the one hand, mechanism, which maintains that action is the mechanical effect of the constraint of external causes; on the other, finalism, which, notably with the theory of rational action, maintains that the agent acts in a free and conscious manner, with full understanding. . . . [43]

The overcoming of Cartesian dualism is a primary motive for the turn to Pascal by contemporary philosophers. This appeal also includes the absence of a universal ground for the construction of knowledge, whether of the natural or social world. For Bourdieu, Pascal offers the "revocation of the ambition of [establishing] a foundation."[44] Indeed, Pascal's admonition that we are embarked, caught up in engagements and interests that we have not explicitly initiated or consciously selected, presents the viewpoint of the social sciences, which Bourdieu contrasts with the universalist claims of Cartesian rationalism: these are sciences "that cannot presume to have a foundation in reason, but are through and through historical sciences [and as such] defeat any foundational claims. They remind us that everything is historical, even our common cognitive dispositions."[45] From this perspective Bourdieu undertakes a critique of abstract universalism, in which he examines the historical conditions of the emergence of the concept of scientific rationality and the significance of the distinction between the theoretical and the practical.

As we saw earlier, it is Pascal also who provides a physics and a system of mathematics free from the appeal to universal laws of nature or to a prior ground of certainty. Chevalley sheds light on this distinction between Cartesian and Pascalian science: whereas, for Descartes,

> the ideal of a unitary, certain knowledge, rooted in the evidence of intuition and universal validity . . . implies the recourse to an external guarantee of universality and necessity of the "laws of Nature" . . . [in Pascal], Geometry (arithmetic, geometry and mechanics) is a discourse that is rooted neither in "the essence of things," nor in our "natural sentiment," but rests on consensus regarding definitions; instead of deriving from the evidence of intuition, truth is obtained here through demonstrating the falsity of the contrary of a given proposition.[46]

For the unity of Cartesian method, Pascal substitutes a plurality of practices, suited to the domain of experience at hand. The strategies of exploration and organization dispel the illusion of an isolated system that could be observed without at the same time being perturbed, affected in some way. "The possibility of knowledge is not eliminated by the fact that what is known depends on the conditions of its observation," Chevalley insists, "it is simply freed from the obsession with certainty."[47]

Descartes's single path, his universal method, was also his gateway to knowledge of himself—first the certainty of his own existence, and then the essence of that existence: "a substance whose whole essence or nature is simply to think, and which does not require any place, or depend on any material thing, in order to exist."[48] The simplicity and transparency of thinking substance allows it to be "easier to know than the body."[49] "Surely my awareness of my own self is not merely much truer and more certain . . . but also much more distinct and evident?"[50] It is here, confronting the issue of self-knowledge, that Pascal most vehemently rejects Descartes's straight and steady path. If our nature were simple, Pascal muses, we could know simple beings; if our vision were guided by the pure light of reason (Descartes) or faith (M. de Sacy) then we could know directly, all at once. However, the complexity of our nature, permeates every aspect of our being: "Instead of receiving idea of . . . pure things, we color them with our qualities and imprint with our composite being all the things that we contemplate."[51] This existence makes us "the very thing we least understand. Man," Pascal explains, "is to himself the most prodigious object in nature, for he cannot conceive what the body is, still less what the mind is, and least of all how a body can be united with a mind. This is the greatest of his difficulties, and yet it is his own being."[52] The complexity of this being is not resolvable into simple, separate units that could be categorized in isolation from one another. To understand the human person, we would have to master this "monster, this chaos, this contradiction. . . . Who can untangle these twisted threads?"[53]

Grene concludes her study of the "Errors of Descartes" by rejecting the underlying Cartesian premise that our knowledge is the product of "a cogitating mind divided in nature and substance from the extended body in which it happens to be housed. Knowledge is an achievement [of the whole person]"[54] interacting throughout a life in a spatio-temporal world. In contrast to Descartes's construction of the machine ("the laws of mechanics are . . . identical with the laws of Nature")[55] from the sovereign viewpoint of thinking substance, Pascal considers that the limits and conditions of human existence set the framework for the possibility of knowledge:

> Man, for example, is related to everything he knows: he needs a place in which he is contained, time through which he endures, motion in order to live, elements out of which he is composed, heat and food to nourish him, air to breathe. He sees light; he feels bodies; in short, everything has a connection with him. . . . [56]

Rather than severing the connection between knowledge and human experience in the spatio-temporal world, Pascal insists that knowledge depends intrinsically on these physiological, intellectual, and affective conditions. This, in turn, places human knowledge for Pascal in the mostly uncharted region between nothing and totality, between ignorance and certainty, making it, as Grene describes knowledge in the conclusion to her critique, "neither an end nor simply a beginning, but a 'stage on life's way'."[57]

KATHLEEN BLAMEY

CALIFORNIA STATE UNIVERSITY AT HAYWARD
OCTOBER 2000

NOTES

1. In particular, Marjorie Grene's book, *Descartes* (Minneapolis: University of Minnesota Press, 1985) and the article cited below, "The Errors of Descartes" in *The Knower and the Known* (Washington, D.C.: University Press of America, 1984).

2. *Discourse on Method*, in *Philosophical Writings of Descartes*, translated

and edited by John Cottingham, Robert Stoothoff, and Douglas Murdoch (Cambridge: Cambridge University Press, 1985), 2 vols; I, p. 148. Quotations from Descartes are from this translation (abbreviated as CSM).

3. *Principles of Philosophy*, Principle LIII, CSM I, p. 210.

4. Cathérine Chevalley, *Pascal: Contingence et probabilités* (Paris: Presses universitaires de France, 1995); Pierre Bourdieu, *Méditations pascaliennes* (Paris: Le Seuil, 1997); Louis Marin, *Pascal et Port-Royal* (Paris: Presses universitaires de France, 1997).

5. Grene, "The Errors of Descartes," p. 78.

6. Ibid., p. 79.

7. Second Meditation, CSM II, p. 16.

8. Pascal, *Pensées*, edited by Ph. Sellier (Paris: Bordas, 1991), Fr. 230, pp. 246–55. The Sellier edition of the *Pensées* is the most recent of the efforts, preceded in particular by Louis Lafuma (1951) and Léon Brunschvicg (1897), to organize the bundles of paper strips left by Pascal. Louis Marin discusses the significance of this fragmented text as it portrays the existence of the author, reduced to a pure structure of utterance whose primary character is instability, lability. See "Un texte nommé 'Pascal'" in *Pascal et Port-Royal*, op. cit., pp. 11–70.

9. *Pensées*, Fr. 230, p. 249. The translations from the French are mine.

10. Ibid.

11. Ibid., pp. 250–51.

12. Ibid., p. 251.

13. Ibid., pp. 251–52.

14. *Pensées*, Fr. 452, p. 361: "Stepping out of the middle is stepping out of our humanity."

15. *Pascal: Contingence et probabilités*

16. Ibid., p. 37.

17. *Pensées*, Fr. 230, p. 253.

18. *Discourse on Method*, CSM I, p. 127.

19. Ibid., p. 121.

20. Ibid., ("if a child who has been taught arithmetic does a sum following the rules, he can be sure of having found everything the human mind can discover")

21. *Meditation V*, CSM II, p. 49.

22. Pensées, Fr. 680, in the section, "Discours de la machine," p. 468.

23. Chevalley, pp. 61–62.

24. Pascal, *Lettre à Le Pailleur*, *Oeuvres complètes*, 210a; quoted by Chevalley, p. 63.

25. *Pensées*, Fr. 445, p. 352.

26. Grene, "The Errors of Descartes," p. 87.

27. Pascal, *De l'esprit géométrique* (Paris: Flammarion, 1985), p. 75.

28. *Pensées*, Fr. 680, p. 467.

29. Ibid., Fr. 670, pp. 459–60.

30. Ibid., Fr. 91, p. 183.

31. Ibid., Fr. 92, p. 183.

32. Chevalley, p. 58.

33. Ibid., p. 59.

34. Ibid., p. 74.

35. Grene, "The Errors of Descartes," p. 79.

36. Pascal, *Entretien avec M. de Sacy* (Paris: Flammarion, 1985), p. 111.

37. Ibid.

38. *Pensées*, Fr. 214, p. 241.

39. Bourdieu, p. 40.

40. Ibid., p. 157. The passage quoted from *Pensées* is Fr. 145, p. 204.

41. "What are our natural principles, if not our accustomed principles? . . . A different custom will produce other natural principles. We see this by experience" (*Pensées*, Fr. 158, p. 207). "Custom is a second nature, which destroys the first . . . I truly fear that this nature is itself but a first custom, just as custom is a second nature" (Ibid., Fr. 159, p. 208).

42. Bourdieu, p. 163.

43. Ibid., pp. 165–66.

44. Ibid., pp. 9–10.

45. Ibid., p. 137.

46. Chevalley, p. 108.

47. Ibid., p. 112.

48. *Discourse on Method*, CSM I, p. 127.

49. Ibid.

50. *Meditation II*, CSM II, p. 22.

51. *Pensées*, Fr. 230, p. 254.

52. Ibid., p. 253–54.

53. Ibid., Fr. 164, p. 211.

54. Grene, "The Errors of Descartes," p. 88.

55. *Discourse on Method*, CSM I, p. 139.

56. *Pensées*, Fr. 230, p. 253.

57. Grene, "The Errors of Descartes," p. 91.

REPLY TO KATHLEEN BLAMEY

For a comparison between Descartes and Pascal, Kathleen Blamey turns to a chapter from *The Knower and the Known*, a book I wrote a good four decades ago. It contains several chapters I now strongly disagree with—including one I'm deeply ashamed of!—but looking back at the points I made in "The Errors of Descartes," I find myself, happily, on the whole still in agreement with them. They are inadequate, however, I believe, in failing to stress adequately the most fundamental, and insidious, of the Cartesian themes that have so long misled us, and that is the turn to subjectivity: to the inwardness of the *cogito* and the implicit solipsism that follows from it. Perhaps that is included in the very concept of dualism, but I'm not sure. In any case, Blamey very neatly uses the four points I did make: indubitability, total clarity or self-evidence, the unity of science, and the duality of mind and body, to stress the analogous counter-Cartesian theses urged by Descartes's younger contemporary, Blaise Pascal.

In attempting to comment on her very interesting essay, if I partly wonder about my own emphasis in my presentation of Descartes's doctrines forty years ago, as a possible interpreter of Pascal I must plead almost total ignorance. It's odd. Although I am about as far as one can get from being a high-powered analytical philosopher who cleverly seeks out logical slips in what look like scrupulously structured arguments (since they are all so good at logic, I wonder why they all find so many flaws in one another's deductions)—since, as I said, I am no such mighty analyst, I don't know why it is that I simply cannot bring myself to read more than a little or to enjoy at all writers of epigrams. Where are they going, and how are they getting there, I want to know. Nor, faced with the need to reply to Dr. Blamey's essay, can I, even if long habituation would allow it, take time to try to reshape my character and devote myself to the study of Pascal in order better to comment on her remarks. So I just have to plead ignorance, or near-ignorance, and respond to what I find within the four corners of the document. My apologies to *Pascalkenner*, and especially to the recent interpreters whose views Blamey is reporting, as well as to Dr. Blamey herself.

On first reading, it seems paradoxical that in resisting the Cartesian program, I should be echoing so deeply religious a thinker as Pascal. When I wrote *The Knower and the Known*, I had been working for some years with Michael Polanyi, chiefly while he was formulating his theory of commitment, and later the concept of tacit knowing. Polanyi used to say that he was adopting the Pauline view that the proper attitude for human beings was neither arrogance nor despair, but hope. This seemed to me an illuminating view, and I took its religious connotations sufficiently seriously to agree that scientists seek only through faith, and find only through grace. Even then, I meant this in a very broad and metaphorical way that would satisfy few true believers. Nor did I realize till many years later how literally Polanyi had taken his religious commitment. I, on the contrary, in my stages on life's way, have come to believe that on the whole organized religion does more harm than good. As Hume recognized, it encourages "superstition and enthusiasm"—the latter, in its eighteenth-century meaning, amounting almost to what we would now call fanaticism, with its attendant intolerance. Yet I still find much in Polanyi's approach convincing. Can one be an atheistic Augustinian?

So much for a general impression. Let me venture a few remarks about the four particular points in question.

First, indubitability. If Pascal recognizes "the anthropological nature of all knowledge," that is indeed a welcome insight. Yet, oddly enough, one can in a sense say the same of Descartes. As Jean-Luc Marion has emphasized, Descartes can achieve certainty in his reading of nature only if he is first assured that nature's code as he reads it is indeed the code according to which God made it.[1] Indeed, Descartes certainly shares Pascal's awareness that he is a creature of "the middle," partway between nothingness and perfection. That is implicit in the very structure of his argument, from the Third Meditation onward.

To be sure, the rhetoric in the two cases is certainly very different. But if we abjure Descartes's smug confidence in God's assurance of our certainties, Pascal's agonized outcries—"our entire foundation cracks and the earth opens up to the abysses"—hardly seems to offer us a good commonsensical starting point for investigating, modestly and conjec-turally, the nature of the nature in which we find ourselves embedded. True, Pascal did do both mathematical and experimental work, through the latter stressing his rejection of something like a "universal mathematics" (more of that shortly). But his characterization of the human situation often sounds more like an anticipation of Søren Kierkegaard than of the kind of historically oriented philosophy of science some of us envisage.

On the second point, total self-evidence, Pascal as presented by Blamey sounds more reasonable. I would only warn against characterizing Cartesian science as "deductive," if deduction is taken in its now current sense. Deduction for Descartes is an orderly movement of the mind from one clear and distinct idea to the next, not the logical inference from one or more element(s) to another in an axiomatized system. Besides, Descartes did do experiments, and in his debate with Harvey he shows a sound awareness of what experiments can and cannot do in testing an hypothesis. (Compared to Harvey, he just didn't do them very well!) But he did indeed declare that all his physics was geometry, and to that Pascal rightly objected.

As Blamey points out, my second point is closely related to the first. I presume that I singled it out for separate treatment because I wanted to emphasize Polanyi's distinction between focal and subsidiary awareness—an anticipation of his later recognition of the from-to character of all knowledge, from everyday perception to the most abstract recesses of the developed, and developing, sciences. Whether there is any equivalent in Pascal, I have no idea—though perhaps his insistence (see point four) upon the embodied nature of our search for knowledge suggests something like it.

Our third point is the unity of knowledge, something Descartes emphatically asserts and Pascal as emphatically denies. So far so good. But I must confess to being deeply suspicious of Pascal's three orders. Of course we all know the heart has its reasons that reason doesn't know; an eloquent maxim, useful to allude to in some argumentative situations. But the pluralism needed to defend the practices of the sciences does not allow categorization into two or three or any definite number. Competent practitioners of any discipline need to learn their way, first gropingly, then with increasing confidence, in the language, techniques, traditions of their discipline. Ultimately, if they are creative as well as competent, they may find their way into new avenues of exploration demanding the acquisition of new perspectives, new techniques, newly developing traditions. The process is open-ended, and though always limited in what it seeks to encompass—never infinity!—, it cannot be cribbed, cabined, or confined within any precisely or exhaustively specifiable set of domains. That is one of the themes Polanyi developed in connection with his investigation of "the unspecifiable in science." It is one of the themes that Pierre Bourdieu appears to be defending in the passages from his *Méditations pascaliennes* that Dr. Blamey refers to in connection with our fourth point, still to come, and that Bourdieu had already discussed persuasively and eloquently in his earlier *Outline of a Theory of Practice*.[2] The "three orders" fall badly short of such a program.

Finally we come to dualism. Here Blamey's references to Bourdieu make me feel thoroughly at home—the primacy of history, of course; thinking with the body, of course. And the two are connected. Every human being is where (s)he is. A human life is something that takes place. So does any life, for that matter, but what seems to be odd about our sort of life is that is takes place not only somewhere on (or above) this planet in the geographical sense, but culturally. When I go on a cruise to the Antarctic, I am still a retired philosophy teacher, an American with ties to Ireland in the last two thirds of her life, and so on. We carry our houses with us, not as visibly as snails do, perhaps, but just as necessarily.

That's all very well, but then here comes that Pascalian rhetoric again. Man, he says, in Blamey's rendering:

> is to himself the most prodigious object in nature, for he cannot conceive what the body is, still less what the mind is, and least of all how a body can be united with a mind. This is the greatest of his difficulties, and yet it is his own being.[3]

Pascal is taking Descartes's "third common notion"—the mind-times-body as distinct from the mind or the body separately—as fundamental. But he makes of it an even greater mystery than did Descartes. Mind—or better, minding, as Ryle put it—is something some bodies are capable of doing. But seeing the two as separate—each unintelligible—and then mysteriously put together? This is triple obscurantism. Yet it appears to me, admittedly a rank outsider, what one would expect from the inventor of Pascal's wager. However improbable it appears, personal immortality is supposed to be worth betting on. Did Pascal accept the even more improbable doctrine of the resurrection of the body? If not, immortality does seem to entail the separability of the soul—Descartes's real distinction after all. To echo Polanyi's favorite Pauline phrase again, in our search for knowledge we have substituted despair for arrogance; but where is hope?

M. G.

NOTES

1. See my *Descartes* (reprinted by Hackett, 1998), pp. 78–83, and J. L. Marion, *Sur la théologie blanche de Descartes* (Paris: Presses Universitaires de France, 1981), *passim*.

2. Pierre Bourdieu, *Outline of a Theory of Practice* (Cambridge: Cambridge University Press, 1995).

3. Pascal, *Pensées*, edited by Ph. Sellier (Paris: Bordas, 1991), Fr. 230, pp. 253–54.

21

Helen Hattab

HANDMAIDEN, NURSEMAID, OR SISTER TO PHILOSOPHY? THE ROLE OF THE HISTORY OF PHILOSOPHY TODAY

I am very honored to have been asked to comment on the work of someone who has lived through and participated in over a half a century of philosophical activity. I apologize in advance for the informal tone in which this commentary is written. It is not a sign of irreverence, but rather a result of two factors. One is that Marjorie Grene herself writes in what she refers to as a "chatty style."[1] This brings me to the second, more important reason. The whole point of the Library of Living Philosophers is to engage in a dialogue with a well-known philosopher, while he or she is still alive. I have proceeded as though I were initiating a conversation with Marjorie Grene (or rather continuing a conversation we began when I gave a paper at Virginia Tech). My hope is that this conversation among historians of philosophy will raise some questions, and perhaps cast some light on the role that the history of philosophy plays within philosophy.

When I first told Marjorie Grene that I had accepted an invitation to write a commentary on her work in seventeenth-century philosophy for this volume, she responded with the exhortation: "Be critical!" This proved to be a difficult task to fulfill, as our approaches to historical philosophical texts are fundamentally in agreement. I could have taken issue with some subtle point of interpretation with respect to her work on Descartes, but that would seem to miss the point. Grene's contribution to Descartes studies, and to the history of philosophy in general, lies not primarily in detailed textual analysis or even in painstaking historical detective work, although she has contributed plenty on this front as well.[2] In some cases her historical scholarship has already been superseded by more in-depth studies, and no doubt any quibbles I have with her reading of the texts and understanding of the historical context will be as well.[3] While that does not diminish the importance of this aspect of her writings, criticizing them on the basis of current research does not seem like the best way to engage with, and celebrate them.

So what then is Grene's primary contribution to this field? Well, for one thing, at a time when philosophers had been going back and forth (or should I say around and around?) on the Cartesian circle and giving logical reconstructions of the "cogito," Grene put together a book that took seriously the context of Descartes's philosophy—both the context in which philosophers approached it in the twentieth century, and Descartes's own intellectual context. As she put it in her introduction to the 1998 edition: "What I wanted was to give a more global view of our recent and, I'm afraid, our present philosophical situation in relation to the tradition that Descartes initiated."[4] Grene drew on recent French scholarship to place Descartes's philosophy within the context of seventeenth-century debates, as well as reveal how *our* context (by which she meant Anglo-American analytic philosophy) can lead us to misread Descartes. Her assessment of the state of the history of philosophy at that time was as follows: "much that has been written recently, especially on Descartes and especially in English, it seems to me, is so narrowly confined to the terms of late twentieth-century debate that the real Descartes is simply left aside altogether. And, since we are products of our past, that means we miss not only Descartes in his own terms, but ourselves, too."[5]

The contextualist approach Grene advocates, which was a rarity in Anglo-American philosophy at that time, has now blossomed into a healthy "cottage industry" (to borrow a phrase from a fellow historian of philosophy). But is this trend simply a knee-jerk reaction against the previous ahistorical, analytic approach to philosophical texts (in which case the next generation is likely to rebel against our historical excesses and return to some form of analysis), or is there more to it? In Grene's case, there is definitely more to it. Her contextualist approach to the history of philosophy is itself a philosophical statement, one which can radically transform the way we think, not only about canonical texts in the history of philosophy, but also about current philosophical problems and practices, insofar as they themselves are shaped by our historical philosophical traditions. Therefore, it seems to me, we must read her work on Descartes as an outgrowth of her insight that our current ways of philosophizing are rooted in the history of philosophy, and can only be transformed by our becoming conscious of, and gaining a deeper understanding of that history. As she puts it, "In the narrowness of our own perspective we miss not only our historical target but the reflective awareness of our own beliefs that should be the aim of philosophy."[6]

What I propose to do here is to examine critically the basis for such a claim in order to assess its strengths and weaknesses. My critique stems not from any credentials in the philosophy of history or theory regarding historical forms of knowledge (I have none). I come to this issue as a practitioner of the history of philosophy. The question I pose to Grene concerns the philosophical justification and future of this field. What makes doing the historical work so important to the future of philosophy and what distinguishes this particular trend in the history of philosophy from those fields in philosophy of which Grene writes: "the more fashionable they become, the more likely it is that they're phony"?[7]

Most historians of philosophy I know take for granted that there is a historical reality to learn about, much as the scientist in the lab takes for granted that there is a physical reality. It can be exceedingly hard to pin this historical reality down, and the further we are removed from it in time, the harder it gets, but we tend to believe that a careful study of documents and other artifacts that survive from a historical era can teach us something about what was really going in terms of philosophical and other intellectual developments. Furthermore, we can and do distinguish between more or less accurate accounts of what was really going on. Yet we also recognize that historical texts are complex things that have to be interpreted, and that there are often several different interpretations, each of which constitutes a plausible way of understanding the text. When studying a historical text we are immediately confronted with unfamiliar terms, strange arguments, seemingly bizarre assumptions, as well as terms that sound deceptively like our own, and yet are used in very different ways. Does this mean that one guess as to the best interpretation is as good as another? No. One can narrow down the range of possible interpretations in various ways, but it often requires going beyond the text at hand and comparing it to related documents from the same period. This method can not only reveal the meanings and assumptions at work in the original text, but also often inspire new interpretations one may not have thought of before. In short, by a careful reading of a historical text, and other texts surrounding it, the historian of philosophy can gradually learn the language spoken by those of past times, in much the same way that one assimilates the language and customs of a foreign land if one lives there long enough (although in some sense one also always remains a foreigner).

So far I don't think I have said anything that would engender heated debate in most circles. I think it is widely accepted today that to be a good *historian* of philosophy, you have to get your hands dirty, that is, you have to rummage around in dusty archives, hunt for interesting texts, pour over them with a fine-toothed comb, and mine them for clues that can help you give a more or less accurate reconstruction of the historical meaning of a philosophical text from the past. Where philosophers disagree is with respect to the question whether this is properly speaking an activity that belongs to the discipline of philosophy rather than intellectual history. Another way of putting it is to ask whether being a good *historian* of philosophy is necessary, or even related to being a good historian of *philosophy*, and is there a difference? Marjorie Grene acknowledges that there is a difference between doing what she refers to as the history of ideas and the history of philosophy, in that the history of philosophy is not just about reconstructing the history of our discipline for the sake of knowing what went on in the past. We don't study the history of our discipline as an end in itself, but "we want on the one hand to put our questions into historical context and on the other hand to illuminate history, to comprehend and criticise the arguments of dead philosophers in the light of what seem to us live issues here and now."[8] Grene's work on Descartes also implies that she thinks that approaching Descartes's texts historically is indispensable to doing a good job on philosophizing about certain issues today. So the history of philosophy for Grene is neither an end in itself nor just a means to advancing specific ends in contemporary philosophy.

That doing the history of philosophy is in some sense related to current philosophizing is undeniable. In my own case, I did not spontaneously decide to write a dissertation on Descartes's views on causation because I just had to know what he wrote on this topic, but rather because I had questions about the nature of causation and Descartes's views seemed to represent an influential shift in the way causation was conceived, one which still has ramifications today. I did not read the Scholastic commentaries he studied out of some antiquarian desire to know what else was being written in the seventeenth century, but because, in order to make sense of Descartes, I had to know what he was responding to and drawing on. So of course there is always some contemporary concern that motivates the historical work we do in philosophy. We all come to historical texts with initial questions and assumptions that arise from our contemporary context (some say we never fully overcome them, but my experience has been that one's initial questions and assumptions are transformed by historical inquiry). But this is a trivial sense in which the history of philosophy is related to current philosophy. Grene sees the history of philosophy and philosophy as related in a deeper sense. It is this deeper relationship that interests me.

One of the questions that frequently came up when I was interviewing for jobs, and which I always found very difficult to answer, is the one that takes roughly the following form: "How does your historical research relate to contemporary debates about x?" (where "x" can stand for any number of things but in my case stands for "causation"). The reason I found this such a difficult question is that if you take the history of philosophy seriously, that is, if you are immersed in your particular historical period, as a conscientious interpreter of historical texts should be, you know that your historical research does *not* relate in any direct or straightforward way to contemporary debates. You cannot just take Descartes's concept "x" and graft it onto a contemporary discussion of "x." After all, Descartes meant something quite different by "x." He developed his view of "x" in response to a different set of questions and concerns, many of which were peculiar to his time. If your commitment to intellectual honesty outweighs your desire to get or keep a job, you acknowledge the lack of any direct relevance but say that, notwithstanding, Descartes's view of "x" is still relevant in the sense that it led to developments "y" and "z," which presuppose "p," and that while "p" is problematic, it was accepted for reasons "a," "b," and "c," and this kind of reasoning eventually engendered "r," which forms the basis for "q," which is still presupposed by contemporary accounts. By this stage your interviewer's eyes have glazed over and you might get a question along the lines of, "What are you going to do when you're done with Descartes?"

I am not telling this deliberately exaggerated story to poke fun at the interview situation. Far from it. I think the concern underlying the question posed by my fictional interviewer is a legitimate one. As philosophers, we want to know what doing the historical research can contribute to our attempts to resolve current problems in philosophy. Having said that, there are two related skeptical challenges one could raise to this enterprise. The first one is that, because our interpretation of historical texts is always mediated by our current assumptions and concerns, we can never know the historical reality in itself. The converse of this challenge, the one implicit in my interview scenario, is that should we succeed in shedding our current assumptions and concerns and come to understand the historical text on its own terms, then we have adopted an entirely different set of concepts and can no longer relate the historical text to our contemporary philosophical problems in an interesting way. Grene wants to maintain, and rightly so I think, that we *can* know the historical reality in itself. As I indicated, I think most historians of philosophy would tend to agree with this claim. She also seems to hold that once we have come to know the historical reality, we can judge it and relate it back to our current predicament in more than a causal way. This is the more controversial claim. Since both claims respond to versions of what is fundamentally the same skeptical concern, I will examine Grene's justification for each of these claims in turn.

Grene's answer to the first skeptical challenge must be understood in light of her view of what knowledge is. Insofar as we are talking about genuine *knowledge* of a historical reality, our question is an instance of the broader question concerning the possibility and nature of human knowledge. While knowledge of historical reality may raise its own peculiar problems, Grene does not seem to think it is intrinsically different from knowledge of any other reality, including knowledge of physical reality. This is not the place to go into a detailed examination of Grene's work on the nature of knowledge, but let me briefly sum up the central tenets of the view she presents in *The Knower and the Known*. Knowing, for Grene, is an active process of seeking which involves focusing our attention on certain clues in our environment and interpreting their meaning. Since we can always change our focus and make explicit what was previously tacit, our interpretations are always changing and so "no subject, no concept is ever self-evident and indubitable."[9] Knowledge is thus always open to doubt and criticism. Furthermore, we can never focus on and make explicit everything at once, and so knowledge is always limited in its scope. As Grene puts it, there is thus "no one universal wisdom."[10] We can increase the scope of our knowledge by progressing to ever higher levels of abstraction, as in mathematics, which is an example of highly abstract knowledge. Grene seems to imply that the more abstract our knowledge becomes the more removed from reality it is, and yet, it always remains a human knowledge, not a god-like point of view. This is clear from the way she describes mathematicians: "But in their strange ethereal world they are still groping, seeking, and finding understanding: not *the* truth, but a claim to truth, still anchored in their personal intellectual situation, in their orientation in the world."[11] For Grene, all knowledge, no matter how removed from the everyday reality, is always personal "because it is an achievement of the whole, inalienable psycho-physical person, making sense of one aspect or another of his situation, of his world. It is not the work of a disembodied intellect."[12]

Implied by this view that knowing involves focusing on clues and interpreting them is the further claim that there is no direct unmediated knowledge, whether it takes the form of the direct intellectual perception of *nous* one finds in the Ancients, Descartes's clear and distinct ideas, or the sense impressions of the empiricists. According to Grene, whether we are talking about sense perception or abstract thought, our contact with reality is always mediated by our perceptual focus, our concepts, and our language. Grene acknowledges that this creates problems for the correspondence theory of truth (although she does not want to give it up) because, "We are in the world, yet not of it; our immersion in it is mediated by the very instruments through which we understand, or misunderstand it. We are always reaching through thought to reality, but since mediation is always inherent in the process, there is always the chance we may have gone astray."[13]

It may well be the case that Grene changed her mind about these matters in the decade between publishing *The Knower and the Known* and *Descartes*, and she may even have developed new views in the past fifteen years. Nevertheless it seems to me that the view on knowledge I have just outlined, can make sense of her approach to Descartes, which continues to be contextualist, as well as her substantive claims about Descartes's philosophy and its relation to contemporary philosophy. So I would like to take this view of knowledge and explore its implications regarding the possibility of genuine historical knowledge that has contemporary relevance.

First, on this view of knowledge, there is no particular difficulty in explaining how we can come to understand a historical text. Since all knowledge involves interpretation, we are simply focusing on a set of clues that historical texts afford us. The knowledge we gain from them is never indubitable and complete, but it does correspond in some way to the historical meaning of the text, and we can advance in our knowledge by refining our interpretations. Recall the first skeptical challenge raised: the very fact that our historical understanding of the text is mediated by our current concepts and language invalidates it. Grene's response would be that *all* knowledge is mediated in this way, and so there is no intrinsic difference between historical knowledge and other forms of knowledge that we rely on every day. Therefore, historical knowledge must stand or fall with all other knowledge.

Even if we accept Grene's view of knowledge, one might still object that our current context poses a greater obstacle to understanding the historical meaning of a text than it does to understanding a present reality because, in addition to all the usual mediating factors, we face the additional problem that the clues we are interpreting are removed from us in time. There seems to be an additional layer of interpretation here. Not only must we interpret the clues, but we must also first find the clues and translate them into our terms—not an easy task given that the words and the meanings they are meant to convey do not match up to our current language. To make an analogy to vision, when dealing with a historical text, not only are we wearing spectacles that cause us to see things in our terms, but these spectacles also have blinders on them that prevent us from noticing and focusing on certain clues that are there in the historical text.

I will shelve this objection for the moment and come back to it later. Right now I just want to question an assumption implicit both in this objection and the previous one, namely, the assumption that whenever knowledge is mediated, it is invalidated, or at the very least, distorted in some way. Grene seems to accept the assumption that mediation implies a loss of information or at the very least distortion, but saves knowledge by redefining it as something that can never be absolutely true, indubitable and complete. In other words, it is not a problem that knowing is a mediated process because the imperfect product of this process still counts as knowledge, albeit not in the traditional sense of absolute knowledge. But why should we suppose that this imperfect product has any correspondence to reality? Why should we rely on it? Grene's response might be something along the lines of, "It's all we have got." But is that a reason to assume its reliability? I think it would help Grene's case if she rejected the assumption that mediation necessarily distorts, and I think there is enough evidence to question this assumption. There are plenty of everyday examples of information being actively processed and transformed without any important loss. Take the example of a fax machine. The letters on the page are translated into vibrations which are transmitted through the phone line. At the other end these vibrations are reconstituted as letters and out comes a document that looks almost exactly like the original one. Despite being a highly mediated process, there is little or no loss of information, provided the fax and phone line are working properly.[14] We could say the same about our perceptual apparatus. Of course the senses take in information which then gets transformed and has to be reconstituted and interpreted, but why should that imply that crucial information is thereby lost or distorted? The fact that we get around in the world perfectly well using our senses indicates the contrary.

So far, I think Grene might be willing to accept my point, but extending this analogy to higher forms of cognition is difficult because now we are dealing with concepts and language, and here there is a lot more variation among individuals and groups of individuals. Unlike the case of perception where, once we decide to focus on something, we have little choice about what we see, the development and use of concepts and language seems to involve a great degree of choice. True, we all grow up learning the concepts and language of our particular culture, but the choice of learning other languages, and questioning or developing accepted concepts, is always open to us. Language is itself a growing, ever-changing phenomenon. As knowledge-seekers, we continually discover new things that we have to conceptualize and for which we devise words. What then ensures that our ever-changing use of concepts and terms corresponds, more or less, to reality?

This brings me back to the second objection which I shelved above. Doesn't this extra level of mediation create additional difficulties with respect to one's ability to know the meaning of a historical text? One must rely on one's grasp of a historical language to make sense of the words on the page. Given that language is always changing, how can one be assured that the meanings one associates with the words on the page correspond to the historical meaning (even when reading a historical text written in one's own tongue)? After all, when learning a historical language, do we not rely on concepts and meanings particular to our time in order to form a conception of what the historical term might mean? It is true that our initial attempts to understand a foreign language (and this goes for a historical language too) consist in finding equivalents in our own language for the foreign terms. But as our knowledge of the other language advances, we come to realize there are often no strict equivalents, and when we finally become fluent in that language, we no longer translate from that language to our native one, but we actually think in the terms of the new language as we formulate sentences.

Something similar happens when one learns to interpret the peculiar philosophical terminology of a historical text. For example, when I first began to read Latin commentaries on Aristotle I probably substituted the term "power" for "potentia," and "act" for "actus" and thought of their meanings as roughly analogous to the contemporary meanings of "power" and "act." Had I continued to do so, I would have been blinded to the fact that "potentia" also means "potentiality," and that it must be understood relative to "actus," which itself does not simply denote an action, but the actualization of a thing's natural capacities. Had I stuck to the meanings I originally associated with these terms, I would have missed important clues in the text and ended up with a completely perverted version of Aristotelian natural philosophy. But that is not what happened. One inevitably realizes, from the sentences and arguments in which these terms get used that they have a whole range of meanings of which one was not initially conscious. In reading several different texts which drew on this terminology I was able to refine my understanding of what "potentia" and "actus" meant in this historical/philosophical context. The point is that we have to start some-where, and of course the starting point is heavily informed by our present language, and of course it posed a barrier that one could compare to blinders. But the nice thing about blinders is that one can remove them. In dealing with a historical text one develops a set of interpretive techniques that enable one eventually to overcome the barriers that are initially there.

In other words, by means of our own language, we can learn another language and the mediation of our own language is only temporary and thus only temporarily distorting. But there is a deeper problem here, the skeptic would say. What about the fact that *some* language always mediates our knowledge, even our scientific knowledge of natural phenomena? Doesn't this mean that even scientific knowledge is as variable and potentially arbitrary as our use of language? Grene tries to get around this problem by means of her realist theory of perception. Perception is the starting point for all knowledge, including abstract scientific knowledge. As she puts it,

"Scientific investigations and extrascientific explorations alike begin with the use of the organism's perceptual systems, [and] move to higher levels of abstraction through processes analogous to perception, . . . for their substantiation."[15] Following J. J. Gibson, Grene holds that "the environment of any organism is highly structured. It has a definite layout, including objects, occurrences, and in particular, affordances—real features of the world that have a bearing on the organism's way of being in its world."[16]

Grene implies that the scientist does not deal with isolated bits of observed data which then become the matter for theoretical statements and logical inferences. Rather, the observations scientists make are already highly structured because their environment is structured. In addition, like all knowledge-seekers scientists interpret and refine the knowledge gained by perception and so inevitably their observations are mediated by their concepts and language as well. But presumably the concepts the scientist uses have to have some grounding in an objective perceptual reality. By anchoring knowledge in a realist theory of perception, Grene avoids the view that science is an arbitrary product of noncognitive drives and desires and is therefore subjective. However, she agrees with those who take a sociological approach to science to the extent that she holds the conceptual framework and language the scientist draws on to be products of the history of scientific practice as well as broader cultural history. This is simply one instance of the general principle that Grene takes to apply to all human endeavors: "To fulfill our capacities, we need, within the constraints set by our genetic endowments and our natural and cultural environments, the medium of a culture, a language, social rituals, the discipline of social practices, through participation in which we develop the human histories that constitute our lives."[17]

Now we are finally in a position to understand Grene's answer to the converse of our first skeptical challenge, that is, it is beginning to become clear why she thinks knowing the historical Descartes can speak to contemporary philosophical questions, and is in fact indispensable to contemporary philosophizing. For Grene, a person is constituted by his or her history. A discipline of knowledge, being but a set of human practices and activities, is similarly constituted by its history. Therefore, the concepts we rely on in our current philosophical endeavors are themselves products of our philosophical past. Let me illustrate this point with an example from Grene's book entitled *Descartes*.

In providing a foundation for his mechanistic physics while leaving room for the immortality of the soul and free will, Descartes found it necessary to draw a real distinction between the mind and the body. Thus in place of the Aristotelian multitude of individual substances with their different forms and qualities, he posited two kinds of substance, each defined by one principal attribute: extension, on the one hand, and thought on the other. And yet, as Grene points out, Descartes is quite happy to retain, as common notions, principles that depend on the Christianized version of Aristotle's philosophy developed by his predecessors. The prime example Grene points to is his reliance on a self-evident causal principle in arguing for the existence of God in the third Meditation. The principle that a cause must possess at least as much reality as its effect presupposes a cosmic scheme of hierarchically ordered degrees of being which is itself inconsistent with Descartes's own stark ontology.[18] Grene's point is that Descartes's strategy was to overthrow "just so much of what his teachers had taught him as would enable him to construct a metaphysical foundation for the new mathematical physics. . . ."[19] This accounts for the delicate balance between seemingly inconsistent old and new elements in Descartes's philosophy. What subsequent generations have done is focus primarily on the new elements and their implications. According to Grene:

> What has held us captive in his thought is its innovations: the alienation of mind from nature, with its consequent subjectivism, and the denial of life, with its reductivistic consequences. But Descartes' concept of substance and the notion of a hierarchically ordered series of causal powers associated with it: these concepts, which furnished the ontological foundation for his proposed reform, had become, through his own originality in transforming them, too abstract, too impoverished, to survive.[20]

Furthermore, Grene contends that philosophy today is still under the yoke of Descartes's dualism and the impoverished views of perception and life it generates: "The albatross of modern thought has been, not in Descartes' own ontology, but items adopted from it and read into new contexts, contexts generated at least in part by those very items taken without their original and idiosyncratic setting."[21] In other words, an ahistorical approach to Descartes which severs his dualism from the context of the rest of his philosophy and modifies it to fit a new context, is at least partially responsible for our false assumption that knowledge, as the product of a disembodied Cartesian mind, is acontextual and impersonal. This assumption in turn is responsible for the analytic approach to historical texts and philosophical questions in general.

We now have Grene's answer to our question, what makes the history of philosophy indispensable to current philosophizing? Our current assumptions and concerns are products of philosophical ideas originated in response to a past philosophical problem, and then modified by subsequent generations to fit their needs. Only by recapturing the context in which these ideas were originally developed can we assess whether it is legitimate for us to sever them from that context and continue to rely on them today.

But here's the rub—on what basis do we decide this? I don't think Grene wants to say that it is never legitimate to rely on ideas that grew out of a different historical context because in the same work where she denies the Cartesian separation of mind and body and the view of perception it implies, she reaffirms the older Aristotelian thesis that "sensory immediacy has its directness, its reliability, not from its being cut off, 'in my mind,' but from the very fact that it is out there."[22] So some insights made by historical philosophers are worth preserving and adapting to our current context, while others need to be rejected altogether. The problem is, since we must judge the value of these past insights in light of our current philosophical concerns, which are themselves constituted by philosophical ideas we have inherited from the past, aren't we just going to reaffirm whatever historical view has been most influential and thus most constitutive of our present philosophical practices? If we do end up rejecting a philosophical principle or idea that seems central to our current philosophical endeavors, as Grene does, then isn't that because it is now becoming explicit that a different intuition, also generated by past developments, is really more central to and constitutive of philosophy today?

Grene addresses a version of this kind of circularity in her article, "Paradoxes of Historicity":

> If human beliefs, attitudes, actions are primarily historical, then they are wholly amenable to covering law type causal explanations, and nothing is left to be understood. All diachronic explanation is causal-deterministic; . . . If this is a defensible or, worse, an inescapable, inference, then the thesis of the primacy of historicity destroys itself. The reliance on historicity, rather than providing adequate ground for a philosophy of the person, proves to be yet another form of intellectual suicide.[23]

In other words, if we and our activities are simply inevitable effects of our past activities and the cultures we grew up in, then our current philosophizing is determined to take a certain course and there is no point in judging it or trying to change it. Or rather, any choice we make to change the course of our lives will itself be predetermined. This point can be applied to developments within the discipline of philosophy as a whole as well as the philosophical activities of any individual person and so we can apply it to the current trends in the history of philosophy and philosophy.

Grene offers a solution of this problem on an individual level that might likewise apply to the development of our discipline:

> my point here is simply that each of us, however pervasively an expression of his society, does exist within his own hermeneutical circle, which must somehow be saved from predation by causal thinking. We cannot get outside

that circle, whatever argument we may use to make it more habitable. We have to ask, then, from within the hermeneutical circle, if there is any way to answer the critic who chooses to interpret historicity in purely causal terms. Only, I think, by reinstating the *natural* foundation of the historical in a way that modern philosophy has largely failed to do.[24]

Let us briefly examine this solution and see how it applies to our problem of the relationship between the history of philosophy and current philosophizing.

Grene wants to affirm the primacy of history while seeing historical existence as one form of natural existence. She asks: "Remaining within the hermeneutical circle, can we found it on nature?"[25] The way she proposes to do this is to see us as historically situated beings who constitute our world by historically conditioned categories and principles. At the same time, the world that surrounds us is not a phenomenal world, but we are in touch with, and trying to make sense of things in themselves. Those real things form the environment for our constituting activities, "in such a way that the person is seen to be a unit in the very nature he seeks to know. *We are real things, too, not only constituting, but constituted.*"[26] What Grene seems to be trying to insert into this historicist picture is our biological nature. It constitutes us as much as our historically conditioned categories do: "We, like other animals, have our ecological niche, not all of which is artifactual and human."[27] Not only that, Grene suggests that our biological nature comes first: "Unless nature is prior (*ontologically* prior) to personal history, our account of the latter seems self-defeating and ephemeral."[28] However, Grene cautions that "a personal history is not just another life history, like a baboon's or a goldfinch's, nor indeed is it a life history plus some other superadded something, but it *is* a *life* history, though of a peculiar kind."[29] The problem with other forms of historicity (and Grene takes Heidegger and Wittgenstein as prime examples) is that they seem "to entail ignoring nature, if not demoting it to a human artifact."[30] Grene identifies the dichotomy between the scientific and the historical or human as the root of this problem.[31]

Grene proposes we reject this dichotomy and suggests that, in place of the opposition between historical and scientific explanation, we acknowledge levels of explanation that are complementary, not contradictory with each other. In keeping with her view of knowledge, Grene claims "We need to show, from within the hermeneutical circle, how both its own level of interpretation, which relies on culture-based meanings and their interpretation and reinterpretation by human beings in their worlds, and poorer but indispensable levels of explanation, causal or otherwise scientific, can, and do, coexist and cooperate."[32] She elaborates that historicity, as a "necessary condition for, and defining principle of, human being, can be within, not over against, nature, in a way superior to, while at the same time dependent on, the possibilities left open by the organization of the natural world within which man as an artifact-needing, culture-dwelling *animal* has become a possibility and, for the moment, an actuality."[33]

How does this provide for a solution to the inherent circularity and determinism involved in judging and changing our current philosophizing in light of its history, when the very concepts informing in our interpretations of history and judgments are supposed to be determined by the historically constituting philosophical activities of the past? Grene's answer seems to be that, while there is no way out of the circle, we are not solely constituted by our history—our biological nature also comes into play. That does not mean we should understand all human forms of development in terms of biological evolution, but our biological nature determines the boundary conditions within which our personal and cultural histories take place. Just as Grene's realist theory of perception allows her to deny the extreme sociological view of scientific knowledge and maintain that science is still the pursuit of truth about some natural process, so her emphasis on our biological nature is intended to get her around the cultural determinism that would seem to result if we are *just* constituted by our personal histories.[34]

An analogous move can then be made with respect to our current philosophical activity. It is not *just* constituted by the history of our discipline (although it is) but first and foremost, all our activity (including philosophical activity) must be understood as the activity of a natural organism, trying to make sense of and get around in its environment. I presume Grene takes this biological fact that we are natural organisms of a certain kind to be accessible to us no matter what our personal and cultural histories. If that is the case, then we have a criterion, not itself dependent on our historically constituted current philosophical categories, for deciding whether to retain or reject philosophical concepts that originated in a different historical context. The criterion would get applied roughly as follows: if a philosophical principle or idea gets in the way of our activities as organisms trying to make sense of our environment, then we must reject it, no matter how historically defining it has been. And according to Grene, Descartes's real distinction between mind and body, and the theory of knowledge it supports, despite all the progress in science it engendered, does ultimately get in the way of our attempts to make sense of our world, in all its richness.

Interesting though it is, I think this answer is problematic. If I have understood Grene correctly, then she is still implicitly relying on a fundamental distinction between nature and history, in that the constraints of our biological nature provide checks and balances with respect to our "historically constituting and constituted natures." If there is such a divide, then it would be reasonable to conclude that the kind of knowledge appropriate to grasping our biological nature is different from the kind of knowledge appropriate to our historical nature. In fact, if knowledge of our biological nature is to provide us with a criterion by which to judge philosophical ideas, then it would seem that we must know our biological nature independently of our historicized philosophical categories. If this is so, then we are back to square one. Not only does scientific knowledge then seem to be different in kind from historical knowledge, but it would seem to be more fundamental than historical knowledge. If this is the case, then the history of philosophy would not seem to be indispensable to current philosophizing. We could figure out what was wrong with our current philosophical activities by judging them in light of our knowledge of our biological nature. Descartes's dualism would be worth studying only insofar as we might need to be reminded from time to time of past mistakes.

I don't think Grene would want to maintain this, and perhaps this is an indication that I have misunderstood her somewhere along the way (in which case I am sure she will correct me). However, it does seem to me that there is a tension between Grene's historicism, and what I read as her implicit privileging of scientific knowledge, in particular, knowledge of the science of biology. If we emphasize Grene's historicism, then we can make sense of her claim that studying the history of philosophy contextually is indispensable to understanding ourselves as philosophers today, but it is hard to find a basis (one that is not itself historically determined) for rejecting some ideas that we have inherited from a different historical context, but not others. On the other hand, if we emphasize Grene's reliance on our biological nature and our knowledge of it as somehow more fundamental, then we have a justification for her claim that Descartes's dualism and its ramifications for knowledge must be rejected, despite its historical influence, but some of the fundamentals of Aristotle's view should be retained, albeit in modified form. However, if we can know that Descartes was wrong strictly on the basis of what we know about our biological nature, then what need have we for a detailed historical study of Descartes's philosophy? Studying the context of Descartes's philosophy would seem then to be relegated to the history of ideas, not the history of philosophy.

Despite this tension, I still think that Grene is onto something. There is and should be more to the history of philosophy than simply accepting or rejecting past philosophical systems according to how well they match up to our current assumptions and criteria. I also agree that a deeper historical knowledge can and does transform the way we think about current philosophical problems. Discovering the historical context in which a problem arose can make us realize that what we previously took to be a genuine problem (usually because it was for previous philosophers) really turns out to be a nonproblem given our context. In other words, doing the history of philosophy in a serious way can teach us to stop regurgitating the problems we have inherited from past generations and begin formulating new philosophical questions that arise from the present. On the other hand, studying the history of philosophy can also reveal problems where we previously thought there were none. We may take a certain philosophical problem to have been resolved until we study the context in which it was solved in the past and realize that the solution no longer works given our current context. Fruitful philosophizing thus involves constantly going back and forth between our context and the history behind it, as Grene has done in her philosophical career.

I also think that Grene was on the right track in the sense that she recognized that explaining how we are able to do this requires a rethinking of what knowledge is. We need a theory of knowledge that can account for objective and relevant historical knowledge as well as objective scientific knowledge. It is clear that the old positivist model of knowledge, with its strict division between causal/scientific explanation and historical explanation is too narrow to account for more interpretative forms of knowledge employed in the humanities and social sciences. Despite attempts to impose this model, which was inspired by the physical sciences, on what we call the social sciences, this endeavor seems doomed to failure as well. The idea that causal/scientific explanation has to be formulated in terms of universal, mathematizable laws has led to a disintegration of knowledge among and even within disciplines (e.g., friends who are professional economists tell me that the theoretical, mathematical models developed by macro-economists have very little to do with, and cannot predict, the actual human behavior in the marketplace observed by microeconomists). Even if we restrict the positivist model to the physical sciences, it fails to capture how scientific knowledge actually progresses and has progressed historically.

Grene is thus right that we need a richer theory of knowledge to account for our ability to gain objective knowledge about human action and human history, as well as the physical world. (I would add that we need a richer notion of causation to account for the fact that we can have genuine causal explanations of human phenomena that are not lawlike and deterministic). Grene tries to accommodate interpretive forms of knowing employed in the humanities and social sciences by arguing that all knowledge is but interpretation, and thus there is no division between knowledge of nature and knowledge of history. But this seems to me to swing too far in the other direction. There are peculiar difficulties involved in gaining knowledge of everchanging human and historical realities created by volitional agents acting over time, difficulties which are not present in our efforts to know a present physical reality (although the latter presents its own difficulties). This may account for the fact that methods which led to tremendous advances in physics do not seem to be producing equivalent results in economics and other social sciences. Even Grene seems implicitly to recognize that there are such differences when she appeals to our biological nature as providing boundary constraints for our personal and cultural histories and to our perceptual knowledge as grounding higher forms of interpretation.

In conclusion, Grene has been well ahead of her time in recognizing that a contextualist approach to the history of philosophy is indispensable to understanding and transforming current philosophizing. She also realized early on that such an approach to the history of philosophy goes hand in hand with a new account of knowledge, in general. While I think that Grene's account of knowledge falls short of explaining how present philosophical thinking can be historically constituted while yielding meaningful ways of evaluating and transforming itself, she certainly provides a starting point for reflection on questions that, sooner or later, every historian of philosophy has to answer to his or her own satisfaction.

HELEN HATTAB

WABASH COLLEGE
APRIL 2001

NOTES

1. Marjorie Grene, *A Philosophical Testament* (Chicago and La Salle, Ill.: Open Court Publishing Company, 1995), p. 1.

2. See in particular: Marjorie Grene, *Descartes* (Indianapolis: Hackett Publishing Company, 1985); "Descartes and Skepticism," *The Review of Metaphysics* 52 (March 1999): 553–71; and two articles co-authored with Roger Ariew, the first on "Ideas, in and before Descartes," *Journal of the History of Ideas* 56 (1995): 87–106, the second on "The Cartesian Destiny of Form and Matter." *Early Science and Medicine* 2, no. 3 (1997): 300–325.

3. See in particular: Daniel Garber, *Descartes' Metaphysical Physics* (Chicago: University of Chicago Press, 1992); Dennis Des Chene, *Physiologia: Natural Philosophy in Late Aristotelian and Cartesian Thought* (Ithaca, N.Y.: Cornell University Press, 1996); by the same author, *Life's Form* and *Spirits and Clocks* (Ithaca, N.Y.: Cornell University Press, 2000) and Roger Ariew, *Descartes and the Last Scholastics* (Ithaca, N.Y.: Cornell University Press, 2000).

4. Grene, *Descartes*, p. xi.

5. Ibid., p. 3.

6. Ibid.

7. Grene, *A Philosophical Testament*, p. 3.

8. Grene, *Descartes*, p. 3.

9. Marjorie Grene, *The Knower and the Known* (Berkeley: University of California Press, 1974), p. 86.

10. Ibid., p. 81.

11. Ibid., p. 77.

12. Ibid., p. 82.

13. Ibid., p. 84.

14. This example was given by Dr. Harry Binswanger during a lecture on perception I heard several years ago.

15. Marjorie Grene, "Perception, Interpretation, and the Sciences: Toward a New Philosophy of Science," in *Evolution at a Crossroads: The New Biology and the New Philosophy of Science*, ed. David J. Depew and Bruce H. Weber (Cambridge, Mass.: MIT Press, 1985), p. 3.

16. "Perception, Interpretation, and the Sciences," p. 4.

17. Ibid., p. 7.

18. Grene, *Descartes*, p. 102.

19. Marjorie Grene, *Descartes Among the Scholastics* (Milwaukee: Marquette University Press, 1991), p. 5.

20. Grene, *Descartes*, p. 104.

21. Ibid.

22. Grene, *The Knower and the Known*, p. 50.

23. Marjorie Grene, "The Paradoxes of Historicity," *Review of Metaphysics* 32 (1978): 15–36, p. 24.

24. Ibid., p. 28.

25. Ibid.

26. Ibid.

27. Ibid., p. 32.

28. Ibid.

29. Ibid., p. 28–29.

30. Ibid., p. 29.

31. Ibid., p. 30.

32. Ibid., pp. 30–31.

33. Ibid., p. 31.

34. Grene, "Perception, Interpretation and the Sciences," p. 17.

REPLY TO HELEN HATTAB

It is difficult to comment on Dr. Hattab's essay for two reasons. First, there is little I can disagree with in her generous account of my views on the history of philosophy as represented in my book on Descartes and in *The Knower and the Known* (the latter a work with which I do now in part disagree, but the passages quoted by Dr. Hattab still seem to me reasonable). Secondly, on the other hand, in looking for other places in which I have spoken of history, she has chosen a piece that has to do with the alleged historicity of the person, but not with the profession of history, let alone with the more restricted discipline of the history of philosophy.

About her own major argument, which comprises two-thirds of her essay, I have only a couple of rather minor problems. I don't think I meant to suggest that the fact that knowledge is mediated (chiefly through language) means that it is distorted. Mediation, it seems to me, entails incompleteness: no approach to any complex subject matter can take it all in at once. If it did, it would be the reality itself, or a mirror image of it, and not a perspective on it. But that does not mean that such mediation distorts its object; it just doesn't say everything there might be to say. True, mediation does imply the possibility of error; but what's wrong with that? I don't believe much in John Dewey; but he was surely correct (as correct as any one can be!) in insisting that the quest for certainty is, or should be, over. Michael Polanyi referred to what he called human "lore"—the whole of the accumulated knowledge won by human efforts and insights—as everything in which we might be totally mistaken. But that didn't keep him from arguing that scientists, or other responsible persons, when they put forward knowledge claims, are confident that they are coming into contact with reality. Of course, they may be wrong; but often their confidence appears to be borne out in unexpected, as well as expected, ways. The possibility of error gives us no reason for despair, or even for skepticism.

Still on the question of mediation: I must confess I find the example of a fax machine as mediator very misleading. Such a mechanism doesn't mediate, any more than my printer does; it just copies.

My problems with Dr. Hattab's discussion of "The Paradoxes of Historicity" are more serious. When I reread that paper, in order to deal with her reference to it, I found it quaintly "continental" and wondered at the dear, or not so dear, old days when I wrote that sort of thing. But then I noticed the occasion for which it had been prepared: the context, which both Dr. Hattab and I think essential to the interpretation of texts. I presented that paper at a conference in the Werner Reimersstiftung in Bad Homburg, in Germany, a conference on the topic of philosophical anthropology. Even apart from that context, indeed, it is clear that in that essay I am talking about the question whether a human person is to be understood *as a history*. The term "history" is ambiguous. It can refer to the discipline of history, the attempt to recount and explain, in a responsible way and according to certain professional standards, what happened at some time somewhere. Or it can refer, at what one could call a lower ontological level, to what happened itself. It is the second of these meanings that was involved in the Bad Homburg conference. When philosophical anthropologists, or philosophers with interests allied to theirs, speak of historicity, they are thinking of the problem of saying what a human being is, and insisting that it is our life stories—not as told, but as lived—that make us who or what we are. This inquiry has no connection with the problem of history as a discipline, let alone with so esoteric a sub-discipline as the history of philosophy. The late Alan Donagan, for example, was a committed Cartesian dualist, who was skeptical of the less than dualistic approach to human nature exemplified by the kind of philosophical anthropology with which that essay of mine was concerned. But at the same time he was a very gifted and careful historian of philosophy.

What I was trying to do in that essay, to put it briefly, was to ask two questions about such an approach to human nature. First, does treating our lives historically after all mean reducing them to a sequence of linear cause-effect relations, and so, it seems, removing our humanity? And secondly, can we correct what appears to me the misguided emphasis of some writers who have reflected on human historicity, when they neglect our natures as beings within nature—as alive, much as other animals are alive, though with a difference? In my presentation of this problem in the essay here under consideration, I have used some expressions that suggest, at least to Dr. Hattab, that I am insisting on everybody's knowing biological science. Of course that would have nothing at all to do with anybody's competence as a professional historian; nor is it what I mean to convey about the "biological" perspective needed in philosophical anthropology. We need to recognize that we are alive; that's all. Admittedly, for educated members of our society, that probably means recognizing that we have come into existence through the processes of biological evolution, and that, for each of us, our genetic make-up has some bearing on our characters, our capabilities and our destinies. But that certainly doesn't mean that people have to be biologists in order to understand who they are. And any relation between biological science and the practice of history, or of the history of philosophy, would be even more remote. It was good of Dr. Hattab to search so far afield to find some texts of mine on history, but, as the Irish would put it, there's history and history in it!

M. G.

22

Charles M. Sherover

ON GRENE'S PRESENTATION
OF HEIDEGGER

Since I find myself in general agreement with the summaries which Grene presents of her own work and ideas, it is difficult to understand why I find almost a sense of anger arise in me as I read Grene on two philosophers—Heidegger and Kant—or the philosophical movements with which they are generally associated. Like her I would describe myself as having a lifelong devotion to Kant's First Critique—yet I wonder why we read it so differently. Like her, I firmly believe that an "authentic" thinker must locate himself or herself in the history of philosophy. And like her I have the highest respect for Michael Polanyi[1] from whom I have learned much.

Yet I find myself puzzled and dismayed by her attempt to introduce existentialist thought, not so much by her efforts to present an exposition as with the slowly withheld explosions of "arrogant!" or some such similar condemnatory expletive. And I am completely puzzled by her generally antagonistic approach to Heidegger. One usually writes an introduction to a thinker, or a movement, because one thinks that something worthwhile is being said, useful admonitions offered, or new insights provided into a question of concern. But Grene, despite an occasional curtsy to a 'good point,' is antagonistic from the outset. I understand that these writings were undertaken more from necessity than for love, but can one not do more to make a virtue of necessity? Let me briefly offer some remarks about the *Introduction to Existentialism* (Chicago: 1948, 1959), and then turn to the book on Heidegger.

The preface to the 1959 edition of the existentialism book graciously concedes, at the outset, that a chapter should have been added on Paul Tillich (who came out of the Reformed Church tradition) because he "has shown how existentialism can issue in a living Christian philosophy."[2] But this concession raises some questions: Didn't Kierkegaard, whom she

regards as the father of existentialism, think of it in terms of a very
personally felt kind of Lutheranism? Didn't Martin Buber tie his deeply felt
loyalty to Judaism to his own form of existentialism? Indeed, Marcel saw
a close relationship between his development of an existentialism that
displayed its roots in German Idealism at the same time as it was closely
tied to his own conversion to Catholicism; he also saw the kinship between
Royce's pragmatic form of German Idealism and the new ways of thinking
that came under the rubric of existentialism. Didn't Berdyaev manifest a
profoundly thought-out existentialist approach that was virtually inseparable
from his deeply felt loyalty to the Russian Orthodox tradition? And, for that
matter, didn't Karl Jaspers assimilate a general European Protestantism to
the general run of European existentialism? The remark about Tillich seems
to suggest that Grene has generalized Sartre's explicit atheism to cover all
varieties of what passes for "existentialism." What makes a philosophical
viewpoint a variety of existentialism for Grene? While more might be said
on this score, perhaps it would be better simply to request from Grene an
account of her thinking then, and how she sees today her earlier approach
to bringing existentialism to the English-speaking world.

   Another point along the same line that requires an explanation is this:
Why does Grene insist upon pairing Heidegger with Sartre as an exemplar
of "atheistic existentialism"?[3] Heidegger, for one, made it clear that while
he believed that some reconstruction of the theistic conceptualization was
necessary, his very call is an implicit continuity of a theistic commitment
(beyond the scope of *Being and Time*). In a footnote, toward the end of that
work, he says:

   If God's eternity can be "construed" philosophically, then it may be understood
   only as a more primordial temporality which is "infinite [unending]." Whether
   the way afforded by the *via negationis et eminentiae* is a possible one, remains
   to be seen.[4]

Certainly his only argument is with one traditional theological formulation.
But any disputation about it or alternatives must presume the theistic
hypothesis. No atheist would word the contest in this way. To charge
Heidegger with atheism seems groundless. After he left the seminary, he
consorted with Protestant theologians, such as Barth and Brunner and, at the
end of his life and at his own request,[5] Heidegger received a Catholic
funeral. What, then, was Grene's reasoning in former times on this point,
and what is it today? Is Heidegger an atheist in her view? It seems that long
life and her own achievements now avail her of an opportunity to clarify her
view, if she is willing.

   It is clear that the "existentialist" writers come out of a tradition—and thus ask certain kinds of questions instead of others—questions with which Grene had, apparently, little sympathy in the '40s and '50s. Clearly she preferred the English tradition of "commonsense" inquiries and answers —for example, consult her quick comparison of Mill and Jaspers.[6] Rather than dismissing Heidegger because of the language he uses, which annoys her, Grene might have attempted to come to terms with the reasons for that obscure language. This language does come out of a tradition, reaching back to Wolff and Kant, of seeking precise German words for concepts that had generally been previously named in French or Latin or Greek. But this had not proven satisfactory, as Heidegger became aware. He explained, "we lack not only most of the words but, above all, the 'grammar'."[7] The Western languages are not only substance/predicate languages but also have difficulty in dealing with a verb as the subject of a sentence. Yet this is precisely what Heidegger believed he needed to do in building what he called a "fundamental ontology of human existence." I would think that anyone who comes to Heidegger from what is professed as a deep attachment to Kant, as Grene says of herself, should have little trouble in making the transition from transcendental structures to ontological structures, and from the empirical to the ontic.

Heidegger's work is built around a vocabulary derived from Kant and themes that come out of moral and religious discourse. Somehow, it is in the "call to conscience" that Grene stumbles over the German word *schuld(ig)*—which can mean "responsible" or "responsibility" as well as "guilt," both deriving from the word for "shoulder," as in, "to take something upon one's shoulders," or "to shoulder something"—and then, without thinking of any of this, protests "Heidegger's weird language."[8] What is weird here? The German language in general? Or does Heidegger's way of appropriating layers of sedimented meaning bespeak a problem? Heidegger had made it clear that his project of seeking out the fundamental structure of human existing necessitated a liberation from the grammatical strictures of our Western languages. This is hardly novel in Heidegger. The dissatisfaction with the grammar of the Western languages can be traced back at least to Leibniz, whose interest in Chinese had not only led him to develop binary arithmetic but also to suggest that the Chinese character (which does not change with grammatical function or pronunciation) could conceivably serve as the model for his sought-for "universal characteristic." Is there something in this general approach to philosophy that annoys Grene, or is there some problem with the way Heidegger, in particular, carries the tradition onwards? It would seem that this point might provide Grene with an opportunity to make clear what limitations she might place upon the role that language, and perhaps other products of culture, plays in constructive philosophy.

Grene further complains of Heidegger's insistence on the ontological character of his human existence while rejecting the "ontic"[9]—when Heidegger repeatedly in *Being and Time* insists on their necessary correlation. It is not uncommon in philosophical circles to hear Heidegger interpreted as having condemned the ontic and exalted the ontological, but perhaps it ought to be less common than it is. Does Grene still accept her characterization of Heidegger's view of the relation of ontic and ontological, or have the intervening years modified her views on this issue? What would be the reasons for either a modification of her view or an absence of it? And what importance does Grene place on Heidegger today, both for her own thinking and for the wider world? How does it compare with his importance, in her view, fifty years ago?

In the existentialism book, Grene speaks of Heidegger's "single-minded arrogance," his "solitary arrogance," and his "punning" of history and destiny.[10] She peppers her paragraphs with acid comments and then goes on without any development, any attempt to understand the author she has charged herself to explain or any consideration of a possible rejoinder or reply. Her encounter with what she calls "existentialism" was not a happy one, and certainly one that serious people should not take seriously. But we all have our youthful indiscretions and things we ought not to have said or written, and I discern in Grene's autobiographical writings a fairly pronounced ambivalence regarding her encounter with existentialism. Yet, she did not forestall the urge to write two more books along these lines, one on Sartre, regarding which others would be better suited to discuss than I am, and a book on Heidegger. These are not long books, but they came upon the scene at important times, before the major works of Sartre and Heidegger were available in English. The decision to write on these figures beyond *Introduction to Existentialism* seems to commit Grene to a serious responsibility as a scholar and as a philosopher. Even forced opportunism, born of the necessity to survive in a "man's discipline," does not absolve one of the duty to treat with due seriousness the subjects one has chosen to study. With this in mind, let us turn to her book simply entitled *Heidegger*.[11]

II

The short book on Heidegger was written several years after *Dreadful Freedom*, or *Introduction to Existentialism* (the same book; one assumes the change in title may have been driven by market pressures). My discussion of it is divided in two parts. First I want to speak of the general presentation, and then, second, of the Kantian heritage which she finally acknowledges (but acknowledges in a way that seems to distort what I see as its legitimate foundation).

Heidegger's first major part of *Being and Time* is entitled "Preparatory Fundamental Analysis of Dasein." The second is entitled "Dasein and Temporality." One chief point of the first part is to demonstrate that every facet of human thinking and acting is grounded in some notion of time and temporality. The first part is often referred to as "The Existential Analytic." It consists of an examination of virtually every aspect of human action: it shows how these are always interrelated with other aspects and with their temporal roots. This important aspect of the book is generally ignored in Grene's analysis. Here she may have neglected the responsibility of a scholar bringing an untranslated work of major importance to an audience that cannot read the work at first hand. Grene's account would have to leave such a reader wondering why Heidegger's prime work should have been entitled *Being and TIME.* At no point in her exposition or analysis does the prime import of time for Heidegger even get allowed to suggest itself—a serious weakness by any reckoning.

What Grene seems instead to have done, is presume that Kierkegaard's psychological studies are the ground of Heidegger's work. She discusses what she takes as three prime *Kierkegaardian* concepts as if this were a discussion of human psychology. There are biographical reasons that make this a likely course for Grene to have followed, although she now seems relieved that her book manuscript on Kierkegaard never saw the light of day, but biographical reasons aside, is reading Heidegger through Kierkegaard's psychology a well warranted strategy for exposition of Heidegger's views? Strangely, Nietzsche is rarely mentioned or alluded to. Would this not have been a more promising approach?

Another issue is that Grene translates Dasein as "existence." Certainly that is its ordinary English equivalent, but most Heidegger interpreters keep it in the original so as to designate the individual human being facing the world and its problems, avoiding thereby "existence" as an abstraction. If she cares to comment, perhaps Grene could clarify how she sees the idea of Dasein now.

A key to Grene's alienation from Heidegger's work is perhaps most succinctly expressed in two sentences: "This—Heidegger's description of the mind's activity as purposeful and animated by possibilities—the psychology of the empirical tradition is unable to admit. Mind viewed on a mechanical model is happy or miserable, not guilty or innocent."[12] If I rightly understand what she is advocating, with this flourish of the pen any and all of Kant and the Kantian foundation of Heidegger's thought is swept aside. After this assertion of the priorities of Utilitarianism, if that is what she intends, there is little room for any empathetic interest in what Heidegger is trying to do, in my judgment at least. And here I am in the minority, but perhaps in stating my view of this I will be drawing closer to Grene's own views, if further from her understanding of Heidegger. In a way that few commentators have recognized, one of Heidegger's concerns is to follow Kant and construct a "metaphysic of morals," one that Heidegger insists emerges out of the nature of human temporality. This yields a concern for the foundational nature of Freedom, of responsibility, a continuity of forward-looking assessment of open options and possibilities—and a foundational concern for the possibility of being-concerned itself. Here, if Grene has for Kant the degree of respect she professes, perhaps I can persuade her that Heidegger's task has more to do with the moral life than she allows. The argument would be a long one, so the suggestion that follows will have to suffice here.

Grene's expository points succeed in showing that for "the first time since Plato . . . death has been given central philosophic significance in the interpretation of life."[13] And she shows that "through the isolation of the individual . . . we can come to see clearly the ethical importance of the concept of personal integrity or authenticity. . . ."[14] As for Kant, moral integrity is bound to moral freedom, so Heidegger goes forward to see that "freedom [is] a venture as well as a fact."[15] One result is that by actively trying to transform one's world by understanding one's own worldly situation, one "transforms" oneself "by the very act of philosophizing."[16] Although she sees well into what Heidegger had regarded as the essential circularity of all thinking, I think that her subsequent reduction of this to egocentricity is wrong—but to demonstrate this would require a separate essay. Instead of facing Heidegger's project of building a "fundamental ontology" of human existence, she reduces all this to a variety of "existentialism" and reiterates themes from her earlier book. Yet, at the end Grene somehow raises Heidegger above the garden variety by noting "the validity of Heidegger's central concept: of the responsible person, whose Being is grounded in the tension of facticity, forfeiture [fallenness] and freedom."[17] Is this project not more closely akin in spirit to Kant's aspirations than to, say, Kierkegaard's?

One problem lurking in the background of Grene's account is the failure to fully recognize Heidegger's picture of himself in the philosophic scheme of things, and to recall Heidegger's training in the Southwest neo-Kantian school of thought.[18] Rather than regarding Heidegger's Kant book as an attempt to justify *Being and Time,* we should take seriously Richardson's suggestion that it was conceived earlier.[19] If so, it serves as a necessary preface and requires that its conceptual structure and argument be taken seriously in trying to come to terms with *Being and Time*. The foundation of *Being and Time*, then, is Kantian, not Kierkegaardian, and needs to be understood as such. And it is not unreasonable to imagine that Grene was in a position to read Heidegger so, given her penchant for Kant. Having had five years to prepare the English-speaking public for their reading of *Being and Time*, Grene's interpretation created some habits that had to be broken and some expectations that still need some unmaking, since her book is still often read by students encountering Heidegger for the first time.

Regarding the reasonableness of Grene's having taken a Kantian line from the start, I note that in 1929, Heidegger had published a short work entitled *Vom Wesen des Grundes*.[20] This essay, listed in Grene's bibliography, is a virtual philosophical genealogy in which Heidegger sees himself as following in the footsteps of first Leibniz and then Kant. It was really Leibniz, in his arguments with Newton, who rejected any equal pairing of space and time (as well as the geometric basis for the calculus) and found himself describing both space and time as not only phenomena but as relational concepts that can only be defined in temporal terms. What Kant seems to have done in the "Transcendental Aesthetic" is but to internalize what Leibniz had done. Later in the First Critique, Kant incorporated Leibniz's reversal of the traditional priority of actuality before possibility. Without some explicit recognition of these two fundamental philosophical reversals, it is hard to see how one can begin to come to terms with Kant's First Critique.[21] Had Grene chosen to follow out the "time" aspect of *Being and Time*, she might well have seen and presented to her readers a far more Kantian Heidegger.

Yet, perhaps the most fundamental error of Grene's attempts to make some sense of what Heidegger has done is to ignore the very method of philosophical reasoning which Heidegger, from the beginning, proclaimed. Whatever Grene may think of Husserl's phenomenology, *Being and Time* claims to be, and thereby must be judged as, a phenomenological treatise. Undertaking this task is something she abjures in her book; to treat it as "existentialist" instead of phenomenological is an easy way out—and one which the author she is criticizing rightfully maintained is illegitimate. Heidegger's rejection of the label "existentialist" is not coyness. The phenomenological method is that by which his efforts stand or fall.

A full defense of Heidegger would take a book to state, of course. And I believe that I have supplied such a defense in my *Heidegger, Kant and Time*, which I grant is not an appropriate subject for this essay.[22] But if I may be permitted to retrieve one argument from that book, it may shed some light upon the issue that I think most hinders the interpretive project of Grene's book. I argue, in agreement with Richardson, that Heidegger's *Kant and the Problem of Metaphysics* is, indeed, *the philosophic* introduction to *Being and Time*. One central theme of Heidegger's early work is his focus on Kant's idea of the Transcendental Imagination, which Heidegger argued is central for Kant, and which he seems to have transformed into his own foundational ontological existential of Care (*Sorge*). That this was not peripheral to Kant may be seen by the way Kant introduced the categories of the pure understanding, which must be synthesized with sense experience to produce specific cognitions. Kant explained:

> Synthesis in general, as we shall hereafter see, is the mere result of the power of imagination, a blind but indispensable function of the soul, without which we should have no knowledge whatsoever, but of which we are scarcely ever conscious.[23]

If one is to take Kant seriously, as Heidegger sought to do, we must acknowledge that Heidegger felt bound, at least in his earlier phase before "the turn," to take the entire First Critique seriously—and not just its first 200 pages. This means that it is *not* merely a theory of knowledge, but also an attempt to found morality in an ontologically grounded Freedom. Here the questions of Heidegger's Kantian roots and whether his project has a moral dimension come together. This would seem to have been a natural course for Grene to have followed. But perhaps it is asking too much to wish she had written a different book than the one she wrote, no matter how much the course of action seems to suggest itself to us in hindsight. Perhaps it is fairer to assume that Grene had decided Heidegger must be criticized, for whatever reasons she may have had at that time.

But this still leaves a question. Supposing one wants to criticize a thinker while still fulfilling the duty to present him responsibly, what vulnerabilities did Heidegger have that Grene might well have taken him to account for? In this regard I think she overlooked what would seem to be the prime question: Why has Heidegger's main work remained unfinished (in 1957, when Heidegger was still very much alive and Grene was writing)? If one is to point out some fundamental error in Heidegger it seems to lie in the fact that the book *Being and Time* is explicitly *unfinished*. The author's preface to the seventh German edition tells us that

> While the previous editions have borne the designation "First Half" this has now been deleted. After a quarter of a century, the second half could no longer be added unless the first were to be presented anew. Yet the road it has taken remains even today a necessary one, if our Dasein is to be stirred by the question of Being.[24]

The intriguing philosophic question is just *why* Heidegger did not or could not finish *Being and Time*? That is the philosophic question which, it seems to me, any critic who seeks to offer an answer on a fundamental level must offer. But to do this the critic must have some kind of fundamental empathy with what Heidegger tried to do. Grene does not seem to have even sniffed out the problem. But if I am still guilty of imagining books that Grene might have written and did not, I am still brought round eventually to wondering how she understood and understands her responsibility as a scholar as it relates to these two books. Does she wish she had not written them, today? Or does she wish she had written them differently? I stated at the outset my general sympathies for Grene's own philosophical views. This agreement makes the two books in question all the harder to understand. So, at the end I ask the same question I asked at the beginning—whatever her contributions may have been made in other areas, why did she go to the trouble of these two largely unhelpful volumes?

CHARLES M. SHEROVER

CITY UNIVERSITY OF NEW YORK,
  HUNTER COLLEGE
MARCH 2002

NOTES

1. In preparing my own book, *Time, Freedom and the Common Good: An Essay in Public Philosophy* (Albany: State University of New York, 1989), I extensively used Polanyi's *The Logic of Liberty: Reflections and Rejoinders* (Chicago: University of Chicago Press, 1951) for one crucial chapter.

2. Marjorie Grene, *Introduction to Existentialism* (Chicago: University of Chicago Press, 1948, 1959), p. v.

3. Grene, *Introduction to Existentialism*, n.1, p. 41

4. Martin Heidegger, *Being and Time,* trans, Macquarrie and Robinson (London: SCM Press; New York: Harper, 1962), n/xiii, (H427) p. 499.

5. On the authority of Professor Joan Stambaugh who translated another English version of *Being and Time* (Albany: State University of New York Press, 1996) as well as several of the later essays and who knew him personally.

6. See Grene, *Introduction* to *Existentialism*, p. 125.

7. Heidegger, *Being and Time*, p. 63 (39).

8. See Grene, *Introduction to Existentialism*, p. 65, n. 9.

9. Grene, *Introduction to Existentialism*, pp. 68–69.

10. See ibid., pp. 70, 135 and 71.

11. Marjorie Grene, *Martin Heidegger* (London: Bowes & Bowes, 1957).

12. Ibid., p. 35.

13. Ibid., p. 44.

14. Ibid., p. 45.

15. Ibid., p. 47.

16. Ibid., p. 49.

17. Ibid., p. 59.

18. For a thorough account of Heidegger's neo-Kantian background in his broader philosophical context, see Michael Friedman, *A Parting of the Ways* (Chicago: Open Court, 2000), pp. 25–61.

19. William J. Richardson, *Heidegger: Through Phenomenology to Thought* (The Hague: M. Nijhoff, 1974 [1967]).

20. Halle: Max Nieymeyer.

21. For a fully documented presentation of these (and related) themes, see my "Kant's Evaluation of his Relationship to Leibniz," in *The Philosophy of Immanuel Kant*, ed. Richard Kennington (Washington: The Catholic University of America Press, 1985), pp. 201–28. A more succinct version of this argument is presented as "Kant's Debt to Leibniz" in Sherover, *From Kant to Heidegger: Essays in Modern Philosophy*, ed. Johnson (Washington: The Catholic University of America Press, forthcoming).

22. Published with a preface by William Barrett (Bloomington: Indiana University Press, 1971).

23. *Critique of Pure Reason*, trans. N. K. Smith (London: Macmillan and New York: St. Martin's Press, 1968), A78=B103 (NKS p. 112).

24. Heidegger, *Being and Time,* p. 17.

REPLY TO CHARLES M. SHEROVER

Dr. Sherover finds himself (almost) angered by my work on Heidegger, or what he has read of it, and I can't say I blame him. Were I an admirer of Heidegger, I would be angry, too. If he knew both my earlier and later discussions of the same thinker, he would probably be even angrier; more of those shortly. In fact, I must admit, most of Sherover's objections to my *Introduction to Existentialism* are entirely justified. It was a hasty and superficial study. If I really suggested, in the introduction to the 1959 edition, that all "existentialists" except Tillich were atheists, that was idiotic. I did for a time find Tillich's perhaps rather thin theism attractive, and Kierkegaard's breast-beating supersubjectivity much less so, to put it mildly. But if I gave the impression Sherover says I did, I can only apologize. In any case, I think I spread the label "existentialism" too widely in those days, as many did. Neither Jaspers nor Heidegger welcomed such a title. That there's any genuine theism in Heidegger I very much doubt, and if there's some esoteric sense in which he invoked some kind of De- ity—well, I really don't care. Let him add that to all the rest of the word- play on German *tiefere Bedeutungen*. That's a con game to which I long ago developed an immunity, and not because I preferred some glib Millian empiricism.

Sherover's remarks about Heidegger and Kant I find bewildering. What has Heidegger's quest for Being to do with Kant's transcendental ques- tions? They seem to me at opposite poles in their attitude to philosophy. One plunges headlong into obscurantist ontologizing, while the other seeks the necessary presuppositions for the experience we do in fact have. In my little book on Heidegger, I did acknowledge that I had learned something from his early Kant book, and the later one is, oddly, just a good scholarly piece of work: a kind of lucid interval in the interstices of its author's usual bombast. To identify Heidegger's *Sorge* with Kantian productive imagina- tion, as Sherover wants to do, seems to me nothing short of impious. As to his question: no, I don't think my first book was a good one. Would I write it differently today? Well, I just wouldn't write it.

As to the little Heidegger book, which, again, shocks Sherover by its negative relation to its subject: the truth is that in a first draft it was so vicious that the editor asked me to tone it down. So it's the milder version that was published. Again, I find some of my critic's points apposite. If I neglected the priority of temporality, that was a bad error. If I attributed much of Heidegger's thought to Kierkegaardian souces, that was also badly mistaken. Heidegger took from Kierkegaard the term "Existenz," to which he gave his own special meaning. He also made important use of the concept of dread (*Angst*), but since that term appears in such diverse contexts in Kierkegaard, Heidegger, and Sartre, it is probably unwise to speak of it as derived in the later cases from the Danish thinker. It was also unwise of me to call *Dasein* existence. I have sometimes spoken of "human being," which is a little better. Further, if I appeared to favor what Sherover calls "the priorities of Utilitarianism," I don't recognize my own voice in that statement. On the other hand, the very idea of a Heideggerian "metaphysic of morals" seems to me nothing short of impossible. Kantian freedom is everyone's; Heideggerian freedom belongs to the German hero, alone, risking his life for the Fatherland. The rest of us, addicted to the everyday, are doomed to perpetual enslavement. If, and I agree, the foundation of *Being and Time* is not Kierkegaardian, it is, it seems to me crystal clear (if anything is clear about that murky work), emphatically *not* Kantian. I admit that *Vom Wesen des Grundes,* in which Sherover finds evidence of Heidegger's Kantian roots, has always seemed to me especially perverse and obscure, even for the sage of the Schwarzwald. Nor can I see *Sein und Zeit* as a phenomenological treatise. It's *ontological*, for goodness' sake.

Sherover wants to know how at this late date I see my responsibility for those two early works. As I said, I think the first was a poor job, and the second a little better. Nor, as Sherover believes I should have done, could I pretend a respect I did not feel. If he is inclined to be angry with me, I may say in return that I have been angry with Heidegger ever since I heard the Heidelberg version of his *Rektoratsrede*, "Die Rolle der Universität im neuen Reich," in 1933—an anger renewed when I read the still Nazified *Einführung in die Metaphysik,* published twenty years later. In the little Heidegger book, I did try to say something positive about his work, as I did also in an essay called "Heidegger: Philosopher and Prophet," in 1958—although that piece also comes, eventually, to a rather negative conclusion. But the first article I published on this subject, "A Note on the Philosophy of Heidegger," in 1938, was less conciliatory. (Both these essays are included in my *Philosophy in and out of Europe*, 1976.) In the reprinted version, I subtitled it "Confessions of a Young Positivist." Although I have long since lost any enthusiasm for the positivist creed, I still find my remarks there not only amusing, but appropriate. Heidegger is a worthy successor to Hegel as a master of German philosophical fraud. And "arrogance" is certainly an appropriate term to apply to his attitude, not only to other philosophers (except Parmenides), but to practically every one. When in one of his lectures he sneered at some commonsensical attitude, a member of the audience is said to have remarked: "Warum sagt er nicht 'hundsgemeiner Menschenverstand'?"

It does occur to me, I confess, that the anger I expressed in that early work on Heidegger may have been intensified by my own frustration, exiled as I was from teaching and from any contact with an intellectual community. The return to teaching and collegiality many years later may have made my voice less shrill. Be that as it may, I have stated my considered view of Heidegger in 1995 in *A Philosophical Testament* (pp. 70–79), and since Dr. Sherover asks me about my later opinion, I take the liberty of summarizing it here.

First, I listed some positive features of Heidegger's doctrine as set forth in *Sein und Zeit*: the critique of Cartesian *res extensa*, the description of human "mentality," if you like, in terms of *Dasein* or human being rather than consciousness, the stress on the priority of the future (though, as I remarked, this fades in extreme old age), historicity, and with it, the hermeneutical circle, perhaps also the contrast of the everyday with authenticity (though not Heidegger's particular account of authentic freedom). Over against these positive items, I listed three features of Heidegger's account of being-in-the-world which I find basically unacceptable. First is his philosophical style: the way in which he plays back and forth with the "ontic" and the "ontological." As I put it, "human being is essentially being-to-death (ontological). But you mustn't suppose that this is the case because we all have to die (ontic). Dear me, no; on the contrary, we all have to die because we are being-to-death" (p.75). And so on and on. Second, in the face of Sherover's defense of German profundities, I have to say, his language is also unacceptable. No one has a right to toss neologisms back and forth as Heidegger does, and my suspicions of the tortured, and torturing, rhetoric of *Sein and Zeit* are reinforced by the patent fact that most of his later writings are simply pretentious nonsense. Third, I have two objections to the substance of Heidegger's message. One is his neglect of life, of the biological basis of our existence, and the other is what I now see as his deep and fanatical German nationalism. I conclude:

It has taken me a long time—nine pages or sixty years—to come to terms with Heidegger. I have had to acknowledge some philosophical lessons of *Being and Time*—and I should also have acknowledged . . . the approach to reading Plato that I learned from his proseminar on Plato's *Phaedrus* in the spring semester of 1932. . . . On the debit side, however, the deficiencies even of his one truly significant published work (defects only intensified in his later writing) make his account of being-in-the-world so deeply misleading that one can only regretfully take the themes one must from it, assimilate them to what one finds a more adequate framework, and leave the rest severely alone. Any other course I am afraid I find both intellectually and morally reprehensible. (pp. 78–79)

Sorry, Charles Sherover. Hier steh' ich; Gott hilf mir, ich kann nicht anders.

M. G.

23

David Detmer

GRENE ON SARTRE

Marjorie Grene played a major role in introducing the philosophy of Jean-Paul Sartre to the English-speaking world. Indeed, it was due in large part to her early writings on Sartre,[1] models of clear, well-informed exposition and of fair-minded criticism, that many English-speaking philosophers first came to view Sartre as a serious thinker, and not, as the prevailing caricature would have it, as a sensationalistic, irresponsible purveyor of overly dramatic literary clichés about absurdity, despair, and the meaninglessness of life.[2] Grene's achievement in this regard can only be seen as remarkable given her lack of sympathy for Sartre's philosophy,[3] and even more so in light of the fact that her engagement with Sartre's thought seems to have stemmed as much from expediency as from a genuine interest on her part.[4]

In this essay I will briefly summarize some of the distinct features of Grene's interpretation of Sartre, calling attention especially to the ways in which her work helped to establish his reputation in the Anglophone world as a genuine philosopher. I will then conclude by offering a few criticisms of Grene's account.

I. GRENE'S INTERPRETATION OF SARTRE

To keep the discussion to a manageable length, I will focus on just ten aspects of Grene's approach to Sartre's philosophy.

a. Sartre as a Logically Consistent and Rigorously Coherent Philosopher

In the initial discussions of Sartre's thought in English, a common complaint was that he failed to offer a coherent philosophy, or even to defend his views with arguments. Rather, so the accusation went, he succeeded solely by means of his literary skills, and because his message fit the mood of the times.[5]

Grene's position, in quite radical contrast, is that Sartre, if anything, is consistent to a fault, as he refuses to acknowledge any truth that does not square with his premises, and relentlessly pursues the logical consequences of those premises, no matter how unsettling or offensive to common sense they might be.[6] Similarly, she would find the charge that Sartre disdains argumentation to be quite spectacularly wrong, as she repeatedly praises him, not for the truth or wisdom of his conclusions, but rather for the "wealth" of "subtle," "detailed," and "ingenious" argumentation to be found in his work.[7]

b. Sartre as Grounded in the History of Philosophy

Another early criticism of Sartre's thought held that it failed to connect meaningfully with the work of previous philosophers. According to this line, Sartre's "philosophy" was better understood as a literary phenomenon, cultural fad (more fit for discussion in cafés and trendy Parisian nightspots than in academic departments of philosophy), or short-lived product of the crisis conditions in Europe during World War II.[8]

Grene's approach, once again, could not differ from this more dramatically. Indeed, she suggests that "[t]he greatness of Sartre as philosopher lies," in part, in "the rigor with which his conclusions follow from theses of the philosophers who have most influenced him . . . "[9] Moreover, she claims that

> Sartre . . . appears to the philosophically schooled reader as, not only an original thinker, but, in a more humdrum way, a thoroughly competent professional philosopher with a sound historical schooling. For this reason, the relation of his own thought to the philosophers he most relies on comes through to the reader with unusual distinctness, and his own method appears, not indeed simply as eclectic, but as an idiosyncratic interweaving and re-making of familiar concepts and themes.[10]

c. Sartre's Conception of Freedom as Cartesian

Sartre has long been excoriated for advancing an unprecedentedly extreme view of freedom.[11] But Grene argues that Sartre's "concept of freedom is Cartesian through and through"[12]—indeed, that "*Being and Nothingness* may . . . be considered a long paean to Cartesian freedom."[13]

d. Sartre as Non-Heideggerian

If Sartre's originality with regard to Descartes is sometimes overstated, it is often understated in connection with Heidegger. It has even been suggested that Sartre's early philosophy is merely a bad translation of Heidegger into French, with lots of misunderstandings thrown in.

Once again, Grene offers a corrective account. While acknowledging, as Sartre himself had, Sartre's great debt to Heidegger, she nonetheless shows how the two philosophers differ on issue after issue, most notably on consciousness, temporality, freedom, the body, authenticity, and philosophical method.[14] Grene suggests that Sartre has grafted a number of central Heideggerian themes onto a Cartesian framework that is wholly alien to his thought, as are the dialectical techniques by which Sartre weaves together the disparate strands of his philosophy.[15]

e. Being and Nothingness *over* Existentialism is a Humanism

Being and Nothingness is a long, technical, difficult work of philosophy. Moreover, while it was published in the original French in 1943, it was not translated into English until 1956. *Existentialism is a Humanism*, on the other hand, is a short, accessible lecture to a general audience—an attempt by Sartre to popularize his philosophy. Furthermore, it was translated into English in 1947, just one year after its initial appearance in French. Not surprisingly, vastly many more philosophers (let alone general readers) have read the latter work than have ever attempted the former. And this disparity was, understandably, especially pronounced in the English-speaking world between 1947 and 1956.[16]

The results, with regard to the reception of Sartre's philosophy in the Anglophone world, have been unfortunate. The problem, in part, is that *Existentialism is a Humanism* was presented at a time when Sartre's thought was undergoing a rapid transition, so it contains many ideas that are not defended in any of his other works, and thus it fails to be representative of his thinking. But far worse is the fact that it is carelessly presented and poorly reasoned.[17] Indeed, it is my opinion that the principal reason for Sartre's poor reputation among philosophers is that so many of them have read only *Existentialism is a Humanism*, and have concluded, much too hastily but otherwise quite reasonably, that he is an incompetent philosopher.

But the situation would probably be much worse than it is were it not for Grene's efforts at making accessible the content of *Being and Nothingness* while warning against the distortions and confusions of *Existentialism is a Humanism*.[18] In this connection it must be recalled that *Dreadful*

Freedom was one of the very few works in English containing a substantial discussion of *Being and Nothingness* to be available prior to the translation (eight years later) of that work into English.

f. Sartre as Dialectician

Sartre's thought is often misunderstood, and undervalued, because readers miss the dialectical element in his thought. For example, readers might confuse a position which Sartre describes and develops over hundreds of pages with his own final position, since they fail to realize that the former represents just one stage in a dialectical movement toward a more adequate view. Or they might see his thought as contradictory, since he seems to say "A" at one point and "not-A" at another, if they don't see that he is moving toward a position which would reconcile and comprehend both of these seeming opposites.[19] Or, finally, they might consider a work such as *Being and Nothingness* to be redundant, since it appears to say the same things over and over again, if they miss the fact that the claims mean something different (and something more) the second time around than they did at first. After all, as Grene puts it, Sartre "opens up avenues along which he can let his basic concepts move—in a movement which is also to alter them, so that they become, at the end of the argument, different and richer than they were at the beginning."[20] And, in general, Grene has led the way in explaining the dialectical strand in Sartre's thinking to an English-speaking audience that tends not to be well-schooled in dialectics.[21]

g. Sartre as Seeker after Necessary Truths

It has been widely believed, especially during the early years of Sartre's reception in the English-speaking world, that his attitude toward evidence and truth is casual to the point of being cavalier. Perhaps because Sartre speaks so extensively of subjectivity, choice, and freedom, some have read him as saying that we are free to believe whatever we might choose to believe, without thereby offending any legitimate philosophical scruple.

As against such a reading, Grene argues that

the ideal of philosophical knowledge, with Sartre, as with Descartes and Husserl, is absolute certainty: "apodeicticity," that is, *necessary* truth . . . The necessary truth of the phenomenologist from Descartes through Husserl to Sartre must be luminousness itself: the self-evident . . . [T]hey seek the self-guaranteeing, the pure light of reason illuminating itself by its own rays . . . [O]nly the self-evident is worthy of acceptance as philosophical truth.[22]

h. Sartre and Religion

Sartre's atheism is often thought to be of the sneering, hostile sort that one might associate with Nietzsche or Bertrand Russell. This has, understandably, led to his work's receiving a hostile reception from some religious thinkers. But Grene points out that "the human reality of genuine religious feeling is not, as it is by most antireligious philosophers, simply dismissed as nonsense by existentialist writers."[23] Indeed, she suggests that much of Sartre's thought can be understood as an attempt to work out, in nonreligious terms, the meaning of those human experiences, many of them universal, that have given rise to religious belief.[24] His view, as she expounds it, seems to be that religious beliefs, though false, are responses to something significant in human experience, which we are unwise to dismiss out of hand.

i. Sartre and Biology

A common criticism of Sartre, and a reasonable one, is that his work seldom engages with, or appears to be informed by, modern science. Grene thus performs a major service by putting her expertise in biology to work in analyzing Sartre's scattered references to biology in his *Critique of Dialectical Reason*.[25]

j. Sartre as the Maker of Mistakes, Just Like Every Other Philosopher

While I have been stressing the ways in which Grene's interpretation of Sartre rescues him either from criticisms or from misreadings, it is far from the case that Grene herself is uncritical of Sartre. But Grene's criticisms are, for the most part, not of the sweeping, denunciatory kind, but rather are addressed to specific claims and arguments, leaving many other claims and arguments untouched, and still others to praise.[26] And even when she does offer a sweeping objection, such as that Sartre's philosophy leads to a dead end, and does so as the inevitable result of its Cartesian premises, she still makes it clear that his work

> repays close and repeated attention. One may disagree with it totally, but if one likes philosophy and is patient, one will find in it a surprising wealth of subtle and ingenious argument. What more can a philosophical reader ask? Truth, perhaps. But for us smaller fry . . . one way to the truth is through the errors of one's great predecessors and contemporaries. Such is the case with Sartre. His work embodies, I believe, more incisively and more ingeniously than any other, the intellectual crisis of our time.[27]

II. OBJECTIONS

The major objection to Grene's account of Sartre that is most likely to suggest itself to the Sartre scholar is that she has offered an excessively Cartesian interpretation. That is, while she certainly acknowledges the many ways in which Sartre departs from his great predecessor, and also gives due attention to several other figures who have profoundly influenced his thought, in the final analysis she regards him as a Cartesian, and seems to see this as the controlling element that determines the development and final destination of his thought. Moreover, she suggests that Sartre's failings stem primarily from his allegiance to Cartesianism, but also that his major contribution has been to demonstrate that Cartesianism must fail. In short, she holds that Sartre's Cartesianism is the key both to the understanding of his thought and to the proper appreciation of its achievements and its shortcomings.[28]

For my part, I am not inclined to criticize Grene on this score, in spite of my conviction that an at least equally plausible and compelling reading of Sartre could be constructed in which Husserl or Hegel would displace Descartes as the figure who holds the key to understanding his thought. But there is certainly room for a Cartesian Sartre, and Grene, a distinguished Descartes scholar, is well-equipped to present him to us. I think she does it well.

But this does not mean that I find her interpretation to be beyond criticism. Here I will limit myself to three objections, all of them drawn, broadly speaking, from ethics. I place my focus there not only for reasons of personal interest, but also because Grene, in her earliest writings on Sartre, also chose to focus primarily on ethics.[29]

a. Radical Conversion

Grene complains that Sartre's frequent moral pronouncements in his work subsequent to *Being and Nothingness* are at best gratuitously added onto and at worst fundamentally at odds with the gloomy impasse to which he consigns us in that book. For example, in a discussion of *Existentialism is a Humanism*, Grene writes:

> [I]n dealing with the objection that the existentialist cannot criticize the morality of others, Sartre replies that, besides the criticism in terms of bad faith, the existentialist can also demand that one choose for the sake of freedom itself, not only for one's self but generally, since "the freedom of one involves the freedom of others." . . . [T]his is superficially logical; but . . . it is too easy; and nothing in the much more detailed analysis of [*Being and Nothingness*], or in the novels and plays for that matter, bears it out. One must admit . . . that,

given as foundation the general principle of freedom for its own sake, of human liberty in general as an absolute value, one can construct upon it an ingenious and, at least superficially, consistent philosophy of revolution. But the question remains: how from the solitary creator of a world who dares to bear his lonely freedom, who decides "alone, unjustifiable, and without excuse," one can deduce so easily an agent of universal freedom, a proletarian inheritor of the French libertarian tradition.[30]

The problem with such criticisms, in my judgment, is that they rest on an insufficient appreciation for two elements of Sartre's thought: his idea of radical conversion and his employment of a specific dialectical strategy in dealing with ethics. What I have in mind is this: At several points in *Being and Nothingness*—after seeming to suggest that it is impossible to escape bad faith[31] or hellish interpersonal relations[32] or the utterly futile project of becoming in-itself-for-itself or God,[33] in short, whenever he appears to consign us to a bleak fate—he appends cryptic remarks, often in footnotes, to the effect that there is a way out after all, provided that we undergo a "radical conversion," which "cannot be discussed here." The clearest indication of Sartre's meaning comes at the very end of *Being and Nothingness*, in the first and only section of that book devoted to "Ethical Implications." There Sartre speaks of the possibility of renouncing the project of being-God, a project from which, he had seemed formerly to suggest, we could not escape. Thus, with regard to the "value of the ideal presence of the *ens causa sui*," Sartre asks, "[w]hat will become of freedom if it turns its back upon this value? . . . [W]ill freedom . . . be able to put an end to the reign of this value? In particular is it possible for freedom to take itself for a value as the source of all value . . . ? All these questions . . . can find their reply only on the ethical plane. We shall devote to them a future work."[34]

So ends *Being and Nothingness*. While the projected ethical work in which Sartre promised to take up these issues was never completed to his satisfaction, his subsequent writings make his meaning clear, at least in very broad outline. The radical conversion is the rejection of the project of being-God and the adoption, in its stead, of the project of taking freedom, both my own and that of other people, as a fundamental value, indeed, as the source of all value. Thus, when Sartre states, in *Existentialism is a Humanism*, that "freedom . . . can have no other end and aim but itself," and that "freedom is the foundation of all values,"[35] he is writing from a post-conversion standpoint, and answering the questions posed at the end of *Being and Nothingness*, a work which describes, not the human condition *simpliciter*, but rather the condition of humans who, in bad faith, attempt to be God.[36]

Thus, Sartre's dialectical strategy emerges. Rather than arguing directly for the adoption of an ethics based upon the pursuit of freedom, Sartre attempts to persuade us to do so by showing us the hellish consequences of doing otherwise. His freedom-ethic is neither in contradiction with nor unconnected to his earlier descriptions of the gloomy impasses in which those embracing other values are trapped. *Being and Nothingness* implicitly argues for the necessity of radical conversion. Sartre's later works tell us, admittedly much too sketchily (except for the posthumously published *Notebooks for an Ethics*, which does fill in some of the details), what this entails. They, in general, are written from a post-conversion perspective.[37]

b. Ethical Subjectivism and the Alleged Impossibility of a Sartrean Ethic

Grene interprets Sartre as holding that "[v]alues are created . . . only by the free act of a human agent who *takes* this or that to be good or bad, beautiful or ugly, in the light of his endeavor to give significance and order to an otherwise meaningless world."[38] Indeed, it seems to be her view that Sartre's philosophy precludes the development of any ethical theory beyond this weak, open-ended subjectivism:

> Sartre never wrote his ethic, for the very good reason that his philosophical principles forbade him to do so. If you start, as he did, from consciousness as for-itself, as the negation of its objective target, the in-itself, concepts like "good" or "right" are either pure negations or bad faith. There is no foundation available to him on which an ethic could be built.[39]

I will make three points by way of reply. The first is that while there are indeed many passages in Sartre's writings which appear to support Grene's reading of him as a value-subjectivist, there is also an abundance of textual counterevidence from all periods of Sartre's career, including the earliest. For example, in an early article on Husserl's doctrine of intentionality, Sartre writes:

> All at once hatred, love, fear, sympathy—all these famous "subjective" reactions which were floating in the malodorous brine of the mind—are pulled out. They are merely ways of discovering the world. It is things which abruptly unveil themselves to us as hateful, sympathetic, horrible, lovable. Being dreadful is a *property* of this Japanese mask, an inexhaustible and irreducible property which constitutes its very nature—and not the sum of our subjective reactions to a piece of sculptured wood. Husserl has restored to things their horror and their charm.[40]

Or again, in a 1939 entry from his posthumously published *War Diaries* (unavailable to Grene when she published her criticism), Sartre states his full agreement with the value-objectivism of the phenomenologist Max

Scheler: "Scheler made me understand that there existed *values* . . . (I) understood that there existed specific natures, equipped with an existence as of right, and called values; . . . (I) understood that these values, whether proclaimed or not, regulated each of my acts and judgments, and that by their nature they 'ought to be.'"[41]

My second point, in reply to Grene's claim that "there is no foundation available to [Sartre] on which an ethic could be built," is that the obvious candidate for such a foundation is phenomenology. Phenomenology is, among other things, concerned to describe the objects of experience without accepting the empiricists' prejudice that all experience is sensory experience. Thus, there is an experience of the hateful, the horrible, and the lovable, and of justice and fairness, of the good and the right. These are not physical objects and they are not perceived through the senses, but they are objects of our experience nonetheless, and we do not typically encounter them within our experience as having been created, invented, or arbitrarily chosen by us.

Finally, if Grene's point is that Sartre's philosophical principles make it unclear what ontological status values could possibly have, I would suggest that they have the same status as do absences. For, just as Pierre's absence from the café cannot plausibly be said to exist as part of the furniture of the universe without the introduction of a consciousness looking for (and failing to find) Pierre, so do values perhaps emerge only as a consequence of the concerns and pursuits of conscious beings. But that does not render judgments about what is or is not valuable any more subjective than are judgments about whether Pierre is or is not absent from the café. I might mistake Pierre for someone else and consequently think that he is not absent from the café when in fact he is, and thus I can be objectively wrong in my judgments about absences even if absences do not exist in a world devoid of consciousnesses. Similarly, I can be objectively wrong in my judgments about what is or is not good, or fair, or just, even if all of these depend upon the activities of consciousnesses for their existence.

c. Revolution and Play

In response to Sartre's call for political revolution, in such works as "Materialism and Revolution," Grene asks,

What of the revolutionary after the revolution? The philosophy of the free man in its political aspect is the philosophy of transcendence as such, of going beyond the present society to create a new one. At present, in Sartre's picture, it is the dichotomy of oppressor and oppressed that motivates such transcendence. But what of the free man in a free society? If he is still free, he still transcends his situation to a new one; he is still, by definition, a revolutionary, but against what? Against freedom itself? That is absurd.[42]

Sartre would later admit, though he was not addressing Grene directly, to being unable to provide a satisfactory answer to her questions: "As soon as there will exist *for everyone* a margin of *real* freedom beyond the production of life, Marxism will have lived out its span; a philosophy of freedom will take its place. But we have no means, no intellectual instrument, no concrete experience which allows us to conceive of this freedom or of this philosophy."[43]

Still, Sartre does offer a sketch for an answer in *Being and Nothingness*, when he offers an analysis of "play" as an ideal for those who have undergone the radical conversion. He defines play as "an activity of which man is the first origin, for which man sets the rules, and which has no consequences except according to the rules posited."[44] As examples of play, Sartre cites "sports or pantomime or games,"[45] and provides a lengthy analysis of skiing.[46]

In Sartre's later works he doesn't talk much about play, but he also says nothing to suggest that he has abandoned it as an ideal. My sense is that he realized that so many people are hungry, poor, and politically oppressed, that the immediate task at hand is to alleviate these injustices and bring about "a margin of real freedom" for everyone. But what comes after that? If play is the ultimate goal, it is clear why we can't answer that question with much precision. What comes will be whatever we decide to bring forth. The revolutionary who in such a society is devoted to play is guilty of no contradiction, for in choosing to be a revolutionary in our world or a devotee of play in the world to be made, such a person is acting consistently on behalf of the same value: freedom.

III. CONCLUSION

I trust that the reader will have noticed that each of my three criticisms of Grene involves very difficult issues of interpretation, over which there is ample room for reasonable people to disagree. While in some cases I think there is a better way of understanding Sartre's project, and one which, at the same time, acquits him of some of her objections, I do not accuse her of any blunder. To the contrary, I find that Grene's pioneering (and subsequent) work on Sartre exhibits the same accuracy, clarity, and scrupulousness that we find in her other philosophical writings. Sartre was fortunate to find such an able expositor and critic to help introduce his thought to the often indifferent, if not hostile, world of Anglophone philosophy.

DAVID DETMER

PURDUE UNIVERSITY CALUMET
FEBRUARY 2002

NOTES

1. I have in mind primarily her *Dreadful Freedom: A Critique of Existentialism* (Chicago: University of Chicago Press, 1948). She had written a few articles on Sartre prior to the publication of that book, but they were not published in major philosophy journals, and thus failed to exert much influence among philosophers. However, the articles were largely incorporated into *Dreadful Freedom*, and this book, as one of the first on the subject to be published in English, and as one of the few to be available before Sartre's major philosophical works (most notably *Being and Nothingness*) had been translated into English, led the way in setting the agenda for Sartre scholarship in America for many years. (*Dreadful Freedom* was later reissued as *Introduction to Existentialism* [Chicago: Phoenix Books, 1959] without alteration, save for the addition of a two-page preface. I will cite this later addition in the remainder of this essay.)

2. Hazel E. Barnes, who was later to translate *Being and Nothingness* and to become a major Sartre scholar, reports that, before she looked into it directly (in 1948), she had been led to believe that existentialism was "a somewhat sensational attitude toward life and a philosophy of defeatism and despair" (*The Story I Tell Myself* [Chicago: University of Chicago Press, 1997], p. 143). Despite the fine efforts of Grene, Barnes, and many other scholars, this caricature is still not dead. For example, George F. Will writes:

> For those who have not read the classics of existentialism (for example, Sartre's *Being and Nothingness*), let me explain: existentialism often seems to be the belief that because life is absurd, philosophy should be, too. Sartre is the patron saint of those people in black turtlenecks and black moods who used to frequent the Boulevard St. Germain, comparing notes on the emptiness of life. ("Jean-Paul Sartre Discovers Democracy," in his *The Pursuit of Happiness, and Other Sobering Thoughts* [New York: Harper & Row, 1978], p. 20)

3. Grene seems to view Sartre's philosophy as a magnificent, perhaps even heroic, failure. For example, she says of *Being and Nothingness* that "it is one of the transcendent works of our philosophical tradition which show how, given inadequate premises, a particular movement of thought works itself into an impassable dead end. On the way to its dismal conclusion, it is brilliant" (*A Philosophical Testament* [Chicago: Open Court, 1995], p. 79). Similar remarks can

be found in *Introduction to Existentialism*, p. 149; and in *Sartre* (New York: New Viewpoints, 1973), [pp. 28, 136]).

4. As Ann Fulton (in *Apostles of Sartre: Existentialism in America, 1945–1963* [Evanston, Ill.: Northwestern University Press, 1999], p. 80) reports, "[w]hen asked why she had written so much on a strain of philosophy that she basically disagreed with, Grene remembered, 'It was simple really. After I lost my job, I thought I should do anything more or less respectable I was given a chance to do.' And being a woman in an almost all-male discipline made her more willing to accept anything that was offered. Grene recalled: 'Women of my generation, like those of countless generations preceding us, did what we had a chance to do, not necessarily what we were inwardly committed to doing.'" Grene's comments are cited in n. 79 of ch. 3, *Apostles of Sartre*: ("In and Out of Friendship," in A. Donagan et al., eds., *Human Nature and Natural Knowledge* [Dordrecht: Reidel, 1986], p. 361) and (letter to Ann Fulton, 6 December 1988).

5. For example, Justus Buchler asserted that Sartre's success had "been in narrative, semi-biographical and dramatic contexts, where standards of explication and rigor are irrelevant" ("Concerning Existentialism," *Nation* [October 25, 1947], p. 449).

6. See, for example, *Sartre*, pp. 136, 267–68 (in which she contrasts Sartre with Locke in this regard); "The Career of Action and Passion in Sartre's Philosophical Work," in her *Philosophy In and Out of Europe* (Lanham, Md.: University Press of America, 1987), p. 108; and *A Philosophical Testament*, p. 79.

7. See, for example, *Sartre*, pp. 6, 28.

8. See Fulton, p. 28.

9. Grene, "The Career of Action and Passion in Sartre's Philosophical Work," p. 108.

10. Grene, *Sartre*, pp. 34–35. Grene then proceeds to explicate Sartre's thought largely by means of explaining his creative appropriations of earlier thinkers, the most important of which, she argues, can be divided into two groups: Descartes and the phenomenologists (Husserl and Heidegger) on the one hand, and the dialecticians (Hegel, Kierkegaard, and Marx) on the other (pp. 32–104). Incidentally, she compares Sartre favorably to Heidegger in this regard, accusing the latter of being, "in the main, a scandalous historian" (p. 34).

11. See my *Freedom as a Value: A Critique of the Ethical Theory of Jean-Paul Sartre* (La Salle, Ill.: Open Court, 1988), pp. 36–39.

12. Grene, *Sartre*, pp. 64–65.

13. Grene, *Sartre*, p. 45. Though Grene does not make the point, it can be argued that Sartre's theory of freedom is also anticipated in Husserl's work. On this point see James M. Edie, "The Roots of the Existentialist Theory of Freedom in Husserl," in his *Edmund Husserl's Phenomenology* (Bloomington: Indiana University Press, 1987), pp. 60–77.

14. This list could be extended at length. The two philosophers disagree significantly on intersubjectivity and on death, for example, not to mention their political differences.

15. Grene, *Sartre*, pp. 61–67, 85–86.

16. See Fulton, pp. 26–27.

17. To give just one example, consider that throughout most of this work, and to a degree not to be found in any of his others, Sartre presents atheism as central to his thought. Indeed, he speaks of its being "necessary to draw the consequences of [God's] absence right to the end"; chastises a kind of secular moralism which asserts that the question of God's existence is not important; declares that it is because of God's nonexistence that we are "abandoned" and "forlorn"; insists that the one doctrine allegedly uniting all existentialists—that existence precedes essence—can only be affirmed with perfect consistency by atheists; declares Dostoievsky's dictum that "if God did not exist, everything would be permitted" to be the very "starting point" of existentialism; and defines "existentialism" as "nothing else but an attempt to draw the full conclusions from a consistently atheistic position" (*Existentialism & Humanism*, trans. Philip Mairet [London: Methuen, 1973] pp. 26–34, 56). And yet, quite incredibly, at the very end of the piece he seems to forget all of this: "[Existentialism] declares . . . that even if God existed that would make no difference from its point of view" (p. 56).

18. See, for example, *Introduction to Existentialism*, pp. 72–74; *Sartre*, p. 253; and "The Reception of Continental Philosophy in America," in *Philosophy In and Out of Europe*, p. 35.

19. See Detmer, *Freedom as a Value*, pp. 93–132.

20. Grene, *Sartre*, p. 80.

21. See, for example, Grene, *Sartre*, pp. 70–104.

22. Grene, *Sartre*, pp. 39–40.

23. Grene, *Introduction to Existentialism*, p. 64.

24. See, for example, *Introduction to Existentialism*, pp. 65–66. This thesis is also worked out quite fruitfully in Thomas M. King's, *Sartre and the Sacred* (Chicago: University of Chicago Press, 1974).

25. See *Sartre*, pp. 230–39. It should be noted in this context that Grene is the author of several acclaimed works in the philosophy of biology.

26. To mention just one of many examples, she argues, based on a careful analysis of one of his own examples, that Sartre is wrong to claim that it is material scarcity that throws human beings into serial relations with one another (*Sartre*, p. 251).

27. Grene, *Sartre*, pp. 6–7.

28. See, for example, *Sartre*, p. 287; and *A Philosophical Testament*, p. 79.

29. See, for example, *Introduction to Existentialism*, p. iii.

30. Grene, *Introduction to Existentialism*, pp. 75–76. For similar arguments, this time in connection with Sartre's adopting a more sanguine view of human interpersonal relations in his later works than he does in *Being and Nothingness*, see *Introduction to Existentialism*, pp. 87, 119.

31. Sartre, *Being and Nothingness*, trans. Hazel E. Barnes (New York: Philosophical Library, 1956), p. 70, note 9.

32. Ibid., p. 412, note 14.

33. Ibid., p. 581.

34. Ibid., pp. 627–28.

35. Sartre, *Existentialism & Humanism*, p. 51.

36. Though it was not available to Grene when she issued her criticism, Sartre's posthumously published *Notebooks for an Ethics*, trans. David Pellauer (Chicago: University of Chicago Press, 1992), sheds a great deal of light on these issues. See, for example, pp. 20, 280–90, 414, 499.

37. See Detmer, *Freedom as a Value*, pp. 102–31.

38. Grene, *Introduction to Existentialism*, p. 11.

39. Grene, "The Reception of Continental Philosophy in America," p. 35.

40. Jean-Paul Sartre, "Intentionality: A Fundamental Idea of Husserl's Phenomenology," trans. Joseph P. Fell, *Journal of the British Society for Phenomenology* 1, no. 2 (May 1970): 5.

41. Jean-Paul Sartre, *The War Diaries of Jean-Paul Sartre*, trans. Quintin Hoare (New York: Pantheon, 1984), p. 88. For additional quotations in which Sartre defends ethical objectivity and attacks ethical subjectivism and relativism, see Detmer, *Freedom as a Value*, pp. 179–80.

42. Grene, *Introduction to Existentialism*, p. 114.

43. Jean-Paul Sartre, *Search for a Method*, trans. Hazel E. Barnes (New York: Vintage, 1968), p. 34.

44. Sartre, *Being and Nothingness*, p. 580.

45. Ibid., p. 581.

46. Ibid., pp. 582–85.

REPLY TO DAVID DETMER

Dr. Detmer has presented a very flattering account of my work on Jean-Paul Sartre. I can demur to it only in two respects. First, my early *Introduction to Existentialism* was a first, relatively weak, effort to understand the thinkers I was dealing with. If I started there from an ethical point of view, it was because I did not grasp sufficiently clearly the ontological import of their arguments. Secondly, I was surprised to find Dr. Detmer praising my acknowledgment of Sartre's interest in biology in the *Critique*. Looking back at those pages, I find the upshot of my analysis there to be that it was precisely the biological aspect of human nature, the concrete lived aspect of our existence, that Sartre was unable to assimilate. We have still on the one hand consciousness over against being, and on the other totalization. When I think of Sartre and biology, I think of the time he thought lobsters were following him along the street. That's about it!

When it comes to Detmer's criticisms of my work on Sartre, I have to beg, respectfully, to disagree in principle. As to the radical conversion, I still see no evidence that it happened. The notes on ethics of 1947–48, unpublished when I was writing, in part predict the dialectic of the *Critique*. They, like the *Critique* itself, are much too Hegelian to permit a viable ethics. History as Mediator of the Absolute too easily takes over. In my reading of the unfinished *Idiot of the Family,* I did predict a possible move, not to a radical conversion, but to a modified conception of human existence, perhaps in answer to Merleau-Ponty's attempts to speak to his fellow-*normalien.* But the work remained unfinished, and no such change took place.

So I still see Sartre as a radical Cartesian: even a pre-reflective *cogito* is still a *cogito*, and, deprived of God and substance, man is still a useless passion. Freedom, to be freedom, must be total, like God's freedom. But the task of freedom fills us with dread, and we collapse into bad faith: into turning ourselves into things. I am a retired teacher of philosophy, a grandmother, an American with Irish connections, because I am afraid to be free.

It is not, as Detmer suggests, by trying to become God that I fall into bad faith, but by *not* trying—hopeless though that trying be. Granted, God, if He existed, would be for-itself-in-itself, and what I am is the for-itself confronting an alien in-itself. But in trying to be purely for-itself, I am attempting in effect to deny the in-itself, and so, all by myself, to be the for-itself in-itself. Or else I hang there as pure for-itself over an unbridgeable abyss, and that's what I dread to face. I see no way out of this impasse consistent with Sartre's premises.

Detmer, on the contrary, envisages a happy dialectic of Sartrean freedom, moving between absence and play. Neither of these seems an adequate foundation for ethical values. Nor am I impressed with the hope of salvation from phenomenology, which appears to me to be plainly one of the disasters of the recent century of philosophy. A twentieth-century philosophy still claiming to be *"apodiktische Wissenschaft"*? And pretending to the go back to the things themselves by bracketing their existence? Nonsense! The note about Scheler that Detmer quotes is interesting, but I can't believe Sartre did much with it. That does not mean, however, that I am ascribing to Sartre a "weak" subjectivism, rather a very strong one, so strong as to be inescapable.

It is many years since I worked on Sartre, and I confess to being ignorant of much of the secondary literature. But I have consulted Dr. Detmer's book, *Freedom as a Value,* to which he alludes a number of times. Sorry; it has not led to my radical conversion! I have the evidence of Sartre's own later works to support my position: there is a vacillation, or if you will a dialectic (with no synthesis) between freedom and totalization, but no such benign reconciliation as Detmer envisages. So we can only agree to disagree.

M. G.

A brief postscript. I regret that the discussions of my work in the history of philosophy should have been confined to Descartes, Heidegger, and Sartre. There would have been a comment on my excursions in Aristotle, had not my colleague, Mark Gifford, been prevented by illness from writing it. But I have had other interests, too, and in recent philosophy the work conspicuously missing is Merleau-Ponty's *Phenomenology of Perception*, which I read, foolishly, only in 1960. In commenting on my work in the philosophy of biology, both Sloan and Beatty have stressed my belief in the primacy of history, but the primacy of perception has been short-changed. The intellectual autobiography that opens this volume should supplement that omission.

PART THREE

BIBLIOGRAPHY OF THE WRITINGS OF MARJORIE GRENE

BIBLIOGRAPHY OF THE WRITINGS OF MARJORIE GRENE

A. BOOKS

Dreadful Freedom: A Critique of Existentialism. Chicago: University of Chicago Press, 1948. Reissued as *Introduction to Existentialism*, 1959; Midway Paperback, 1984.

Heidegger. New York: Hillary House, 1957; London: Bowes & Bowes, 1957.

A Portrait of Aristotle. Chicago: University of Chicago Press, 1963. Reissued as Phoenix paperback, 1967; Midway paperback, 1979; Bristol: Thoemmes Press, 1998.

The Knower and the Known. New York: Basic Books, 1966; University of California Press, paperback, 1974. Reissued by University Press of America, 1983.

Approaches to a Philosophical Biology. New York: Basic Books, 1969.

Sartre. New York: Franklin Watts, 1973. Reissued, Washington D.C.: University Press of America, 1983.

The Understanding of Nature: Essays in the Philosophy of Biology. Boston Studies in the Philosophy of Science, vol. 23. Synthese Library, vol. 66. Dordrecht: D. Reidel, 1974.

Philosophy In and Out of Europe. Berkeley and Los Angeles: University of California Press, 1976.

Descartes. In the Philosophers in Context Series, ed. S. Körner. Brighton: Harvester Press, 1985; University of Minnesota Press, 1985. Reissued by Hackett Publishing, Co.: Indianapolis, Ind., 1998.

Descartes Among the Scholastics. Milwaukee: Marquette University Press, 1991.

With Niles Eldredge. *Interactions: The Biological Context of Social Systems*. New York: Columbia University Press, 1992.

A Philosophical Testament. Chicago: Open Court, 1995.

With David Depew. *Philosophy of Biology*. In the Cambridge University Press series, "The Evolution of Modern Philosophy," forthcoming.

B. BOOKS EDITED

With T. V. Smith. *From Descartes to Kant: Readings in the Philosophy of the Renaissance and Enlightenment.* Chicago: University of Chicago Press, 1940. Reissued 1951 as two-volume paperback: *From Descartes to Locke*; *Berkeley, Hume, Kant.*

The Anatomy of Knowledge: Papers Presented to the Study Group on Foundations of Cultural Unity. London: Routledge and Kegan Paul; Amherst: University of Massachusetts Press, 1969.

Toward a Unity of Knowledge, Study Group on Foundations of Cultural Unity. New York: International Universities Press, 1969.

Knowing and Being: Essays, by Michael Polanyi. Chicago: University of Chicago Press, 1969. Reissued 1973.

Interpretations of Life and Mind: Essays Around the Problem of Reduction. New York: Humanities Press, 1971.

Spinoza: A Collection of Critical Essays. Garden City, N.Y.: Doubleday, 1973. Reissued, Notre Dame: University of Notre Dame, 1979.

With Everett Mendelsohn. *Topics in the Philosophy of Biology.* Boston Studies in the Philosophy of Science, vol. 27. Synthese Library, vol. 84. Dordrecht: D. Reidel, 1976.

Dimensions of Darwinism: Themes and Counterthemes in Twentieth-century Evolutionary Theory. Cambridge [Cambridgeshire]; New York: Cambridge University Press; Paris: Editions de la Maison des Sciences de l'Homme, 1983.

With Debra Nails. *Spinoza and the Sciences.* Dordrecht and Boston: D. Reidel, 1986.

With Roger Ariew. *Descartes and his Contemporaries: Meditations, Objections, and Replies.* Chicago: University of Chicago Press, 1995.

C. ARTICLES, COMMENTS, INTRODUCTIONS, AND REVIEWS

"Relativism and Philosophic Methods." *Philosophical Review* 46, no. 6 (1937): 649–56. (As M. Glicksman)

"A Note on the Philosophy of Heidegger." *Journal of Philosophy* 35 (1938): 93–104. (As M. Glicksman)

"Discipline and the Efficacy of Ideals." *Journal of Higher Education* 9 (April 1938): 175–82. (As M. Glicksman)

"Theories of Interpretation in the Law of Contracts." *University of Chicago Law Review* (1939): 374–98.

"Hume: Skeptic and Tory?" *Journal of the History of Ideas* 4 (1943): 333–48.

"Gerard's Essay on Taste." *Modern Philology* 41 (1943): 45–58.

"An Implicit Premise in Aristotle's *Ethics*." *Ethics* 56, (1946): 131–35.

"Kierkegaard: The Philosophy." *Kenyon Review* 9 (1947): 48–69.

"L'Homme est une Passion Inutile: Sartre and Heidegger." *Kenyon Review* 9 (1947): 167–85.

"Two More Existentialists: Karl Jaspers and Gabriel Marcel." *Kenyon Review* 9 (1947): 382–99.

"On Some Distinctions Between Men and Brutes." *Ethics* 57 (1947): 121–27.

"Sartre's Theory of the Emotions." *Yale French Studies* 1 (1948): 97–101.

Review of *The Philosopher's Way*, by Jean Wahl. *Kenyon Review* 10 (1948): 688; *Ethics* 58 (1947/1948): 311.

"Authenticity: An Existential Virtue." *Ethics* 62 (1952): 266–74.

"Men and Ideas: David Hume." *Encounter* 4 (1955): 54–60.

"Two Evolutionary Theories." *British Journal for the Philosophy of Science* 9 (1958): 110–27; 185–93. Reprinted in *Man and Nature: Philosophical Issues in Biology*, ed. Ronald Munson. New York: Dell Publishing Company, 1971.

"Heidegger: Philosopher and Prophet." *Twentieth Century* 164 (1958): 545–55.

"The German Existentialists." *Chicago Review* 13, no. 2 (summer 1959): 49–58.

"The Faith of Darwinism." *Encounter* 13 (November 1959): 48–56.

"Statistics and Selection." *British Journal for the Philosophy of Science* 12 (1961): 25–42.

"The Logic of Biology." In *The Logic of Personal Knowledge: Essays Presented to Michael Polanyi on His Seventieth Birthday, 11th March 1961*. London: Routledge and Kegan Paul, 1961, pp. 191–205.

"The Theory of Evolution." *Philosophy* 37 (1962): 268–72.

With J. R. Ravetz. "Leibniz's Cosmic Equation: A Reconstruction." *Journal of Philosophy* 59, no. 6 (March 1962): 141–46.

"Karl Jaspers: A Philosopher of Humanity." *Times Literary Supplement* 62 (12 April 1963): 241–42.

"Causes." *Philosophy* 38 (1963): 149–59. Reprinted in *The Understanding of Nature: Essays in Philosophy of Biology*, Marjorie Grene.

"Two Evolutionary Theories: A Reply." *British Journal of the Philosophy for Science* 14 (1963): 152–54; 349–51. Reprinted in *Man and Nature: Philosophical Issues in Biology*, ed. Ronald Munson. New York: Dell Publishing Company, 1971.

"Biology and Teleology." *Cambridge Review* (February 15, 1964): 269–73.

"Beyond Darwinism: Portmann's Thought." *Commentary* 40 (1965): 31–38.

Review of *The Narrow Pass: A Study of Kierkegaard's Concept of Man*, by George Price. *Philosophical Review* 74 (1965): 96. Shorter Review, *Philosophy and Literature* 3 (Fall 1979): 239.

Review of *Esthetique de Martin Heidegger*, by Joseph Sadzik. *British Journal of Aesthetics* 5 (1965): 91.

"Descriptive and Prescriptive Statements." *Proceedings of Seminar, Institut für Wissenschaftslehre*, Salzburg (1966): 38–54.

"Positionality in the Philosophy of Helmuth Plessner." *Review of Metaphysics* 20 (1966): 250–77.

"Discussion: Mr. Manier's 'Theory of Evolution as Personal Knowledge': A Quasi-Reply." *Philosophy of Science* 33, nos. 1–2 (March–June 1966).

"Straus's Phenomenological Psychology." *Review of Metaphysics* 21 (September 1967): 94–123.

"Martin Heidegger." *Encyclopedia of Philosophy* 3 (1967): 459–65.

"Biology and the Problem of Levels of Reality." *New Scholasticism* 41 (1967): 427–49. Reprinted in *The Understanding of Nature*, Marjorie Grene.

"Tacit Knowing and the Pre-Reflective Cogito." In *Intellect and Hope: Essays in the Thought of Michael Polanyi*, ed. Thomas A. Langford. Durham, N.C.: Duke University Press, 1968, pp. 19–57.

"Hobbes and the Modern Mind: An Introduction." In *The Anatomy of Knowledge*, ed. Marjorie Grene, pp. 1–28.

"Bohm's Metaphysics and Biology." In *Towards a Theoretical Biology*, vol. 2, *Sketches*, ed. C. H. Waddington. Edinburgh: Edinburgh University Press, 1969, pp. 61–69.

"Notes on Maynard-Smith's 'Status of Neo-Darwinism.'" In *Towards a Theoretical Biology*. Edinburgh: Edinburgh University Press, 1969, pp. 97–98.

"Sartre: A Philosophic Study." *Mind* 78 (January 1969): 143–53.

"Philosophical Anthropology." In *Philosophy 1955–65*, ed. R. Klibansky. Paris: International Institute of Philosophy, 1969, pp. 215–20.

"Hierarchy: One Word, How Many Concepts?" In *Hierarchical Structures*, ed. Lancelot Law Whyte et al. New York: American Elsevier Publishing Company, 1969, pp. 56–58.

"Die Erkenntnistheoretische Grundlage der Anthropologie." *The Human Context* 2 (1970): 221–32.

"The Aesthetic Dialogue of Sartre and Merleau-Ponty." *Journal of the British Society for Phenomenology* 1 (1970): 59–72.

Foreword to *Laughing and Crying: A Study of the Limits of Human Behavior*, by Helmuth Plessner. Evanston: Northwestern University Press, 1970, pp. xi–xiii.

"Sense-Perception: Philosophy's Step-Child?" In *Aisthesis and Aesthetics*, ed. Erwin Straus. Pittsburgh: Duquesne University Press, 1970, pp. 13–30.

"Believe-In-What?" *Main Currents* 27 (Sept–Oct 1970): 26–28.

"Reducibility: Another Side Issue?" In *Interpretations of Life and Mind*, ed. Marjorie Grene, pp. 14–37.

"Aristotle and Modern Biology." *Journal of the History of Ideas* 33 (July–September 1972): 395–424. Reprinted in *Topics in the Philosophy of Biology*, ed. Marjorie Grene and Everett Mendelsohn, 3–36.

"Jean-Paul Sartre: French Existentialism and Politics—The New Revolutionary." Reprinted in *Political Obligation and Civil Disobedience: Readings*, ed. Michael P. Smith and Kenneth L. Deutsch. New York: Thomas Y. Crowell, 1972.

"On First Reading *L'Idiot de la Famille*." *California Quarterly* (June 1972): 33–55.

"Polanyi et la Philosophie Française." *Archives de Philosophie* 35 (1972): 3–5.

"Sartre and the Other," (Presidential Address delivered before the 46th Annual Pacific Meeting of the American Philosophical Association, San Francisco, March 24, 1972), *Proceedings of the APA*, 1973: 22–41.

"People and Other Animals." *Philosophical Forum* 3 (1972): 157–72; *Philosophia Naturalis* 14 (1973): 25–38. Reprinted in *The Understanding of Nature*, Marjorie Grene, pp. 346–60.

"Is Genus to Species as Matter to Form? Aristotle and Taxonomy." *Synthese* 28 (1974): 51–69.

"Darwin and Philosophy." In *Academie Royale de Belgique: Connaissance Scientifique et Philosophie*, Colloque Organisé les 16 et 17 Mai 1973. Brussels: Palais des Academies, 1975, pp. 133–45.

"Three Aspects of Perception." In *The Understanding of Nature*, Marjorie Grene, pp. 13–34.

"Explanation and Evolution." In *The Understanding of Nature*, Marjorie Grene, pp. 206–27.

"Immer Noch Philosophie?" In *Sachlichkeit*, Festschrift for Helmuth Plessner, 1974: 93–100; reprinted in *Philosophy In and Out of Europe*. Berkeley and Los Angeles: University of California Press, 1976.

"Means, Ends and Functions." Editorial, *American Review of Respiratory Disease* 112 (1975): 325–28.

"Life, Death and Language: Some Thoughts on Wittgenstein and Derrida." *Partisan Review* 43 (1976): 265–79.

"Merleau-Ponty and the Renewal of Ontology." *Review of Metaphysics* 29 (1976): 605–25.

"Mind and Brain: The Embodied Person." In *Philosophical Dimensions of the Neuro-Medical Sciences*, ed. S. F. Spicker and H. T. Engelhardt. Dordrecht: D. Reidel, 1976: 113–29.

"To Have a Mind . . ." *Journal of Medicine and Philosophy* 1 (1976): 177–99.

"Imre Lakatos: Some Recollections." In *Essays in Memory of Imre Lakatos*, ed. R. S. Cohen, et al. Dordrecht: D. Reidel, 1976: 209–12.

"On the Use and Abuse of Deconstruction." *Journal of Philosophy* 74 (1977): 682.

"Philosophy of Medicine: Prolegomena to a Philosophy of Science." *PSA 1976* 2 (1977): 77–93.

"Tacit Knowing: Grounds for a Revolution in Philosophy." *Journal of the British Society for Phenomenology* 8, no. 3 (October 1977): 164–71.

"Individuals and Their Kinds: Aristotelian Foundations of Biology." In *Organism, Medicine, and Metaphysics: Essays in Honor of Hans Jonas on His 75th Birthday*, ed. S. F. Spicker. Dordrecht: D. Reidel, 1978: 121–36.

"The Paradoxes of Historicity." *Review of Metaphysics* 32, no. 1 (1978): 15–36.

"Knowledge, Belief and Perception." The Andrew W. Mellon Lectures, Fall 1978. New Orleans: The Graduate School, Tulane University, 1978. Reprinted in *A Philosophical Testament*, Chicago: Open Court, 1995.

"Sociobiology and the Human Mind." *Sociobiology and Human Nature*, ed. M. S. Gregory, A. Silvers, D. Sutch. San Francisco: Jossey-Bass, 1978: 213–24.

"Comments on Pellegrino's 'Anatomy of Clinical Judgments.'" In *Clinical Judgment: A Critical Appraisal*, ed. H. Tristram Engelhardt Jr., Stuart F. Spicker, and Bernard Towers. Dordrecht: D. Reidel, 1979: 195–97.

"Discussion: Comment on Desmond Clarke, 'Teleology and Mechanism: M. Grene's Absurdity Argument.'"*Philosophy of Science* 46 (1979): 326–27.

"A Note on Simberloff's 'Succession of Paradigms in Ecology.'" *Synthese* 43 (1980): 41–45.

"The Sense of Things." *Journal of Aesthetics and Art Criticism* 38 (1980): 377–89.

"Changing Concepts of Darwinian Evolution." *The Monist* 64 (April 1981): 195–213.

"Sartre and the Tradition." *American Philosophical Quarterly* 18, no. 4 (Oct. 1981): 355–59.

"Landscape." In *Phenomenology: Dialogues & Bridges,* ed. R. Bruzina. Albany: SUNY Press, 1982, 55–60.

"Empiricism and the Philosophy of Science or, *n* Dogmas of Empiricism." *Epistemology, Methodology and the Social Sciences*, ed. R.S. Cohen and M.W. Wartofsky. Dordrecht: D. Reidel, 1983, pp. 89–106.

"Philosophy of Biology 1983: Problems and Prospects." *Proceedings of the 7th International Congress for Logic, Methodology and Philosophy of Science* VII, ed. R. Barcan Marcus, G.J.W. Dorn, and P. Weingartner (Elsevier Science Publishers B.V., 1986), 433–52.

"Comments." *PSA* 2 (1984): 378–88.

"Idea and Judgment in the Third Meditation: An Object Lesson in Philosophical Historiography." *Independent Journal of Philosophy* (1985).

"About the Division of the Sciences." In *Aristotle on Nature and Living Things*, ed. A. Gothelf. Pittsburgh: Mathesis, 1985.

"Perception and Interpretation in the Sciences: Toward a New Philosophy of Science." In *Evolution at a Crossroads: The New Biology and the New Philosophy of Science*, ed. D. Depew and B. Weber. Cambridge, Mass.: MIT Press, 1985, and in *Philosophy in Its Variety*, Belfast: Queens University, 1987, 107–129.

"In and On Friendship." In *Human Nature and Natural Knowledge*, ed. A. Donagan, A.N. Perovich, Jr., M.V. Wedin. Dordrecht: D. Reidel, 1986, pp. 355–68.

"Die Einheit des Menschen: Descartes unter den Scholastikern." *Dialectica* 40, no. 4 (1986): 309–322.

"Introduction." In *Integrating Scientific Disciplines*, ed. W. Bechtel. Dordrecht: Martinus Nijhoff Publishers, 1986, pp. 145–48.

Introduction to *Spinoza and the Sciences*, ed. Marjorie Grene and Debra Nails, xi–xix.

"Puzzled Notes on a Puzzling Profession." Invited Panel: The Future of Philosophy, Sixty-first Annual Pacific Division Meeting of the American Philosophical Association, San Francisco, California, 1987, pp. 75–80. Reprinted in *Through Time and Culture: Introductory Readings in Philosophy*, ed. A Pablo Iannone. Englewood Cliffs, N.J.: Prentice Hall, 1994: 462–65.

"Hierarchies in Biology." *American Scientist* 75 (Sept.–Oct. 1987): 504–10.

"Darwin's Great Tree of Life: Roots and Ramifications." *Barnard Alumnae* (Fall 1987): 9–13.

"Historical Realism and Contextual Objectivity: A Developing Perspective in the Philosophy of Science." In *The Process of Science*, ed. Nancy Nersessian. Dordrecht: Martinus Nijhoff (Kluwer Academics), 1987, pp. 69–81.

"Hierarchies and Behavior." In *Social Behavior and the Concept of Integrative Levels*, ed. E. Tobach and G. Greenberg. Hillside, N.J.: Erlbaum, 1987, pp. 3–17.

"Wahrnehmung und Wirkleichkeit: Die Gibsonsche Angebotstheorie in ihrer Beziehung zum Leib-Seele Problem." *Studia Philosophica* 46 (1987): 98–112.

"Descartes and His Contemporaries." *The Monist* 71 (1988).

"Interaction and Evolution." In *What the Philosophy of Biology Is: Essays Dedicated to David Hull*, ed. Michael Ruse. Dordrecht: Kluwer Academic, 1989, pp. 67–73.

"A Defense of David Kitts." *Biology and Philosophy* 4 (1989): 69–72.

"Perception and Human Reality." In *Harré and His Critics*, ed. R. Bhaskar. Oxford: Blackwell, 1990, pp. 17–22.

"Is Evolution at a Crossroads?" *Evolutionary Biology* 24 (1990): 51–81.

"Evolution, 'Typology' and 'Population Thinking.'" *American Philosophical Quarterly* 27, no. 3 (July 1990): 237–44.

With Richard Burian. "Wilhelm Roux: Early Historical Inferences Regarding the 'Why?' of Nuclear Division Patterns, with a Translation of Roux (1883)." *Evolutionary Biology* 25 (1991): 427–44.

With Richard Burian. "Philosophy of Biology in Historical and Cultural Contexts." *Synthese* 91 (1992).

Review of *Le Principe de vie chez Descartes*, by Annie Bitbol-Hespériès. *Isis* 83, no. 1 (1992): 132.

"Editorial Introduction." *Synthese* 91 (1992): 1–7.

Review of Steven Nadler, *Malebranche and Ideas*, ed. G. Rodis-Lewis, Malebranche *Oeuvres* 2, *Isis* 84 (December 1993): 800–802.

"Aristotelico-Cartesian Themes in Natural Philosophy: Some Seventeenth Century Cases." *Perspectives on Science: Historical, Philosophical, Social* 1 (1993): 66–87.

"Recent Biographies of Darwin: The Complexity of Context." *Perspectives on Science* 1, no. 4 (1993): 659–75.

"The Primacy of the Ecological Self." In *The Perceived Self: Ecological and Interpersonal Sources of Self-Knowledge*, ed. U. Neisser. Cambridge: Cambridge University Press, 1993, pp. 112–17.

"The Heart and Blood: Descartes, Plemp, and Harvey." *Essays on the Philosophy and Science of René Descartes*, ed. Stephen Voss. New York: Oxford University Press, 1993, pp. 324–36.

"Qualified Freedom." In *Perspectives in Philosophy*, ed. M. Boylan. New York: Harcourt Brace Jovanovich, 1993, pp. 277–89.

"The Objects of Hume's *Treatise*." *Hume Studies* 20, no. 2 (Nov. 1994): 163–77.

"Résponse à Jean Louis Chedin." In *Descartes, Objecter et Répondre*. Paris: PUF, 1994, pp. 179–84.

"Epilogue." In *Descartes and his Contemporaries: Meditations, Objections and Replies*, ed. Roger Ariew and Marjorie Grene, pp. 227–37.

"Animal Mechanism and the Cartesian Vision of Nature." In *Physics, Philosophy and the Scientific Community: Essays in the Philosophy and History of the Natural Sciences and Mathematics in Honor of Robert S. Cohen*, ed. Kostas Gavroglu, John Stachel, and Marx W. Wartofsky. Dordrecht: Kluwer Academic, 1995, pp. 189–204.

With Roger Ariew. "Ideas, In and Before Descartes." *Journal of the History of Ideas* 51 (Jan. 1995): 87–106.

Introduction to Part Two of *Malebranche's First & Last Critics: Simon Foucher and Dortous de Mairan*. Carbondale, Ill.: Southern Illinois University Press, 1995: 61–67.

"The Personal and the Subjective." *Tradition and Discovery* 22 (1995/1996): 6–16.

Review of *William Harvey's Natural Philosophy*, by Roger K. French, and *Die Mechanisierung des Herzens: Harvey and Descartes—Der vitale und der mechanische Aspekt des Kreislaufs*, by Thomas Fuchs. *Isis* 87, no. 4 (1996): 724–25.

Review of *The Cambridge Companion to Spinoza*, ed. Don Garrett. *Isis* 88, no. 1 (1997): 145–46.

Review of *Discipline and Experience: The Mathematical Way in the Scientific Revolution*, by Peter Dear. *The British Journal for the Philosophy of Science* 48 (March 1997): 113–16.

"Current Issues in the Philosophy of Biology." *Perspectives on Science* 5, no. 2 (1997): 255–81.

With Roger Ariew. "The Cartesian Destiny of Form and Matter." *Early Science and Medicine* 2 (1997): 300–325.

Review of *Physiologia: Natural Philosophy in Late Aristotelian and Cartesian Thought*, by Dennis Des Chene. *Archiv für Geschichte der Philosophie* 79, (1997): 343–48.

Review of *Representation and the Mind-Body Problem in Spinoza*, by Michael Della Rocca, *Journal of the History of the Behavioral Sciences* 34, no. 2 (Spring 1998): 218.

Review of *Aristotle on Perception*, by Stephen Everson. *Review of Metaphysics* 52, no. 1 (1998): 142–43.

"La Philosophie de la Biologie dans les Pays Anglophones." *Annales, d'histoire et de philosophie du vivant* 2 (1999): 9–13.

Review of *Descartes and Augustine*, by Stephen Menn. *Review of Metaphysics* 52 (March 1999): 711–13.

"Descartes and Skepticism." *The Review of Metaphysics* 52 (March 1999): 553–71.

"What Have We Learned from Philosophy in the Twentieth Century?" *The Proceedings of the Twentieth World Congress of Philosophy: Vol 8, Contemporary*

Philosophy, ed. Daniel O. Dahlstrom. Bowling Green: Philosophy Documentation Center, 2000, pp. 257–61.

"Recent Work on Aristotelian Biology." *Perspectives on Science* 8, no. 4 (2000): 444–59.

"The Philosophy of Science of Georges Canguilhem: A Transatlantic View." *Revue d'histoire des sciences* 53, no. 1 (2000): 47–63.

Review of *Spirits and Clocks: Machine and Organism in Descartes*, by Dennis Des Chene. *Philosophy in Review* 21, no. 4 (2001): 251–53.

"Darwin, Cuvier and Geoffroy: Comments and Questions." *History and Philosophy of the Life Sciences* 23 (2001): 187–211.

D. TRANSLATIONS

C. F. v. Weizsäcker. *The World View of Physics*. Chicago: University of Chicago Press, 1952.

Jahnheinz Jahn. *Muntu*. London: Faber and Faber, 1961.

Helmuth Plessner. *Laughing and Crying: A Study of the Limits of Human Behavior*, with James Churchill. Evanston, Ill.: Northwestern University Press, 1970.

Dortous de Mairan. "Correspondence with Malebranche," in *Malebranche's First and Last Critics: Simon Foucher and Dortous de Mairan*, with Richard A. Watson. Carbondale, Ill.: Southern Illinois University Press, 1995.

Thomas Fuchs. *Mechanization of the Heart: Harvey and Descartes*. Rochester, N.Y.: University of Rochester Press, 2001.

INDEX

(by Kathleen League)